BUChairPORTS

1995

by Martin S Harrison

3rd edition

ISBN 1 898 779 05 8

16 colour photos

published and distributed by:

BUChair (UK) Ltd
P O Box 89
Reigate, Surrey RH2 7FG
England

phone: 01737 224747
fax: 01737 226777

Printed in Great Britain

Where to obtain products of BUCHair (UK) Ltd and Bucher & Co Publications

If you cannot obtain our products at your local bookstore or if you need information about publication dates or prices, please contact the following organizations in, or nearest to, your country:

AUSTRALIA

Mr James L Bell
BUCHER PUBLICATIONS (Australia)
P O Box 70
Ridell
Victoria 3431

Phone: (054) 28 63 12

CANADA

Aviation World
195 Carlingview Drive
Rexdale
Ontario M9W 5E8

Phone: (416) 674 5959
Fax: (416) 674 5915

DANMARK

NYBODER BOGHANDEL ApS
114 Store Konensgade
DK-1264 Copenhagen K

Phone: 33 32 33 20
Fax: 33 32 33 62

DEUTSCHLAND

BUCHER & Co PUBLIKATIONEN
Postfach 44
CH-8058 Zurich Flughafen
Postcheckkonto
Zurich 80-30353-6
Schweiz
Telefon: 0041 1 874 1 747
Telefax: 0041 1 874 1 757

FINLAND/SUOMI

AKATEEMINEN KIRJA-KAUPPA
Keskuskatu 1
SF-00101 Helsinki

Phone: (80) 121 41
Telefax: (80) 121 44 41

FRANCE

LA MAISON DU LIVRE
76 Boulevard Malasher
F-75008 Paris

Phone: (1) 45 22 74
Fax: (1) 42 93 81

GREAT BRITAIN

orders only:
BUCHair (UK) Ltd
P O Box 89
Reigate
Surrey RH2 7FG

Phone: 01737 224747
Fax: 01737 226777

GREAT BRITAIN

pick up:
BUCHairSHOP
Spectators Terrace
Gatwick Airport

ITALIA

LA BANCARELLA AERONAUTICA
Corso Duca degli Abruzzi, 12
I-10138 Torino

Phone: (011) 37 79 08
Fax: (011) 37 79 08

JAPAN

NISHIYAMA YOSHO Co Ltd
Takin Building 3F
4-7-11,Ginza, chuo-ku
Tokyo 104

Phone: (03) 3562 0820
Telefax: (03) 3562 0828

NEDERLAND

BOEKHANDEL VENSTRA BV
Binnehof 50
Postbus 77
NL-1180 AB Amstelveen

Phone: (020) 641 98 80

NORGE

SCANBOOK NORWAY
AUTOMOBILIA A/S
Postboks 7035
Homansbyen
N-0306 Oslo

OSTERREICH

BUCHER & Co PUBLIKATIONEN
Postfach 44
CH-8058 Zurich Flughafen
Postcheckkonto
Zurich 80-30353-6
Telefon: (01) 874 1 747
Telefax: (01) 874 1 757

PORTUGAL

Mr Paulo Nuno
Marques Mengo
Apartado 413
P-2405 Leiria Codex

SCHWEIZ / LEICHN

bestellungen:
BUCHER & Co PUBLIKATIONEN
Postfach 44
CH-8058 Zurich Flughafen
Postcheckkonto
Zurich 80-30353-6
Telefon: (01) 874 1 747
Telefax: (01) 874 1 757

SCHWEIZ / LEICHN

abholer:
BUCHER & Co PUBLIKATIONEN
BUCHairSHOP
Schaffhauserstr 76
CH-8152 Glattbrug

Telefon: (01) 874 1 747
Telefax: (01) 874 1 757

SOUTH AFRICA

The Aviation Shop
Mr Karel Zayman
P O Box 316
Melville 2109

Phone: (011) 472 32 55

SPAIN/ESPANA

LA AERTOTECA
Librearia Miguel Creus
C/Congost, 11
E-08024 Barcelona

Phone: (93) 210 54 07
Telefax: (93) 210 59 92

SVERIGE

ESSELTE BUKHANDEL
Gamia Brogatan 26
Box 62
SE-101 20 Stockholm

Phone: (08) 23 79 90
Telefax: (08) 24 25 53

NORTH AMERICA

World Transoprt Press
1224 NW 72nd Avenue
P O Box 521238
Miami, FL 33152-1238

Phone: (800) 875 6711
Fax: (305) 599 1995

NORTH AMERICA

BUCHair USA Inc
P O Box 750515
Forest Hills
New York 11375-0515

Phone: (718) 349 4828
Fax: (718) 263 8748

INTRODUCTION

The 1993 edition of this book featured over seven hundred airports. At the time, this seemed a lot. There are now details of well over eight hundred, and coverage continues to increase. A report for yet another country, not previously included, arrived too late for inclusion. Without the active assistance from readers, there is no doubt that this book would not have been possible. With each additional entry comes the responsibility of keeping the record up to date, In many instances this is not possible.

Improvements are continuous, mostly made possible by information technology. In order to include more airports in the minimum space, the text is now printed in 8 point Arial. This keeps down the number of pages, an important consideration when paper prices have risen steeply over the last year or so. Last year's listings at the rear of the book, complete with radio frequencies, proved to be popular. They have now been rationalised to incorporate the index.

The pace of change continues at an alarming rate. Two brand new airports have been opened: Denver International and Kansai, and the fullest details are supplied within the constraints we were set. Airlines have come and gone, as they do, and apologies are made for any names which appear belonging to defunct operators. Readers will appreciate that 200,000 words amounts to a lot of work. From the writer's point of view, it's like painting the Forth Bridge: as soon as work is complete at one end, it's time to start at the other. The publication deadline puts a stop to modifications and improvements, no matter how desirable.

Readers, as stated above, have made this book possible. Recommendations for improvements have been made, studied and all suggestions have been incorporated where possible. The last edition appealed for better information about Russia. Readers will see for themselves that the Moscow entries arose from that request. By the time the book is published, some of its information is already out of date. Much happens over two years, and readers are invited to provide any information they think might be appropriate. For instance, one short letter merely stated that the entry for one airport in the Far East was still correct - useful to know. The book contains information, and it is either right or wrong. Any assistance to convert wrong information into something better is always warmly received.

Almost fifty people contributed to both this and the last edition. Reports are taken at face value and checked for accuracy wherever possible. They can't always be checked for originality. One person, in the belief that it would be helpful, submitted a report which was not original, which led to complications regarding copyright, good manners and so on. The only publications which are knowingly used comprise the following:

Airport and airline publicity material, the Red Book of Aviation (America's airport directory published by Sales Directories Inc), British Airways Aerad Flight Supplements (listing airport data), Airlines & Airports Coding & Decoding (published by Airnieuws) and BUCHair's JP Airline Fleets International. Additional sources include the George Philip University Atlas and the Collins/Rand McNally Road Atlas of the USA.

Contributors, without whom this book would not have been possible, are: Andrew Abshier, Graham Alliance, Mark A Bates, Falk-Christian Bender, Piet Biesheuvel, Chris Boyde, George Brigham, Paul Chandler, Oto Chudy, Neil A Clarke, Martin A Cooper, Martin Davidson, David Dowling, Chris English, Marco Finelli, Felix Gasser, Claude-Patrick Giraud, Howard Griffin, Lars-Inge Grundberg, Geraint Hayward, Andy Holten, Dave Hose, Chris Hughes, Ton Jochems, Neil Jones, Alan Lord, Takanori Maeda, Michel Magalhaes, Adam J Marshall, Marshall C Morris, Per Olufsen, John Palmer, Ewan Partridge, Hanno Plastounik, Alex Rankin, Robert Rennert, Brett Robinson, Brian Roffee, R J Rogers, Stephen Rudge/ANR, Vik Saini, David Shephard, Kajetan Steiner, Thomas Stuenkel, Henry Tenby and Simon Wills. It will be appreciated that much of the previous edition's information appears again but it is not possible to acknowledge its sources.

Work usually starts on compilation every other January but many people supply information while it's still "hot", as soon as they return from trips. It's all welcome and can be mailed or faxed to the author:

Martin S Harrison, P O Box 12, Atherstone, Warks CV9 3RX, England, or by fax on 01 455 233 066.

DEAR READER,

Welcome to the third edition of **BUCHairPORTS**, published by BUCHair (UK) Ltd. We hope you like the many improvements which this edition features.

The Airport Data section, introduced in the last edition, includes IATA and ICAO codes, country designator (and state, where applicable), goeographical location, runways, runway lengths and radio frequencies. One feature of the last edition, missing from this, is information regarding Airpasses. Airline policy on these is currently under revision, and it would be misleading to publish data which might rapidly become outdated.

Other books published by BUCHair (UK) Ltd include *jp Biz-Jet*, *jp Biz-Jet Production List*, **BUCHairHELICOPTERS**, and the **BUCHairLOG**.

BUCHair (UK) Ltd produces database systems from *jp Biz-Jet* and **BUCHairHELICOPTERS** and from the *jp airline-fleets international*, published by Bucher & Co Publications in Zurich.

The database systems are fast becoming an essential tool of the world's leading aircraft brokers, dealers, insurers, manufacturers, maintenance companies, airline operators and government agencies. etc.

> Ronald P Harman   Frank E Bucher

April 1995   BUCHair (UK) Ltd

ILLUSTRATIONS

Front cover:
Dublin Airport
Terminal B from the air. Photo supplied by Aer Reanta.

Rear cover:
Phoenix Sky Harbor
A view from the multi-storey car park, showing America West 757-200 N907AW in the colours of the Phoenix Suns' basketball team. Photo supplied by Martin Hollier.

AP PAKISTAN (Islamic Republic of Pakistan)
GILGIT
GIL   OPGT

The delightful, colonial-style, passenger terminal is served by PIA F.27s but only when the weather is fair. The landing aids, which are taken for granted in western countries, are expensive and beyond the means of the Third World, especially when they aren't needed too often. When it rains, it rains, of course. Being ten thousand feet up in the Karakoram Mountains means that it can snow a bit, too. In this part of the world, passengers learn to live with inconvenience.

A footpath, at the tree line, leads along the western perimeter of the field. Anyone who really must have a photograph of an F.27 can, in theory, take one here. There are no military aircraft based, so security precautions are not as strict as at other Pakistani airports.

This note applies to all airports in the country: Pakistan is surrounded by Iran, Afghanistan, China and India. The dispute over Kashmir means that a state of near-war exists with India. Little needs to be said about the perceived threat which its other neighbours pose. The people are extremely friendly and outgoing but they are held in an iron grip by the police and the military. Foreigners, under these circumstances, represent a genuine threat which must not be under-estimated. Aviation photography is therefore not something to be explained after the event. It will fall on deaf ears. However, the situation is not all gloom and doom.

ISLAMABAD
ISB   OPRN   Chaklala   5m/8km NW of Rawalpindi

Officially known as Islamabad, the airport complex is in fact closer to Rawalpindi, the two cities being very close to each other, and combines civil and military activity, both of some significance. To the left of the Islamabad Airport terminal and stands is Rawalpindi base, used by the Pakistani Air Force.

Islamabad has one feature which is almost unique in the country: a viewing balcony which is open to the public. Anyone wishing to record registrations, rather than take photos, will enjoy a couple of days here. All representative types of the PIA fleet can be seen, in the company of domestic carriers. The departure lounge is large and modern, and can also be used for watching the activity.

To the left are the numerous military C-130s and 707s, plus some trainers. Showing anything but passing interest will, almost certainly, be misunderstood. When security precautions are as tight as they are in Pakistan, it is sensible to take one or two of your own. From the comfort of your living room, it may sound strange to use an airport toilet cubicle for writing down civil registrations. Before dismissing this as being silly, consider answering, in a strange country, the question: what are you doing?

KARACHI
KHI   OPKC   Quaid-e-Azam International   10m/16km N

The main passenger terminal is modern, air conditioned and clean. It has three levels: arrivals on the lower, departures in the middle, the restaurant and viewing gallery on top. The external viewing gallery is, of course, permanently closed.

Projecting from the terminal are two rotunda satellites: one for international flights and the other for domestic. Once inside the departure area, it's possible to walk around, and see most of the aircraft, very much like Pier 3/the Satellite at Gatwick (which they closely resemble). With binoculars, all movements can be logged from either terminal but discretion is essential.

Photography is to be considered as reckless.

Nothing will ever stop the local populus from going to the airport to meet and greet, or to wave off. The gallery might have been closed to them but the people congregate instead in large numbers on the elevated departure level road. It's possible to blend into the masses, without drawing attention to one's self. Anything other than casual note-taking is bound to draw attention. If anyone contemplates taking a camera out of the gadget bag, and locking a 200mm zoom lens onto the front of it, it's best to think of it like dropping your pants. The effect will be pretty much the same!

This is the country's principal international airport, so visiting airlines, a predictable assortment of Asian and European long-hauls, may not be as interesting as the chance to see most of the PIA fleet and the other domestic carriers. These include Aero Asia ROMBAC 1-11s, Bhoja Air and Shaheen Air 737s.

Karachi is also served by another (all-civil) field, called Shara-e-Faisal, of which nothing has been reported. Apart from a nominal military presence at Quaid-e-Azam, there are two other military fields in the area. Detailed exploration is not recommended!

LAHORE
LHE   OPLA   2m/3km NW

Probably best for the smaller airliners used by PIA and the other domestic carriers, Lahore has a pleasant passenger terminal. Its main problem is that larger aircraft use remote stands, about a mile away, where they are completely hidden by trees.

It is advisable to be content with reasonably good views of some of the aircraft on stands adjacent to the terminal, rather than be tempted to venture along the perimeter, by the runway, in the vain hope of logging all the movements.

The lack of any significant general aviation at this airport is probably explained by the existence of WALTON airfield, of which nothing has been reported.

PESHAWAR
PEW   OPPS   2m/3km NW

PIA operate domestic and international flights from this airport, though not in any great number. The runway is used by a mixture of fighters, trainers and strike/attack aircraft, so self-discipline could be the rule of the day. Leave the camera in the hotel room - that way there's more chance of returning there in the evening!

For anyone who wants to see the Pakistani Air Force, Peshawar's passenger terminal is probably the safest location in which to do it. Standing at a window for three hours, in full view, is not a good idea, though!

SKARDU
KDU   OPSD

If watching foreign airliners on their home turf is interesting, Skardu airport is no more interesting than any other tiny regional airport. In theory, this is just a quiet little airport: set close to the River Indus, in the high desert, and surrounded by 20,000 feet high mountains. In reality, the war zone of Kashmir is only 80 miles away. As if that weren't enough, China is even closer.

The scenery is, of course, breathtaking. And getting there is one of the best white-knuckle rides in the world. Brown trousers are essential! Anyone who thinks he has travelled the world, and can't get excited by any of it, has not landed at Skardu. The PIA 737 descends to the airport through twisting mountain passes, and the captain is just earning a living. This is Living on The

Edge. That's when the weather is good.

There is normally no active military presence at the airport but it is geared up to act as a forward operating point. The authorities are trained to be on constant alert for anyone who might be doing a spot of reconnaissance.

Also in this part of the country, and situated in the Swat Valley, is SAIDU SHARIF (SDT OPSS), an idyllic rural airport at which to witness the arrival and departure of the twice-daily PIA F.27 flights to Peshawar or Islamabad. It will not be a hurried activity, however. It is difficult to blend into the background in such a small airport, so no attempt should be made to record the scene for posterity.

A4O OMAN (Sultanate of Oman)
MUSCAT
MCT   OOMS   Seeb International   25m/40km

The Sultanate of Oman has quite a lot to offer as a destination and the relaxing of visa restrictions is meant to encourage tourism, so entry is much easier than in the past. Anyone who visits is probably making a one-hour technical stop on their way to or from the Far East, under cover of darkness. Most of this traffic now uses alternatives to Muscat, such as Dubai, or is operated by B.747-400s which can fly direct.

Taxying to the normal departure runway threshold means passing the hangars. Next to the terminal is the ramp for visiting military and general aviation movements, followed by the Sultan of Oman Air Force facility, with at least one Hercules close to the taxiway (50-135mm will do), a collection of helicopters, and probably a 1-11. The next apron is that of the Royal Flight but their aircraft are usually hangared, as well as being a fairly common sight at Heathrow. The last hangar is that of the para-military Royal Oman Police Air Wing, and one or two of their fleet may be outside.

Viewing is possible from the refurbished terminal, though only after passport control. The escalator which gives access to the Duty Free Shop also offers the rest of the upper floor for exploration. There is now a large seating area with windows overlooking the eastern end of the apron. On some occasions, security personnel can prevent anyone but passengers entering the terminal, probably due to local activities such as the arrival of a VIP. VIPs in the Gulf tend to be seen as rather more important than elsewhere in the world.

For the visitor staying in Muscat, it will be worth a short description of the facilities: to the right of the terminal is the OAS hangar and ramp with a collection of Twin Otters and F.27s. The limited amount of traffic handled at the main terminal is mostly Gulf Air, Air India and PIA, whose F.27s and 737s are among the more interesting. Ethiopian Boeings and Thai A300s supply the other notable arrivals. Much of the traffic passes through between 10:00pm and midnight.

All the separate facilities here are individually accessed from entrances off the main road and each has its own security checkpoint. Some form of introduction to the company would lead past the Omani guard to a small, friendly group of British expatriots, particularly at ROPAW and Oman Air Services. Between those friendly expats, who would welcome talking to someone new, is the guard who probably welcomes talking to nobody, and certainly not in anything other than Arabic!

A5 BHUTAN (Kingdom of Bhutan)
PARO
PBH   VQPR

The capital city of Bhutan is Thimpu, served by Paro airport, into which Druk Air's BAe146s fly from various points in Asia. Photos of a Druk Air (Royal Bhutan Airlines) 146 are rare indeed.

Photos at Paro are as rare as hens' teeth.

The government has limited foreign tourists to a maximum of 2,250 annually. The other restriction is that tourists must guarantee to spend a certain amount of money in the country. Bhutan, in travellers' terms, is very exclusive indeed - and very expensive. The airport is situated in a narrow valley, surrounded by extremely steep mountains. Approach, in poor weather conditions (it gets a lot of cloud at 7300 feet above sea level), is not exciting at all - it's terrifying!

The passenger terminal building is tiny, as it would be. It only has to accommodate the people who can fill a 146, not many. Stepping through one of the patio doors, there are small gardens, surrounded by two feet high fences, painted green. How quaint! There is absolutely nothing to do except wander around and view the magnificent scenery. Taking a superb photo, once at the apron's edge, couldn't be easier. The trick is getting there in the first place. Anyone who makes the trip can see some of the most wonderful scenery and architecture in the entire world. Bhutan is, quite simply, the ultimate.

A6 UNITED ARAB EMIRATES
DUBAI
DXB   OMDB   International   3m/5km SE

Unlike most other airports in the Gulf, Dubai handles many long-haul flights as well as the usual regional traffic. About forty scheduled passenger airlines use Dubai plus a growing number of cargo operators. Due to its location, halfway between Europe and the Far East, Dubai handles an interesting mixture of movements: Thai and Singapore International Airbuses, Eva 747s, Air China 767s and Finnair DC-10s. Traditional links between Central Europe and the Middle East mean that Balkan A320s and 767s, LOT 737s and Tarom A310s are regular visitors but there are also Olympic 737s, Air Malta A320s and Turkish A340s. South African and Ethiopian 767s visit, and Federal Express use 747s and MD-11s. For daily up-to-date schedules, a copy of Emirates News, an English language newspaper, is recommended.

Passenger aircraft park on the main apron, facing away from the two parallel runways, aligned 12/30, with the terminal building at the western corner, closest to town. Next to the passenger terminal, and almost directly opposite the thresholds of Runways 12L/R, is the apron used for cargo and general aviation.

The main apron consists of twenty three stands, with a planned extension of another twenty. Unlike Sharjah and Abu Dhabi, Dubai's arrivals park nose-in, instead of at air bridges.

The cargo apron is easily seen from the staff car park. The six bays, each big enough to take a 747, are planned to be doubled to twelve. Beyond the cargo area is the general aviation facility, which usually contains two or three corporate jets each day. Delivery flights, when passing through, also park here.

Between the cargo and GA facilities is the Emirates' maintenance area, comprising three hangars. One, capable of holding a couple of 747-400s, is used by the airline, while the others are mainly occupied by Air Force C-130s. Aerogulf Helicopter Services have their own hangar, usually with about a dozen Bell 212s to be seen, plus the occasional police MBB 105.

At the eastern end of the field is the royal hangar, where the sheik's aircraft can be seen, often in the company of visiting Gulfstreams and other private jets, owned by the privileged. Showing undue interest is obviously not wise.

Security precautions in the Middle East mean that viewing the movements from outside the passenger terminal can be fraught with difficulties. A pass is required from the airport authorities, just to stand near the car park and record the registrations. Permission to take photographs, without some good reason, is out of the question. High fences surround the field, and comprise two barriers, about 5 metres apart, making ground level photography impossible.

The airport road passes close to both the main apron and the royal hangar. Parking in a layby is not unusual, to watch movements on the taxiway, for instance. Staying there for four hours and using a camera or binoculars (worse still, a telescope), however, does invite attention.

ABU DHABI
AUH   OMAA   International   23m/37km SW (bus 40 minutes)

This is the Emirates most modern airport, with a new satellite pier in front of the arc-shaped passenger terminal. Movements are similar, in terms of colour schemes, to those visiting Dubai. Abu Dhabi is, however, the capital city, so there are more corporate jets to be seen. Most of these use the stands to the right of the satellite. An ornate state reception building, also to the right-hand side of the apron, is used to welcome the sort of people who expect to be welcomed by more than a chauffeur carrying a board with their name on it.

The terminal's cafe and seating area, from which the apron can be watched, are predictably to the left. The view is good, if not ideal: if anything moves, it can be seen. The runway is about half a mile away, at the far side of two taxiways, thus making photographs difficult. Security presence might be expected to make matters worse but this is not so. Negotiations to take photos through the glass are normally successful.

The airport is developing, with service roads to the different aprons. At the far end, towards the threshold of Runway 31, one apron is shared by Emirates Air Service and a small general aviation terminal. To see anything parked here, the occasional Cessna, Piper or jet, a walk is necessary but not necessarily recommended! The cargo apron, halfway between the passenger and GA terminals, is hidden from view by the cargo terminal.

In the opposite direction, the Gamco apron can be seen from a couple of vantage points at reasonably close quarters. Apart from the usual Gulf Air aircraft, the stored ADC Airlines TriStar 5N-BBB has spent a good part of 1994 here.

ABU DHABI
OMAD   Bateen   3m/5km S

What was Abu Dhabi's first airport is now Bateen Air Base, passed on the road to the present airport. An unmarked ADAF Mirage guards the entrance but is unlikely to prevent a determined enthusiast gaining entry. Guards, standing in its shadow can, AND WILL, do that!

Close inspection of the resident UAE military aircraft and the Presidential Flight, barely visible from the road, is unlikely.

The only hope of access is by negotiation with Abu Dhabi Aviation, whose extensive fleet of helicopters is based here. Even if access be arranged, permission to take photographs should be obtained separately from the security office.

SHARJAH
SHJ   OMSJ   International   15m/25km SE

Sharjah's appeal is cheap electrical goods, which can be bought in some quantity and shipped back to Russia for sale at a profit. This means that as many forty Russian aircraft can be seen in a single day, many of the flights no doubt officially sanctioned.

A typical day's haul at Sharjah can include movements by any of the following airlines: Armenian, Azerbaijan, Belarus, Estonian, Kazakhstan, Kyrgyzstan, Latvian, Lithuanian, Moldova, Moscow, Tajik, Tojikistan, Turkmenistan and Uzbekistan. Few of these movements park at the passenger terminal, however. A few people can arrive in a Yak-42, Tu-154, Il-62 or Il-86. Their purchases often require at least an additional Antonov of some kind, or even an Il-76.

The single runway, 12/30, is served by a taxiway, off which are four apron areas. Arriving by road from town, the clover-leaf flyover leads, via a roundabout, to the passenger terminal, at the far (eastern) end. In front of the terminal is the main apron, with air bridges, plus an additional stand, for use by the Royal Flight 737, A6-ESH. To the left are three more stands which will, in time, no doubt become part of one main apron. A hangar was being built in 1994, to the right of the main terminal, to hold the sheik's 737.

Visiting scheduled traffic features a good range of operators, including all Gulf Air types, Kuwait A320s, Alyemda A310s, Algerian, Iranian and Syrian 727s (plus other types), as well as Uzbekistan and CSA A310s, and a variety of Air China aircraft. The main charter airlines are, predictably, Britannia (767s) and Condor (757s and 767s). Details of each day's aircraft movements are to be found in Emirates News.

A service road leads west from the roundabout. Along it are several vantage points. The first overlooks the passenger aprons and, beyond the fuel compound, another offers a view of the cargo apron. Lufthansa and German Cargo Airlines occupy the far building, where daily movements are regular. At least a couple of 747s can be expected, as well as up to four DC-8s.

At the far end of the service road are, respectively, the service and military aprons. Whilst security at Sharjah is not as strict as at Dubai, procedures are still necessary if confrontation is to be avoided. The Airport Security Office (in the main terminal) grants permission to take photos and record registrations, which can include a ramp pass. The perimeter road seems to allow views without red tape but, having travelled this far, it might be wise (and polite) to take a few minutes to observe the niceties. Arousing the interest of one of the army guards is certainly going to be more time-consuming in the long run, and parting as the best of friends is unlikely.

The perimeter fences are not in the best condition, and offer temptation to an ardent photographer. Crossing them, where they have fallen down, might look like a good idea. One minute, it feels like you're all alone. The next minute, your telephoto lens reveals a bayonet! Think about it.

AL AIN
AAN   OMAL   International   15m/24km SW

The Ruler of the Abu Dhabi Emirate (also the President of the UAE) needed access to this oasis, so Al Ain airport was built. The enormously long runway (2.5m/4km) is little-used, and rarely by traffic needing the full length.

The main terminal building, which has to be seen to be believed, is for the Ruler's own use. There is also a small general aviation centre, which houses the passenger terminal used by ordinary folk. Only a few resident Cessnas and Pipers are to be seen, unless the Ruler is visiting. In that event, security becomes proportionately strict.

Even the most dedicated aviation enthusiast may find more interest in the local camel market.

RAS AL KHAYMAH
RKT   OMRK   International   10m/16km SE

A Gulf Air 737 daily links this airport to Abu Dhabi. Occasional visitors can be seen but not enough for even the most serious enthusiast to plan a trip here. Thus the airport sleeps in the sun most of the time, while the local population goes about its business of trading.

The only unusual aspect of this airport results from local trade, predictably in cheap electrical goods, and therefore enough reason for the arrival of ad-hoc shopping flights from Russia and the CIS states.

A7 QATAR
DOHA
DOH   OTBD   International   5m/8km SE

Almost all the scheduled services (about 90% in fact) are supplied by Gulf Air 737s, with the more interesting PIA A300s and Egyptair 767s passing through at night. The only residents of any note are the government's fleet of Boeings, a reasonably common sight at Heathrow. From the town centre, the passenger terminal is at the end of Airport Road. Heading east from town instead, along Ras Abu Aboud Road, the northern end of Runway 16/34 is passed. This leads to the Qatar Emiri Air Force, a right turn off the road. Stopping and taking photos are not recommended!

A9C BAHRAIN (State of Bahrain)
BAHRAIN
BAH   OBBI   Muharraq International   46km NE of Manama

The days of glory for Bahrain have now gone, as Dubai has successfully attracted the air traffic in transit between Europe and the Far East. Some interest was generated by a residue of carriers but PAL and Korean moved out, Iran Air was banned for political reasons, and the remaining foreign scheduled flights are on their way to, or from, Heathrow. The only worthwhile airliners are the Gulf Air fleet, whose 747s and 737s don't visit the most of Europe, and one or two Saudia 737s each day. DHL are building up a package cargo service with (Saudi-registered) Metros and Merlins. A Saudia Citation flies nightly services into Bahrain for DHL, but the other visitors each day are probably fuel-stopping. Military movements are most likely to be USAF C-141s or Australian C-130s, and a US Navy C-12 is normally present.

Executive traffic is down to a trickle and only the Royal Flight 727 and Gulfstream are based. With the arrival of the fighter aircraft, operating from a new base opposite the terminal, restrictions on photography were increased. The days when it was permitted to take photos from the excellent rooftop terrace are over, though passable shots of airliners taxying past the airside departure area could be obtained with a 135-200mm lens.

At the ends of the runway are good vantage points, the better probably being that next to the sea and the military parking area, but guards here prevent any thoughts of using a camera. At the opposite end, just after the old and new roads meet, the other viewing point is close to the holding point and was never guarded, but that was prior to the arrival of the fighters.

B CHINA (People's Republic of China)
BEIJING
BJS   ZBAA   Capital   16m/25km NE

Most of the enthusiasts visiting Beijing (and much of China) still take advantage of the excellent specialist tours. Because organised tours have more likelihood of gaining access to some of the airside areas of Chinese airports, the lone traveller will continue to be exceptional. His log and photo collection will certainly be thinner. There have been several reports from this airport, but few give anything more than a list of aircraft seen.

The old terminal was the original, positioned at the end of a ceremonial way. Beyond its apron lies the new terminal, used by international flights, and served by its own access highway. The splitting of CAAC into regional operations has created more interest, as there are more airline schemes to be seen. In time, Beijing will become as familiar to western enthusiasts as Jakarta or Singapore but, as yet, those who have visited seem reluctant to share their experiences.

GUANGZHOU
CAN   ZGGG   Baiyun   8m/13km SE

China Travel has offices in Hong Kong, where package tours are offered to Guangzhou, still better known as Canton. These comprise return rail travel, two nights' hotel accommodation and a visitor's visa, for about $US50. A more expensive option is to book a day return flight from Hong Kong. One of the problems is that the route between Hong Kong and Guangzhou is popular with tourists and so a flight of less than twenty-five minutes costs rather more than is reasonable. Affordable, nonetheless, but beware of the overbooking, especially if hoping to catch the last evening flight home.

Now China's busiest airport, Guangzhou might have almost as much to offer, in its way, as Kai Tak. Anyone who doubts this fact can study a China Southern fleet list, as this is their base of operations. There are two separate passenger terminals, and the international building is reported to have no viewing facilities. The previously reported open viewing terrace, which gives an uninterrupted view of the ramp, is probably located in the old domestic terminal.

Based aircraft include, apart from China Southern, a few An-2s, though it is unlikely that they can be approached at anything like close quarters. Also to be expected are three or four An-24s, often with the occasional one crew training. Stored on the far side of the field are (were?) three Tridents B-2216/7/9, Il-14 611 and Li-2 324.

GUILIN
KWL ZGKL   7m/11km SE

There are few pictorial images as powerful as the bizarre domed peaks rising over the mist and flat river valley at Guilin. Mists and mountains don't mix easily with landing aircraft: it is a dangerous place, as a few Trident captains could testify, if they had survived to tell the tale.

Spellings are also a problem. Guilin is also Kueilin and the Yangtze River can be anything from the Xiang Jiang to Hsiang Chiang. A tour of southern China would be incomplete without a boat trip on the river, and it is a photographer's dream.

Many of the short trips from Hong Kong, organised by China Travel, involve a two night stay. Arrival by air is sometimes after dark and the Holiday Inn, probably the town's biggest building, is a likely resting place. Some rooms overlook a MiG-15 in what looks like a cabbage patch. After a memorable day on the river, and possibly a second night at the hotel, departure can mean the only chance to sample the airport.

Wandering about, outside the terminal area, for a half hour or so may not be a good idea but there is little to see anyway. There may be another aircraft on the apron, such as a Y7 or a Tu-154, but even this might be asking too much. The departure area offers the chance to see what little there is. However, at the end of the taxiway by the end of the runway are a couple of dozen assorted MiGs. Cameras should be at the ready!

WUHAN
WUH ZHWT   Wangjiaddun   3m/5km

Wuhan is a major city, the capital of Hubei Province. It sits on the Yangtze River, which is now known as the Ch'ang Chiang. Chinese names are something of a problem for the average westerner, and even reference to official documents doesn't clarify the situation. Wangjiaddun is also known as Hsukiapeng and has an extremely interesting range of movements. Quantity is another matter, however. Anyone wishing to witness the action will need to be an early riser, as a good number of Guangzhou Regional An-24s and Yunshuji Y7s depart before 0800.

WUHAN
ZHHH   Nanhu

Nanhou, or Nanhu, is the city's other airport, also quoted as being called Hankou, and there are reports of Air Wuhan/Wuhan Airlines Il-14s operating from here. It is certainly the airline's centre of operations but the airfield is also used as a military base. Visits here are therefore more likely to be by escorted tour parties, rather than the lone traveller trying to 'pole off' a few goodies!

XI'AN
XIY   ZLXY   Xianyang

Xi'an has become a major tourist destination, to be found in some holiday brochures and atlases as Hsian or Sian. To present the right image to the world, the new Xianyang airport has been built. Airline traffic is still modest, though interesting of course. The China Northwest base has a number of Tu-154s and An-24s to be seen.

XI'AN
SIA   ZLXG   Xiguan   2m/3km

The opening of Xianyung meant that all traffic was moved there. All that remains at Xiguan are a pair of old Ilyushins: an Il-14 and an Il-18, both of which could be moved to another location (or broken up) by now.

B CHINA/TAIWAN (Republic of China)
TAIPEI
TPE   RCTP   Chiang Kai Shek International 25m/40km SW (bus 90 min)

Anyone who has visited Washington's Dulles International will see the resemblance with Taipei's main passenger terminal. Given that Taiwan has maintained, with strong political and economic support from the USA, that it is China, a visible link with Washington DC is easy to understand. Taipei is reported to be the world's Number One destination for hi-jacked aircraft - about twenty a year. No prizes for guessing where most of them come from.

Taipei's main airport is, from a spotter's point of view, best described as generally user-hostile. The airport layout is similar to Changi with an approach road between the parallel runways. The terminal and car parks are predictably placed.

The terminal is used for checking-in and inbound passport and customs clearance. It is linked to two ranks of departure lounges, again like Changi, with China Airlines on one side and evryone else on the other. There is nothing else to say. There are no panoramic views from any part of the buildings. Access to a departure lounge, after entering passport control, allows views of two or three stands only. It is possible for departing pasengers to walk the length of the lounges and record what is parked on one side of the apron. It's tedious and it doesn't reveal anything that can't be seen just as well elsewhere around the Pacific.

Visitors to Changi will also recognize the similarity between the location of the Singapore Airlines maintenance base there and China Airlines' version here. Maybe the designs come cheaper by the dozen. Eva Air also have a maintenance base, beside Runway 06/24, inside which is normally housed a Falcon 900, the personal hack of Evergreen International's owner.

Located at the entrance to the terminal complex is the Airport Hotel, where a room costs about US$85 per night. It's good value in this part of the world, and much used by aircraft crews. The food is, quite literally, a matter of taste. Some upper level rooms allow views of one runway.

Close to the hotel is the air museum, open between 9:00am and 5:00pm, mistakenly reported in the last edition as being at Sung Shan. To get there, it's best to take the hotel bus and stroll across the grass. The reward for the effort is rather a lot of propaganda, such as: "the aviation industry was introduced to China in the late Ching Dynasty stemming from the far-sighted policy of Dr Sun Yat Sen in developing the Chinese Air Force." etc etc. Much of the information is in

Chinese so it might not be understood by everyone. A lot of stuff about defectors from Communism and how well they're doing in the Free World. Among the exhibits are C-47 B-126 and fighters such as an F-100, RF-101A and F-104.

The larger exhibits are parked in the open. Immediately to the north, and on the other side of the road, is a line of trees and a fence, beyond which is the taxiway to Runway 05L. Zoom lenses allow good photos from along the fence, especially in the mornings, when the sun can be most helpful. Opposite the museum entrance is the entrance to a six-storey observation tower, which gives an impressive view over the airfield. Photos are a bit of a problem, not made any easier by the dirty glass from which observers are kept at a distance.

TAIPEI
TSA   RCSS   Sung Shan   3m/5km N

Failure to see anything at Chiang Kai Shek might encourage the spotter to try his luck at Sung Shan, the domestic airport located very much downtown. High walls have been built to make things no easier here. Along the northern perimeter, Sun Yat Sen Freeway is hardly the place to walk in the hope of seeing something and the terminal area (departure lounges apart) is no better. Whenever airport buildings offer nothing in the way of windows, the experienced eye scans the area for a suitably elevated observation point. Multi-storey car parks usually offer one.

Sung Shan's car park offers an excellent view but, it must be remembered, the top floor isn't always the best. When the weather is hot, there is no shade, whilst one floor down there is plenty. Security officers expect to see people standing around, if they patrol the roof, so it may be possible to blend into the background with greater ease by staying in the shade. The view of the ramp is as good as anything that most spotters, and indeed photographers, would want.

Mintsu Road, which runs parallel to the freeway, is believed to be one of the best places where aircraft can be seen on final approach. Anyone seeking directions should look for its intersection with Sungchiang Road.

Traffic, to western eyes, is undoubtedly good, offering a mixture of Far Eastern and China Airlines 737s, plus Fokker 100s and BAe 146s. Prop-driven traffic is very much in evidence, including Foshing ATR-42s and Formosa SF340s. Dash 8s and D0228s add extra variety.

Taiwan's other main airport, located at the south of the island, is Kaoshiung International, a few miles down the coast from the town, but no reports have been received.

C CANADA (Dominion of Canada)
ABBOTSFORD BC
YXX   CYXX   8m/13km SW

Not an airport where many scheduled services are operated, but few visitors to the Vancouver and Seattle area would miss the opportunity to have a look. Apart from a moderate amount of general aviation, this airport is entirely dominated by one famous operator: Conair.

Fire-fighting is just as important in heavily-forested Canada as in the western United States, and Conair's headquarters at the airport demonstrates that it treats business seriously. The offices are modern, and the reception area is up the stairs. A request for a look at the aircraft causes few problems, so there is no excuse for walking around without permission.

Depending on the time of year when a visit is made, the number of residents can vary, late summer being when fire risk is greatest, and inmates therefore at their lowest. The A-26s ended their useful life many years ago, and were stored here. The fleet is quite varied, and one or two representatives of each type, ranging from Grumman Firecats to DC-6s, plus the more modern F-27s and CL-215s can be seen.

CALGARY AL

YYC   CYYC   International   7m/11km NE (bus 30 minutes)

Edmonton is the provincial capital but Calgary is the centre of aviation activity, with one of the busiest and most interesting airports in Canada. Anyone spending time watching movements from the terminal will learn that the scheduled traffic is remarkably repetitive, and only a small percentage of the general aviation movements can be identified. For a broader picture, travel southwards, towards the city, but this need not necessitate the use of a hire car, despite the distance. Two hotels, the Port o Call (expensive) and the Airliner (affordable), operate courtesy buses and both are within walking distance of the southern complex.

The Calgary International Airport which most visitors know about is the new, modern terminal, located well to the north of the field. The building is split into two: the northern annex being almost exclusively the preserve of Canadian Airlines and offering no views of the apron. The upper level of the main building is faced with smoked glass and offers a good view between the two main piers, international on the right and domestic on the left. It should be noted that, since the last edition was published, a commuter airlines pier has been added to the north/right end of the passenger terminal.

Any airline traffic which doesn't park within sight of the glazed area of the main building will pass beyond the end of the right hand finger. Since this usually comprises most of the American operators, some of which (like Continental and American Trans Air 727s) can be interesting, it may be worth the walk to the glazed link between the two halves of the building. Photography is possible here but some skill is necessary to judge the critical moment when an incoming aircraft will be just at the right angle as it turns.

Air Services Way, the approach road to the passenger terminal, crosses 78 Avenue, where new facilities have been built. Apart from Hertz and Tilden car hire, Canadian have a maintenance base next to the new cargo area. 21 Street, which crosses 78 Avenue, leads towards the threshold of Runway 28 (used relatively infrequently) and offers a view of the air tanker base. Anyone staying in Calgary for a few days, and wishing to investigate the local aviation scene thoroughly, might want to ring 291 3503 and ask if a visit to the base is possible.

The real action at Calgary is down at the southern end, though there can be more than one runway in use at any one time. Down south, at the 'old' end of the field, there are two centres of activity, at either side of the threshold of Runway 34. MacKnight Boulevard is the main road which links the two aprons, the western of which is shared by the executive customs ramp and Fields. A fairly steady trickle of biz-jets uses the customs ramp before dispersing, either to Fields or, across the runway, to Hudson General. What will be seen at Fields is strictly a matter of luck. They do, however, seem to specialise in DHC aircraft, which can be anything from Buffaloes of the Mexican Navy and the NWC at China Lake, to a couple of CAF Twin Otters. The Amoco HS748 is also based here in the company of a good number of Citations.

The East Hangars comprise a selection of aprons worthy of a visit in their own right. Traffic to be seen here is extremely varied and can feature CAF F-5s and Tutors, and the Mobil Canada fleet (including the Dash Eight). Based here, apart from Federal Express, are a number of operators; Alpine Helicopters have an apron with at least one handsome Bell 212 present, whilst Highland Helicopters usually only have one or two JetRangers on their ramp.

The Kenn Borek hangar is large but can stay firmly closed, with nothing parked outside it. On the apron behind, however, should be at least one North Cariboo aircraft and a good selection of prop-jets and biz-jets, ranging from King Air 200s to the Esso 737. A short access road leads to the closest vantage point for the threshold of Runway 34. With the sun behind in the morning, this is a rewarding location for the photographer, subject to wind direction. In the afternoon, some vacant ground next to the customs ramp also faces the threshold but is probably too far away for good photographs. In the corner of the field, next to this spot, is a small helicopter compound/graveyard containing the wrecks of about twenty JetRangers; not much good to those in search of registrations but quite interesting. The Lancaster, which used to be parked beside

McCall Drive, has now been moved to a museum, close to the helicopter bases.

Calgary is a large, busy airport with a range of vantage points and a commendable variety of traffic. To get the best out of what is there, it will be necessary to spend two or three days moving about between the different parts of the field. It will be a well-travelled enthusiast with extremely bad luck who leaves Calgary without being impressed.

CASTLEGAR BC

YCG   CYCG   Ralph West   3m/5km E

The Crowsnest Highway from town offers a panormaic view of the airport, though it disappears from view as you approach the perimeter. The field is on a plateau between the Columbia River and the mountains. A turn to the right leads to the passenger terminal, where scheduled activity consists of the usual commuters. Continuing past the terminal, the road leads past the general aviation ramp, used also by a few air taxi operators, to the control tower and an air tanker base.

CRANBROOK BC

YXC   CYXC   Kimberley   10m/16km N

Without doubt a scenic part of British Columbia, which is saying something, Cranbrook is a small community right in the heart of the Rockies. Actually, around these parts, they are the Selkirk Mountains. It's only a few miles to the US border, and nearer to Calgary than to Vancouver. The town is served by a commuter airport. Scheduled services are operated, on a like-for-like competitive basis, by Canadian and Air Canada. Activity is minimal but there are air tanker bases, on the right of the approach road.

DAWSON CITY YT

YDA   CYDA   Municpal   11m/18km W

The facilities comprise a gravel strip for the runway and a passenger terminal, plus customs facilities in a cabin, so this is an international airport. The scheduled link is with Alaska, operated by an Air North C-47, whose daily service goes to Fairbanks or Old Crow. The aircraft climbs out, then makes a 300 degree turn as it gains height at the same time as missing the surrounding hills. All interesting stuff! Make the most of it because that's all there is, apart from ten or so light aircraft.

EDMONTON AL

YXD   CYXD   Industrial   3m/5km N

There have been many subjective reports from Edmonton and there is unquestionably a worthwhile range of aircraft to be seen. The terminal is immediately in front of the multi-storey car park and, from the top deck, the whole field is visible as indeed are the high rise offices of the downtown area, not far away. Officially the airport is three miles out of town, but the view from the car park suggests it's rather less. Behind the car park is a hangar and apron, where maintenance is (was?) carried out. The scheduled airline visitors are Dash 7s and 8s, but NWT Air make regular appearances.

General aviation traffic, up to DC-3 size, is quite modest and the urban location of the field is sure to cause restrictions on noisier visitors. It has two runways, 12/30 and 16/34, and a line of hangars and aprons along the far side includes one for the Alberta provincial government and, in the southeast corner, the Hudson General FBO terminal. Below the car park, to the right of the small passenger terminal is a small viewing terrace at ground level, very conveniently placed for some of the biz-jets and small airline visitors, when they do not use Hudson General. For those with the time to circumnavigate the field, there should be something to justify the effort. Best known are Northwest Industries, who carry out maintenance work on CAF aircraft, with one or two T-33s or C-130s present. Also visible from the top of the multi-storey car park are occasional C-130 circuit bashers at the nearby CAF base.

EDMONTON AL
YEG   CYEG   International   21m/33km S (bus 45 minutes)

The few enthusiasts who have ventured the trip out to this airport have found a good roof top viewing deck. However, there is only a modest amount of traffic, and a good proportion of it can be supplied by one international visit from a Northwest 727. Any length of time spent here will seem very heavy going, despite the good facilities. The RAF often use this airport for VC-10s and Hercules movements, usually connected with activity at Cold Lake, to the east.

    A visit to Edmonton could be at the expense of some very good movements at nearby Calgary, which is in a different league for most types of aircraft. If searching for all the airfields in the area, SAINT ALBERT is worth the effort, despite being an airstrip. It usually has a couple of B-25 fire bombers based. Take Primary Highway 2 north from Edmonton, pass through the town, and the strip is about 5km further on, signposted to the left.

FORT SIMPSON NT
YFS   CYFS

The airfield is situated in a forest clearing beside the Mackenzie River, on the south side of the road from town. The apron, beside the single runway, is used for the passenger terminal and an airborne fire-fighting base. As can be expected in this part of the wrold, security measures cost considerably more than the threat represents, so fences only tend to be erected if the moose or bears get too friendly. There is very little to see, apart from the occasional Ptarmigan or Buffalo Airways flight.

GATINEAU PQ
YND   CYND   16m/25km ENE of Hull

The Ottawa River divides the capital city, in Ontario, from Hull in Quebec. The divide is also a cultural one in many ways, as it forms the frontier of the French speaking Canadians. Some miles down river from Hull is a small airport which serves Hull and the scenic Gatineau area.

    As befits an airport in this location, its scheduled air links are mainly with French-speaking Canada, with a few commuter services being operated. The facilities are modern and well laid out, but not over-used. The glass fronted terminal overlooks the ramp, and vantage points at either side reveal alternative views of what few aircraft may be seen here. Since these aircraft are unlikely to be seen anywhere else on the average itinerary, other than considerably further east, it is worth the trip if seeking to fully cover the aviation scene in this part of Canada.

HALIFAX NS
YHZ   CYHZ   International   25m/40km NE (bus 50 minutes)

The return trip from town costs C$18 and the journey is worthwhile, because Halifax is a busy regional airport. The passenger terminal is located in the standard Canadian manner, at the intersection of the two runways, 15/33 and 06/24. It makes life a little difficult for the spotter, and almost impossible for the photographer, though there are alternatives. At the right hand end of the terminal is a limited view but it's worth the walk along the perimeter fence for photos of the movements on the taxiway. The various ramps and hangars used by the smaller operators are reached by walking from the terminal towards the threshold of Runway 06.

Air Canada DC-9s and CAI 737s dominate the arrivals board but regional services mean plenty of Air Atlantic Dash 8s and Air Nova BAe146s. The nearby Shearwater CAF base open house day can combine reasons to visit.

HALIFAX NS

YAW	CYAW	Shearwater CFB	8m/13km SE

Anyone intending to visit the Maritime Provinces might care to plan ahead, for the trip to coincide with the Open House here. The base is near Dartmouth, on the far side of the harbour. Simple headings, such as eight miles east, are misleading. The road from Halifax heads northeast, but the base itself is to the southeast of town.

Once across the bridge in Dartmouth, take a right onto Pleasant Street, Highway 322. The road passes the base entrance. It's mostly used by helicopter units. At any time other than when an airshow is being held, the only sure way to gain access to the base is to write (or possibly phone) beforehand. Even this cannot guarantee success, of course.

HALIFAX NS

YWF		Downtown Heliport

When staying in the Halifax area, it is worth noting the existence of the heliport, even though it is unlikely that anything will arrive there. No matter how remote the chance, a close up view (and photo) of a CAF CH-124, otherwise known as an S-61, should always be borne in mind.

HAMILTON OT

YHM	CYHM	Civic	6m/9km SW

Airline traffic is mostly commuter schedules, a few charter flights and one or two package delivery services. Anyone driving between Toronto and Niagara Falls may consider a detour. The airport is well away from the direct road but the sign-posting is good. With so few scheduled services during the day, the main appeal is probably the Canadian Warbirds Museum, well stocked with a good variety of interesting aircraft. The field is also home for a considerable number of light aircraft.

HAY RIVER NT

YHY	CYHY

This is not a name that many of us recognize, and few would imagine that the airport had two runways. The town is on the southern shore of Great Slave Lake and it has a railroad link as well as being at the end of the Mackenzie Highway. The airport is about a thirty minute walk from the motels, in town, and well worth the effort. Just after the road and railway cross the river, the airport is on the left. The passenger terminal is located in a rather typical Canadian position, facing the main runway.

It is probably the aprons which face the cross runway which of some interest, as they are occupied by the general aviation (half a dozen aircraft), Buffalo Airways and an air tanker base (often empty when aircraft are active elsewhere). Buffalo Airways' centre of operations provides somewhat more permanent consolation for enthusiasts of piston power: The C-47s stored in the open vary from complete to fuselage only.

Airline traffic is sparse, ranging from modern Dash 8s of Canadian to good old C-47s. Anyone with an interest in general aviation will need to investigate the nearby floatplane base, which explains the lack of light aircraft at the airport. Water is in far greater supply, in this part of the world, than runways.

KELOWNA BC
YLW   CYLW   Ellison Field   9m/15km NE

Scheduled commuter operations do include Fokker 100s, as well as the usual Dash 8s, but most visitors will probably be seeking the Kelowna Flightcraft base. A service road runs between, and parallel to, the runway and Highway 97. At the far end of it, from town, are hangars and their resident general aviation, plus several Kelowna CV-580s in storage. The airline's building is at the other end of the road, next to the passenger terminal. Unlike Penticton, this is not the sort of place that will please the family on holiday, as it's located in a rather wide valley and surrounded mostly by farmland.

LONDON OT
YXU   CYXU   7m/11km NE

With the growth of STOLports, London has witnessed significant growth in the last few years. The small passenger terminal has an upper level observation deck, most of which is now closed. A hole, about four feet square, was the observation point in summer 1994!

Anyone staying in Ontario will nevertheless find that London does offer chances to get close to commuter airliners but it requires quick reflexes. The chain link fence at either side of the passenger terminal offers limited views of the ramp. Good photos of aircraft on the move are possible. Getting close to the other aircraft on the field necessitates a car or an awful lot of walking.

MONTREAL PQ
YUL   CYUL   Dorval International   14m/22km W

Montreal's two airports share the traffic on the basis that the smart modern Mirabel handles transatlantic flights while domestic, and some US, schedules use Dorval. The passenger terminal is not new by any standards but it is light and pleasant, with a glass front overlooking most of the apron. There is an extensive observation deck along the front, but this has been closed for many years, and is now falling into disrepair.

To accommodate the extra stands needed by a busy airport, a tunnel gives access to the satellite of departure lounges on the far side of the ramp. This is only accessible to passengers who present boarding cards. It is wise to delay passing through passpost control, if travelling to the USA, because the viewing facilities are not the best. Without recourse to exploration, nearly all the activity can be satisfactorily monitored from the seats in the main hall. A good proportion of the airliners taxi by on their way in or out. The installation of air jetties has made life more difficult and it can need skill to get an acceptable photograph of Air Canada 767s, which congregate at the right hand end of the terminal, out of sight.

On leaving the main terminal, a right turn leads to the maintenance area, where a variety of aircraft normally includes one or two of the Transport Canada fleet. Next to this apron are the cargo sheds and the Province of Quebec CL-215 facility. These are seen at close quarters from the cargo area, as is the Innotech ramp, where new Challengers are fitted out prior to delivery. A short drive round to this apron may result in the sight of a new aircraft rolled out of the hangar, in pristine condition; close scrutiny may be possible.

Backtracking to the Cote de Liesse, the main highway to Montreal, there are several roads which lead to a variety of aprons and facilities on the southern perimeter. It is extremely difficult to negotiate the turn to this area from the eastbound carriageway, so a visit on the way from the city would make life easier. There are two separate sections to the southern complex, reached respectively by 43rd and 55th Streets. The former reveals a quantity of operators and types, ranging from cargo and courier airlines to plenty of executive aircraft, with general aviation in quantity to swell the numbers.

Each apron has its own office/hangar and all can be seen at close quarters without needing access to the other side of the fence. At the northern end of 55th Street is a car park for employees, often frequented by local watchers, and the end of Jenkins Avenue has been a traditional place where traffic landing on Runway 28 or using 06R/24L can be watched.

Nearby CARTIERVILLE, once a major general aviation airfield, is now to all intents and purposes closed.

MONTREAL PQ

| YUL | CYUL | Mirabel International | 33m/51km NW |

Over thirty miles north of Montreal and this on a toll motorway, Mirabel allows plenty of time en route to savour the delights of a day's spotting before providing its great disappointment. Depressing, too, is the prospect of having to pay to drive back to Montreal with the camera unused. Those using only binoculars and logbooks can sit on the upper level of the terminal in the afternoon and watch a good range of wide-bodies arrive from Europe.

The facilities are modern and cater for passengers only, even the lounge area being nowhere near the glass overlooking the large apron. Apart from the Cubana Tu-154s, daylight hours don't offer anything which can't be seen easier elsewhere in North America.

MONTREAL PQ

| YHU | CYHU | Saint Hubert | 12m/19km S |

Also in the Montreal area and worthy of a short detour is St Hubert, close to the main highway link with New York State. St Hubert is a large airfield used by the Canadian Armed Forces, though the resident fighters left long ago. What remains is army activity, supported by the Caribous and Otters, with occasional weekend visitors of a more spectacular nature. Also to be seen are the Helicraft base, on the perimeter, and a good selection of the Canadian general aviation scene, on the south side.

For anyone who feels the need to log as many registrations as possible in the Montreal area, St Hubert is worth the trip. An interest in airliners is not repaid here nor, it has to be said, is the need to see something out of the ordinary. It is, of course, comments such as these which draw howls of protest from people who swear that the sight of a Jinsen PJ-2600 is special.

NANAIMO BC

| YCD | CYCD | Cassidy | 10m/16km S |

When crossing by ferry to Vancouver Island, Nanaimo is the normal port of entry. On the way south, towards Victoria, is the community of Cassidy and at the eastern side of the road nearby is a small airport. Hardly likely to be the high spot of any trip to Canada, it does offer a chance of a portrait photograph of aircraft up to SD3.60 size, operating a regular shuttle to Vancouver.

NANAIMO BC
ZNA   Harbour   1m/1.5km E

In such a small port, it is difficult to miss the harbour, and the regular drone of (mostly Beaver) floatplanes. Scheduled services are operated by Baxter Aviation Beavers. Daytime activity doesn't reach fever pitch, but it makes an interesting change to witness one of these movements. Anyone heading north from Nanaimo (to Comox for example) would be well advised to seek out Sproat Lake, near PORT ALBERNI, where Forest Industries Flying Tankers still operate a pair of Martin Mars flying boats.

OSHAWA OT
YOO   4m/6km NW

Thirty miles or so east of Toronto, Oshawa airport is only a small diversion if motoring from Ottawa or Montreal. It is a pleasant airport to visit, especially at weekends, when activity is minimal. Since the local airline is primarily a commuter operation, it doesn't fly much at weekends, so its aircraft can be seen at leisure. An L-shaped ramp has most of the general aviation on one side and Skycraft on the other. Skycraft's fleet includes a few small twins as well as Bandeirantes. The ramp is open to all sensible folk, and the airliners to be seen undergoing servicing mingle with some other interesting types, including a Pembroke.

OTTAWA OT
YRO   Rockcliffe   6m/9km NE (bus 55 minutes)

This is a small general aviation field but few enthusiasts would visit Ottawa and not call here. The field is shared by the general aviation community, the armed forces (who don't normally fly from here) and the National Aeronautical Collection museum. Leaving Ottawa city centre north, Wellington and Rideau Streets ultimately become Montreal Road. A left turn at St. Laurent Boulevard leads to the airfield.

The museum is housed in a splendid new pyramid building, instead of the old hangars on the southern edge of the field. Some of the inmates are rotated occasionally, to the science or war museums, both in the city. The larger exhibits are stored externally, including the Trans Canada Airlines Viscount.

A drive round the field, past the forces base, leads to the general aviation. There is surprisingly little action, especially during the week, and a stroll around the inmates is possible. Apart from a variety of home-produced hardware, there are floatplanes to be seen and a walk down the ramp to the Ottawa River may reveal more, tied up.

For anyone relying on public transportation, Rockcliffe needs a little time and patience. The No95 bus operates from Ottawa to Blair, with a change to the No198 for Rockcliffe. The journey takes about an hour.

OTTAWA OT
YOW CYOW   Macdonald-Cartier International   11m/17km SSE

Canada's capital city doesn't generate the quantity of traffic that may be expected and is beaten by many other cities in the country for the number of flights and passengers. Movements are dominated by Air Canada and Canadian Airlines, but other operators include First Air, Voyageur and Air Ontario, all of whom have some interesting aircraft. The many recent renovations have, effectively, created a much improved Macdonald-Cartier airport compared with the enthusiast-unfriendly Uplands. There is now a glazed observation area in the centre of the passenger terminal, offering views of all airport movements by being opposite the intersection of the two main runways.

Transport Canada has a significant fleet of aircraft based at Ottawa, ranging from Viscounts and JetStars to King Airs and Dakotas, all in perfect condition, and the Canadian Armed Forces base, immediately to the north of the terminal, offers additional interest. The Transport Canada hangar is only one part of the facilities which are now line the north side of the taxiway to Runway 25. Next to it are two FBO's: Shell and Esso Avitat. First Air's hangar, at the far/eastern end, is reached from Thad Johnson Road, outside the terminal complex. To reach it, take the exit road (Airport Parkway) and pass under the taxiway before leaving at the first intersection, Alert Road. This can offer a golden opportunity to see at close quarters their 727s, showing off their rainbow livery. There are views from Alert Road of the hold for Runway 25 and, by passing the end of the runway, of traffic on the runway, though a long lens is needed for photographs.

Anyone arriving by way of the Parkway could leave without ever knowing that there is another self-contained airfield at the northern end, beyond the CAF facilities. Riverside Drive in Ottawa leads to a separate and self-contained airfield, complete with its own runways, accessible from Hunt Club Road. The facilities at the northern end are excellent and a good number of light aircraft are based here. Also to be seen are the Department of Mining and Resources aircraft and one or two old DC-3s and Cansos.

Ottawa's appeal is broad, with something to please everyone; old, rare types rub shoulders with a good selection of airliners, and CAF operations include Cosmopolitans, Falcons and Buffaloes with some regularity, plus the occasional Chinook and T-33. With the right runways in use, half a day spent in the either the terminal or Employee Parking Lot 3 can produce a delightful variety, though the pace can be unhurried. From this external vantage point the parked Delta Connection/Business Express Saab 340s can be seen and, on certain afternoons, Martinair's 767 is fully visible on its stand. Whether or not this service continues to operate for the life of this book can't, of course, be guaranteed.

PENTICTON BC

YYF	CYYF	Municipal	4m/7km S

Most parts of British Columbia are scenic but Penticton is better than most. It is a resort in its own right, so motels are plentiful. The Skytel is one of the cheaper examples, with the bonus of overlooking the runway threshold. Aircraft noise is, however, rarely a problem! The town nestles in the beautiful Okanagan Mountains, with the lake and National Park to the north and Skaha Lake at the southern end of the runway.

Scheduled traffic comprises mostly Dash 8s and Jetstreams but there are other movements to be seen, including fire bombers and air tankers. A holiday stay of a few days will allow the family to enjoy Canada at its prettiest (which is saying something) including a day on the beach. This is to be recommended, as the beach is actually at the end of the runway, and just across the road from the Skytel. A canalside footpath runs parallel to the runway, offering photographers the chance of different mountain backdrop. Whichever way the camera points, east or west, there's no getting away from the mountains!

PETERBOROUGH OT

YPQ	CYPQ		1m/1.5km N

The name of Air Atonabee, who were based in Peterborough, is now the only link with its historic past. That airline, which became City Express, is now long gone. When travelling by car from Montreal or Ottawa to Toronto, it may be worth the detour as the airport is easily reached from Highway 401, and does contain a reasonable selection of general aviation residents.

QUEBEC CITY PQ
YQB   CYQB   Aeroport de Quebec   9m/15km W

The modern terminal is light and airy, with the domestic apron laid out in front of the windows. Most of the traffic is feeder-liners, though one or two Air Canada jets do appear. A need to see jet traffic means travelling west to Montreal. A modest amount of international traffic is supplied, predictably, from the United States. This can be seen to the left. Air Alliance (it helps to say Air Al-yonce) has a maintenance base, and their hangar usually has something inside.

Next to the approach road, at the threshold of the cross runway, is a generous general aviation ramp, with a reasonably good selection of residents, all seen with ease. It is always tempting to say that Quebec is good for logging, but lumberjacks normally do that!

A quarter of a mile from the main terminal is the Quebec Province Government fleet of CL-215s. There is a lot, most of them parked outside, together with the odd PBY and Conifair DC-4 or DC-6.

RED DEER AL
YQF   CYQF   Industrial

The relatively large passenger terminal invites optimism but there is next to nothing, in terms of scheduled airline activity, to be seen most of the day. This airport could, however, be an essential stop for propliner fans. The airfield is at the edge of a military area, and it stages an annual air show, of sorts. Beside the runway are aprons and hangars used by Buffalo Airways and Air Spray, either or both of which can contain something of interest. Apart from that, there are only a few twin-engined aircraft among the general aviation residents. When travelling by road, the field is off Primary Highway 2A, about half way between Red Deer and Penhold.

REGINA SA
YQR   CYQR   Municipal   3m/5km SW

Like many cities miles away from anywhere else in Canada, Regina is a regional aviation centre and thus somewhat self-supporting, but its scheduled links with the rest of the country are not very exciting. The terminal is red brick with glass brick panels to let in the light. Unfortunately, it doesn't allow views of the main apron. However, the occupants of this ramp are unlikely to be of particular interest, and some of the regional cargo operators can be seen from the fence, just to the right of the terminal. To the left is the general aviation visitors' terminal and ramp but it only handles a few light aircraft from across the border.

In front of the terminal is the only runway, 12/30 and, at right angles to it, and to the right of the cargo terminal, are the general aprons, hangars and quite a lot of aircraft. Anyone spending more than a day here will be in serious pursuit of a quantity of Canadian registrations, rather than interesting types which can be seen easier elsewhere.

About forty miles west of Regina is MOOSE JAW, where the Canadian Armed Forces 2CFFTS is located. Since this is a major training base, a visit on a summer weekday should reveal a lot of CT-114 Tutors.

ROCKY MOUNTAIN HOUSE AL
YRM   CYRM   80m/130km W of Red Deer

Anyone travelling across Canada in search of air tankers might care to make a telephone call before driving all the way to Rocky Mountain House, as the journey can be wasted at certain times in the season. Only when the fire risk increases are aircraft certain to be posted here, sometimes up to four A-26s. Their base is at the end of the runway, some distance away from the general aviation. You have to be dedicated to make the trip. It's about 130 kilometres west of Red Deer, along Highway 11. Having driven through town (blink and you'll miss it), head towards Nordegg. A turn to the north, onto a parallel road, leads to a signpost and a right turn. After about 5 km, make a left turn.

SAINT JEAN PQ
YJN   CYJN   2m/3km SW

Highway 10 is called the Autoroute des Cantons de l'Est, and heads out of Montreal across the St Lawrence River at Champlain Bridge. It links up with Interstate 91 in Upper New York State. Once over the river, St Hubert is to the north and, a few miles further, St Jean is to the south. Turn south off Exit 9 and the road is signposted to the town. It is better to leave at St Luc and by-pass the towns. The airfield is at the side of this road.

St Jean is quieter than St Hubert but it was famous for being an almost permanent residence for the Constellations of Conifair. Still to be seen are a few C-54s and Forestry Commission Cansos but visits should be made during normal working hours to ensure that hangars are not locked up, as their contents can yield some more interesting residents.

SASKATOON SA
YXE   CYXE   5m/8km NW

Certainly more interesting than Regina, this was the base of Norcanair, with its fleet of sky blue aircraft, ranging from King Airs (used for airline operations) to CV-580s and an F.28. That was long agao, and there have been many changes to the airline scene since those far-off days. There is therefore now less to make Saskatoon unique, apart from some Athabaska Airways and West Wind King Air operations.

There are two runways, 14/32 and 08/26, and the terminal is near the intersection, facing 14/32. Whilst the building has a considerable amount of glass facing the apron, only passengers get to see the view, so no photos can be taken from the building. Like Regina, the general aviation terminal is to the left and normally has one or two small American visitors present.

Facing 08/26, and quite a walk from the terminal, are the main hangars and aprons. Anyone intent on walking here from the passenger terminal is advised to keep to the road, rather than attempt a short-cut across the grass. Since there is often a NWTAir aircraft parked by this fence, it is often tempting to head across the grass but the whole area is fenced off at its perimeter and the only way from one side of the fence into a different area is to crawl under it.

A considerable variety of aircraft can be seen in the hangar complex, including the provincial government fleet and one or two King Airs. A T-33 has been mounted on a pole at the entrance. A leisurely stroll around the ramps should be rewarded by plenty of interesting aircraft, most of which can be viewed at close quarters.

TORONTO OT
YYZ   CYYZ   Lester B Pearson International   18m/29km WNW

The multi-storey car park towering above the oldest of the main buildings, Terminal One, is still the best place for a view of the airline ramps, and remains accessible to all despite generally increased security precautions at Toronto. It should not be assumed that the top storey is the best, especially in winter, when it might not be accessible to cars. Try instead levels 8 or 9 for a slightly lower view of the aircraft, certainly better for photography. The rooftop is now occupied partly by Transport Canada's ground movement control tower.

Security has become tighter than previously but this doesn't mean that the authorities are heavy-handed. The patrolling officers know that spotters and photographers make much use of the car park and, as long as common sense prevails, nothing should spoil the fun. It is now widely accepted that, at an international airport, security is a modern requirement so the patrols are for everyone's protection.

Speculation about Toronto's new facilities included whether or not Terminal 3 would improve the lot of the enthusiast. To quote one publication on the subject, passengers who arrive at Terminal 3 really make a debut. Coming in at roof-top level of the glassed-in transfer corridor, they can survey airport activity and the surrounding landscape in full daylight . . . on the way to customs and immigration.

Thus, departing passengers and others can expect business as usual! This, at Toronto, means disappointment, as none of the passenger terminals offer any views at all to the general public, with all airside windows being monopolised by those awaiting embarkation.

There can be no doubt that Toronto now ranks highly, compared with other international airports, as the quantity and variety of movements continues to grow. Canadian Airlines International occupy half of the new terminal. Additional operators like PIA, Thai, Aerolineas Argentinas and Korean with 747s, Finnair with DC-10s and SAS with 767s, ensure there is no shortage of interest. Cubana Tu-154s, Varig 767s and Cargo Jumbos provide a supplement to the already significant string of European arrivals, and Aeroflot operate summer charters.

It should also be borne in mind that Toronto handles a large amount of domestic traffic: Air Ontario Dash 8s and Jetall Metros are still to be seen but commuter operators do seem to come and go with surprising rapidity. Names which are taken for granted one year are frequently replaced by others, suggesting that operating profits are, at the best, low.

To handle the increase in traffic, particularly commuter carriers, Terminal 2 has a new pier which screens much of the apron from the link road to the south side. This road continues past the threshold of Runway 24L and is popular with local watchers. The Worldways hangar, on the south side, appears unoccupied and, next to it, what was the Wardair facility, now sports Canadian Airlines titles. Both can be reached via Convair Drive.

To the north, the picture is just as interesting and lively. On the way along Airport Road to Derry Road and the general aviation area, it is worth making a turn at Orlando, where the road passes very close to Air Canada's maintenance ramp: Air Jamaica 727s can be seen doing engine runs right next to the road. Just to the west of Air Canada's hangar is Cargo Corner, used mostly by parcel carriers.

For executive aircraft enthusiasts who still wish to keep an eye on the airline traffic, the East Service Road in the general aviation area is extremely popular, being close to the thresholds of 24R, 15 and 10. The parking area/waste ground opposite the Met Office is close to the taxiway used by bizjets and, with luck, the occasional propliner on the move.

A small aircraft, the size of a Citation, would need a 200mm lens, so airliners are well within reach. Afternoons and summer evenings offer the best lighting conditions, due to the southerly aspect. For those in search of cargo operators in action, some disappointment awaits, as they tend to move mostly at night, along with the other numerous courier-related aircraft which now fly from Toronto, so action shots are less likely than static ones, taken through the fence.

The car parks servicing the McDonnell-Douglas plant still offer a good vantage point for landing shots, and it is either here or by the Met Office that Toronto's small, but growing, enthusiast population can usually be found. Security personnel are keen to deter use of the McDonnell-Douglas car park, however. The general aviation area, off Derry Road, is now totally fenced in and, for the most part, generally inaccessible. The occasional friendly security guard has been known to allow entry to Skycharter and Hudson General (previously Innotech) hangars.

Fields' apron is always that most likely to contain an interesting visitor. Apart from the part of the apron visible from the approach road, a service road leads round the hangar, revealing the rest, and other aircraft parked on it. The staff at Fields have earned a reputation for being hostile to the enthusiast. They actively pursue camera-carrying enthusiasts who show an interest in aircraft. A request for a look round is definitely a waste of breath!

With the increase in traffic at Pearson, the use of runways has started to follow the American model: aircraft can often be seen on approach to both parallel runways at the same time. Thus, unlike Heathrow, there are no designated runways for arrivals and departures. To relieve pressure on slots, a new runway is currently under construction, parallel to the existing 15/33.

Propliner fans associated YYZ for many years with Millardair. Carl Millard's fleet of immaculate (mostly) C-117Ds and C-54s was accessible and extremely photogenic. Times changed but, it seems, Millardair didn't. Magazines will no doubt update the ongoing situation but the aircraft were last reported to be stored at Toronto, awaiting buyers.

TORONTO OT
YTZ   CYTZ   Island   1m/1.5km SW

The emergence of STOLports owes much to de Havilland Canada and their range of commuter-liners built for this purpose. Toronto Island was a notable front runner among this new generation of airports, its traffic dominated by the colourful City Express. With the introduction of Dash 7s and 8s in their chic paint schemes, the image of flying into Toronto Island took a leap forward, the job being done now by Air Ontario Dash 8s. The terminal facilities, however, still need a matching facelift. City officials approved the construction of a new control tower but they are still squabbling over proposals for a suitable passenger terminal.

A little ferry called Maple City crosses the narrow channel, on what is reputed to be the world's shortest ferry ride, to the airport, which has no shortage of runways or hangars. Fortunately, this is still an informal place where a request at the control office, to the left of the terminal, should result in access to the hangars being gained.

The CN Tower dominates the backdrop and can be fitted somehow into a souvenir photograph, while the view from the top gives a very good idea of the airport's layout and the considerable number of its residents. Ontario Place, also on the lakeshore in downtown Toronto, hosts major exhibitions in summer. Kiowas and Tutors have been noted and, not to be missed close by, there is a Lancaster permanently mounted on a pole.

TORONTO OT
YZD   CYZD   Downsview   8m/13km N

Downsview may not handle scheduled traffic, nor have many residents but it is nevertheless worth a visit. This is the home of Boeing Canada's DHC-7 and DHC-8 production plant, where a vast field is shared with a small CAF base. Reached from Exit 50A off the Macdonald-Cartier Freeway (Hwy 401), Dufferin Street crosses Wilson Avenue and leads to the employee car parks at the edge of the ramps. There is normally very little activity to watch here but there should always be one or two aircraft which have been rolled out of the paintshops, awaiting delivery to some exotic customer.

TORONTO OT
YKZ   CYKZ   Buttonville   20m/32km NE

West of Downsview on the MCF/401, Exit 56/Woodbine Road (Hwy 8) leads north to Markham. For anyone travelling to Buttonville from downtown Toronto, it should be borne in mind that Woodbine is the continuation of the Don Valley Parkway.

Buttonville is a busy field with a smart little terminal and a nice aviator's book store. There are several operators, especially those with helicopters, so interesting photos are always possible.

TRENTON OT
YTR   CYTR   3m/5km

Not to be confused with its more famous namesake in New Jersey, this is a major base of the Canadian Armed Forces. The quantity of personnel generate some demand for civilian air transport, and Voyageur Airways provide links with Kingston and Toronto, with King Air 100s. The short detour off the highway would not be worthwhile for most, except for the presence of the CAF transports also to be seen. Since these include Buffaloes as well as the more common Hercules, and their ramp is next to an accessible road, it may be considered as a stop, even for those in a hurry, between Montreal or Ottawa and Toronto. Airline activity, such as it is, is largely curtailed at weekends, which applies also to military business. A visit during the week is therefore more likely to yield results.

VANCOUVER BC
YVR   CYVR   International   9m/15km SW (bus 30 minutes)

Sea Island is shared by the airport and the small, quiet community of Burkeville, with two arms of the Fraser River to the north and south and, to the west, the great expanse of Georgia Strait. The southern half of the island is occupied by the airfield, and Runway 08/26, extending west into the bay, splits the field in two, with the main passenger terminal and cargo to the north and the general aviation and marine terminals to the south.

The diagonal Runway 12/30 is remote from all accessible parts, a shame since it handles a lot of traffic, even when 26 is in use. The busy main terminal is centrally located, reached by a long highway with only the CAI maintenance hangar on the right/north. A new runway is now being constructed on the north side, and will be completed about the same time in 1996 as the new international terminal. This means that the situation will alter significantly during the life of this book.

A service road to the south gives access to rather more facilities but vantage points aren't numerous. There is usually an NWT Cargo aircraft present until about 5:00pm every day when, like the Federal Express 727, it leaves with its parcels. Next to the cargo terminal is the Air Canada maintenance hangar, where the occasional foreign military visitor parks. Some open land next to the apron means that photography is possible but the fence interferes with these close-ups unless viewed from a higher level like, say, the roof of a car.

The emergency access point here gives one view of the many biz-jets lined up in front of Hudson General on the opposite side of the runway. By continuing down the access road to the traffic lights and turning right (a right turn on red is permitted in Canada) Russ Barker Way leads to the end of the runway, and another right turn, posted to Burkeville, reveals the holding point and a different view of Hudson General's apron. This long hangar is also used by Transport Canada, and a proportion of their fleet is towed out in the morning; this is the best place to identify them. For anyone who enjoys watching and logging, this large expanse of grass offers an ideal location, as many aircraft land on Runway 26. The holding point is too far away for photos, however. Airport Road South offers no views of the Hudson General ramp but other large aprons are close at hand, on the other side of the road. Continuing down Russ Barker Way, a series of large aprons offers prospect after prospect of all sorts of aircraft: an Air Canada Viscount still with its engines, most of a CF-100 Canuck and a Sea-Bee in British Airways colours have been (and maybe still are) some of the more memorable. To the left is the river and the marine terminal with several Twin Otters, Beavers and Cessnas tied up at the water's edge.

Sunny days are not particularly welcome at this point, as it faces south and the photographer will have to be up early in the morning and return in the evening to get acceptable shots. A light overcast sky is much to be preferred. Beyond the seaplane base are the Air BC apron and the

Executive Air Craft terminal. There is also a short track which leads to the edge of the South Terminal apron. Air BC's fleet is a busy one, so few aircraft spend much time at the base during the day. Watching the South Terminal apron requires patience if the fine selection of Islanders, Navajos, Aztecs and even Apaches in airline service are sought after. Biz-jets are plentiful at Executive Air Craft and it is one of the few places where the Victoria-based British Columbia government fleet can be seen regularly at close quarters.

Anyone relying on public transport in Vancouver can visit all parts of the airport: a shuttle bus operates a link between this area and the main terminal.

After the bustle of the south side, the main terminal can seem tame. Three fingers project like an incomplete 'X' and security procedures include checking boarding cards. Thus the best of the visiting airliners stay out of reach. The incompleteness of the 'X' does at least allow ground level views of the north apron. Traffic here includes the Air BC Jetstreams, Dash 8s and BAe 146s, plus a good selection of US airlines some of which can be too close for photographs. The nearby staff car park looks promising but usually a quantity of freight containers obstructs the view. Inside the terminal, the glazed front overlooks a wide expanse of ramp but, if a wide body parks close in, it completely obscures the view. Visitors to Vancouver will also have to travel to other airports in Canada if they are to get vaguely close to some of the traffic seen here: Victoria can be particularly good.

The overall verdict for Vancouver is mixed: for wide-bodies, 737s and the like, there are many better places to go but, for those in pursuit of local carriers and a different selection of executive traffic, it has few equals. Under these circumstances, it is difficult to make an objective assessment. In an area where scenery and aircraft abound, remembering that Seattle is not far away, Vancouver is a superb destination.

VANCOUVER BC

CXH	Harbor Heliport	1m/1.5km W

Anyone visiting this picturesque city will almost certainly see Stanley Park which projects into Burrard Inlet. From here, the distant movements of Helijet Airways S-76s can be seen. The base is believed to be on the site of the old Cold Harbour seaplane base, one and a half blocks east of the Bayshore Inn. Anyone trying to get there by public transport will be seeking the Seabus terminal.

Other fields which may be of interest to anyone staying in the area for a while: DELTA AIR PARK is south of Ladner Trunk Road, on the north side of Mud Bay. Further east, on the north side of the Fraser River, is PITT MEADOWS, another field used by general aviation.

VANCOUVER BC

YDT	Boundary Bay	14m/22km S

Delta Air Park is a very small field overlooking Boundary Bay. To the west of it, along Ladner Trunk Road, is this larger airfield. Roads give access to the north and west sides, from which it is possible to see a good number of the residents and movements, most of which are light singles.

VICTORIA BC

YYJ	CYYJ	International	17m/27km NE

It's difficult to visualise Victoria as the capital of British Columbia, since it is totally overshadowed by Vancouver on the mainland. It can also be difficult to find the airport as it's almost in Sidney, rather than anywhere near Victoria. Patricia Bay Highway (17) passes close and a turning leads to the passenger terminal. To its left is a customs/baggage reclaim area, and a fence next to this keeps the apron safe from intruders but allows decent views of all visiting aircraft. Air BC Dash 8s and Jetstreams, the odd Canadian Airlines 737 and a selection of commuter carriers can all be seen at quite close quarters from this corner. From here, the threshold of Runway 02, often used, is within reach of a 200mm lens. Continuing past the entrance to the main terminal, a dirt road leads to Butler Aviation but only for a handful of light aircraft.

From Highway 17, by following signs to the industrial area, the general aviation side of the field is reached, with fifty or so light aircraft, plus hangars for Flying Firemen and the British Columbia government. It is difficult to see the BC Government fleet well, even when they are out of the hangar, but permission for a closer inspection may be sought at the tower. The registrations of these official aircraft are placed very tastefully in the cheatline, so they are difficult to read. Note that the last letter is shown on the fin.

Because of the enormous amount of flights between Victoria and Vancouver, this airport offers a real chance for the photographer to obtain first class pictures of many smaller aircraft which remain out of reach at the larger airport.

VICTORIA BC
YWH   Inner Harbour   1m/1.5km SE

The city centre is perhaps a little quaint, especially to British eyes. It is a caricature of Britain, aimed at tourists from Seattle who arrive on the ferries. The grey stone buildings are, in the main, handsome as they surround the harbour, and close to the centre of things is the small jetty where the seaplanes operated. Helijet S-76s, rather than Twin Otters, are the modern mode of transport. What a shame!

Victoria is a ferry terminal, and anyone travelling to Seattle will find that check-in can be very early indeed. If this necessitates an overnight stay, it is wise to shop around for hotel rooms, which can be ridiculously expensive downtown. Bed and breakfast accommodation, in private houses, sounds like a suitable alternative but not everyone likes getting up at 4:00am to cook breakfast for departing guests.

WHITEHORSE YT
YXY   CYXY   3m/5km E

Yukon Territory is not the sort of place one calls into, while passing. Whitehorse is a reasonably pleasant drive north from Skagway, in Alaska. Both take a lot of getting to! The Alaska Highway follows the Yukon River valley, and passes the airport, just after the turn into town and the C-47 weather vane. The field, on a plateau overlooking the town and the river, boasts no less than three runways.

Not much happens here. From the short approach road, the passenger terminal is directly in front, beyond the car park. To the right is the transport museum and to the left, Canadian's cargo shed. The museum mostly tells the story of how the highway and the oil pipeline were built. The car park is level with the terminal's upper floor, so it leads directly into the check-in area. Passengers then descend the stairs to the ramp. The main apron is likely to contain little or nothing of significant interest most of the day. Three Canadian flights are operated daily to Vancouver, there is an occasional Ptarmigan service to Yellowknife, and one or two Air North movements. Exploration of the rest of the field is therefore normal. Passing the cargo shed, the service road leads to a smoke jumper's base, where something might be parked. From their car park, the runway and main apron can be seen through the fence, but movements require a 300 mm zoom lens.

Unless there is something to be seen at the terminal, it is necessary to return to the highway and take the next exit, which leads around the threshold of the diagonal runway, to Air North, a tanker base and the air taxi ramp. The pace of life is normally slow enough for ramp tours to be possible. Normally, this should include an intimate relationship with at least one A-26. A car park next to Air North's base offers a view of the runway thresholds, but through a fence.

Lodging is affordable and tolerable: the Roadhouse Inn, for example, charges something like C$45 for a room but there are others to choose from. For a complete picture of Whitehorse aviation, the next turning off the Highway, South Access Road leads down to the town. Watch out for a right turn before reaching the river. This is Miles Canyon Road, which leads to the floatplane base on the edge of where the river widens enough to be called Schwatka Lake.

WINDSOR OT
YQG   CYQG   6m/9km NE

This is Canada's version of Detroit, with a car plant of its own and all the charm that goes with it. The airport is worth the small detour from the road between Toronto and Detroit, if only to get quite close to visiting Canadian Airlines 737s, Air Canada DC-9s and a growing selection of commuter operators. The terminal is not one of the finest in Canada but the car park to the right is close enough to the ramp for anyone standing on a car roof to be able to do some useful work with a camera. Anyone calling in after 3:00pm should be rewarded with one or two movements but a protracted stay isn't likely. The general aviation hangars and aprons don't often contain much excitement but odd rarities pass through with some regularity.

WINNIPEG MN
YWG   CYWG   International   4m/6km W

It is a long time since Detroit's Willow Run lived up to its reputation and yet here is a pleasant, reasonably busy, airport with active DC-3s and C-46s, small interesting operators, a military base to share the runway, and a superb museum. Usually, in these cases, there is a catch but Winnipeg's only shortcoming is the fact that the observation deck is closed, thereby rendering airline operations from the terminal out of sight. In fact, these movements amount to CAI 737s and a lot of Air Canada aircraft, all by far the least interesting of what can be seen here.

A car isn't essential to get around Winnipeg but it does save a lot of time. The general aviation and local operators' ramps are quite close to the main terminal but it is a circuitous route to get there, especially when short cuts have a habit of turning out to be dead ends. Ellice Avenue (not Sargeant) leads to the aprons and a right turn at Ferry Road reveals a delightful assortment of aircraft: the Hudson Bay Fur Trading Company, known in Canada as 'The Bay' (essentially a large chain of department stores) has a hangar where their aircraft are based. Next door neighbours are Canada's Department of Transport with King Airs, a Beaver and a DC-3, next to which are two buildings used by Perimeter for their Beechcrafts and Metros.

At the end of the road is the Aero Centre, a general aviation terminal where a number of visitors should be seen, and a left turn leads to the museum entrance and its car park. The view from here is tantalising, with C-46s and DC-3s and, across on the far side of the runway, the CAF base and ramp.

For those on foot, the rest is extremely frustrating, as all the aircraft seem so close but it takes time to get around to where they are. Early risers will find that a lot of the more interesting residents will all be leaving at the same time and it can be hard to decide where to go first. The museum's apron is shared by other operators and all of them are of interest to any enthusiast. The CL-215s normally spend more time on the apron than anywhere else and they sit side by side with Perimeter's fleet of ageing Barons and Queen Airs.

Perhaps the most spectacular airline here is Air Manitoba. Their corner of the field features Curtiss Commandos and HS748s plus one or two smaller types, an engineless ex-Air Canada Viscount and, nestling in the long grass, the surprisingly complete remains of a few Bristol

Bolingbrokes. These hulks are only a stone's throw from their birth-place, as the Bristol Aircraft Company built countless examples of these machines here during the war. Manitoba is littered with them!

The CAF base is active and training sorties are carried out in a variety of machinery. No recent reports have been received but regular visitors are known to include Canadair Tutors, T-33s, C-130s and the all-yellow Beech Debonairs. Together with a CC-137 visiting every afternoon and the odd Cosmopolitan and RAF Hercules or VC-10, there is plenty to delight the enthusiast.

The Western Canada Aviation Museum is actually quite famous in North America but it hasn't really attracted European interest. This is a shame, since the volunteers have done an incredible job with their relics, and the CF-101, Viscount and Bristol Freighter are in pristine condition. The WCAM justly claims to be one of Canada's largest and most complete aviation museums - a close and tangible link with their flying history. For a modest entrance fee, most visitors will find the boast to be well-founded but the closing time of 4:00pm must be borne in mind when planning a visit.

Anyone in search of photographs of airline movements will probably be much better rewarded elsewhere in Canada but a drive north and a left turn along Notre Dame Avenue leads to a viewing point, good in the mornings when Runway 18 is in use, but photographers will get closer by heading a little further north. The road and runway converge and the holding point is opposite Logan Avenue, where the aircraft are within range of most cameras.

For those staying in the area, about fifty miles west of Winnipeg is PORTAGE LA PRAIRIE, home of CAF's 3CFFTS base and its CT-134 Musketeers. It does receive a good range of military visitors from elsewhere in Canada.

YELLOWKNIFE NT
YZF   CYZF

The passenger terminal occupies its traditional Canadian spot, facing the intersection of the two runways, 09/27 and 15/33. Whilst the main ramp faces Runway 15, interest focuses very much along the northern side of Runway 27, for this is where the maintenance hangars are to be found.

The prime attraction of Yellowknife is its large, and thriving, population of propliners. Buffalo Airways' DC-3s, DC-4s and C-46s are maintained in airworthy condition at the NWT Air hangar, often in the company of NWT's own L-100-30, the only example of its type in Canada. Next door are the DND hangar, which houses several CAF Twin Otters, and Echo Bay where First Air look after their four locally based HS 748s.

Add Air Tindi Beavers and Twin Otters, Ptarmigan Airways, Canadian North's 737s and Canadian Regional F.28s, and it's clear that a trip to Yellowknife is worth the journey. Whilst ramp access at the terminal isn't allowed officially, it is possible to walk across for a quick photo, with the help of staff at one of the maintenance bases.

Unfortunately, the prevailing winds make Runway 33 the most used, which has no nearby accessible road. Fortunately, the runways offer less interest than the parked aircraft. Between early June and the end of August, a couple of government-operated CL-215s are based for the fire-risk season. These are regularly augmented by contract fire-fighters, such as Conair Trackers or DC-6s in the past. Between 1995 and 1999, the contract has been awarded to Buffalo Airways, whose DC-4s will be in evidence.

Given that the main terminal is less interesting than the hangars, a view of the main apron is best from the cafeteria/bar. The windows are not tinted and aircraft park close enough for a standard lens to be used.

The Old Town floatplane base is also worthy of inspection, as Ptarmigan and Air Tindi use it. During the summer, a dozen or so Twin Otters and Cessna 185s take off from the lake each day, best seen from a rocky hill at Air Tindi's base on Latham Island. It's a couple of kilometres from downtown and, according to someone who should know, it's about the best place to take

such photos in the whole of Canada.
Yellowknife is not the sort of place to visit at the drop of a hat. Travelling this far requires some sort of arrangements. For £550, Henry Tenby offers a round-trip from Edmonton or Calgary, plus accommodation and a round trip in a Buffalo DC-3 to either Hay River or Fort Simpson. Bearing in mind that a peak season return fare between Edmonton and Yellowknife costs £325, the package should be attractive to genuine propliner enthusiasts. Mr Tenby, who works for NWT Air, shares the enthusiasm and takes personal care with visitors. For further details, contact Mr Tenby at Postal Service 9000, Yellowknife, NT X1A 2R3, Canada. The fax number is (403) 873 4274 and the telephone (403) 920 4358.

CP BOLIVIA (Republic of Bolivia)
COCHABAMBA

CBB   SLCB   Jorge Wilstermann   2m/3km W

At only 7000 feet above sea level, this is one of Bolivia's lower airports. To read the entry in ABC World Airways Guide, it would appear that there is little excitement at Cochabamba. Scheduled traffic is a slow procession of Lloyd 727s. What makes the airport interesting doesn't appear in ABC. Firstly, there is a B-25 (FAB-542) preserved, in the middle of a roundabout on the road from town. The approach road passes the threshold of the little-used cross runway and leads past the terminal to the hangars and aprons of Lloyd and Canedo. Lloyd's facility is surprisingly large but only one or two aircraft may be present.

After such a long journey, to such an exotic location, the first question could be: where is everything? The cargo apron, on the opposite side of the cross runway from the passenger terminal, invites inspection. Permission is needed. The reward for the effort is a selection of C-46s and DC-3s. Cochabamba's reputation has been built up so that reality can be a disappointment. An early arrival is one way to make the best use of the day. It is reported that many of the aircraft depart in the early morning and do not return until late afternoon. The word "many" should not be interpreted as a vast quantity. This is Bolivia, not O'Hare!

The small military base, round the corner from the cargo ramp, operates PC-7s, and is located so that it doesn't interfere with civil operations. This is a bonus for photographers, whose activities are therefore less likely to be misinterpreted.

LA PAZ

LPB   SADL   El Alto International   8m/13km NW (bus 40 minutes)

Perhaps one of the most exotic destinations any enthusiast can find in the world, everything about La Paz is truly memorable. 'El Alto' means 'the high one' and, at 13,000 feet (4,000 metres) above sea level, it is certainly an accurate name. The federal capital of Bolivia is Sucre but La Paz has always been the commercial heart of the nation, high on the Altiplano. The Trufi bus from Plaza Isobel la Catolica serves the airport.

Communications in this part of the world, thinly populated by a poor nation, dominated by the Andes and with sparse ground links, place a great dependance upon aircraft for many essentials. Cheap aircraft have found their way here and the DC-6 can be considered as being the latest word in luxury. Any piston engined airliner which can be pressed into service may find its way here, to operate the most unusual of cargo flights.

Meat is an essential food and it arrives at La Paz in these old airliners, ranging from C-46s and Martin 404s to DC-3s and DC-4s. This activity is not related to any scheduled passenger traffic, and the enthusiast can negotiate his way, with a smattering of Spanish, around the aprons. Piston engined aircraft, even in Bolivia, do have a limited lifespan, and several examples now lie around the field in disrepair. They make a sad sight.

The airfield lies in a very flat, open Altiplano landscape but with the Andes in sight. It is not busy, by any stretch of the imagination. The airport's essential appeal is the cargo ramp, and scheduled passenger airline flights are neither exciting nor frequent. They can be seen from the restaurant but photographers will experience problems with the glass, which is neither clean nor optically correct. The window at the top of the stairs also offers a view.

To the left of the terminal is the cargo area and, to the right, Fri Reyes is beyond the military compound. Arriving from town, the approach road to the terminal passes the entrance to the cargo apron, where a sentry is posted. A separate road leads past the military base to Fri Reyes. Old propliners are to be found on both the cargo ramps in some numbers, ranging in condition from serviceable to component parts. Don't expect concrete or tarmac - the surface is a mixture of dirt and oil. The buildings are generally in poor condition, though Fri Reyes has a more conventional appearance. Activity is, at best, moderately paced, the busiest days being reported as Thursdays and Fridays.

Political activities in many parts of South America are sudden and unpredictable which can mean that military uniforms often represent power to the populus. This can have unfortunate consequences for an unsuspecting enthusiast who thinks that a souvenir photograph of a Lloyd 727 at the terminal is no big deal. When visiting the Fri Reyes area, the military compound can be seen, and its inmates are close enough to log. Instead of concentrating 100% on the aircraft at La Paz, it's also worth keeping an eye on the guards. They are keeping an eye on you! The use of cameras should be accompanied by exaggerated, even theatrical, displays so that it can be seen, from a distance that nothing suspicious is happening.

SANTA CRUZ
SRZ   SLCZ   El Trompillo

This is the city's old airport which, in this part of the world, suggests things will be interesting: less so than at other remote South American destinations, but there is a little action to see. Cargo aircraft are thin on the ground, and most of the residents are general aviation and the Air Force's T-33s. If half of these aircraft appeared at Frankfurt or Gatwick, there would be a stampede to see them. In Bolivia, they are slightly disappointing.

SANTA CRUZ
VVI   SLVR   Viru Viru International   10m/16km E

The most interesting scheduled operations here are the occasional para-military, and incredibly cheap, TAM services. The rest of the traffic is virtually undiluted Lloyd 727s. Bolivia is an interesting country to visit, and it is tempting to want to see everything. Santa Cruz seems to offer, from fleet lists in JP, plenty of scope. The reality, even in this part of the world, is something of a let-down. There are about seven scheduled movements a day, and the quantity of aircraft on the cargo ramp can be disappointing.

Along one side of the runway are the passenger terminal and a US Government facility next door, outside which a twin-engined light aircraft is normally parked. At the other side of the terminal, beyond the fire station and control tower, is the cargo terminal and apron. Propliner fans travel the world, seeking quality, rather than quantity. The result is mouth-watering photographs of old aircraft with others in the background. What is often forgotten, by other aviation enthusiasts, is that all the other aircraft could be in the background. If the prospect of seeing six DC-3s on their home ground is appealing, then Bolivia might be the country to visit. This is not the land of Holiday Inns and Burger Kings on every street corner. It is South America: poor, often barely accessible and always thinly populated.

CS PORTUGAL (Portuguese Republic)

FARO

FAO   LPFR   4m/6km W (bus 30 minutes)

The variety of movements at Faro continues to increase, and most of them can be seen from the spectators terrace in the terminal. A 200mm lens is usually adequate. Charter flights are operated in groups, each relating to the country of origin. The British arrive on Thursdays, the Dutch on Mondays and the Germans on Wednesdays. Weekends are a mixture, though British aircraft predominate.

For British spotters, Wednesdays are good and, for the Germans, Thursdays possibly. Most of the arrivals are turned round between 9:00am and 1:00pm, though the evenings witness a repeat display. The airport information desk in the arrivals hall offers a schedule of the day's visitors, though registrations are not included. It should be assumed that sod's law applies: if an aircraft is small and/or rare, it could park at a remote stand, so it usually does!

Since the terrace offers a bar and TV monitors, showing flight information, alternative vantage points should not be necessary. However, for those who wish for something different, immediately after leaving the airport compound, a left turn to Praia de Faro leads to a causeway over a lagoon, directly under the flightpath to Runway 11. The fence is high enough to cause problems for photographers without something on which to stand. Parking places are lacking on the causeway, but they are to be found at both ends.

At one end of the runway is a campsite and hotel, offering a choice of ideally located accommodation. Photographers will need at least 200mm focal length to capture a 737 on the move. At the opposite end is the old market square in Faro. Aircraft on approach pass the southern edge of this dusty square, and a limited range of photographs is possible.

Most days start with a northerly cross wind and end with a south westerly breeze, which makes a change of runway at some point necessary. After a lot of walking, the intrepid photographer may find something different from the view in the terminal but, if the runway direction is changed, it can be hard, hot and thirsty work.

FUNCHAL

FNC   LPFU   Santa Cruz/Madeira   14m/22km NE

Madeira is a Portuguese-owned island out in the Atlantic. Like the Canaries, which are slightly further south, Madeira is not one island but a small archipelago. Also like the Canaries, Morocco is the nearest country. Islands that stick out of the Atlantic are rarely flat, as they are volcanic in origin. Experienced pilots are required for landings here.

At the end of the runway is a hill which makes approach decidedly tricky. It would help matters if the runway was flat. Accidents, however, don't happen too often so there's no reason to avoid a holiday here. The airport is small, with a passenger terminal and apron on the coastal side of the runway.

The observation deck has a cafe and offers an excellent view of the traffic. Anyone arriving in a hire car should prepared for a walk, as the car park is sometimes full. Like Faro, charter flights are rostered by country of origin, with Mondays and Thursdays the busiest. British arrivals are a feature, though Transavia and several Scandinavian carriers also visit. The German presence on a Thursday can include three LTU flights and four or five Condor. Aerocondor's Do228 operates local flights to Porto Santo, Madeira's other island some distance to the northeast.

For an alternative view of proceedings, without visiting the airport, the surrounding hills are very close indeed, offering opportunities for unusual photos of aircraft taking to the air. It can, however, be hard work on the feet. The Atlantis Madeira Hotel, in Machico, overlooks Discovery Bay from the hillside and offers a good view of the movements from the comfort of the swimming pool.

LISBON
LIS   LPPT   Portela de Sacavem   5m/8km N (bus 35 minutes)

Since the terminal complex offers little opportunity to see what is happening, it is normal to investigate other locations. There is a terrace and snack bar, above the domestic area, offering a limited view, and the 100 escudos entry fee allows access between 8:30am and 11:00pm. It is quite remote from the aircraft, and reflections on the glass cause some problems for a photographer. Whilst the general aviation and military areas can't be seen from here, ex-Onyx CV-880 N8806E has been noted as visible on the east side. This was a surprise, as it was previously reported as scrapped.

With open ground to the south, it would appear that a better chance is offered by walking in this direction. The bushes on the other side of the fence make things frustrating, particularly for photographers, around the threshold of Runway 36, but a walk to the end of Runway 03 results in the chance to take photos of aircraft as they land. Through the fence, movements approaching the hold for 03 can be recorded, with the sun being quite helpful; a 200mm lens is needed for a 727. Any time spent here will be at some risk to the health, as the busy highway produces offensive fumes.

On the eastern side of the field, Estrada des Amoreiras is considerably higher than the airfield. Bushes have been planted to provide a screen between the aircraft noise and the housing, but there are gaps in the hedge, from which it should be possible to watch the runway and take photos, particularly in the morning with the sun behind.

A walk north from the terminal area is recommended if Runway 21 is in use: a spot next to the fence allows good watching, though an airband radio is needed to be sure of being ready for arrivals. They are often seen before they are heard! Because it faces west, this location is ideal for photographers in the mornings, with a 135mm lens needed for an Air Portugal TriStar 500.

OPORTO
OPO   LPPR   Francisco sa Carneiro   6m/9km N (bus 20 minutes)

Oporto is geographically remote and economically depressed. The airport is north of the city on the N107, about 10km from where it joins the A1. The N107 passes right along the southern perimeter, where there is ample room to pull off the road and watch aircraft on approach to Runway 36. Beyond this is a left turn, leading to the airfield and a fork some 100 metres after means bearing left again. On the right is a residencia where a bed for the night can be found at reasonable prices (food is a different matter). At the end of the approach road is a roundabout. To the right is what looks like a cargo building or hangar, and to the right is the passenger terminal.

Accessible from inside the terminal is the open viewing deck from which all the action can be watched and photographed, particularly in the morning, due to the south westerly aspect.

It would be easy to underestimate this airport as just another charter destination. The majority of flights are domestic, most of them going to Lisbon, but any airport worthy of direct Varig connections to Brazil should be taken rather seriously.

CU CUBA (Republic of Cuba)
HAVANA
HAV   MUHA   Jose Marti International   11m/17km

The idea of planning a trip to Cuba to see aircraft used to seem to be a contradiction in terms, as it was always assumed that Communist countries took a dim view, at best, of this type of activity. This is no longer the case in Central Europe, and a reasonable interest in civil aviation is also possible here. The camouflaged bowsers give a military air to the place but there is no visible sign of the base from the terminal.

The international passenger terminal has been modernised. It is on the south side of the runway, at the eastern end, with the domestic terminal on the north side. The large viewing area along the front of the international terminal has been refurbished, and both its glass front and open deck offer fine views. It's also possible to see most of the action from the restaurant/bar on the first floor. From here, the ramp, runway and remote parking area are all visible, with most aircraft taxying past the terminal.

Photography is permitted officially but a 300mm lens is essential to capture anything which is on the runway. Times can change, and it would be prudent to seek official guidance before having a go. If permission is not going to be granted, it is better to find out politely, than to suffer a long interrogation, possibly risking the confiscation of some possessions.

The domestic terminal offers better facilities for the photographer. The observation deck is external and overlooks the action. Anyone spending a few days in Havana, with time to visit the airport, will no doubt take advantage of what is on offer on both sides of the runway, leaving with an impressive collection of photos. The logbook might lack variety but it will certainly contain a considerable quantity of Cuban registrations. The average day at Havana offers a really interesting selection of airliners, few of which are likely to be seen outside Cuba, except by well-travelled (and frequently lucky) spotters. Most of the common Soviet-built types are much in evidence, including Yak-40s and many Antonovs. The Aero Caribbean Britannia is stored and their active aircraft still include Il-18s and one remaining Il-14.

In the city are one or two sites worthy of exploration: Revolution Square has a Hawker Fury and a Vought Kingfisher, and Lenin Park has a selection including a couple of An-2s, a MiG-21 and a Yak-18T. No serious airliner enthusiast is likely to miss the chance of a visit to the Expo Cuba site, as it features Caravelle HI-499 in full, but rather fictitious, Cubana colours.

SANTIAGO DE CUBA
SCU   MUCU   Antonio Maceo

Santiago is on the south coast, not far from the US base at Guantanamo Bay. A visit here is normally only possible when staying on Cuba for a reasonable length of time. Preserved Il-14 CU-T816 wears Cubana colours, and it is here that most of the Volo Turistico An-2s are to be found. One or two of them sport Cubana colours. Most of the scheduled traffic is made up of Yak-40s but, as is to be expected in Cuba, there are always oldies and goodies to be seen.

VARADERO
VRA   MUVR   J G Gomez

This is becoming a significant charter airport but there still a few days when nothing at all is likely to be seen. Cubana have a maintenance base here, for work mostly on the Aerotaxi An-2s and their own An-26s, but it isn't visible from the passenger terminal. Photography is allowed, but most opportunities come from the departure lounge windows.

C5 GAMBIA (Republic of the Gambia)
BANJUL
BJL   GBYD   Yundum International   18m/27km S

A taxi from the town passes the main gate to the airport, some two miles from the terminal, with little to see on the way. No spectator facilities are provided but most of the apron is visible from the car park and departure hall. Once through the customs check, there is a good viewing area but the going is decidedly slow, with only two or three flights each day. Scheduled airlines visiting include Nigerian 737s and Ghana DC-9s, with charters becoming regular, attracted by the good beaches and sunshine: Condor DC-10s accompany Conair and Britannia Airways. The flying club has one or two interesting aircraft, and its entrance is via the security post next to the terminal. Being close to the runway, it can be the best place on the airfield.

D GERMANY (Federal Republic of Germany)
BAYREUTH

BYU   EDQD   Bindlacher-Berg   6m/9km

The smart modern terminal has a roof terrace, glazed at the front, which offers a very good view of the field. To the right of the terminal, from the landside, is a chainlink fence where an alternative ground level view is reasonable. To the left of the terminal are the main hangar and some general aviation hardstands. The general aviation terminal is to the right of the main terminal.

Nobody would dream of spending a whole day at Bayreuth; traffic is much too slow. The only scheduled operations are NFD Do228s, which occasionally serve Frankfurt and Hof.

BERLIN

SXF   ETBS   Schönefeld   12m/19km SE (bus/train 55 minutes)

The rooftop observation deck normally offers a comprehensive view of proceedings. On the other hand, the proceedings now amount to only a dozen or so daily movements. It can be a waste of time, so it might be best to contact the airport for a timetable. For advance information and anyhting else that can be elicited, contact: Berlin-Brandenburg Flughafen Holding GmbH, Flughafen Schönefeld, D-12529 Berlin. Renovations to the terminal might mean the deck was temporarily closed at the time of writing.

When this was the capital of the German Democratic Republic, it was the centre for Interflug's scheduled operations with, on the far side of the field, the maintenance base and many aircraft parked outside it. All there is to be seen these days is the occasional charter flight, operated by Condor, Aero-Lloyd or LTU, plus the occasional visitor from one of the former Eastern-bloc countries. Everything else has moved to Tegel or Tempelhof. It would be unwise to travel to the airport, in the belief that some exotic arrival, such as Air Koryo, Cubana or Vietnam Airlines was due. Such scheduled movements have a nasty habit of being cancelled or, just as likely, arriving a day or so late.

Anyone with only a restricted amount of time would do well to forget about a trip out here, as it can be an extraordinary disappointment. Its reputation survives mostly because of the old DDR days, which are long gone.

BERLIN

TXL   EDBT   Tegel   5m/8km NW (bus 30 minutes)

Tegel Airport is modern, with a drum-shaped terminal, reminiscent of the Worldport at Kennedy. Except in winter, its roof is almost completely accessible, with views of all the stands plus, in the distance, the two parallel runways and possibly one or two military aircraft parked at their own terminal on the far side. Before deciding to investigate the observation deck, beware the security check includes the requirement that cameras be opened up. Film should, if possible, therefore be loaded only after arrival.

This is going to cause problems for a few people, so it would be sensible to pack something which can be used to clean glass. The glass which will, almost certainly, need cleaning is at the top of the glazed stairwells which lead to various offices. One overlooks a part of the ramp, and can offer a glimpse of something photogenic. The other, which faces the taxiway, is better. That's the one that gets the smeared glass! Needless to say, the airport staff are quite used to seeing photographers, especially in winter, using this vantage point.

There is a small technical area, for maintenance and cargo but, on the average daytime visit, it is unlikely to yield anything of note. The number of airlines operating scheduled services into Tegel has grown but, realistically, there is still little to be seen here that can't be witnessed just as easily at many other European airports. However, for the intrepid, Tegel does offer the chance of good photography, though from on high.

BERLIN
THF   EDBB   Tempelhof   4m/6km SE (bus 40 minutes)

The quadrant of enormous hangars, built in 1926, occupy the northwest corner of the field and once housed 60% of Germany's commercial aircraft. Times have indeed changed. Inside the passenger terminal, there are no views except from the departure area, so whatever can be seen is from the fence. Scheduled traffic is augmented by the occasional American military movement, the most notable of which may be an Army Pilatus UV-20A Porter.

Templehof's name has a very nostalgic sound to it, by association with the blockade. One corner is occupied by the immense hangars used by the US Military base, and their segmental arrangement ensures that aircraft parked on the ramp are very difficult to see. The museum's C-54 is parked in the northeast corner, and so close to the fence that a good quality souvenir photo is difficult to take.

Tempelhof's fortunes have been revived by the introduction of scheduled traffic. Since there are no more Conti-Flug BAe146s, all commercial movements are prop driven, and include Lufthansa, Sabena, Crossair, Luxair, CSA, Eurowings and SAS among others. Being close to the city centre, it is popular with businessmen, who make use of the S-bahn (look for the big green S). Paradestrasse station is closest to the passenger terminal but spotters will find Tempelhof just as convenient. Between the two stations are the thresholds of Runways 09L and 09R. The perimeter fence at this, the western, side normally offers the best views.

When the 27 runways are in use, Leinestrasse station is nearest to the perimeter, a short walk down the street of that name. Frequent use of the S-bahn will make use of a block of five tickets, which can be the cheapest way to travel.

BRAUNSCHWEIG
BWE   EDVE

A magnificent old building, built to impress, the terminal has a huge upper level terrace plus another at the edge of the apron. This latter is ideal for photos of the occasional biz-jet, or to log the many parked aircraft.

The flagpoles can make some photos from the deck difficult, but they are unlikely to feature a scheduled airliner because it leaves early, very early, in the morning.

BREMEN
BRE   EDDW   Neuenland   2m/3km SSW (bus 20 minutes)

Bremen is situated to the southwest of Hamburg and, as such, is a likely port of call for anyone passing. The airport is moderately busy, handling Lufthansa 737s and the usual regional commuter carriers. To the left of the terminal is the Roland Air hangar and, to the right, a ramp for executive visitors and the Lufthansa Flying Club. This is probably the main attraction of Bremen, with King Airs in the full Lufthansa scheme and the bright yellow Bonanzas. Over the field to the right is the remaining general aviation, and there are adequate places for viewing most of the residents from the perimeter of the main apron.

COLOGNE/BONN

CGN EDDK   9m/15km S/ 12m/19km W (bus 30 minutes)

The terminal building is tucked away in a corner of the airfield, though this isn't apparent when arriving on the autobahn. The first impression might be of a modern bustling airport, and the main concourse overlooks the apron so that one can form an idea of what is happening very quickly. Because the view is so good, it is disappointing to find that the windows have a slight colour tint, which does have a noticeable effect on photos.

The viewing deck, now re-opened, is ample and overlooks the apron and the nearby runway threshold. The front of the deck is glazed, making photography a little tricky, but the ends are left open. There are only limited chances to use these side areas, but they do produce better results. Opening times in Germany are normally good, which is helpful, as the busiest times at Cologne/Bonn are between 7:30am and 10:00am, with another spell from 4:00pm to 7:30pm. The rest of the day can be very quiet. If runway 14L is being used, it can be an excellent airport to visit, as all traffic taxis past the main terminal, but other days can give a totally different impression of the place.

Because economic considerations have established Frankfurt as Germany's premier airport, nearby Cologne/Bonn only receives a sprinkling of scheduled traffic from around Europe. Apart from the infrequent Lufthansa wide-body, it seems quite parochial, though early morning charter flights help to keep up the numbers. Occasional cargo flights by Affretair or Seagreen and Russian charters can make a visit an interesting one but, most of the day, there may be little to see, apart from the regular trickle of Lufthansa domestic flights plus the occasional Condor or LTU Sud charter.

More variety is provided by the Luftwaffe transport fleet, which shares the runways. The base is to the right of the passenger terminal, and some distance away beyond the WDL F.27s, so that only aircraft on the move can be identified. These will include 707s, Challengers and Hansas during the week, plus occasional Transalls in the circuit and foreign VIP flights. Expectations should not be high, especially at weekends.

During the night, TNT's parcel hub operation is at its busiest, with as many as a dozen aicraft arriving from all over Europe around midnight. UPS have built a hangar in the expanding cargo area, and a 727 is usually parked on their apron during the day. Unfortunately, these parcel carriers are difficult (if not impossible) to identify from the passenger terminal, as they are generally parked so as to be seen nose-on.

To the right of the terminal is the ramp for light aircraft (many of which park on the grass), and Runway 14R/32L, which these smaller aircraft normally use. Executive movements use the Lufthansa Cityline terminal on the far side of the apron, where a selection of Fokker 50s share the ramp with some of the larger general aviation types.

Directly in front of the terminal is the cargo apron, some distance away, but any occasional visitors will need to be on the move if they are to come within range of a camera. At each side of the field are trees, giving a clear indication that the forest had to be cleared to build the airport.

DORTMUND

DTM EDLW   Wickede   6m/9km NE

This is a very quiet airport but it may be of interest to anyone wanting a good portrait of RFG's aircraft. Metros, ATR-42s and Saab 340s all visit, and can be seen at close quarters from the ramp level viewing area. Access is free and there are a few light aircraft to be seen. Also worth watching out for are LGW's Cessna 404 and Islander.

DRESDEN
DRS   ETDN   Klotsche   6m/9km NE (bus 30 minutes)

Dresden will no doubt be an interesting and busy airport in the future, as the economy of what was East Germany strengthens. Meanwhile it can be rather tedious. The majority of movements are domestic services, and there is little action during the day. The spectator deck (flughafenterrasse) faces north . . . probably the only good news for the photographer. Entry costs DM2 and the facilities are rather basic but there is also a restaurant to the left.

An interest in general aviation from the DDR days is satisfied by what remains of the old Dresden aircraft factory. The apron is located, across the runway, directly opposite the terrace. A 300mm lens or a long walk are needed. From the terminal take the first turn past the hangars. At the end of the lane is the entrance gate, on the left. The apron can contain as many as a dozen An-26s.

At the far end of the field, next to the threshold of Runway 22, is a military base which housed (and may still do so) An-2s and MiG-21s/23s.

DÜSSELDORF
DUS   EDDL   Rhein-Ruhr   5m/8km N (train 15 minutes)

The modernisation of Düsseldorf was effectively complete with the opening of an additional new runway, and passengers use one terminal with its three radiating piers. Many international flights arrive at the centrally placed Pier/Flugsteig B, and its roof forms the observation deck. To the right, Flugsteig A handles mostly Lufthansa and Air France whilst, to the left, charter traffic uses Flugsteig C.

Pressure for slots at Frankfurt has meant that Düsseldorf had to grow as a viable alternative, and the departure board shows that most European capital cities and many other international destinations are served direct.

Enthusiasts travelling around Europe often need a car to sample some of the better locations, but Düsseldorf can be enjoyed by anyone arriving by air or train. The S-bahn links the city with the airport, and the observation facilities have few equals in the world. The train costs DM8 and entry to the terrace another DM2.50. The ticket encourages a return visit, as it features a colour photo and technical details of an airliner. It might show an Olympic 737 or a CSA ATR, or many others. The tickets are, in other words, collectible.

Strict noise abatement regulations are enforced, with no flights being permitted between 11pm and 6am, and no departures after 9pm. Between midnight and 5am, the terminal building is closed. Opening shortly after the airport, at 6:15am, the observation terrace, (zuschauer-terrasse) has a commanding view of the airfield, with only aircraft parked on the far sides of the lateral piers being out of sight. An early start is essential, as the based LTU fleet leaves for holiday destinations soon after the airport opens. Unlike Frankfurt, there is no longer a security check before going onto the roof. When the weather is unkind, a walk up to the next level leads to the cafeteria and its many tables overlooking the ramp, and there is also a standing area behind the glass.

In front of the zuschauer-terrace are the parallel main runways 06/24 (L and R), and to the left is Runway 16/34, used mostly by general aviation which has its own terminal on the west side of the field. All movements can therefore be seen from the roof, and most airliners pass within range of the camera lens when taxying. The photographer will find Düsseldorf the ideal airport for definitive portraits of a wide selection of airliners, both scheduled and charter. The LTU Sud

757s and 767s, despite being operated from Munich, do visit Düsseldorf. Viva Air, Nortjet and Instanbul Airlines are all regular operators.

It is sometimes assumed, by the unknowing, that Germans have a love for Turkey as a holiday destination. This may be so, but the majority of Turkish flights carry guest-workers (mostly employed in the more menial jobs, including working in car assembly plants) home to see their relatives. Because the terrace faces north, the patient photographer is sure to leave with good results. Before leaving the airport, however, a little exploration may be worthwhile. Anyone using the terrace has probably parked the car in one of the three multi-storey car parks (Parkhaus 1-3). A complex circular road system surrounds this area, and a road at ground level (NOT Kalkumer Strasse) leads west. The hangar is at the western end of the apron is labelled Thyssen, and its doors can be firmly shut some days. Just beyond, the free car parks P5 and P20 are located. Close to P20 is the general aviation terminal and its own apron. The aircraft parked here often include something unusual, and photographs are best taken in the afternoon. The three hangars are occupied by Rheinland Air Service, Krupp and Jet Aviation. SD3.60s are parked on the apron in the company of a few corporate and visiting executive aircraft.

It is a long walk west to the maintenance hangars at the opposite end of the field. From the road a few aircraft can be seen. Since these might reasonably include a few A330s and MD-11s, the journey is necessary for anyone who wants to check out everything on display. Even without these aircraft in the log book (they probably won't make good photos on the maintenance ramps) a day at Düsseldorf offers splendid variety and good quantity - certainly one of Europe's most interesting airports.

ERFURT
ERF   ETEF   3m/5km NW (bus 15 minutes)

The small, two storey terminal building overlooks the apron. At either side, the chainlink fences are doubled. This makes photography impossible because, although the lens can be poked through the first screen, the second is only a few metres away. Fortunately, there is rarely . anything extraordinary to be seen. Apart from a handful of light aircraft, the main scheduled services are operated by NFD which can be seen better at many other airports in Germany.

FRANKFURT
FRA   EDDF   Main International   6m/9km SW (train 10 minutes)

Frankfurt has been a favourite airport with enthusiasts for many years, and its appeal continues, especially for spotters, though photographers are less likely to applaud all the recent changes. There are few airports in the world (except nearby Düsseldorf) which offer a complete package to match Frankfurt. If the whole complex could be rotated through 180 degrees, so that the sun shone from behind, it would probably be perfect!

Having arrived at the airport, it will be worth curbing enthusiasm to get onto the roof. Once in the terminal, a visit to the basement (Level 0) supermarket will ensure a good stock of drinks and snacks at moderate prices (by German standards). What is available at the sales kiosks on the roof is very expensive and has little variety. Not everyone is prepared to pay Dm3.50 for a coke, even on a hot day. Arrival at the airport for about 8:00am ensures time to stock up with food and drink before queuing for the baggage search. The deck opens at 8:30am and closes at 7:30pm, just before when a polite man on a bicycle tells you to put the binoculars away, forget about the 747 on approach and go home.

Access to the roof deck necessitates a security check, after which the payment of Dm7 allows a walk onto Pier B. There is much similarity in the layouts of Düsseldorf and Frankfurt, the main exception being that the central pier at Frankfurt has two diagonal extensions. Slight disappointment awaits regular visitors, as the eastern half of the roof has been closed off. Because this offered very good views of many stands, with the sun at a good angle, this is bad news for photographers. The entry ticket should be kept somewhere safe because it can be used for re-entry if, for example, making a quick trip to the supermarket. It also has another use.

Once through the security check to get onto the observation deck, even old hands will feel some excitement: the constantly widening vista of airliners as each corner is turned reveals a variety of operators as well as much of the Lufthansa fleet. On the far side of the runway is the USAF's Rhein-Main base, with one or two transports but the many Hercs that used to be based here have gone. One or two aircraft on nearby stands will only be photogenic once they are on the move. Despite the deck having a southerly aspect, it is often possible to find somewhere for a good photo. The commuter carriers have been forced out of the central terminal area, so that these aircraft are now parked some distance to the east. This can sometimes make identification a problem, and photographs very difficult. There is a rule at Frankfurt which states that the more interesting the aircraft, the less likely it is to offer a good photograph. Immoderate language, in several languages, can be heard as a Mauritius A340 or a Tyrolean Dash 8 turns away at the last minute. It happens regularly, so get used to it.

Because almost all arrivals land in full view, on Runways 25L/R normally, it must not be assumed that they will all taxi out and take off in the same direction. Many departures use Runway 18, at the western extremity of the field. Those wishing to log all the visitors would do well to remember this fact, and ensure that all incoming movements are logged.

Traffic to be seen from the deck is of the highest order, being a representative collection of airliners from all parts of the world. Heathrow no longer offers anything like the same opportunities to gain close access to such a variety of airliners, and the range of angles to take photos means that most of the shots will have a pleasant choice of backgrounds. On the distant north side of the field is the Ratioflug hangar and ramp, with its F.27s beyond the reach of most binoculars, and to the west are Lufthansa's enormous maintenance and cargo facilities. The cargo centre is already Europe's largest, and still growing.

At the western end of the field is Runway 18, used only in that direction, with a viewing area close by. Photographers with cars will have a very rewarding time here, particularly in the afternoons, when the sun has moved round. Those on foot must take the No.77 bus from the airport bus station to the cargo centre, and it is a fifteen minute walk around the perimeter. There is a small car park, and a slightly elevated platform ensures that photographers have a first class view. A 200mm zoom lens will ensure good photographs of aircraft down to about 737 size. The road passes through a tunnel below the runway, and Tor (Gate) 31 is the last accessible point to the perimeter. This faces south and might be of use to photographers with long lenses. Clearly seen from here is the DC-3, reportedly that which used to be on display on the roof terrace.

Linking Terminals 1 and 2 is a people mover called Sky Line. It can be considered essential transport for spotters when Runways 07L/R are in use. The escalator leads to McDonalds and the viewing balcony. Opening times are the same as the main deck and the one ticket is good for both, so don't lose it. During most days, the spotting from here is excellent, though landing from the opposite direction are not unkown. Terminal 2 handles many of the morning transatlantic arrivals, so this may be a good place to start the day. At other times its apron might only hold a few commuters.

The guided airport tour (flugfahrt) parties meet on the Terminal 1 roof, by the front fuselage section of the DC-8 on Pier B. The DM9 is expensive and some say it's worth every pfennig. Not everyone agrees, however. The full tour takes about 45 minutes and includes Lufthansa Cargo and their maintenance hangars for 737s, 747s and A310s. The bus does not pass the general aviation ramp but offers a chance of photos as aircraft line up at the hold for Runway 18. Frankfurt Airport is constantly developing and the authorities are making every effort to accommodate the needs of the enthusiast. Sometimes compromises are necessary but nobody would deny that it is still one of Europe's finest airports. A day's stay here is over all too soon.

HAMBURG

HAM   EDDH   Fuhlsbüttel   8m/13km N (bus 20 minutes)

Hamburg has witnessed some very major changes over the last few years. As is normally the case in Germany, it isn't all bad news. General aviation interest is much more difficult to satisfy, as the parking area has been moved to the centre of the field, remote from all vantage points. However, an airline enthusiast has almost nothing but good news.

The main passenger terminal has been modernised, and a new terminal has been added, further south on the apron. The new observation deck now occupies almost exactly the same position as the old one. The new version is better. Entry to the deck costs a reasonable DM3, and there is a security check. It should be noted that cans of drink are not permitted past the security check. Anyone who has been to an open air pop concert will know the reason, and it has nothing to do with security.

The deck overlooks the threshold of Runway 23, where most arrivals land, and even moderate camera equipment allows some very good landing shots. Many of the movements pass the deck on their way to stands on other parts of the apron, many out of sight, and they may take off on Runway 33. When Runway 23 is being used for departures, everything is wonderful. All aircraft must pass very close to the deck, within reach of all cameras.

At the left-hand (southern) end of the main apron are the new terminal and the cargo area. Behind the new terminal is a circular multi-storey car park, eight floors high. For anyone who only wants to log the movements, the top of this car park has advantages: it is free and there are no security checks or restrictions on what can be carried.

Beyond this terminal and car park, facing the threshold of Runway 33, is a hangar area for commuter airlines, occupied by Hamburg Airlines. Parked in front during the average day are a DLT F.50, one or two Dash 8s and NFD ATR-72s plus a FedEx F.27 and a DHL CV-580.

A walk along Zeppelinstrasse, from the main terminal, leads to a roundabout and a right turn onto Weg beim Jager. This road heads for the Lufthansa maintenance base and is where traffic landing on 33 (occasionally) can be seen at close quarters. From the fence, aircraft parked on the southern apron can be seen with ease. It was once full of general aviation, as were the hangars, but now the same aircraft can be seen in the distance, in the centre of the field.

Without a car, that is probably all the average enthusiast needs to know about Hamburg. It is busy, it offers variety and the sun in the morning makes the photographer a very happy person. Local enthusiasts, who had to endure the lack of observation facilities for some time, made use of the many alternative viewpoints around the perimeter. A car is essential to reach most of them, especially if runway changes occur.

HAMBURG

XFW   EDHI   Finkenwerder   11m/17km NW

Crossing the River Elbe from the city, or from Fuhlsbuttel, by way of the tunnel, a drive north following the west bank leads to the village of Finkenwerder, with the airfield on the northern edge of the houses. A high bank/levee obscures the field from view but a walk to the top reveals the MBB hangar where the Airbuses are fitted out. Visits at weekends are usually fruitless because everything is locked up.

HANNOVER

HAJ   EDVV   7m/11km W (bus 20 minutes)

Famous for the Air Show, the amount of apron used for this purpose allows some very good views of the scheduled movements but, at all other times, this is a very frustrating airport. There are two runways, on opposite sides of the field and, between them, the terminal with an absurdly high observation deck. This is bad news, as (a) the majority of the movements are small and, by the time they come within range of the camera, they are almost in plan view, and (b) the escalators are often not working, necessitating a long climb to the roof!

Between the runways, and beyond the passenger terminal, is a significant area for general aviation, though much of it is difficult to see. Although the multi-storey car park is not as high as the terminal, it does allow a different, and better, view of the many light aircraft. Without a car, exploration of the hangars off the approach road involves much time for little or no reward.

When the Air Show is under way, there is usually a good selection of aircraft on display, plus the chance to take a photo of a DLT Fokker 50 or NFD Metro at ground level as they taxi by.

LEIPZIG
LEJ   ETLS   Halle   8m/13km WNW

This airport has the almost obligatory, by German standards, observation deck. The East German heritage also means free admission at the time of the last visit. Perhaps this will change, but any fee will be worth paying. It is a good airport. Everything which moves passes within range of a 200mm zoom lens. The only drawback is the southerly aspect. Behind the air traffic control building is an 'Aeropark' where some relics of Interflug have been moved. It is a comprehensive collection: apart from the Il-62 DDR-SEF and the Tu-134 DDR-SCF, there is an Il-18 DDR-STA and a couple of crop-sprayers. The Il-14 which completes the collection is by the ice rink in the town of Halle, 15 km to the west. Latest news from Leipzig is that the Interflug passenger aircraft serve as restaurants and the Il-14 is used as a travel agency, which should help their survival.

Outside the terminal area, another photo opportunity exists at the east end of the runway. By following the road towards Schkeuditz, there is a small village called Kursdorf, just north of the airport boundary. The runway is easy to find!

MANNHEIM
MHG   EDFM   Neuostheim   4m/6km E

What makes Mannheim airport worth a detour, when driving past, is the presence of Arcus-Air. Apart from their many smaller aircraft, the airline operates Do228 scheduled services to Erfurt, Dresden and Leipzig. These flights operate only occasionally, so reference to a timetable is important. On Sundays, the Dorniers might not be seen at all, as they are often confined to their hangar. The airport is more accurately described as an airfield (flugplatz rather than flughafen) and has a (free) car park from which the apron can be seen. The low hedge doesn't hamper the view but the sun can be a nuisance around midday. The best times to see the Dorniers on their home patch is before 8:00am, so early starters might have less problems.

Finding the airfield can be difficult. When coming from the Karlsruhe - Frankurt autobahn (A5) take the A656 exit (Mannheim Neckarau) and follow the signs for Mannheim-Neuostheim or Mannheim-Flugplatz. From the city, head out in the direction of Heidelberg and turn left at the planetarium, following the signs for Neuostheim and Flugplatz. Take care not to follow the tram tracks. When they bear off to the left, go straight ahead or you'll finish up in the village.

MUNICH
MUC   EDDM   Franz-Josef Strauss   13m/20km NE (train 25 minutes)

Every opportunity to get maximum publicity when the new airport opened was taken, and every enthusiast around the world knows about it. The letter M has been used as its logo, and the old designation of Munich II has been overtaken by the name, Franz-Josef Strauss. This Bavarian politician was once the head of Airbus Industrie as well as being a private pilot.

Between the two parallel runways are all the main facilities, including the railway link. The airport has two stations; one for the passengers at the terminal area and another, reached before it, for spectators called Besucher-park. The airport shuttle train from the city's main station is service No. S8. In the southern part of Bavaria are the Alps, so people don't mind climbing. This is good, because the observation point is an enormous pyramid, and there are plenty of stairs to climb. The view from the top is excellent but there is no shade. Like the central theme building at Los Angeles, everything can be seen, but from a distance. Photographers who don't have 300mm lenses will find that many of the movements aren't worth the effort. The kiosk which sells food and drink is at the bottom of the hill, so it's worth thinking ahead before the climb.

Everything which used to be seen at Riem is now at Munich II, and there is no shortage of variety to the movements. These include quite a selection of Turkish airliners, once again used mostly to take guest-workers home to their families for a few days.

MÜNSTER OSNABRUCK
FMO   EDLG   Greven   16m/26km SE

This is mainly a general aviation field. Its appeal to the enthusiast is the fleet of Hansa Luftbuild light aircraft known, because they are painted bright yellow, as Banana Airways.

NÜRNBURG
NUE   EDDN   4m/6km NE (bus 20 minutes)

The internal viewing facilities are spoiled by the tinted glass which makes colour photography a waste of time. However, anyone engaged in only logging movements can enjoy a visit here. The rooftop deck can be even more frustrating, particularly on a sunny day, as the reflections in the glass make photography of any worth almost impossible. The charter terminal is to the left of that used for scheduled flights and at either side are the cargo apron, to the right, and the hangars and general aviation, to the left. Aero Dienst and NFD occupy the two hangars closest to the passenger terminals, and light aircraft are housed in lock-up hangars out on the grass.

Traffic during the week is slow, being restricted to a handful of Lufthansa 737s and the based NFD fleet. Summer weekends offer increased variety, with additional charter flights. Nearby military bases mean that British and American visitors are often seen, with C-130s making regular troop flights.

PADERBORN
PAD   EDLP   Lippstadt   11m/18km W

It is a dedicated enthusiast who will go far out of his way to visit Paderborn. It is extremely quiet, though the observation deck is free. What can be seen, and then only occasionally, is an RFG ATR-42.

SAARBRÜCKEN
SCN   EDRS   Ensheim   8m/12km E

Apart from the occasional Hamburg Airlines Dash 8 and, less so, a Luxair Brasilia, there isn't much scheduled traffic to see. The cost of parking a car for a short while can seem poor value, but there are other places across the road which might be worth the effort. The terrace at the front of the terminal costs DM1 (sometimes) but the view is good, despite facing south.

To see the Jet Aviation apron, the restaurant has windows, though the car park next to it is also close. This is at the western end of the apron, beyond which the lands slopes down from the end of Runway 09. The road in this direction is inaccessible but things are different to the west. Instead of heading out to the autobahn, a right turn passes Contact Air and a hangar, where one or two aircraft can be worth a stop for a photo. The road enters a deep valley, passing below the threshold of Runway 27, after which it continues around the perimeter towards Ensheim. At the top of the hill is a good view of the field, through the wire mesh fence.

Weekend scheduled traffic is non-existant, so a visit during the week may be best. From the Mannheim - Saarbrücken autobahn (A6), leave at exit St Ingbert West and follow the signs for the airport.

STUTTGART
STR   EDDS   Echterdingen   9m/15km S (bus 35 minutes)

The large apron is not dominated by the passenger terminal but by hangars and general aviation facilities. The new terminal has been built, to the right of the existing one, in the corner of the apron. Parked well out into the middle are usually Condor/Lufthansa aircraft, many of which are wide-bodies, and the terminal is tucked away in the northwest corner. The viewing facilities are not really adequate, and enthusiasts have found other vantage points, though some ingenuity and effort is involved. Pink sector car parks are short-term, and can be used to pick up arriving passengers (not in THAT sense!). The ticket allows 20 minutes of free parking, so it's possible to go into charter terminal 3, ask the security officer for the day's schedule (tagesflugplan) and drive off to Bernhausen. Taking longer than 20 minutes costs DM2.50.

Apart from most German operators, with a good variety of aircraft types, many European airlines are regular, so that while Stuttgart is not as busy as Frankfurt or Düsseldorf, it has does have plenty to choose from. Traffic has been bolstered by a host of charter flights, and there is no shortage of operators from abroad, such as Egyptair with anything from 737s to 767s and A300s, plus American Transair, Arkia and Pegasus, to name but a few. The US Military base on the south side of the field also attracts some sporadic visitors, including MAC charters.

The observation deck, which faces south, costs DM3 and many of the more interesting aircraft, such as charters, cargo carriers and general aviation, park a long way from it. The cheapest car parks are P9 and P0, which cost DM12 per day. The S-bahn rail connection, indicated green S, leaves from the city's main station and costs DM4 each way.

Guided tours of the airport are offered to parties, usually local, and it is possible to be added to the list. Advance notice can be obtained of tours, and bookings made, by ringing Public Relations on 0711-948-2326 but they need to know at least a day before, if a name is to be added. At peak times, two tours are operated each day, so there should be no problems.

The new approach road still passes commendably close to part of the apron but the occupants are shielded from view by a glazed wall. Anyone arriving by car can pass the main entrance and continue 200 metres or so beyond the last buildings. A track leads across the fields to the perimeter, and a very close view of the holding point for Runway 08. From here, all movements can normally be seen, though traffic on 26 turns off well before reaching this end. When Runway 26 is in use, the road at the opposite end of the field, leading into Bernhausen, has an alternative vantage point. At the southern end of the underpass, a walk up to the fence gets reasonably close to the runway.

The really energetic can also follow footpaths around the eastern perimeter for a view of the 08 holding point. Not only is there access from the north but the road out of Bernhausen towards Echterdingen passes the entrance to the USAF base. Parking the car around here means a walk to the perimeter fence. Neither the police nor the American security personnel mind spotting from this fence, but they can get upset if stepladders are used to see over it.

The last runway extension involved the realignment of part of Autobahn A8/E11 slightly to the north. Work in 1995 is scheduled to be more dramatic. It has been reported that the new runway extension will involve closing the airport for two months in summer.

DQ FIJI
NADI
NAN   NFFN   International   6m/9km S

The passenger terminal is divided into two: international passengers use the right-hand side (viewed from landside) and domestic passengers the left. The observation deck, on the roof of the domestic terminal, is reached by an unmarked staircase next to the snack bar, and faces the intersection of both runways. The deck lacks facilities (there aren't even any seats) but it is possible to go downstairs to the snack bar for a drink and a spell out of the sun. The wire mesh doesn't prevent photos using a standard lens - things do come that close. To the right, and out of sight from the deck, is the Air Pacific hangar which faces the international part of the terminal. The cargo area is to the left and also out of view.

What can be seen, however, is everything which moves. Traffic is fairly brisk, mostly due to the comings and goings of the small Sunflower movements. All their commuter aircraft can be seen in one day (or less!), as the airline's hangar is directly opposite the deck, on the far side of the cross runway. What remains to occupy the time is only about a dozen movements a day. It might not sound much but each one is likely to be of much interest: mostly 737s of Air Nauru, Air Marshall Islands, Air Vanuatu and so on, though Air New Zealand 767s call regularly.

Anyone staying on the island for a while should also bear in mind that Suva, on the eastern side of the island, also has an airport, called NAUSORI (codes SUV/NFSU) which is certain to be worth a visit.

EC SPAIN (Kingdom of Spain)
ALMERIA
LEI   LEAM   5m/8km N

Apart from a small number of 'alternative' holiday destinations, there is little to support this airport. Occasional Aviaco DC-9s and foreign charter flights visit, and these can be seen by passengers from the rampside patio. Other landside visitors must content themselves with a view of the taxiway from the side of the terminal. Before lunchtime, the sun only offers the chance of improving a tan; it certainly spoils photographs.

BARCELONA
BCN   LEBL   9m/15km SW (train 20 minutes)

The 1992 Olympic Games meant the reorganising of communication services in the city, most of which could be seen on the television, and the new airline terminal was a major part of that investment. The Costa Brava was one of the first package holiday destinations, but tourists' needs have changed. Package holidays by air now go elsewhere, to the Costa del Sol, the Canaries and the Balearics. Younger, and livelier, folk now come to Catalonia, usually on the bus, to keep costs down. Barcelona is a major Spanish business centre, and the future of the airport may be related more to European Community business travel than to tourism.

At the city end of the airport, the fence at the threshold of Runway 11/29 offers good views of the traffic, though the range of movements is less exciting than elsewhere in Spain. A stay of more than four hours, from early morning, means that many of the Iberia and Aviaco movements put in a second appearance.

Inside the new terminal, where cool is often welcome, there is a huge window between gates 39 and 40. This faces the main runway and, as at Frankfurt, all incoming movements should be logged. The other runway is sometimes used for departures. The double glazing makes photography a little tricky. Worth watching are the monitors which show the day's movements. The occasional Varig 767 or Egyptair 737 can help boost a rather lacklustre log, and it would be a shame to miss it from lack of warning.

BILBAO
BIO   LEBB   Sondica   6m/9km N

Perhaps one of the most scenic of all Spanish airports, the mountainous background could make the various vantage points extremely good for a photographer. The problem is the distinct lack of subject matter, with Iberia jets being the only regular visitors. Even the light aircraft are appear regularly at other European airports.

FUERTAVENTURA
FUE   GCFV   Puerto del Rosario   7m/11km SW of Corralejo

The terminal area isn't as good as Coleta del Fuste for reading off registrations. The problem with this location is that many of the charter flights are German, mostly on Saturdays and Mondays. Since they don't have underwing registrations, they pose a problem. One of the quieter of the Canary Islands, neither the facilities nor the quantity of movements stand comparison with Gran Canaria, Tenerife or Lanzarote.

GRAN CANARIA
LPA   GCLP   Las Palmas   14m/22km SSE (bus 30 minutes)

The large terminal offers passengers a very good view of almost every aircraft to visit, and the balcony is a bonus. Traffic is an extremely good mix, and anyone with a hire car could justify a couple of visits to the airport during a holiday. Transatlantic flights between Spain and South America often refuel at Las Palmas, though most of these movements take place after dark. Scheduled traffic includes inter-island services by the locally based Iberia subsidiary, Binter Canarias, with ATR-72s and CASA 235s. Charter traffic shows how popular the island is with the Scandinavians: almost all the charter airlines from that part of the world, and from West Germany, are regular visitors, with wide-body movements being a regular occurrence.

On the far side of the field, though quite some distance away, is the military base, used by some CASA 212s, and a Search and Rescue facility. The Aviocars are seen at an oblique angle and can therefore be identified but the SAR F.27s usually park so that they are seen end-on, frustrating any attempts at identification, unless on the move . . . a rare occurrence!

IBIZA
IBZ   LEIB   5m/8km SW

The new passenger terminal is large and modern, and good views are available at the right-hand side, through the tinted glass of the domestic departure area windows. Most of the apron can be seen but the general aviation ramp is out of sight. In the lounge area, the bar serves drinks and snacks at reasonable prices.

The original terminal is now used for general aviation. The adjacent wire fence to the left, near the control tower, offers a limited view of executive movements, which normally include several from various European countries. It is useful to contact someone in authority at the terminal, so that suspicions are not raised.

At the opposite end of the new terminal are Iberia Cargo and a staff car park, where fences allow other views. At Ibiza, there are a few places to see most movements but no single spot allows everything to be seen on the ramp. To be able to monitor the situation better, there is a well-used track leading from the main road to the end of the runway, which may offer something more comprehensive for both watchers and photographers.

The resort of Playa d'en Bossa is fairly close to the airport, and lies under the flightpath of aircraft on finals. Anyone planning a visit may consider staying at the strategically placed Hotel Club Bahamas, and hiring a cycle from one of many shops, thereby reducing travelling time to the airport at a moderate cost.

The quantity and variety of visitors to Ibiza are not in the same league as Palma but the facilities in the airport complex are better. As is to be expected in Spain, most of the action takes place in the mornings or after dark.

LANZAROTE
ACE   GCRR   Arrecife   4m/6km

The passenger terminal is adequate for anyone noting registrations but photographers will make their way to Playa de Matagordo. A car is essential, however, and the road between Arrecife and Puerto de Carmen has a turning where it can be parked. From here, a five minute walk is all that is needed, even with the children. Anyone who must take holidays with the family will find Lanzarote a good destination.

The family can sit on the beach, facing the sea, and the enthusiast can turn round and see the threshold of Runway 03. From the tops of the sand dunes in the morning, it is possible to follow the angle of the sun so that, by about 4:00pm, the high ground on the west offers a splendid view of aircraft turning to line up for take off. Traffic is modest, but photographers will be rewarded by first class shots, rarely needing the full range of a 200mm zoom lens. Military activity is minimal, so the police take little interest in aviation enthusiasts.

MADRID
MAD   LEMD   Barajas   10m/16km ENE (bus 30 minutes)

Madrid's only airport is just ten miles out of the city, and is easily reached by a special bus service which operates every five minutes from the underground bus station at Colon, at a cost of about 200 pesetas. There are two crescent-shaped terminals side by side, for domestic and international flights respectively.

The upper level of the domestic terminal (at the extreme left-hand end) offers a reasonable but limited view, overlooking both principal runways, 15/33 and 01/19, and the taxying aircraft. It is officially forbidden to take photos (through glass) but the police may turn a blind eye to foreign nationals. This should not be taken as permission, of course. Discretion, and a 200mm zoom lens, will be useful. Large helpings of patience are also at a premium . . . this is a frustrating airport.

To the right, and beyond the international terminal, is the cargo ramp, an area of much activity. Aircraft parked here can be seen from outside the international terminal, some of which should be within range of the zoom lens. Cargosur, who operate Iberia cargo flights, still operate some DC-8s. In the far corner of the ramp, the Post Office CASA 212s and TNT BAe146 await their evening's work and beyond them are the Falcons and 707s of Grupo 45, the Spanish Air Force VIP Squadron.

A well-stocked general aviation ramp, comprising mostly Falcon 20s and Corvettes which deliver packages at night, is to the left of the domestic terminal. Views are only possible from inside the North Terminal, now reserved exclusively for general aviation passengers.

The steady stream of Iberia A320s, DC-9s and 727s dominates the activity, as much of the long-haul wide-body fleet generally leaves at night to arrive in South America at dawn. Domestic services are operated by Aviaco's F.27s and DC-9s, so visits by other Spanish airlines are rare. Foreign operators are standard European fare, except for SAS MD-87s, though Spain's links with Latin America mean that more interesting visitors are regular. Cubana, LANChile, Aeronaves del Peru and Pluna can be seen, though their movements can be weekly, rather than daily.

The chances to enjoy Barajas are so limited, it must be stressed that it is not an airport to be considered as a destination in its own right, involving a long drive or an expensive flight.

MADRID
LEVS   Cuatro Vientos

The superb Spanish Air Force museum is to be found here, containing among its exhibits a Do.24, two CASA Azors and a British Rapide, G-ACYR. Admission is free, though photography is forbidden. Indeed it is forbidden anywhere on the airfield, due to CASA and the active military presence. There are some 150 light aircraft and helicopters based here. The railway station at Vientos is far enough from the entrance to the field to need a taxi. These are rare. Permission for ramp access should be sought at the control tower. Military activity, and the security which often accompanies it, can occasionally lead to difficulties. Madrid's other general aviation field is GETAFE, but little is known about it.

MAHON
MAH   LEMH   Menorca   4m/6km SW

Minorca is the quietest of the islands but its popularity is increasing, with the airport expanding to handle the traffic. Most of the charter traffic is British and of interest to only a few enthusiasts but Aviaco do operate scheduled services to the mainland. Because the terminal area is poor for watching, and worse for photography, the perimeter fence is the only place to exercise serious interest. A hire car is useful as there are some very long walks otherwise.

To the right of the terminal, the view is across the apron, and from the car park, the main apron and light aircraft can be seen. Cameras should be used with discretion. Resorts are spread across the island, particularly on the northern coastline, so a visit to the airport will probably involve a taxi ride or the hire of a car.

Light aircraft from Europe are quite prominent here, though the local residents are based at the Mahon Aero Club airfield, some six miles away. As there is only one road across the island, the Aero Club grass strip is easy to find, and there is rarely any trouble gaining access, for some photos of unusual types.

MALAGA
AGP   LEMG   6m/9km SW (bus/train 10 minutes)

The view from inside the terminals is only possible once departing passengers have gone through passport control. Car parks at either side of the terminals allow good views of the aprons, and they are widely used by holidaymakers catching their last sunshine before departure. Anyone walking about taking an interest in the movements arouses little attention.

To the left of the international terminal are the Jet Aviation facility and aeroclub hangars. It is probable that a request for a close inspection will be refused: in this event, all except hangared aircraft can be identified from the main road, next to the threshold of Runway 32. On the opposite side of the runway, in the southwest corner of the field, is a military base which attracts a few visitors. Traffic, mostly charter operators, is generally brisk, though a couple of Iberia 747s call each week. The airport is served from resorts and Malaga city by buses and trains.

PALMA
PMI   LEPA   Son San Juan   6m/9km E (bus 30 minutes)

The only public transport to the airport is bus service No.17, which runs from the Plaza España in the centre of Palma every half hour. The twenty minute journey costs about 120 pesetas. When alighting at Terminal B International, the first stop (the observation point) is to the right of the terminal, but only part of the apron is visible. The platform is quite high and there is no rail, so care should be taken or legs will be broken!

The next stop is Terminal A Domestic, where the coach park was a popular location for viewing. A lounge extension now occupies this ground, used by passengers on delayed flights.

At the far side of the field, once visible from next to Terminal A, is a patch of waste land which offers superb views of the movements. From here, 75% of the airport, and virtually all traffic, are visible, often at close quarters. To reach this haven, much used by the local community, take the road from Palma to Manacor (or the No.15 Palma to El Arenal bus) and a right turn at San Ferriol towards Col d'en Rebasa and the Continente hypermarket. A very sharp bend had the Bonpas Bar (now closed) on the corner and, from here, a track leads to the fence. Close to the threshold of Runway 06L, on the opposite side of the field, is a concrete track with access to the fence and from here afternoon photography is possible.

The resort of C'an Pastilla is near the airport, and aircraft are close to touchdown as they pass overhead. Rooms facing traffic at the Helios Hotel are popular. The new runway, 06R/24L, is gradually coming into use, but its use is restricted (not least by local hostility) to landings on 24 and take-offs on 06.

The airport is moderately active all week, siesta time apart, but the weekends are busiest. Any enthusiast who records airline movements at major airports will probably witness only a small percentage of charter operators, so Palma offers a very real opportunity to see a range from all over Europe, including as many as three Scanair DC-10s on Saturdays.

The general aviation field of SON BONET is a 15 minute drive from Palma, and thirty or so aircraft are normally present. The local staff are bothered by lots visitors, particularly in the peak summer period. Most of what is there can be seen from the fence but anyone wishing to gain access should telephone the airfield on 264 670 beforehand.

TENERIFE
TFS   GCTS   Reina Sofia   37m/59km SW (bus 40 minutes)

The new airport and its terminal were completed with some urgency, and the decaying balcony offered evidence of the hasty construction. Now that the balcony has been repaired it is leased by a catering company, who provide refreshment for those who wish to catch the last of the sunshine before going home. It is, once again, the best place to see the apron and get good photos of all the movements. Some of the aircraft which park out on the apron may require longer lenses.

A service road leads past the Texaco filling station to the perimeter, where the needs of photographers are met. Bushes next to the fence by the threshold of the runway mean that aircraft landing on 07 are easier to see than those on the ground, especially as distance and heat haze make life difficult. Runway 25, when in use, offers much better prospects, however. By going all the way round the south side of the field, all movements can be seen, and photographs are of a high quality, with the sun behind the camera and the hills behind the aircraft. The small beach east of El Medano has a cafe and offers good spotting.

Traffic is predictable, as with most Spanish resort airports: charters dominate the movements board, and weekends are particularly busy. Like Las Palmas, the island is popular with the Scandinavians, and their numbers supplement the German and British flights.

TENERIFE
TFN   GCXO   Los Rodeos   8m/13km NW (bus 30 minutes)

The airport is now surrounded by fences, making it difficult to take photos on the left side. In front of the terminal is a small (free) car park and, inside, there is a cafe with lots of seats and views of the movements. Photography is good, but through glass, and subject to the limited amount of traffic. There are (still?) two ex-LAC Viscounts stored in the maintenance area.

At the perimeter, it's only by the Aero Club entrance that decent shots are possible, with the aid of a 200mm lens. For an elevated view, La Esperanza road offers the best opportunities, again with a 200mm lens, but the only scheduled traffic are the inter-island flights, operated by Aviaco F.27s and Binter Canarias CN-235s.

EI IRELAND (Republic of Eire)
CORK
ORK   EICK   3m/5km S

A small airport, with the occasional scheduled visit by Aer Lingus SD3.60s and 737s, it's difficult to find any good views from the terminal. Exploration is worthwhile, as the hangars contain a good number of residents, and general aviation arrives from abroad in quantity during summer.

DUBLIN
DUB   EIDW   5m/8km N (bus 30 minutes)

Aer Reanta, who operate Dublin Airport, have taken a lot of trouble to ensure the best compromise between the (reducing) need for security and the needs of the many spotters. The general feeling is that they have been quite successful. The viewing gallery on the third floor is fully enclosed and overlooks the apron between the main terminal and Pier A. Movements on Runways 10/28 and 16/34 are also visible. In the distance, aircraft parked at Iona and the flying club can be identified. Runway 05/23 appears to be out of use.

At the far end of the gallery, the cargo ramp can be seen and, at the other end, by the lifts, there is a partial view of the Team and Aer Lingus hangars. The daily flights bound for America mean the gallery gets busy for a while but, as soon as the aircraft depart, so do the people. The concourse between the terminals is now strictly for passengers only, due to the provision of additional shopping facilities. The Sky View Bar has a good view of the apron, especially facing towards Ryan Air but the purchase of an appropriate beverage is essential. This is Ireland, and it would be a foolish man who went near a bar without partaking of a bevy or two. Anyone who doesn't understand this fact of life would probably be wasting his time visiting Ireland!

Outside the terminal, Car Park 4 overlooks the Ryan Air apron, with additional views of Aer Turas and any cargo aircraft which might be present, a UPS DC-8 being the most likely. From the nearby roundabout, a link road passes the Aer Lingus headquarters, beyond which is a footbridge. Even from the top, only a part of the Team and general aviation area is visible. There is little reason to find somewhere out in the open to spend any amount of time and doing so can cause the security personnel to show undesirable, and probably unnecessary, interest. The advice is therefore to see whatever there is to be seen, keep moving, and get back into the terminal for a longer stay.

A car allows use of the popular perimeter road. To get there, make a left turn at the roundabout onto the main road in the direction of Drogheda and Belfast. After another left turn at the next roundabout, posted Swords, the road passes close to the runway. There are lay-bys where it is possible to sit and enjoy life, a popular pastime in Ireland. Photos of aircraft landing, complete with tyre smoke, need only a 200mm zoom and departing traffic is just as easily seen, subject to runway in use, of course.

Also seen from here is the giant Team Aer Lingus hangar and maintenance area and some general aviation. A left turn at the corner of the field, at the thresholds of Runways 11 and 16, the road continues to the hangars of Iona National Airways and Aer Lingus Commuter. By following the road, the main runway (10/28) is reached, and there are views along both sides.

Irish light aircraft are thinly spread so anyone with an interest in the country's civil register will certainly want to visit to WESTON, on the N4, where a good proportion of all the nation's aircraft can be seen.

GALWAY

GWY EICM   Carnmore   4m/6km E

This airport is tucked away on the western extremity of Europe. Anyone who visits will note that the people like it that way. The pace is, even by Irish standards, relaxed. There is no equivalent in Galway of the Spanish word 'mañana' (meaning they'll get round to it tomorrow) as the same sense of urgency is not felt! Carnmore is somewhere to chat to people about aviation, rather than experience a lot of action.

SHANNON

SNN   EINN   16m/25km W of Limerick (bus 45 minutes)

Shannon is famous for its small number of quality movements, ranging from Aeroflot crew training and delivery flights to . . . almost anything.

Comparable in many ways to Prestwick, Shannon handles some trans-atlantic traffic, with the last chance of fuel before crossing the ocean, but the main runway, 06/24, is generally quiet enough, and long enough, to be of use for wide-bodies in the circuit.

The spectators' enclosure in the old terminal offered fine views of the traffic but it can remain closed for part, if not all, of the day. This may be due to the alternative facilities now on offer. The new terminal features an observation area, behind glass. The reflections can cause problems for photographers. Any visitor will need a large slice of luck, or prior warning, to leave Shannon with a photographic record of one of those really extraordinary movements. Anyone touring Ireland in a car will also be able to park at the appropriate end of the runway.

Between the passenger terminal and Runway 06/24 is a small Aer Lingus maintenance hangar. Most of the interest is generated by aircraft on the ground, seen by travelling in the opposite direction. A road leads past the cargo terminal and the Omega facility, round the end of Runway 31. Just beyond it are an Irish Air Corps base and Guinness Peat. A long walk (or short drive) through the industrial estate is worth the effort. After passing the threshold of Runway 24, the road leads to the massive Shannon Aerospace hangar.

F FRANCE (French Republic)
ANNECY

NCY   LFLP   Meythet   2m/3km NNW

One of France's many quiet backwaters, where the only scheduled link with the outside world is an early morning commuter flight from/to Paris. During the rest of the day, some of the two dozen residents may venture out of the hangar, next to the terminal, but things are otherwise very quiet indeed. Only seekers of French registrations will bother to make a detour here, probably on their way to Geneva or Chambéry.

AVIGNON
AVN   LFMV   Caumont   4m/6km SE

Linked to Lyon by a couple of commuter flights per day, this is another example of France's many quiet regional airports. There is normally one TAT Fokker 100 parked on the ramp during the day, but no other airliners to be seen moving. A short detour from the A7 Autoroute, at the Avignon Sud exit, can result in a ground level portrait shot of an F.27, with the only other likely subjects being the displayed ex-Air France Caravelle and, on the far side of the runway, a B-26. Access to this is normally achieved by a request at the control tower.

BEAUVAIS
BVA   LFOB   Tille   3m/5km NE

A roof terrace offers a splendid view of the apron but few enthusiasts want to see, or photograph, aprons. Traffic is at its busiest at weekends, such as Friday evenings and Sundays, when passengers are transferred between aircraft and buses. Scandinavian flights are not unknown but seeing their charters can be a matter of luck. Apart from them, Air France 737s might be crew training or a cargo charter may be present.

BELFORT
BOR   LFSQ   Fontaine   9m/15km E

One of several regional airports in France which is suffering a sharp decline in its fortunes. Scheduled services operated for some time, though not profitably and these have now been dropped, leaving only a small number of (mostly general aviation) movements to keep the alive. With only a handful of light aircraft to log, it might not be worth a detour.

BEZIERS
BZR   LFMU   Vias   6m/9km E

Even in summer, scheduled traffic is a rarity, though the occasional charter flight is attracted by the nearby Cap d'Agde. Anyone visiting this part of the world would be well advised to stay at the beach, where the view is famous for being far more interesting than that at the airport.

BORDEAUX
BOD   LFBD   Merignac   7m/11km W (bus 35 minutes)

As the regional capital of southwest France, Bordeaux handles quite a quantity of traffic, and a better variety than most other French airports have to offer. Many of the movements are Air Inter but they do include representatives of each type in the fleet. Apart from its many domestic flights, Bordeaux is important enough to warrant an en route stop by wide-body flights, including Air France 747s and Air Afrique Airbuses. Sadly, these most interesting visitors arrive in the early morning or late afternoon, so the middle of the day has little excitement.

The French Air Force base is quite active, with plenty of Mirages and Jaguars on the move during the week. Another presence here is that of GAM-Dassault and its Falcon production line. There is more chance of a customer despatching a Hercules, for example, to pick up spares, than that of a sporadic Falcon flight but both are bonuses to bear in mind.

Inside the passenger terminal is a lift which serves the spectators' terrace. Next to the lift button is a very permanent-looking sign which reads, "Closed Terrace". The first floor level restaurant offers the only real view, though it gets very warm in summer. The adjacent toilet windows face the ramp though, once again, the heat is a problem. One would have to be extremely dedicated to make the trip to Bordeaux for the chance to peer out of a toilet window for two or three hours!

CARCASSONNE
CCF LFMK   Salvaza   2m/3km WNW

It is now debatable as to whether this exceedingly quiet airport is worth even a detour. Even Aigle Azur SF.340s are now a rare sight, so this can be considered as merely an airfield with a small selection of French light aircraft in residence.

CHAMBERY/AIX LES BAINS
CMF LFLB   Voglans   5m/8km N/ 4m/6km S

The decision whether or not to visit this airport means deciding on which road to take, usually when travelling between Geneva and Lyon or Paris. It's a choice between the scenic route and the autoroute. Worth the detour from the scenic road, Chambéry has a few hangars and a good number of residents. The far hangar is often used for maintenance on some aircraft with exotic foreign registrations. Scheduled traffic can be seen at close quarters and a souvenir photo of a TAT movement, FH-227 or F.28, will be taken at breakfast or tea time. During the rest of the day, the field has that typical French air of peace and tranquility.

CHATEAUROUX
CHR LFLX   Deols   3m/5km NNE

Some way south of Paris, this airport has become worthy of a visit for anyone passing in the car. Aero Technique Espace is a company which carries out subcontract work for Airbus Industrie. Since some of the newly built aircraft are ferried here for painting, it is possible to see some surprisingly exotic colour schemes outside the hangar.

The airport owners are looking for an operator who needs to develop a cargo (probably parcels) hub in this part of France. If they succeed, a passing visit could be even more worthwhile.

CLERMONT-FERRAND
CFE LFLC   Aulnat   4m/6km NE

The roof deck is far too high to be of use to the enthusiast, since the majority of visitors are relatively small aircraft. At Toronto or Hannover, a telephoto lens can ensure that larger aircraft are seen from something approaching side view but here the aircraft are too small.

Since Air Inter flights are operated by A320s (at wide intervals during the day) it would be worth hoping for the right runway in use. The holding point for Runway 27 is very close to the D54e local road, and photos of aircraft on the taxiway are likely to be of high quality, though there may be few opportunities.

COLMAR
CMR   LFGA   Houssen   2m/3km NNW

The airport is small, and quite informal. However, it has lost its battle to retain scheduled services, being not too great a distance from Basel/Mulhouse. Air Inter's regional services operated at an intolerable loss. Since only a short detour from the road between Strasbourg and Basel is involved, the effort might be worthwhile, and there are some interesting residents in the hangars. Military enthusiasts will associate Colmar with Mirages but attempts at close inspection will involve meeting a security representative.

DINARD
DNR   LFRD   Pleurtuit   4m/6km S

The airport is signposted from the Dinard - St Malo road, and has a small, well appointed terminal. The cafe overlooks the stands and the runway, and there is a balcony complete with tables and chairs. As is normal in such circumstances, all that is lacking is the aircraft. There are no commuter services but occasional flights from the Channel Islands are operated by Jersey European SD3.60s and Aurigny Trislanders. The TAT maintenance hangar is clearly visible, usually with one or two FH-227s outside. Any notable sighting at Dinard will probably be a foreign visitor to the TAT facility.

GRENOBLE
GNB   LFLS   St Geoirs   24m/38km NW (bus 45 minutes)

Yet another small provincial airport but business picks up in winter, when the skiing season gets under way. Many of the charter flights are operated from Britain, but there is a rampside enclosure between the control tower and the terminal from which the view is first class. A daytime visit during summer will usually result in little or nothing to see, apart from some resident light aircraft.

LE HAVRE
LEH   LFOH   Octeville   3m/5km NNW

Brit Air, Transvalair and Regional operate services from Brittany to several parts of France, and foreign summer charters are growing in number. Because their aircraft can be seen with less trouble elsewhere, le Havre may not warrant much interest but the residents do feature a Coastguard Alouette. Access to the ramp may offer better chances of photos but the chainlink fence doesn't obstruct the view for those without a camera.

LE TOUQUET
LTQ   LFAT   Paris-Plage   2m/3km N

Everything about this airport suggests it's seen better times. When it was fashionable for the English to cross the Channel for a holiday, this was a flourishing town. It was also an early express link for onward travel to Paris. The railway tracks can still be seen next to the terminal, and the buildings around the perimeter tell of more prosperous times. Apart from a handful of light aircraft, there is little to see unless another attempt is made to operate scheduled cross-Channel flights. It is a long time since Lydd to le Touquet was a viable proposition.

LILLE

LIL   LFQQ   Lesquin   9m/15km SE

The observation deck offers good views of the small apron but most of the scheduled traffic operates rarely during the day, except for some charter flights at weekends. Apart from an Aeropostale F.27 parked all day remote from the terminal, there may be one or two Flandre Air King Airs to see at a separate apron, next to the approach road, close to which are helipads for the Gendarmerie and, on the opposite side of the road, a couple of Army Alouettes.

LYON

LYS   LFLL   Satolas   15m/23km ESE (bus 45 minutes)

Perhaps on a par with Marseille, this is one of France's busier airports, outside Paris. The roof terrace, situated between the two terminal wings, is open on Sundays but the view is an elevated one. The car park beside the domestic terminal overlooks much of that apron and a similar view from the taxi stands, at the opposite end, allows the freight area to be inspected.

Traffic is made up mostly of flights by Air France and Air Inter. The only operator based at Satolas is Air Exel, whose Brasilias use the domestic terminal. When Runway 36 is in use, it is worth leaving the terminal area and following the signs for 'Fret et Fatton'. Two left turns lead past the fret/ freight sheds to Ets Fatton, where the taxiway and holding point can be seen at close quarters. Photography here is at its very best in the afternoon, with the sun perfectly placed.

Satolas seems to be a perpetual building site. Development work has meant many additional facilities, and the construction of a TGV rail link has resulted in major upheaval to the road layout. It will take a while for this major work to be completed.

LYON

LYN   LFLY   Bron   3m/5km E

Despite the pressures for space around this field, it has survived. Close to town, and totally surrounded by commercial development, it is the base for several business aircraft operators, though few may be present on a weekday. The old terminal area, closest to the extremely busy main road, was decaying away in 1982, so redevelopment is probable. The main hangar area is in the opposite corner, a short drive away.

MARSEILLE

MRS   LFML   Provence International   15m/23km NW (bus 30 minutes)

Summer means increased traffic and another chance for the observation deck in Marignane's international terminal to be open again. The entrance fee pays the cost of the security check but it is a very dedicated enthusiast who stays all day. The lack of shade means that the heat of the afternoon gets wearing, and there are no facilities for buying a much needed drink or, perhaps more important, for going to the toilet.

Opening hours are, reportedly, between 10:00 and 6:00 on weekends, public holidays and during the school holidays. Weekends, and Saturdays in particular, are rather quiet. Photos of movements on the apron suffer from having a sepia tint, imparted by the bronze coloured glass of the two metre high security screen.

Carriers are varied, though movements by the Securité Civile CL-215s are few and related mostly to fire-fighting emergencies in late summer. Since their compound, and that of

Aerospatiale, are out of bounds and generally out of sight, it would be wise not to pin hopes on seeing anything of the inhabitants. Other vantage points include the top level of the multi-storey car park, P6, though some distance away from the ramp for photos, and the general aviation terminal to the northwest, where smaller aircraft can be seen at close quarters. The adjacent taxiway is rarely used, as the opposite direction runway is favoured by the prevailing winds.

The dedicated and intrepid might be prepared to brave the summer heat and explore. From Merignac town the road to Le Jai passes the far end of the field, where an alternative view of the hangar areas allows most of the inmates and other residents to be seen.

MONTPELLIER

| MPL | LFMT | Frejorgues | 5m/8km SE (bus 20 minutes) |

Quiet for scheduled movements, the majority of the traffic is dedicated to the commuter. Air Littoral have their base of operations here, and the visitor may be rewarded by close-up views of their increasingly varied fleet. The terminal offers no facilities but there are other places from which the ramp can be seen with ease. General aviation is quite brisk, especially at weekends, and much of the resident population can be seen from the fence. Photos are another matter . . . very rare at Montpellier.

MULHOUSE

| MLH | LFSB | EuroAirport | 16m/26km SE |

This is the French part of Basel-Mulhouse. Unless there is a specific reason to visit the French side, it is best to arrive at the airport (landside) from Basel, in Switzerland. For further details, see under the entry for Basel.

NICE

| NCE | LFMN | Cote d'Azur | 4m/6km SW (bus 15 minutes) |

Terminal 1 is light, airy, modern and pleasant for passengers. Casual visitors, such as spotters, have nowhere to go in this building, apart from the toilet. The construction of Terminal 2, next to the large general aviation ramp, has enabled a different view of the field to be opened up. The access roads and Zone 3 car park serving the new building are close to the taxiway, and photographs in the late afternoon make the most of sun. Much of the interest at Nice is generated by general aviation, and biz-jets from all over Europe can be seen. Saudi Arabian and American businessmen also feel the need for the occasional trip to Nice, especially when major events, such as the tennis or Formula One Grand Prix are taking place in Monte Carlo, or the Cannes International Film Festival.

Other interesting movements are regional ATR-72s and Securité Civile Firecats, as the jet airliners tend to be much as can be seen at any other major European airport. The cargo area usually contains, during the daytime, an Aeropostale F.27.

An alternative vantage point, also on the western side of the field, is very popular, as it is close to the taxiway between the apron and Runways 05L/R. This is the shopping centre with parking provision for 3,000 cars, hence the name CAP3000. Leaving the terminal on the busy main road in the direction of Antibes, it is only a ten minute walk to the far/western side of the river, where the car park overlooks the airport. The facilities include seats and a general view of the entire airport. Afternoons and evenings are the best times to visit.

At the far end of the field, where the road passes close to the holding point for Runway 23R, aircraft landing and those on the taxiway are seen at close quarters. Again the sun can be a major problem to the photographer. The conifers, planted along the edge of the Boulevard des

Anglais, were meant to provide an effective screen between the airport and the road. They are now mature enough to be doing their job rather well, and views through them are best described as glimpses.

NIMES

FNI	LFTW	Garons	7m/11km SE

One of Aeronavale's main bases shares the runway with this minor regional airport, so the majority of activity is of more interest to the military enthusiast. The dozen or so Atlantics and a couple of preserved Caravelles are all that most passing visitors will see, because scheduled passenger services are few and far between. Photographs taken here are rare. This applies to weekdays. At weekends, things are even quieter!

PARIS

Those with a car will do best if they are accompanied also by two maps: Michelin produce Environs de Paris, No.96, and Plan de Paris, No.10. The former is essential to discover the various fields located on the outskirts, while the latter makes it possible to visit Issy without fights breaking out between driver and navigator. The latter also details all the one way streets, which ease the problem of passing some time in the city centre.

Travel by bus is more economical when carnets of tickets are pre-purchased for RATP journeys. To get to le Bourget and Charles de Gaulle, buses Nos. 350 and 351 leave from the Place de la Nation, Gare de l'Est and Gare du Nord, while the SNCF train serves Charles de Gaulle by line B.

Travel to Orly involves catching an Orlyrail train, from Quai d'Orsay, Pont St. Michel or Gare d'Austerlitz, to Pont de Rungis, where a bus connects with the airport. SNCF line B also serves Denfert-Rochereau and Antony, from where the Orlyval people mover (a two-car tram without a driver) completes the journey to Orly Ouest.

Light aircraft can be seen in number at several fields, all of which offer good opportunities for the enthusiast but travel will probably be by car. Close to Versailles, and not far from Orly, is TOUSSUS-LE-NOBLE with a large number of residents, while VILLACOUBLAY, nearby, is essentially a military field on the southern edge of the N186. At one end of this road is Orly and at the other is Versailles, with ST CYR L'ECOLE close by. To the west is the last field to complete the short tour, CHAVENAY, and a day's trip around these fields will make an impressive log, but no significant impact on the French register!

Aéroports de Paris (ADP) is the company which operates Orly and Charles de Gaulle. They prepare, for daily use, photostat documents entitled 'Prévisions des Mouvements'. It doesn't need a degree in French to know that these are the movement timetables. They are known to be available for Charles de Gaulle, with sheets coloured separately for CDG1 and CDG2. It is probable that similar sheets are also supplied for Orly Sud and Orly Ouest. The airport information desk is the obvious place to ask.

PARIS

CDG	LFPG	Charles de Gaulle	14m/22km NNE (bus/train 30 minutes)

Charles de Gaulle's traffic is shared between the two terminals and keeping track of both is a problem. Air France occupy Terminal 2, effectively four terminals: A, B, C and D (with two more under construction) and the views from here are minimal. Air France passengers in transit will say otherwise, pointing out that gate A40 offers a fine view of a large percentage of the arrivals and departures, as well as overlooking the domestic ATR/146 area and the 747Fs on the cargo apron.

Between Terminal Areas 1 and 2 are a few other buildings of significance: the railway station, with a bus link for passengers, the splendidly located Ibis Hotel (previously Arcade) next to it, with some rooms offering restricted views of movements, and the control tower near which was one of the best locations for the serious photographer.

Terminal 1 is the original drum-shaped building, which handles non-Air France movements in some quantity, but has no views from within. The road at Arrivals Level 2 does allow a popular view of the proceedings. The battle between spotters and gendarmes has been won, it seems, by the spotters as there are no recent reports of conflict. Continued sensible behaviour on this road level of the terminal should ensure that the victory becomes permanent. Bus drivers in particular are keen to remind spotters that they do stand perilously close to such obects as passing wing mirrors - one false step, easily made, can end in serious injury.

The roadside, particularly for spotters, isn't necessarily the best place to stand. The views from within the building through the full height windows beside, say, doors 8, 10 and 12 is equally good. Photographers will need to stand at the parapet. The same area, 8 to 12, is probably as good as anywhere. It overlooks Satellites 2 and 3 but allows views also of movements on the northern Runway 09/27, which means a few of the aircraft, mostly Air France, which can't be accommodated on 10/28. Beyond the taxiway is the apron for Terminal T9. (What happened to 3-8?) This is the charter terminal, which features an increasingly good variety of visitors: Pegasus 737s, Air Jet 146s and Air Alfa A300s for instance. For the spotter, and many photographers, this is probably as good a place to take up temporary residence as any at CDG.

Having established that neither terminal offers comprehensive viewing possibilities, the alternatives have to be pursued. The Zone Technique car park has acquired a renown for its proximity to the northern edge of the apron. The authorities are becoming less tolerant to this use, and the vacant area between car park and fence can be out of bounds, depending on the nearby gate-keeper. Whilst the appearance of a coachload of Salon-bound spotters will keep the gendarmes' hands full, they have more time to deal with one or two people in a car. The use of the ventilation shaft, a much-loved perch for photographs, now encites a reaction from officialdom, so life can be difficult at CDG.

Bearing in mind that the road layout is quite confusing, alternative spots can be found and one of the best was, more or less, below the control tower. To screen off this vantage point, a row of tall conifers now obscures the view. Anyone who shins up the bank on the western side of the main approach road to Terminal 1 can get a portrait of one or two of the airliners parked nearby. At least one French government aircraft, often an A310, is normally parked within range of a camera. Extended stays at the fence are not a good idea! Out to the west is Entretien Nord, and the Air France hangars. There is usually something parked outside to justify the detour.

CDG is a modern airport, and it was designed for the convenience of its passengers. Air France has its own facilities, including effectively its own runway, and the competition gets everywere else. As is always the case, things are not quite that simple: Air France also plays host to a small number of foreign operators, such as Aeromexico. This can mean that an arriving star visitor, such as a 767, can go unidentified. Instead of cursing bad luck, anyone with some knowledge of flight numbers (gleaned from either an ABC Airways Guide or a radio) might care to contact the ADP Aéroports de Paris information desk. In most instances the aircraft's registration can be supplied.

PARIS

JDP   Issy les Moulineaux   5m/8km SW (bus/train 30 minutes)

Paris is ringed by the busy Boulevard Périphérique. In the southwest corner of the city, just east of the river, is the heliport, living in the shadow of this main artery but not easily found without a map. The Porte de Sèvres exit (NOT Quai d'Issy) leads to the front door. Metro users will alight at Balard and walk under the Périphérique overbridge.

Heli Union have a base here but the majority of their helicopters are away earning their living, so that only a few can be seen at any one time. Another operator is the Gendarmerie, usually with an Alouette on the ground. It is unwise to expect vast quantities of helicopters but a few examples will offer variety to a trip log otherwise dominated by light aircraft or airliners.

A footpath along the perimeter is marked 'no entry' to deter motor vehicles, so the sign can be (and is) ignored by pedestrians. Proof of this for the wary, who may be afraid to venture this way, is offered on the ground: there is sufficient squashy evidence left by dogs for walkers to divide their concentration between what they can see on the airfield and what they should see under their feet.

PARIS
JPU   la Défense Heliport   1m/1.5km W

Situated at the heart of the spectacular new development of la Défense, this pad may be of interest to the very dedicated enthusiast. In reality, any visitors seen here normally come from one of the local airports, so nothing new is likely to be seen. Photographers may, however, make the trip here in the hope of being able to take a souvenir photo with a difference.

PARIS
LBG   LFPB   le Bourget   9m/15km N (bus 20 minutes)

During the Paris Air Salon, the ramps to the north are crammed with biz-jets, and many of them can be seen by anyone investigating all the nooks and crannies. Photos are being made more difficult by the erection of more and more temporary buildings, but it is possible to get up to many fences, and gates, for a chance to look at this spectacular array. Through the year, this part of the field is where the action is concentrated, and all roads between the buildings are worth exploring, as the different angles can yield one or two aircraft.

North of the old UTA hangars, FBO's handle plenty of traffic and the service road passes around Europe Falcon Service to a gate by the fence. There are several windows in the EFS hangar, revealing some exotically registered Falcons, but few aircraft pass on the taxiway, just beyond, during the day. Even the length of the grass, enough to spoil photos by obscuring wheels, conspires against the photographer. The EFS area is at the extreme northern end of the ramp area. Close to it is a quasi-military base. Restrictions imposed unilaterally by EFS on photos and spotting are often enforced by someone in a uniform. To what extent the law is on their side is debatable but it doesn't need a law degree to figure out who will have the last say. In several instances, 'the last say' means confiscation of log books and film. Try arguing that in a court of law during a weekend trip to Paris!

South of the main terminal area is the famous Musée de l'Air, with its many exhibits. Other aircraft are stored on the remote Dugny side of the field. As there may be someone with nothing better to do than take a couple of guys over there, it may be worth showing an interest.

PARIS
ORY   LFPO   Orly   9m/15km S (bus/train 35 minutes)

Despite the amount of traffic which uses Charles de Gaulle, there are enough interesting operators to ensure that Orly is still worth a visit, and often a lengthy stay. Many major international operators use Orly, though these are now mainly European, plus a good variety of North African traffic.

Because some of these more interesting visitors are sporadic, there are afternoons which seem interminable, with only a procession of domestic commuters to be seen. Reference to a timetable is therefore necessary to ensure that Orly repays the interest. The two terminals are

Orly Ouest, mostly used by Air Inter and Orly Sud, effectively the centre of the action. The spotter can stand at the windows on the left hand side of Orly Ouest's Departures level and identify a fair number, but by no means all, of the Air Inter airliners. Once this is done, it's best to head to the northern end of the building and take the people mover shuttle to Orly Sud.

There are two platforms: that to the left is the Orlyval link which goes to Antony. It costs FFr76 for a ticket into central Paris. The free transfer to Orly Sud leaves from the right-hand platform.

For the spotter, there are windows on the first floor and mezzanine levels. The terrace is considerably higher, and it offers a much greater area from which to watch activities. A loose mesh is hung over the entire enclosure, which allows in the pleasant sunshine, and the glass is only a minor irritation to most photographers. Watching is good but work with a camera can be a little more difficult, especially due to facing south though, with care, good results can be obtained.

Any of the vantage points chosen in the terminal should follow a visit to the most important level of all: the basement, where a supermarket offers a good range of snacks and drinks at affordable prices. A shop at this level stocks aviation postcards, with a selection for those who seek souvenirs, or additions to the collection.

Elsewhere on the field, there are some other places worth a look. Just north of Orly Sud is the cargo terminal, handling a variety of operations, many of which are C-130s of foreign air arms. The guardians of the gate don't offer any assistance to those wishing to take photos, and ground clutter can compromise the quality of portraits. Further north are the Air Inter and Air France hangars and ramps, in which can be found a good selection of operators and types.

On the opposite side of the N7, and best reached from remote parking area P7, there are two areas which can yield plenty of interest. Close by the road is the VIP terminal, and a line-up of French Government Falcons is not uncommon. When foreign dignatories are expected, this area is at its best . . . and out of bounds. The best way to know if this is a likelihood is to look out for a proliferation of flags. The tall timber fence hides the taxiway to runway 25 but another, lower, fence abuts it, and can be scaled for good views of airliners taxying. This is by far the best spot to obtain those ground level shots, without having recourse to telephoto lenses.

Photographs taken from the roof deck can become repetitive, despite the subject matter, because the rows of trees and buses appear so often. Another feature of Orly photos is the clock on the control tower; first time visitors may not notice these considerations through the viewfinder but they are very noticeable in the results. Time often goes quite slowly at Orly, especially in the afternoon. Attention then turns to the details. Directly opposite the Orly Sud terminal, on the southern edge of the field by the threshold of 02L, are the Concorde prototype painted in Air France colours, and an ex-Corse Air Caravelle. Out to the east are another two Caravelles (one ex-Catair and the other ex-Air Inter) plus 727 F-BPJU.

Much of the traffic is Air Inter which normally lands on the same arrivals runway as the other traffic, 26. Runway 25 is normally used for departure, so all incoming traffic should be logged and, if possible photographed. In many instances this is not possible from the deck. Corsair 747s and Alia A310s might taxi past to a stand but Air Outre Mer DC-10s and Egyptair 747s tend to use stands at the western end of the ramp. Blast screens between Orly Sud and Orly Ouest mean that many interesting visitors might not be photographed, without a visit to the fence opposite car park P5. This is only a two-storey building but the roof might offer the chance to take a photo of something exceptional as it taxis to the hold for Runway 25.

PAU

PUF   LFBP   Uzein   6m/9km NW

A reasonably large, and very modern, passenger terminal contains a lounge, a bar and viewing facilities. There are also shops and a restaurant, and a visit in mid summer can be a mystifying experience. Having parked in the enormous car park (with their confusing ticket machines), entry into the terminal may reveal only two signs of life, both of them gendarmes! During the day, everything can be closed with, needless to say, not a single aircraft in sight. Pau is one of France's many regional airports which cater for a small number of commuter movements in the early morning and evening, with no traffic during the day.

PERPIGNAN
PGF   LFMP   Rivesaltes   4m/6km NW

Anyone driving to Spain will call in at France's most southerly airport and be rewarded by an Aeropostale/Air France F.27 awaiting the evening mail flight, and possibly an Europe Air Service 737 or 727. The good view from the terminal rarely offers any subject matter but the EAS ramp can be seen from the D117 (that's a road, not a Jodel!) close to the junction with the approach road.

POITIERS
PIS   LFBI   Biard   3m/5km NW

The passenger terminal is distinctive in the extreme, being a circular building, with a balcony around the front. If only there were more aircraft to see, this could be a memorable airport for reasons other than the shape of the terminal. There are occasional Transall flights, related to the nearby military academy, and one or two TAT ATR-42s.

ROANNE
RNE   LFLO   Renaison   3m/5km NW

Yet another regional airport where activity is restricted to breakfast time or in the evening, the occasional commuter flights to Paris will only be seen by the extremely lucky, or dedicated. The only other airliner worth noting is an ex-Air France Caravelle, but most French airports seem to have one now.

STRASBOURG
SXB   LFST   Entzheim   6m/9km WSW

Another ramp with only an Aeropostale F.27 to be seen, though there is a little more traffic here than at some similar airports. The runway is shared by a military base on the far side, with plenty of Mirages present. Any thoughts of a stop at the end of the runway here may be dispelled by signs which warn of 'Danger of Death', though this probably refers to the possibility of being hit by a landing aircraft, rather than the penalty for taking photographs! Nevertheless, there is an official eye kept open for people involved in this pastime, and a meeting of the minds could take time. While there is some general aviation based at Entzheim, another field, closer to town, handles most of this traffic.

TOULOUSE
TLS   LFBO   Blagnac   6m/9km NW (bus 35 minutes)

It should not be overlooked that Toulouse is an active airport, and not just the home of Airbus Industrie assembly. The passenger terminal handles a good number of charters, especially in summer, with such remarkable movements as Portugalia F.100s, Egyptair wide-bodies and Trans-Med 737s plus a good variety of aircraft from North Africa. In the absence of an observation deck, the upper level restaurant is the only place to see them, but the view is good. For nostalgia-freaks, the Air Toulouse International Caravelles offer a link with the past.

The increasingly wide range of products rolling off the Airbus Industrie lines do make this an interesting airport to visit. The only guided tours of the plant are offered to parties, which must be pre-booked. There are two versions, French and English, and the latter must be booked at least four weeks in advance. About a week's notice is adequate for the French tours. The A330 and A340 production lines are included, as are the all-important flight lines and paint shops. For further details, telephone 61 154 400. Anyone with a real interest in Airbus Industrie, travelling to Toulouse by car, will no doubt pass Chateauroux on the way, as a company subcontracts some of the Airbus finishing work there.

Airbus Industrie do not go to extreme lengths to advertise their presence, and the approach is signposted in a rather low-key fashion. In other words, directions are necessary.

Leaving the upper level of the terminal, a right turn and a walk down the ramp lead to a roundabout. Take the road marked 'Fret' which passes the cargo area, where a couple of interesting aircraft might be present. At the end of the road is another roundabout, and another right turn onto the bridge over the main highway. The dusty road down the near side of the highway leads to the No.66 bus stop. Where it goes, and how much use it is, nobody knows! At the far end of the bridge is another roundabout and a walk alongside the highway, past the Airbus building, to the far end of the airport. It is now time to get to the other side . . .

At the traffic lights, follow the sign which says St Martin. The D124 leads there and any turns from now on will be to the right. The high grassy bank inside the perimeter fence prevents views of the field. The first available right turn leads past the FedEx building to the Airbus factory. Here is the security gate and a large car park from where a selection of nearly finished wares can be seen, though a souvenir photograph will probably be less than ideal.

TOURS
TUF   LFOT   St Symphorien   4m/6km NNE

The significant size of the TAT fleet is not to be seen to any degree here, in spite of this being the headquarters of the airline. The centre of operations is mainly Orly, with other aircraft based all over the country. Apart from a chance to see a TAT ATR-42 in operation, the only other appeal lies in the prospect of a rarity being present for maintenance. TAT handle some quite exotic airlines but they are to be considered exceptional. French Air Force Alpha Jets offer consolation for anyone intent on making the journey.

VALENCE
VAF   LFLU   Chabeuil   3m/5km ENE

Chabeuil is quiet and served by only a few scheduled commuter flights. There is an enclosure between the tower and the terminal but, apart from the odd charter flight in summer, there is little to see. The light aircraft population is augmented here by some military Pumas and Alouettes. Rhonavia's small fleet of executive aircraft are more often seen at Lyon Bron.

F-O FRENCH OVERSEAS DEPTS and PROTECTORATES
GRAND CASE
SFG   Esperance

The Air Guadeloupe flights fly regularly to the 'other' part of St Martin, owned by Guadeloupe, and French-speaking. Literally a few miles from Princes Juliana airport, Esperance is so small, it could best be described as a strip. As befits a place of this size, the three Do228 flights each day can be witnessed on the ramp, with a souvenir portrait easily obtained.

G UNITED KINGDOM (U.K. of Gt Britain and Northern Ireland)

This section has been divided into the countries and principalities. The first is England, followed by Scotland, Wales and Northern Ireland. The Isle of Man and the Channel Islands appear last.

BIGGIN HILL
EGKB   1m/1.5km N

This is probably one of Britain's, and possibly the world's, most famous airfields because of its World War II history. Now it houses Britain's largest collection of general aviation. The main road passes the western boundary, and many aircraft can be seen. The southern apron area has its own access and there are several hangars, all crammed full of light aircraft. At the far end of Runway 11 is a (restricted) access road across the threshold of Runway 29, to more aprons and hangars. Nowhere else in Britain is it possible to log so many aircraft at one go.

Interest in the larger visitors is centred further north along the main road. Passing the threshold of Runway 03, and the RAF base with its Spitfire, the general aviation terminal sits next to the western apron. It is here that the biz-jets arrive for customs clearance. The apron can be seen from the terminal windows and from the fence, where photos are possible, though both the view and content are often slightly limited.

BIRMINGHAM
BHX   EGBB   International   6m/9km SE (train 10 minutes)

England's second city now boasts an airport to match the status but, even in summer, traffic is only moderate. The main passenger terminal, past British Airways Eurohub, has a viewing deck but there is all too little to see. The completion of the Eurohub terminal, on the south side of the apron, has not restricted the excellent view from the spectator's grassed area. Most, if not all, jet traffic passes this area as it taxis in or out. Some of the commuters tend to use the runway best suited to their destination, when prevailing winds blow across, rather than along, the field.

British Airways dominate the movements but, during the summer especially, there is a fair variety of charters, including some from across the Atlantic. But Birmingham offers some of the best opportunities to get portraits of smaller aircraft, such as an Aer Lingus Fokker 50. Many of the business flights betwen Birmingham and Europe take place in the very early morning or late evening.

On the west side of the field, on the site of the original Elmdon Airport, are the domestic general aviation, cargo and Maersk Air facilities. A staircase at the corner of the old terminal is popular for a view over the wall, and it would appear that attempts to seal it off have not been entirely successful. At weekends, there can be one or two aircraft parked here, including the occasional interesting cargo carrier. The screen wall separating this ramp from the road has, next to the hangar, a gate: now the only vantage point, though it is normally possible to take a photo of one or two of the Maersk residents, parked close by.

BLACKBUSHE
BBS   EGLK   6m/9km NW of Farnborough

More a reasonably large airfield than an airport, Blackbushe is on the north side of the A30 trunk road, a few miles north of Farnborough. Most of the time, the only action is light aircraft in the circuit, most of which operate from the old terminal area, next to the main road. It is probable that every resident and visitor can be identified from the car park or from the perimeter fence.

On the north side of the field, some distance west, is a modern facility where the larger aircraft, including some Beech jets, are to be seen. The access road passes the western end of the runway and leads to car parking areas immediately next to the ramps. Those who wish to see inside the hangars will possibly find difficulty. Unlike the occasional visitor to a remote field in, say, a rural part of France, this is England, and close to London, so there is no shortage of spotters who could make a nuisance of themselves.

BLACKPOOL
BLK   EGNH   Squire's Gate   3m/5km S

In some ways, Squire's Gate can be considered to be two separate airports, functioning side by side. The main passenger terminal is used mostly by holidaymakers bound for the Isle of Man. To its left is a car park which also serves as the viewing area. This is convenient, as it is situated between the terminal and the gas rig heliport, where it is usual to see one or two Bond Dauphins on the ground.

Beyond the heliport are hangars and ramps used for general aviation, with Westair occupying the farthest one. Another viewing area here ensures that all the light aircraft are visible without any real need for ramp access. Bond's hangar can be seen in a separate area, reached by turning left at the Vulcan, next to the Aero Club. By heading east, past the terminal, and then turning right a few times, there is a road leading to a new housing estate. This road runs parallel to the runway and aircraft using it are within range of a 200mm lens.

BOURNEMOUTH
BOH   EGHH   Hurn   4m/6km NE

Hurn airport boasts an extremely pleasant modern terminal, and what could be described as a viewing garden next to the ramp. Movements not using the terminal may not be seen on the move from here as the runway is partially out of sight. Traffic is very slow but the runway does offer occasional movements of the Flight Refuelling (FR Aviation) Falcons and some additional rarities. Access to the far/north side of the field is restricted, due to FRA activity, and security measures are tight. Anyone intent on a visit to the north side should make arrangements beforehand.

The B3073 road, which runs along the southern perimeter, offers excellent views across the airfield. Taxying aircraft, depending on the runway in use, pass very close to the low fence. A turning to the north at the roundabout in the southwest corner of the field leads to another vantage point which can be particularly good in the late afternoons.

BRISTOL
BRS   EGDD   Lulsgate   9m/15km SW

The airport is southwest of the city on the A38. Important road connections with the M5 motorway are tortuous, to say the least. The charter flights at summer weekends boost the movements total but a visit during the week in winter must be scheduled to coincide with one or two of the international commuter flights. Since these include DLT or RFG, Cityhopper and Aer Lingus Commuter, a souvenir photo can be easily obtained.

Bristol airport has the car parking sewn up, so that it's almost impossible to find anywhere that's free. The perimeter road to the south is good for ground level shots and the small observation deck is well-placed. As an alternative, a left turn onto the A38 followed by the first left and another left turn after about a mile, along Cooks Bridle Path, gains access to the runway's edge. Just before the road turns right, there is a track leading to the aero club where a few light aircraft are parked.

The service road to the east of the passenger terminal is posted as no access to unauthorized traffic. Pedestrians can (in theory?) walk along here for close-up views of the occasional JEA Fokker or Brymon Dash 8 which may be parked awaiting its next flight.

BRIZE NORTON
BZZ   EGVN   1m/1.5km S

It may come as a surprise to some readers to learn that scheduled services are indeed operated from Brize, but the RAF needs to maintain a constant link with its remote outpost in the Falkland Islands. This is where a TriStar departs for its long journey. Being a military base, access is restricted but the majority (if not all) the parked aircraft can be seen from the perimeter. TriStars are not the easiest of aircraft to hide among the relatively small buildings.

CAMBRIDGE
CBG   EGSC   2m/3km NE

All that can normally be seen from the main road are a few parked light aircraft. The dedicated follow a road at the western end of the field, between the A1303 and Sainsburys, and try to identify some of the visitors to Field's technical facility. The ramp beside the super hangar can be seen and there are places to see if something interesting, such as an LTU TriStar, is parked outside. Vantage points along the A1303 on the northeast side of the field, and around the village of Teversham allow the runway to be seen. Most of the time, the traffic amounts to little more than the occasional Cessna in the circuit.

CARLISLE
CAX   EGNC   Crosby   5m/8km E

There have been several attempts to operate scheduled services, but few have lasted long. There is only a modest collection of residents to justify a visit.

COVENTRY
CVT   EGBE   Baginton   4m/6km SSE

Coventry is a major industrial city, but so close to Birmingham International Airport that any real hope of growth of its own airport is strictly limited. A few links are operated regularly but they are unlikely to be enough to draw serious interest. There are other features, however. The terminal area and its car park next to the taxiway are far less interesting than the Air Atlantique ramp, with its handful of Islanders, DC-3s and even a couple of DC-6s. Helicopter movements are also quite plentiful but not enough to warrant a prolonged stay. The road between the city and the airport passes the splendid aviation museum and the hulks of a few abandoned Daks can also be see through the trees. A playing field and a rugby pitch can be crossed for close access to the Air Atlantique facility, for those who can't be bothered to try the simple method of gaining entry: asking.

Coventry Airport achieved fame in 1994/95 by allowing the operation of cargo flights, carrying live calves to Holland for the veal trade. The operator of the charter flights used some unusual aircraft, including an Air Algerie 737, which crashed one morning in the woods to the north.

Protests by local (and other) animal rights activists led to the death of a woman, ensuring that Coventry received more than its fair share of publicity, compared with the amount of traffic it handles.

EAST MIDLANDS
EMA   EGNX   Castle Donington   9m/15km SE of Derby

The spectators terrace is easily found, and well-placed, for a good view of the entire apron and anything using it. However, the mesh screen makes photography impossible. There are less scheduled services than charters to the sun. Britannia Airways are almost as common as British Midland. To the east of the terminal area is a separate viewing park which overlooks the threshold of the runway and is also the home of the aviation museum. Apart from the almost obligatory Vulcan, the most notable inmate is the Elan Argosy, still in good condition, and reasonably photogenic. Dotted around the field elsewhere are the remains of Vanguards which became Merchantmen, and ended their days here.

To the west of the terminal, things can more interesting. Not only is there a BMA maintenance base but quite a few stored aircraft have found their way here, as worldwide passenger figures dropped. BAe 146s came home to roost, and long term residents included several in Meridiana colours. Fields have their own apron and hangar where aircraft up to VC-10 size are regularly seen. Jetstreams receive their paint here, and it is often possible to see something exotic on the ramp, prior to delivery.

As an alternative to the officially approved viewing park, which is on the south side of the runway, some people are still tempted to find other places at the perimeter. A footpath runs along the northern perimeter fence, and is reasonably close to the runway. Fortunately, the British climate means that the sun is not usually a problem.

EXETER
EXT   EGTE   7m/11km E

Close to the M5 motorway, Exeter airport handles occasional commuter, regional and charter movements, and there is a viewing area next to the road which overlooks the apron. Anyone heading to the southwest of England in pursuit of aircraft will learn the law of diminishing returns. Bristol is the last airport of any size. Exeter, further west, is smaller. Beyond it lie others, where light aircraft registrations are probably the only reason to keep going. What lie beyond Exeter are the following:

PLYMOUTH Roborough is one of Brymon's bases, and a few flights are operated from here. Also in the extreme southwest are other departure points for the Scilly Isles in summer: NEWQUAY shares the runway with RAF St Mawgan and handles the occasional aircraft on the ramp, It can be a desolate place in winter, when there is nothing to see, and everything is locked up, giving the appearance that life has been suspended.

PENZANCE is used by a British International S-61. The destinations are the Isles of Scilly, where two of the islands, ST MARY'S and TRESCO, have landing facilities.

HUMBERSIDE
HUY   EGNJ   6m/9km NE of Brigg

A modest regional airport but the ramp can be seen in part from the terminal. British International Helicopters base a Westland WG.30 here, seen at close range, if access to the service road is gained at the right time. Beyond their apron is a line of hangars and buildings used by the general aviation fraternity.

LEEDS/BRADFORD
LBA   EGNM   8m/13km NW of Leeds

The passenger terminal is modern, the only view from which is at the first floor level, in the lounge/cafeteria. Movements are not particularly lively but photographers may find consolation by having a closer look around the Northair facility on the far/south side. Bayton Lane leads to a hill which overlooks the airport. From here all movements including those of Northair are visible.

The main A658 road heads south towards Bradford. A left turn, towards Leeds, is followed by another, leading to the golf course. This is where photographers go, though some walking is involved. The footpath runs along the south side of the runway, accessible from a lane next to the golf course. Extremely good north-facing portraits can be taken from here.

LIVERPOOL
LPL   EGGP   Speke   8m/13km SE

The bar/cafeteria area on the first floor of the new South Terminal offers a good view of the apron and taxiway. Scheduled services operate to Dublin, Belfast, Isle of Man, Southampton, Aberdeen and, in summer, Jersey. A range of chartered services also operate in the peak summer months. Emerald Airways' fleet of HS 748s is based here and, during the day, several examples are parked on the apron, awaiting night freight services. Bond Helicopters also have a base for Irish Sea gas and oil exploration support services. The airport is particularly busy at night, being a hub for: the Royal Mail Skynet first class letter post, freight and newspaper flights to Ireland and the Isle of Man, TNT and Ford Motor Co freight charters.

A large light aircraft resident fleet (private and flying schools) is still based at the old northern airfield but all their movements can be seen from the new terminal.

LONDON

With the exception of the new dockland airport, all are located well outside the city and the cost of getting from the City Centre to Heathrow or Gatwick will quickly give some indication of how far out the airports are. The British Airports Authority is responsible for the main airports, and they are taking very seriously indeed the IATA security recommendations. Both airports have formal viewing facilities, and much effort has been put into ensuring that only these are used by enthusiasts.

The use of alternative sites around both fields is deterred. Other airports close to London are Luton and Stansted, both of which have their attractions, but neither of which come close to the Big Two for the number, or variety, of movements. Total journey times for City (underground, Thames Light Railway and shuttle bus), Gatwick (via Waterloo), Heathrow (underground - Piccadilly Line) and Stansted (via Liverpool Street) are given from Charing Cross, rather than just the time taken by the train once leaving the station.

LONDON
LCY   EGLC   City   4m/6km E (train/bus 75 min)

Like most of Docklands, the boom time for redevelopment came during the 1980s. Unlike the rest of Docklands, life didn't come to an end with the crash of Olympia & York. London City airport continues to grow, particularly with the introduction of more and more international STOL commuter services.

Without a car, London City can be a pain, though the authorities go to great lengths to stress

66

otherwise. This is because London's businessmen can take a taxi from Plaistow tube station. There is a bus service from West Ham, and a shuttle bus link from the Docklands Light Railway station at Canary Wharf. British Rail's Silvertown (reached from Liverpool Street) is the closest, and the riverbus service from Central London is the classy (but far from the cheapest) way to arrive.

The runway and terminal area occupy a patch of land between the disused Royal Albert and King George V Docks. The airport sees little use at weekends, and could not be described as busy during the week. It is possible to watch the moderate action from the terminal area but the view is just as good from the perimeter. Just after crossing the bridge between Victoria and Albert Docks, the road passes the end of the runway. The roundabout here is only a few steps away from Silvertown station. As arrivals drop steeply onto Runway 28, they can be seen clearly, and the turn off to the apron is only 200 metres away.

LONDON
LGW   EGKK   Gatwick   32m/50km S (train 60 minutes)

Almost all alternative vantage points have now been closed to the enthusiast, in an attempt to control their movements. All that remains is the observation deck which does allow a very good general view of the proceedings but photographers may quickly tire of the limitations. There is the chance of shots of wide-bodies as they taxi to a stand, or as they push back, but a large percentage of movements never come within range. Facilities are, however, good. Not only is there a large cafeteria but there is also the excellent BUCHair UK shop, stocked with plenty of specialised items for the aircraft enthusiast.

The variety of traffic is excellent, as charter flights now form a much smaller proportion (though still a growing number) of movements, which now features many intercontinental, European and commuter services.

Most of the favourite haunts have now gone: the north side car park, for example, was replaced by the new North Terminal. At the opposite side of the field, development and deterrents have put an end to the use of several spots on the south side of the runway. It may still be possible to witness landings from the road at either end of the field but that at the eastern (most frequently used) end is too distant for photos of any worth.

LONDON
LHR   EGLL   Heathrow   15m/23km W (train 75 minutes)

"Heathrow Airport Ltd welcomes spotters and amateur photographers so long as they use the facilities provided on the Queens Building Roof. The problems arise when unauthorised areas are used. For instance, parking cars on the airfield emergency access points is potentially very dangerous because it could delay the arrival on site of a fire appliance. Parking illegally anywhere along the perimeter is a hazard to other road users, especially when photographers climb on the roofs of cars, distracting other drivers. Gathering in the cargo area may infringe Customs regulations and spotters there run the risk of having themselves and their cameras checked.

The greatest problem is simply that, in these dangerous times, groups of people stopping in unauthorised places have to be checked-out by police or security staff. If their time and vigilance is being constantly diverted by plane spotters, it makes life a little bit easier for the terrorist."

The above statement was made formally by Heathrow's Airport Security Manager and contains everything necessary for the enthusiast to see the problem from the opposite point of view. Indeed it applies to most, if not all, other airports in the world.

The Terminal 2 roof (which used to be accessible from the Queen's Building) offers only a general view, with very few opportunities for the photographer. Compensation for restricting the size of the spectators' area is that (a) entry is free and (b) the opening hours have been extended. Apart from aircraft taxying onto the stands in front, used mostly by A320s of Iberia, Lufthansa and Air France, all other movements are out of range for good photography.

More frustrating still is the southeast corner of the deck. This is closest to the taxiway used normally by the long-hauls leaving Terminal 3. The gap between a lamp pole and Stand 12 is so narrow that when something (normally an Olympic A300) is parked, there is just too little room for photos. With so many exotic 747-400s passing this close, it's clear that user requirements took a distant second place to other considerations when the screen fence was planned. Another ten feet of room would have made all the difference.

There are several multi-storey car parks in the central terminal area. The most popular was that serving Terminal 2, as it overlooked part of the Terminal 3 apron, and good photos were quite easy to take. Screening put an end to this on all floors, but viewing is still possible. Much the same applies to the other multi-storeys though none of the others have protective screens because distances are greater.

The area next to the enormous British Airways maintenance area, close to the threshold of Runway 27R has always attracted spotters as it is one of the few places that ensures all landings can be monitored. A lengthy stay here is unlikely, as parked cars are moved frequently. The alternative spot, for use when Runway 27L is used for landing, is off the airport complex, and the collection of parked cars in side roads on the south side of the A30 readily identifies the better spots.

The entire perimeter fence has now been enclosed by screening, the specific purpose of which is to deter viewing. The odd gap in these 'defences' comes under a lot of pressure from those wishing to take photos, particularly the access point next to the threshold of Runway 27L. Regular stops are made by the police, to ensure that anyone standing here is moved on, so most of the good vantage points can now be disregarded. Anyone who considers the security measures to be extreme must bear in mind that terrorists did manage to land a few mortar bombs very close to an active runway.

Elsewhere around the perimeter, on roads accessible to the public, there are views of British Airways' maintenance areas, some of which reveal airliners in reasonably photogenic spots. The traffic lights where the taxiway and road cross has been used by photographers but airliners on the move in or out are very infrequent. The cargo and executive aprons on the south side are partially visible. There is a lay-by next to the main cargo ramp but blast screens and multiple layers of fencing are sure to prevent activities other than logging one or two aircraft.

LONDON

LTN   EGGW   Luton   2m/3km E of Luton (bus 15 minutes)

Luton is now a very modern and often busy airport. Well placed relative to the M1 motorway, it handles a significant quantity of charter traffic, much of which is by British airlines. Monarch and Britannia Airways have their maintenance bases here but their operations are spread through the entire country, so few of their aircraft are in evidence on the average visit.

The international terminal offers no views at all. Beyond this terminal, where the taxiway enters the apron, there is a viewing area, very close indeed to passing aircraft, but the fence makes photography very difficult. Part of this viewing area has been developed to form a small domestic terminal.

Many enthusiasts visiting the field will make a tour of the perimeter and be on their way, as the central apron is large enough to contain a quantity of varied aircraft, including biz-jets and cargo carriers.

On the opposite side of the approach road from the main apron is the general aviation area, where quite a number of light aircraft are parked, all visible from the fence. Before this ramp is reached, there is a road to the right which leads round to a remote car park. This road is now used as a direct link, and passes the Hotel Ibis. The fences on this side, around the McAlpine hangar, have been much strengthened, so that it is now difficult to see the aircraft, let alone note their registrations.

Instead of entering the airport complex by turning right at the roundabout, it might be worth driving on to the next roundabout and turning right. After the hotel, bear right and watch for a small turning to the right. The road, which winds past the end of the runway, leads ultimately to an emergency access gate. It might be necessary to walk part of the way but the sunlight and the view for photographers are good until the middle of the afternoon. This location can be accessed directly from the main road from the M1 by leaving it at a roundabout and passing under the new road. A series of left turns is necessary.

LONDON

STN   EGSS   Stansted   34m/46km N (train 110 min)

This airport has undergone a major transformation, with a new cargo centre and passenger terminal. Traffic was encouraged to build up quickly, with American Airlines being the first notable transatlantic carrier to be wooed, for a while, in the hope that others would follow. Stansted is moving quite quickly towards a reasonably prosperous future but its past, when Scandinavian charters arrived for shopping sprees, was better for the spotter.

The "old" side of the field is worth exploration. Large, unoccupied car parks allow close access to a few aircraft parking areas where something exotic might be parked. Exotic, at Stansted, can mean very exotic. The business terminal and the CAA hangar will be of interest to any non-regular visitor to the airport. The road to Tye Green passes waste ground and a grass bank, both of which allow overall general views of the airfield and runway.

The new passenger terminal is on the south side of the runway, beyond the cargo facility when arriving by road. The views around the terminal are minimal. The roundabout from which a road leads to the cargo area also has a sign for Self Storage. This road is a dead end but it overlooks the runway, albeit at some distance. The taxiway is, however, closer and many aircraft are within range of a 200mm lens. A prolonged stay here will, in the course of time, attract attention. The police may ask to see some form of identification, while they size you up. The private security personnel, however, tend to take a more direct approach. It may be counter-productive to argue that the police take a lenient view!

MANCHESTER

MAN   EGCC   International   11m/17km S (bus 35 minutes)

Definitely the busiest airport outside London, the traffic still includes a good number of international carriers linking the north of England with many business centres around the world. The additional number and variety of charters in summer can be as good as anywhere else in the country except for Gatwick. With its new passenger terminal, the airport is now also served by its own direct rail link from the city.

It became clear that the multi-storey car park was used by enthusiasts, and all areas offering a view were screened off. As compensation, the roof terrace was re-opened, though with no access to the piers. To the left of the terrace is the domestic Terminal 1A, and to the right the international Terminal 1B. To ensure the best chance of knowing what is happening in the airport, an initial visit to the terrace allows all aircraft on the main apron and those in the maintenance areas to be seen.

Some legwork is needed to identify aircraft hidden from sight: those on the far side of Terminal 1A are visible from next to the pay-desk on the first floor of the car park. A walk back towards Terminal 1B reveals, on the left-hand side of the corridor, a lounge with seats next to the large window. From here, the arrivals and departures can be seen, as it is directly beneath the roof terrace.

There are several alternatives around the perimeter. When the ground next to the old brickworks was closed, all the cars went to Moss Lane, where spotting was as good as anywhere, but photography wasn't. The death of the old brickworks land was temporary. It is now the Aviation Viewing Park, with a small raised platform for photographers, an enthusiasts' shop run by The Aviation Society and some rather primitive toilet provisions. Close to the South Side hangars, an overspill viewing area is located rather closer to the centre of the runway, particularly useful when the predominant Runway 24 is in use.

The A538 to Wilmslow passes south of the airport and, just after the tunnel beneath the runway, a turning to Styal reveals, on the left, the nicely landscaped car park. Aircraft on the move can be seen well from here but standing space on the platform is limited. The next turning on the left is signposted as another viewing area and, beyond it, Moss Lane allows runway movements to be seen as well as many of the residents of the south side. The contents of the hangars cannot be seen at all without permission to enter.

The new cargo terminal, west of the central terminal area, is accessible but the continuous sheds do not allow the aircraft to be seen, except from the western corner of the ramp. The new passenger terminal was not designed to improve matters for the enthusiast but is located in the northern corner of the terminal area, away from much of the activity.

Prevailing winds mean that Runway 24 sees most use, so many of the movements do not come close to the Viewing Park. What is often needed therefore is somewhere nearer the active end of the runway. The Airport Hotel, diagonally opposite is probably as good as anywhere. The car park and open ground mean that aircraft taxying to the hold pass close enough for photography but the sun is not always at its most helpful from this angle.

NEWCASTLE
NCL   EGNT   International   6m/9km NW (train 30 minutes)

England's most northerly airport handles a good number of airlines in the summer, when the charter traffic is at its peak. It has, over the years, attracted some extremely interesting services. Whilst the region may have suffered economic decline, the airport's catchment area is large enough to support almost continuous growth.

The terminal has a roof deck, though quality photography is difficult once aircraft are parked. The aero club and GillAir facilities are visible, but distant, on the far side. Restrictions are imposed on access to the aero club, but not necessarily strictly enforced. A car park next to the club house overlooks the apron.

Scheduled traffic is slow by most standards but varied. Compensation may be provided by occasional military diversions and crew training flights. The nearby ranges mean that quite a few fighter pilots are tempted to make a short detour and carry out a 'practice diversion'. This often involves a short but impressive diplay to please the sightseers on the roof.

Over the years, Newcastle has hosted plenty of airliners on delivery across the Atlantic, often to quite exotic operators. These movements are hardly to be considered daily (or even weekly) but the presence on the apron, in front of the tower, of something extraordinary shouldn't come as a surprise.

NEWQUAY
NQY   EGDG   Saint Mawgan   5m/8km NE

Even on a pleasant day, St Mawgan can be a bleak place to visit. Close to the Atlantic Ocean, this part of Cornwall is exposed to the elements, and the countryside is not flat. The passenger terminal is, on the average day, likely to be firmly closed, so there will be nothing to see, other than one or two RAF Nimrods in the distance. Even the airfield isn't flat, so it can't all be seen from the terminal.

NORWICH
NWI   EGSH   4m/km N

Norwich, which used to be called Horsham St Faith many years ago, now has a terminal bright enough to be seen from 20 miles out in Category 3 conditions. It handles Air UK and other airlines but most of the real interest is generated around the site of the old terminal area, for this is where Air UK carry out maintenance on F.27s. The industrial estate is reached from Hurricane Way and, from the road, a glimpse of something extraordinary is always possible.

PENZANCE
PZE   EGHK   Heliport

Anyone visiting Penzance, with an active interest in aviation, is almost certainly bound for the Scilly Isles for a holiday. The heliport offers a convenient, and comfortable, link across the water. Whether the single S-61 is recorded at Penzance or St Mary's is a matter of choice. This is how scheduled air services peter out at the tip of Britain!

PLYMOUTH
PLH   EGHD   Roborough   4m/6km N

This is one of Brymon's bases, and scheduled services are operated from here. Apart from a selection of locally-based light aircraft, there is no other reason to travel such a long distance to the southwest of England. However, anyone wishing to fill a logbook with UK-registered aircraft will doubtless make this a destination as part of a regional tour.

SHOREHAM BY SEA
ESH   EGKA   2m/3km W

Quite the most delightful passenger terminal reminds visitors what Shoreham must have been like in its rather modest heyday. It is like a scene setting for a 1930s movie. The elevated railway line passes the airport, though there is no station. Parked on the grass and the small apron are plenty of light aircraft and there are, on either side of the terminal, enough hangars to contain plenty of registrations, plus some interesting aircraft. Permission for a closer look should be sought.

SOUTHAMPTON
SOU   EGHI   Eastleigh   4m/6km N (train 10 minutes)

Eastleigh has been undergoing major refurbishment for the last few years. If it was to succeed as a stepping stone to the Channel Islands, such investment was essential. The moderate amount of cross channel flights continues all year round, but holiday traffic builds up during the summer. The Genavco facility carries out maintenance on executive jets, with some interesting examples often present. Extensive car parks surround the building and the far corner is close to the taxiway, so the movements here should pass within the right sort of range for any photographer, regardless of the runway in use. The largest scheduled movements are Air UK, Jersey European and Cityhopper Fokkers, and portraits of a high order are possible in the sun. Air France ATR-42s and Aurigny Trislanders comprise the rest of the airline traffic.

SOUTHEND
SEN   EGMC   Rochford   3m/5km N

Anyone with a car will find it is a deceptively long drive from London but there is much to make the effort worthwhile. The old rooftop enclosure has now gone, replaced by a small viewing area in the gap between the tower and the terminal. There is a new bar in the terminal which has an excellent view of the ramp, though there is often little on it to see. To the left of the terminal is the base of British World Airlines who, at quieter times, have allowed ramp access for photography of their Viscounts and 1-11s. Maintenance work for other carriers means that some interesting aircraft visit Southend. The ramp can be seen by driving past the terminal area, along a service road past the many parked cars and offices. A turning on the right reveals a small aero club and the maintenance ramp. On the far side of the runway, the tails (but, in most cases, not much more than the tails) of the stored 1-11s can be seen.

The railway bridge, on the road to Rochford, offers an elevated view of the main apron. Traditionally, one or two 707s have stood close to this road, often in the company of the mortal remains of scrapped Belfasts.

The remote cargo and hangar area is not easily found, as access is not via the perimeter road. Although a manned security gate now prevents access to this area, there is a bank from where some of the withdrawn Viscounts and 1-11s can be seen and, to a very limited extent, photographed.

TEESSIDE
MME   EGNV   6m/9km E of Darlington (train 15 minutes)

Too close to Newcastle to become a major airport, as they compete for many of the passengers. Newcastle's inter city rail and Metro services ensure better connections for holidaymakers, many of whom can fly direct to America in summer. Teesside therefore handles mostly commuter links with Heathrow, Air UK and British Midland providing the scheduled traffic. In summer, there are a few charters to the sun. There is a south facing roof deck, which overlooks the apron but subject matter is often lacking for the casual visitor. To the left are several hangars and aprons, and ramp access is often possible.

ABERDEEN
ABZ   EGPD   Dyce   5m/8km N (bus 20 minutes)

The old terminal was located in Dyce, and has been replaced by a modern building on the far/western side of the runway. The peak of oil-related movements is over but the helicopters based here are still numerous and active. Totally exposed to the elements is a viewing area to the south of the terminal/ramp, which looks down the length of the apron, faces north, and offers quite good opportunities for photographers, though only of the fixed wing movements. A notice on the wire fence states that it's in accordance with government standards and they realise it's a problem for photographers. It's a pity, but hardly surprising, that nobody has thought of finding a solution.

There are no real views from inside the building but, to its left/north, the grass bank is higher than the fence and an excellent place to watch, and photograph, the movements. What is to be seen from here is the Bristow apron, with half a dozen or so Super Pumas and S-61Ns in various stages of operation. Security personnel can be increasingly concerned about people standing for long periods on this bank, so any close encounters with officialdom should be treated politely.

The access road leading north from the terminal passes the hangars of Bristows and BIH, though glimpses of inmates are few. The photographer who is more anxious to get a good portrait than to log all the residents will be rewarded at Aberdeen, and the operators can be welcoming to parties of visitors, if trips are properly organised.

On the far side from here is the old airport, whose ramps still exist but are now occupied by Bond Helicopters and Business Air. Visits in summer allow the most to be made of the long daylight hours and there are plenty of vantage points next to fences to suit most needs. The concentration of so much specialist operation makes Aberdeen one of Britain's most interesting airports. For a close-up view of activity on both runways, head north from the old terminal area into a housing estate, where a grass mound on the edge of some wasteland offers a good view. It's almost directly opposite the control tower.

DUNDEE

DND	EGPN	Riverside	2m/3km W

Various attempts at scheduled operations through Dundee have not always proved successful. A dozen or so light aircraft are the only reason to call here, and anyone doing so may also have a look at PERTH Scone, the home of Airwork and (still?) an ex-Air Inter Viscount.

EDINBURGH

EDI	EGPH	Turnhouse	7m/11km W (bus 25 minutes)

Technically, Turnhouse is the name of the old facility on the north side of the field, where the small military base is still active. The new terminal has a roof deck which is good for photographers; it overlooks the entire field but the capital city of Scotland generates a rather limited amount of scheduled traffic. The British Airways 757 shuttle flights are augmented by British Midland DC-9s, Loganair and Air UK flights, plus a selection of charters in summer.

The executive facility is separate and accessible only via a security gate, but the inmates can be identified (with some difficulty) from the north side. Leaving the main terminal and heading east towards the city, a left turn at the first roundabout leads to the old apron. Weekends can reveal a few commuter airliners parked but photos are difficult, as the aircraft park close to the fence. The gate to RAF Turnhouse is usually open, as it is the only way to gain access to the aero club residents, parked next to the railway line. Occasionally, military visitors can be present but a request for a look in the hangar at the resident Bulldogs is always worthwhile.

Driving towards the airport perimeter from Kirkliston leads to the north side of the field. There is, almost directly opposite where the two taxiways join (from cargo and the passenger terminal), an emergency access road leading to a grass bank. A 200mm lens in the late afternoon can provide some good photos.

GLASGOW

GLA	EGPF	International	9m/15km W (bus 25 minutes)

Once known as Abbotsinch, this is the premier airport for Scotland, and by far the busiest for fixed-wing aircraft. Once, it was possible to walk along the pier roof and get very close to the movements but life is more difficult now. The central ramp can be seen from the terminal, and some photos through the glass can be of an acceptable quality.

Development to the west/left of the main terminal may one day spoil the view from the multi-storey car park. Popular though it has been with anyone logging, photographers find the many apron lighting columns to be a problem. To the west is one hangar occupied by Loganair and another for flying club aircraft and the UAS Bulldogs. From the fence, the interior of Loganair's facility is visible, though not the other.

When leaving the airport by road, a left turn at the roundabout before the access road to the motorway leads to a T-junction, and another left turn will take the photographer to a vantage point overlooking the taxiway. As the view is westwards, the morning offers a better prospect but Glasgow isn't famous for its all year sunshine. Another road passes around the western edge of the field, offering an alternative general view of the field, and of movements on the runway.

INVERNESS
INV   EGPE   Dalcross   10m/16km NE

It is a long way north to Inverness, and the roads are not made for fast driving. Only the dedicated in search of G- registrations will be prepared to make the journey as the movements don't normally justify the visit. Also north of Aberdeen, up the east coast, is PETERHEAD, which is used mostly by Bond Helicopters for their smaller helicopter operations.

PRESTWICK
PIK   EGPK   1m/1.5km NE

Prestwick is well-placed to receive transatlantic traffic, having a long runway, and being on the west coast of Scotland. However, the regular strong westerly breeze on this coast can make landing on the north-south runway an experience to remember. Occasional crew-training, transatlantic deliveries and military flights stopping for fuel make up a portion of the meagre traffic. The long runway and large terminal only serve to increase the impression of quietness.

A dedicated enthusiast could spend all day on the balcony but see few movements to record. The BAe Jetstream production and the Sea King base on the eastern side often provide the only interest. A road on the east side of the field ends at the perimeter fence, almost directly opposite the main terminal. Also, an area of waste land in the south east corner, near the control tower, gives a good view of both the runway and taxiway. Finding something to see can be the problem.

CARDIFF
CWL   EGFF   Wales   12m/19km SW (bus 30 minutes)

A fairly small airport for a fairly small principality, the passenger terminal is pleasant and it has a roof deck. There is more to see on summer weekends, when charter flights operate, since scheduled movements are modest. During the week, an SF340 in Air France or Cityhopper colours may be of interest. Also visible is the museum, with a significant collection in a very tight space. This has been shoe-horned into a tiny site, to make way for the new British Airways maintenance facility. Heathrow regulars will be used to the sight of several 747-400s parked at Terminal Four, but these aircraft have a more startling effect when they arrive at such a small airport.

On the far side, viewed from the observation deck, are the aero club aircraft and, to the left of the terminal, an apron is used occasionally by executive visitors but not in large numbers. Photography of aircraft on this ramp is difficult, as vantage points are limited.

Between the terminal and the aero club is the Cambrian Airways Viscount. By taking the road from the airport to Rhoose, a mile or so, the second right turn in the village leads to a playing field. At the far side is the perimeter fence and, awaiting the photographer, the Viscount. Also visible from here may be one or two light aircraft at the aero club which could not be seen from the terminal.

BELFAST

BFS   EGAA   International   13m/20km NW (bus 40 minutes)

Investment to match the international tag has certainly brought Aldergrove, as it used to be known, up to date. F.28s in the colours of Air France and Cityhopper add a businesslike air to the movements though, with such an enormous catchment area, summer charter flights include transatlantic carriers. At the mention of Belfast, considerations of security still come to mind, and it may be a surprise to find that it does not prevent viewing or photography.

The viewing area has lightly tinted glass through which all scheduled movements can be photographed. The traffic on Runway 07/25 is within range of a 200mm lens and an F.27 or HS748 on the apron my need 28mm as they park very close. The aircraft can, in theory, be watched from roads at the perimeter but it is hoped that there are few foolish enough to do so.

Traffic throughout the year is varied, though not busy. An enormous proportion of passengers travel to/from London, and there are some very busy days around Christmas, Easter and July. Indeed, 5,000 passengers can be carried in just one day on the British Airways shuttle at Christmas, ferrying expats home to Northern Ireland. At such peak times BMA and BA will press any aircraft into service that is available. On these occasions, even 747s are to be seen.

The cargo and executive terminals handle a small amount of traffic, though nothing extraordinary, and there is an RAF base. Fixed-wing visitors (from Beavers to TriStars) taxi past the balcony, and helicopters overfly within range of cameras and binoculars.

BELFAST

BHD   EGAC   City   2m/3km E (bus 10 minutes)

Known generally as either Belfast Harbour or Sydenham, this is where Shorts' assembly plant is located. Completed SD3.60s parked outside are well beyond the range of even a 300mm lens. Heavylift Belfasts collect Fokker 100 wings for delivery, and scheduled airlines include Loganair, Manx, Capital and Jersey European (there being no charters).

The main car park fence is right beside the apron and taxiway. A standard lens is ideal for taxying aircraft, and a 200mm zoom necessary for those on the runway.

ALDERNEY

ACI   EGJA   The Blaye   1m/1.5km S

The airport is known locally as Alderney International but the title is a little grandiose, even if there are customs and immigrations facilities. Anyone who has an interest in smaller airline operations will enjoy Alderney as the diet is undiluted Trislanders, those of Air Sarnia and Aurigny. A good airport for a classic landing shot of each colour scheme but, after half a day, a log book will yield no further surprises.

GUERNSEY

GCI   EGJB   4m/6km SW (bus 20 minutes)

As is to be expected of a holiday island, traffic is busiest in the summer, when it becomes (at best) moderately busy. To any British national, what visits is generally considered mundane but European enthusiasts often have a different perspective. Apart from the occasional German charter, most of what visits can be seen in greater volume, and better, at Jersey. The perimeter offers the photographer more than the free roof terrace. From here some stands are seen well but the runway is not.

JERSEY

JER   EGJJ   JERSEY   5m/8km W (bus 30 minutes)

This is the fifth busiest airport in Britain and much of the traffic only visits in summer. Consequently, July and August weekends are very busy times indeed. Afficianados of prop-liners (though not necessarily piston, of course) are sure to enjoy Jersey. As long as British World Airlines continue to fly Viscounts, this will be the best place to see, and photograph, them. Viscounts, F.27s, ATPs, HS748s, and SD3.30/60s in a good mixture of British colour schemes, plus occasional Maersk, Braathens and DLT movements, and its appeal to European enthusiasts is obvious.

Additional jet traffic features a predictable mix of Britannia, BMA and British Airways, so a Saturday spent at Jersey has much to offer. It is common for such an interesting airport to lack some essential feature like, for example, an observation deck. Jersey has two: both excellent, with views across the stands and the west end of the runway. There is no charge for admission, and refreshments are available in the nearby departure hall.

Bus service No.15 runs past the airport, between St Aubin and St Helier, so a hire car is not necessary. Since the observation decks are preferred by most photographers, exploring the perimeter is not essential though this too offers further variety. Perhaps the most difficult aircraft to photograph are the Aurigny Trislanders, and their staff can be helpful in the occasional quiet moment.

Taking the road west to St Ouen's Bay, a track leads close to the perimeter where taxying aircraft pass close on their way to Runway 09. A 70-200mm lens may be needed for aircraft landing, but movements on the taxiway pass much closer. East of the terminal, next to the aero club, taxying aircraft still pass within range of the camera, but the bonus is a large quantity of light aircraft, including many foreign visitors. Walking further east, a footpath leads under the threshold between the approach lights, and photos of landing aircraft are also easy to take.

A long stay on the island, with many visits to the airport may be another matter. Most of the aircraft to be noted on the first day will be seen many times, as they shuttle back and forth between Jersey and various airports in Britain.

ISLE OF MAN

IOM   EGNS   Ronaldsway   14m/22km SW (bus 55 minutes)

A visit to the Isle of Man would probably make an enjoyable break, but the airport would not be the main reason. The Manx Airlines fleet operates most of the services, with occasional daytime appearances by the Business Air SD3.60. There is a bus service from Douglas and the steam train runs to nearby Castletown Station. On the northwest side of the field is the main terminal, and to the southwest, the coastline of Derbyhaven.

There are no views from the terminal, apart from through the restaurant windows, but low fences between the car parks and apron at each side of the building allow close encounters with arrivals. All three runways, 04/22, 09/27 and 18/36, have places where photos can be taken, though the best location is probably next to the aero club, in the northeast corner. Road A12 runs to the aero club from Castletown, between the perimeter and the coast, and the coastal footpath is ideal for photos until mid-afternoon.

The hangars, on the north side, are worthy of investigation as it is here that the world's only Percival Q6 is housed. Airliner enthusiasts may not show much interest but unique and historical craft are rare, and this one only leaves its hangar occasionally. Also to be noted is the Manx Airlines maintenance base, used also for work on Loganair and BMA ATPs.

By hiring a cycle in Castletown, one morning trip to the aero club could be combined, another day, with an afternoon trip to the terminal car park. To spend a full day at Ronaldsway would necessitate nice weather and a very good book.

HA HUNGARY (Hungarian Republic)
BUDAPEST

BUD   LHBP   Ferihegy   10m/16km SE (bus 35 minutes)

It is possible to get to the airport by underground train and take a No. 93 BKV bus from Kobanya-Kispest but the express Volan bus from Engels Square is the simplest way and takes about the same time. Another reason to take the Volan bus is that tickets, costing about 70 pence, are paid for once on board. Using ordinary public transport, it must be remembered that tickets must be bought before travelling. With heavy penalties for anyone hitching a free ride, even by accident, a simple mistake can have unfortunate consequences.

Hungary has endured a miserable existence over the last years, and one of the old rules was that talking on public transport was forbidden. As most foreign visitors are unlikely to speak much of the language, casual conversation would be rare. If the locals seem unfriendly, at least this information offers a reason. A car can be the most difficult means of transport, as direction signs aren't exactly numerous.

There are two terminals and, to all intents and purposes, two entirely separate airports. Ferihegy 1, the old terminal, is closest to the road and does have a spectating facility. It is covered and double glazed, which makes photography a little difficult. Without prior permission, photography can still be more than just difficult! Using this terminal are most of the international carriers, except for Lufthansa, plus general aviation.

To the right of the deck, and visible, are the maintenance hangars and, in the distance, the cargo apron. Further away, quite a long way, is the more modern Ferihegy 2 terminal. The main concourse has a striking resemblence to Frankfurt, though on a rather smaller scale. The observation deck is best described as a rooftop cafe, and it has the advantage, compared with Frankfurt, that entry costs next to nothing. It is relaxed and enjoyable place to sit, especially with Hungarian prices being so low, and the view is of Malev's Tupolevs and Boeings plus, rather more distant, some Yak 40s and Let 410s.

Budapest is strictly for the type of enthusiast who has seen everything at the usual European destinations, and needs something different. The journey to Hungary takes time and money. Excitement is not a word which readily springs to mind when describing Ferihegy.

The approach road to Ferihegy 2 has on display Il-18 HA-MOA plus an Il-14 and another aircraft. Scattered around the field are a few relics of the old days. Tu-134 HA-LBG is now used for fire practice and Il-18 HA-MOG is reported to be a ground instructional airframe. The museum compound repays interest, as it contains a number of unusual types, to western eyes.

To complete coverage of Budapest's aviation scene, it's necessary to visit BUDAORS, which is a major general aviation field. The old connections with the CIS will endure for a while, and such types as An-2s, Yak-18s and Zlins can all be seen in the company of one or two Turbolets and the ABKS Turbo Porters. North of the city, DUNAKESZI is the home of the Malev Flying Club, whose light aircraft all wear full airline colour schemes.

HB SWITZERLAND (Swiss Confederation)
BASEL

BSL   LFSB   EuroAirport   7m/11km NW (bus 15 minutes)

While operations here are considerably less in number than Zurich or Geneva, this is still a very interesting airport to visit. Arrival from the Swiss city of Basel/Basle ensures that the most interesting parts of the field can be visited, whilst anyone driving from the French side will be faced with nothing but confusion.

Fences line both sides of the roads to form what must be the most complex international boundary in the world. After some time, it becomes apparent that access is not possible to the

Swiss facilities. Having been so close to the goal, it will be necessary to give up, and drive away. Returning from the Swiss side takes a disheartening length of time.

Scheduled movements have increased in quantity and variety in recent years, with Crossair's fleet being regular visitors. The terrace to the left of the terminal is only open between 1pm and 7pm, precisely the time when the sun shines from the wrong angle. The SFr1 admission fee is hardly money well spent but the adjacent cafeteria, where the view is little different, is very expensive indeed. Anyone visiting in a car will drive to the far end of the central complex for views of the general aviation.

Jet Aviation has a large hangar, whose inmates normally include a varied selection of biz-jets. Maintenance work for small operators means that their ramp can contain some extremely unusual types, but the construction of the Crossair hangar has restricted viewing.

BERN

BRN	LSZB	Belp	5m/8km SE (bus 20 minutes)

Switzerland's capital city nestles in the Bernese Oberland, the mountainous backdrop being most picturesque, but causing severe restrictions on movements, due to the steep approach. STOL airliners, such as the Air Engiadina fleet and some Crossair SF.340s, operate the only scheduled services here.

The terminal is surrounded by several hangars, the contents of which are varied, and interesting, and the photographer can have a very rewarding hour or so, roaming around the residents. At the centre of things is a grass enclosure, and the entire proceedings can be witnessed from here. With the right weather, this can be a very enjoyable experience indeed.

The passenger terminal appears, from the outside, rather primitive. This is Switzerland, so it comes as no surprise to find it is very pleasant inside. Its next door neighbour is Air Engiadina's hangar. At weekends, when commuter flights are rare, this is where the fleet can be seen and photographed. Heliswiss, Alpar and Eagle Air are all based here, but anyone planning a visit may find that there is more action to be seen during business hours on a weekday, as the field is essentially devoted to general aviation at weekends - on one hand, the Heliswiss hangar is normally locked up but, on the other, there could be three Do328s and a Jetstream, all waiting to be photographed at closer range than anywhere else in Europe.

GENEVA

GVA	LSZB	International	3m/5km NW (bus 20 minutes)

Switzerland's second airport is better known to most people by its old name of Cointrin. Its variety of traffic, and the places from which to see it, mean that many photographers rate Zurich quite a long way behind Geneva.

The observation deck has been an essential feature of the airport for several years, offering a panoramic view of almost all the apron, the satellite terminals, and the runway beyond. It does not offer toilet facilities, however. Anyone parking in the undergound car park (costing SFr1 per hour) will note the position of the toilets before going through the security check and paying another Swiss Franc for admission to the deck. It opens at the relatively late time of 9:30am.

The wide body movements park at the extreme right of the apron, so some of these movements must be captured whilst they are on the move. The deck stretches the full length of the passenger terminal but it doesn't quite reach the remote stands 14-19. Visible from the eastern end of the deck is DC-7C 45187 which used to carry fictional HB-SSA markings. It started life with KLM as PH-DSH and saw its last service as VR-BCW and N9498.

There are three circular lounges for gates numbered accordingly: 20+, 30+ and 40+, where most of the scheduled airliners park, always passing so that a photo can be taken. On the far side of the runway are the general aviation ramps, offering mostly twi-engined aircraft, many of which are identifiable. To the left, the original passenger terminal is now used for charter traffic, especially in winter. Skiing holidays mean Britannia 767s, though there are visitors from other parts of Europe, notably Scandinavia. Beyond it, in the southwest corner of the field, is the apron occupied by Aeroleasing and Jet Aviation, but it is out of sight from the balcony. A walk is necessary. An access road off Route de Meyrin leads to the terminal/hangar and the fence where the parked biz-jets can be seen at reasonably close quarters. The access road to Aeroleasing reveals a cycle track. Take the short walk along it, as the view from here is good, overlooking the Aeroleasing ramp and the holding point for Runway 05. There is a grass bank, for an elevated view, and the fence has suffered damage, where holes have been enlarged for camera lenses.

Route de Meyrin heads north to the community of the same name. A right turn, after passing the end of Runway 05, is followed by a few more right turns as directed by the signs. The road leads to the general aviation facility. Opposite the army vehicle store is a high concrete wall, and things look bleak. Don't panic! In the corner is a gateway marked public access. It leads to an aero club which has its own viewing area. From here, all movements in and out of the complex pass very close, though not with any great regularity. The apron's residents can be identified, as can some of those in the hangar to the right. Nestling among the trees and the buildings beyond the hangar are the remains of an Italian Gulfstream 1. Some say it's I-GGGG, c/n 51.

Follow the concrete wall and more aircraft can be seen. The first hangar has windows so its inmates can be seen, and its car park allows another vantage point. The apron is part of the facility for hangars 2 and 3, both of which are inaccessible, beyond a gate. Normally parked in the corner, very close to the fence, is the strange-looking (Dewoitine?) C-552/HB-RBJ.

Because both the car park and the viewing area offer a broad view of the runway and the main terminal area, it is tempting to take photos of airliners on the move. Before doing so, it might be worth considering two items: the angle of the sun and the background. Experienced photographers know that the quality of portraits from here, even in the afternoon, is not as good as they would wish and certainly not as good as can be taken from the terminal's observation deck.

Geneva handles an inspiring selection of scheduled movements, many of which are rare at other European airports. Added to the international movements are the increasing commuter flights by Metros, Saab 2000s and SF340s, to give Geneva that rare combination of good movements and no shortage of vantage points from which to see them. It is likely that travellers with a European itinerary will wish to stay overnight at Geneva.

Switzerland is not a cheap country in which to stay but France offers better value. The border is just north of the runway. Heading east from the airport, one of the first exit roads passes under the runway on its way to the customs post and Ferney-Voltaire. At the roundabout, a left turn along the Route de Meyrin leads up the hill to another roundabout. Here are the Novotel and Formule 1 hotels, the latter offering basic accommodation (for up to three people in a room) for only FFr140 a night.

A return trip to the airport, next morning, involves passing through the same customs post, as it's the easiest route to take. The photographer's view of the taxiway from the southern side of the tunnel is excellent. Parking the car and walking all the way back to it is, however, something to be considered as the quality of photographs is of the highest order . . . by anyone's standards.

LUGANO

LUG   LSZA   Agno   5m/8km N (bus 10 minutes)

A twenty minute bus ride from the town, or less than an hour by car from Milan, taking motorway exit Lugano Nord. The airport is small, modern and pleasant, though car parking is expensive. As befits an Alpine resort, biz-jets are regular visitors, and scheduled services are offered by Crossair SF.340s. Photography is easy, especially with the weather enjoyed by this area.

SANKT MORITZ
SMV   LSZS   Samedan   3m/5km NE

This airport is in the very heart of world-famous, and rather exclusive, skiing country. Anything which needs to be purchased in this area is therefore expensive. Unless travelling overland to the airport by car, the only alternative means of getting there is by taxi. The relatively short journey from town is by no means cheap! At 5600 feet above sea level, this is Europe's highest airfield (comparable in height to Denver) and certainly one of the most spectacular for its surrounding scenery.

The airport is at its busiest between December and April, with many corporate aircraft, up to 1-11 and DC-9 size, visiting for part of the season. Some remain for the duration of the owners' holidays, sometimes flying away for a couple of hours, or days.

Samedan is linked to Geneva and Zurich by Air Engiadina's Jetstream, though Aeroleasing Lear Jets have offered competition on the routes. Charter operations in winter include Maersk Dash 7s from Copenhagen. Samedan's railway station is close to the airport, just a short walk away, past the Heliswiss hangar.

Close to the threshold of Runway 03, not far from the passenger terminal, is a level crossing with automatic barriers to warn of movements. Since the field is surrounded by a cross country skiing circuit, sporting and spotting can be enjoyed by a privileged few. Photography is not a problem at Samedan, and the terminal has a cafeteria, where one can meet the pilots or other aviation buffs. The added bonus is that, quite remarkably, car parking is free! To enjoy the threshold of Runway 21, a little energy or a car are needed. Places to take photos are obvious and easily found.

SION
SIR   LSGS

This is a small field, primarily serving a military purpose. The car park is free and viewing facilities are good. It is reasonable to expect several helicopters and plenty of general aviation. The Swiss Air Force presence during the week can mean that a variety of types are active.

ZÜRICH
ZRH   LSZH   Kloten   8m/13km N (train 10 minutes)

As mentioned in the entry for Geneva, there are many reasons for considering the No.2 Swiss airport as being better than Zürich from the enthusiast's point of view. Despite Zürich's roof terrace, open in summer from 9:00am to 7:00pm (cost: SFr2 entry before the security check), Terminal A's pier extension has restricted the view. There are so many stands out of sight that the dedicated onlooker would probably find the facilities relatively meagre. This would be to deny that it is still very good indeed.

This is all relative, as what can be seen from the deck does represent a broad picture of the proceedings, since most movements can be seen as they pass from one part of the field to another. Because the roof deck has its limitations, the various multi-storey car parks attract attention for alternative vantage points. Car Park B allows the stands for that terminal to be seen, and many of the others. Car Park F, to the right, is lower and overlooks the cargo and Crossair ramps, Terminal A, and the aircraft taxying to Runway 28. With several runways in use, Car Park F does not allow all movements to be seen. The view from Car Park A has been blocked out by the construction of an office building.

Detailed advice about the observation deck will be of use. The SFr2 entry fee is paid into the turnstile, where change machines are provided. They even take banknotes. Each visitor is supposedly only allowed three items of luggage: one *fotoaparat*, for most people, might mean the Instamatic but it must also include a couple of single lens reflexes and a selection of lenses. One *handtasche* means a bag, which isn't necessarily just a ladies' handbag. One *schrim* is not a surface-to-air-missile. If security personnel decide a visitor has too much baggage, there are left luggage lockers, but it would be wise to take only what is needed. Something to eat and drink might be wise. Paying SFr2.60 for a cup of coffee isn't everyone's idea of good value for money. The cafeteria is, however, the only place on the terrace where smoking is allowed.

Despite its shortcomings, the deck really is excellent. Most of the residents on Swissair's maintenance ramp can be seen, if not identified. The remote stands, at the far side of the Flughafenbahn building, usually contain a number of charter airliners, and aircraft landing on Runway 14 can be seen with binoculars. Operators are identifiable but that's all. Many of the MD-80s and Fokker 100s only come into sight again when departing on 28, which is the annoying frustration. This also applies, of course, to virtually all the Crossair movements, and there are many.

Between Runway 16/34 and the taxiway is a remote general aviation parking area, probably about as secure as they get. The residents are beyond the reach of most binoculars and telescopes. Beside the threshold of Runway 16 is a DC-8 still wearing faded Air Afrique colours. It is reported to be c/n 45568, previously TU-TCP.

Swissair's maintenance area is usually worth close scrutiny. To reach it from Terminal B, walk to the main concourse, at the same level as the Pou-de-Ciel hanging from the roof. To the right is a door which leads straight into the Parkhaus. Stairs at the far side lead down to a short tunnel and the road to a ground level car park. The two Classic Wings C-47s are normally visible, plus anything else which may have taken up temporary residence. At Easter 1995, for example, there were a couple of A310s: Diamond Sakha F-OGMY and Air Club C-GCIV.

Without recourse to time-consuming exploration, the movements at Zürich can all be seen from somewhere in the central complex. One of the extra attractions is the tour bus (rundfahrten), which leaves from the observation deck pier, and costs SFr3. This offers a comprehensive look at the airport and a stop is often included at the intersection of Runways 28 and 16/34. This viewing area is ridiculously close to the aircraft and, after leaving the bus, some incredible opportunities exist for anyone wielding a camera. Between April and October, the tours operate hourly on Wednesdays (1:00pm to 4:00pm) and at weekends (12:00 to 4:00pm). They are subject to the weather conditions, and at all other times they are only available for parties who have booked in advance.

For the energetic in search of light aircraft, the Wanderweg has much to offer. This is reached by walking to the eastern corner of the field, past the cargo terminal, and following the yellow signs. It takes twenty minutes to reach anywhere with a view but the reward should be something in the region of a hundred registrations. When Runway 28 is in use, which is regularly, photographers can also obtain ground level portraits of a wide variety of departing aircraft.

With Runway 14 used mostly for landings and 28 for departures, the Wanderweg leads to one of the better spots but transport is essential for the other. A car park next to the thresholds of Runways 14 and 16 is used by most serious photographers. Reference to the photos in any recent JP Airline Fleets will demonstrate that the results are first class. Rümlang is a village worthy of note, as a road from it leads to another popular vantage point, complete with its own car park. It overlooks Terminal B, Runway 16/34 and the taxiway to Runway 10.

As long as the shortcomings are borne in mind, and the visit is combined with one to Geneva, the trip should result in the best of both airports producing a comprehensive cover of Swiss movements. While Geneva specialises in shorter range aircraft, Zürich has the Swissair widebody fleet on display (in the morning, prior to departure) and a varied assortment of Asian 747s rub shoulders with Dash Sevens, Metros and SF.340s: a unique combination. On summer Saturdays, there can be a good selection of Spanish charter flights. Display boards on the observation deck show the colour schemes of seventy-two operators. A prolonged stay will, almost certainly, allow most of them to be seen at close quarters and there aren't many airports in the world that claim that. Perfect it isn't, but it does come pretty close!

HC ECUADOR (Republic of Ecuador)
QUITO
UIO   SEQU   Mariscal Sucre   5m/8km N

The let-down and approach to Quito are, like Hong Kong, considered fun or terrifying. Arrival by White Knuckle Airways is an achievement which, to pacify the faint of heart, happens many times without incident every day.

The airport is an anti-climax, as there are very few movements (sometimes three only) on the average day, so it takes dedication for Quito to be on an itinerary. There are some interesting aircaft parked around the tarmac, and there is also a military base with, it is reported, a small museum. Photos from the terminal windows seem to pose no problems. The Noratlases move only rarely, and the Caravelle hulks not at all. Quito is an airport to tell your friends about . . . it's more fun than being there!

HI DOMINICAN REPUBLIC
PUERTO PLATA
POP   MDPP   La Union International   15m/23km W

On the north coast of the island, Puerto Plata is a growing tourist area, with charters coming from the United States and Canada, and even from Europe. The appeal is obvious: hot climate, exotic surroundings and gallons of cheap booze. Viewed from the other side, wages are so low that profits are astronomical. Most of the flights are mundane, coming from Miami and New York, but Turks and Ciacos Airways Islanders and Trislanders make it an airport with a difference. They are best seen from the edge of the apron.

SANTIAGO DE LOS CABALLEROS
STI   MDST   Cibao International

Less than 100 miles north of Santo Domingo is Santiago where another airport, Cibao, is to be found. Like Herrera, sightings of general aviation and executive aircraft are more likely, though there are occasional scheduled operations to San Juan by LIAT Dash 8s. Reference to distances in this part of the world may mislead, as roads are generally in very poor condition: this is not a wealthy country.

SANTO DOMINGO
SDQ   MDSD   Las Americas   19m/30km E

The Dominican Republic is still good for two stored Super Constellations, HI-548CT and HI-583CT, and that, in these modern times, can be reason enough for propliner fanatics to visit. Las Americas has aprons on either side of the terminal but with little chance of viewing. The main apron is best seen from next to the Dominicana hangar, to the right. A separate access road leads to the cargo terminal, and the maintenance base of AMSA and Aerochago, where the Connies are stored. Scheduled traffic includes Aeropostal DC-9s and ALM MD-80s, though Air Aruba's YS-11 often fails to keep its appointment.

The exotic assortment of piston types, including C-46s, Martin 404s, Convairs and DC-6s, make Las Americas unique. A few quiet words with a worker may help gain admission to the cargo ramp. A few dollars may be a greater help, however, though it must be noted that photographers are becoming more commonplace, and therefore better understood.

SANTO DOMINGO
HEX   MDHE   Herrera   4m/6km SW

The reason that general aviation is distinctly lacking at Las Americas airport is because it uses Herrera, closer to the town. Most of the residents can be seen from the perimeter, and anyone with a reasonable amount of Spanish (or good sign-language) may try to negotiate access to some of the hangars, where many of the more interesting aircraft lurk, out of sight. Portraits of President Hamilton are greatly appreciated by art-lovers in this part of the world. His face appears on a $10 bill.

HK COLOMBIA (Republic of Colombia)
BOGOTA
BOG   SKBO   Eldorado   8m/13km E

A visit to Eldorado airport is exciting, and extremely exotic. With the jungle is all around, this is life on the edge, in more ways than one. Guns are numerous and very visible.

There are still C-46s and DC-3s flying cargo, and their numbers are swollen by a wide range of other propellor types: Twin Otters, Bandeirantes, F.27s HS748s and CASAs. There are plenty of colour schemes, too, including Satena who operate the el-cheapo domestic flights. Subject to availability, this is the way to see Colombia.

RIO NEGRO
MDE   SKRG   Jose Maria Cordova International   4m/6km S of Medellin

---

The passenger terminal at this new airport, formerly known as Medellin, has an excellent spectator's terrace. There is some jet traffic but lots of the flights are operated by propellor-driven aircraft, and all of them rather exotic. Twin Otters and Fairchild F-27s of ACES rub shoulders with Aries Bandeirantes and Satena HS748s. Every movement needs a photograph, or so it seems. Traffic is only moderately brisk, but each aircraft is something rather special, and very exotic.

MEDELLIN
      SKMD   Olaya Herrera   23m/37km SE

The old airport is further down the valley, and this is where the old piston airliners are still to be found, and in reasonable numbers. Movements are cargo-related, so the passenger terminal is of little relevance. For access to the cargo ramp, a reasonable knowledge of the Spanish language is useful, though there is always somebody around who wants to show off how well he speaks American English.

MIRAFLORES

Miraflores does not have an airport at all but nevertheless deserves a mention in this book. The town is linked to the outside world, mostly by DC-3s, which land on the main street! This is very much frontier-land, as the airstrip is policed by the anti-narcotis police by day and by guerillas at night. The street is not paved, so the aircraft often touch down on/in red mud. The television programme mentioned below, featured the cargos carried by the visiting aircraft, which included mini-skirted prostitutes. Climbing into and out of a DC-3 requires a helping hand from one or two men - no shortage of willing hands! This is the sort of place that intrepid aviation photographers will find subject matter with a difference.

VILLAVICENCIO
VVC   SKVV   la Vanguardia   4m/6km

Colombia is a large country with a significant undeveloped region. The best way to get to Villavicenzio is by Satena, with their Aviocars and HS748s, at a ridiculously low cost by western standards. Anyone who has an interest in piston aircraft would do well to consider a $10 trip from Bogota to Villavicenco, where the small airport's traffic is free of the sound of jet engines.

Because the jungle was cleared to make this airport, photographs of old airliners with an equatorial background take on a truly exotic appearance, and there is no shortage of subject matter. The single storey passenger terminal is adequate for the purposes, and has a cafeteria and a few shops. More important, the security staff do allow photos to be taken, with access to the ramp. Many small airliners are based here, though operations tend to be ad-hoc, with little regard to timetables. Such operators as AVESCA, El Dorado and Transamazonica all base aircraft here, plus several others, and there are plenty of operators of Cessna/Piper fleets.

One edition of the British TV programme, Pertpetual Motion, featured the DC-3. Very much in evidence were the many DC-3s, C-46s and C-54s standing around at Villavicenzio. Few other airports in the entire world do as much maintence work on DC-3s. Anyone visiting might care to contact Aliansa, the airline which was featured. Also prominently featured was Nubia Alvarez Rodriguez, Jorge's (big?) sister. She might welcome the chance to talk to people who watched the programme.

HL SOUTH KOREA (Republic of Korea)
SEOUL
SEL   RKSS   Kimp'o   16m/25km W

The magnificent new passenger terminal created for Korean Air and Asiana has been built next to a new apron, in a corner a little remote from most of the action on the field. Facing the runway is the old international passenger terminal, and between them is the small domestic building. The quantity of sky blue airliners is hardly surprising but there are numerous small aircraft to be seen in these colours: to the left of the new terminal, a pair of hangars house the Korean Air biz-jet fleet.

The older terminals at Kimp'o must be explored, to enable the large quantity of aircraft to be seen, as the view from the snack bar in the new building offers only a distant view of the runway.

The airport and city are linked by two bus services. One operates to each side of the Han River: No.600 to the south side and No.601 to the station and most of the major hotels. The fare is Won700.

HS THAILAND (Kingdom of Thailand)
BANGKOK
BKK   VTBD   Don Muang International   15m/23km NNE (bus 20 minutes)

Construction seems to be an almost permanent feature of this airport. Work to bring the passenger terminal areas up to modern standards has been completed, and already there is a need for more investment.

The cost of living in Thailand is, by western standards, low. Nevertheless one or two words of advice before arriving may be in order. There is a courtesy bus service into town but tickets must be purchased before leaving the Arrivals area. Failure to do this leaves a tired traveller at the mercy of extremely keen taxi drivers. Alternative number one is to stay somewhere such as the highly-recommended Asia Hotel. Thai Airways operate a courtesy bus between the International Terminal and the hotel every 30 minutes, at a very reasonable Bht 60 (about £1.50) each way. Alternative number two is to catch a train. These are very cheap (Bht 6) though infrequent.

The two lower levels of the International Terminal are for arrivals, while the two above are for departures. The observation deck is on the fourth floor, and is best described as a corridor linking dining facilities. All views, whether from the 'deck' or the cafe/restaurant, are behind glass but very good. To be sure of seeing what is parked on all the stands, it is worth walking from one extreme to the other. Photography is another matter, very much subjective: opinions vary from good to hopeless. Suffice to say that a pictorial record is possible but, in many instances, the photos are not likely to be of the highest quality.

The apron which is visible is that between Piers Two and Three, and is restricted in both content and area. The flat roof of the departure hall below extends forward, to block out aircraft parked on the closest stands, and such movements as Vietnamese Tu-134s and Laotian An-24s often only appear at night.

Beyond the apron is a view of the runway threshold, so inbound or outbound aircraft can be seen passing along one of the taxiways. On the far side of the field is the military base, though distance and heat haze conspire to ensure that serials can not be read, except in the early morning. This is probably a good thing, as the pleasant Thai temperament does not extend to the military personnel who patrol the airport.

The domestic terminal is not without its merits. For a start, its visitors are unlikely to be seen on the average day at Düsseldorf or Liverpool. Leaving the international terminal at ground level, turn left and walk along by the chain fence. Through it can be seen whatever is parked on one side of Pier 4 and on part of the domestic ramp. Once inside the domestic terminal, a security check is followed by a flight of stairs leading to a small snack bar. The view is excellent of both the domestic ramp and international movements on the taxiway.

Between the two parallel runways is what must be a unique feature for an international airport: a golf course! It must not be assumed that, by packing a No.5 iron and a putter in the holiday luggage, a round of golf can be used as a way of getting close to the movements. Anyone who feels that a round of golf, between two of Asia's more interesting runways, is essential should contact the Royal Thai Air Force Golf Course on 5236441. (I can't believe I'm writing this!) Weekday green fees are Bht 100, and all equipment, shoes and clubs included, can be hired. Eighteen holes on a Saturday, with everything thrown in, costs Bht 500.

Cameras in the hands of the average tourist excite no interest and it is possible for the security presence to be low-key. Low-key can be plain clothes, of course, and the use of a 300mm zoom for a close up of something exotic, even a civil airliner, could be risky. Also conspiring against the serious photographer is the cleanliness (or lack thereof) of the glass. Bangkok is an ideal airport for watching, and even noting, a fine variety of movements but any photographic record, other than tourist 'snaps', will be the result of luck, in more ways than one.

The good news: ramp access is possible! The bad news: it costs Bht 750 to take still photos for up to three hours (no problem) and another Bht 900 an hour for an 8-seater bus. In other words, this is for organized tour parties only. Further details from Wing Commander Tawatchai Rachawat, Airport Operations Department, Airports Authority of Thailand, Vibhavadi Rangsit Road, Bangkok 10210, or fax on (code plus) 531-5559.

The temptation to think: "so far so good" might be halted abruptly by another requirement, that you must also submit written permission from each airline if wishing to take a photo of their aircraft. That really is the tricky bit! Imagine having paid your money and standing on the ramp when something extraordinarily exotic taxis into view. No piece of paper, no photo! Local contact with Ops might yield different results. Try 535-1650 or 535-1705 or, at weekends, the duty officer on 535-1566.

CHIANG MAI
CNX   VTCC   3m/5km

The best way to reach the airport from town, is to take a Tuk-tuk, a three-wheel motorbike. Depending on your abilities to bargain with the driver, the journey should cost about Bht 40 (about £1). On arrival at the passenger terminal, it's worth asking at the information desk for a timetable of the day's events. Don't expect too much. Traffic is only moderate, featuring mostly a few Thai A300s and ATR-72s. Kumming, Hong Kong and Bangkok Airways are all reported as regular visitors. In the evenings, a Silkair A310 could also be likely.

To the left of the terminal is a fence where it's possible to overlook the apron and the runway. The late afternoon sun makes things quite difficult for photography however. At the other side of the passenger terminal is the cargo building, and between them is a gate which offers another view of the apron. Visible from here are aircraft at the Thai Air Force's Chiang Mai Base. If any military aircraft are parked outside, the guard at the gate can make life difficult for anyone showing (unwelcome) interest.

This is northern Thailand, less than 100 miles from both Laos and Burma, neither of which might represent the best neighbours. Unlawful activities in this part of the world are best left to the imagination but it would be naive to pretend that westerners are always regarded as friendly and harmless.

CHIANG RAI
CEI   VTCR   Ban Du   5m/8km N

A visit to northern Thailand is not like a holiday jaunt to Bangkok or Phuket. This can seem quite hostile territory, unless you know what you're doing. This airport, probably the country's northernmost, is quite close to the border but is not a military base. A Thai A300 visits two or three times a day, and a photo is easily taken. Otherwise, the journey is hardly worthwhile, in civil aviation terms.

PHUKET
HKT   VTSP   International   18m/30km N

Several shuttle buses link the airport with the resort's different hotels. Patong Beach, about 20km to the south, is probably the best served. Officially, this is Thailand's second busiest airport but it comes a long way behind Bangkok. Anyone considering a day's spotting at the airport might do well to contact the airport's information desk by telephone before making the journey. The number is 327230-7 and, for public information, try extension 1111 or 1122.

Traffic is mostly Thai A300s, which park at the air jetties but there are also ATR-42s and 737s, which normally park out on the apron. Variety may be offered by the occasioal day-time Malaysian 737 or a Silkair A310.

The airfield has been built beside the coast, the 09 threshold being virtually on the beach. To the south of the runway are the aprons and the passenger terminal, which faces the coast. Parallel to the runway, and separating the passenger and cargo terminals, is a fence. This overlooks the apron used mostly by turboprops. At the side nearest a house and garage stands a group of trees, ideal for shade when staying any length of time. The view from the fence is excellent, as it also allows photos of aircraft on the runway. If extra height is needed, there are some old posts to stand on. They also make a good place to sit.

Jet aircraft taxi round and park at the other side of the passenger terminal, so are normally out of sight unless they move. When Runway 27 is in use for landing, incoming movements are hidden by a hill on top of which are the ATC aerials, so a radio is useful to ensure that the camera is ready for use.

As is to be expected in this part of the world, the airport is surrounded by lush vegetation. Palm trees abound. It is possible, for the adventurous and energetic, to explore other vantage points around the perimeter. The most obvious is the beach, reached by walking through the national park. There is no fence at this side of the field, so security officers keep watch for anyone trespassing near the runway. It is also worth noting that walking along the beach is hazardous, as the tide can cause one or two problems. Rather than run unnecessary risks, it might be best to take other people's word for it: the fence next to the apron faces north, has good views and isn't risky at all.

HZ SAUDI ARABIA (Kingdom of Saudi Arabia)
DHAHRAN
DHA   OEDR   International   8m/13km SE

Apart from limited views from the departure lounges, there is little scope for observing the fairly busy traffic here. The upper levels of the Dhahran International Hotel (near the terminal area) provide panoramic but distant views of the 'civil' runway and taxiways. Good landing shots could be obtained from the airport - city road, just by the northern threshold but the aircraft normally land in the opposite direction!

Even in normal times, there is much fighter activity here, many visiting C-130Hs and the occasional USAF C-5 and C-141 but the military facilities are not visible from the civil side of the airport. Most long-stay executive movements park on the cargo ramp and others go in front of the main terminal. Airlines feature many of the usual European carriers but of note are Airbuses of Air India, PIA and, a long way from home, Korean Airlines. PAL and Thai International A300-600s are also regular visitors while Gulf Air 737s visit frequently on the 'Air Bridge' from nearby Bahrain, as does Yemenia's 737. Saudia are naturally busy and the ramp usually contains two or three A300s as well as a few 737s.

The international and domestic terminals face the 'civil' runway and all aircraft visiting park nose-in. Across the runway is the cargo and general aviation long-term parking and, to its right, the ARAMCO facility, with a good number of aircraft normally present. At the southern end of Runway 34R/16L, that most remote from Dhahran, is a large air force dump. Being close to a missile site, approach must be avoided. Anyone with the slightest interest in military aviation would be advised to make do with the consolation Lightning, Sabre and T-33 on poles by the main road. It would be unrealistic to imagine that Dhahran has returned to normal after the Gulf War, and it can be assumed that the military presence is always on a high level of alert, with activities and attitudes to match.

JEDDAH
JED   OEJN   King Abdulaziz International   11m/17km N

Jeddah is located on the Red Sea coast of Saudi Arabia and is the closest city with an airport to Mecca, the most important place in the world for muslims and one of pilgrimage (the Hadj) for any who can make the trip. The annual influx of aircraft to Jeddah has repercussions throughout the world for airlines, with short-leases being sought for almost anything which can carry lots of economy passengers. At these times, the Hadj terminal is the gateway to Mecca and close scrutiny by non-muslims is unwise.

A vast airport, with three parallel runways although one would easily be able to handle the amount of movements for most of the year. The civil operations take place on the western and central runway, with all the terminal facilities between them. Beyond, and to the east, is the military base, with its own runway. The RSAF base about half their C-130s here at any one time, with the rest at Riyadh's old airport. The two all-white VIP C-130Hs and various examples painted in Saudia colours are also often parked here, totalling about twenty, just visible in the heat haze, and otherwise inaccessible. Between the eastern and central runway is the King's 747 hangar, though there is rarely any activity to be seen around it.

The terminal and general aviation areas are situated between the western and centre runways, as is the impressive Hadj terminal. There is no viewing area in the Saudia terminal but, inside, one gets a good view of the airlines' aprons. All the Saudia aircraft are parked neatly in lines according to aircraft type and are served by (unpopular) mobile lounges from the terminal. Foreign airliners are parked along the western side and are served by mobile lounges from the 'Other Airlines' terminal, to the north. Photography is an extremely risky business and is probably best done from the aircraft as it taxis in or out.

The general aviation ramp is within walking distance from the Saudia terminal and is accessible to someone who has a plausible reason to get past the reception area at Arabasco (the Fixed Based Operator). Although most of these aircraft are regularly seen in Europe, they make an extremely impressive, and highly photogenic, sight in the constant sunshine and backed by the scenic hills in the distance. When Saudia's Special Flights fleet is taken into account, there can be few other places in the world where fifteen or more Gulfstreams are almost always present at any time. An interesting collection of local operators with hangars in this area are Petromin (with Twin Otters and F.27s) and Saudia Special Flights/Ministry of Resources (with Skyvans and JetRangers). At least forty executive jets could be expected here on a typical day.

Visiting airlines include all the major European carriers, several from Asia and a few from Africa. Many schedules are operated in the middle of the night and the more interesting aircraft to operate here are Ethiopian and Kuwaiti 727s, Yemenia and Gulf Air 737s, and PIA A300s.

RIYADH

RUH   OERK   King Khaled International   22m/34km N

Not a particularly interesting airport for visitors but the beautifully maintained and visually stunning passenger terminal is worth a visit for its own sake. The loop road from the city has the airline terminal, split into domestic and international, on one side and the VIP terminal on the other. In the middle is a mosque.

Foreign airlines increase in number, having been unwelcome until recently, but they are still limited to a selection of major European national carriers. Gulf Air 737s do visit several days a week.

Viewing is good from the airside of the terminal, with the cargo ramp some distance to the left, and the general aviation terminal directly opposite, across one of the two runways. Unlike Jeddah, there are no hangars, and far less residents but the g.a. terminal is signposted clearly from the main airport highway. It is a long drive round the perimeter for perhaps twenty or so inmates, ranging in size from 727s to HS125s.

The large VIP terminal is impressive, to say the least. Its ramp hosts either nothing at all or, frequently, a fair number of Middle Eastern executive jets when there's a major ministerial gathering in town. Typical sightings include a Syrian Tu-134, Yemenia's VIP 727 and the usual array of Gulfstreams. The idea of going near this area with a camera would be ridiculous and using it even more so! Only small compensation, the Saudi TV channels diligently record all important arrivals and departures, so close-ups of various interesting executive aircraft appear almost nightly on the news.

Riyadh's old airport is now a military base, a couple of miles out of town. It is used by the RSAF and also very much by the USAF since the Gulf War. The views from the road are only distant and anyone who wants to find out more about the movements will check in at the Marriott Hotel. The upper floor rooms allow the E-3s, KC-10s and KC-135 movements to be seen, plus a selection of the local military aircraft in the circuit.

I ITALY (Italian Republic)
BERGAMO
BGY   LIME   Orio al Serio   3m/5km

The signposts give clear directions from the Milan to Verona Autostrada (A4). Sceduled passenger services amount to very little but cargo and charter activity are a little livelier. The car park, next to the passenger terminal, offers a good view of the cargo ramp though the aircraft can be parked head-on. On the far side of the field is the general aviation facility, with about thirty light aircraft to be seen from the fence.

BOLOGNA
BLQ   LIPE   Guglielmo Marconi   4m/6km NW (bus 20 minutes)

Better known locally as Borgo Panigale, Bologna offers the enthusiast everything that's required. The roof terrace in the brand new terminal is normally open from 7:00am to 11:00pm and there is no glass to make life difficult for photographers. Even the car parking is free. If this isn't enough, there is even better spotting by leaving the terminal and turning right at the traffic lights. Another right onto Via dell' Aeroporto leads past a wall behind which the army helicoppters sit, and after another right turn, past the fire department with a couple of Agusta Bell 206s, to the Aeroclub, which also has a north-facing roof terrace, close to the taxiway. If this isn't enough, carry on west along Via della Fornace, which leads to Via della Salute. A side street leads to the perimeter, and even closer views of the taxiway, close to the holding point for Runway 12.

Alternatively, leave the terminal and head north on Via Triumvirato, where an embankment beside the river allows a view of the end of Runway 30. A series of left turns, into the community of Lippo, leads down the Via Surrogazione to the fence by the runway. The holes in the fence were apparently created by photographers but it would appear they used high explosives for the job. In other words, you can't go wrong. From here a DC-9 requires a 200 mm lens, and 767s rather less.

The airport is quite close to the city centre, on the far side of the Tangenziale Austostradale Kennedy (ring road). The passenger terminal is in the southwest corner of the field, close to the threshold of Runway 30. International flights are relatively few, and limited to 737s of British Airways, Lufthansa and Air France. Apart from that, it's best to have a serious interest in DC-9s, as Alitalia, ATI and Meridiana make up the bulk of the movements. In summer, the variety of foreign operators increases, and can include such visitors as Olympic 737s. The cargo apron, tucked away in the eastern corner of the apron normally receives only only a couple of regular visitors: a TNT BAe 146 which arrives at midnight and stays for a couple of hours, and another 146 which spends all day on the ramp during the week.

CATANIA
CTA   LICC   Fontana Rossa   4m/6km SSE

A modern airport, and one which may be of more interest to military fans. Less than a hundred miles north of Malta, a shipping line offers affordable day return services which allow seven hours ashore. This may be of interest to anyone who has negotiated a visit to Sigonella. To fill in the rest of the day, the No.24 bus runs regularly between the town and the airport. The large balcony allows views of only half of the two ramps, for scheduled services and general aviation. Opposite is the military base, with several helicopters and some CL-215s. As there is only the occasional ATI or Air Malta arrival, plus infrequent charters, it may be tempting to take a hike in search of the two withdrawn Trackers. The result should be a polite warning from a guard against such an activity.

CUNEO
CUF   Levaldigi   13m/20km N

Unlikely to be a destination for anyone but the most dedicated enthusiast, Cuneo might be worth a short detour fro someone intent on comprehensive coverage of Italian airports. It can be found, for those who must go, off the Strada Statale SS20, north of town. The only scheduled service is an Air Capitol Beechjet 400 to Rome (Urbe) but the runway has been extended to allow ATRs. The passenger terminal has an observation deck, from which can be seen anything present. Normally, it doesn't amount to much. Perhaps the occasional biz-jet will share the tarmac with the Linbergh Flying School's small fleet of light aircraft. The ex-Italian Search and Rescue Grumman Huiga, which is displayed on the field, is in poor condition.

FLORENCE
FLR   LIRQ   Peretola/Amerigo Vespucci   3m/5km

The best place for photos is by the fence, where the sun is at its best until about 3:00pm. Since this also coincides with most of the action, this can't be bad. The majority of the movements are on the small side, which means they can be very attractive subjects. Carriers such as Avianova, Air Dolomiti, Eurowings and Meridiana are all regular visitors and, with BAe146s being considered large, photographers can add some excellent portraits to their collection. There aren't many places in Europe where it's possible to get so close to these Dash 8s, ATRs and Do228s.

GENOA
GOA   LIMJ   Sestri/Cristoforo Columbo   4m/6km W

The coastline on the Gulf of Genoa slopes steeply to the sea, so this airport is packed very tightly into its space. From town, SS1 is the easiest road to take, but the Autostrada to Savona (A10) has an exit for the airport. The modern passenger terminal features a lot of glass and bright red steel. The single runway, 11/29, is built on reclaimed land in the bay so that movements cause the least noise nuisance to the local population, many of whom live very near.

The observation area is on the upper level, next to the restaurant and bar. The whole area is behind glass and every movement on the runway can be seen. Behind the terminal is the aero club, with the general aviation and Piaggio plant next to it. Because most of the scheduled movements are operated by ATI, it is Piaggio which often provide the most interest. Because of the sun, afternoons are best for photographs, and it's worth remembering that the air jetties are usually only occupied by jet traffic. ATRs and Saab 340s need long lenses, and should be caught while on the move. It isn't always easy.

MILAN
LIN   LIML   Linate   6m/9km E

When Linate is busy, it is very busy. During the week, there can be a movement every two minutes, but it would be foolish to arrive after lunch and expect the pace to be brisk. Early mornings are best. The viewing gallery has been closed for some years, but none of the locals use the terminal area anyway. Apart from the predictable quantity of Alitalia movements, there is variety, provided by Alisarda, ATI and an increasing amount of third-level flights. Because the city centre is so close, business traffic is frequent, with several biz-jets being based, or operating from, the airport. Almost all the international traffic is now handled by Malpensa.

Movements can still be witnessed from Canzo cemetary but the fence has been repaired. The holes in the wire mesh are now very small and will remain so for a few months until the regular visitors change the situation. Italian photographers have a way of winning their battles with fence-builders, but this one might take some time! From the terminal, a short way along Viale Forlanini is a turn to the right, to Rivolta, which leads to the Idroscalo. This artificial lake was once used as a seaplane base but now forms part of a public park. Keeping the Idroscalo on your right means following the sign for Idrascalo Est, then Crema. Follow the small blue direction signs for Canzo, which means travelling parallel to the perimeter fence. A small square leads to the cemetary, the fence, and a fine close-up view of the taxiway. On the far side is the town of Linate. With sun behind, it's best for the photo-grapher in the mornings, when traffic is busier.

As the sun moves round, the photographer can do the same. A footpath follows the fence to the threshold of Runway 36R and, after a short walk along the road there is another footpath heading back north. The runway is now seen from the western side. By heading north into Linate, it's only a short distance to the general aviation area on the west side of the field. Whilst there is usually a lot of interesting aircraft, there are no places around the g.a.terminal (ATA) from which to see them. Runway 36L is used only by light aircraft, due to its length. Traffic using this is best seen from Viale Forlanini, but it means missing more exciting movements on the other side.

MILAN

| MXP | LIMC | Malpensa | 29m/47km NW |

A long way out of the city, on Autostrada A7, Malpensa's open air terrace was closed in October 1985 and remains so. The whole passenger terminal, at the north end of the field, is to be replaced by a new complex on the west side of the field. Construction work has suffered delays while legal wrangling resolved who was bribing whom. The completion date is now believed to be some time in 1995.

Malpensa handles the larger movements, but is much less busy than Linate. For this reason, local knowledge makes use of the perimeter road essential for a short time. It passes commendably close to the hold for Runway 35R, with the opportunity to enjoy close encounters with a range of Alitalia movements, including the wide-bodies, mostly before lunchtime. Occasional tourist charter flights are operated, and the summer season is supplemented by a good variety of ski charters in winter. Interest rapidly turns to Linate, as it's busier and normally handles a wider variety.

Worth watching out for are military cargo flights which feature C-130s of many European air forces and, until sanctions, the odd Iraqi Il-76, the reason for their presence being the Agusta/SIAI production facility.

The general aviation field, BRESSO, is hemmed in by housing, and its single runway, again north/south, sees very few movements. The hangars and apron are on the western side, but there is little to see.

NAPLES

| NAP | LIRN | Capodichino | 4m/6km NE (bus 25 minutes) |

A regular bus service is operated to the airport from the city centre. It leaves from the railway station and the Piazza Garibaldi. The passenger terminal has a glazed spectator's gallery. From it can be seen everything that moves. The majority of scheduled traffic is operated by Alitalia and ATI but there are some regional carriers to add a little spice. The far side of the field is reserved for non-civilian use. The US Navy has its own ramp, as do the police helicopters and the Italian Air Force, whose G222s are extremely difficult to identify, due to the distance and the heat haze.

PISA

PSA   LIRP   Galileo Galilei   2m/3km NW (train 5 minutes)

Pisa is an hour by train from Florence. Competition is fierce between the airports of Pisa and Florence to develop international services to Tuscany. The runway is used primarily by the Italian Air Force's San Giusto base, with plenty of G222s in evidence. There is a C-119 on the gate. Though its identity wasn't confirmed in the report, it could be MM61922/SM-26 which first saw service with Linee Aeree Italiane as I-LADY.

RIMINI

RMI   LIPR   Miramari   4m/6km

Despite being so close to the resorts on the Adriatic, traffic is slow. Photos in the morning are possible but the subject matter is likely to be a solitary Avianova ATR-42. Due to the presence of the military base which shares the runway, photographers need to show a little more caution than might be necesary at other Italian airports.

ROME

CIA   LIRA   Ciampino   10m/16km SE

Located in the city's southeastern suburbs, Ciampino has a large general aviation facility, a small terminal for inclusive tour charters, and a military base featuring VIP executive aircraft. There are different vantage points at the perimeter, one being in Ciampino itself, on the eastern side of the runway, remote from the terminal. The road to Ciampino passes round the northern edge of the field, and photos of landing aircraft are possible.

Whilst there is an extremely good selection of interesting types and operators to be logged, including civil biz-jets in number, photographers can expect frustration. No attempts should be made to take photos from the terminal area, inside or outside the building. Arrest is very likely, due to the security measures which result from the VIP movements. Any knowledge of Italy's turbulent politics, and massive corruption means that precautions must be strict, and be seen to be strict.

ROME

FCO   LIRF   Fiumicino   22m/34km SW (train 40 minutes)

Also known by its official name of Leonardo da Vinci, the roof terrace extends across the front of both terminals and along the top of the linking pier, but it was closed permanently many years ago.

The international terminal allows no views at all, and the domestic terminal is only marginally better. The occasional tantalising glimpses through ground floor windows are supplemented by a slightly better view from the two first floor restaurants . . . but beware prices which are treble those in what is already an expensive city.

Most of the ATI fleet can be seen, particularly in the evenings, in the company of the majority of Alitalia's European operations airliners, while some of the movements taxying to/from the international terminal pass within range.

At various points outside the two terminals, there are more glimpses of aircraft, the upper level road overlooking the cargo apron. Other aircraft are visible from the road which passes Alitalia's maintenance area but not adequately so, from a photographer's point of view.

The airport is close to the coast, but there is a road between the sea and the perimeter.

Signposted to Focene, it runs alongside 16R/34L where there is parking and an excellent view. To see most of the movements, it is best to settle close to the intersection between this runway and the threshold of 07, which heads away from the fence. A right turn at the end of the runway is marked 'Fregene'. A close-up view of aircraft at the hold for 16R is at its best in the early morning. As the sun moves round, photographers experience a range of problems. Beyond a bend in this road, where it heads north again, is a turning to the right. At the end of it is Runway 16L/34R and the holding point for Runway 25. A footpath across open ground leads there, though the aspect is better for spotters than photographers.

TREVISO
TSF   LIPH   San Angelo

Only the occasional KLM Cityhopper livens this airport up. The passenger terminal is small and, beside it, the fence allows anything on the apron to be seen. Normally this means something like about twenty light aircraft.

TURIN
TRN   LIMF   Caselle   10m/16km NW

Also known as Citta di Torino, the airport is undergoing a major modern-isation programme, with a complete new passenger terminal due to open in October 1993. Delays are possible, of course.

The layout is similar to Bologna, with the passenger terminal in the southwest corner of the field and the single runway, 18/36. However there is far more activity along the western side of the field. Alitalia Cargo 747s are a regular sight, most of which are used to ferry Cadillac bodies to Detroit. Alenia (formerly Aeritalia) has a production plant where work is carried out on the AMX and Tornado. It was here that Italian F-104s were assembled.

Hangars contain an interesting assortment. Turin is famous all over the world for being the home of FIAT, so their fleet of biz-jets is based here. In an adjacent hangar are Euro-Fly's biz-jets, plus a few small helicopters and other aircraft. Euro-Fly's DC-9s are rarely seen here, as they normally operate from Malpensa or Bergamo.

Traffic is increasing, and there are places around the perimeter from where it can be seen at close quarters. In the mornings, when things are quite brisk, it's best to leave the terminal area and make left turns, past Caselle cemetary and the Alenia plant, in the direction of Malanghero. Before reaching the village, a playing field with a football pitch is seen on the left. The footpath goes past the far side to the perimeter.

In the afternoon, coming out of the terminal area, take a right turn for San Maurizio. On the edge of town is a right turn at the ERG filling station. This leads to the airport perimeter, with a close view of the taxiway and, just beyond, the runway.

VENICE
VCE   LIPZ   Tessera   8m/13km NW (boat 20 minutes)

Even the most hardened enthusiast will make the airport only a secondary reason for a visit to Venice, such is the nature of the city, steeped in history and unique beauty. The most unusual feature at Tessera (or Marco Polo) is the boat service linking it with the city and Lido. The journey across the lagoon is the quickest way, and definitely the most scenic.

The airport follows the common Italian layout, with its terminal area at one end of the runway, in this case aligned 04/22. The passenger terminal has the bus station and harbour to its right, seen from the landside, and a terrace area to the left, where the best view is found. There is a new passenger terminal, occupying what was the car park area immediately in front of the old terminal.

The scheduled traffic includes Alitalia, ATI and Alisarda as well as Air Littoral, and these are complemented by a steady charter programme in the summer. A series of right turns from the terminal leads to the general aviation apron or, alternatively, a drive to the cargo area ensures that anything present can be seen with the bonus of being able to log all the landing aircraft.

VERONA
VRN   LIPX   Villafranca Veronesa   7m/12km SW

Anyone touring Italy by road might consider a stop at Verona, as it is at the intersection of two major highways: Milan to Venice and Modena to Innsbruck. The civil scene is decidedly quiet for much of the day, with a handful of mostly Meridiana flights, though there are occasional visits by British Airways, Air France, Air Dolomiti and Lufthansa. The runway is shared with the air force, VRN being the civil airport code and LIPN being that of the Boscomantico base.

The passenger terminal does have an observation gallery but the glass is tinted. Photographers may therefore prefer to walk half a mile or so, parallel to the runway, where the view and the sunshine are at their best all day. The military presence means that caution really must be exercised.

JA JAPAN
FUKUOKA
FUK   RJFF   Itazuke   6m/10km E

The southernmost main island of Japan is Kyushu, linked by both a causeway and Shinkansen (bullet train) to cities on Honshu. Fukuoka is a major city, with its own international airport. Apart from the regular wide-body visitors, like those of ANA and JAL, there are plenty of other movements which are of interest. They range from Japan Air Charter DC-10s to Nagasaki Koku Islanders. Most of the surrounding Pacific Rim countries operate wide-body services to Fukuoka.

The passenger terminal features an observation facility on level four. From it, all movements on Runway 16/34 are visible, the threshold of 16 being quite close. However, photographers will not be thrilled to read that the deck is fronted by an acrylic screen, which makes photos of any quality almost impossible to take.

KAGOSHIMA
KOJ   RJFK   18m/29km S

Whilst Kagoshima is essentially a regional airport, it does handle some international flights. The vast majority of flights are, of course, domestic though, in Japan, this represents an extremely interesting array.

Access to the substantial roof terrace necessitates a small admission charge but it is value for money. Traffic is not brisk but each movement would be regarded by most to be of interest. During the course of the average afternoon, for example, all principle Japanese carriers are seen. A couple of dozen Japanese airliners in the space of two hours or so is probably adequate reward for the trip, but it must be remembered these include the complete range, from ANA 747s to a dozen or so YS-11s.

Add a Korean Air 727 and a Dragonair 737, and the fact that they can all be adequately photographed with, at most, a 135mm lens and Kagoshima becomes a significant airport. The most basic photographic equipment will achieve results for aircraft on the apron and those on the runway are within reach of the average telephoto lens. To ensure that the leisurely pace doesn't get too boring, the terrace has vending facilities.

The Maritime Safety Agency maintains a couple of King Air 200s here, and other light aircraft can be seen. A short walk from the terminal past the apron leads to some hangars where the photos can be taken.

KUMAMOTO
KMJ   RJFT   5m/8km E

Most European aviation enthusiasts probably know little of the southern island of Kyushu, though it features three major airports, apart from Kagoshima (qv). Without some prior knowledge, arrival here would be a very pleasant surprise. Unlike its European and American counterparts, where the viewing facilities seem to be good only if the subjects are poor, Kumamoto has a deck and plenty to see from it.

In return for a 50 yen admission charge to the roof deck, the excellent view features mainly wide bodies. The choice of airlines and number of movements may be limited, relatively speaking, but all the domestic airlines are to be seen, including a number of local ANA YS-11s.

Although Kumamoto is not widely known in Europe, it is an expanding gateway to Japan, but only Korean Air calls regularly at present. Other foreign carriers are likely to be attracted here, to ensure that it can be regarded as a truly international airport. As a bonus, general aviation is also to be seen, with a dozen or so light aircraft on the apron, to the left of the domestic terminal.

MIYAZAKI
KMI   RJFM   2m/3km S (bus 10 minutes)

One of Kyushu's smaller airports, Miyazaki is on the east coast of the island, though arrival here leaves no doubt that plans are afoot. The ultra-modern terminal was opened in March 1990 and, unlike its counterparts in almost every other country, here is a new airport terminal with ideal facilities for the enthusiast.

The very reasonable admission charge to the first class observation deck allows easy photography of both the apron and movements on the runway. To be realistic, traffic is limited though, once again, wide body aircraft are featured. The opportunity to take perfect photos of ANA 767s and YS-11s sounds wonderful from a few thousand miles away. The reality, it has to be admitted, is perhaps not quite so exciting.

Variety is provided by the occasional Korean Air flight from Seoul, together with some general aviation movements: the helicopters which call in for refuelling include Maritime Safety Agency Bell 212s, and the circuit usually features one or two training Bonanzas.

NAGOYA
NGO   RJNN   Komaki   12m/19km N

As expected at a Japanese airport, the observation deck is first class, offering a good view over the entire airfield. At the entrance to the deck is a small museum display: nothing special but nice to see. Most of the airliners are 767s of All Nippon and JAL but the occasional Korean and China Eastern Airbus add some variety, as do the Air Micronesia 727s. Runway 34 sees most use, and its threshold is only about ten minutes' walk from the terminal. Photographers are strongly recommended to take the trip, as the light conditions are almost perfect.

Whilst traffic can be described as moderate at best, there are normally several C-130s to be seen opposite the terminal. A stay in Nagoya does not mean spending a fortune. This isn't Tokyo, and there is a good selection of inexpensive hotels around the station area in town.

OKINAWA
OKA   ROAH   Naha   2m/3km SW

Two and a half hours' flying time southwest of the main islands which make up Japan are the Ryukyu Islands, the biggest of which is Okinawa. Naha, at the southern tip, is the biggest city. Whilst the airport is very much regional, the majority of its scheduled movements comprise JAL and ANA wide-bodies, the various Japan Transocean (previously Southwest Airlines) aircraft for which Okinawa is the main hub, plus a few international flights, such as Northwest 747s, Continental 727s and China Airlines 737s. In other words, Okinawa offers pretty much the same fare as can be seen at Tokyo or Osaka, apart from Ryukyu Commuter Islanders and Twin Otters.

One or two intrepid travellers have made the trip, with high quality photos being published. What still isn't known for certain is whether ramp access made them possible. There are some people who, having taken the time and trouble to discover new places, are not always willing to share their information with others. Thus Okinawa remains quite an expensive destination, though with the chance that something a bit different can be seen.

OSAKA
KIX   Kansai International   18m/30km SW (bus 60min train 25min)

It took two mountains to build the island on which this airport now stands. Apart from Denver's new masterpiece, few airports have been the subject of so much rumour. The runway is not, contrary to some reports, sinking slowly into the bay. Its rate of descent is less than one millimetre annually. There are, however, lots of stories about money. The sums are staggering, and most of them are probably true.

For a start, the airport cost something in the region of about fifteen billion dollars to build. That money has to be repaid and airport tax is, without doubt, slightly on the high side. Stick a piece of plastic in a machine, pay it, and forget about it until the monthly payment slip arrives. A cup of coffee doesn't cost £5 - it actually costs £1.90, which isn't cheap, and a hot dog can set you back £2.20. So what if a burger and fries cost £5?

Kansai is, to be realistic, the sort of place where normal standards are put to one side. The terminal really is something special. Instead of paying the taxi fare (a ridiculous £120 one way) into Osaka, take a bus for only £8.20. The Nankai Railways dark blue trains are something of a problem, if you are a nervous woman. At first glance, it appears they are called Rapists, but closer inspection reveals the word is actually Rapi:t. Fares might be expensive but at least three or four girls stand at the end of the platform to wave you off. Maybe that was just for the inauguration!

If you like modern architecture, you'll love Kansai. A giant wing of a roof, with steel tubes, cables and huge nuts and bolts all over the place. There is more than enough glass to ensure the place feels light. Being inside Kansai is at least as good as travelling and, in many cases, better.

New airports usually mean bad news for the spotter, but not so in Japan. At one end of the airport complex is a purpose-built observation hall, open between 10:00am and 9:00pm. It's a short ride from the international arrivals area in a dark blue coach. The bus journey costs 800 Yen but the ticket includes admission and the return journey. The best way to find the bus stop is on the free Terminal Guide brochure. Leave the passenger terminal on level 1F, preferably by door F at the far end. To the left are the "group bus" stands, two of which are reserved for the observation hall buses.

Before leaving the passenger terminal, it might be worth a visit to the basement level, B1, where the convenience store is to be found. Snacks and cans aren't cheap here but they're cheaper than any of the alternatives.

The observation hall is a five storey building, the top floor of which is completely open giving a view of the entire airfield and, on the floor below is a McDonalds-type fast food restaurant. It's best to be extremely hungry before going there, so that the prices don't hurt so much. All movements can be seen from the deck, though photography is only at its best in the mornings. Prevailing winds are also important, because not all runway movements are easily photographed.

To reach Osaka's other airport, Itami, the bus leaves from Stop No.8 on level 1F (outside door BC). Journey time is about an hour, depending on traffic, and the fare is 1800 Yen (about £10). Alternative transport into town, and several other nearby towns, is offered by high speed catamaran, which leaves from the airport's ferry terminal. Journey time is less than forty minutes. A regular jet-foil service also operates to Kobe, which takes only half an hour.

OSAKA
OSA   RJOO   Itami   10m/16km W

As Kansai opened, the international terminal at Itami was closed, and all flights transferred. The future of domestic movements through Itami is a matter for speculation, as all flights may one day be moved to the new airport. Land suitable for building is expensive in Japan, hence the need to move mountains into the bay. Flights over populated areas cause much local opposition, so Kansai is the logical airport for the future.

The observation deck is on the roof of the domestic (effectively the only) terminal, and offers views of all movements, between 7:00am and 9:00pm. Centrally located on the first floor (that immediately above the airline check in desks) is a staircase which leads to a turnstile. Pay the 50 Yen and have a nice day.

For closer views of the JAS YS-11s and SF340s, it is worth investigating the departures area, as there are numerous windows which allow eye level photos, rather than looking down on them from the roof.

Traffic used to be brisk though, because most of it was (and all of it now is) domestic, a day's spotting is still quite lively. General aviation is modest, as befits a modern airport. The occasional rotary movement by one of the residents can be seen, though somewhat remote from the deck. Anyone in search of closer encounters must walk past the cargo sheds for a view of the hangars. A left turn outside the terminal leads to several hangars at the corner of the field and, beyond, this walk ends at the access point to the fuel farm, served by many tankers during the day. From here, the end of the runway is close enough for the photographer in need of an alternative vantage point.

While much has been said about the cost of almost anything in Japan, things at Itami are more affordable. This applies particularly to hotels, many of which are only a short walk from the airport. Expect to pay £25 a night. The inexperienced traveller is warned about the alternative type of accommodation: these are called "love hotels", where rooms are normally paid for by the hour. The decor is usually the quickest, and least embarrassing, way of telling the difference. If it's pink and fluffy, it might not be what you want.

TOKYO
         RJTF   Chofu   18m/30km SW

This is Tokyo's executive airport, handling much of the air taxi and other business flights. Even the most ardent airliner fan will probably make the (difficult) journey to take a few photos of the various types to be seen here. The hundred or so light aircraft also feature a handful of helicopters and Saturday is probably the best day for a visit when, as befits a businessman's airfield, not much flying takes place.

Before leaving the hotel, it is wise to ask someone to write in Japanese characters 'Chofu

Airport' as it will come in handy later. The underground train goes to Shinjuku and the Keisei private railway operates a service to Chofu. Normally, the booking clerk will be English-speaking but not so the taxi driver on your arrival. Here, the piece of paper will be of use and the fare should be about 800 Yen (£3). The journey takes ten minutes, and a request at the control tower for ramp access may result in an interrogation session. The permission which should follow the questions is best augmented by requests at the flying clubs around the apron. The Japanese are a very polite nation.

TOKYO

HND   RJTT   Haneda International   12m/19km S (train 20 minutes)

From Tokyo's main station, local trains take the traveller to Hamamatsu-cho and, from here, a monorail link goes to Haneda, on Tokyo Bay. The trip takes about half an hour and costs 480 Yen (less than £2), a small price to pay for getting to one of the more interesting airports in Asia, especially as the facilities for the enthusiast are of a high quality. Photographers will, however, consider life has not improved lately. A complete new terminal, on the far side, is now open. It's called "The Big Bird" and is not only popular with enthusiasts but also dating couples who like to see the culturally important (propitious?) Mount Fuji. The terminal's top level, 6F, has what appears from the plan to be two separate and centrally placed observation decks, which face southwest. This means that top-quality photos are best taken before about 11:00am.

Entry to the deck(s) is free and the view is obstructed only by a fence which doesn't seriously hamper photography. Japanese people tend to be generally shorter than Europeans, so cameras can be placed on top of the fence, or lenses can be placed so that it doesn't intrude. As is to be expected, there are toilet and eating facilities close by. Expect the observation decks to be crowded, especially on holidays.

All aircraft movements can be seen but anything by the old terminal can be difficult to identify. To make matters worse, China Airlines, the sole user of the old terminal, tend to use the distant Runway 04 for departures. It would appear that, already, the new terminal is lacking in sufficient stands. This means that many of the YS-11s, 737s and A320s park some way from the terminal, making photography almost impossible.

Traffic is generally domestic, except for China Airlines who still operate one or two 747s a day. Not surprisingly, Japan Air System and All Nippon fleets dominate, but JAL's presence features aircraft unlikely to be seen in Europe: 747SRs and 767s as well as DC-10s. Most enthusiasts probably associate Haneda with YS-11s, though developments have obviously changed the situation for the worse.

To get the most from Haneda, an early start is recommended. The opening times for the new terminal deck are not yet known for certain. They are likely to be similar to the old one: 6:30am to 8:00pm. Counting up, a typical midweek day should yield the following: JAL - 13 747s, 6 DC-10s and 6 767s; JAS - 15 A300s, 14 DC-9s and 5 YS11s; ANA - 16 747s, 27 767s and 3 737s, making a total of over one hundred aircraft operated by the main carriers. Taking into consideration that there are several other operators, a full day at Haneda is indeed a full day! Since the opening of the new terminal, nobody has reported investigating whether or not the old terminal deck is still open. Somehting else to be considered by the adventurous: a taxi will be needed to get to Keihin Jima. This is an industrial area, and good for photographs of aircraft using Runway 04/22.

TOKYO

NRT   RJAA   New Tokyo International   40m/64km E (train 55 minutes)

Japanese farmers continue to make life difficult at Narita. One tiny plot of land, close to the airport is owned by about four hundred farmers, making its aquisition virtually impossible. This doesn't help get the new runway built, which is exactly the farmers' intention. When the Japanese don't like what's going on they do something more positive than getting themselves killed under the wheels of trucks. The new Terminal 2 is open at last. It cost $1.5 billion, and has observation decks at both ends of level 4, but close-wire fences make photographs impossible. Airlines using the new terminal are mostly JAL, JAS and ANA, with occasional visits by the likes of KLM, Aeroflot, Garuda and Thai. The departures area inside the new terminal can become extremely congested. A twenty minute queue is not unusual, after which access to the departure areas allows the chance to take photos and a clear sight of other parts of the airport. A shuttle train operates to the satellite, which contains gates C81 to D99.

Until the new runway is opened, all movements to Terminal 2 are visible from the observation deck on Terminal 1. Departures can be airborne before they pass which can sometimes make photography a little tricky.

For the present, then, Terminal 1 is still the place to go, though frequent shuttle buses operate between the two arrivals levels. Below the main observation deck, there are windows with views of the aprons, so most of the action can be seen, and photographed, with ease.

Being the country's main international gateway, the range of aircraft visiting is restricted largely to major operators, with a surprisingly large amount of Northwest Airlines activity. Most of the activity takes place in the afternoons and, disappointingly, evenings, although the Chinese movements in daylight hours offer ever-increasing variety. The Japan Asia and JAL wide body fleets operate from Narita, and the occasional Qantas 767 visits in the evening. A collection of wide-bodies from other parts of the Far East ensures variety, and Continental 727s are regular movements.

At the far (southern) end of the field are the large maintenance facilities of All Nippon and JAL. Located in this area is an aeronautical museum, open between 10:00am and 5:00pm. Admission is Y500 and among the smaller aircraft are a Puma and a YS11. The perimeter fence is worth detailed exploration, as the authorities have realised that photographers really do want to poke their lenses through the fence. Rather than allow acts of vandalism to take place, these holes are now formed properly and provided by the airport management for the job.

Ground transportation between the airport and the city is, for most folk, a choice between the cheaper On Liner bus, which takes two hours, the so-called Airport Limousine to/from Hakozaki-cho Air Terminal or the Japan Railways Narita Express (N'EX) for Y2900. A Japan Railpass, giving seven days of unlimited travel for about £150, is good value for the tourist, and is valid on the Narita Express. Travel between Narita and Haneda is most straight-forward by taking the Limousine Bus.

JY JORDAN (Hashemite Kingdom of Jordan)
AMMAN
AMM   OJAI   Queen Alia International/QAIA   20m/32km S (bus 30 minutes)

An efficient airport for the traveller but not an overwhelming place for enthusiasts, the observation deck has been closed and only a mediocre view of the ramp is possible through the windows of the upper (landside) restaurant/bar in each terminal. There are runways on either side of the approach road and the two crescent-shaped terminals are for Alia, on one side, and foreign airlines on the other. Also between the runways are the cargo terminal and Alia's maintenance base, though both are difficult to see from inside the terminal. Good landing shots, with a 200mm length zoom lens, can be taken from the airport approach road but only with caution.

Since Royal Jordanian developed a hub-and-spoke operation, several arrivals in the middle of the morning from points in the Middle East are followed by departures for Europe/USA shortly afterwards, with virtually nothing until the whole procedure follows in reverse in the evening. Apart from Royal Jordanian A310s, Saudia A300s and a few Gulf Air/Egyptair 737s, there is little here to stimulate the interest of the average enthusiast.

AMMAN
ADJ   OJAM   Marka   3m/5km

The proximity of the old Marka airport to the city and the limited space were prime reasons to build QAIA. This is, however, a busy little airport with most of the activity being provided by Royal Jordanian Air Force C-130s and CASA 212s, all of which are resident. The government's aircraft are based here, and the Gulfstreams have been augmented by the arrival of the spectacular TriStar. Other aircraft to be found here include the Flight Academy Bulldogs and the Falcons' Pitts Specials, with the odd biz-jet and USAF Starlifter visiting. There are limited views from the perimeter but, once again, photography is not recommended.

LN NORWAY (Kingdom of Norway)
BERGEN
BGO   ENBR   Flesland   12m/19km S (bus 40 minutes)

A new circular terminal has been constructed, complete with air bridges, close to the old terminal building. The Scandinavian climate doesn't justify external observation decks but the military presence, with F-5s and F-16s, is such that watching aircraft at Bergen isn't actively encouraged, anyway.

The merger between Lufttransport and Helikopter Service has had little effect on the operation of Super Pumas from Bergen. Their hangar is visible from the old terminal, whilst that of Norving is tucked away, out of sight. Airline operations are slow but the ramp can contain a Wideroes Dash 7, a Norving Dornier and a Norskair Brasilia, all at the same time!

BODO
BOO   ENBO   1m/1.5km SW

The uninviting and implacable wall which confronts the landside visitor is not a spotter-deterrant. On the other side of the road are the comfortable suburbs of the quiet town, and the screening deflects much of the noise. Norway, like the rest of Scandinavia, is extremely environment-conscious. Traffic is modest but interesting. Domestic services are mostly operated by propellor-driven aircraft, with only occasional 737s and MD-87s of Braathens and SAS to be seen. The semi-circular passenger terminal is modern, and even features air jetties. The cold winter season is long, and passengers must be sheltered from the elements. Viewing is possible from the upper level gallery but most of what can be seen is the roof below! Photographers will need a long focus lens to capture one of the many Dash Sevens taxying. Once on its stand, it is almost hidden from view.

The lack of flat ground on Norway's coasts means that runways must be used to their maximum capability. This usually means sharing with a military base. Movements by helicopters and Twin Otters are rare but the Skv 331 F-16s make use of the runway for crew training and other exercises.

OSLO
FBU   ENFB   Fornebu   5m/8km SW (bus 20 minutes)

Only ten minutes' drive from the city centre along the E18, Drammensveien, the airport is on the left, on a peninsula between the city and the fjord. The approach road, Snaroyveien, passes the Park Royal Hotel, and the general aviation facility is reached by making a right turn here. The scheduled airlines terminal is straight on, at the far side of Runway 06/24. Next to the cafe is the entrance to the spectator's terrace (now closed). The view from the windows here is adequate and seats are provided so that, on the odd day when the weather isn't kind, it's still possible to watch the movements. The airlines using this terminal are European, and all operations, including those of SAS, are limited by the lengths of the two runways.

Modernisation has been a major project, and one of the few which has made life easier for the photographer. The new multi-storey car park brings aircraft using Runways 06 and 24 comfortably within range of a 200mm zoom lens. Because the city is so close, 06 is preferred for landings and 24 for departures. The background, being densely forested hills, makes the most ordinary aircraft, such as SAS DC-9s, at Fornebu look good.

As an alternative, the fence next to the fire station can be good but the view is sometimes blocked by the parked snow-moving equipment. The sun is at its best after 5:00pm but, in summer, good quality photos are possible until very late in the evening.

The general aviation terminal has its own ramp, where executive movements can be seen. To the right of this small terminal are the hangars of Braathens and Fred Olsen and, between them, the Oslo Aero Club overlooks most of the apron and Runway 01/19. For light aircraft, Fornebu is rewarding, even more so in summer when the floatplanes are parked at the water's edge, but anyone with an interest in airline operations will prefer the passenger terminal area. Movements worth bearing in mind are Braathens and Busy Bee, plus the occasional Scanair charter and Wideroes Dash 7, whose movements are not uncommon here.

OSLO
GEN   ENGM   Gardemoen   32m/50km NE

A long way out of the city, this airport has a runway long enough to take wide-body movements, so it is the capital city's transatlantic gateway. The other civilian movements are charter flights, dominated by Braathens and Scanair, though there are based Air Force C-130s and Falcons as some compensation. The Norsk Teknisk Museum is dedicated to military history, although outside is Caravelle LN-KLH (c/n 3), painted in SAS colours.

STAVANGER
SVG   ENZV   Sola   9m/15km SW (bus 30 minutes)

The new terminal, completed early in 1987, is even further from the runway than its predecessor, though it may contain similar facilities for seeing movements taxying. The old terminal had a cafe with very adequate windows for this purpose.

The far side of the runway is taken up by a military base of some significance, the F-5s being quite active, and can be seen on the runway. Also based here are Sea Kings and Lynxes but identifying any of these movements can be an extremely frustrating business.

The pursuit of an interest in aviation is not an ideal pastime in Scandinavia, as the terminal facilities are designed to beat their winter climate. Any visitor engaged in watching aircraft will probably be in the country on business and the airport will be an item of interest on the trip.

LV ARGENTINA (Argentine Republic)
BUENOS AIRES
AEP   SABE   Aeroparque Jorge Newbery   5m/8km NE

This is Argentina's busiest airport, with over four hundred movements a day, and can be compared to New York La Guardia or Rio's Santos Dumont for its waterfront location, beside the Rio del Plata or River Plate. The important difference is that the perimeter is separated from the water by the Lugones Highway, which means that the entire airport is visible from one point or another, and there are even recommended observation points.

Facilities here are, by European standards, rather out of date and primitive. Seen from another perspective, Aeroparque has character. The single runway, 13/31, is shared by the commercial airport, the military air base (Base Aerea Militar) and a museum.

Commercial operations are handled in a complex of three terminal buildings: Austral for domestic traffic, Aerolineas Argentinas which handles domestic and international flights and a separate facility for cargo operations. There are no special facilities as such for observation but there are two terraces, the better being above the Austral area, which allows a good view of the ramp and taxiway. Photographic opportunities are good, with quality shots being possible of most of the operations. What can't be seen close enough from the terminal will be better observed from the perimeter.

Access from the city centre by bus requires a short ride on either the No 33 or 56, from Retiro Railway station, some two miles to the south.

The roads surrounding the field are all close to the perimeter fance: Rafael Cantilo and Sarmiento Avenues are the links at each end, between la Pampa Street and Lugones Highway, and it is by making this circuit that almost everything to be found at Aeroparque can be seen. The northern end of the runway is close to the south side of Rafael Cantilo Avenue, and this is where the best ground level photos are to obtained. The majority of the movements are demonstrably domestic, and the only foreign presence of any regular kind is that of Pluna 737s operating frequent flights from Montevideo and Asuncion, in nearby Uruguay and Paraguay.

The museum is worth a visit, since it houses such interesting pieces as a Viking and a Bristol Freighter among twenty or so other exhibits. General aviation at Aeroparque is mostly biz-jets and larger twins. Smaller aircraft use the nearby DON TURCUATO field, where up to three hundred can be seen without any trouble.

BUENOS AIRES

EZE   SAEZ   Ministre Pistarini   32m/50km SW (bus 45 minutes)

A much larger airport, reserved almost solely for international traffic, is the main gateway, known locally as Ezeiza. All Aerolineas Argentinas wide-body operations are to be seen here, in the company of almost all other flights from abroad. Excluded are Aerolineas Argentinas 727s, which operate a significant amount of international flights, and are the largest aircraft to be seen at Aeroparque. The blue bus service No 86, marked Fournier, serves the airport, but only if they are also marked 'Aeropuerto'.

The Aerolineas Argentinas terminal nestles between the other two, so the panoramic view from it is limited. To the left is Terminal 2 for international flights, and to the right is Terminal 1, for domestic. It doesn't take much imagination which is the better one to try.

The gate guardian, seen from the approach road, is a C-47 in naval colours. The serial, reported as CTA-15, may be correct though one source says 5-T-15 is more likely. The military base is at the north end of the field, beyond the Aerolineas Argentinas maintenance apron. Armada Argentina's transport wing is, by definition, purely military, but there are other semi-official operators which carry passengers to supplement the income and to help develop the country's economy in the regions. Many of the services are therefore scheduled to operate on a regular basis. To reach vantage points on the perimeter, a car is essential as distances are too great for walking.

USHUAIA

USH   SAWH

For an aviation enthusiast, this one of the most remote destinations. Like many others in distant corners of the world, Tierra del Fuego is a remarkable place. The scenery is quite splendid but, with the stormy waters of Cape Horn close at hand, the weather can be unpleasant at times. With the Beagle Channel on the southern perimeter and mountainous scenery all around, photos at Ushuaia take on a magic all their own. Despite the naval air arm presence sharing the runway, it is a relaxed place and photos at the taxiway edge are easy to take. Aerolineas Argentinas 737s are the largest regular visitors and F.27s make one or two calls during the course of the avreage day.

LX LUXEMBOURG (Grand Duchy of Luxembourg)
LUXEMBOURG

LUX   ELLX   Findel   3m/5km ENE (bus 20 minutes)

A small country with a small, pleasant capital city, the arrival of much EC administration has had little effect on aviation. Diligent research by the fanatics wishing to complete national registers may lead to the impression that Findel and a small strip near Wiltz, in the north of the country, should contain a good proportion of the nation's aircraft. A visit to both proves otherwise.

Findel has a reasonably new terminal, with all the usual conveniences, including a roof observation deck. If this is not open, alternative views of the modest ramp can be had from the terrace at each side of the building. Indeed, for some photographers, the terraces may prove to be more suitable. Movements are decidedly slow, featuring the Luxair fleet, of course, occasional Icelandic 757s, and not much else.

Down the road is the old terminal building, together with a couple of other facilities worthy of close attention. The Cargolux complex allows close inspection of the aircraft on the ramp, and photos in the afternoon can be of a very high quality indeed. Whilst what can be seen at Cargolux is often very unusual, it is also possible that nothing at all will be present. It is worth asking permission for ramp access at Cargolux for a good photograph, if something is parked on their ramp. The staff can be helpful. Beyond this is the aero club hangar, situated on top of quite a steep bank, making it difficult to see any of the inmates. For anyone on foot, the long walk to this general aviation facility his hardly worth the effort, as any aircraft which may be parked outside can be seen just as easily from the bus, which passes on its way between the city and the airport terminal. Without permission to have a look around, departure from Findel can be accompanied by some disappointment for lovers of smaller aircraft.

LZ BULGARIA (Republic of Bulgaria)
BOURGAS

BOJ   LBBG   International   8m/13km NE (bus 20 minutes)

The passenger terminal is small, outdated and frequently overcrowded. It does, however, handle a good selection of mid-European carriers. As befits an old terminal, it has an observation deck on the roof and there can be much to see.

Naturally, the majority of movements are Balkan: An-12/24s and Il-18s supply prop power. A rather predictable procession of Tu-134/154s makes up the majority with some Yak-40s for variety. The political changes which have swept through Central Europe have not adversely affected old relationships, so visiting airlines will be dominated by Aeroflot, Malev and CSA for some time yet. Aeroflot visitors are mainly Tu-154s but An-12s are seen, and there can be as many as three Il-76s visiting per day. The local nature of Hemus Air operations means that their Yak-40s and Turbolets are rarely seen outside the country, though they are regular visitors to Bourgas. With beaches so close to the airport, it is possible to keep an eye on the traffic during the course of a holiday. Regular patrols are operated along the beach by various types of aircraft: the An-2s, Mi-8s and Ka-26s which are most frequently seen are based at the airport, on the far side of the field from the passenger terminal.

SOFIA
SOF   LBSF   International   6m/9km E (bus 20 minutes)

Organised package tours are probably the only way to visit Bulgaria, though they are very rare to Sofia. Enthusiasts tours are occasionally operated, and these undoubtedly allow much of the difficult paperwork to be sorted out by others, preferably beforehand. Hotels should be pre-booked but not pre-paid, as there can be severe complications if the money has not been received.

The No.84 bus leaves from the University, close to the city centre. The 0.30 lev fare is so cheap, it can barely be converted into most currencies. One of the sights en route is that of Il-18 LZ-BEV which is supposedly preserved in a residential area. Its state was so poor, by the end of 1991 that it may not exist for much longer.

The airport passenger terminal has an observation deck on the top floor but this is, almost certainly, permanently closed. Other parts of the terminal offer only one alternative: the restaurant on the upper level of departures,which is inaccessible, except to passengers. To the left of the terminal, a wire fence separates the viewer from the VIP transport stands where interesting aircraft are normally parked. Inside the building, to the right, is a view of the main apron, at the side of the luggage deposit.

To the right of the terminal, a security gate at the end of the wall gives access to the facilities and, from this gate aircraft parked in front of the hangars can be seen. The derelict remains of Il-18 LZ-BET are also visible, parked on the grass next to the taxiway. On the opposite side of the runway, effectively out of sight, are government aircraft. These include anything from An-2s and Mi-8s to Yak-40s and Tu-134s. The most interesting visitors, to western eyes, are almost certainly the Central European carriers and military movements. What is seriously lacking is a vantage point from which to see them. Don't expect help from the local people. The recent political changes mean that their attitude has changed, and friendly encounters are uncommon.

One recommended hotel is the Novotel, which is located 5 miles from the airport, and in line with many departures (with the right wind). An upper floor room facing the airport allows underwing registrations to be read off, as the aircraft bank away from their take-off heading.

VARNA
VAR   LBWN   International   5m/8km NW

Varna's place in the sun seemed assured, in more ways than one, ten years ago. With Black Sea resorts in summer and ski slopes in winter, Bulgaria made inroads into the tourist market but western tastes, it would seem, demanded something a little more sophisticated. The regular charter flights from all parts of Europe have shrunk back, and Varna now caters mostly for eastern Europeans.

The airport's passenger terminal is adequate for the purpose, and a small terrace overlooks the apron. Most of the movements in summer are charters, several of them by German airlines, plus a few scheduled services to nearby countries. The Bulgarian Navy has a small presence, mainly Mi-8s, but activity is rare.

N UNITED STATES of AMERICA

This country occupies a significant amount of the book. To enable airports to be found with some ease, the entries have been placed according to their states, starting with Alaska and ending with Wyoming. The standard two-letter codes are used, so AK for Alaska means that it appears in front of AL for Alabama. Puerto Rico, whose aircraft use N registrations, appears at the end of the USA section. The index offers details of states, enabling entries for airports to be found with ease.

ANCHORAGE AK

ANC   PANC   International   7m/11km SW

Alaska is a vast state which would rate as a large country if it were independent. Small communities are separated by bleak, though beautiful, scenery and roadbuilding is a difficult process under such climatic conditions. Since there are so many lakes throughout the state which can be used by floatplanes, roads are not essential for survival. They are needed for growth, of course.

Alaska is also one of the most misunderstood locations on earth as it is considered to be cold and remote. Anchorage is very close to the Pacific Ocean, so it does not suffer the climatic extremes associated with, say Stockholm or Leningrad (both at similar latitude). It is no further north, in British terms, than the Shetland Isles but it does enjoy the benefits of a warm ocean current. In summer, the days are long and the temperatures very pleasant. The seeming remoteness arises mostly from the way we say a map of the world, with Alaska in the top left hand corner. As can be seen on a globe, rather than a map, Anchorage is actually about the same distance from Western Europe as Houston.

The enormous area which can loosely be termed Anchorage International Airport includes a number of features which would each offer very attractive prospects in their own right. The importance of the airport as an intercontinental staging post dwindled rapidly with the advent of 747-400s. The ability to fly non stop between Europe or America's East Coast and Eastern Asia has taken a fair slice out of Anchorage's economy. This is a shame. International movements still include a large quantity of cargo flights, and it will be some time before all these can operate non stop. The 747Fs of FedEx, Northwest and the Asian carriers grace the aprons as usual but the lunchtime rush, when up to two dozen Jumbos used to pass through, is over. What is left is still rewarding, especially since the movements are local, and therefore likely to be seen in normal circumstances nowhere else in the world.

There are two main terminals at the the heart of the airport, for domestic and international traffic. Access is possible to the domestic building, though photography even through glass is often difficult. Some of the best vantage points are from lounge areas with glass on both sides, making bright reflections a major problem. Markair and Alaska Airlines, in that order, dominate the traffic, though Reeve Aleutian and ERA/Jet Alaska add variety.

Visible from the domestic terminal are, to the east, the various cargo aprons, each of which features some very interesting aircraft. On the opposite side of the field is the South Air Park, again with its own specialities. To the north, not visible from the centre of activity, are remote ramps used for parking some of the more exotic visitors. To the northeast, and almost to be considered as a separate airport, is the lakeside annex known as Lake Hood. A taxiway just north of the international ramp links this to the main field.

Between the two main terminals is an employees' car park which overlooks a large apron. Through the fence, photographs of the cargo 747s are taken, with completely uncluttered backgrounds. Taxying jumbos also pass within range to and from the international terminal. Many pleasant lunchtimes can be spent here, often in the warm sunshine.

Without a car, the mile-long journey to the furthest apron needs time, especially with all the intermediate stops. A letter prior to a visit is normally met by appropriate enthusiasm. Reeve Aleutian's pioneering spirit is demonstrated by their downtown museum. Northern Air Cargo operate DC-6s, with the company's approach to business bringing back memories of how aviation used to be. An Argosy here, an Electra there: the aprons offer a string of interesting airliners. The various operators are Alaska Airlines, Reeve Aleutian, the FAA, Markair Cargo, Van Dusen FBO and Northern Air Cargo. Sadly, some of the museum-piece Packets associated with this area have been shipped away to more lucrative locations.

Good quality food is to be found opposite the Delta/JAL etc cargo shed, at the Fly In Restaurant, similar in style to Denny's.

The drive round to South Air Park passes a C-123 on a pole, in front of Kulis ANG base. The C-130s on the ramp can be seen from the fence. The southern apron has operations at each side, many of the more interesting movements requiring an early start, if they are to be seen. On the eastern side of the ramp are the Era Aviation terminal, Alaska Helicopters and Air Logistics. The Era car park offers close views of the Convair and Twin Otter movements, though the helicopter fleets are generally based upstate, earning their keep. The most interesting operator on the other side of the ramp was Troy Air, with its small fleet. A casualty in 1989, Troy Air may have now disappeared without trace, but another casualty, the fire-blackened hulk of a 727 fuselage, was dumped here after an accident.

Anchorage can be a hard, and unforgiving, place on winter nights. The Airport Authority has kept a gruesome photographic record of some of the worst accidents, though the average passenger would probably prefer not to know some of the details. As a last resting place one famous airliner, the TWA Starliner, merely slipped out of active service and into a ground training role. Its condition in 1988 was very poor, worse than its neighbour, an ex-Reeve DC-6, and their continued existence is in doubt. They are only visible from the perimeter road, and access will be by arrangement with the Airport Authority. From the main terminal area, travelling north, the road crosses the taxiway to Lake Hood on its way past the main Post Office. A C-119 and a couple of C-82 hulks occupy this corner, though the road offers views of other items of aviation history. The Cargomasters which are resident include one in airworthy condition. Its arrival on a runway is memorable!

The aprons further north have been developed and include a facility for UPS and Fed Ex, across the road from the Post Office. Beyond the new cargo ramp is an apron worth inspection, as it normally contains a couple of C-119s and a C-97. Postmark Drive, the public road which passes the aprons, ends at a T-junction. Two left turns in quick succession lead to a hill, ideal for taking photos of aircraft taxying to the hold for Runway 14.

The road continues round the end of the runway and offers more elevated views on the other side. This is West Access Road, which leads to a right turn more or less opposite the end of Runway 6L. Look out for turnings, any of which could result in standing on banks, overlooking Runway 6R. In other words, if you want photos of aircraft on the runway, Anchorage offers plenty of alternatives.

Lake Hood, without a car, will occupy at least one full day. It is a mile long and almost half a mile wide at one point. With all the various jetties and docking areas, it has a very long coastline indeed. Lovers of phalaropes and piston-engined aircraft on floats could wish for no better lake. DHC Otters and Beavers abound, plus large numbers of Cessnas. Paint schemes tend to be as colourful as possible to attract custom and to aid visible location, if necessary. Salmon fishing from mid July is very big business, and movements are frequent. Without suggesting that aircraft are ever overloaded, some of them do labour to get off the lake!

Operators which come close to airline status at Lake Hood are Penair, with a servicing base in the southwest corner, and South Central Air, whose tiny freight shed is south of the taxiway link. Occasionally, the Islander can be seen scurrying across, and its irregular visits here represent the few opportunities to take its portrait.

On the southern edge of Lake Hood is the aviation museum, which pays homage to the part played by aircraft in developing Alaska. Opening times may not be regular, but a visit is recommended. Also close to the lake are the International Airport and Clarion Hotels, neither of which can be classed as inexpensive.

Accommodation is not to be treated lightly in these parts. Make reservations early and be prepared to say you're only staying one night. The cost could use up a week's allowance anywhere else. For $45, try the Midtown Lodge but don't expect en suite facilities. Access to an indoor toilet can be considered a luxury in Alaska.

ANCHORAGE AK

MRI	PAMR	Merrill Field	1/1.5km E

As befits a city on the edge of a vast and empty country, Anchorage has good air communications for light aircraft. The only significant operator at this field is Wilbur's, whose terminal supports the airline's activities at the main airport. Access by car, or foot, to the various ramps is easy. It should be noted that the Markair Express fleet undergoes servicing here, so a Twin Otter or Cessna Caravan may be seen. The small terminal next door to this maintenance hangar belongs to the optimistically-named Airlift Alaska whose Cessna Stationairs may perhaps prove too small for a real airlift. The An-2s are normally the largest residents. Nearby is the Red Ram Motel, cheap at $49 for a room.

ANCHORAGE AK

EDF	PAED	Elmendorf Air Force Base	8m/13km E

Elmendorf is a main diversion field for Anchorage, when bad weather strikes. Anyone visiting Anchorage will be anxious to record as much of the aviation scene as possible, as frequent visits are few. Guided base tours are operated, normally from the Post Road gate. Post Road, from the city centre, passes through the evocative yards of the Alaska Railroad, beside the river. In July, many evenings are spent by local folk watching vast numbers of enormous salmon leaping on their way to their spawning grounds. Inside the base, the two flights of F-15s occupy separate ramps and hangars. A tour normally includes the C-130s and helicopters on the far side, but access to the interesting visitors ramp may not be possible.

FAIRBANKS AK

FAI	PAFA	International	5m/8km SW

It's a long drive north from Anchorage, and one which may be out of the question to many, even with a hire car, as mileage is normally charged separately in Alaska, as in Canada. The airport has passenger and cargo terminals, plus several hangars and ramps on one side of the main runway, 1L/19R, and the general aviation facility with its own runway, 1R/19L, on the other. Between them is a lake, accessible from the general aviation side, which is used by a considerable quantity of single-engined aircraft. Most of what can be seen on the move at Fairbanks can also be seen at Anchorage except on those rare occasions when Anchorage is closed. Fairbanks is the main diversion field, and the ramps can look extremely impressive, when occupied by a large quantity of wide-bodies. In summer, Fairbanks gets better summer weather than Anchorage but the sun sets quite early, 9:00pm or so, due to the hills.

The facilities lined up west of the main runway are just across the road from the Golden North Motel. Expect to pay about $65 for a night but the standard of accommodation is worth the extra money, compared with what $38 buys. A service road leads to the Everts Air Fuel ramp at the north end, though their hangar is further down the road, beyond Brooks Air Fuel. Active aircraft include a number of DC-4s/6s and C-46s, though often only a small part of the fleet. Stored aircraft, by the UPS facility at the southern end, include some intersting hulks. These included, in July 1994, three C-46s and three C-118s.

Markair and Northern Air Cargo have their own facilities, next to the terminal building, though nothing may be visible outside during the average day. Follow the road round the end of Runway 1L for access to the general aviation and, from it, the floatplane base. The main runway is visible from here but too distant for photography. For more light aircraft, it's worth investigating Metro Field (MTX) on the south side of town.

FAIRBANKS AK

FBK	PAFB	Fort Wainright	1.5m/2km SE

For some reason the entrance to this field is at the eastern end, that most remote from town. On weekends this military base can be "open post", without entry restrictions. Before attempting to inspect the resident aircraft, permission should be sought. The rampside dispatcher's building seems to be as good a place as any.

The Bureau of Land Management has a base here, with a few CASA 212 smoke jumpers and a civil OV-10 Bronco observation aircraft. The air tanker base amounts to nothing more than some wooden huts, behind which are stored spare engines. What air tankers are to be seen is obviously variable, though three or four could be a realistic expectation in summer. On the opposite side of the runway are the Army helicopters.

KENAI AK

ENA	PAEN	Municipal	1m/1.5km N

When driving from Anchorage, especially on a summer weekend, patience can be needed. The road is used by many RVs, and overtaking isn't easy. The first part of the journey, through the Chugach National Forest, offers views of the Kenai Mountains across the Turnagain Arm, and a stop at Portage Glacier is worth the sort detour. After that, it's great, if you like trees. The Kenai (pronounced keen-eye) Peninsula projects southwest from Anchorage, with Cook Inlet on its north side. The area is scenic with a capital S: tall fir trees forest the hills, mountains form much of the backdrop and, on clear days, Mt McKinley is visible, almost 200 miles away. It's a bit like being able to see Heathrow from Manchester, in terms of distance!

Salmon fishing is big business in these parts. The season starts in early July. DC-6s ferry huge quantities out of the airport and the floatplanes bring the fishermen. By the end of June, salmon fishing is not what everyone calls sport. Up river at this time of the year there are often more fish than water - they're probably glad to get out. They're all going to die after they've spawned anyway. More advice, about Alaska's national bird: mosquitoes round here grow to something about the size of a king salmon. To kill them, take a baseball bat.

The airport has one runway, 1/19, at the south end of which is a cemetary. The residents are not likely to complain about aircraft noise. They are also unlikely to take exception to anyone standing around, camera in hand, awaiting the next aircraft moving up the taxiway. As they say in these parts, folks is less hassle when they're dead.

Markair and ERA operate hourly from Anchorage but scheduled air traffic is the least of the airport's attractions. On one side of the runway is the centrally placed main terminal and ramps for South Central, at the southern end, and the fish hauliers at the north. On the western side, accessible by a road junction immediately after passing the end of Runway 1, is the floatplane canal, with the take-off area at the north end. The canal is, in effect, a long stretch of water for the aircraft to park.

Accommodation is not cheap in Anchorage. Kenai is no different. The airport's information board suggested The Place might be a good bet. At $60 for a night, this was relatively inexpensive. A room in Soldotna starts at around $85.

PALMER AK
PAQ   PAAQ   Municipal   1/1.5km SE

On the edge of town, some forty miles from Anchorage on Glenn Highway, is this small airport. Apart from one or two light aircraft in the circuit, not much happens. This is because almost any stretch of water is bounded by houses, many of them quite grand. At the bottom of the garden is the Cessna 185, as normal as the Ford Escort in Europe. Among the fifty or so residents are the Woods Air Service fleet, which includes C-47s and C-118s. From the Glenn Highway, turn left just before reaching the runway. Across the railroad track is Woods' hangar, almost big enough to hold one of their C-118s. Lots of zig-zagging leads to the rest of the field, with little in the way of reward.

SKAGWAY AK
SGY   Municipal   1m/1.5km S

Assuming there is no history of insanity in your family, you have to be a serious aviation enthusiast to visit Skagway. There is little to justify the trip. At one end of the runway is the fjord called Lynn Canal, with mountains on the opposite shore. All very scenic and all very historical. Unless you are particularly interested in Cherokee Sixes and the occasional Islander, there is nothing of any significance. The White Pass and Yukon Railroad might be more exciting, as it links historic downtown Skagway with Bennett, the gold rush ghost town. Great stuff, but not really in aviation terms.

SOLDOTNA AK
SXQ   1m/1.5km SE

From Anchorage, follow Highway 1 for Kenai, and Soldotna is just a little way down the road past Kenai. The airfield, on the far side of town is posted. Apart from fifty or so light aircraft, there is nothing to justify the effort, though it can be used as an air tanker base.

WASILLA AK
WWA

From Anchorage, Glenn Highway parts company with the road to Wasilla, George Parks Highway, before reaching Palmer. There are only fifty or so light aircraft to be seen but possibly worth the trip is the Museum of Alaska Transportation and Industry, moved from nearby Palmer. Anyone who relishes rooting around relics will be rewarded by by an Alaska ANG C-47, 0-315200, C-123 N98 in FAA colours and H-21 Workhorse 34362, plus several other pieces of interest.

BIRMINGHAM AL
BHM   KBHM   Municipal   5m/8km NE

Birmingham's passenger terminal is an excellent place to witness what happens on the runways. Driving around the perimeter is even better. On the far side of the runway are the Alabama Air National Guard, using the main runway like the other traffic, only the jets deploy chutes for increased braking. To one side of the base are the hangars and fixed base operators where a good assortment of biz-jets is to be found, and on the other helicopters in some variety.

The cargo ramp is closer to the terminal, where the usual Federal Express, UPS and Airborne Express aircarft can be seen. Beyond them, on the far side of the cross runways, is the general aviation apron where the light aircraft are housed. Among them are a few larger twins and biz-jets. PEMCO have their own separate ramp where work is carried out on C-135s amongst other types.

DOTHAN AL
DHN   KDHN   6m/9km NW

Birmingham-based PEMCO Engineers is one of America's largest companies to be involved with converting passenger airliners into cargo configuration. The facility at Dothan usually has several 727s waiting their turn, many of the most recent examples wear United colours.

MOBILE AL
MOB   KMOB   Pascagoula Regional   14m/22km W

Known locally as Bates Field, this airport is rather slow going but, in the afternoons, it offers the best opportunities for photographers. The low fence next to the old terminal allows standard lens shots of anything that passes on the taxiway. A small number of redundant airliners have found their way here in recent years but the current state of affairs is unknown. Mobile Aerospace is also a facility on the field, where airliners can often be seen either awaiting their turn for work or being made ready for delivery.

The US Coastguard have a major base, used for aviation training. The variety of aircraft, including Guardians and helicopters, makes it worthwhile seeking permission for a visit.

FAYETTEVILLE AR

FYV   KFYV   Drake Field/Municipal   5m/8km S

A pleasant little airport, with a surprising quantity of regional activity, including no less than five airlines. In the afternoon, a standard lens is required to take photos of the movements, the fence being only about four feet high. Ramp access isn't really necessary but, if morning photos are required because of tour itineraries, the staff are friendly and happy enough to accompany you out onto the apron. The autumnal colours of the leaves make this a very colourful location, as the tree-covered hills form a perfect backdrop.

An interest in biz-jets makes this an attractive airport. The Tyson Foods fleet is based and there are also many visitors during the week, due to the retail giant Wal-Mart being located in nearby Bentonville.

Admission to the small aviation museum costs a couple of dollars, though it covers mostly older general aviation. There is a display about Skyways Airlines, which was based in Fayetteville.

FORT SMITH AR

FSM   KFSM   Municipal   4m/6km SE

If you like Jetstreams, you'll love Fort Smith. Being only a modest regional airport, traffic is slow during the day but TW Express, Northwest Airlink and American Eagle all call. Photos of aircraft on the apron can be taken, over the fence, presenting no problems. The Arkansas ANG F-16s need the full extent of a 80-200mm lens, when being taken on the move. The base is guarded by a photogenic F-4D and access will be needed to log or take photos of the ramp.

LITTLE ROCK AR

LIT   KLIT   Adams Field   4m/6km SE

The main concourse of the passenger terminal is fine for spotters but the windows have tinted glass. Photographers will quickly discover that the perimeter offers little as an alternative. Airline traffic is mostly Air Midwest (USAir Express) Beech 1900s but one or two USAir F.28s and Conquest Metros do visit. British Aerospace have a facility here, which always worth a look, and handles its fair share of visiting biz-jets.

CHANDLER AZ

Memorial   10m/16km SW

Heading south from Phoenix, on Interstate 10, bound for Marana and Tucson, it is worth watching the eastern horizon for the shimmering shapes of the aircraft parked at Chandler. The next exit leads to the airfield, over some atrocious dirt roads, but the diversion will be worthwhile for any lover of piston power. Fences are unnecessary and free access is available to all the inmates, which include the Biegert Aviation DC-4s and T & G's selection of DC-7s, two of which once served with BOAC, as well as Privateers, Lodestars and C-119 Packets. Activity is usually restricted to a few men doing maintenance work, so a wander around the apron should result in a memorable collection of photos, and all in the Arizona sunshine.

Since the community of Chandler is due south of Mesa, Country Club Road may be used as an alternate means of getting to the airfield. Beware signposts for the aerodrome, as these refer to the general aviation field Stellar Air Park, not a location for lovers of piston power.

CHANDLER AZ

P19   Stellar Air Park   4m/6km SE

Stellar Air Park will no doubt have many fans, as general aviation fields are good for quantity. In this case, the quality is elsewhere. The road due south from Mesa is one to be avoided by some, and taken in anticipation of good logging by others.

FLAGSTAFF AZ

FLG   Pulliam   4m/6km SE

Anyone travelling by car to the Grand Canyon and other scenic places in the west may pass through Flagstaff and consider it to be a major town in the region. Its fame stems mostly from being on Route 66 (now effectively replaced by I-40) but its importance is not reflected in the size of its airport, nor the amount of traffic handled. In fact, the air links are quite local, with the majority of the flights being to Phoenix. These scheduled services are operated by Sky West Metros and the airfield has precious little other traffic. A small terminal is surrounded by plenty of vantage points, so that anyone in need of a photograph of the occasional visitor will be accommodated. It is unlikely that a diversion here will result in any great surprises, or reward of any kind.

GOODYEAR AZ

GYR   Municipal   25m/40km W of Phoenix

Known to most enthusiasts as Litchfield Park, Goodyear is worth a visit for anyone passing on the way to/from Luke Air Force Base. The field is used for major crew training programmes, due to its good weather all year round. One of the airlines to make the use of the field for this purpose has been Lufthansa, who used Debonairs and Barons. The Caravelle is now at the Pima County Air Museum. To see if anything is still stored at Litchfield, a bit of walking is necessary. The last report mentioned only a couple of VASP 737s but that was some time ago.

GRAND CANYON AZ

GCN   National Park   7m/11km S

Located on the South Rim of the canyon, the village is predictably picturesque and served by two aviation centres. The airport handles twin engined aircraft (some of them jets) operating scheduled services, mainly from Las Vegas, and a separate helipad is used for scenic flights over the canyon.

The airport is south of the village and a pleasant terminal building is usually bustling with day trippers intent on sampling the awsome view of this natural spectacle. The ramp at either side of the terminal often contains some interesting aircraft but numbers are low. A request to stroll onto the apron for a photograph or two is normally successful, though few would consider the airport as being anything other than a very distant second placed feature of the trip. On the way through the village to the South Rim, the helipad is on the right-hand side, close to the road.

On the North Rim, another helicopter pad handles the occasional visitor, as the distance between the two communities by surface transport is enormous. It should be remembered that the South Rim is 8,000 ft above sea level (and the North Rim even higher) so it can be inaccessible due to snow for a prolonged winter period. Anyone intent on visiting the Canyon in April or November should check conditions before departure. In November, 90 degrees in Las Vegas or Phoenix can be matched by freezing temperatures at the Grand Canyon, despite the short distance between them.

Right next to the road leading to the rim of the canyon, in the middle of South Rim's spreadeagled village, the heliport is used for regular sightseeing trips over the canyon. Normally there are three of four helicopters, JetRangers and Ecureuils, to be seen. At high season, the amount of movements is surprisingly high. Business is sufficiently informal to allow a stroll onto the ramp. A request is not only polite, but it acknowledges that the company's insurance policy may be liable in the event of some mishap.

KINGMAN AZ

IGM	Municipal	9m/15km NE

The airport still provides the town with a link to the outside world but its fame stems from its almost nil humidity and, as a result, its suitability for storing redundant airliners. The days when considerable numbers of 707s and DC-8s could be seen are over, Marana and Las Vegas being used these days, but the remains of the odd airframe are still present. The last reported visit yielded 707 N7515A plus a DC-4 and a C-123 Provider.

MARANA AZ

MZJ	Pinal Air Park	22m/34km NW of Tuscon

Visible from I-10 between Tucson and Phoenix are the shimmering airliners stored in quantity at this remote airfield. There are two distinct storage areas: the apron, with many 'active' Evergreen aircraft among the hulks, and the central runway compound, where a large number of bigger airliners are parked. The range of colour schemes to be seen here is vast, more than could be expected at the average active airport. Movement isn't a feature of Marana, apart from the A-10s from Davis-Monthan crew training, but a proper tour of the stored aircraft needs prior arrangement with Evergreen International.

Caution must be shown when compiling a book such as this, especially when suggesting that aviation enthusiasts can always expect a warm welcome at some airfields. The staff at Evergreen Air Center have jobs to do. Some days they might be very busy, which could mean having to turn even the most polite requests down. Anyone wishing to visit the Air Park is strongly advised to write beforehand (enclosing an international reply coupon) to the Marketing Department, Evergreen Air Center Inc, Pinal Air Park, Marana, Arizona 85653-9501.

There is no doubt that many requests have been successful but, over the space of two years, the situation can change. It has been suggested that the comments in the last edition showed inadequate research. This is not so. What is printed in this book can cause unwelcome attention, to the point that staff find themselves spending too much time doing jobs they are not paid to do. For anyone who cannot understand the situation, it is suggested they read the entry for Hong Kong, where enthusiasts at the Aero Club have become so numerous that visitors cannot be made as welcome as might be wished.

Even if nothing more than a walk along the apron's edge results from a visit, this will yield a remarkable variety of interesting (to put it mildly) aircraft, though this will be overshadowed by the disappointment of not getting close to the main storage area.

MESA AZ

MSC	Falcon Field	12m/19km NE

East of Phoenix, this is the home of the Champlin Fighter Museum. For anyone in search of old aircraft, particularly well restored, there are Fokkers and Sopwiths, Wildcats and a MiG-17. The number of Confederate Air Force residents adds to the specialist interest. A few biz-jets and C-54s can be seen but S-1 Trackers are most numerous, awaiting conversion into water/borate bombers. The Hughes H-64 Apache assembly plant offers very little parked outside, to indicate what goes on inside the buildings.

PAGE AZ

PGA	Municipal	1m/1.5km E

The rapidly developing recreation area of Glen Canyon and Lake Powell is centred on the town of Page, which is still in its infancy. Civilisation has arrived, though Page Airport shares little of the growth, so far. This is probably because so many people arrive in campers and other recreational vehicles, usually towing boats. Aviation serves only a small proportion of the needs, and Lake Powell Air Service have a Twin Otter and some Cessna 207s, used most of the time for scenic overflying. Close by is Monument Valley, and the Twin Otter can often be seen next to the strip at Kayenta, waiting to take a party over some other very impressive scenery. Scheduled services, operated by Skywest Metros, are rarely seen in the daylight but they link the town with Phoenix, Flagstaff and St George.

PHOENIX AZ

PHX	KPHX	Sky Harbor International	4m/6km SE

America West's hub operation has ensured that Sky Harbor has become a busy airport, with two runways in use all day. The growth of traffic mirrors that of Phoenix/Scottsdale and the climate is the main reason. Apart from high summer, this part of Arizona has lovely weather and a trip in late autumn or early spring is very enjoyable.

The airport's passenger terminals are located between the two parallel runways and the best view of the proceedings is from the top of the multi-storey car park, though this can present some problems. Many of the airline movements will be seen to the south or southwest, so the sun does cause trouble to the serious photographer.

Despite Scottsdale being a leisure-oriented community, with its own general aviation field, Sky Harbor does have a very significant general aviation presence, mostly in the centre of the field. These aircraft include many executive types, and biz-jets are quite numerous. The access road from 24th Street passes the hangars and aprons, and it is possible to see most of the based aircraft on their ramps. This approach to the airport gives a better guide to the general layout than the 40th Street access, at the eastern end, with the cargo and commuter areas being visible on the way to the car parks. Expansion at Phoenix has revolved round the based airline, America West, who opened a new terminal and a maintenance hangar, both found to the east of the central complex. Like Air Florida, America West grew with tremendous speed, and their resources were stretched. Operating under Chapter 11 protection from their creditors, They have been poised for some time on the brink of failure. Like Continental, however, they still weather the storm.

Access to the Arizona ANG is from 24th Street, just north of the I-10 intersection, after passing the threshold of Runway 8R. This road used to be one of the finest spots in the USA for the aviation photographer, but this corner has been developed, with a consequent reduction in appeal.

Apart from getting access to the F-104 on a pole, there is now little point in going to the ANG base, as the KC-135s are all identifiable from the main terminal area. With its variety of domestic traffic, and the occasional foreign movement like a Moroccan Air Force C-130, Phoenix rates extremely highly and the added local attractions of Litchfield Park, Mesa, Scottsdale, Chandler Memorial and the Air Force bases of Luke and Williams, plus Tucson not far away, make this part of Arizona very attractive to the enthusiast.

SCOTTSDALE AZ

SCF	Municipal	9m/15km N

There is enough money in Scottsdale for its residents and business interests to consider themselves as a serious community in their own right, rather than as a suburb of Phoenix. The airport is small, though it bristles with large numbers of small aircraft plus a good selection of executive aircraft. There are many hangars and aprons to be explored.

The passenger terminal reflects a community on its way up in the world: it is rather elegant. However, the enthusiast is more likely to drive around the accessible part of the perimeter and make notes of the more interesting inmates, before passing on elsewhere.

SEDONA AZ

SDX		2m/3km SW

Travelling between Phoenix and the Grand Canyon means passing through the scenic Oak Creek Canyon. At the top (north) is Flagstaff and at the bottom (south) is Sedona. The airport is a modest affair, to be kind, but it may be worth a detour for anyone interested in saturation coverage of Arizona's aviation scene.

TUCSON AZ

TUS   KTUS   International   10m/16km S

Tucson is synonymous, in the aviation world, with Davis-Monthan Air Force Base. It is nevertheless a destination for civil enthusiasts as the airport has much appeal in its own right. Even here, the military presence extends its arms, with the north side of the field being occupied by the Arizona ANG, with an accent on training. The passenger terminal offers only limited viewing facilities but the movements are merely a diluted version of what can be seen better at Phoenix. Since few enthusiasts visit Tucson for the chance to stand around in the terminal and log scheduled airliners, it might be appropriate to concentrate on what can be seen elsewhere.

The perimeter holds many delights which can't be sampled anywhere else. To enjoy them, a car is essential. Valencia Road, on the north side, has a few places off it where the ANG A-7 serials can be identified, and a little further west of the base is what was once one of the largest Viscount collections in the world. Go Air, later Jade Point, owned this fleet, many of which provided spares for the others. Even if there is no longer any activity, it could take some time for all the hulks to disappear.

Continuing west along Valencia to South Park Avenue, a left turn here offers more delights for the lover of older airliners. Hamilton's work on Convairs is slow, and many aircraft are parked, still bearing the colours of their last operator, awaiting conversion to turbine power and other rumoured modifications. This area bristles with interesting aircraft, a C-133 Cargomaster, several UH-1s and C-54s which have escaped from D-M, and a selection of types which have included in the past (and may still) an ex-Thai Air Force C-123 and a Boeing Stratocruiser whose rear end was removed, reportedly by mistake, plus many more. Star resident is the immaculate L-1049 (C-121) N494TW.

AMARC, the Aerospace Maintenance and Regeneration Center, at Davis-Monthan Air Force Base casts a long shadow across Tucson and the southeast sector of the city is almost totally occupied by the vast storage compound. Tours at the height of summer are best avoided, as the heat is excessive and, even in October, the heat is wearing by lunchtime. Tours of Davis-Monthan are now restricted to Wednesdays only, and booking ahead requires three months notice to avoid disappointment. Do note that no tour covers the entire vast aircraft disposal area, so further investigation may be required from the fence.

The main entrance to the base is at the southern end of Craycroft Road, and anyone assembling for a tour will probably come here from downtown Tucson, having seen nothing of the enormity of the place beforehand. A better idea can be gained when travelling to the Pima County Air Museum on the south side, down the Tucson-Benson Highway (I-10) as most of the compound can be seen, on the left, before the Wilmot Road exit is reached. A left turn, on Wilmot Road, leads to the southern edge of the field, to the museum, and to a collection of scrapyards. Lovers of airframes for their own sake have hours of pleasure, hunting through vast numbers of derelict helicopters etc.

The museum houses a superb collection of aircraft, though some may still carry their spraylat protection on windows, spoiling authentic photos. Last admission is at 4:00pm, but an earlier arrival would be wise.

The perimeter of D-M provides hours of investigation, and obtaining a record of the serials will provide much hard, but extremely enjoyable, work. The eastern perimeter is easier to check, though many of the B-52s have had their tails removed, which makes life difficult.

TUCSON AZ

| E14 | Avra Valley | 20m/32km NW of Tucson |

A close neighbour to Marana, this field is nevertheless classified officially as Tucson. Off Interstate 10, drive through Marana village, then follow your nose through the maize and cotton fields. Eventually the airfield is signposted. The reason for making a detour on the way to/from Pinal Air Park is Mr Vern Raeburn's famed CV-240 and ex-MATS Connies. Permission should be sought to take photos but there should be no problem.

A dirt road, marked "Parachute Club" leads to their Beech 18 and a variety of stored piston types which, at the last report, included a P-2, a Mexican DC-3, a couple of C-54s, ex-Nantucket Marine Timber Company C-118 and three CV-440s. Well worth the detour, but do watch out for the security guards which take action instead of asking questions. Rattlesnakes are not the sort of security guards that bother with niceties.

YUMA AZ

| YUM KYUM | International | 5m/8km S |

Strategically located as a stopping place on the long drive between Tucson and San Diego, there's a good selection of motels for an overnight stay. Most of these are located on the Motel Loop Road. The airport has customs facilities for the occasional movement from Mexico, which justifies the 'international' status, as the only scheduled services are occasional Metros. The terminal has a car park next to it, and photos of the ramp are possible here. What is also seen is the US Marine base, with considerable numbers of aircraft. On the opposite side of the runway is the small McDonnell-Douglas test facility. The extreme length of the runway, and the equally extreme temperatures endured by Yuma, made this an ideal testing place for prototypes, and the compound may contain the odd aircraft.

From the terminal, on the north side of the field, 32nd St leads to a left turn and closer proximity to the runway and McD-D. A sandy track at the side of this compound allows any inmate to be identified and/or photographed but a reminder about the depth, and softness, of the sand next to this area should be heeded. It is easy to continue driving along the perimeter until it is too late. Beyond the McDonnell-Douglas area, the road passes close to the runway, and it's possible to take photos of aircraft on the move. Since the base is often used by Top Gun crews, there is some understandable concern over security and any casual watching of interesting F-5s or A-4s is often misunderstood. The units visiting from Miramar are a considerable attraction, though low-visibility schemes make serials difficult to read. Without access to the base, aircraft on the ramps are almost impossible to identify, due to distance and heat haze. The VMFAT-101 are the most likely hosts for a visit, and they normally keep a comprehensive stock of reasonably priced souvenirs.

BAKERSFIELD CA

| BFL KBFL | Kern County/Meadows Field | 6m/9km N |

Anyone travelling west from Nevada to San Francisco will pass Bakersfield. It is best remembered by the unlucky as where the California Highway Patrol starts to do an effective job. The speed limit, across the desert, is left mostly to the driver's discretion (or otherwise). At Bakersfield, the grip tightens. Instant fine . . . have a nice day!

Meadows Field is easy to find, as long as it's borne in mind that it is also known as Bakersfield Municipal Airport and Kern County Airport. Getting out of the car is not compulsory. One or two commuters might be visible on the ramp at a busy time, all just as easy to see at LAX. Perhaps the rather ugly (but unique) XF-84H on a pole will justify the visit. The other airfield in the area is Shafter Airport, also known as Minster Field (!), where a selection of more light aircraft reside.

BISHOP CA
BIH   1m/1.5km NE

Long ago, this was the home of Sierra Pacific Airlines. Their aircraft were rarely seen at the little airport. Now it handles one or two commuter flights during the course of the average weekday. Timing a visit to coincide with one of these movements can be a matter of luck. Most people keep driving, on their way to or from Yosemite.

BURBANK CA
BUR   KBUR   Burbank-Glendale-Pasadena   3m/5km W

This was once quite a busy field, with the scheduled traffic being supplemented by numbers of P-3 Orions nearing completion at Lockheed's assembly plant. The factory has been closed for a long time, and is the proposed site of a new passenger terminal. Not before time. The existing terminal has served passengers for many years and is more pleasant inside than its exterior suggests. Airline traffic is mostly Southwest, American, United, Skywest and Alaskan, and there are windows within the terminal which allow photos of aircraft being pushed back.

The multi-storey car park offers views of runway activity but, to see the contents of the various ramps (Lockheed, Warner, Disney, MCA and Universal), a car is essential. For access to the perimeter, the airport operations department might be helpful.

CARLSBAD CA
CLD   Palomar   2m/3km E

On I-5, between LA and San Diego, this quiet airport may be worth a detour. There is a dozen or so difficult-to-photograph Air Resorts Convairs, rotting away in the sun. Flight International also base a part of their large fleet here. Apart from that, not much happens.

CHICO CA
CIC   KCIC   Municipal   6m/9km N

The journey takes some dedication, as it is a long drive northeast from San Francisco. Leaving I-5 at Orland, Chico is about 20 miles east. Aero Union's operation is separated from the main airport by a road, and the base is at the eastern end of the field. A high wire fence surrounds the facility, with signs saying that loitering, trespassing and photography are not permitted. This would not appear to be an inherently welcoming operator. Nevertheless, a request for ramp access still produces results, though it must be borne in mind that straying off the Aero Union patch is not permitted.

The chance to take photos of the DC-4 fleet may not be for much longer, as turboprop power is becoming affordable. This is generally in the shape of P-2s and P-3s at present. The rest of the field is also of interest, though not necessarily the scheduled traffic, which comprises mostly United Express Bandeirantes and Ameriflight Pipers. The museum is worth a visit, if only to see the delightful Viscount 700 parked there. There are, however, other exhibits worthy of interest.

CHINO CA
CNO   4m/6km E

It is not true that half the fun of Chino is finding it. The directions are simple . . . when you know. Pomona Freeway (Hwy 60) skirts the southern edge of Pomona and Ontario. The community of Chino is immediately south, but the airport exit is two or three miles east. Take Euclid (Hwy 83) south and the airport is difficult to miss, on the left side of the road. The Euclid exit was, and might still be, only accessible to eastbound traffic.

Arrival at Chino is confusing, as there are many ramps and hangars. Several compounds look inviting but may be no-go areas, due to the presence of a C-130 maintenance facility. The Planes of Fame Museum became famous as a centre of excellence for restoration, so more warbirds were attracted. The last reported visit, however, suggested that there was nothing to be seen. Evidence of the old fire-bomber days also seems to be consigned to the past.

COMPTON CA
CPM   10m/16km ESE of LAX

Security is tightening here, but there are not enough residents of note for the serious enthusiast to bother the authorities. Now less than a dozen light aircraft contain nothing outstanding, so attention need not be diverted from other pleasures, to be enjoyed in the area, such as LAX, Long Beach or Orange County.

CULVER CITY CA
CVR   Hughes   2m/3km N of LAX

The main road heading north from LAX, Sepulveda Boulevard, has a right turn, Lincoln Boulevard, which skirts the northern perimeter of the airport. It is also only a short drive along it, across Manchester Boulevard, to Hughes Airport. Passing the western threshold of the single runway, a right onto Jefferson reveals very quickly if there will be anything to see on the far side. Apart from one or two corporate visitors, there are usually a few Hughes helicopters to be seen on the ramp. Everything else is safely hidden behind closed doors.

FRESNO CA

FAT   KFAT   Air Terminal   5m/8km NE

The airline traffic here is not very brisk but the variety is adequate for most enthusiasts. Views from the terminal are restricted and photos are hard come by. The California Air National Guard has an almost road-side apron, in front of which stand a selection of older jets. Across on the far side is a base for TBM Tankers but only the occasional water bomber is present, close to a small Army UH-1 base. Interest in the TBM ramp can be misconstrued as prying into the Army area and there has been the occasional misunderstanding here. The rows of Trackers, visible from the passenger terminal, have been stored for many years.

Westair's maintenance base features a substantial number of United Express commuters undergoing checks. A trip to Fresno is more likely to be a quick recce of Westair and TBM than a prolonged stay. Interest in the area's general aviation means a call into Fresno Chandler, west of Highway 199, and closer to town.

FULLERTON CA

FUL   Municipal   24m/38km E of LAX

Leaving the noise and other splendours of Los Angeles International Airport for the joys of Fullerton is not many people's idea of a good time. Ignore this warning, make the journey, and try it. The route is south on Sepulveda to Hermosa Beach, then left/east along Artesia. Fullerton Airport is at the end of the road. Its residents were once rudely described as being a hundred and fifty spam cans . . . extremely accurate, however. Access to the field is (sometimes grudgingly) offered, with a warning not to venture past the windsock, unless prepared to pay a $1000 fine!

HAWTHORNE CA

HHR   KHHR   Municipal   3m/5km E of LAX

At least it isn't far from LAX to Hawthorne. Take Imperial or El Segundo. Apart from a hundred or so light aircraft to see, there are helicopters and a small museum which includes a Sea-Bee and an A-4 Skyhawk. For access to the field, the Security Aviation building is on 120th Street, off Crenshaw, just north of its intersection with El Segundo.

INYOKERN CA

IYK   Kern County   1m/1.5km E

Travelling north from Edwards Air Force Base on Highway 395, the town of Inyokern can be seen from miles away. So can the airport. Directions are unnecessary. Metroliners operate regular links with Los Angeles, so it's usually possible to see one at close quarters on the little apron. Most of the time, Inyokern bakes in the sun and, even during the week, there is very little activity to witness.

LANCASTER CA
WJF   General William J Fox Field

A little way to the north of Palmdale, and visible from a long way off, this airfield may contain something worth the detour. most likely a couple of Aero Union DC-4s on duty. Some extremely unusual aircraft ended their days here, including the prototype F-111 (is it still there?) and an airworthy Argosy was noted on the last visit.

LONG BEACH CA
LGB KLGB   Daugherty Field   3m/5km NNE

The airport's main tenant is McDonnell-Douglas, with its vast assembly plant for MD-80s and MD-11s. The airline terminal handles a few Alaska Airlines and TWA MD-80s, though traffic is modest. However, this is a useful alternative way of getting charter passengers into the Greater Los Angeles area, and therefore Disneyland etc, taking advantage of reduced landing fees. Anything at the terminal will therefore be considered a bonus, as this is just one of the points worth a stop on a tour of the perimeter.

The McD-D facility is large indeed and much of the airport's boundary is taken up by its buildings. There are several access gates and that most likely to yield results is Gate Four, with its car park behind the blast screen of the main ramp. This used to be a remarkable place, with exotic colour schemes adorning MD-11s as they were finished for delivery. Several visitors have attempted to find viewing points around the McDonnell-Douglas plant but given up, with little or nothing to show for their efforts. Every accessible road is worth investigation, as it could offer the one chance to see something out of the ordinary.

Photographers are not officially welcome at this ramp but hurried attempts to snap something interesting here may not be as successful as asking for permission of the gatekeeper. At quiet times, it may be that his/her indifference on the matter may allow a better quality photograph to be taken, especially if it is pointed out that the picture will only form part of a personal collection.

The apron surrounding the FAA control tower is always full and many of its inhabitants are business aircraft with the occasional military visitor to be seen. A parking space around here is usually hard to find but persistence will be rewarded by a good variety of interesting types. Also visible, near the terminal on the far side of the runway, is the AiResearch ramp, now used to complete assembly of Gulfstream 4s, and for servicing older models. A side road allows close inspection of this apron and hangar but access can be difficult, and Long Beach is acquiring a name for security measures. These are quite strict, and little attempt is made to be friendly, thereby increasing the deterrant.

The Airport Operations office has confirmed that logging registrations from the fence is not a problem but undue interest, especially with a camera, can lead to over-zealous action by their own security personnel. Nobody's suggesting they should be put firmly in their place because they have the advantage of knowing where their company's private land starts.

Guided tours round the McDonnell-Douglas production plant, the subject of much conflicting correspondence, suggests they are offered, not offered, have been offered, or might be offered. Given that this book is published every two years, the situation can change several times during its useful life, so no advice can be given.

LOS ANGELES CA

LAX   KLAX   International   15m/23km SW

Arriving by road at LAX, the third busiest airport in the world, the terminals are seen to be arranged in a U-shape, at the centre of which is the striking Theme Building, offering a panoramic, though distant, view of all movements. The restaurant in this building offers reasonably good value and, for this reason, is used by airport employees. When the Theme Building is closed, the alternative vantage point is the multi-storey car park next to the Tom Bradley Terminal, which handles international flights.

Construction is scheduled to start, some time in 1996, of a new midfield terminal which will have 24 international and ten domestic gates. The tunnels which give access to some of the terminals are still there and a security check is followed by quite long walks, some close encounters with the aircraft being the prize for the effort. Each of these terminals is served by a limited number of airlines, so any photographs will be at the expense of many movements being missed. On the other hand, airliners moving around adjacent terminals can also be seen at close quarters, so a systematic circuit should result in a comprehensive collection of photos.

The building of the Tom Bradley Terminal obscured from view the cross-field taxiways, the source of many good photos in the past. The terminal's apron is now disappearing from view behind a screen of rapidly growing trees.

To sum up the situation in the central complex, it is no longer possible to get within reach of many of the more interesting aircraft but those who are content to play the percentage game will do well. The end of Runway 24L was, for many years, a popular place to stand. An elevated roadway has now been constructed which makes this location inaccessible. An access road, close to Sepulveda, and opposite a police pound (full of beat-up hulks) is now as close as it's possible to get. For consolation, there is a friendly taxi rank with a couple of drinks stalls.

Whilst it is quickest to get to the south side by way of Sepulveda, under the runways, at least one trip round the eastern end is recommended. Leaving the airport on Century Boulevard, and ignoring the direct Sepulveda route, a right turn after the Delta maintenance base, at Avion Drive, is followed by a relatively circuitous route, most of which is close to all the eastern cargo ramps. The range of aircraft to be seen around here is good, as it features mainly carriers who operate only occasional flights, as well as Emery Express and Evergreen International.

This road joins Aviation Boulevard at the threshold of Runway 25R, and a right turn leads to Imperial Highway, where there are more busy aprons than many quite interesting airports could boast. Devoted mainly to cargo operations, there are many ramps to be explored, most of which can be seen from under-used car parks and emergency access roads. That next to the Imperial Cargo Terminal offers a tremendous, and northerly, view to the thresholds of Runways 25L/R, regarded by many well-travelled enthusiasts as being one of the best photo-locations in the USA.

Before reaching Sepulveda Boulevard, Imperial Highway serves one large general aviation terminal, part of whose ramp is visible from the car park. There is a good number of biz-jets to be seen at close range but photographs are hard to obtain. West of Sepulveda are a few more aprons, including that of Federal Express, and the last area worthy of inspection is the Imperial Terminal, which handles American charter flights, including some of the smaller commuter operations. The car park here, being quiet, offers good views of Runways 25L/R.

It is unlikely that even the serious photographer will leave Los Angeles with a portrait shot of every type of aircraft seen but patience and time spent around the perimeter should make it possible to record a fine selection, particularly when so many major airports seem to offer variety seriously reduced by hub operations.

The Los Angeles Department of Airports does have a public relations bureau. Its telephone number is (310) 646-5260.

122

LOS ANGELES CA
VNY   Van Nuys   24m/38km N of LAX

Van Nuys is some distance north of Los Angeles, just off San Diego Freeway. It is a very large general aviation field, split into two unequal parts by Sherman Way. A look at the southern portion reveals one or two items of interest, and a drive round the entire perimeter should reveal everything present. The airfield has always featured something of interest, and the last report mentioned a Caravelle, a Delta DC-9 plus a Jet Provost and a Canberra among the other war (and post-war) birds.

The California Air National Guard unit has a separate little corner, where its C-130s sit, all close to the fence. The entrance to the base is on Rubio Avenue, where their F-104 gate guardian can be seen.

MADERA CA
MAE   Municipal   1m/1.5km S

Conveniently close to the highway, when driving between Los Angeles and San Francisco, Madera once provided the pleasant surprise of a few withdrawn piston airliners in storage. They have gone, and with them went any real reason for the detour. Traffic during the day is negligible.

MODESTO CA
MOD   Harry Sham Field   3m/5km E

The journey along I-99 can be broken by a stop at Modesto. It is a quiet little airport, which is used for commuter flights to San Francisco and San Jose. For the chance of a photo of a Metro or Jetstream, it may be worth the trouble, but there isn't much else of note.

MOJAVE CA
MHV   Kern County   5m/8km E

Another field worth a detailed look is not far from Edwards Air Force Base; Dick Rutan worked on his Vari-Eze and Long-Ez projects here and it was also the base for his around-the-world Voyager project. Stored aircraft and test facilities have always made a visit here an interesting proposition, usually with something extraordinary to be seen.

Itineraries which feature California and Nevada or Arizona could involve passing Mojave, but never without a stop. The far side of the runway became the storage area for ex-TWA CV-880s, and a pair of C-133 Cargomasters also became famous residents. The dry weather is ideal for storage, and also for flying: Canadair did much testing of the Challenger prototypes at Mojave, losing two in the process, and Flight Systems Inc have many military aircraft for conversion to drones.

A walk around the apron reveals a remarkable selection of fighters converted to civilian use: T-33, F-104 or Meteor . . . nothing is too extreme to be considered as recreational transport at Mojave! The stored aircraft are a different matter: over the years, Mojave's role has changed, and a wide range of airliners destined for many carriers spend some time here before delivery. MDC Finance MD-80s, USAir 146s, lots of Continental and Boeing 747-400s of national airlines can be seen from a distance. Neither access nor tours, however, are available any more. Interest in the far side inmates can result in a checklist, if requested at the admin office.

MONTEREY CA

MRY   Peninsula   5m/8km ESE

In Del Ray Oaks, and next to Highway 68, the airport has the Del Monte heights to the south. Confusion of terminology regarding the direction means that the last edition said WNW and this states the exact opposite. The airport is ESE of the town and the town is WNW of the airport! The name of Del Monte is famous to anyone who has ever bought canned fruit and it is here that the Del Monte Aviation fleet of business aircraft is based. The terminal allows good views of the apron, and the runway beyond, with United and Delta being the most regular of scheduled visitors. There is also plenty of commuter traffic and a considerable number of executive movements.

The executive ramps are east of the main terminal and the road is elevated above the level of the airfield, allowing good but distant views. To the north of the field is Fort Ord and a naval college, both of which justify a fair amount of military visitors. Anyone who intends to investigate this airport should consider doing so in the afternoon as it is prone to fog in the mornings.

NAPA CA

APC   County

A few miles north of San Francisco Bay, Napa is worth a detour for anyone interested in seeing something different. Several Beech 36s and King Airs are based here for use by Japan Air Lines' pilot training school.

OAKLAND CA

OAK   KOAK   International   10m/16km SW (bus 20 minutes)

On the opposite side of San Francisco Bay from its more prestigious neighbour, a selection of scheduled flights can be viewed from the terminal, but only by taking a walk down the long pier and looking out of the various windows at the gates. Passenger operations are not generally exciting and traffic is slow, so the main interest lies in the maintenance and general aviation aprons up the eastern side of the field. These should be visited in the morning, if serious attempts at photography are going to be made.

Once famous for being the main bases for World Airways and Transamerica, present day operations owe much to that history. This is still an active airport for MAC charters which, once upon a time, was how those two airlines earned much of their living. Freight operations result in a relatively large number of aircraft, dominated by FedEx, though there are normally a few UPS, Airborne and Burlington Express examples.

Most of the cargo carriers can be seen from outside the passenger terminal, at the commuter gate. The quantity of airliners has never been Oakland's main strength; its speciality lies in there usually being something present out of the ordinary. Maintenance bases carry out work for unusual operators, and it is along the eastern perimeter that a line of hangars and ramps can produce rarities. Identifying everything is a problem, so the photographer can suffer very real frustration. Large numbers of executive aircraft use the terminals here, and much more can be parked on the airside of the large hangars, out of sight from the road. It is quite normal for a morning at Oakland to result in a fascinating and varied collection, and what can be seen here is usually more interesting than San Francisco International.

The airport is located on Bay Farm Island, just a few miles from Nimitz Highway (I-880). A bridge at the north end of the island leads to Central Avenue and Alameda. At the northwest tip, overlooking San Francisco Bay, is Alameda Naval Air Station. Heading south on Nimitz, it's a short journey to HAYWARD Air Terminal (HWD), usually worth a look.

ONTARIO CA
ONT   KONT   International   3m/5km E

Promoted to some sort of international standing by being used as a West Coast version of Newark. Ontario's name is often synonymous with Red Eye Specials, where no-frills bargain flights operate. During the daytime, when cut-rate fares are not possible, the moderate traffic contains little out of the ordinary. The pleasant terminal building has a walkway next to part of the ramp, where airliners can be seen, though over the modest blast screens. Low walls permit enough height to be gained for photography.

Lockheed have a C-130 service facility here, to the right of the terminal when driving in. Due to the presence of foreign military aircraft, there is no shortage of posted notices warning against photography. To ensure that heed is taken, there should be more personnel to enforce it.

Ontario's largest operator is UPS, though their parcels traffic reaches its busy peak after dark. All types of their aircraft, including the elusive 747s visit the parcels sorting facility here. Union Flights are also to be seen, and anything from their Buffaloes to one or two Beech 18s are a common sight here.

OXNARD-VENTURA CA
OXR   County   1m/1.5km E

When travelling along Highway 101 between Los Angeles and San Francisco, this is one of the airports close enough to the road to be considered as a detour through the orange groves. Scheduled traffic through the neat little terminal is minimal, and strictly limited to commuters. However, Oxnard has been known as the last resting place of one or two airliners. The field is quite open, so there is no shortage of vantage points from which to see interesting aircraft.

PALMDALE CA
PMD   KPMD

This used to be an exciting place to visit, in the days when Lockheed rolled out their finished TriStars. Airline operations are negligible but the other claim to fame lay down a track, in a secluded corner. This was the last resting place of the airframes built in the A-11/YF-12 project.

PALM SPRINGS CA
UDD   Bermuda Dunes   24m/38km E

Surrounded by thousands of square miles of desert and scrubland, Palm Springs is an emerald green cushion of golf courses, where enough water is sprinkled every day to supply a good-sized town. Bermuda Dunes is a new community (using the term loosely) and the residents enjoy a lavish lifestyle. Naturally the airport houses a fair number of corporate transports. Any interest in them is not always welcomed.

PALM SPRINGS CA
PSP   KPSP   Regional   2m/3km E

Literally a few paces east of City Hall, the municipal airport was essential to the growth of Palm Springs but it was a major blunder in planning terms. So close to the town, its use is now greatly restricted and it has largely outlived its usefulness. Only light aircraft now use it, and there will be ever-growing pressures to develop the land in future.

RIVERSIDE CA
RIR   Flabob   4m/6km NE

When atmospheric pollution first hit Los Angeles, it was fashionable to move up into the Sierras for the better quality air. San Bernardino and Riverside are the results. Time has caught with the inhabitants, as the smog is blown up the slopes by the coastal breezes. This is as far as it gets . . . the worst of both worlds. Two Convairs were reported as rusting away by the control tower at Riverside. This may refer to Flabob or its near neighbour . . .

RIVERSIDE CA
RAL   Municipal   3m/5km N

Like Flabob, there are no scheduled services operating here, but it is a general aviation field which may be worth a detour for number-crunchers on their way to see something a little more exotic. To the north east are the USAF's large transports operating from Norton Air Force Base and, a similar distance to the south east, the bombers and tankers at March AFB.

RIVERSIDE CA
HMT   Hemet - Ryan Field

Hemet, home of Hemet Valley Flying Service, is officially called Riverside Hemet. It is not a major field by any stretch of the imagination and the distance between Riverside and this airport is over sixty miles. Leaving I-10 at Beaumont, Highway 79 winds it way south. For anyone interested in older transports it's worth the drive. The setting is lovely and the aircraft are interesting: plenty of tankers are to be seen, ranging from stored aircraft to the newly configured C-130s. Also in the area is PERRIS, a small airfield but anyone who wishes to add a couple of Twin Otters to a day's log can find them here, used for para-dropping.

SACRAMENTO CA
SAC   KSAC   Executive   4m/6km S

The state capital of the most buoyant (though almost bankrupt!) of American states is bound to attract some business and the airport which handles the scheduled movements is Metropolitan. Traffic is seen to be relatively slow, with most of the operators being nothing out of the ordinary. The power and the money is demonstrated by a visit to the Executive Airport where, during the week, good numbers of business aircraft can be seen from the fence on either side of the terminal. The airport's most important resident is Union Flight, for it is here that their opeations base is found. Among the Buffaloes and Beech 18s (and C-45s) are several withdrawn aircraft which greatly add to the appeal and interest.

SACRAMENTO CA
SMF   KSMF   Metropolitan   10m/16km NW

The Metropolitan airport is relatively disappointing, with no views from the terminals, and not much activity to see, apart from the occasional military aircraft in the circuit, having come from Beale, McClellan or Mather, all of which are nearby. Walkways along the edge of the apron are close to the aircraft, indeed too close when some of them are pushed back, but photography is not at its best here. The commuter terminal, on the right, does have a rampside observation area but this can be out of bounds when there is an aircraft to be seen!

SAN DIEGO CA
SDM   Brown Municipal

Aviation heritage is strong in San Diego and the tradition continues at Miramar. It was the Ryan Aircraft Company of San Diego who built the Spirit of St Louis, used by the intrepid Charles Lindbergh. His name is commemorated at the city's main airport. Brown Municipal airport keeps the tradition alive, too, in its way as it plays host to regular light aviation spectaculars. For the rest of the year, it is quiet with one or two executive aircraft among the light planes. The odd Mexican visitor can be noted, just a few miles from its home country.

SAN DIEGO CA
SAN   KSAN   Lindbergh International   2m/3km NW

The airport, like the city, has a lush air about it, with close attention having been paid to planting greenery. The passenger terminals offer no quality vantage point but there are three alternatives, one of which is so good, they must have put a stop to it by now. If it's accessible at all, it will be strictly for pedestrians. Leave the east terminal and turn left. At the intersection, a road to the left gives access to the ramp for cargo vehicles. The gate here overlooks much of the ramp and certainly ensures that everything taxying in or out passes within view. Some sort of ladder may be necessary for perfectionists, which is just the sort of thing to attract the wrong kind of attention.

A journey down North Harbor Drive will reveal the Coast Guard air station, with a couple of Guardians based. Because the station was originally used for HH-3s, they could take off over the harbour, where aircraft carriers can be seen. The fixed wing Guardians need a runway, so a policeman stops the traffic when they need to cross. Very convenient for the lucky photographer!

Just beyond this crossing, Laurel Avenue begins. This is almost directly opposite the end of the short Runway 31 and very close to the threshold of 27. The city fathers, in their infinite wisdom, have caused a public viewing area to be built next to the fence. Being California, a car park is essential but the bus stop is close by, on North Harbor Drive. Lots of people turn up, especially at weekends, to watch the action. Apart from close access to taxying aircraft, the general aviation can be seen on the (relatively nearby) far side of the field. A number of fixed base operators handle good quantities of executive movements during the week. For the best photos in winter time try also early mornings next to the fence on Pacific Highway, which is an ideal place for aircraft as they turn at the hold to Runway 27.

SAN DIEGO CA
MYF   Montgomery Field

An interest in airports means an interest in airliners. On this basis, a visit to Montgomery Field could be essential for one of the few remaining Ford Trimotors is to be found there. There are no scheduled services, and the airfield is dedicated largely to general aviation but it makes an interesting detour for number crunchers.

SAN FRANCISCO CA

SFO   KSFO   International   13m/20km S (bus 30 minutes)

This airport dominates the aviation scene in the area and has seen much extension and refurbishment since the days when it was possible to stand on the deck by the control tower on the original terminal building, watching PSA and Air California Electras, and Hughes DC-9s. This has all been swept away to make room for a new international terminal and views from this are hard come by. Generally, the only way to see what is on the stands is to walk from one end of the terminal area to the other, as many windows overlook the extensive aprons. The shuffling around of various airlines operations to suit the completion of work in the terminals means that San Francisco may always be in a state of flux, and even recent reports may still be subject to regular updating.

United's presence at San Francisco is substantial, and its numbers are boosted by the many Westair Jetstreams and Brasilias which are constantly on the move. USAir, and to a lesser extent, Delta and American make up the rest of the movements, though Alaska Airlines are regular arrivals. The American Airlines presence is reducing, due to their development of the nearby San Jose as a regional hub.

Despite the upheavals in the centre of the airport, the perimeter has changed little and one of the best spots, adjacent to the threshold of 1R is still good for views of aircraft taking off. Photographers sometimes have a problem with the fence, because the ditch prevents close access to the chainlink. The mobile means of gaining height will help, but it can lead to undesired attention from police.

The maintenance areas to the north of the terminal area offer many different viewpoints and the best of these is probably the car park next to the Butler Air Terminal, where many executive movements can be seen at reasonably close range.

The facilities at the north end of the field are not easily accessible and anyone who penetrates this area will have obtained some written authority to pass through the security gate which guards it.

SAN JOSE CA

SJC   Municipal   3m/5km NW (bus 15 minutes)

The main entrance to the airport is off Coleman Avenue, in the southeast corner, though a less interesting entrance is off Guadeloupe Parkway from the north. Entering the complex off Coleman, it is possible to achieve some idea of the layout before reaching the passenger terminal. Airport Boulevard loops around the eastern, busiest, part of the field, passing the general aviation ramps and terminal, and the FBOs on the north side.

Despite being close to San Francisco, there is enough local demand for an alternative airport to justify a very wide variety of schedules here. International services are handled by SFO but San Jose is intent on capitalising on being a small and convenient airport. American Airlines plan to change things by the extension of hub operations to include their long-haul Pacific Rim flights. The new terminal, for American and USAir, is operational and the observation deck in the old one remains open. It offers a limited view of the proceedings, being a little low, and set back behind the extended building to the right but scheduled airline movements do pass within range.

An alternative vantage point for the main apron is to the right of the tower, in the parking lot, though others are also available: a spot next to Fire Station 20 is close to the taxiway, and opposite the ramp where biz-jets are parked. Also, at the eastern end of the airport, the general aviation terminal usually contains a free parking space. From here, approaching and taxying aircraft can be seen. In the southeast corner is Aris Helicopters. Their fleet contains a number of S-58s, and the friendly staff usually allow ramp access for photography.

128

SAN LUIS OBISPO CA
SBP   Municipal   3m/5km S

The existence of this airport is not doubted but it has confused one or two visitors. There is almost nothing of any interest to be seen. Thus arrival at San Luis Obispo, followed by immediate anti-climax almost certainly means this was the place. All is not lost . . .

SAN LUIS OBISPO CA
CSL   McChesney Field

If the confusion from having two airports serving such a small community were not enough, McChesney Field is also known as County Airport! The majority of scheduled services are commuter flights, so most of the action is concentrated into the early morning and evening. During the day, there are still a few notable residents, up to Metro-size, so all the effort to leave San Luis Obispo with something to remember is not completely wasted.

SAN PEDRO CA
SPQ   Catalina Island Seaplane Base   3m/5km E

The road bridge sweeps high over the docks of San Pedro, and some very large ships are to be seen. From the highway, it is an interesting car journey to the ramp at the water's edge which was once Briles seaplane base. It was here that the Grummans plied to and from Catalina Island, a few miles off shore. Briles, based at Long Beach, have moved with the times, and their operations now use a range of helicopters. One of them, parked on the dockside, can make an unusual photo for the collection.

SANTA ANA CA
SNA   KSNA   John Wayne International   5m/8km S

Officially Santa Ana, John Wayne/Orange County: ABC World Airways Guide sticks to the old name of Orange County but the locals have adopted the new one. You pays your money and you takes your choice. An interest in general aviation, hardly the main topic of this book, makes this an attractive airport in theory as it houses countless light aircraft. Only the Pan Western GA Terminal is yet to post signs around its car parks, warning against spotters popping in for a good look. Lots of aircraft, and so few places to see them: expect to leave with only a small proportion, and Santa Ana won't be too frustrating.

The newer terminal, east of the old one, has no observation deck, but car parks at each end do overlook the commuter ramps. USAir Express and United Express are at the western end, with American Eagle and Skywest at the other. Midway's MD-87s have added some spice to the movements, so the terminal is worth visiting in the morning.

The afternoon is best enjoyed by taking a series of right turns from the terminal, a long drive, but worth it. Having taken a look at the occupants of the Million Air FBO, the road reaches, in the northeast corner, a spot close to the end of the runway. From the car park here, approach photos are easy to come by, but the construction of fuel tanks has stopped views of aircraft on the ground. Anyone in need of portraits of 757s in the colours of America West, American or Delta might spend some time here. East of the airport, and worth a detour for the military-minded, are Santa Ana and El Toro Marine bases, the former having helicopters easily seen from Barranca Road.

SANTA BARBARA CA
SBA   Goleta Municipal   10m/16km W

Most of the scheduled traffic is commuters, plus the occasional 727 or MD-80. On either side of the passenger terminal are mesh fences, where it is possible to see the parked aircraft. The car park to the left overlooks the ramp where commuter traffic stops, and photographs are no problem. Further left is a selection of general aviation, which makes up 90% of the movements.

Tracor carry out modification work on a variety of airliners, and what can be seen on any visit is a matter of luck. The graveyard contains withdrawn Jetstreams, bearing a variety of colour schemes, and serving as a reminder of the days when the airport was served by Apollo and later Pacific Coast Airlines. Santa Barbara is a pleasant airport and usually has something present to justify the small diversion off the main road.

SANTA MONICA CA
SMO   Municipal   7m/11km NW of LAX

The desire to investigate Hughes Airport in Culver City can be combined with a trip a little further up Lincoln Boulevard to Santa Monica. It is a general aviation field, with rather a lot of aircraft. The place oozes money, as it is the closest airport to fashionable Beverly Hills and Bel Air. Olympic sprinters who wear the T-shirts help, of course. As is to be expected, there are a few expensive toys waiting for their owners to take some time off from earning their millions.

Logging numbers from the fence is permitted but the far side of the field offers untold numbers, which elude the binoculars. The end product is between 100 and 150 light aircraft registrations, which might be the law of diminishing returns for anyone with only a limited amount of time. Apart from the biz-jets, the large museum features six outdoor exhibits and, of all things in California, a Tornado simulator!

SANTA ROSA CA
STS   Sonoma County   8m/13km NNW

The small passenger terminal handles a few commuter airline movements, similar to Stockton (q.v.). Most aviation-minded visitors made the journey for one reason only: Macavia. The demise of that airline may mean that propliners may no longer be in evidence. This is not the only airport north of San Francisco, so a journey by road will probably feature Santa Rosa on a day trip with visits also to Napa and Sacramento. Before including Chino on the itinerary, it's worth bearing in mind that it can make for a long day from San Francisco.

STOCKTON CA
SCK   KSCK   Metropolitan   6m/9km S

This is one of California's quieter airports, though hardly surprising when it is so close to San Jose and Oakland. Local scheduled services link it with the Bay, operators being American Eagle and United Express, with Wings West Metros and West Air Bandeirantes respectively. The only reason it will receive visits from enthusiasts is the presence of the Hemet Valley base, which usually contains a selection of aircraft, some of which are being serviced. The Trackers and Boxcars are now being augmented with more modern types, though the age of the C-130s hardly makes them young. A request at the office for a look at the ramp will probably meet with success, and the bonus of a couple of C-97s in storage.

TORRANCE CA

TOA	Municipal	13m/20km S of LAX

Sepulveda Boulevard runs due south, past Los Angeles Airport, and reaches the sea at Redondo Beach. Here it turns inland and becomes Pacific Coast Highway. After a couple of miles heading east, the airport is on the left, on Airport Drive (from Crenshaw). It is the spiritual home of all Robinson mini-helicopters. Robinson warn of danger from getting too close, mostly to satisfy their insurance underwriters. Access to the rest of the field is easy enough, via the desk in the building next to the control tower. What you get is numbers, in both senses of the word: a couple of hundred light aircraft can take about an hour and a half to log, for those who like that sort of thing.

ASPEN CO

ASE	Pitkin County	4m/6km NW

The playground of the rich in Colorado is, quite definitely, Aspen. In some parts of the world, it seems like only poor people take the bus, but in Aspen, it would appear that the poorer folk have to take scheduled flights. There is no shortage of executive transport at this airport.

Leaving Aspen on Hwy 82 to Glenwood Springs, the airport is next to the road, on the left. The airline terminal is immaculate, as the rich expect, but the apron to the north is where the private transport is parked. The selection is good, and has been known to include a SIAI Marchetti S205 in full Yugoslav Air Force markings!

With the alpine scenery on the other side of the runway, most photographers will wish to leave with at least one record of their visit. Anyone heading west from here by car is strongly advised to ensure that the tank is full before tackling Independence Pass. At 12,000 feet above sea level, the drive is hard, and fuel goes quickly!

AURORA CO

FTG	Front Range

From I-70, take exit 295 and head north into the village of Watkins. From here signs give directions to Front Range Airport. The road north, numbered 25A, is paved as far as the turn-off, beyond which a dirt road leads to the airport. It may also offer views of nearby DIA.

This is a new general aviation airfield, built to replace the now-closed Skyline Airport. It's very modern and open plan, with no fences (yet). Enquiries about ramp access are met favourably, though there were, in January 1995, only one or two heavier residents likely to be of interest: Continental Express Dash 7s are stored here in the company of a Colorado ANG A-7E.

COLORADO SPRINGS CO

COS	KCOS	Peterson Field	7m/11km SE

The new passenger terminal, on the south side of the field, opened in 1994. The road from town is near-DIA proportions, and views from it of the airfield are good. What is distinctly lacking is any volume of traffic. Apart from a couple of Reno Air flights a day, most of the airlines and aircraft are also Denver visitors. Photographs taken facing west have a mountain backdrop. The air cargo facilities remain unchanged, being just north of the old terminal. Across the field are the hangars and C-130s of Peterson Air Force Base, which shares the runway.

DENVER CO
APA   Centennial   11m/17km SE

This field used to be called Arapahoe County, hence the code. When travelling on Highway 87 between Denver and Colorado Springs, there is an enormous airfield on the east side of the road. Whilst there is a reasonable amount of larger general aviation types at Stapleton, it's clear that there is more to be found elsewhere.

DENVER CO
DEN   KDEN   Stapleton International   6m/10km NE

By the time these words are read, Stapleton will not exist as an airport. Indeed, events have been much delayed (and much publicised) at the new airport because October 1993 was supposed to be the date when everything changed.

Stapleton will become, increasingly, like an enormous ghost town until a use is found for the site. Anyone attempting to land there will see, painted on the runways, huge crosses suggesting there is something wrong. Everything has moved, at long last, to Denver International, Better known as DIA.

DENVER CO
DIA   KDIA   International   25m/40km E

What does three billion dollars buy, in the 1990s? A lot of superlatives, that's for sure. DIA, it must be said, is splendid. Its area is reported to be twice that of Manhattan, in other words about ten times as big as Heathrow. Thus, not only is a hire car essential to see the perimeter, unlimited mileage might be a good idea also.

On the day it opens, DIA becomes the eighth busiest in the world, which puts it on a par with Frankfurt. However, for a few years it will be surrounded by almost nothing, apart from prairie. They said that about what was known as Stapleton's Folly in 1929. It can safely be assumed that the price of the wide open spaces will be very high indeed, so that even the nearest house, some five miles away, will increase in value. Major airports attract business and DIA will be surrounded, for many years, by an enormous building site.

It takes between half an hour and forty five minutes to reach DIA from the city, along Peña Boulevard. What greets the eye, as it was meant to, are the thirty-four fibreglass peaks of the terminal roof, designed to mirror the Rockies on the skyline.

The control tower is, of course, the tallest in the world. It overlooks the five runways, none of which intersect and each of which is at least a mile from its neighbour. This is important, as it ensures the waves of United and Continental can arrive and depart without undue conflict.

The elevated bridge which links the terminal with the outside world offers views of the Rockies and of the aircraft which can taxi beneath. However it is not designed for spotters to stand on all day. A moving walkway sees to that.

Information is, as yet, speculative. The good news is that, unlike Atlanta, the three concourses have plenty of glass, albeit tinted. There is, however, a lot of space between the concourses, so it may be difficult to find a good spot which allows movement on all the runways to be monitored. The mutli-storey parking garage will certainly offer a view but the sheer size of the place means it will be distant. A fence next to the service road just north of the main terminal is where the south side of A Concourse can be seen, together with the taxiway to/from the parallel Runways 17/35L/R.

The perimeter is enormous. The first exit off Peña Boulevard, when leaving the main terminal area, leads to the airport services and cargo area. UPS and Fed Ex are encountered first, after which comes AMR Combs FBO which will no doubt contain a fair quantity of biz-jets. Leaving this area westbound, past the rental car lots, there is a distant view of Runway 7/25. Back on Peña Boulevard, the next exit is Tower Road which leads in turn to 56th Street and a long drive, at the end of which is TRACON. Beyond here is the perimeter fence with a view of the taxiway and approaches to Runways 3L/R.

Tower Road also leads to 88th Street, where a public viewing point was created, but only for watching the construction. The opening of the airport and the closing of this facility will probably coincide, not that it would be much use: it's a very long way from any of the runways. Further north, however, is somewhere more promising. Take 96th Street. A long drive west eventually leads to the United and Continental maintenance hangars. The road ends, after passing under the approach for 16L, with a view of Concourse C and the outer parts of Concourse B. Several runways can be watched from this general area.

Nothing can be said as yet about what spotting and photography are like at DIA because, as this book was written, the airport was yet to open. Traffic is expected to be more varied than Stapleton's, with Markair, Vanguard and Frontier coming onto the scene, the latter with its colourful 737s each sporting unique schemes on the fin. Mesa and Air Wisconsin operations, from Concourse B, feature the usual array of colour schemes, ranging from pure United to almost anything else. GP Express, the Continental Connection, share Concourse A with the host airline drastically cutting back its operations (they have enough troubles already).

Considering that the airport wasn't opened when this entry was placed in the book, the information is about as hot as can be managed. All this, and no mention of the baggage handling system which will, in time, no doubt deliver the goods!

GRAND JUNCTION CO

GJT   Walker Field   6m/9km NE

A prosperous town on the Colorado River is served by a modern airport. There is a Sabre on a pole in front of the terminal, but action on the tarmac is confined largely to commuter flights in the morning and evening, with little action during the day. Hawkins & Powers have an operational base here, to the left of the terminal, and access to the ramp, to photograph the resident P-2V Neptune, or similar, is readily granted at the office.

HAYDEN CO

HDN   Yampa Valley   25m/40km W

This runway is long enough to allow 727s to land, usually en route, and so the community offers a gateway for the rich on their way to the ski slopes. It is probable that a close-up view of a Continental Express Dash Seven at the smaller airport may provide more excitement than a few American, America West and Northwest Boeings calling at Hayden. Variety is provided by smaller types which commute from Denver during the day.

STEAMBOAT SPRINGS CO

SBS   Municipal   3m/5km W

This winter resort has already split into two, the old town along the main street, and a separate upmarket village at the foot of the ski slopes. The airport barely qualifies for the description but the small terminal handles the occasional Continental Connection Dash Seven. The gate next to the terminal allows ideal photos to be taken as the aircraft taxis past. The almost compulsory FedEx Feeder Caravan is parked with a dozen or so light aircraft. The airport which serves as the resort's link with major centres of population is further west along I-40, at Hayden.

GROTON-NEW LONDON CT
GON   Trumbull   6m/9km S

Trumbull's terminal handles a number of movements, including some US Navy executives, associated with the submarine base. The Army Guard has its own facility, with a number of UH-1s and, rather more interesting, some AVCRAD C-7 Caribous. It is possible to stand next to the fence for photography but a request at the gate may result in closer inspection, during the week.

HARTFORD CT
HFD   KHFD   Brainard   2m/3km E

East Hartford lies beside the Connecticut River. Its importance to the American economy cannot be overstated, for the Pratt & Whitney division of United Technologies is here. It would be easy to dismiss East Hartford as a small general aviation field without this item of information. Executive aircraft are always to be expected in number and variety. Weekends can be a disappointment, of course.

NEW HAVEN CT
HVN   Tweed   4m/6km SE

Tweed is a small airport, by any standard. Fortunately it is appropriately informal. Access to the ramp is usually available on request, but the casual visitor may not find anything to see. Always worth a detour from the highway, Tweed occasionally plays host to one or two (literally) interesting aircraft.

STRATFORD CT
BDR   KBDR   Sikorsky Memorial   2m/3km SW

Heading east by car from New York City, there are a few airports along Connecticut's southern shore. The first used to be known as Bridgeport but there is so much economic influence in Stratford, the name has been hi-jacked. Stratford really is one of the most important industrial centres on the aviation scene. Sikorsky Memorial airport offers a clue: it is here that production of S-76s and the various H-60 variants are assembled. What can be seen, at the edge of the field, are only massive buildings and car parks.

Next to the small passenger terminal is a viewing area at ramp level. The Business Express Beech 1900s can be seen at close quarters, and good photographs of aircraft taxying on the ramp are easy to take. The southerly aspect towards the ramp can make sunny days a nuisance for the photographer. With so few opportunities to get this close to New England's commuter aircraft, it can be very disappointing to leave with a silhouette on film.

WINDSOR LOCKS CT
BDL   KBDL   Bradley International   14m/22km N

Connecticut's state capital, Hartford, is quite close to the town of Springfield, in Massachusetts so a location about halfway between the two was chosen for a joint airport. This is Bradley Field, at Windsor Locks, whose growth is testament to local prosperity. The passenger terminal is split into two: the new Terminal A is linked to the two halves of Terminal B by an elevated corridor, in front of the Sheraton Hotel.

The entrance to the airport is from Highway 20 (off I-91) and terminal facilities offer little of interest. Since there are so many alternative points from which to see the action at close quarters, this is no problem. To the left of Murphy Terminal B is the FedEx cargo building, and this gives access to large, under-used car park very close to the taxiway for Runway 6. No matter how small the aircraft using this taxiway, it is within reach of the camera. Beyond the runway, some of the ANG A-10s are visible, and the base attracts a small number of military visitors.

Leaving the terminal area via Schoephoester Road (instead of Highway 20), there is a left turn just before Route 75. It leads, ultimately, to the Aviation Museum, but passes some very interesting aprons on the way. A left turn at the 4-way stop sign leads to Corporate Air, a FBO with a car park close to one of the taxiways to Runway 33. The new taxiway on the other side of this runway has drastically reduced what can be seen passing close by, but it still good for executive movements. AMR Combs owns the other hangars and terminal, where more biz-jets are to be seen. The next left off the perimeter road leads to Business Express, whose movements dominate activity at Bradley.

The next ramp is an extraordinary place, for it is here that the Army Guard has a base, complete with UH-1s and CH-54 Tarhes. Several examples can be seen quite easily from the low fence, and a request at the office, on the far side of the building (off the car park) usually yields results. The road winds round the end of Runway 24 to the museum. It is now one of the biggest in America, with two new buildings, and some of the larger exhibits are parked outside. There are twice-yearly open-cockpit days, when visitors can scramble around inside such aircraft as a B-29 or a B-47. The road terminates at the Connecticut ANG base but general access is barred, just beyond the museum.

Traffic is very mixed, ranging from Delta TriStars to the many Business Express Beech 1900s and SF.340s, and the delightful Air Ontario Dash 8s. The cargo terminal, next to Passenger Terminal A, also sees plenty of traffic but the evening package operations are when most of the aircraft move. Bradley deserves better renown among enthusiasts, as it offers a wide variety of movements, most of which will result in high quality photographs. A day spent here may not be hectic but it is usually pleasant.

WASHINGTON DC

IAD KIAD Dulles International 27m/42km W (bus 50 minutes)

Congestion at Washington National is now as bad as La Guardia, both landside and airside, and other airports have attempted to capitalise on this fact. The distance between the city centre and Dulles (in Virginia) is compensated by the freeway and the journey time should not exceed half an hour. As a change from DCA, it is worth making the effort. A car is not essential, however. Orange Line Metro trains serve West Falls Church Station, from where a shuttle bus operates to the airport, at a cost of $7 one way.

The airport is becoming increasingly busy, and its highly-regarded observation deck can reward the patient with quality photos of taxiing aircraft. It should be noted that the observation deck is not necessarily open all year round. When the deck is closed, Concourses B and C allow views of all the aircraft except those on the cargo and general aviation ramps.

Many airline visitors park well away from the main terminal, at the midfield concourse, primarily used by United and American. Although these movements are visible from the observation deck at the front of the main terminal, they are really too far away for good quality portraits. Nevertheless, aircraft on the taxiways closer to this deck do make for good photographs, though patience is needed. Prior reference to United's timetable is also useful. Arrival at the wrong time can mean seeing thirty or so United Express commuter-liners but nothing at all of United's own fleet. When in evidence, examples of just about every type of airliner that United operate can be seen, so a prolonged stay does have its rewards. Also visiting are Saudia, KLM, Swissair and ANA 747s, TACA and Transbrasil 767s, Markair 737s and Valujet DC-9s. Daily Lufthansa and Air France A340s are also worth a mention, as is the fact that DCA is now the USA's fifth most important international airport.

Previous comments regarding admission to airside appear to have been ill-researched. Strong protests resulted, from several friends of DCA. There are plenty of landside shops and other facilities, and access to many of the boarding areas, even by the so-called moving lounges, is possible. Boarding cards have not been required for access to the midfield area, Concourse C/D, but the ongoing situation cannot be taken for granted.

A billion dollars buys a lot of building, and that's what's being invested at IAD. Until 1997, when the work is due to be complete, work could cause short-term changes in the situation. When work finishes, the changes will indeed be long-term! The main terminal is to be doubled in length. The International Arrivals Building will eventually be demolished and a much larger replacement built elsewhere. Visitors should expect, for the next couple of years, that the observation deck might be the only place offering a view.

To the east of the terminal is a general aviation area (the other being in the northwest corner), which handles a fair amount of business traffic, with the occasional foreign official aircraft, RAF and Luftwaffe representatives being regular visitors. As long as smaller aircraft don't block the view, it is often possible to obtain fairly close-up shots of these aircraft through the fence. Airborne/Fereal Express aircraft, parked at the cargo terminal, are visible from the parking lot next to the Post Office.

WASHINGTON DC

DCA	KDCA	National	5m/8km S (train 20 minutes)

If subjective criteria sometimes affect reporting of airports, Washington National can best be described as a matter of taste. There are now enough young readers, with no idea of the way things used to be, for previous remarks about DCA to cause howls of protest: the way things are, that's what counts and, in many people's opinions, things are fine at DCA.

The quantity of movements at this airport is enormous, with influential companies having sufficient political·clout to retain parking space and slot times, so that their own movements are now causing serious delays to the scheduled traffic. It is not uncommon for airliners to wait at the holding point for over half an hour while half a dozen or so corporate jets land in a continuous procession. Even the most ardent DCA supporters would concede that airline traffic is limited in variety - pretty much Delta and USAir.

It is possible to find views in the terminal buildings, and a viewing terrace exists at the front of the old Eastern Airlines terminal. This has been closed for some time and is unlikely to re-open because the security risks would be too great. In the event of inclement weather (it does rain in Washington!), the balcony at the back of this building allows quite a good view of the proceedings but obviously no chance to use a camera.

Construction of a new 35-gate Delta/USAir terminal means that information for this part of the airport can become out of date quite rapidly. Readers/travellers will discover for themselves how events unfold. The general aviation which used the apron seen from the bank has now been moved to Butler Aviation's new terminal, at the southern end. Delta's Gates 10 and 11 in the temporary building, a converted hangar, are probably the best for getting some idea of the proceedings (somewhat like gate 85 at Newark). Aircraft land, stop, turn round and taxi back, all in front of you.

Alternative locations at DCA are restricted in their nature: to the north is Daingerfield Park, with its wildfowl sanctuary and marina. The boat landing area offers extremely close up views of traffic landing on Runway 18, regarded by some as being as good as anywhere in the world for photographers. If the runway is in use, this location is certainly worth serious investigation. When Runway 36 is in use, photos of aircraft on take off are to be considered. A car is not needed to reach the marina, since it is closer to the temporary Delta/USAir terminal than many of the other terminal facilities.

When the weather is a problem, or time is tight, consider also the city-bound platform of the Metro station, which has a roof. The view of the airport is comprehensive, though a long lens is needed for photographs. The cost of access to the Metro station is just $1, although it could be part of the cost of a ticket for a journey into town, in which case the view is a free bonus.

For access to the quantities of biz-jets, try the Northwest/Continental terminal or, for a more general (and more distant) view, the top level of the multi-storey car park.

WASHINGTON Airfields

There are so many true major airports, the subject of this book, in the Washington area that the need to look for general aviation fields may be ruled out of the average itinerary, if only due to restrictions of time. To complete the picture, there are some fields which may repay attention: COLLEGE PARK is north Washington's main g.a. field, with over 150 residents including many antiques, homebuilds and warbirds. The Metrorail isn't recommended on this occasion, as the station of the same name is nowhere near the airfield. Also north of the capital is BALTIMORE (q.v.) whose airport is near enough to Washington for it to claim to be an alternate international port to Dulles.

To the east of Washington is ANDREWS Air Force Base, where tours are arranged for visitors on a regular basis during the summer months. These are subject to cancellation and written details should be obtained prior to departure from home. In the event of the Public Affairs Department turning down an application for a visit, an alternative may be contact the Air National Guard Unit, located at the end of a road which passes the Naval facilities on the base.

Silver Hill is not a famous place in its own right but it deserves to be. Anyone visiting the Smithsonian Air and Space Museum in Washington should note there is an annex, served by a free shuttle bus. The annex, at Silver Hill, has some extremely impressive exhibits, including a YF-12 to complement the SR-71 housed in the downtown building. Silver Hill is southeast of the city, on the way to Camp Springs and Andrews.

Also close to Andrews is HYDE FIELD, with some items of vintage interest among the Pipers and Cessnas. Forty-five miles south is FREDERICKSBURG (SHANNON) which is well worth the mileage for its collection of pre-war aircraft, including Bellanca and Northrop airliners in flying condition.

GREATER WILMINGTON DE
ILG   KILG   6m/9km SSW

The city is the home of the du Pont Chemical Company, owned by about 1600 very wealthy adult family members, few of whom bear the surname. The extraordinary quantity of biz-jets to be found here is a tribute to their prosperity, though many are used as company jets by du Pont, its suppliers and customers.

Not far off Interstate 95, between Philadelphia and Baltimore, Highway 141 from the north gives a first, stunning impression of the airport and its well-heeled residents. Apart from two ramps and hangars of these private aircraft, there is very little activity. A quick foray onto the tiny roof deck will rarely reveal more than one airliner on the ramp, as most of the movements are used for commuting.

Also visible on the far side of the field is the Delaware ANG base, with its own ramp of C-130s, their serials just readable through the average binoculars. Also worth looking out for here are half a dozen or so 'pre-owned' aircraft, waiting to start a new life with some shoestring operator or, just as likely, end their life under the breaker's axe.

BOCA RATON FL
BCT   KBCT   1m/1.5km W

Between Fort Lauderdale and West Palm Beach, and next to Interstate 95, is the business aircraft field of BOCA RATON. Despite being so close to the highway, finding the entrance to the field can be difficult, as a right turn has to be followed by skillful navigation through the community. The apron usually contains a good number of biz-jets and, during the week, the occasional visitor from Latin America.

CLEARWATER FL
PIE   KPIE   Saint Petersburg   10m/16km ESE

The alternative airport for Tampa Bay comes a very distant second to the busy international field of Tampa. Airline traffic is mostly of a modest nature but the terminal does also handle occasional charters from Canada. Sun Jet International DC-9s, Canada 3000 A320s, American Trans Air 727s and Air South 737s are the most regular visitors. The amount of interest (or lack of it) in Clearwater as an active airport is evident from the total absence of any reports about what can be seen through the tinted windows of the new passenger terminal.

Off the main highway, the terminal and general aviation facilities are side by side, and one or two interesting smaller aircraft can be seen. There is normally a couple of UPS 727s parked all day but often too close to the fence for a photograph of any quality. Another access road leads to the business terminal and a few biz-jets park here, though often difficult to see from the fence. Close to this executive terminal are the US Coastguard base, with Hercules and HH-53s, and an aircraft museum, with one or two interesting exhibits including an A-4 Skyhawk. Pemco carry out work on 727s mostly, and one or two can sometimes be seen.

It is unlikely that anyone would visit this airport for more than a casual look around while passing, because of the lure of Tampa and more lively runway activity. The aviation enthusiasts' shop is worth a visit, specialising in all sorts of publications for the light aircraft flyer as well as a selection of T-shirts and suchlike.

DAYTONA BEACH FL
DAB   Regional   3m/5km W

Another small airport where not much happens, it is well worth the detour, if only to see what is present at Trans Florida Airlines. A couple of their CV-240s have been withdrawn from use for some time, and are unlikely to move in a hurry. If the gate is closed, ask at the FAA tower for access to take photos. The aircraft may have a slightly South American air to them but the immaculately cut grass gives a very different impression.

FORT LAUDERDALE FL
FLL   KFLL   Hollywood International   4m/6km S

Florida is a growth area of the United States and the economy continues to move away from traditional centres, like Miami. Examples of where major investment can be seen at its peak are Fort Myers, Orlando and, most of all, Fort Lauderdale.

Despite being so close to the northern edge of Greater Miami, Fort Lauderdale handles a prodigious amount of traffic, with surprising quantities of Delta TriStars and other widebodies. The traffic to the extremely busy terminal is similar to the domestic airliners visiting Miami, and

Runway 9L/27R is used for the majority of it. Fortunately, both ends are accessible for the photographer, with SW 39th Street offering an impressively close vantage point at the western end, and Marriotts Catering car park at the east. There are two economy car parks, north and south, which cost only $3.50 a day, for anyone intending to spend time in the terminal.

Three pasenger terminals are arranged in an arc. Delta's Terminal 1 is also used by Icelandair. Terminal 2 has been described, dismissively, as being used by the usual airlines and not very interesting. Few would disagree with that verdict. Terminal 3 offers variety. If photographs are not essential, this might be the place to spend a day, especially if visiting on an air pass. Between the terminals, the upper level road offers the chance to wield a camera to some effect. Sadly, the best view is not of the best aircraft but that's life!

Before leaving for a tour of the perimeter, ramp access at some of the facilities would be useful, and this may (not will) be obtained at the Aviation Department, on the western side of the field. A clockwise tour starts by leaving the passenger terminal and taking the first exit, marked for car rental returns. The employee parking lot, accessible from the perimeter road running parallel to Griffin Road, overlooks the threshold of 9R. The first ramp of note on this circular tour is that of Paradise Island, just beyond the threshold of 9R.

A series of right turns leads to the FAA tower and, next to it, the Combs-Gates Lear Jet facility. It is this area which is being transformed by much modernisation. Thus the scene is constantly changing, and reports rapidly become out of date. The number of biz-jets handled here and at Hudson General is large, and there are gateways close by which allow good views of traffic landing on the diagonal 13/31 runway, when in use.

The next vantage point is at a gate by the threshold of the busy Runway 9L, on SW 39th Street, particularly useful when the sun is behind the camera, as it faces north. This corner of the field is extremely popular with photographers. The fence shows signs of slight wear as it continues to lose the battle.

The elevated road along the northern boundary, above SW 34th Street, dominates the many ramps full of all sorts of airliners, many of which have been here for some years. The first ramp, World Jet Center, is used by Florida Aircraft Leasing but redevelopment may be changing the sitaution. Several of the ramps are accessible after a request at the office and some of the more interesting newer types can be seen on the Embraer apron. The Walkers International ramp has a reputation for holding more than its fair share of interesting aircraft. DC-4s/6s are becoming a rarity, as are CV-440s, but Dave's Airplane Repairs can usually be relied upon to offer something out of the ordinary.

To anyone who hasn't visited Fort Lauderdale for two or three years, the cargo terminal comes as a surprise. It has enjoyed much growth, and it isn't finished yet. The overnight parcels traffic operators spend the day here, with a couple of Burlington 727s being a regular feature, though usually parked too close to other aircraft to make good subjects for the camera. At the end of the northern perimeter is the Marriott car park but with the disadvantage that the prospect is southwards, into the sun.

FORT LAUDERDALE FL

FXE   KFXE   Executive   6m/9km N

Continuing north along Interstate 95 from Fort Lauderdale-Hollywood, the next port of call is likely to be Fort Lauderdale Executive airport, accessible from NW 50th Street. Most of the facilities and aircraft are on the southern edge, with many ramps and hangars containing a good variety of general aviation. Apart from a huge number of light aircraft and a fair number of biz-jets (including one or two from Latin America) there are some specific items to note. The ramps most likely to hold something of special interest are probably World Jet Center and Renown Aviation.

FORT MYERS FL
FMY   KFMY   Page Field   4m/6km S

Despite the rise of the new airport, Page Field is still worth a visit. It achieved fame from the Modern Air Transport DC-7 which ended its days here. With scheduled traffic using Southwest Florida, the accent is on general aviation. It is a strong accent. From occasional pistons up to DC-3 size and an array of biz-jets, the Fort Myers community needs a lot of aircraft. This is where to find them.

FORT MYERS FL
RSW   Southwest Florida Regional   14m/22km SE

Some miles away from Page Field is an impressive new airport with a very long access road. The darkened glass of the passenger terminals overlooks a quantity of stands but the operators are a rather mundane lot. There are a few vantage points, one reached by an emergency access road which ends very close to the runway, though a car parked at this point could attract attention, being easily seen across the expanse of flat grassland, when parked in what is, in all probability, a prohibited place. The alternative would be to walk to the spot, a long way on a warm day, and very likely to generate the interest of several thousand mosquitoes.
   A grassy bank overlooks the commuter ramp, where Beech 1900s park within reach of any camera, though the sun can be a problem. Better views are to be enjoyed at NAPLES (q.v.). Also in the Fort Myers area, due east, is LEHIGH ACRES. The exit north from Highway 82 leads to the field. The main reason for visiting is probably the chance to see the DC-3s of Lee County Mosquito Control.

FORT PIERCE FL
FPR   Saint Lucie County   2m/3km NW

One of several stops on the road along Florida's east coast, St Lucie is only likely to reveal an occasional Aero Coach Cessna on the little ramp and, parked all day, a Federal Express Caravan.

GAINESVILLE FL
GNV   KGNV   J R Alison Municipal   6m/9km NE

An indication of how busy this inland airport gets: seeing a Delta 737, a USAir Fokker 100 and a USAir Express Beech 1900 in the space of two hours is about average during the day. However, the detour might be worthwhile if only to see and photograph the Gators' F.27. Florida University's basketball team use it as their hack. The field is mostly surrounded by trees, so the apron is where to see whatever is present. Most people do so, and move on.

HOLLYWOOD FL
HWO   North Perry   6m/9km W

Only a short drive east from Opa Locka, to Highway 817/NW 27th Avenue, North Perry is easy to find, even without a map. It is also only a short distance east of Fort Lauderdale. Apart from a lacklustre selection of light aircraft, North Perry is the home territory of Pelican Express. One or two of their Hansas, or their DC-3s, might be present. For anyone who likes to fill a notebook, the Army National Guard offer a number of UH-1s.

JACKSONVILLE FL

JAX	KJAX	International	14m/22km N

Since the traffic which visits this average-sized regional airport is fairly ordinary, the military activity is likely to be of greater appeal. Identifying these movements from the passenger terminal's observation deck is difficult, usually due to the heat haze.

The ramps next to the approach road have an interesting selection of aircraft, up to DC-3 size, but the end of the runway may have to suffice for most of the photographers intent on capturing an Air National Guard aircraft on the move. Prior contact with the base is worth a try, for a tour of the flightline.

KENDALL-TAMIAMI FL

TMB	KTMB	Executive	8m/13km SW of MIA

West from Miami International is what used to be called New Tamiami. It is reached by following the South Dade Tollway/Highway 874. A turn at North Kendall Drive and a drive westwards leads to Lindgren Road/SW 137th Ave, the entrance being on the right. Fences have now appeared, spreading like weeds, so free access to the ramps is no longer possible. Requests are necessary.

The Kermit Weeks Museum has attracted a growing collection of rarities, some of the larger ones merely using cheap storage space. At the last count, there were two DC-3s and DC-6s plus a CV-240. The most recent report suggests that the museum suffered devastation in the 1992 hurricane. To what extent it is still open, or closed, may change with the passage of time.

KEY WEST FL

EYW	KEYW	International	3m/5km E

The customs facilities justify the International tag. Once the dawn flight of an ASA Brasilia has left for Freeport in the Bahamas, there is little else during the day to cause excitement. The rest of the traffic includes only the occasional foreign light aircraft to augment the types seen further to the north. For lovers of spectacular scenery (and Florida doesn't offer much) the drive to Key West may be worthwhile. It may also be nice to reach the tip of the country but the journey is of little value for the aviation enthusiast.

For those intent on the trip, the airport is small and has adequate opportunities for taking photographs from the fence next to the apron. General aviation, to the left, occupies a crowded ramp, so that photos can only be taken with access. The right side of the apron is used for freight but little arrives or leaves during the day. The Naval Air Station is not renowned for giving casual tours and it is a long way to drive without confirmation, views of the field from the perimeter being impossible.

MARATHON FL

MTH		1m/1.5km NE

On the way from Miami to Key West is Marathon, still surviving as an airport with some scheduled commuter traffic, which can be easily seen. As befits a local airport of this size, activities are quite informal and photographers are satisfied. Apart from the occasional scheduled visitor, DC-3s of the Monroe County Mosquito Control can also be inspected at close quarters.

MARCO ISLAND FL
MRK   3m/5km NE

A country club resort was developed several years ago and, to encourage visitors, Marco Island Airways was set up, operating from Miami. This was found to be uneconomical many years ago, and the Martin 404s passed into storage. Not far from Naples, it may be worth a detour. At least one of the 404s remains in store there, with little chance of seeing active service again. Due to the nature of the well-heeled customers using this quite remote resort, occasional biz-jets use the airport. A request for ramp access is normally successful, as the staff are friendly and generally unhurried.

MELBOURNE FL
MLB   KMLB   Regional   3m/5km NW

The new passenger terminal is tiny and very quiet. Melbourne's catchment area is limited, due to Orlando being only a short drive away. As is often the case with the smaller airports, it is possible to get closer to the aircraft and this has certainly been the case at Melbourne. Airline traffic, though by no means busy, features surprisingly large aircraft for such a small region. The opportunity for one or two, at the most, photos will compensate the detour but a stay in excess of an hour will only be due to the wait for something interesting on the arrivals monitor.

Grumman have a systems division base here, which is used for carrying out radar modifications to a variety of aircraft. The security which is inevitable around USAF E-8As means a casual request for a look round is sure to be met with an equally casual response. One such reply was cropped to the bare minimum of two words: they referred to sex and travel!

MIAMI

Aviation enthusiasts instantly recognize the name of Miami as being synonynous with a feast of immense variety. Few other places in the entire world offer so much in such a conveniently tight geographical area. The international airport is justly famous for its piston types, parked around the perimeter (though they are declining in number) and WATSON ISLAND offers the rare chance to see a Turbo Mallard take to the air from the harbour. OPA LOCKA boasts a spectacular array of general aviation, and other small fields have their own specialities.

Considered as being part of Greater Miami is Fort Lauderdale, though it is a centre in its own right and only a few miles to the north. Whatever specialist aviation subject is chosen, Miami is a springboard to the rest of Florida, and the trip is certain to be a memorable one, and will probably lead to a return visit at a later date.

Readers have their own preferences regarding small airfields in the area. All probably justify some exploration but only a few are mentioned in the text as being known to have some items of specific interest. Air passes meant that a number of visitors arrived at Miami International with no intention of investigating either the perimeter or neighbouring fields. Each to his own, as they say, but this corner of Florida has so much to offer that logging numbers from a car park roof is only a small part of the enjoyment. Many visiting aircraft don't come within range of the terminal, and most of them won't be around for ever, so a trip to Miami could be the chance to record for posterity the declining number of piston airliners and older jets.

MIAMI FL

| MIA | KMIA | International | 7m/11km W (bus 40 minutes) |

The international arrivals satellite has considerably improved the appearance of the airport, when first impressions count so much. From the time when Miami looked rather dowdy, and out of date, it is now a modern airport, offering every amenity to today's discerning traveller.

Despite the modernity of the central terminal area, it is the perimeter which attracts the enthusiast, and each part has different features. The sun deck on the international satellite is only available to passengers with a boarding card, though the windows in the terminal do offer reasonable views. Security is supposed to be a serious business, and many people earn their living from it. What counts is that passengers feel secure. Boarding card checks look good, in other words. Since any boarding card, issued by any airline (and in the test case, long out of date) was adequate to gain access, it is to be hoped that measures are tightened . . . though not by the spotter, who might fancy trying his luck. Because there are only restricted views from this concourse, keeping pace with the changing scene involves much physical activity.

Boarding passes are now required for all concourses except H, which can be of little use when the wrong direction runways are in use. Without a car, try instead the top level (7) of Car Park 2 or 4, which are linked to each other. "Runway in use" will determine which is better. If you choose the wrong one, it isn't necessary to go all the way down and start again. More than anything else, a good sense of direction is essential. To see the entire field, access will also be required to Car Parks 3 and 5. This is where the fun starts. Level 7 is an island in these two car parks, offering direct connections nowhere else. Level 4 becomes that for all interchanging. If it all seems too complicated, hire a car! American Eagle movements, in particular, are something to be seen but probably not recorded, as they are too far away.

Prolonged stays out in the hot Florida sunshine, like on a rooftop car park, can become very tiresome. Without soft drinks, or water, dehydration and sunstroke are genuine health hazards. A large bottle of Diet Coke, no matter how warm it becomes, is much cheaper than a few minutes in an American hospital. Baseball caps, worn backwards, offer more than street cred. Red faces, no matter how uncomfortable, are less dangerous than red necks.

From inside the air-conditioned comfort of a hire car, the visitor will need to plan a tour of the boundary, starting at the main terminal. The huge car parking blocks are now topped with a heliport, and the tunnel-like roads thus created can make it difficult to understand the road layout. A right hand exit leads away from the main road to the city and into some minor service roads. The ramp to be seen on the right is used by Delta, USAir and for some charter flights, and an adjacent ramp has been used for storage in recent years.

Passing the thresholds of Runways 27L and 30, the southern perimeter offers superb views of the aircraft using the southern runway (in one direction or another) with several parking places. The height of the fence is just enough to make photography difficult, and something to stand on will be of use. There may be signs of previous attempts to solve the problem, with a pile of stones, wood or even an old tyre being left for further use.

Much of the international traffic uses this runway and it is only necessary to get into position at one end or the other to watch a procession of some extremely exotic airlines. Even movements on Runway 9R can be photographed at the eastern end, as they taxi a long way parallel to the runway before turning into the terminal complex. A 300mm lens may be necessary for good shots on the taxiway, however. The carriers normally using this runway include many Latin American airlines, ranging from TACA 767s to TAN Electras, Mexican DC-10s to Ecuatoriana 707s. Added interest at the eastern end was the presence of the Agro Air C-97s. Florida West are now the main occupants. A problem with photographs of aircraft on this runway is the background can appear too 'busy' unless some care is taken.

Parked at the old Airlift hangar are 707s and DC-8s of several operators, some American and some foreign, and all too close to each other. Runway 9R, Miami's longest, sees a lot of use and photographers may find themselves settling in the NW 72nd Avenue area. Keep an eye open for the excellent aviation enthusiast's shop, called Just Plane Crazy.

A drive around the western end of the runway gives closer views of these aircraft but photos are still difficult to obtain. Cargo World looks a little long in the tooth these days but modern extensions are always under way, none of which seem to make things better for the enthusiast. Before leaving Cargo World for other ramps to the north, note should be made of one vantage point off NW 25th Street which has given good service over the years, overlooking the thresholds of both Runways 9L and 12. The Department of Agriculture has a car park which seems to be freely available. With the sun behind, aircraft taking off from this corner are extremely photogenic, especially as exotic oldies are often best seen on the move from here. Aircraft landing on 9L also make good subject matter for the camera.

Passing the thresholds of 9L and 12, a right turn leads into a small cargo complex, used mostly by Latin American companies, Tampa Colombia being a regular visitor as well as a number of piston airliner operators.

Returning to the perimeter, and heading to the north eastern corner, the famous 'Cockroach Corner' is reached. To be seen at the terminal in this corner is an assortment of cargo carriers, usually related to Latin America in one way or another. Continuing along the northern perimeter road, the next right turn leads past the Trans Air Link ramp and a considerable number of DC-6s, all of which are parked too close to the fence and buildings to be easy to photograph. At the end of this road is a small terminal used for customs clearance by cargo and executive flights arriving at the north side. Views from here are a matter of luck but the Aeromar and Pan Aviation presence can be enriched by the occasional sight of a parked TAN Carga Electra.

Miami is still synonymous with piston aircraft, though obviously on a reducing basis. Conner, Aerial Transit and Regal Air, all names associated with old airliners, have gone, to be replaced by others for a while, no doubt. DC-6s are traditionally in evidence along the northern perimeter. Perhaps the saddest sight, in November 1993, was the breaking up of Dyn-Air's C-97s.

The next street offers closer views of Pan Aviation and a few derelict airliners, and the confined space of the Department of Commerce apron, often with an Electra and/or Hercules. Other aircraft to be seen here can include a Varig wide-body parked for the day before its evening departure. Leaving this street, the first real view of the general aviation activity is seen, with a ramp used by a good number of biz-jets. The next two hundred yards can be a delight to the eye, often with a good selection of Central American executive aircraft, behind which is an enormous apron. The inhabitants of this stretch of tarmac can be the most exotic to be seen in Florida, featuring VIP aircraft of many Latin countries, some of them military, in the company of small airliners old and new. This is not always the case, however. The perimeter tour ends, effectively, at NW 57th Avenue, where a right turn at the lights leads ultimately to the northern taxiway. This road gives access to some large car parking areas and there should always be something of interest to be seen. Some folk have been known to make use of the hire car roof as a vantage point for good photos but it should be remembered that the police have quite a presence on this street, and this sort of activity arouses the wrong sort of interest. The Page Avjet terminal here is not always busy. Disappointment has sometimes been expressed at the lack of long rows of parked biz-jets.

NW 36th Street is a divided highway and turns to the right are numerous. Only one or two are worthwhile, these being at either side of the former Pan Am Training Center. The huge car parks next door overlooked the Eastern maintenance facility, and still offer a good view of the threshold of 27R and executive aircraft taxying along to the holding point as a bonus.

A right turn at the end of NW 36th Street leads onto NW 42nd Avenue (also known as le Jeune Road) and under the approach to Runway 27R. A little further along the road is the entrance to the passenger terminals and the tour is complete.

On the northbound side of le Jeune is the George T Baker Aviation School, which should be of interest to first-time visitors, with its ex-Belize 720 and other interesting types. Apart from the views of aircraft which are the reason for visiting, there are other buildings which may be worth noting. Breakfast in America is one of the joys of the holiday and The Grand Slam at Denny's is highly recommended: their local restaurants are just south of George T Baker and north of

NW 57th Avenue. Lovers of fast food will find the Burger King just across the road from Page Avjet, and good value lunch can be found at Jerry's Catering next to Cargo World. Hotels abound on all sides except the west but those on the north side are of variable quality. Comfortable and quiet is the Ramada Inn in the southwest corner, close to Dolphin Expressway.

Miami International enjoys a reputation as being one of the most interesting airports in the entire world. It is busy, it offers variety and there is no shortage of vantage points. To get the most from it, a car is essential, as most Florida itineraries require independent mobility.

MIAMI FL

OPF   Opa Locka   7m/11km N of MIA

Opa Locka is easily reached from Miami International by heading north up le Jeune to NW 135th Street and following the signs from there. Opa Locka is nurturing its image as a user-friendly airport. There has been a campaign to monitor its success, necessitating answering a one-page questionnaire, in return for which a bag is/was handed over. It contains/contained an Opa Locka T-shirt, details of other local airfields and some other goodies.

There can be few visitors to Florida who would omit a call at Opa Locka from their itinerary. The open plan has gone and fences are now in abundance but access can still be obtained by being sensible. The subjective opinion of what constitutes an interesting aircraft is countered by Opa Locka's inmates, which range from Dauphins and Falcons/Guardians of the US Coastguard, a varied selection of executive aircraft from several countries, DC-6s and other prop-liners, plus plenty of large jets, in storage or under restoration, or just a lot of general aviation with exotic registrations.

The TPI ramp held a number of Electras for some time, one of which bore ALM Cargo titles. A book, written early in 1995, cannot offer reliable information on what may be seen there a year or so later. One visit can result in seeing a number of Beech 18s whilst another, six months later, can offer something else. The aircraft might change, albeit slowly, but the quality seems to remain fairly constant . . . and that means "good".

Taxiway activity is not brisk, so the possibility of a sensible spotter coming into conflict with aircraft on the move is improbable. Other hulks of note include the ex-Prinair Herons and an ex-Rico Beech 18, all of which have been present for many years.

The airport manager's office may grant permission for a look around, and it is unusual to have to get out of the car, once airside, except to take the photographs and check the contents of the hangars. The three large hangars near the control tower have a good variety of inmates, from the USCG at one end to Twin Otters and Latin American twins in the others. Access to the coastguard is best obtained by walking along the path between hangars and apron to the main office, thereby omitting the gatehouse, where negotiations can take a little longer.

'Hangar One' is also guaranteed to contain some interesting types, ranging from American biz-jets to Latin American twins. Despite the amount of fencing around Opa Locka, there have been no reported instances of difficulty in gaining access to the aircraft. The only exception is the Beechcraft facility, where problems have been experienced. Unless things are hectic, the US Coastguard usually allows visitors to photograph their aircraft, including those inside their hangar. All that's normally needed is a polite request and sensible behaviour.

MIAMI FL

MPB   Watson Island   2m/3km E

Heading east from Miami International, along what is now called Dolphin Expressway, the highway leads across the MacArthur Causeway, to Watson Island, with Chalk's Seaplane Base on the right immediately after the bridge. Apart from good views of the (mostly) Turbo Mallards in action, anyone in need of a souvenir T-shirt should ask at the check-in desk.

NAPLES FL
APF   Municipal   2m/3km E

Situated at the eastern end of Alligator Alley, Naples is well worth the trip, if only to get close to a completely different set of aircraft from those seen at Miami. Renowned for its sunshine and, for many years, for its surprisingly large number of executive movements, Naples has, in recent years, acquired a new passenger terminal and a proportionate increase in scheduled services.

Close to the highway is the old terminal and its ramp crammed with bizjets. The informal attitude here should make access for photographs easy. Usually to be seen is the odd aircraft withdrawn from use, though others have been secreted elsewhere.

The new terminal is very pleasant indeed and now features several operators, compared to the times when all scheduled action was dominated by PBA. Fierce competition at Naples means that commuter flights are regular, and the sight of two jets side by side on the small ramp is quite impressive. The enclosure which separates the terminal from the ramp is an ideal spot for any photographer and a short stay during the week should yield a good selection of portraits not easily obtained elsewhere.

As a bonus to the rampside enclosure, there is another spot, just left of the terminal building which overlooks half of the apron and is also good for some different views, also at close quarters. The C-47s of Collier County Mosquito Control are based in their own secure compound, which is reached by continuing round the perimeter road, instead of turning right into the passenger terminal. Naples' most famous residents were the Martin 404s, one of which, in Marco Island Airways colours, is parked next to the now vacant hangar.

ORLANDO FL
MCO   KORL   International   10m/16km SSE

The expansion of Walt Disney's attractions has produced a massive growth in Orlando's economy and the airport has had to move apace. This has been achieved with much success, the facilities being up to date in every way. The new passenger terminal is modern and is linked to the departure satellites by monorails. The edge of the aprons are protected by scenic lagoons which maintain security without fences. Since the view from the landside is good, it is worth paying to park in the car park to obtain some nice photographs of airline movements. The only drawback is the amount of stands on the blind side, where many interesting operators park, out of sight.

A central location is needed to overlook all the action. Above the main terminal is a multi-storey car park. This must not be confused, by people with cars, with Critters A or Critters B garages. Every level of each of the three multi-storey car parks has its own name. In Disney's make-believe world, leaving your car on Tropical Fish or Manatees is more user-friendly than trying to remember B1 or A2. Level 10 on the central garage is Eagles. It offers, instead of shade, a panoramic view of everything that moves. When it gets too hot, go down a level to Pelicans.

There is no shortage of action on the eastern (terminal) side of the airport and yet it is just a fraction of what is to be seen at Orlando. The western side of the field is worthy of some detailed exploration and care should be taken to avoid the Beeline Expressway as a link. Not only does it cost 75 cents each trip between the east and west sides, it is also time-consuming. Instead, it is best to watch out, on leaving the eastern terminal facilities, for Cargo Road and a left turn. This leads to the perimeter of the field and an anti-clockwise circuit passes close to some interesting features. Alternatively, drive under the Expressway and turn left at the lights next to Lee Vista Center. This is Semoran Blvd (SR436) which has a parking area opposite the threshold of 18R, where landing aircraft pass, at close quarters.

Reaching the northeast corner from Cargo Road, the new cargo facilities occupy the site of the original airport complex. Normally parked here is a DC-8 of UPS and a Burlington 707 keeps it company in the early morning. On the other side of the road is a B-52D and a small car park. By following Ports of Call Street past the thresholds of the parallel runways, a left turn at Tradeport Drive is best followed by patience. Despite views of interesting ramps, it is sensible to head south to the far end, make a U turn and carry out the detailed investigations from the right side of the divided highway.

Freezone Street is the last accessible turn which, apart from giving access to the Citation maintenance hangar, is a dead end. The advantage of this is the ability to park up against the fence all day without obstructing an emergency access point. When the runways in use are 36-oriented, this can be the best location on the airport for watching the movements, although those on the far runway are distant. Page Avjet have a charter terminal served by a fair selection of US carriers, and the taxiway passes indecently close to this vantage point.

Returning north, past the charter terminal and the large Page hangar, the next ramp is used by a good variety of executive traffic, followed by a long low freight facility used most regularly by Airborne Express. The maintenance base on the next ramp was occupied by Florida Express and subsequently Braniff. Ramps here, which would otherwise remain empty, have been used for storage: several withdrawn Eastern aircraft have been noted, all within reach of a camera.

The F-101 Voodoo is prominently displayed as a tribute to McCoy AFB, though it is now in delapidated condition, at the end of the street, with only a peek into what remains of the military base to complete the tour. Inmates are the RU-21s and UH-1s of the US Army, most of which can be readily identified.

Having seen all the residents at close quarters, the business of monitoring the movements now remains to be considered. When the 36-runways are in use Freezone Street is the best vantage point, though it can be an unpleasant experience, with a cool northerly wind. Fortunately, Florida is famous for its balmy (at least) climate when the wind is from the south. Orlando is at its best most of the time as the warm weather and prevailing winds also allow the use of the best parking place on the entire perimeter. A vast, though underused, customs car park takes up most of the space next to the holding point at the northern end of the field. From the roof of a hire car, classic portrait shots with no background clutter are easily achieved. The police patrols pass regularly, without any conflict.

The Park and Ride car park, at Cargo and Bear, allows traffic at the north side of the international terminal to be seen, and photographed though once again some artificial means of getting above fence level is needed. The southerly aspect of this location should be borne in mind by the photographer.

Photographers without transport must make other arrangements. About half of Orlando's traffic now seems to use 17/35, much of it being Delta, bound for the Airside 4 concourse. Aeropostal and Transbrasil are the star arrivals here, and most of the British airlines also use it (though not exclusively). Mickey Mouse is also a frequent sight, though he has yet to be seen boarding a plane!

Airside 3 is almost all American Airlines territory, and Airside 1 USAir and dependents. The last concourse, Airside 2 was, at the last visit, nothing more than a concrete base.

ORLANDO FL

ORL	Executive	4m/6km E

When the USAF quit McCoy AFB, Orlando acquired the site for the new civil airport which we know as Orlando International. This also explains the MCO code. Orlando's old airport, formerly known as Herndon, became used for executive traffic, being conveniently placed closer to town. Whilst there are no scheduled services, anyone seeking biz-jets to boost a day's log should consider the detour. It is only a few miles east of the centre of town, and can be reached by taking Ewell Ave, to the south of Colonial Drive (Hwy 50). The shopping mall car parks, off

Interstate 4, offer good views across the field. What can be annoying is the sight of interesting airliners passing overhead on their way into MCO, almost all of which carry no under-wing registration markings.

PALM BEACH FL
LNA   KLNA   County (Lantana)   8m/13km W

Not to be confused with its big brother, Palm Beach International (which is actually WEST Palm Beach!), Palm Beach County is just west of Interstate 95 and is a busy little general aviation field whose main attraction is the maintenance base of Florida Airmotive and the ramp containing a pleasant selection of types.

PANAMA CITY FL
PFN   Bay County   3m/5km N

The airport is not busy by any stretch of the imagination, but it is worth a detour, if anyone wishes to find out what aircraft Bay Aviation are working on. The only guaranteed inmate is the DC-3 used by a spider-research unit.

POMPANO BEACH FL
PPM   1m/1.5km W

The Old Dixie Highway (Highway 811) passes Pompano Beach, though the residents are strictly general aviation, and not a particularly interesting collection either. The Goodyear blimp base has been moved to the west side and the car park can be full when the airship is due to return to base in the evening.

SANFORD FL
SFB   6m/9km SE

Another airfield on many a Florida itinerary, Sanford provided a last resting place for Air Nevada's Beech 18s. In the company of some converted C-45s, one or two examples are still in reasonable condition. Starliner N974R started its life as D-ALAN with Lufthansa. It could end it here. The huge expanse of tarmac sees remarkably little action. Also to be seen here are numbers of S.55 helicopters, some restored for further action but most heaped unceremoniously in a storage compound.

SARASOTA FL
SRQ   Bradenton   5m/8km N

Not the easiest of airports to find from the average map but it is worth the effort. From Interstate 75, take exits 40 or 41 and head west. Whilst it is not busy, the observation deck is either (a) reasonably well placed or (b) a complete waste of time, depending on who is telling the story. It certainly does allow views of aircraft up to 727 size, as well as the occasional Delta 757, but there are other options which may be better. Photography is certainly hampered by plenty of ground handling equipment and some closely spaced lighting columns. The appeal of Sarasota is the relatively large number of executive aircraft on both sides of the field, and withdrawn airliners directly opposite (and distant) from the terminal. The question is: where to go?

Immediately to the right of the terminal, seen from landside, is an elevated grass bank complete with bench seats, right in front of the commuter ramp. For classic shots with even the most basic equipment of such movements as USAir Express Beech 1900s, American Eagle Jetstreams or Comair Brasilias, this is certainly the place. Photos of some taxying aircraft are also possible, depending on the runway in use.

For a different view of the proceedings, other than that to be seen from by the terminal, leave and turn onto University. After the cargo road entrance, take the first left, past the runway approach light towers. Look out for 15th Street, sometimes known as Old Route 301, where there is a very nice place to watch, only a few hundred feet from the runway.

The Dolphin Aviation facility, half a mile to the north on I-41, is always worth checking out. It is close to the runway and allows good access close to the taxiway. A small selection of biz-jets and one or two Nomads might be enough reward but there is always the chance of something a little special.

STUART FL

SUA   Witham Field   2m/3km E

Driving around Florida, seeking saturation coverage of its aviation scene, means a car is essential. There is little to see between West Palm Beach and Melbourne, except possibly for the declining Vero Beach and Stuart. Witham Field is close to the highway, and possibly worth the short detour because the airport has a toilet.

TAMPA FL

TPA   KTPA   International   5m/8km W (bus 30 minutes)

Photographs taken from Tampa's multi-storey car park are always easy to spot and the results are less than ideal, as the subject matter can be upstaged by palm trees in the foreground. It should be noted that there are many other vantage points worthy of exploration. At the centre of things is a semi-circular concourse area, where four terminals have now been joined by a fifth. The approach road leads north from Spruce Street but it should be avoided unless seeking only the overall view from the car park.

Arrival at Tampa airport by car may be via the Memorial Highway or Interstate 92, both of which lead to Spruce Street and a link road on the southern edge of the field. Taking this link road and then turning left, the road follows the perimeter fence, past some stored rental cars, to the large Post Office building. On the right of the road is a car park, where overspill use is permitted. The right turn at the intersection gives access to the service road which runs parallel to the main approach road.

Once the staff car park is passed, the first terminal to be seen is what will become Airside A, the international concourse, scheduled for completion in summer 1995. Airside B, previously occupied by Eastern, was still vacant (early 95) for lack of a tenant. What can be noted, instead of aircraft here, is the occasional lay-by. They are very convenient for a quick photo. The tow-away warnings have more relevance to long-term parking. The stop-go tour continues past the international terminal and the other three, all of which may have well-positioned aircraft for the photographer. Make a note of Airside D, which is used by newcomer Kiwi. Their 727s use the stand closest to the road, so photography could hardly be easier.

The inner perimeter road can be very useful for photographers arriving by air and therefore without a car. By setting up base under the monorail to Terminal E, familiarisation with what parks where can result in extremely good photos, as the aircraft taxi onto their stands. It does require a certain amount of energy, especially when a couple of interesting aircraft arrive at more or less the same time. Inside the accessible Terminal E, the glass really is far too dark for photography but the view of Runway 36L is excellent.

Leaving the central complex, the close proximity of the taxiway and runway on the right are to be noted before making a left exit for the Post Office car park. A short walk back across the main road, and the aircraft on the taxiway are at the perfect distance for any photographer. Since most of Tampa's traffic lands on 36L and more than half of it leaves the same way, this is the single best place to stand. Sitting has its problems, however: it only takes one fire ant to give you a bite and it's time to look for somewhere else!

Up until lunchtime, when the sun starts to shine down the centreline of the runway, good photos are easy to take but afternoon options aren't quite as clearly defined. Alternative vantage points of such quality are rare and more than one at any airport would be asking too much.

Returning around the southern perimeter, the Beechcraft Executive Center screens many of its inhabitants from view but the ramp still has quite a few executive occupants, best seen from the patch of waste land off West Columbus Drive. Also to be seen from here are the Mosquito Control DC-3s on the far side, reached by way of Dale Mabry Highway (I-92) and Tampa Bay Boulevard.

The internal angle of the field, where West Shore and Tampa Bay Boulevards meet, is occupied by the Suncoast Air Center, a fixed base operator handling more bizjets, but views along the West Shore Boulevard are hard come by. For a good view of the departures of feederliners, the vacant ground next to Beech Exec is convenient but, once again, only in the morning.

Hillsborough Avenue, at the north of West Shore Boulevard, forms the northern airfield boundary. Look out for the large blue sign for the bowling alley. The car park is almost directly under the flightpath, when traffic is landing on 18R. During the mornings, this is an ideal place to take approach shots, with the bonus of there being less ants than at the other end of the field. A left turn leads into the cargo complex, which is a dead end. Whilst none of the aircraft parked at the cargo centre are visible from the road, the southern edge of the car park overlooks the main terminal apron. Perhaps a little further from the action than the Zone Technique car park at Charles de Gaulle, it does offer a reasonably close (but not comprehensive) view of aircraft moving around the taxiways and apron.

Tampa's international movements aren't quite as common as one might hope. The majority of these are Air Canada A320s, but Air Jamaica and Cayman Airlines 727s are regular. Northwest's acquisition of Republic increased the airline's share of the traffic but the number flights reduced after rationalisation. Delta and USAir are starting to enjoy near-monopoly status here, as at many other airports, but America West 737s, Omni Air Express and Kiwi 727s offer some variety.

TITUSVILLE-COCOA BEACH FL

TIX   Space Center Executive   2m/3km S

Known to old Florida hands as Tico, a visit is usually made because it isn't far from Patrick AFB or Cape Canaveral. The reason for the diversion used to be the presence of the ex-Danish Air Force Dakotas which might still be there. Apart from these, there is normally little or no traffic of note.

VERO BEACH FL

VRB   KVRB   Municipal   1m/1.5km W

This small airport was the home of Piper Aircraft's Cheyenne assembly plant. Today it is better known as a ghost town. The last report referred to the workforce numbering a mere twenty. All the activity that remains to be seen, as a reminder of better days, is the big training school's fleet of Piper twins.

The small airline passenger terminal building handles the occasional feederliner and the ramp is seen at close quarters from the grassed enclosure between the building and the apron. If the commuter flights are few and far between, the ramp does offer a small collection of executive aircraft as consolation.

WEST PALM BEACH FL

PBI   KPBI   International   3m/5km SW

The affluence of West Palm Beach is conspicuously displayed along the southern perimeter of the airport. While the terminal is quaint, with views of the ramp through the fence between the buildings, the presence of the airliners is totally eclipsed by the prodigious quantity of biz-jets. The various Fixed Base Operators handle an astonishing array of aircraft and a log of fifty biz-jets was considered the norm, though this was before the deepening of America's recession.

Apart from a good selection of airline traffic, up to 767 size, the south side of the field has two enormous ramps, both offering much, and both worth exploration. Unique to West Palm Beach is the regular presence of the US Navy's C-27, which may be parked with little consideration for the photographic fraternity, close to the Jet Aviation FBO. Lovers of older aircraft are not usually disappointed, as Renown Aviation Convairs are usually to be seen.

ATLANTA GA

FTY   Fulton County   2m/3km N

A lengthy stay in the Atlanta area means that Hartsfield will not be the only airport visited. For a change from Delta's fleet, there are two other fields of note. The first is Fulton County, some ten miles north of Hartsfield. Though there is a general aviation terminal on the north side of ATL, clearly it does not accommodate anything like the number of aircraft likely to be used by such a prosperous community as Atlanta.

A drive around the perimeter gives the impression that Fulton County contains most of Atlanta's (indeed Georgia's) general aviation. Travelling a few miles further north proves this not be so.

ATLANTA GA

PDK   de Kalb-Peachtree   12m/19km NE

Situated to the northeast of Atlanta, off Interstate Highway 85, is a general aviation field much used by the business fraternity. Anyone with an interest in executive transport should ensure a visit here. The observation area is popular enough for a commentary on the public address system.

ATLANTA GA

ATL   KATL   William B Hartsfield   9m/15km S (train 15 minutes)

Hub operations are now becoming a common way of operating airlines, with many airports in the United States being dominated by one or two carriers, just as they are in Europe. The main difference is that, in Europe, the hub is usually the base for the national airline, such as British Airways at Heathrow and Air France at Charles de Gaulle. Atlanta was very much a forerunner of this practice in America, with 75% of all movements (and there are a lot) operated by Delta and Eastern. ASA included, Delta's share of the movements at Atlanta currently stands at an astonishing 81%. Whether time spent at such an airport as Atlanta is an enjoyable experience is subjective, and reports suggest that it is highly regarded by many. The concourses are served by an underground people-mover, and many visitors will choose to investigate the situation fully for themselves. There are now five to choose from, but only one is reserved for 'Other Airlines'. Other airlines now include Aeropostal MD-83s, Lufthansa A340s on Saturdays, Swissair 747-400s and new operators, like Kiwi and Valujet.

It will be apparent very quickly that comprehensive logging (if such a thing is possible at all) involves quite a lot of travelling, made worse by the fact that both sides of each concourse can't be seen at the same time. The glass through which everything is viewed is dark - too dark? Photographers will make up their own minds . . . sunny days do help. If any reader is tempted by the prospect of fleet-watching without recourse to touring North America, a visit to Concourses C and D at Atlanta will ensure the best chance, as they overlook the runways and the cargo area, thereby allowing much of the action to be monitored.

Concourse E, for international flights, was opened well in advance of its target date: in time for the 1996 Olympic Games. The former international gates have been redesignated.

At each side of the concourses are pairs of parallel runways: 8/26 to the north and 9/27 to the south. The numbering of gates on each concourse is consistent, so that C1 and D1 are both at the same end though they do not necessarily offer the same facilities. C1 has windows at the end, offering good views of the taxiway and runways, as well as being over-run with commuter passengers. A1 does not have this window feature, so viewing is inferior. There is little, apart from aprons, taxiways and runways to be seen on the southern side, as Delta's base occupies a large area between the runways, with everything else to the north.

Because concourse-based locations for watching aircraft only offer limited possibilities, alternatives are bound to be sought. Since photographic subject matter is limited, a central overview would be ideal. Multi-storey car parks are often suitable, and Atlanta offers a choice of two such elevated vantage points. The South Deck overlooks the thresholds of Runways 9L/R, but looks into the sun, and prevailing winds mean that the 27 direction is most used. The North economy parking lot offers a view of landing aircraft, suitable for many photographers. Riverdale Bridge, over I-85, offers an alternative view of aircraft landing on the southern runways. This spot is only for the fit and dedicated - it's a long walk, the nearest legal parking being half a mile away.

The northern perimeter contains substantial cargo facilities, the vacant Eastern maintenance base and Hangar One, though photographs are only possible at the executive facility, with a car park allowing a decent view of the inmates. Watching the aircraft at the thresholds of Runways 8L and 8R offers some variety to the day, but photographers will be disappointed by the elevated aspect of the runway's end. Delta's maintenance hangars are centrally placed at the eastern end of the field but portraits of aircraft parked here are rare.

Opened in late 1992, the Stouffel Concourse Hotel overlooks Hangar One, and south facing rooms on the upper floors will prove attractive, though the cost of such rooms may be out of reach to some.

West of the terminal complex is the MARTA (Metropolitan Atlanta Rapid Transit Authority) railway station, which supplies the link with the city, some fifteen minutes away. Though the airport sits in the middle of three Interstate highways, I-85 is that which actually serves the passenger terminals. :

Atlanta is now a major transatlantic gateway to much of America and, as such, it ensures that vast quantities of registrations are collected at the start of a holiday. The return trip with Delta often entails the use of Cincinnati, thereby allowing two airports to be sampled en route.

AUGUSTA GA

AGS   Bush Field   10m/16km S

Though this is the city's main gateway, its traffic is mostly Jetstreams operating feeder services to Atlanta for Delta. Jet traffic is mostly restricted to DC-9s plus some USAir F.28s, whose

SD3.60 feeders are also in evidence. Augusta is still quiet enough for the casual observer to be able to pursue his interest without problems being encountered.

AUGUSTA GA
DNL   Daniel Field   5m/8km W

Very much Augusta's 'other' airport, it is small but densely packed with light aircraft. The passenger terminal is used mostly by executives travelling in corporate and chartered air taxi aircraft, a good proportion of them being jets.

GRIFFIN GA
6AZ   Spalding County   2m/3km S

About halfway between Atlanta and Macon, the airfield is on Highway 155, and worth a detour. If it moves, it probably has only one engine: it's all Cessnas and Pipers - well, nearly all. A lot of trees were cleared to make the airfield possible, so open views aren't to be expected. The single runway is surrounded by light aircraft and trees but arrival here gives an altogether different impression. The first sight, to the right, is the Academy Airlines hangar beside which are a couple of Carvairs, N83FA and N89FA. The airfield reception area is housed in the hangar next door. Ask and it shall be given.

Only N83FA was operational, at the last report. Close attention to detail around here will reveal several component parts of another Carvair, N155243, the fin still bearing its Pacific Air Express titles. If future visits to Griffin reveal no sign of N83FA, it may have been relocated permanently to Bear Creek (q.v.).

Before getting back in the car, photos safely in the camera, take a look down the far end of the airfield. At either side of the runway are a couple of grassed clearings. Half a dozen C-47s have been seen here. Two of them are used by Academy Airlines but the others are unlikely to leave under their own power. A few Beech 18s can also be expected, parked around here.

LA GRANGE GA
LGC   Callaway

Not an airport at all, though no apologies are made for including La Grange. There aren't too many places in the world where a Carvair can be seen. Make the most of it while it lasts. Some way southwest of Atlanta, and quite a long way out of town, the road leads to a crossroads at the perimeter. Instead of turning left and heading for the general aviation terminal, go straight ahead. The road stops at a gate next to a hangar. Beyond the garages in 1993 was N103, wearing Pacific Express colours but no titles. Since the parking fees were being paid, this aircraft is considered an asset by its owner. Whether it will remain at La Grange is another matter. It's been here since 1989 - so far so good.

MACON GA
MCN   KMCN   Lewis B Wilson   8m/13km S

This airport is also known as Middle Georgia Regional, and should not be confused with Herbert Smart Airport, at Wheeler Heights, some 6 miles east of town. Neither the map nor an airline timetable give any impression of what the airport is like, and it would be easy to underestimate its status.

An F-86 Sabre on a pole is displayed at the airport entrance, in recognition of the Air National

Guard base, seen to the right. This is not Warner-Robins, which is further out. The passenger terminal handles a modest amount of feeder traffic, many of which are ASA Brasilias. The ASA maintenance hangar is in the southwest corner of the airfield, across the runway from Zantop's facility, which can prove a disappointment. Reports suggest that the hoped-for Electras are nowhere to be seen, and a DC-8 might be all the only consolation.

SAVANNAH GA

SAV   KSAV   International   9m/15km W

The name of Savannah means only one thing to the biz-jet afficionado: Gulfstream Aerospace Corporation. The scheduled 727s and DC-9s may come and go, albeit thinly spread, all day, but people come to Savannah to see completed Gulfstream corporate jets. The facility is located, not surprisingly, on Gulfstream Road, so there can be no excuse for missing it. This is where the construction process is completed, and the aircraft are rolled out.

The other operators of any note at Savannah are Key Airlines with their small hub for 727s, and the Georgia Air National Guard. To be seen on the far side of the field from the passenger terminal, there are normally half a dozen or so C-130s on the ground.

HANA HI

HNM   PHHN   Municipal   4m/6km NW

Reports from the Hawaiian Islands are so infrequent, it took some time to confirm this was the only airport at the eastern tip of Maui. The confusion arose from the two designators: normally three-letter IATA designators in the Pacific are prefixed with a letter P, for the four letter ICAO code. This does not apply to several of the Hawaiian airports.

Apart from a small number of light aircraft, the only visitors here are the regular Aloha Island Twin Otters. It is probably the least interesting of the three airports on the island, the others being Kahului and Kapalua.

HILO HI

ITO   PHTO   General Lyman   2m/3km SE

Hawaii Island's Hilo International (Lyman Field) used to handle a selection of long-haul traffic but this now uses Honolulu almost exclusively. Inter-island services are mostly a restricted range of DC-9s and 737s, operated by the competing Aloha and Hawaiian Air.

HONOLULU HI

HNL   PHNL   International   6m/9km NW

This extremely large airfield is to be found on the south coast of Oahu, between the evocative Waikiki Beach and Pearl Harbour. Runways 04/22L/R are placed diagonally to the main passenger terminal, whilst Runway 8L/26R is aligned roughly parallel with the terminal. Reclaimed land in the bay was used to construct Runway 8R/26L, totally remote from any vantage point.

The international terminal is new, and very impressive, especially when its open-fronted first floor observation level is first seen. This main terminal has one central pier projecting into the apron and, at both ends, L-shaped piers pointing outwards. The prospect which is offered is considerably better than what can be seen, however, because the traffic is essentially the same wide-body movements at Los Angeles or San Francisco, the view is due south, and four of the stands are arranged for the aircraft to park nose-in. For much of the time the view can be restricted by at least one large aircraft in the foreground. At either side of the terminal are maintenance and cargo facilities where a good range of aircraft is to be seen, and the ramp immediately to the left/east of the terminal contains quite a number of smaller aircraft.

An inter-island terminal has been opened. The building is fully enclosed, with air bridges. Behind is a six storey car park, from which the activity can be seen, though long lenses will be needed for photos.

Leaving the terminal area, the enthusiast makes his way to Lagoon Drive, at the eastern end of the field, for the other ramps. These are on the far side of Runway 4R/22L, and it is here that most of the local operators will be found. The essential hire car will enable the considerable length of these ramps to be explored, with many interesting operators to be seen, though the fence obstructs the view, and use will have to be made of the car's mobile elevated vantage point. Quite frustrating at times, this is a very individual part of the world, and what is seen (and photographed) here will be a peculiar mixture of old and new types in strictly local colours.

Gone are the YS-11s and most of the old piston aircraft. The two Carvairs, N5459M and N5459X, were still present early in 1992, together with one or two Skyvans used for Federal Express parcels services. Movement is not a feature on Lagoon Drive: Islanders, Shorts, Doves and Herons can still be seen, together with the inevitable Beech 18s. Their days are numbered.

The western portion of the field is occupied by military bases, Hickam AFB and the ANG, both having their taxiway access at the threshold of Runway 8L. Without authorised access to one or other of these bases, identification of military aircraft is difficult and photography almost impossible.

For the most spectacular view of the airport, a trip to the Aloha Tower is essential. This overlooks the harbour and Runway 8R/26L. Through a long focus lens, the departing aircraft seem to be aiming for the tower. Admission is free, and there is a car park which officially allows only thirty minutes parking. The alternative is to take 'The Bus'.

Also on the island of Oahu is Dillingham field. This could be dismissed as a glider-towing strip, were it not for the presence of the O-1s which do the towing. A hangar contains a Voodoo and an H-52 plus some other antiques.

KAHULUI HI
OGG   PHOG   Maui Island   5m/8km E

Now largely eclipsed by the busier West Maui airport, there are few movements of any interest here. However, to anyone wishing to record Hawaii's aviation scene, it will be an essential destination. For the rest, it is barely worth the time and trouble.

KAPALUA HI
JHM   West Maui   4m/6km S

Until 1987, Maui was served only by Kahului airport but it is more than an hour's drive from the major resort area on the west coast of the island, considerably longer than the flying time. Hawaiian Airlines formed a subsidiary company to develop this rival airport, on the west side. The impact on local aviation was significant: Aloha bought Princeville Airways and Mid-Pacific did a deal with Reeves Aviation, to be sure of operating the short-field airliners which were needed.

The small terminal building has views through glass, and space at either side from which to watch a very restricted number of aircraft operating shuttles. The ultimate in personalised licence plates: the designator code is JHM, as in John H Magoon, the airline's chairman who masterminded the project.

LANAI HI
LNY   PHNY   City   4m/6km SW

Another coastal strip which, like Hoolehua, wakes occasionally to the sound of an Aloha Island Air arrival.

LIHUE HI
LIH   PHLI   Municipal   2m/3km E

The island of Kauai is the only other, apart from Hawaii to be served from Honolulu by jet traffic with any regularity, although the same DC-9s and 737s visit Hilo. These schedules are operated to Lihue Municipal Airport, whilst elsewhere on the island, the Twin Otters use Princeville.

MOLOKAI HI
MKK   PHMK   Hoolehua   10m/16km SW

Another island, for those hopping about with an airpass. Once again, the scheduled Twin Otter flight will cause the biggest stir until it leaves, and everything goes quiet again. The Hawaiian Islands are exotic but they don't offer excitement at every turn.

PRINCEVILLE HI
HPV   1/1.5km E

The last entry for Hawaii is, like several others, about a small coastal airport, carved out of some fairly dense forest on Kauai as a landing strip for the Twin Otter service. The jungle has now given way largely to farmland for growing the inevitable pineapples.

BOISE ID
BOI   Air Terminal   3m/5km S

A real reason is needed to visit Idaho. Nice scenery is not enough, as the Rocky Mountains offer plenty of attractions in neighbouring states. Boise is, however, an extremely memorable airport. Gowen Field, as it is still known locally, is obviously scenic and it does offer a variety, though not quantity, with Horizon Air supplying many of the movements. Larger jet traffic is modest but nice. There can be few better places in the USA to see an America West 737 at close quarters. The general aviation terminal also handles a few biz-jet movements.

The Idaho Air National Guard base sees little activity during the week but, at weekends, part-time fliers climb into their jets for a spot of fun at the tax-payer's expense. The Army National Guard also has a base here, and their helicopters can be seen from the adjacent car park.

COEUR D'ALENE ID
COE   10m/16km NW

Empire Airlines. That name sums up the airport. Twenty miles east of Spokane, just across the border in Washington State, Couer d'Alene is eclipsed by it bigger neighbour. The Empire base can be relied upon to provide close contact with their small fleet, especially at weekends, when many of their F.27s are present. Some wear Federal Express colours, for whom services are operated.

IDAHO FALLS ID

IDA   Fanning Field   2m/3km NW

The smart, modern terminal offers no views of the apron and, for the greater part of the average day, this is quite appropriate, as there is little to see. Occasional movements by Skywest and Horizon Air link Idaho Falls with the outside world, and a FedEx feeder Caravan occupies a separate cargo apron, awaiting its evening flight to Salt Lake City.

CHICAGO

World-renowned as a major centre of aviation activity, Chicago is served by three airports: O'Hare is obviously the main gateway, while Midway handles an increasing amount of traffic, due to its relative proximity to the centre, and Merrill C Meigs is literally downtown and therefore handy for executives to get to the business district. These three airports are separated by relatively short distances which take a disproportionate time to cover. Traffic in Chicago is never light and the route between Midway and O'Hare passes through some of the rougher parts of the metropolitan area, on terribly maintained roads.

A trip to Chicago will normally involve at least one night's stay, and the choice of hotel will be an important consideration. Des Plaines, Park Ridge, Rosemont and Schiller Park are neighbourhoods close to Orchard Place (hence ORD) where hotels are handy (yet reasonably priced) but the Holiday Inn at Schiller Park is only recommended for the deaf, being close to the end of one runway and also to a busy highway!

CHICAGO IL

CGX   Merrill C Meigs   1m/1.5km E

This small airport is located on the shore of Lake Michigan, with Soldier Field (home ground for the Chicago Bears) behind it. Because this airport is so close to the business district, and because its (short) runway is quite remote from noise-sensitive areas, there is a reasonably good selection of executive movements, and some scheduled services are operated here during the week.

Closely comparable to Toronto's Island airport, where the STOLport capability has been used to the best effect, Meigs still seems under-used but its charming little terminal does have an observation area, very close indeed to traffic parking at the terminal.

CHICAGO IL

MDW KMDW   Midway   10m/16km SW

Midway is the home of one of the very first 'no frills' airlines to operate in the States and the Midway Airlines fleet has grown considerably from its humble beginnings. It is also served by Southwest, the Texas counterpart of Midway Airlines, and traffic is quite brisk. A map shows the field to be a square reservation bounded on all four sides by residential development. Because it is such an old airport, the layout is perimeter-oriented, which is quite good news for the enthusiast.

Arrival by car at the passenger terminal can be followed by investigation of vantage points there, and it becomes obvious that these are few. A photo of a Midway airliner on its home territory is something of a rarity, though the view from next to gate C5 reveals a limited angle of vision through which airline traffic passes. For those without a hire car, this may represent the best location to log, and photograph, a proportion of the executive traffic.

A clockwise tour of the perimeter ensures an easy access to each turning, road traffic being on the right, and the western side of the field is occupied mostly by hangars filled with executive aircraft. The ramps, too, contain a worthwhile assortment, though not all the aircraft are going to be seen. The north side is where most of Chicago's general aviation is to be found; considerable numbers of single-engined aircraft are present, though few are very interesting. In the southeast corner is another batch of executive and light aircraft but access to this FBO is difficult, since the majority of the eastern side is bordered by buildings. The runways are in the middle of the field and there are no vantage points close to them, where a camera can be used to any great effect.

CHICAGO IL

ORD   KORD   O'Hare   21m/33km NW

Chicago's premier airport has the reputation of being one of the busiest in the world and its name needs no introduction to most enthusiasts. The central terminal area is surrounded by runways on all sides, and traffic lands and takes off on almost all of them, regardless of wind direction. Since there is no single point where the bewildering number of movements can all be seen, it is an extremely difficult business to gain a complete picture of what is going on. If ever the enthusiast needed a guide to an airport from his own point of view, O'Hare is a real example, since research and decisions should prove to be essential before arriving.

The spotter, armed with binoculars, notebook and pen, can spend a day here and be certain that his log will be a considerable one. Selectivity as to what particular movements are most sought will determine a single vantage point, and a number of aircraft (and even a number of airlines) will not be seen at all. The notebook will be full but by no means complete, and the more discerning visitors are advised to have a plan of action.

Photographers who prefer taxying and ramp shots, and who don't like taking photos through glass, need not bother coming to O'Hare as the many views of the aprons are all from the terminal windows, and close access to taxiways is rare. The multi-storey car park shares centre stage with the expensive Hilton Hotel, and arranged round these buildings are the passenger terminals in a large semi-circle. Even from the windows of Terminals E, F, H and K, there is more to see than at most other airports in the world but it is still frustrating to think how much activity is missed.

What were known as Terminals Two and Three are Y shaped, leading to piers now called Terminals E and F (in 2) H and K (in 3). This means that the gates, and aircraft parking at them, in the fork of the Y can remain hidden from view so they can park, and leave, without being seen. The plan of the central area shows the general disposition of the buildings and detailed notes of what can be seen are quite spurious: all the major operators in the USA have scheduled flights to O'Hare, so their aircraft are to be seen, somewhere or other. By walking from one end of the complex to the other (often several times a day) all the various windows can be found, and many offer good views of the ramps.

Constant motion from one end of the terminals to the other makes for a long day, so a permanent base must be found. Perhaps the most likely candidate is a seat near Gate C2 in the United satellite terminal. It offers comprehensive coverage of all movements passing round the north side. Delta's Gate L10 serves a similar function at the other end. L10 has the possible advantage of facing the international terminal, though at the expense of missing virtually all of the considerable quantity of United movements.

On the north side of the terminal area is a large limousine park, bigger than most airports' taxi ranks, and this offers a north facing view of one of the inner taxiways, where some good photographs can be obtained. To the east of the international terminal is a small general aviation ramp and a cargo area used by TWA and Continental. In the northeast corner of the airfield are bases for the USAF and Illinois ANG, who operate KC-135s, and there are a few locations in the airport where the serials can be read off. Closer inspection is impossible without having made prior arrangements for a visit.

The main cargo area occupies the southwest corner of the field, and is occupied by UPS, FedEx, United, American and Northwest. Identification of aircraft, once they have entered this area, can be difficult from the passenger terminals. Also visible, from some parts of the terminal area, are the various maintenance hangars, in the northwest corner of the field. The drive to this area is a long one, and the reward for the effort is nil. Few aircraft are normally present in the daylight hours, and the whole area is only accessible through a security gate.

CHICAGO IL

| PWK | Pal-Waukee Municipal | 7m/11km N of ORD |

Midway is linked to O'Hare by helicopter services, and other fields may be worthy of a visit, since they are now profiting from downtown congestion with similar helicopter links. One of these is Pal-Waukee, seven miles north of O'Hare at the intersection of Highways 45 and 21, where a selection of the region's general aviation can be seen at reasonably close quarters.

A serious interest in airliners will probably mean that the drive north from O'Hare is not considered. Biz-jet buffs will need to make the trip, to be sure of the chance for another twenty or so for their logbooks. This is easy to achieve without taking the trouble to negotiate entry to any of the hangars.

DU PAGE IL

| DPA | County | 30m/48km W of Chicago |

Time to spare in Chicago may also make a visit to Du Page possible. It is west of the city on Highway 64. Much like Pal-Waukee, this is a destination for the enthusiast anxious to visit all the local fields for quantity, regardless of the interest (or lack of it). This is by far the largest general aviation field in the Chicago area, though only half a dozen biz-jets are likely on the average visit. It is the scrap compound opposite the main field which invites some real scrutiny. Among many other wrecks are the mortal remains of Falcon 20 LN-FOE which was written off in 1973. Also present, ex-TWA 707 N742TW, the active life of which came to an abrupt halt at Cincinnati in 1967.

GARY IN

| GYY | Municipal | 2m/3km W |

Accessbile from, and close to, I-90 is Gary Municipal Airport, just across the state border from Chicago and Illinois, in Indiana. It may be close to the highway but a river runs between the road and the airport. To get there, take the Hwy 12 exit north, along Columbus Drive and Industrial Highway. Scheduled traffic is limited to the occasional Navajo Chieftain.

INDIANAPOLIS IN

| IND | KIND | International | 8m/13km SW |

Exit 11 off I-74 leads to Airport Expressway. Arrival by car normally means leaving it in the Remote Lot, which only costs $5. The free shuttle bus takes you to the passenger terminal's upper level. The large, spacious terminal building is arranged in a twisted W shape, with two piers extending from the centre tip. The layout is so open that the moderate traffic seems very thinly spread. There isn't one single spot which allows all the aircraft to be seen at close quarters but there is no shortage of windows from which to see particular movements. Most of them are slightly tinted but many of the doors are clear glazed.

The reference, in the last edition, to the observation deck did it a severe injustice. There have been protests! It is located where Concourses B and C meet, and almost everything can be seen, though much of it from rather a distance. In winter, only the indoor portion is accessible. The railings to the outdoor deck are just at the wrong height, making work with a camera difficult. Something to stand on, like a solid camera case, is an advantage. Whilst a 200mm zoom lens is good enough for most shots, some of the movements, particularly on Runway 5L/23R, needs 300mm. A loud-speaker relays Air Traffic Control's conversation with the aircraft. Not far from the American Airlines gates, the deck allows most aircraft on the move to be witnessed though the sun can be a problem in the afternoon. Mornings are definitely best.

About half the traffic is USAir, the remainder being thinly divided between the other domestic carriers. Daily scheduled departures total something like two hundred. For close-up views of American Trans Air, gates C7 and C10 can be worth the walk, though A1 to A3 are also used. Gate C6 is used by Valujet, and C8/9 are for Southwest Airlines. Concourse D, used by USAir, overlooks the distant executive apron and cargo areas. American Trans Air's maintenance base and the general aviation ramps are visible from various parts of the terminal area.

LIBERAL KS

LBL	George Welch Municipal	2m/3km W

The three runways form a triangle, and the facilities are positioned on the east side of the field. Only the bare minimum of scheduled operations, however: Mesa operate three Beech 1900s during the week. To the south of the passenger terminal is a museum with exhibits inside and out, spaced to allow photography.

WICHITA KS

BEC	Beech	6m/9km E

Wichita is peppered with airports and airfields, all of which are worthy of exploration. Beech Aircraft Corporation is a very major aviation constructor, yet it isn't the only show in town. Beech Field is on the north side of Highway 54. Webb and Greenwich Roads are the western and eastern boundaries. The drive up Webb possibly as far as JABARA Airport (for general aviation) on 29th Street, then back down Greenwich. What can be seen will include King Airs and Beech 1900s. Log them and go, as that's all there is to do at this field. It is not the end of Beech's presence in Wichita, however, because there are two maintenance areas at Mid-Continent.

If the circuit of Beech doesn't include Jabara, it can be done separately!

WICHITA KS

CEA	Cessna Aircraft	7m/11km SE

The Cessna finishing centre is close enough to the northern boundary of McConnell Air Force Base to be almost part of it. Because of this, the view from Cessna Finance is more interesting to military enthusiasts. The F-16s can be seen and their serials, or most of them, can be logged. From Beech Field, a few blocks towards town leads to Rock Road. A left turn (south) along Rock Road passes under the turnpike, Interstate 35. Cessna Aircraft is on the right, and can't be missed.

McCONNELL Air Force Base is the other enclave of the military base to the western end of the field. The city's link with Boeing goes back a long way. The B-47 on the gate reflects this, in the company of an F-105 and other ex-Kansas Air National Guard fighters. To reach Boeing skirt round the perimeter or reach it direct from town by George Washington Boulevard. Apart from leading to McConnell this road also passes the aptly named Planeview Park. Boeing is to the south.

WICHITA KS
ICT   KICT   Mid-Continent   6m/9km W

At the opposite end of town from Beech, the airport entrance is also off Highway 54. To the north of the road is Lear Jet Inc, previously Gates Lear Jet. For a view of what is out in the open, there are a few places on the perimeter. Weekends are definitely good for visiting and viewing. Much the same applies to Cessna's facility. The factory area is enormous, with several assembly plants. The road marked 'Shipping' off what is believed to be Tyler, has no security check. It offers the best view. The purpose of production lines is to complete aircraft for delivery. This means that they are not supposed to spend weeks parked outside on the tarmac. Numbers of pre-delivery aircraft at Lear Jet and Cessna are not great.

Jet traffic at the main airport is a good mix, though the pace during the day is only moderate. There are plenty of 737s and DC-9s plus an assortment of commuters serving Kansas City. At O'Hare and Atlanta, it's possible to let the aircraft come to the airport. At Wichita, what is to be seen needs exploration. Cargo carriers at Mid-Continent supply a range of aircraft but, once everything has been logged, it's time to move on.

CINCINNATI KY
CVG   KCVG   Northern Kentucky International   12m/19km SW

The city may be in Ohio, but the airport is on the south side of the Ohio River, in Kentucky. Its scheduled traffic is brisk, though limited to mostly a mixture of Comair and Delta. The twin runways are aligned 18/36, with the terminal area facing south, towards Runway 9/27, directly into the midday sun. To the west of the passenger terminal is a large cargo ramp, and to the east is a small Delta hangar. The main Comair base is on the south side, though a long way from the passenger terminal's windows.

There was once an observation deck but it has been closed for several years and the only chance to witness the movements at close quarters is to pass through the security check and watch from one of the lounge areas. An early start is recommended, to witness the departure of Comair's rather large fleet of Metros, Bandeirantes, Brasilias and SF.340s on their first flights of the day. Some may not return before dark, which happens early, due to the strongly tinted windows. Terminal 1 gave a very good view of the Comair ramp but the airline has subsequently been reported to have a new terminal for its own use.

For a general view of proceedings, the top level of the car park oppsite Terminal 3 is probably as good as anywhere. Two of the three runways and the cargo ramp can be seen. The new international building, an island on the far side of the main apron, obscures much of the action. Being international, it's the usual story: passengers only, of course.

LEXINGTON KY
LEX   KLEX   Blue Grass   6m/9km W

Don't be tempted to use the free 15-minute parking, as a visit here can take longer than seems likely at first. By road from town, take Versailles Road (US 60). The main passenger terminal is surprisingly good for anyone who wants to stick around all day, log and photograph a selection of aircraft, without demanding huge quantities in the logbook. Most of the traffic is

Delta and USAir 737s, but American Eagle and USAir Express Jetstreams, ASA Brasilias and United Express BAe 146s are also regular movements.

The upper level of the terminal is glazed, and the view from it is panoramic. Photography through the glass presents no problems (if you like that sort of thing) yet there is more good news: not only are the gates, on the floor below, accessible for close-ups, there is also a staircase, to the right-hand side of the concourse, which leads up to an observation deck.

Movements on Runway 26 and its taxiway are seen at close quarters from the area around Gates C4 and C5 - everything else, including the Southern Jet Hangar and Island Creek, from the central area of the main concourse. Outside the Aviation Museum of Kentucky are a C-46, B-24 and B-29. Lexington might not be the busiest airport in the world but it is certainly one of the more enjoyable.

NEW ORLEANS LA
MSY   KMSY   International   13m/20km NW

An Airpass makes New Orleans a good destination. Obviously the city has more character and tourist attractions than many others, and the airport (known locally as Moisant) offers plenty to see for a limited amount of time. Interest wears off after a lengthy stay, and only photographers with patience enjoy stays of more than a day. Inside the passenger terminal, the Delta area is poor for photography but the large windows elsewhere make up for this. Miami, Carnival and American Airlines all come commendably close to the camera, with even a chance to get a photo of the elusive American Airlines F.100s. West of the terminal, but out of view, is Lafon Air Park. Used by general aviation, this apron is worth the walk for close-up views.

Outside the terminal area, the perimeter is at its most attractive to the east. Airport Access Road offers everything. Traffic on all three of the runways, subject to normal wind conditions, passes (or passes over) this road. For the photographer, this road is what Americans call a turkey-shoot. You can't go wrong, assuming you park your car in one of the side streets, rather than on the main road. The No Stopping signs are strictly enforced.

In the mornings, something will be needed to stand clear above the perimeter fence, to allow high quality photos. In the afternoons, Washington Street, on the other side of the runway, is an ideal spot when Runway 19 is in (normal) use.

NEW ORLEANS LA
NEW   KNEW   Lakefront   6m/9km NE

A brief geography lesson might be in order: New Orleans actually faces north, onto Lake Pontchartrain. The Mississippi passes round the south side of the city in a loop, hence the term Crescent City. Lakefront Airport sits on a promontory, just north of I-10. Take exit 240 or 243.

This is the old airport, where the majority of the region's biz-jet population is to be found in the company with plenty of other general aviation. Most of the action can be seen from the fence.

BOSTON MA
BOS   KBOS   Gen E L Logan International   4m/6km E (train 10 mins)

Almost completely surrounded by water, like Vancouver and San Francisco, Boston is similarly frustrating for the enthusiast in offering very little in the way of compensation. For someone without a camera, the multi-storey car parks offer panoramic views of the proceedings, though even a good pair of binoculars may be inadequate to read off every registration.

Obviously the best view of any airport is from the top of the control tower. The top may not be accessible at Logan but the 17th Floor is. Probably of no use at all to a photographer, it is quite superb for comprehensive coverage of activity . . . truly fantastic! To the front is a view of most of the airport, with the biz-jets and Federal Express to the right. At the back are the other freight and commuter areas.

The value of alternative vantage points will be dependant on the runways in use but Terminal B has its own multi-storey car park, offering what is probably the best chance to get close to much of the action, as it is reasonably centrally located. All traffic can be seen, and most of it identified, the bonus being it is reasonably close to the executive terminals. Terminal A, formerly used by Eastern, is the commuter terminal. Construction is scheduled to start in 1995 of a completely new landside terminal on this site, with a fourteen-gate airside terminal.

After discovering that none of the car parks allows close scrutiny of a fair proportion of all the movements, it may be worth considering walking through the terminals, the darkened glass of which allows reasonable views of most aprons.

On leaving the central terminal complex, it is wise to look out for a right turn after the Hilton Hotel. This leads to the cargo area and often features a healthy selection of visitors, ranging from Electras to 727s. Since the small-package business is founded on departure times between 5pm and 6pm, the aircraft which have been parked all day too close to the fence for photography, should move into a better position on the way out.

Boston's excellent selection of aircraft now features a quite remarkable quantity of European-built feeder-liners, Do228s, ATR-42s, SF.340s and Shorts especially, but some of them, like the Northwest Airlink Dorniers, can be very difficult to identify, even from Terminal B. It can be an extremely frustrating airport for the enthusiast. Alternative vantage points will be sought, though the water makes the perimeter inaccessible.

Highway 1A north leads to Bennington Street, where the beaches overlook 4L/22R and 4R/22L. By subway train from the airport, the station is Orient Heights, followed by a walk. Alternatively, Route 45 in Winthrop passes the yacht club, where a car park allows a reasonable view of traffic on 9/27. None of these locations are ideal for a photographer, and what is seen from here will almost certainly be at the expense of movements on other runways.

HYANNIS MA

HYA   Barnstable   1m/1.5km N

___

Anyone touring New England will soon find out that Cape Cod is the region's recreation area, and considered by the locals to be extremely scenic. It is, without doubt, heavily forested but the heavy hand of American development isn't always kind. Barnstable is at the gateway to the Cape Cod peninsula and its airport sees considerable traffic in summer.

Permission for a walk around the apron is normally granted at the control tower and there is a good selection of smaller types to be seen. PBA's ability to survive was under threat year after year, and only by moving to Florida for the winter did it keep two seasonal traffic peaks viable. Gull Air was an attempt to do the same. After their demise, operations became more diffuse, with a good range of commuters to be seen, including Nantucket Airlines with Cessna 402s and the locally-based Hyannis Air Service, which operates as Cape Air. With patience, a fine collection of quality photos can be assembled here, representing types normally seen only at a distance at larger airports.

BALTIMORE MD

BWI   KBWI   Washington International   10m/16km S

___

This airport continues to benefit from substantial investment, capitalising on the overcrowded nature of Washington National and the relative remoteness of Dulles. Being very modern in terms of planning and convenience to the traveller, it has much to offer, with road connections entailing a relatively short journey time to the city.

Modernity is usually the last feature of an airport which best serves the enthusiast but Baltimore's brand new observation area, scheduled for completion in March 1995, represents a significant investment. It even includes an exhibit area with the cockpit of a 737. The three thousand square feet of glass ensure a wide angle of view from directly above the old south passenger lounge. Of the five piers, only Pier E is inaccessible, as it's the international departures area, used by Air Aruba, Air Jamaica, El Al, Icelandair, Ladeco and charters.

The other piers offer close encounters with aircraft at their stands but the glass is heavily tinted. Even on sunny days, quality photographs are hard to come by. This, of course, is a highly subjective matter. For many, it's some consolation that the majority of its traffic can be seen just as well elsewhere. Work on Pier C, used mostly by American, Continental and Northwest, is scheduled to finish in the second half of 1995.

The Roy Rogers family restaurant windows give a good view of the many cargo aircraft. Gates D7 to D18, at ground level, are dominated by the many USAir Express Dash 8s in the busy commuter area.

Since the airport is so close to the Baltimore-Washington Expressway (Interstate 295), a small diversion will at least be rewarded by a good selection of executive aircraft parked at the terminal to the north of the main passenger buildings. Leaving the terminal on Elm Road, a car park allows views of most of the executive aircraft as well as a glimpse of the cargo facility immediately to the north. An access road, Aviation Boulevard (Hwy 170/162) leads around the northern perimeter of the cargo ramp, where parked aircraft can be seen easily, to the extensive general aviation area, east of Runway 15L/33R. On the southern edge of the field, Friendship Park is an external viewing area, close to the threshold of Runway 33. Follow Aviation Boulevard until it joins Hollins Freery, make a right and turn right again onto Dorsey Road (Hwy 176). You can't miss it.

The information desk in the passenger terminal is worth a visit, if only to obtain one of the free Maryland highway maps. The scale of the map makes road navigation very easy, and airports in the area are all shown clearly.

BALTIMORE MD
MTN   Glenn L Martin   11m/17km E

Without a road map it would be very difficult to find Baltimore's other significant airport: east of the city, off Eastern Avenue (Hwy 150) is Glenn L Martin State Airport which has historical connections with the production of Martin seaplanes. It is now a general aviation field, shared by a quantity of light aircraft and the Maryland Air National Guard's C-130s and A-10s, most of which can be seen at relatively close range from the road.

When travelling by car from Wilmington, and wishing to avoid the unlovely city of Baltimore, head east from I-95 on the Beltway (I-695) to Eastern Avenue. Care should be taken at Intersection 36 where the highway becomes No 702 for a short distance to its end. Also in the area, a few miles to the south, is Essex Skypark, on the shores of one of the Chesapeake Bay inlets.

COLLEGE PARK MD
CGS   1m/1.5km E

This is north Washington's main general aviation field, with about 200 residents. They include a good number of warbirds, antiques and homebuilts. The Metrorail station, which serves the community of College Park from Washington, is nowhere near the field. It is served by an Amtrak commuter service, however. On the map, the airport is inside Washington's Beltway northeast of the city, reached by going south from Intersections 23 and 25.

BATTLE CREEK MI
BTL   W K Kellogg

The road between Detroit and Chicago is not one of America's loveliest, and the journey needs a break. Battle Creek may be worth a detour. Very little happens at this quiet field, with only a moderate amount of general aviation to be seen but the Air National Guard ramp can be seen from the car park. A good proportion of the inmates can be read off, and more if they are on the move, but this needs more time.

DETROIT MI
DET   KDET   City   5m/8km NE

For many years, aviation enthusiasts who specialised in piston power extolled the virtues of Detroit as if the only airport was Willow Run (q.v.) but the Motor City has other attractions which should be borne in mind by the would-be visitor. Not least of these is the City Airport which handles quite a number of commuter flights, with SD3.30s and SD3.60s being accompanied by SF.340s.

The decline of Willow Run as a centre for piston-engined operations, and the closure of Metropolitan Airport's observation deck has thrust Detroit City Airport forward as worthy of more attention. The main centre of operations for most of the executive movements as well as the commuter operators is now well worth a visit in its own right.

Interstate 94 links Detroit with the north and the City Airport is reached from the Gratiot Avenue exit. Further directions are superfluous for anyone with a car, as all that is necessary is to circumnavigate the field clockwise to gain close access to a real selection of the Midwest's general aviation activity.

Continuing north along Interstate 94 leads to Mount Clemens and SELFRIDGE ANG Base, which shares the field with a Naval Air Station. A letter to the Air National Guard would be almost obligatory for any military-minded enthusiast, as the varied assortment of types present is matched by a very enthusiastic approach to the subject of aviation at the base. A good reason for visiting the base is the reasonably well stocked Military Air Museum.

Heading in the opposite direction from the centre of Detroit are the two airports which most enthusiasts know about, though both are a shadow of their former selves.

DETROIT MI
DTW   KDTW   Metropolitan   20m/32km WSW (bus 45 minutes)

Interstate 94 is Detroit's main artery and the Metropolitan Airport (also known as Wayne) is close to it, west of the city. The northeast corner houses a small amount of general aviation, including Ford's large hangar which is visible from Middle Belt Road. Like Chicago O'Hare, there are several terminals, arranged roughly in a loop but, unlike O'Hare, there is a single, well-located observation deck which, in theory, allows most of the activity to be seen with ease. It was enclosed with wire mesh, to increase security, but the last report, dated February 1995, said the deck was still closed.

Terminals A to G (G being the latest addition) are all accessible without boarding cards. American Airlines Gate B8 overlooks a busy taxiway and one active runway. Fed Ex can be seen and a modest amount of Continental traffic, but the view is restricted. The end of Terminal C is probably about the best place, as it allows almost all the airline traffic to be seen taxiing by. The glass is, in most cases, in rather smeared condition, making photos of any quality unlikely.

Try instead the open air swimming pool deck of the Marriott Airport Hotel. The view is comprehensive, including the cargo ramps, most of the terminals and traffic on Runway 3L/21R. A 200mm lens is adequate for most aircraft. The only problem is that, if enough people take this advice, it becomes self-defeating. No attention is paid to one person every couple of weeks or so. Then, one day, a tour party from Manchester turns up . . .! The sun is most helpful in the mornings and a positive nuisance late in the afternoon.

The adventurous may investigate the employee car parking lots but they are only accessible to vehicles by the driver placing a card in the machine slot, obviously not a problem to pedestrians, and the main lot is very close to the central runway and its taxiway.

A road leaving the airport parallel (and to the right of) the main thoroughfare, leads to maintenance facilities and, ultimately, to the general aviation hangars in the northeast corner. The cargo facilities to the west of the field usually contain the occasional aircraft but daytime operations are quiet.

DETROIT MI
YIP   KYIP   Willow Run   30m/48km W

Willow Run was once Detroit's most famous airport. It is some distance west, on I-94, on the edge of Ypsilanti. Its renown as one of the world's great airfields for piston airliners is historical but, as an airport devoted largely to cargo operators, there is still a reasonable quantity of older types on view, though the C-46s and DC-3s have gone.

What remains is an eerie atmosphere, caused by the looming presence of the nearby GM Transmission Plant and by the fact that very little on the field moves during the daytime. The large passenger terminal still exists, though now occupied mostly by offices of varying sorts. The advantage is that the field is quiet enough for access to the apron to be possible, with little risk of conflict with taxying aircraft. Zantop and Trans International are based here, continuing to use some prop power. Part of the appeal may be the desolate air exuded by the empty car parks, now overgrown with weeds, and the general stillness which surrounds the aircraft.

The Yankee Air Museum is situated off Belleville Road, and might be worth investigating. Among its exhibits there are a B-17, B-52, C-47 and an F-101. For further details, call (313) 483-4030.

KALAMAZOO MI
AZO   County   5m/8km SSE

Take Portage Road, exit 78, from I-78. Little has yet been reported from this airport but it is known to house an increasing quantity of warbirds in a museum, aptly named Air Zoo. Not just short for Kalama-zoo, but also because of the "animals" on display: these are Wildcat, Hellcat, Tigercat and a Flying Tiger, which make up part of a display of about twenty aircraft. Also located there is the Guadalcanal Campaign Veterans Museum. To find the museum, take East Milham Road, a left off Portage hwhen heading east.

MINNEAPOLIS/SAINT PAUL MN
MSP   KMSP   International   10m/16km SSE (bus 45 mins)

Just as Atlanta is dominated by Delta, the reputation of Minneapolis grew from its Northwest Airlines hub operations. The only other major operator here was Republic, who acquired North Central, but they too were absorbed into Northwest's empire to create a monopoly at this airport, offering the enthusiast little more than the chance to log vast numbers of one operator.

A band of dedicated European enthusiasts pass through Minneapolis each year on their way to the biggest general aviation event on the calender, at Oshkosh. Close encounters with aircraft will have to wait until arrival in Wisconsin, as airliners are seen mostly from a distance here, and the multi-storey car park has to be used for the only panoramic view of proceedings on all three runways. The Blue Concourse has an indoor observation facility, between Gates 62 and 68.

From the elevated platform of the car park, the two main runways can be seen on either side, beyond the terminal buildings, arranged on three sides. The cross runway, 4/22, to the west is no shorter than 11L/29R but is used mostly by commuter carriers, dominated by Northwest Airlink. The few international movements use a separate terminal, beyond 29L/11R, which is served by its own access road.

The general aviation hangars around the perimeter are easily seen, though not always their inmates, and the only other features worthy of mention are the AFRES base, the Northwest maintenance base and the Minnesota Air National Guard C-130s tucked away, inaccessibly, in the remote northeast corner of the field.

SAINT PAUL MN
STP   Downtown/Holman Field   3m/5km SE

To reach Holman from Minneapolis, cross the river south on Lafayette Freeway (Hwy 3) and the first exit leads there. It is compact, with the Mississippi along one edge. The general aviation includes many executive types, with no shortage of biz-jets. Remarkably for a downtown location, the Army Guard has a base here, where AH-1s, OH-58s and AH-54s are found.

The rest of the general aviation is dispersed widely around the area. FLEMING FIELD is further down the same road. FLYING CLOUD is ten miles southwest and CRYSTAL is six miles northwest. Leaving town north on Central Avenue leads to BLAINE-ANOKA COUNTY, also known locally as James Field.

KANSAS CITY MO
MKC   KMKC   Downtown   1m/1.5km N

Located on a loop of the Missouri River, the general aviation scene has mirrored the decline at the International Airport. However, there is still a good number of corporate aircraft to be seen during the week, but it would be wise not to expect too many biz-jets. There is competition for the business from several airports. All have a number of fixed base operators, and all are finding times to be tough.

Number crunchers will delight in Central Air Southwest's fleet of Aero Commander 500s but there are also items of individual worth: in addition to their L-1049H Super Constellation, the Save-a-Connie group owns a Martin 404 and a DC-3 which is being restored. There are occasional air shows on summer weekends, and a small museum which is open on weekdays between 10:00am and 2:00pm.

KANSAS CITY MO
MCI   KMCI   International   18m/30km NW

A few years ago, Kansas City enjoyed playing host to Braniff and TWA. Braniff has gone for ever but there are signs that TWA is showing signs of considerably improved health. Because of the passenger terminal layout, a lot of walking is now needed to see the traffic. The hub and spoke operations used to mean periods of absolute dead quiet were interspersed with chaos. Chaos has become little more than occasional bouts of activity.

Of the three round terminals, Terminal A is probably now the busiest, handling lots of Beech 1900s of USAir Express. Just to the north is an employee parking lot, reasonably close to Runway 1/19. A long lens will be needed by photographers.

TWA's redundant 727s and MD-82s are stored at their maintenance base, which is not accessible by public roads, so permission for access will be required. Across the street from the post office is a garishly painted 727-100, used by the Trans World Technical School.

KANSAS CITY MO
OJC   Johnson Executive

Not to be confused with Johnson Industrial, this is one of the many private airfields which compete for market share around the city. Only genuine biz-jet enthusiasts will take the time to visit all the fields but they will be able to record a reasonable amount for their trouble and patience.

KANSAS CITY MO
JCI   Johnson Industrial

Were it not for the different codes, it would be easy to think that there was only one Johnson Airport. This is not so, but most readers will probably consider the matter to be academic. Fairfax Minicipal, on the other side of the river in Kansas State, has been closed and redeveloped as an industrial park.

SAINT LOUIS MO
STL   KSTL   Lambert-Saint Louis International   13m/20km NW

The passenger terminal occupies the southern edge of the perimeter. Its eastern apron is expansive and can be seen by passing through a security check. A left turn at the Y-junction allows the runways to be seen, and the main apron behind. The airport authority might take the purpose of its own notices rather more seriously one day. Having allowed all the world and his dog through the security check, there is then a small sign saying "Ticketed Passengers Only". It was seen, quite by chance, on the the third visit. Clearly, there are not enough non-ticket holders using the concourses for there to be a problem but anyone travelling to STL should bear in mind that the situation can change. In the meantime, head for gates G36 and 38.

Most of the airliners are easily seen, if not photographed, from Concourse C. There could be, however, a strange apparent dearth of Southwest movements. Traffic using Runway 6/24 and parking at the conveniently placed Concourse A can remain a mystery to anyone who stays at Gate 36. It's worth walking around.

Across the field are various facilities: McDonnell-Douglas has an enormous plant on the north side, away from TWA's maintenance base and the general aviation aprons. Between these two hangar areas is the cargo ramp. To see them at close quarters a car is essential. There are one or two vantage points round here that overlook the field but the two main runways, 12R/30L especially, are somewhat distant.

Satellite parking lots B and C are quite close to the approach for Runway 12R, normally the main arrivals runway. Shuttle buses operate to these lots, so it is only a short walk for the dedicated photographer. McDonnell-Douglas has a gift shop on the corner of Lindbergh and McDonnell Streets, just to the north of the airport. Among the mainly military-oriented stock are a few items which may be of interest to the civil enthusiast.

Apart from the terminal and general aviation areas, there are one or two quiet roadside places to watch the perimeter. Care should be exercised when parking the car, as the police are vigilant for anyone who disobeys the 'No Stopping' signs. Rather than pull up at the roadside, wind down the window and point the binoculars at something, it's more sensible to find somewhere to park and do the job properly. It's certainly less hassle in the long run.

GULFPORT-BILOXI MS

GPT   Regional   3m/5km NNE

This is not a busy airport nor, it has to be admitted, a particularly interesting one. One or two Northwest DC-9s and Continental Express Brasilias comprise the only scheduled movements. The opening of gambling casinos on the coast will continue to generate additional flights, the majority of which by early 1995 comprised Viscount Air Services 737s. What the field does have to offer is the National Guard unit. The army presence is very large indeed. Their Mohawks are easy to find but identifying them is a different matter. The extremely rare AVCRAD Caribous can also be seen. An ex-PBA Martin 404, N40413 is now stored here, having been moved from Naples. The military ramp on the east side of the field sometimes holds entire squadrons of Air National Guard aircraft, deployed here for their annual two-week drills. All park close to the fence, and can be logged and photographed with ease.

Nearby, Keesler Air Force Base sees relatively little action but of interest are the Air Force's hurricane-hunting WC-130s which are based. Spotting and photos will require access to the base to be negotiated.

BILLINGS MT

BIL   Logan International   2m/3km NW

A quiet place, this Logan International bears no resemblance to Boston's airport of the same name. The Billings version is served by Continental, United, and Northwest as well as being the base of operations for Big Sky Airlines (Montana is Big Sky Country). Their Metros can be photographed with ease over the car park fence, just next to the terminal. Lynch Flying Service usually have some smart B-26 sprayers parked on the far side of Runway 9L/27R and access to them should not be a problem.

The terminal area sits compactly facing the intersection of 9L/27R and 4/22. This would be enough runways for most small airports but Billings also has 16/34 and, for general aviation only, the short 9R/27L. To the right of the terminal is the airport's fixed base operator, Lynch, with whom it is worth having a short discussion before driving around to the far side.

HELENA MT

HLN   KHLN   3m/5km NE

Apart from Hawkins & Powers, there is very little in the way of civil aviation to justify the mileage but that is not to say that Helena is not interesting. The Montana Army Guard's unit flies AH-1s, UH-1s and H-58s. Preserved here are some 1950s fighters and EC-121T N4257L, c/n 4335. With one or two Metros and the occasional Delta 737, scheduled traffic takes a distant second place to the other delights.

CHARLOTTE NC

CLT   KCLT   Douglas Municipal   8m/13km W

Anyone visiting the United States with a USAir Airpass will get to know Charlotte, as this is a very significant hub indeed. As with any hub and spoke operation, an enormous influx of traffic is followed by similar chaos as they all depart. The sight of fifteen USAir-craft lined up at the holding point, awaiting take-off, is common at Charlotte. When they have departed, calm returns.

Across the diagonal runway, 5/23, from the old passenger terminal, the present one stands between two parallel runways, 18/36L/R, and walkways connect the various concourses.

Concourse A is reserved for all airlines except USAir. The others, B to D are almost the exclusive preserve of the one airline. USAir Express is represented by CCAir, with SD3.60s, Jetstreams and Dash 8s; their ramps are around Concourse D.

This may be the best place to watch the action, though one runway is out of sight. Passengers flood the buildings, so anyone attempting to keep apace with what is moving where will have an energetic time. It will almost certainly lead to frustration, however.

Taking photos through the glass of the feederliners can be followed by a walk round the concourses, to and fro, just to keep track. The end of Concourse C has the advantage of being close to the cargo ramp, and photos from here of the FedEx 727 or UPS DC-8 do not need particularly sophisticated equipment. The end of Concourse B is also good for great views of aircraft using Runway 5. The general aviation apron, close to the dozen or so North Carolina Air National Guard C-130s, is out of sight from the terminal.

Air pass travellers are not likely to hire a car in order to explore the airfield, so they miss out on what is on offer. The present terminal, on the north side of the field, has its own highway access off Billy Graham Parkway. Leaving the parking area by car, instead of taking the main road, make a turn to the left, as if returning to the terminal. Go straight ahead to the T-junction and make a right turn. A left turn at the next T-junction onto Old Dowd Road leads round the end of Runway 18R to the elevated viewing area. This offers a panorama of the airfield as well as a close-up of anything landing on the main (longest) runway.

The road meanders beyond this point and, after a few left turns, leads to the cargo area. Amongst the modern aircraft, Saber Airlines stand out as belonging to a different era: Saber operates C-47s and Beech 18s, a few of which are normally present on the ramp. Next to cargo is what was once the main apron, now used by general aviation. The loop road to the old terminal also offers a glimpse of the main general aviation apron, on the the side of 18L/36R.

A left onto West Boulevard passes the end of 36R before its junction with Airport Parkway. Another left gives access to the FBOs across the road. The apron just beyond, to the north, is used by the Air National Guard, whose C-130s spend most of their time doing nothing. Airport Drive continues to a junction, offering the choice of returning to the terminal or heading into town. Wilkinson Boulevard, at the end, is the easiest way to do so.

Much is happening at Charlotte. The remodelling of the terminal was due to be complete by early 1995, greatly increasing its area. There are plans for a third parallel runway, and nobody's quite sure what the earth-moving equipment has been doing at the end of 36L . . .

ELIZABETH CITY NC

ECG   KECG   Municipal   5m/8km SE

Take Highway 34 out of town, which is on the opposite side of the river estuary from the road leading to Kitty Hawk and the Wright Brothers Monument. Traffic at the airport is negligible but Albatross 7247 guards the gate to the main attraction. The US Coast Guard's main base is here, and its facility is quite large. Maintenance hangars and aprons normally have examples of all types, but access cannot be guaranteed. A letter in advance might help, of course. Most of the C-130s can be logged from outside the gate but the various helicopters and Guardians are mostly hidden from view.

GASTONIA NC

0A6   Municipal   15m/24km W of Greensboro

An interest in propliners and a car are the two essential requisites for a trip to Gastonia. Patience doesn't come amiss, either, as it can be a difficult place to find. It's on the south side of town, farthest from I-85. Take New Hope Road and, if necessary, ask for directions. If you want to find Piedmont Air Cargo, it would be silly to give up, when you're this close! Union Road passes the end of the small airfield. Past the terminal building are the hangars and apron, where a few C-47s and Beech 18s can be seen. Very little moves here during the day, so access to the ramp is relatively easy to obtain.

GREENSBORO NC

GSO   Piedmont Triad International   11m/17km W

Greensboro is quite a major regional capital, and its airport handles a fair amount of scheduled traffic. From town, take US 421 in the direction of Winston-Salem, and the airport is on the north side of the road. It's relatively quiet, and nobody would want to spend a day or so logging the movements, most of which are DC-9s and 727s, plus some commuters. There is no shortage of general aviation, including some biz-jets. To see it, a car is needed. Triad International Maintenance Corp (Timco) works on a range of aircraft, and their centre is on the east side of the field, a long way from the terminal. DC-9s and 737s wait their turn for maintenance, and some of the aircraft appear to have been in storage for a while.

Also worth investigation is the GTCC Aviation Technical School, where a range of airframes can be seen, including T-39s and at least one Hansa. One of the more famous residents of Greensboro is Tradewinds International, whose CL-44s are among the last airworthy examples in the world.

Tradewinds' facility is close to the highway, next to the disused cargo shed, on the south side. It is reasonable to expect anything up to four or five CL-44s. They can be seen from the fence of the abandoned car park, as can a fair number of biz-jets on the other apron. There is now a choice: go west and north to the main terminal or go east and north to TIMCO. Both ultimately go to the north side of the airfield where the cargo terminal can be seen. Don't think that, because it's a dirt road, it can't be the right one.

RALEIGH/DURHAM NC

RDU   KRDU   14m/22km NW

North Carolina is not flat country and, around this airport it's quite hilly. Arrival, from the main road, gives little impression of the airport. There is a choice: park the car and walk into either or both of the passenger terminals, or continue past the car parks, under the two taxiways, to a spectator's area next to the control tower. A grassy bank overlooks both runways, though only 5L/23R is close enough for photography. The majority of the scheduled movements are American Airlines and American Eagle.

Close to the viewing park is the large general aviation apron with its many hangars and residents. The executive movements also pass within range of a good zoom lens, so that Raleigh-Durham does offer some variety in return for a long stay. What will be remembered here, though, is seeing an awful lot of American 727s and MD-80s.

A shuttle bus operates to the terminals from the satellite parking lot, for anyone intent on finding out that there is little to see from inside the buildings. The Army National Guard helicopters are parked, some distance away, beside Runway 14/32. There may be somewhere in Terminal A or B from where the serials can be read.

WINSTON-SALEM NC

INT   KINT   Smith Reynolds   3.5m/6km NNE

The airport, like everything else in town, depends on the prosperity of the Reynolds Tobacco Company. This is an enormous business concern, and it comes as no surprise to find that general aviation includes plenty of corporate aircraft. There is little else of any note.

MORRISTOWN NJ

MMU   Municipal   17m/27km W of Newark

There are no scheduled visitors, and probably very little reason to trek out into New Jersey to see this airport. A band of dedicated biz-jet fans will consider the trip worthwhile, as the general aviation activity includes some interesting aircraft including, it was reported some time ago, a Grumman Widgeon.

NEWARK NJ

EWR   KEWR   International   1m/1.5km S

Because New York's other two airports have now become so busy, particularly La Guardia, Newark has been developed to capitalise on the increasing inconvenience of the other two. None of EWR's three terminals possess observation decks. Despite a good variety of movements, Newark has generally been considered by enthusiasts as the poor relation in this part of the world. This may be due to the terminals facing east, and therefore only at their best in the afternoon. When faced with a choice of watching the world's wide-bodies land at JFK or getting good views of domestic airlines at Newark, most enthusiasts will choose JFK. However, the windows in Terminal C offer such sights as SAS 767s for those who choose this airport as an alternative. The lack of slots at JFK will force more airlines here, and operators and passengers alike will probably benefit. Terminals A and B are accessible only to passengers, most of whom fly with United, USAir and Virgin Atlantic.

As long as the darkened glass doesn't pose too great a problem, most of the aircraft can be seen at reasonably close quarters. Also good for photos are the emergency exit landings at the corners of the terminals, as they offer quite elevated views of aircraft pushing back or taxying in. This additional height is useful as the walk between each terminal is at a level considerably below that of the blast screens.

Gates 85 and 86 in Terminal C offer a good view of the active runways, plus the ability to monitor movements on the taxiways. There is a good variety of food on offer here, though all at New York prices of course, and anyone who isn't intent on taking photos will find the only drawback is that the FedEx/UPS ramp is out of sight. Those without a car who wish to see this area will need to show a boarding pass to visit the United departure lounge in Terminal A.

Brewster Road leads from a very complex road layout (it can be missed easily) to the freight and general aviation areas. Passing close to the parcel cargo ramp, it is possible to make a quick stop for a photo of what may be on the apron, before taking the next right turn. This leads into the cargo complex proper where views of aircraft on the ramp are limited. The loop road leads back to the executive terminal and hangar, both of which can be relied upon for a good selection of biz-jets. The rest of this large ramp is used for parking, mostly by cargo aircraft. The Forbes Magazine all-gold DC-9 is a regular visitor, as is the Presidential 747 which parks next to the tower.

TETERBORO NJ

TEB   KTEB   15m/23km N of EWR

A sortie east of the Hudson River usually combines Teterboro and Newark, both of which make a change from New York's two major airports. Most of the residents are to be seen along the western perimeter. In the southwest corner is the Falcon Jet Center, which overlooks an apron renowned for quantities of biz-jets. The museum on the western perimeter may not contain anything intrinsically thrilling but its presence does allow the casual visitor a valid reason to stroll onto the ramp. It occupies the lower two floors of the old control tower building. (There is incidentally another museum at Teterboro, on the opposite side of the field, by the new control tower.) Passing a large hangar full of executive wares, the apron beyond is laden with more visitors of interest. Due to the number of light aircraft visible along the western edge, it will be somewhere about here that the first misgivings might be experienced by the ardent spotter with a notebook to fill.

ALBUQUERQUE NM
ABQ   KABQ   International   9m/15km NW

___

Not a particularly busy airport but it is interesting for the variety of traffic to be seen here. The small observation deck in the original terminal building has been overtaken by progress, and is now closed. America West, Southwest, TWA, American and United are the most frequent operators, while Mesa Air/United Express Beech 1900s dominate the commuter activity.

Extensions to the original terminal include one pier to the right and another projecting forward, linking it to a new terminal, closer to the intersection of two major runways. The link faces the USAF base and offers some restricted views of airliners on the apron, as does the new terminal. It is now best to take advantage of one of the many places around the perimeter, if a stay of any length is planned.

Much of the field is occupied by Kirtland AFB, outside which is a preserved T-39 on a pole. The C-21As are parked quite close to the passenger terminal, together with any visiting military movements. The A-7s and C-130s are relatively inaccessible at the far end of the field, though landing shots of all movements are possible near the end of the main runway. Regular activity can be interrupted by the arrival of F-4s and A-7s, as well as F-14s and F-18s of the US Navy.

The general aviation area is situated directly opposite the passenger terminal, on the other side of the runway, whilst Ross Aviation, who fly on government contract work, are to be found next to the military installation. The cargo sheds are to the right of the passenger terminal, on the same side of the runway. For more general aviation, in quantity, CORONADO Field should be investigated. It's northeast of town on the Pan American Freeway.

ALAMOGORDO NM
ALM   White Sands Regional   5m/8km SW

___

To the west of town is the vast White Sands National Monument. There are about 150,000 acres of pure white sand, drifted into dunes up to forty feet high. Ten times that area is occupied by the White Sands Missile Range, a playground for Holloman Air Force Base crews.

Based at White Sands is, rather inappropriately, Black Hills Aviation. Their many P-2V Neptunes have been joined by ex-Spanish P-3As. Commuter airline movements are few and far between, so there is little reason for Alamogordo to be more than a short stop between El Paso and Roswell. Some miles to the northeast is Hondo, New Mexico and the Mescalero Apache Reservation. However, the T-41 Mescaleros are based at Hondo, Texas!

IMPORTANT NOTICE:

It is hereby confirmed that a report for New Mexico was submitted for inclusion in the previous edition, which made use of information gleaned from an enthusiasts' magazine, without due accreditation. This resulted in (a) failure to acknowledge the original sourse and (b) a lot of unnecessary correspondence, none of which seemed to appease the person whose information was, effectively, stolen. It is now difficult to determine which entries were thus created, so a general acknowledgment is hereby made to Mr Stephen Rudge of LAAS.

All information is gratefully received and anyone making use of material gleaned from sources other than their own observations might, in future, care to mention the fact! Thank you.

ROSWELL NM
ROW   KROW   Industrial Air Center   3m/5km S

Once upon a time, Roswell was the home of Lufthansa's training school. Though some 737s are to be seen, they are not German. F-5s are also much in evidence, but the most memorable resident is probably JetStar N440RM, in its livid red colour scheme. The rest of the movements amount to a few Mesa Beech 1900s operating for United Express.

SANTA FE NM
SAF   KSAF   Municipal   9m/15km SW

This may be New Mexico's state capital, but the airport is extremely disappointing, especially if driving for a few hundred miles in expectation. What passes through is Mesa Beech 1900s, and even these are quite rare.

CARSON CITY NV
CSN   2m/3km NE

Too close to Reno to generate any traffic of its own, Carson City is only worth a detour if seeking a couple of Albatrosses, which are the only notable aircraft to be seen.

ELKO NV
EKO   Municipal   0.5m/1km W

Commercial gold-mining in northeast Nevada has led to the growth of this airport. Skywest, for example, now operate eleven daily flights to Reno and Salt Lake City. The big attraction is, however, the colourful Casino Express fleet of 737s operating regular charter flights from across the western states. Two are based at Elko. In the mornings, the accessible perimeter fence allows good photos of anything on the taxiway.

HENDERSON NV
HSH   Sky Harbor NV   2m/3km NE

Henderson is on the road between Las Vegas and the Hoover Dam, and this is more than just another private field with lots of general aviation. The two Toa Domestic YS-11s which are stored here will never fly again, and they are stored in the company of a couple of American Eagle SD3.30s.

LAS VEGAS NV
LAS   KLAS   McCarran International   6m/9km SSE

Las Vegas is in the middle of a constant programme of investment and development which will be finished by the end of the century. Reports from McCarran have a way of becoming out of date very quickly.

The main passenger terminal was never of real use for either viewing or photography. Behind it is a multi-storey car park which offers the spotter a view of everything on the move. An awning offers much-needed shelter from the blistering (quite literally) sun, and a zoom lens allows some of the larger aircraft to be photographed with some success.

Access to the new Terminal C is by monorail, and the airlines here are mainly by Southwest, American, United and TWA. Finding somewhere to sit between Gates C9 and C11, for example, allows all traffic on the busy parallel Runways 25L and 25R to be monitored.

On the west side of the field, the old charter terminal is now used for domestic flights only, and it doesn't face the busy Runways 25L/R. However, next to it, the Hughes executive terminal has the Flitedeck Restaurant with an open balcony, complete with seats, tables, sun and refreshments. . . and a view worth having. What can be seen are the ramps and the runways, plus all traffic on the move. However, there is increasing resistance to photography of corporate aircraft, extending even to allegations of it being illegal. Whether or not this is the case may not be relevant: visitors to Las Vegas can be influential in one way or another, and they can be temperamental. Movie stars get upset about being photographed without make-up, and some of the businessmen here have a reputation for being single-minded! Any warnings should be treated politely, and taken seriously.

On the north side, accessible from Tropicana Boulevard, the Scenic Airlines terminal is at its best early in the morning, before flights leave for the Grand Canyon. When nothing is happening, the area can be locked up. Close by here is the C-124 Globemaster, on its own ground. From this part of the field, much of the general aviation can be seen but there is little of any interest. Continuing along the upgraded fence, the nearby storage area holds some USAir 1-11s, Interocean 727s, Continental 737s and, possibly still there, a Eurocity Dash Seven.

The charter and executive terminals do handle the more interesting movements at Las Vegas: American Trans Air 727s and 757s, Worldways TriStars and Air BC BAe146s are all regular visitors, but its appeal may lie more in what is stored . . . and of course the colourful nightlife.

LAS VEGAS NV
VGT   North Air Terminal   2m/3km NW

The city's other field, apart from the busy Nellis Air Force Base, is North Air Terminal. To find it, take Rancho Road (Highway 95) out of town. Like Las Vegas/Henderson Sky Harbor, it is used mainly as a departure point for the many sightseeing flights over the Grand Canyon.

RENO NV
RNO   KRNO   Cannon International   4m/6km SE

For variety, Cannon is worth the long journey, especially if combined with a visit to Stead Airport. Scheduled traffic is reasonably varied, though not brisk during the week, except for the morning and evening peaks. Weekend gamblers provide more activity for the usual airlines. Delta, American and America West are regulars, and so are United BAe146s. Locally-based Reno Air MD-83s are much in evidence. During the daytime, Cannon is an airport with a perimeter to explore. General aviation includes a fair amount of biz-jets and, for once, plenty of places from which to see them.

The passenger terminal is in the northwest corner of the field, facing Runway 16L/34R, with the shorter parallel runway beyond it. At each side of the terminal are large ramps and, to the south, the cross runway. Probably the best place inside the terminal is by Gate C6, which also overlooks the cargo apron. There is no problem finding somewhere around the remote g.a. facility and, during race week, it houses about four hundred aircraft, many of them twins. From here all runways can be seen, and most aircraft taxi by at close range.

The Nevada Air National Guard ramp can be seen, to the right, from the passenger terminal. F-4 numbers exceed F-16s.

STEAD Airport is at its best in mid-September, when the Reno Air Races are held here. Plenty of visitors, and many of them are extremely exotic types and paintjobs. To get there from town, follow Highway 395 for about fifteen miles. What is to be seen all year round is of more than passing interest to many visitors. Aviation Classics have half a dozen Chinese MiG-15s and at least one An-2. The other notables include a couple of Il-14s and various older US military types. Patriot Airways is a new cargo carrier, with 727s which may be operable.

ALBANY NY
ALB   KALB   County   9m/15km NW

The appeal of this small airport lies in its pleasant little roof terrace which overlooks a fairly busy ramp. Despite the mesh which now surrounds it, photography is still possible. Apart from the regular airlines, like USAir and Continental, there is a splendid amount of feeder airline traffic and this is one of the few airports in the north eastern states to feature such a variety of Beech 1900s, Shorts, Dash 7s/8s, Dornier 228s and ATR-42s in the company of DC-9s, F.28s and 737s, all visible at close quarters.

As befits feederliner traffic, a good part of it passes through in the morning and evening rush hours, the middle of the day being somewhat slower. Metro Airlines Northeast (Trans World Express), Command (American Eagle) and Precision (Northwest Airlink) are the local airlines, the first two having maintenance facilities at the far end, off Albany-Shaker Road.

As the IATA Security Advisory Committee advice takes effect through the USA, and major airports are battening down the hatches, the initiative shown at Albany acquires a new significance. A car park next to the main road has been designated as an observation point, where close views of the threshold and holding point are on offer. The Army National Guard AH-1s and OH-58s can also be seen parked on the field, on the far side of the runway. There is also a separate lay-by on Albany-Shaker Road, close to where traffic using the shorter cross-runway lands.

BINGHAMPTON NY
BGM   Broome County   10m/16km N

Better known locally as Edwin A Link Field, it's easy to find from town. Drive north on Airport Road! Scheduled operations are busier than might be expected, with a number of commuter flights during the day. It is not, however, a place to settle down and watch the action. Worth a detour when passing through the area, Binghampton's residents include a few antiques, and biz-jets are regular visitors, though not in great numbers. Permission for ramp access should be sought from Broome County Aviation.

BUFFALO NY
BUF   KBUF   International   9m/15km ENE (bus 45 minutes)

The passenger terminals are divided into two parts, the newly enlarged Western Terminal and its next door neighbour, solely for domestic use, the Eastern. It will come as no surprise to seasoned travellers of the USA that a domestic terminal is usually good news, as only a security check has to be passed to get to the departure lounges. Boarding cards aren't required, so access to close encounters with the aircraft are possible.

Traffic, though busy, is generally lacklustre, being dominated by US Air, whose acquisition of Piedmont included the hub of Empire Airlines. A name which lives on at Buffalo is Flying Tigers, though it refers to the wartime heroes, rather than the airline. This is the name of a restaurant, located close to the intersection of Runways 5/23 and 14/32. To get there, a left turn onto Genesee Street is followed by another left turn at the lights by the Holiday Inn. Two more left turns lead to an underpass below Runway 5/23. Before the tunnel, the restaurant and its car park are on the left. Catering for the enthusiast, quite literally, in more ways than one, some of the tables have headphones tuned to the tower. Since meals start at lunchtime, the car park is usually empty in the mornings. A meal there would certainly repay them for their facilities!

ELMIRA NY

ELM	Corning Regional	7m/11km NW

No busier than any other regional airport, Elmira Corning does handle one or two jet airliners each day. Schweizer Aircraft build their Ag Cats here, so there is usually something to be seen. Crop sprayers find their way to some remote corners of the world, so exotic registrations are always a possibility, particularly in early spring before the seasonal delivery peak. Nearby is the Soaring Society of America, and the field has a strong accent on this activity, with rides and lessons on offer to the interested.

FARMINGDALE NY

FRG	Republic	2m/3km E

Finding Farmingdale on a map of New York State can be difficult. It's on Long Island, about twenty miles east of Kennedy. Exit 32 on Southern State Parkway leads north to the airport. Jetstreams do visit occasionally but the Lockheed Air Terminal handles mostly executive movements, including some jets. Considered as a general aviation field with a fair number of residents, Farmingdale is worth the trip, as almost everything can be seen.

ISLIP NY

ISP	KISP	Long Island MacArthur	8m/13km NE

The residents of Long Island may live close to New York City but they can avoid the traffic jams and check-in queues if they fly from Islip (pronounced eyes-lip). A few commuter airlines seized the opportunity to capitalise on this fact, and the airport witnessed some major growth in the mid-1980s. Unfortunately, investment in the airport failed to keep pace with demand, and travelling via Islip became as much trouble as anywhere else. Facilities were stretched beyond the limit, and the airport has settled back into a comfortable role of offering a limited alternative to New York's major airports.

Facilities for viewing are non-existent but the fence at the left side of the terminal does allow photographs to be taken of the movements. Islip's appeal has always been that it is possible to get close to feeder liners, and the varied selection includes Henson Dash 7s/8s and Precision Do228s, as well as many other types which have been around a bit longer.

Although Islip has two runways, neither are easily reached for close-up photos. The general aviation apron is located separately from the passenger terminal, and houses very little of real interest. However, next to it is the National Guard helicopter base, with numerous UH-1s and OH-6s, all easily seen from the fence at very close quarters without offending anyone, and a bonus here is the proximity to one of the taxiways. If the right runway is in use, the aircraft do pass very close. Success at Islip can be very much a matter of luck.

MONTICELLO NY

MSV	Sullivan County

Nestling in the picturesque Catskill Mountains, Monticello is a quiet and pleasant place. It is rarely troubled by the noise of jets or large aircraft of any kind. It is, however, on the road from

New York City to Binghampton, Elmira and the larger cities around the Great Lakes and may be worth a stop en route.

NEWBURGH NY

SWF   KSWF   Stewart International   4m/6km NW

Close to the West Point Military Academy, Newburgh is convenient for rich dads to visit their sons. The fathers use corporate aircraft and the sons use T-41 Mescaleros. Newburgh's long runway has been the basis for many plans for the field's future. Scheduled flights now total about ninety a day, most of them up to 727 size, related to American and USAir. There is no shortage of feeder services, so that Stewart Field now offers links to almost anywhere.

Probably the most impressive new arrivals at Stewart were the dozen or so C-5s which are used by the New York Air National Guard. There is also a US Marines unit based here with, it is believed, KC-130s. The quantity of general aviation seems to be growing daily.

NEW YORK NY

JFK   KJFK   John F Kennedy International   14m/22km SE (bus 60 minutes)

New York isn't to be used as a barometer for the rest of the country, as its airports handle a disproportionate amount of traffic, especially international flights, and the security precautions have been extraordinarily unimaginative. New York was once the automatic first choice for a first trip to the USA, but it is probably no longer in the Top Ten.

La Guardia is crammed beyond sensible limits with domestic traffic, none of which can be seen in Europe, while JFK handles vast numbers of movements from across the Atlantic. Assuming that the decision is to sample the delights of JFK the first day after arrival, it is quite likely that an early start will be made, getting to the airport before the action starts. It will be a long wait. Apart from some extreme rarities which do pass through in the mornings, interest isn't generated until lunchtime when the first of the international flights start arriving.

Kennedy is a vast airport with all the passenger terminals at the middle, where further growth is just about impossible. Major airlines have their own terminals and there is a separate, large building for international arrivals. This is also stretched beyond the limit in the afternoons and evenings, and many transatlantic flights now arrive at other terminals, which also have customs and immigration facilities. The Worldport also handles international flights including those from Eastern Europe.

The centre of the airport is occupied by five separate car parks, and it is wise not to consider moving the car from one to another as the costs can be frightening. Before leaving the car out here, despite the fact that there aren't many others, a careful note should be made of its location. When returning at dusk the car park will be, literally, full so departure will need time and patience. The alternative was to park on the roof of the Worldport, once the best vantage point in the central terminal area. It is now completely spotter-proof.

Instead, the five-storey car park outside the International Arrivals Building is tall enough to offer a good overall view of proceedings. A security guard is always on duty so, sonner or later, he will become interested in anyone spotting. It is best to discuss intentions, and reach some agreement, as he merely contacts the local police who despatch a car with predictable (though not disastrous) consequences.

A typical stay in New York needs a plan of action, the most common being to arrive at JFK from La Guardia at lunchtime, using the Van Wyck Expressway. The terminals will not contain anything significant yet, so a look around the maintenance areas will save a lot of time. On the right, what were Pan Am's hangars are where the occasional Saudia, Varig and Chinese 747 spend the day, parked quite close to the fence, and easily photographed from the roof of a car. Next is TWA, though there is normally little exciting here. Making a U-turn to get to the opposite carriageway, United and American hangars will contain more aircraft and the use of an employees' car park allows closer inspection.

Continuing, after another U-turn towards the central area, the general aviation terminal is on the right but handles only a small amount of biz-jet traffic so a stop here isn't worthwhile. Faced with the prospect of nine terminals to visit, the advice is simple: assume nothing can be seen from any of them. This includes the Delta Worldport (including what was the Eastern Airlines Terminal), Northwest, American and British Airways, as they offer no facilities at all. The interior of the TWA terminal (including the National Airlines building which they acquired for domestic flights) offers a sight of part of their ramp, but nothing that would justify the trip. Terminal One is, at the time of writing, being completely rebuilt.

Security precautions meant that the Worldport rooftop car park had to be enclosed, and it has now been done in an extremely effective manner. Around its perimeter, there are now two fences, about five feet apart, one of which has the wooden slats - extraordinary precautions which cost money to erect. The number of parking spaces (and the income therefrom) has also been reduced, in order to be rid of spotters and, presumably, any threat of terrorist activity.

The balcony of the International Arrivals building is closed but, on the level below, glass allows good photography of a restricted number of wide-body movements. The authorities have been slow to appreciate that enthusiasts are being denied access to views of aircraft and that they use their imagination to compensate. This leads to unnecessary, but inevitable, conflict and such places as the 150th Street exit, so close to the BA ramp and the threshold of 13L, continue to get more attention, from both parties.

The taxiway between 13L/31R and the American terminals passes over the road next to the Post Office Building and an ample of provision of grassy bank can serve admirably for taking photographs of traffic as it lands on 13L (a regular feature, but not a continual one). Passing very close to this taxiway is another overbridge, used to transport cargo containers into the freight areas, and this vantage point allows ridiculously close views of taxying aircraft as well as a good prospect of the British Airways and TWA ramps. It must be borne in mind that the police also use this bridge and they will not take kindly to anyone standing here.

Standing with camera in hand, awaiting the arrival of a Swissair 747, is taken to be loitering in the USA and there are penalties for this. Anyone tackled by the police should be aware of the fact that 'loitering' is a subjective word. Someone engaged in the legitimate business of aviation photography cannot, realistically, be accused of this, though the purpose is to deter. A positive approach to the situation, if it occurs, would be to inform them that, as a free-lance photographer, one is trying to earn a living.

The central cargo area, near the 150th Street exit, is difficult to see well but there is a major facility on the other side of Runway 13L, where aircraft can be seen more easily from the roof of a car, with photos possible over the fence. Like Lufthansa, JALCargo operate their 747F into JFK at night and these aircraft may be a rare sight unless a special trip is made, possibly at dawn. The second major turning to the right leads to an assortment of ramps, with Northwest Cargo at the end. An early morning visit may be rewarded by a shot of a Lufthansa 747F on the move and a Northwest example with its nose door open.

At the end of this cul-de-sac, the road turns to a large staff car park and, at the turning, it is possible to get high quality shots of aircraft landing on 22R, with the sun on the aircraft, instead of behind. Standing here, even when the runway is heavily used, will mean missing many movements arriving and departing on other runways.

Food and drink are not readily available at sensible prices in JFK and anyone spending any amount of time here should consider the need for nourishment. The 150th Street exit leads to Rockaway Boulevard. This road passes the thresholds of 22L and 22R, so many of the locals pull in here to watch the planes land. Continuing along Rockaway Boulevard, there is a shopping centre and a good selection of eating establishments, with something to suit most tastes. It is possible to read the underwing registrations of aircraft landing on 31L (not American, of course) from the comfort of a seat in Dunkin Donuts or Arthur Treachers.

Buses operate from Kennedy to the other airports: Carey Express to La Guardia and

Princetown Express to Newark. Costs were last reported as $9.50 and $19.00 respectively. For more information and tickets, contact any ground transportation desk. Manhattan by bus costs $11, and the journey takes about an hour. The buses use either Grand Central Station or the Port Authority Bus Terminal. For a few dollars more (well, actually, quite a few dollars more) helicopters serve East 34th Street. The fare, of $65, offers quite an experience but groups of travellers should bear in mind that reduced group fares can apply.

NEW YORK NY

LGA   KLGA   La Guardia   8m/13km E (bus 40 minutes)

La Guardia is reached, without a car, from Kennedy by the Carey bus which costs a maximum of $10 each way. Alternatively, buses also leave Grand Central Station, Rockefeller Center and Penn Station in Manhattan. The cost is, at most, $12 one way. There are alternative means of transportation: a ferry operates from Wall Street Pier, on the East River (11th and 34th) and the journey takes about 40 minutes. From the Marine Air Terminal a bus service, Q47, leaves every fifteen minutes or so, and serves local subway stations. $2.50 is a cheap way to get into Manhattan, though how long the journey takes will depend on the destination station. Anyone who is unfamiliar with New York (and New Yorkers) is strongly advised not to make use of the subway system after the evening rush hour. There are enough stories about muggings, and worse, for the situation to be taken seriously, and alternative travelling arrangements made. It's a tough town, and Brooklyn ain't no quiet suburb!

What readers no doubt want to know, more than anything else, if whether the journey is a waste of time. So, here is the wording on a sign, to be seen in LGA: "Public welcome at gates and Food Court". True, the fabulous rooftop observation deck has been closed for several years, but USAir have shown imagination, largely because it is good business.

Always keen to be a user-friendly airline, USAir has extended its terminal, more or less opposite the threshold of Runway 31. Lots of glass and lots of views. Admittedly most of the views are of USAir's own planes, better than nothing, but anything using this runway passes very close. Wind direction is crucial. When Runway 31 sees heavy use, the situation is very good indeed. American and United might use Runway 4 but almost all the other carriers can be seen passing the USAir terminal.

The restaurant on the top floor is reported to be open again. Here, for the occasional Coke (albeit at New York prices) the aprons and runways can be seen.

The Butler Marine Air Terminal handles many executive aircraft each day. This building is a little piece of history. Inside it are exhibits from the days when this was a terminal for Pan Am flying boats. The art deco interior has been restored, and anyone interested in aviation history will make time to have a look round.

The fence around the Butler apron makes photos of the aircraft difficult, wide angle lenses suffering from vignetting caused by the chainlink being within the depth of field. A quick look from the roof of a hire car, parked in the taxi rank can reward camera users. It would be all the opportunity a terrorist needs but that seems to have been overlooked.

The cargo buildings close to the threshold of Runway 4 have a small car park from which the taxiway is but a small distance. Photography and viewing in the mornings can be particularly good from here if this runway is in use, though most photographers have to restrict themselves to landing aircraft as their subject matter. Most 'alternative' vantage points are now to be found around the threshold of Runway 4.

NEW YORK Heliports

The traffic on Manhattan's overcrowded and chaotic streets makes the use of helicopters essential for some businessmen with tight schedules, and many of the flights are included in the first class ticket to New York. Spotters will gain little by a visit to any of these locations, as the fleets are seen regularly at the three main airports.

For the photographer, the rewards are much greater, as rampside photos are possible at the heliports. The three most famous buildings in Manhattan are probably the Empire State Building, The World Trade Center and the United Nations, and each has a heliport close by. That at the WORLD TRADE CENTER was just to the southwest of the twin towers, on the bank of the Hudson River, and this may be the location of the DOWNTOWN MANHATTAN pad. The other two both overlook the East River. The EAST 34th STREET heliport is well-placed for camera work in the afternoon, as the vantage point for the ramp looks northeast and the traffic handled is similar to EAST 60th STREET, known locally as Metroport, near the United Nations Building.

Anyone venturing into Manhattan with a car would do well to do so at the weekend, when the traffic is tolerable. On the west side of the island, at Pier 86, is the retired aircraft carrier USS Intrepid, and admission allows inspection of a good selection of airpower on the deck and below. The collection is no longer restricted to Naval types, as even an SR-71 has found its way here. On Sunday mornings, Manhattan can be a sane place, and ideal for exploration. An early start allows visits to the Statue of Liberty and many other sights before the serious business of queuing builds up.

NIAGARA FALLS NY

| IAG | KIAG | International | 12m/19km E |

Since airline traffic to this scenic spot of New York State is handled through Buffalo, the airport is only used by general aviation, Bell Helicopters and some military units. Quite a drive out of the town, the airport is at the junctions of Highways 62 and 182, the latter being Porter Road. The terminal side of the field reveals nothing out of the ordinary for most enthusiasts but the southwest corner of the field is occupied by the Army National Guard, who have UH-1s and OH-6s on their ramp.

The Bell assembly plant, at the southeast corner of the field, rarely provides movements of any interest but the next left turn leads to the north side, where the New York ANG and an AFRES unit are based. A written request for a tour of the ramp may be rewarded but there will always be consolation in the camouflaged F-101 gate guardian.

Across the border, in Canada, there is another airport for Niagara Falls but this only has a collection of general aviation to be seen on the ramp.

PLATTSBURGH NY

| PLB | Municipal | 3m/5km SW |

Plattsburgh is best known for its USAF base and the FB-111s which are found there. A lazy hour or two can be passed, sitting on the shore of Lake Champlain, as the swingers fly low overhead on final approach. The airport is not busy but it is pleasant. The apron in front of the tiny terminal often has at least one photogenic commuter. Permission to photograph is worth the request. Commutiar have a maintenance base here, where weekends see work on their Beech 1900s. A few DC-3s are now believed to have been added to the fleet for pleasure flights.

POUGHKEEPSIE NY

| POU | Dutchess County | 5m/8km SE |

If a visit is planned to Plattsburgh, there is really little point in airliner enthusiasts trying to find Poughkeepsie. It is served by only a few Metro Beech 1900s each day. Corporate aircraft are to seen here, however, as IBM's headquarters are close by. Their business relations are enormous, meaning that large corporate customers also visit Dutchess County.

SYRACUSE NY
SYR   KSYR   Hancock Field   7m/11km NE (bus 15 minutes)

Leaving the city north on Highway 11, the airport is on the east of the road and its terminal has been substantially extended, so that it now looks rather more like a modern building. The old roof terrace was a casualty in these improvements but the multi-storey car park has always been the best vantage point anyway. Scheduled traffic is a surprisingly good mixture, though USAir dominates, and other airlines are represented with aircraft up to 727 size. This was, a long time ago, a hub for Empire Airlines, which was taken over by Piedmont, and now USAir. The hub operations have been cut back drastically but the airline is still by far the biggest operator here.

The southern edge of the field has a number of general aviation facilities plus a resident Army detachment of UH-1s and OH-58s, whilst the northern side is home to the New York ANG, which now operates F-16s. Various gates to this base are guarded by a selection of types which have previously seen service with the unit.

UTICA NY
UCA   Oneida County   11m/17km NW

Empire Airlines once used Oneida as their headquarters and maintenance facility, though the hub of their operations was Buffalo. With their absorption into Piedmont and then USAir, the traffic at this small airport has been rationalised to mostly commuter flights which leave very early in the morning for destinations in upper New York State.

Only one or two, at the most, commuter-liners are seen at the small, neat terminal on a visit here, and it is probable that the reason for being in the area will be to take part in one of the guided tours of Griffiss Air Force Base. These are arranged for a 1:00pm start on certain days but it would be worth checking before a long journey, as the tours are subject to annoying cancellation due to a lack of participants.

WESTHAMPTON BEACH NY
FOK   KFOK   Suffolk County   2m/3km NE

It's a long drive across Long Island to this airport, and not worth the effort without a specific purpose. Exit 63 off Sunrise Expressway (Hwy 27) leads south along Riverhead Road to the field. It was once an active military base but all that now remain are a few National Guard Jolly Green rescue helicopters.

WHITE PLAINS NY
HPN   KHPN   Westchester County   7m/11km NW

This airport has a growing timetable of scheduled departures. It has capitalised, like Islip, on the difficulty of getting around New York City. No longer is it necessary to be troubled by the traffic and parking problems which a flight to another major city once entailed. Many major airports in the northeastern states can be reached direct, with even Detroit and Chicago being served non-stop from this airport. Congestion at La Guardia, both landside and airside, is contributing in a big way to expansion here.

Whilst this is one airport where it may be possible to get close to commuter operations, Beech 1900s and SD3.30s being a speciality here, the main attraction is the thirty to forty biz-jets which are based. Not far from the airport is the gigantic estate of Pocantico Hills, owned by the Rockefeller family, and this is the logical place for their fleet of aircraft to be based. Few people have heard of Wayfarer-Ketch, the Rockefeller's private air taxi company, and the first few enthusiasts to have the nerve to walk up to the security gate and ask for directions to this office may be rewarded by being told to take the long walk past all the other hangars, as your destination is right at the end of the apron! The guard would assume that anyone asking for this company must have a good reason for a visit but it would be sensible to be dressed in something more appropriate than jeans and T-shirt or a patch-emblazoned parka (depending on the season) before attempting this audacious move!

AKRON OH

CAK	KAKR	Akron-Canton Regional	16m/26km SSE of Akron

Easily reached by road, the airport is in North Canton, next to exit 113 off I-77. The long-term car park, which costs a couple of bucks, is a short walk from the terminal. On the roof is an open-air observation deck, overlooking Runway 5/23 and most (but not all) of the apron. Views to the sides are rather restricted but access to the boarding gates is possible, to see the others. There are only 35 weekday departures, over half of which are USAir, so traffic can't be described as brisk. Comair, Northwest Airlink and United make up the rest, mostly with feeder-liners, though USAir Fokker 100s make regular appearances.

Rather than stand on the observation deck all day, listening to its sweet music (!), a tour of the perimeter might be more rewarding. From the parking lot, a turn into Lauby Road leads to another right, resulting in views of the general aviation at the Goodyear, Laurence, Ohio Valley and Gordon Aviation facilities. Back on Lauby Road, look for a turning onto Mount Pleasant, which heads west. The 356th Fighter Group Restaurant has nothing on display outside but, by following Waywood, Wales and Massillon, the Military Aviation Preservation Society's C-47 and F-86 hulks can be seen.

Back on Massillon, the turn onto Koons Road brings more hangars and the Army Aviation Support facility into view, after which the next turn, Greensburg, heads east past the Goodrich Hangar alongside West Airport Road, after which Lauby Road heads back to the terminal.

There are plenty of FBOs, most of which handle some executive traffic. References to BF Goodrich and Goodyear will indicate what you should know by now: this is where a lot of tyres are made!

CINCINNATI OH

LUK	KLUK	Lunken Municipal	6m/9km ENE

The international airport is located across the river, in Kentucky, so the city's only airfield in Ohio is used by general aviation. Take exit 9 off I-71 and head south. From Columbia Parkway, you can't miss it. Not just Cessnas and Pipers here - this is quite a busy airfield, with a reasonable selection of business aircraft to be seen.

CLEVELAND OH

CLE	KCLE	Hopkins International	12m/19km WSW

Berea Freeway links the city with its airport and the main terminal's small outdoor spectator deck, open from 7:30 am and no charge, is to be found at the end of Concourse B. Early mornings are best for photographs and, by lunchtime, it's time to look for somewhere else. In winter, the open deck is inaccessible (to prevent juveniles throwing snowballs at the Southwest 737s!) but there is an indoor facility. All the concourses are accessible, and a close-up view of almost any airliner operating a scheduled service is possible. The window at TWA's Gate A5 is worth investigation, as are Delta's Gates B2 and B4. One window on the Connector to

Concourse A offers a good view of USAir's activity.
Continental and its attendant feeder services, operated by Britt Brasilias, accounts for half the scheduled traffic. The remainder consists of the usual American carriers plus one or two Air Ontario movements. In other words, Cleveland offers nothing that can't be seen just as well at other airports. A tour of the perimeter is therefore in order but it isn't possible to drive right round the field. The road ends at Runway 5R where photos are possible.
All the various ramps are easily seen from the road, with a small number of executive aircraft bolstering the considerable quantity of single engined machinery. The Air Services FBO handles the occasional exotic visitor and is worth investigation. Beyond it are the cargo areas, with the usual UPS 727 and DC-8 in evidence. The post office parking lot is useful for photographers. Fed Ex have their own apron, where three 727s normally spend the day. It's necessary to backtrack onto Berea Freeway, in order to get onto IX (International Exhibition) Center Drive. Beyond the IX Jet Center is the threshold of Runway 5R.
North of the field, Brookpark Road (SR17) passes the thresholds of Runways 23L/R. The 100th Bomb Group Restaurant has a P-51 Mustang and a car park. By standing on the car roof, it's easy to take good photos of aircraft turning onto 23L for take off, with the control tower in the background. Accessible from Brookpark Road, on West Hangar Road (the third set of lights after the restaurant) is NASA's Lewis Research Center. The road crosses the taxiway into the NASA ramp, where one or two aircraft can usually be seen. Beyond is 5K Flights and the airport's remaining stock of general aviation.

CLEVELAND OH
BKL   Burke Lakefront   2m/3km N

Anyone interested in general aviation, and staying in the Cleveland area, will investigate Burke Lakefront, once used by weekday Northcoast Executive Metros, but no longer. For those intent on taking a look, it's close to the stadium used by the Cleveland Browns and to the Rock n Roll Hall of Fame. North Marginal Drive, leads past the coastguard base, to the airport. There is a small terminal, the main lobby of which allows the ramp to be seen.
A tour of the perimeter leads first to Million Air and Aircraft Companies, both ramps being behind a high fence which makes photography impossible, even when standing on the car roof. At the back of the Aviation High School is a DC-3 and a few other aircraft.
The best time to visit Burke Lakefront (if there is one) is in early September, when the Cleveland National Air Show is held. Traffic also increases in early July, when the Budweiser Grand Prix takes place.

CLEVELAND OH
CGF   Cuyahoga County   14m/22km ENE

Taking I-90 towards Richmond Heights, the airport is south of exit 182. It is a major general aviation field, handling a fair number of biz-jets among its many executive aircraft. For anyone with an interest in quantity, this is an airfield not to be missed. For saturation coverage of the area, a visit to Lost Nation Airport (LNN) in Willoughby will be essential. Its principal attraction will be the United States Aviation Museum, which is being relocated there, and due to open in Spring 1995.

COLUMBUS OH
CMH KCMH   Port Columbus International   7m/11km NE

The city is not on many touring intineraries because it doesn't lie between two important centres.

Like Cleveland, it is also served by several airports, spread out around the town. The international airport lacks volume of traffic to make it worth the detour in its own right but it's fine for America West A320s.

The passenger terminal sits at the end of its approach road, Stelzer Road off I-670, with the parallel runways 10/28 on either side. Before reaching the terminal in a car, one of the general aviation facilities is on the right. The other, served by its own two short diagonal runways, is on the far side of the field, tucked in the southeast corner.

COLUMBUS OH
OSU   Ohio State University   11m/17km NNW

The airport's name says everything about its location. Much of the general aviation activity is generated by the university, which has its own Aerotechnology program. The number of residents is large though, in the main, somewhat lacklustre. For anyone who wants to log over a hundred light aircraft without trouble, this is useful destination.

COLUMBUS OH
LCK   KLCK   Rickenbacker   11m/17km S

Highway 23 leads from exit 52 off I-270 to what is, for many, the most interesting airport in the area. It is not the exclusively a military field and its status is changing. The ANG's 121st Fighter Wing was due to take its A-7s elsewhere towards the end of 1994, leaving a few C-141s and KC-135s on the base. A small museum could provide the excuse for seeking a short-term pass to get closer to the action.

DAYTON OH
DAY   KDAY   James M Cox International   12m/19km NNW

The airport is in Vandalia, easily reached from either exit 63 off I-75 or exit 32 from I-70. Terminal Drive leads to an impressive building, inside which things are rather good. There are two piers/concourses, B and C (don't ask!) USAir's being on the left. The other is mostly for United and American flights. The concourse windows are not tinted, which is good news for photographers, and almost anything which uses the passenger terminal can be photographed from somewhere. If traffic gets slow, a game of pool next to the restaurant also allows one eye to be kept on events outside.

In 1992 USAir stopped using Dayton as a hub, though they didn't pull out altogether. The effect on movements was instant and drastic. Daily jet departures fell overnight from seventy-three to twenty. Business is starting to get better. Including commuter traffic, there are now over a hundred scheduled passenger flights departing each weekday. USAir accounts for more than a third of the movements, followed by Continental with a quarter. The rest is the usual mix but it must be said that variety of aircraft types is surprisingly good.

Dayton is regarded as synonymous with the major overnight parcels carrier, Emery Worldwide, and their Superhub. Anyone expecting to see large numbers of this airline's aircraft will be disappointed as they arrive from all over the country after midnight and leave again before dawn. Between these times, forty or so DC-8s and 727s are turned round, though it is academic to the average enthusiast. The apron is on the eastern side of the field, next to the threshold of Runway 24L, reached off Peters Pike. A large sign says (shouts?): AUTHORIZED PERSONNEL ONLY, which rather suggests Emery don't want to be bothered with casual visitors. Anyone with a serious interest in overnight parcels handling would be well advised to write to them at their headquarters: 3350 West Bayshore, Palo Alto, California 94303.

DAYTON OH
MGY   Montgomery County

Top Flight Air Service link Dayton with Cleveland, Toledo and Detroit. To keep services attractive to the businessman, they make use of smaller, and more convenient, airports. Their movements, mostly Aerostars and Navajo Chieftains, use this airport. General aviation is also to be found in quantity at Moraine Air Park, some five miles south of the city.

DAYTON OH
FFO   KFFO   Wright-Patterson Air Force Base   9m/15km NE

West of Fairborn, this is the home of the United States Air Force Museum, which is open between 9:00am and 5:00pm. Arrival should be arranged early in the day as there is a lot to see. The museum now occupies two buildings, outside which a white B-1 bomber is parked. The first building is divided into two: the Early Years on the right and the Air Power Gallery to the left. Wow! A B-36 dominates this hall, though the B-29 at the other end also takes up a bit of space.

A walkway leads to the Modern Flight hangar, inside which you are greeted by an F-117. Behind it stands a B-52, with a B-47, SR-71, B-58 and the XB-70 Valkyrie at the back. On the right from the entrance door are, among many others, a C-46, C-47 and C-124. This is one very large building!

Not on show here are the Presidential aircraft, which form part of a separate display, found in the annex. Check in the lobby for the times when the shuttle bus operates to the old hangars. Not to be missed is the IMAX movie theatre: what America does rather well. The usual - 80 feet high screen, six channel stereo that makes the floor move, that sort of thing!

Generally, it can be assumed that if the USAF flew it, the museum has it, and any military-minded enthusiast will find this museum to be exactly what it should be: the best in the world. It can take a whole day to enjoy this museum. Even the gift shop is worth an hour. For details, write to USAF Museum, Wright-Patterson ADB, Ohio 45433-6518, USA. Two telephone numbers which might be of use are the museum on (513) 255-3286 and the movies on (513) 253-IMAX.

An interest in the history of aviation makes Dayton a special place. It all started in a bicycle shop at 22 South Williams Street, where the Wright Brothers thought it might be possible to fly. The area has several attractions, and an information leaflet is avaiable at the museum for those wishing to investigate further.

MANSFIELD OH
MFD   Lahm Municipal   3m/5km N

About halfway between Akron and Columbus, Lahm handles most of mid-Ohio's general aviation as well as being the home of 179 Airlift Group's C-130s. It is worth the detour for anyone passing through.

SPRINGFIELD OH
SGH   Beckley Municipal   6m/9km SSW

Very little happens here in the way of airline activity, as it is primarily a general aviation field. The civil aircraft share the runways, however, with the Ohio ANG F-16s. This may be enough reason for a visit.

TOLEDO OH

TOL   KTOL   Express   14m/22km W

It's wise to avoid the city, without good reason to visit. The airport is best reached from the Ohio Turnpike, I-80/90, off exit 3A. The long term car park is cheapest, and reasonably close to the terminal. Through the doors, go straight ahead to the security check point, after which an escalator leads to the upper level. Windows at either side allow views of the airliners, many of which are commuters, and those at the far end overlook the general aviation and ANG ramp with its F-16s.

Scheduled traffic rarely exceeeds 727-size (Delta, usually), the rest being a mixture of Comair SF.340s, American Eagle ATR-42s, Chicago Express Jetstreams and the like. Photos in the afternoon are reasonable, though the glass is slightly tinted.

For views of the rest of the field, head east along Airport HIghway. An off-road car park allows a good view of the airfield (including the F-16s) but the company might be disturbing. It's a great place for whatever young couples do in cars. Wind down the window, breathe in and smell that pot! East Service Road leads to Express Aviation, for some general aviation, and is a dead end. Off Airport Highway in the opposite direction is Garden Road, which passes the gates of the ANG base. The next right, Eber Road, passes under the runway flightpath on the way to Burlington Express. Usually there is nothing to be seen during daylight hours.

WILMINGTON OH

ILN   Clinton/Airborne Airpark   6m/9km SE

Not to be confused with Greater Wilmington (ILG), this is the Airborne Express hub. Very little happens during the day but the evenings are most interesting, especially with an airband radio. The centre/approach frequency is officially 118.85, 24 hours a day, but the airline's own frequency (unknown) makes better listening, as the crews of the various YS-11s, DC-8s and DC-9s talk to each other. It has been reported that the tower offers no radio assistance at night. This, if be confirmed, would make things very lively indeed!

YOUNGSTOWN OH

YNG   KYNG   Warren Regional   10m/16km NW

Bad news can still be good information: anyone who wants to know about the observation deck at this airport will be displeased. It's outdoors but the wire mesh is perfect for ensuring that photography is all but impossible. That said, the view is reasonable in the mornings. What is lacking is traffic. USAir Express share the work with Northwest Airlink and United Express. Two commuter liners on the ramp at the same time is, at this airport, as hectic as it gets. Visible are the AFRES C-130s, which rarely move, and a couple of FBOs, Cafaro and Am-Air, reached off State Road 193. An entry of this nature could save someone a long, and worthless, journey.

ARDMORE OK

ADM   KADM   Airpark   13m/20km E

This former Air Force Base is about halfway between Oklahoma City and Dallas. Its attraction has nothing to do with scheduled traffic, nor much with general aviation or military movements. Instead what it offers is a view over the fence of something that doesn't move at all. Lockheed's prototype L1011 came to rest here, in the company of an Eastern Airlines example, plus a Pan Am 747 and a Trump 727. They have been joined recently by a number of United 727s and DC-

10s. If access is needed for photography, the fire/security department are likely to be of assistance.

OKLAHOMA CITY OK

OKC   KOKC   Will Rogers World   10m/16km SW

If this is truly a world airport, it must be due to the number of foreign-made aircraft which use it: American Airlines Fokker 100s and ASA ATR-72s being obvious examples. Activity is, to be generous, modest. An observation tower, suitable for spotters, costs 20 cents admission and has speakers tuned to the control tower frequency. An open air observation deck in the passnger terminal faces south, so its popularity with serious photographers is limited. Without a car, afternoons are best, as the east employee parking lot, just north of the old air cargo building, faces the taxiway. The chain link fence has clearly proved problematical to preceding photographers but the problems seem to have been partially solved, judging by the state of the barbed wire.

Within walking distance (ish) from the terminal area are the north cargo ramp and AAR Oklahoma, the FBO. The cargo ramp can boast a good variety of air freighters and the FBO is partially an airliner repair station. Maybe it doesn't handle all that much business but few would turn down the opportunity to see such goodies as an Azerbaijan Airlines 727, a Southeast Pacific Airways (Chile) 737 or a Paradise Island Dash 7, all of which made their first appearances here. Discreet photography over the fence might yield better results than asking, as there is a policy of requiring the owner's permission to do so officially.

A car is required to visit the north end of the field. The Oklahoma ANG C-130s are based here, as is the FAA's Mike Monroe Air Center. For access to the FAA ramp, which can't be seen from the road, contact with the public affairs office is almost obligatory. The other notable presence is a fleet of jets owned by the US Marshal. They are used for flying federal prisoners. Don't even think of asking!

The third weekend in June is a good time to visit Will Rogers, for this is when the west side of the field is taken over by the annual Aerospace America airshow. The line-up is impressive enough for it to be worth seeking written approval for access to the huge static display before the crowds arrive.

OKLAHOMA CITY OK

TIK   KTIK   Tinker Air Force Base   8m/13km SE

A visit to Oklahoma may mean more than passing through on an Airpass. If this be so, then Tinker is worth a look. It's home to the Air Logistics Center, though resident aircraft are few. The occasional B-1 or KC-135, undergoing or awaiting refurbishment, is consolation. TAFB has recently been designated as the overhaul centre for B-2 stealth bombers, so there's always hope of seeing something extraordinary in the pattern. More in evidence are the E-3A AWACS, the Oklahoma ANG F-16s and, most notably, the Navy's TACOMO E-6s. When aircraft land from the south, good approach photos are possible from an open field overlooking the end of Runway 18, just to the north of I-40. The police are used to enthusiasts and are unlikely to bother them but it must be remembered that activity is slow.

OKLAHOMA CITY OK

PWA   Wiley Post   9m/15km NW

The city's principal general aviation field is also the home of the Commander Aircraft production line. Interesting residents include a C-47, restored to 1942 Army Air Corps markings, and an S-

188

2F Tracker in full Navy colours. For spotters, the average weekday should yield a hundred or so light aircraft. Other general aviation fields in the area include STILLWATER Municipal (code SWO), sometimes used by Oklahoma State University for college football charters, and NORMAN University Park which, if nothing else, is close to I-35.

TULSA OK

| TUL | KTUL | International | 9m/15km NE |

The name is rather optimistic as there are no scheduled international flights. Traffic is mostly Comair Regional Jets, ASA ATR-72s and Northwest Airlink SF.340s. The large, spacious passenger terminal faces northeast so photography through the concourse windows is relatively easy.

The perimeter invites exploration and a car is essential. A series of small streets leads round the end of Runway 1 to Sheridan Road. A turn to the north reveals the general aviation hangars and, possibly of interest, Nordam Industries, who make 737-200 hush kits. Their test bed 737 is often present here.

36th Street North is where the interest starts to grow. The first right leads to Tulsa Technology Center, where three ex-Alitalia DC-8-43s languish, now close to dereliction. The 727 wearing TTC titles is ex-Air France. Further along 36th Street North is the Oklahoma ANG unit, with its A-7Es. Look out also for a right turn to Mingo Road, where American Airlines have an enormous maintenance base. The hangars, unfortunately, block most of the view. The Rockwell and McDonnell Douglas plants, further south, are both closed.

Avid spotters should be aware that there are other, general aviation, fields in the area. R Lloyd Jones Airport is probably the most notable, southeast of the city. It has, among its residents, an An-2.

EUGENE OR

| EUG | Mahlon Sweet Field | 8m/13km NW |

Anyone visiting Oregon will probably do so for its outstanding scenery, rather than to see this airport. It is a small, parochial field with a limited offering of flights, the links being to Seattle and Portland with Horizon Air, and elsewhere with United or Delta. The old fashioned terminal is on the east side of the runway and the airliners park in front of it, making photography difficult. The commuter types are easier to get at but the ground level access means that a lot of foreground clutter may spoil the view. The real view here is of the mountains and any would-be visitor would do well to remember the fact, rather than hope for close-ups with a scenic backdrop.

MEDFORD OR

| MFR | Municipal | 3m/5km N |

Ramp access is essential for the photographer, as the more interesting residents are close to the fences. With thousands of square miles of forests all round, Medford makes an obvious base for a few fire fighters during the season. A Catalina, possibly resident, has been noted and one or two biz-jets can normally be expected.

ALLENTOWN PA

| ABE | /Bethlehem/Easton | 4m/6km NE of Allentown |

Three industrial towns have grown into one long conurbation. Their economic fortunes grew with

DUBAI International – photos are possible at the perimeter, with blue skies and brilliant sunshine. THY A340 TC-JDJ is seen here on final approach.   Neil Clarke

HAVANA Jose Marti International – the domestic terminal observation deck overlooks less action but offers good views of aicraft like Cubana An-24RV CU-T1262.   Chris Boyle

FRANKFURT Main International – Runway 18 is normally used for departures and the observation platform allows excellent photography. Lufthansa A340 D-AIBC rolling, under full power.

Michel Magalhaes

BANGKOK Don Maung International – Royal Jordanian TriStar 500 JY-AGC on the international apron, as seen from behind the glass of the observation deck.
Paul Chandler

ROME Fiumicino – the perimeter offers several places to take photos, often with the sun in the right place, as this 747-200 of Aerolineas Argentinas, LV-OPA, clearly shows.   Marco Finelli

SAN DIEGO Lindbergh International – ground level viewing areas at the perimeter ensure good photos. Northwest A320 N211US taxies to the hold.   Andrew Abshier

SAN JOSE Municipal – some viewing decks might offer more panoramic views but photography is good. TWA MD-82 N952Y makes a good subject as it taxies to its stand.   Michel Magalhaes

ORLANDO International – not only are there plenty of viewing points around the terminal area and the perimeter, there are interesting visitors, such as SAM DC-9-31 XA-SHR.   Alan Lord

MINNEAPOLIS-ST PAUL International – Northwest may dominate the activity but photos from the observation area include other subject matter, like American Airlines Fokker 100 N1445B.

Chris English

CLEVELAND Hopkins International – Continental 727 200 N34415 leaves the terminal on departure, seen from the deck, with NASA's facility on the far side of the field. Vik Saini

VIENNA Schwechat – the sun can sometimes be a problem but Eva Air 767-300ER B-16602 makes a good subject on pushback before departure. Michel Magalhaes

PRAGUE Ruzyne – the roof terrace is open all year round, as proved by this photo of CSA 737-500 OK-XGE, being pushed back on a bitterly cold winter's day. Henry Tenby

JAKARTA Soekarno Hatta – observation decks on the domestic side terminals are screened with mesh which does have a slight effect on photos, as might be noticed in this shot of Airfast 737-200 PK-OCF.   Paul Chandler

MOSCOW Vnukovo – the observation deck overlooks wall-to-wall Tu-154s in a variety of colours. Locally-based Alak Airlines RA-85712 is prepared for service.   Alan Lord

MELBOURNE Tullamarine – photos from the domestic terminal can also include aircraft like Air Polynesia 737-300 5W-ILF being towed from the maintenance area to a stand.   Paul Chandler

KUALA LUMPUR Subang International – photos are possible from airside. Cambodia 737-200 N197AL taxies past the terminal on its way to the runway.   Paul Chandler

the steel industry but the decline was abrupt and this became one of America's more depressed areas. A certain amount of regeneration is breathing new hope into the area but the airport, lacking its lifeblood of businessmen on the move, still functions at a fraction of its earlier hey-day. It is linked to all major hubs in the region, with a varied selection of operators and types, up to 727 size. Apart from being a good place to stop for a cheap snack and a good photo of one or two airliners on the ramp, the Bethlehem Steel fleet of biz-jets is based directly opposite the terminal, on the far side of the runway.

Heading northeast from Allentown, another airport rejoicing in the name of MIFFLINTOWN, is worth a visit, if only for its airworthy Lockheed Lodestar.

ERIE PA
ERI   International   6m/9km WSW

Two operators, USAir and Northwest Airlink, serve this regional airport with 737s, DC-9s, Fokker 100s and Metros. It does not get busy. The apron can only be seen from the cafe and the restaurant, so buying a coffee and a donut seems to be the order of the day. What was the observation deck has now been turned into a break room for airport employees, though there is no report of what the view is/was like.

Given that airline operations are not particularly inspiring, a tour of the perimeter is likely. The general aviation is nothing special. The Erie Airways hangar and apron can be empty, not that it gets particularly full, and is reached on Kudlack, accessible off Ashbury Avenue.

HARRISBURG PA
MDT KMDT International   4m/6km SE

The airport shares a runway with Olmsted AFB and is located in Middletown, hence the MDT code. From Harrisburg, cross the river and turn right along Front Street, parallel to the river. After passing under the turnpike, keep straight on, along 2nd Street and the airport is on the north bank. It is hardly worth the effort for photography but the road from the terminal to Middletown reveals the Air Force Base on the right, in the distance. The Pennsylvania Air National Guard EC-130s rarely move and are normally lined up, within range of a 200mm lens.

Scheduled services for passengers are increasing, and there is now a strong cargo presence here. Pennsylvania Airlines, who are based, operate Shorts, Beech 1900s and Dash 8s. Scheduled services are operated to all the region's hubs by a good range of aircraft, up to 727 size. Air Toronto provides the international link with regular Jetstream flights to Canada. The city's bizjet and King Air population are also in evidence, and access to the ramp isn't normally a problem. German Cargo are surprisingly regular visitors, and the local overhaul facility, Stambaugh's Aviation, services FedEx's F.27s as well as US Navy T-39s, A-4s and T-2s.

The new passenger terminal offers good views over the field from its observation deck on the elevated departure level, and reasonable photos can be taken through the glass.

HARRISBURG PA
HAR KHAR Skyport   3m/5km S

From Harrisburg International, backtrack to the Harris Bridge across the Susquehanna River and take Interstate 83 to New Cumberland. Harrisburg Skyport, previously known as Capital City, is easy to find from here. With all the scheduled traffic using the international airport, only general aviation is in evidence, though one or two antiques do make the trip worthwhile . . . but only if staying in the area, with time to kill.

JOHNSTOWN PA
JST   Cambria County   5m/8km E

Take Frankstown Road from town and a right turn leads south to the airport. Alternatively, it can be found just to the north of Highway 219. With only the occasional Beech 1900 commuter/feeder during the day, traffic is light but, for anyone passing on the way across country to or from Pittsburgh, it may be worth a quick visit.

LATROBE PA
LBE   Westmoreland County   1m/1.5km

Once the home of Jetstream Airlines, Latrobe now receives the odd Twin Otter service. Most of these are bound for Pittsburgh and, unless there is a need to see all of Pennsylvania's airports, it might be sensible to do the same thing.

PHILADELPHIA PA
PHL   KPHL   International   8m/13km SSW (train 25 minutes)

Leaving the city of Philadelphia southbound on Interstate 95, the airport is on the left with its eastern boundary being the Delaware River. Alternatively, the train costs $4.75 each way. There are no external viewing facilities (indeed there are no formal viewing facilities at all) but the main terminal is used almost exclusively by domestic traffic, and the fingers of the spread-eagled building all allow close inspection of airliners parked on the apron. Perhaps the most convenient for most purposes are Concourses B and C reached, as usual, via security checkpoints.

An afternoon's patient viewing will be amply rewarded by a good selection of airlines, with a wide variety of local commuter carriers. USAir dominate the proceedings however. The extremity of the piers is very close to one of the taxiways and there are few better locations for high quality photographs than this, after lunchtime. The apron next to Concourse B has been used for storage. Eastern Airlines 727s and Intair Canada F.100s became a notable presence. When airline operators finally succumb to financial pressures, a few debts are sometimes left behind. These can often include significant unpaid landing fees. Substantial sums are involved, and the possession of aircraft is used as a lever to recoup some of those losses. It's a hard world!

Scheduled international traffic does feature the occasional overseas arrival, which parks at the western end of the passenger terminal, and close views of these movements are a matter of luck.

To the north of the main terminal area, off Concourse E, is a ramp where USAir Express carry out their Philadelphia operations. Those wishing to obtain some permanent detailed record of this will need to make the rather long walk between Concourses C and E. It is worth the effort because there is also the biz-jet ramp, where up to ten aircraft are normally to be seen with, as an added bonus, aircraft on the cargo ramp, such as the occasional World Airways MD-11 and Capitol 727. At the opposite extreme, Concourse A might not be quite so rewarding: the parcels carriers can be seen from here but frustration can be in store, as only one or two of the aircraft can be logged.

Access to the Atlantic Aviation facility was once a matter of driving up to the gatehouse and being waved past by the guard. Security arrangements are now generally more stringent and a letter in advance could allow a good look at large numbers of executive jets and turbo-props, plus several Beech 18s operated by smaller cargo charter carriers. Another part of the field worthy of close attention is Cargo City, accessible by Island Road, to the south of the field.

Slightly further south, and visible from the highway, is Boeing Vertol's large hangar and apron. It is not renowned for having helicopter's on show.

PHILADELPHIA PA
PNE   KPNE   Northeast   12m/19km NE

Not an airport for scheduled traffic but the old terminal building remains to give an idea of what the place must have been like in its hey-day. The apron is expansive and is often occupied during the week by a good number of executive aircraft whose operators benefit from the lower handling charges and relative proximity of the city.

Ransome Airlines have prospered for many years, though their image has been subdued because most of them have been spent as a feeder carrier. Currently TWExpress, instead of Pan Am Express, their fleet comprises Dash 7s and ATR-42s. The maintenance base is to the right of the terminal but most of their aircraft will be easier to see at JFK. The corporate headquarters are here, and the reception area features a sales counter worthy of inspection, with numerous souvenirs at very reasonable prices.

Visitors to this part of Pennsylvania may wish to consider a detour to one or two other locations of interest. Lovers of Constellations will take the trouble to locate the suburb of PENNDEL, a few miles northeast on Highway 1, where L-1049E N1005C was converted into Jim Flannery's Restaurant. Leaving the city on Highway 611, the WILLOW GROVE Naval Air Station can't be missed, being next to the road. A selection of museum pieces has been placed next to the road for the spectator's interest and, beyond these, a ramp of two squadrons of P-3s provides an excellent prospect. Because there are so many different types of military aircraft operated from this field, visitors will take advantage, no doubt, of the roads around the perimeter. A left turn off Hwy 611 at County Line Road leads to Keith Valley Road (small and easily missed) and the next left turn is Governor's Road, which peters out into a track before stopping at the fence, overlooking the ramp for A-37s and C-130s. By checking down every lane on the perimeter, views of the various naval/marines helicopters and other types will be possible. Willow Grove's claim to fame is that it has the world's largest bowling alley . . . more than a hundred lanes.

Parallel to County Line Road is Highway 132 which gives access to the Turnpike and passes WARMINSTER Naval Air Development Center. The Turnpike (Interstate 276) crosses the Delaware River northeast of Philadelphia and just before the bridge is Exit 29 to 3M AIRPORT, where the Minnesota Mining & Manufacturing Company (3M) have a terminal for visitors to their nearby plant.

PITTSBURGH PA
PIT   KPIT   Greater Pittsburgh International   16m/25km NW

The massive industrial city of Pittsburgh is in Allegheny County. The local airline took its name from the county and, after several take-over and amalgamation deals, USAir was created.

With Pittsburgh being a major hub for USAir, the movements here are totally dominated by the one airline. In 1990, they accounted for 83% of all landings. The old terminal, like Stapleton airport, came to the end of its useful life overnight. From October 1992, the new Airside Terminal became operational. Without doubt, this is a very large airport indeed. According to one press statement, the field occupies over 12,000 acres - more than Atlanta and O'Hare combined.

The Airside Terminal lies between the parallel runways, accessible from the west. The main building forms a large diagonal cross and most of its gates are, not surprisingly, used by USAir. Concourse D is used by the others, and Concourse C is for international flights. Commuter feeders have their own gates on a small apron in front of the check-in building. A people-mover gives access to the building and entry doesn't require boarding cards. Apart from the international wing, the rest is up to you . Each concourse has twenty-five gates, so there is a lot of walking to do. Concourse E, used by USAir Express, is visible from C or D, so this cuts down the work. Walking to the extremity of Concourse A is essential, to log all the cargo aircraft, many of which park at very inconvenient angles. After that, it might be best to settle down at the end of D, which allows a view of 10L/28R.

A trip to USAir's maintenance base, in the centre of the field, also reveals the general aviation terminal, and a considerable number of business aircraft. Also seen from this part of the field are the Air National Guard movements, with their A-7s in the circuit and the more static C-130s.

PITTSBURGH PA

AGC   Allegheny County

What general aviation is seen at Greater Pittsburgh is clearly only a fraction of the traffic and residents required by the area. Most of it is to be found at Allegheny County, including plenty of biz-jets, the occasional DC-3 and a fair number of warbirds and antiques. Also worthy of investigation, for numbers only, are EAST PITTSBURGH and MONROEVILLE.

READING PA

RDG   Regional (General Spaatz)   3m/5km NW

This is still the home of Allegheny Commuter Airlines, previously Suburban Airlines, and it is the only place to be reasonably sure of an F.27 portrait. For permission to look around the apron, the fixed base operator, Reading Aviation (Suburban in disguise), should be contacted and the reward is seventy or so based aircraft, including some biz-jets and antiques.

STATE COLLEGE PA

SCE   University Park

This should not be confused with College Park, just north of Washington DC. Airline activity using the new passenger terminal is restricted to Pennsylvania Airlines plus a couple of FedEx Caravans, but a half a dozen biz-jets and the Clark Motor Company's vintage and warbird collection make the field worth the visit. Since the museum is in a closed (and spotter-proof) hangar, permission for a look should be sought in writing prior to arrival: the company is welcoming on this basis.

Not far from State College is LOCK HAVEN (W T Piper Memorial), where a number of pre-delivery exotica could be seen on the average visit, though the Taylorcraft Co production isn't the mecca it used to be.

WILKES-BARRE/SCRANTON PA

AVP   Avoca   12m/19km NE

The passenger terminal has a rooftop viewing area with free entry. Since it faces east, it is ideal for afternoon shots of USAir jets and a good range of dedicated commuters. With a 200mm zoom lens, excellent landing shots of visitors are possible, with the bonus of picturesque mountain scenery in the background. The fleet of Pocono Airlines Nord 262s found its final resting place here.

WILLIAMSPORT PA

IPT   KIPT   Lycoming County   5m/8km E

This small regional airport is used solely by Pennsylvania Airlines, as USAir Express, and the car park next to the passenger terminal is ideal for photography of these, and the odd collection of machines belonging to the Area Community College, including a T-29B. Inside the college hangar are more eccentric aircraft, and access is normally possible. A few of the other forty or so light aircraft on the main general aviation ramp, to the south, are also interesting.

ANDERSON SC

AND	KAND	County	3m/5km SW

If scheduled services operate here, none were seen. The approach road, off Highway 24E, features an F-105 directly opposite the terminal. Mountain Air Cargo have a shed here, the first building of any size on the left when arriving. Whether anything is to be seen outside it is a matter of luck. At the far side of the passenger terminal are the FBOs, who normally grant ramp access if requested. At the far end of the ramp is a C-47, N3BA, which last saw service with Academy Airlines. The titles are still to be seen but the missing engine and the collapsed oleo suggest it won't be moving in a hurry.

GREENVILLE/SPARTANBURG SC

GSP	Municipal	11m/17km NE/SW

Busy it isn't but it's extremely popular with local enthusiasts. The authorities, in their wisdom, have created a park in the centre of the ramp, and it's freely open to all visitors. Probably unique in all the USA, this is more like it! The catch? Of course there's a catch. There are very few aircraft to see and something is needed on which to stand to see over the fence, in order to take good photos.

CHATTANOOGA TN

CHA	KCHA	Lovell Field	10m/16km E

The passenger terminal sits opposite the intersection of the two runways, 2/20 and one designated as 33 only. Everything can be seen from it, in theory, as no report has been received to confirm this. Our correspondent was more concerned with the FBOs and the cargo aircraft. Fed Ex use F.27s and Airborne Express station a YS-11 here during the day, both of which can be seen from the fence. The FBOs include the Chattanooga Jet Center and Signal Air Services, among others, where executive aircraft are normally to be seen.

FAYETTEVILLE TN

FAY	Municipal	4m/6km S

There is nothing special about Fayetteville's airport. It handles a few United and American jet movements plus a regular procession of ASA Brasilias. Nearby is Fort Bragg, which generates some of the business. The 82nd Airborne Museum is at the base, and is probably of more interest, since its exhibits feature a number of transport aircraft.

MEMPHIS TN

MEM	KMEM	International	10m/16km SE

By day, a Northwest hub and by night Federal Express. These are the bare bones which need a little more meat. During daylight hours, the passenger terminal offers the chance to see a reasonable number, but limited selection, of airliners. Among these are normally about thirty or so Federal Express 727s. The cargo area also offers plenty to see.

On the far side of the field is the Tennessee Air National Guard, usually with half a dozen C-130s and the odd C-141B on its ramp. Close to their base is Federal Express. A car is essential for close encounters, and these should be restricted to the road. Getting closer means conversation with security personnel. Real interest in the operation should be followed up. A phone call to Fed Ex reveals that a tour of the operation is available, starting at the wholly unreasonable, but highly appropriate, hour of 11:30pm.

Also to be seen at the airport is the Bomb Group Restaurant which, in this instance (there are plenty of others around the country) has an unmarked C-47. Memphis is more than a hub for Federal Express: it was the home of Elvis Presley. His home, Graceland, is west of the airport. The road which passes under the runways is Winchester. A few blocks west is Elvis Presley Boulevard. A left turn leads to the house and his two jet transports, the Jetstar and the CV-880. As good taste can be flushed down the toilet when discussing anything to do with the Elvis legacy, nothing else needs be said.

West Memphis, across the river in Arkansas, is a quiet general aviation field but it does occasionally handle McNeeley's DC-3s, one of which still flies in RCAF colours. The airfield has no fences, so access isn't a problem!

KNOXVILLE TN
TYS   KTYS   McGhee Tyson   13m/20km S

US Highway 129 heads south from town and the airport is signposted. The passenger terminal handles an amount of commuters and up to DC-9 and 737-sized scheduled traffic. Next to the terminal is a car park, lower than the ramp so that nothing can be seen. On the right of the car park is the business terminal, which is accessible and, obviously, at apron level. A request for ramp access should meet with success. A C-47 is parked next to the garage hangars and on the far side of these is a Convair. The Cherokee Aviation hangar is at the end of the apron, where more general aviation is to be seen.

The Air National Guard base is on the far side of the parallel runways (4/22L/R). When leaving the terminal area, a side road to the left passes round the end of the runways, giving access to the cargo shed, where an assortment of aircraft are parked, including the almost obligatory Fed Ex jet. For a general aviation field with a difference, travel into town. Cross the river on Alcoa and double back onto Riverside Drive. By heading east, the Downtown Island Airport can be seen. It is, quite literally, what its name suggests.

MORRISTOWN TN
MOR   Moore-Murrell   6m/9km S

Signposts to this airport are difficult to find. Take US 11E, south from the town, and the airport is tucked away on the right, discreetly behind a housing estate. A memorial to the Reverend M M Murrell, an aviation pioneer, stands outside the entrance to the passenger terminal. One day, there may be a memorial to Morristown's more famous son, who became one of America's most famous drag-racing stars: Mr Conrad A Kalitta - or Connie, as he is better known. Having felt the need to fly his rods all over America, he developed a taste for aviation and the rest is history, as they say.

Off the approach road leading to the terminal is an insignificant turning on the left. Kalitta Flying Services are to be found here, with several Volpar Turboliners to be seen. There is also a C-47 on display, visible en route to the passenger terminal. Behind it are the general aviation hangars and an FBO.

NASHVILLE TN
BNA   KBNA   Metropolitan   8m/13km SE

From Opryland, take Interstate 40 east and Exit 216A to the airport. Next is Donelson Pike which is effectively an approach road to the passenger terminal, though it also passes the threshold of the busiest runway, 31, on its way to Murfreesboro Road and a view of the two parallel cross runways.

Most of the movements are domestic, with only a handful of flights to Toronto and Puerto Rico, so security checks allow access to gates and views. Perhaps the best are at the end of North Concourse, Pier B, for the American Eagle movements which make up a large proportion of the traffic. Gates C22-24 in the South Concourse offer a view of the general aviation and cargo ramps but not of the runway.

Before arriving at Nashville, for a few hours' stay, it's essential to consult an American Airlines timetable. The waves of airline movements mean that two hours can pass with little or no movement. However, for a short period, things get very hectic. Between about noon and 3:30pm (which might not always be a peak time) sixty or so American and American Eagle flights come and go. The monitors also reveal that, between 6:00pm and 7:00pm, fifty arrivals can be expected. For a while, the situation is bewildering. At least two runways in use, and aircraft on the move in every direction. From Concourse C, the American/Eagle aircraft can be seen, plus some of the general aviation. The end of Concourse B allows a view of one of the busiest runways. Parked American Eagle commuters can be logged in passing, and anything bound for Concourse A can be seen from here.

A few stored Metros are also to be seen in the general aviation area, and there is a facility for preparation work on Dornier feederliners. The Air National Guard ramp normally contains about a dozen C-130s. As at Memphis, the Bomb Group restaurant has a C-47.

AMARILLO TX
AMA   KAMA   Air Terminal   9m/15km E

The large, spacious terminal has lots of clear glass through which to see the apron. Movements are, however, relatively few and feature mostly the occasional ASA ATR-72. Under-use of the facilities made Amarillo ideal for aircraft storage. In past years a notable array of aircraft have found their way here: USAir's entire stock of ex-Piedmont 727-200s and the A300s of both Pan Am and Eastern. In January 1995, about twenty stored aircraft were present.

Outside DynAir's hangar are many stored aircraft, most of which can be seen from the fence. Across the field is a large aircraft scrapyard, also run by DynAir. Most of the airframes here, numbering another twenty, are 727s. Access for photography to either of DynAir's facilities is their decision. Only logging is believed to be permitted at the far side.

Hughes FBO, west of the passenger terminal, can play host to some interesting visitors including a few USAF T-38s and T-43s.

AUSTIN TX
AUS   KAUS   Robert Mueller Municipal   4m/6km NE

Austin is the state's capital city but its downtown airport is generally unremarkable, save for one fact: Conquest Airlines' hub means that their Metros visit four or five times a day. Photos can be taken through tinted glass in the rather cramped main concourse but serious photographers will consider the need for ramp access. It could be easier to walk a short distance from the terminal, to the weather service office, across from the municipal golf course parking lot. As long as departures are to the north, good photos of taxying aircraft are easy to take in the afternoon.

This is a fairly large general aviation field, with no less than three runways, and the two Hughes FBOs (one on each side of the field) ensure it gets its fair share of traffic. Biz-jets bring a regular supply of VIPs to lobby the State legislature. The best viewing is from the Signature Air Support Terminal on Airport Road, a long walk from the main passenger terminal. To ensure saturation coverage of general aviation in the area a car is essential, enthusiasts will also need to visit Executive Airpark, Bird's Nest and Lakeway Airpark.

BROWNSVILLE TX
BRO   KBRO   South Padre Island   5m/8km W

With no scheduled passenger services and only one or two parcels aircraft, it might be difficult to understand the appeal of Brownsville. For many people, there is none at all. A Confederate Air Force Museum is enough for some and T-2 Buckeyes (still?) suit others. In other words, Brownsville is a matter of personal taste and preference.

COLLEGE STATION TX
CLL   KCLL   Easterwood

For three seasons of the year, not much happens here: the usual trickle of Continental Express, American Eagle and ASA, so hardly worth a detour. Between September and Christmas, things get busier on Saturdays, when the college football season is in full swing. Plenty of rich Texas A&M University alumni fly into this airport in their private jets to support their team.

CORPUS CHRISTI TX
CRP   KCRP   International   5m/8km W

For anyone in need of ground level photographs of Continental or Southwest 737s, Corpus Christi is a good destination but the number of movements during the day is not great, and supplemented only by occasional United arrivals. Since it is possible to stand at the side of the apron, next to the passenger terminal, any camera with a standard lens will achieve the desired results. However, they will be very similar to those obtained at Houston Hobby or Dallas Love Field, where the majority of flights are bound. Perhaps the only movements that won't be seen elsewhere are the rig support helicopters, though not in great numbers.

DALLAS TX
ADS   Addison   11m/17km N

It's generally thought that a trip to Dallas means Love Field and Dallas-Fort Worth. When pursuing airliners, this is indeed true. Biz-jets are a bonus which, at Love Field, become a very big bonus. The wish to see more, or clean up the area, means that time must be made for a trip to Addison. It is a busy general aviation field with much to see. Hotels around here also tend to be slightly cheaper than near some of the better known locations.

DALLAS TX
DAL   KDAL   Love Field   4m/6km NNW

The home of Southwest Airlines, this is still the only field where their fleet can be seen in numbers. The frequency of movements is such that the fleet can be seen in a couple of days.

The passenger terminal contains some interest. Downstairs is an art gallery, specializing in aviation art and photography. Upstairs, across from the admin offices, a small museum offers something to justify the $2 entry: one of the exhibits is a model of a 727, used by James Calder to design Braniff's Flying Colours. The observation deck was scheduled to re-open some time in 1994. It overlooks some of the Southwest gates and the commuter ramp, but a re-opened deck represents serious progress in the USA.

The south side of the central multi-storey car park offers a panoramic view, and excellent photography in the mornings, when Southwest are at their busiest. The many hangar complexes and ramps can be relied upon to provide a sight of over a hundred biz-jets at any one time.

Between the runways are the passenger terminal and the facilities of Hughes (previously Jet East) and KC Aviation. Accessible from the perimeter is the Associated Air Center and, at the end of this road, a small circular parking area very close to one runway. From this spot, admittedly facing south, the whole field can be seen. To the left are Aviall, Citijet and one of the Associated Air Center hangars. To the right is another, plus Arco and Daljet. Anyone with a car will find these ramps worthy of the time and attention, but not so accessible are Rockwell and Associated Air Center, in whose hangars maintenance is carried out on electronic surveillance aircraft. Photography in the afternoon is probably at its best on Denton Road, next to the southern perimeter. In the southwest corner (where else?) is Southwest's corporate headquarters, quite close to the runway. From here, their aircraft can be photographed at their best. The airline staff are friendly, so it might be worth letting someone know your intentions before setting up for an afternoon's photo session.

Corporate attitudes to interest in their aircraft are now hardening. Anyone hearing a suggestion that photography might be unwise in any particular location would be well-advised to heed the advice given. The United States is the source of many stories about enthusiasts being given a hard time, including successful prosecution. Precautions relax in mid-September, when the NBAA biz-jet show is held. Access to the tarmac for casual visitors is generally easier if they wear something appropriate. Essential luggage should therefore include a pair of slacks and a drip dry short-sleeved shirt. A tie is useful and tie pins add a touch of local colour!

DALLAS TX
DNE   North   14m/22km N

Having made the effort to go to Addison in pursuit of general aviation, Dallas North is the next logical step. A car is essential to get there and to cruise clockwise round the perimeter.

DALLAS TX
RBD   Rainbird   11m/17km S

Rainbird completes the Dallas g.a. itinerary. If airliners are no more interesting than any other aircraft, then Dallas North, Addison, Love Field and Rainbird will provide hours, perhaps days, of entertainment.

DALLAS-FORT WORTH TX
DFW   KDFW   International   15m/23km NW of Dallas

American Airlines' hub-and-spoke operations take on real meaning at DFW where huge numbers of the fleet come and go in waves, or 'banks', as they are known. Within a half-hour period there will be forty or so American flights arriving followed, half an hour later, by these aircraft departing. These banks of flights occur eight times a day and, since American/American Eagle's four hundred movements account for more than half the traffic, they leave a lasting impression.

Delta have also established a hub at DFW, making them the second largest operator, with nearly a quarter of the movements, many of which are 737s, operating a shuttle-type operation between Dallas and Atlanta. The other major presence here is the dedicated commuter carrier, Simmons. Their fleet can be seen sharing American Eagle commuter work with the Delta Connection, mostly ASA Brasilias and Bandeirantes, which are also conspicuous. DFW is, to put it simply, the second busiest commercial airport in the world.

American occupy two entire terminals: 2E and 3E. Delta and ASA use 4E, and everyone else use 2W, originally Braniff's facility.

The facilities of this very modern airport don't cater for the needs of the aviation enthusiast but anyone in need of sample photographs should try Delta's new satellite off Terminal 4E. Regardless of which runway is being used, almost all the Delta and American movements pass within reach of even a standard lens. The tinted glass is, in east and west facing areas, wired to reduce sunlight penetration. The effect on photography becomes very subjective. At one extreme are the people who can live with it and, at the other, protests are loud. Windows facing north and south have no wiring,

Indoor vantage points can be desirable when the Texas sun makes the temperature soar. Those which could be checked include American Terminal 3E, where logging Delta and Delta Connection is good at Gate 38 . . . and Gate 35 for American. Gate 6 in Terminal 2E overlooks American Eagle arrivals and one of the holding points. Terminal 2W overlooks the general aviation terminal. For a closer inspection, leave the terminal at the southern end and follow the service road along the ramp perimeter. Traffic is brisk and most of it can be seen from the fence. Nearby are long-stay airlines, mostly the locally based Express One. Charter action here includes Sun Country DC-10s and 727s plus the occasional AeroExo, American TransAir and Carnival arrival. This is a good area for spotting in the mornings, particluarly as there is more to see than just AA and DL.

To reach the general aviation area by car, take one of the air cargo exits, before reaching the parking ticket booths. Continue north or south (depending on where you entered) and head in the towards 2W. Exploration of the rest of the field requires navigational skills of the highest order. West Cargo, out near American's huge maintenance base, has two small hangars used by Kitty Hawk Air Cargo and GTE's corporate fleet. Whatever is present can be photographed from the fence. Cargo Road, leading west from employee lot 1W, has been closed.

South of the AA maintenance base the fence (but not the road) is close to Runway 18R/36L. To reach it, park in the gravel lot next to the road and hike. There is a high mound next to the fence, so ladders aren't necessary, and the AA base is in view. On the southwest side of the field a viewing park has been constructed. Needless to say, being official, it's next to useless for photography. This applies also to the two employee parking lots, though they are great for spotting. WARNING: spending considerable periods of time out in the Texas sun is extremely hazardous. The heat can be extreme and large quantities of liquid, preferably non-alcoholic, are recommended. Beer is NOT a good idea as it actually helps cause dehydration.

American Airlines has opened the superb C E Smith Museum at their Learning Center, just south of the airport. Outside it is a beautifully restored DC-3 and, inside, the airline's history is presented as only the Americans know how (can afford). The movie theatre is equipped with first class airline seats, and shows "Dream of Flight" on a screen 25 metres high. Not 25 feet - 25 metres! To reach the museum, take the south exit from DFW and head west on Highway 360 southbound, in the direction of Arlington. The FAA Road exit leads to the Learning Center, open between 11:00am and 6:00pm Wednesday thru Sunday (as they say). Admission is free.

EL PASO TX

ELP	KELP	International	7m/11km NE

Approaching this airport from town, the street names have a slight accent on aviation. From Airways Boulevard, a turn onto Convair Drive passes the freight terminal (used by FedEx), the passenger terminal and three hangars. Northrop Drive leads around the southern perimeter, where the general aviation hangars and terminal are found. The road continues past a biz-jet ramp of some size, and with plenty of occupants during the week. A UPS 757 awaits its evening work, and a NASA Guppy normally stands on the tarmac.

A request at the GA terminal for ramp access can result in the ability to photograph one or two visiting Mexican corporate aircraft, plus several older types, which have been known to include such diverse craft as YS-11s, an assortment of DC-3s and even an Il-18.

The Continental pier in the passenger terminal is also worthy of inspection, as it is close to the taxiways and most movements have to pass on their way in or out. Anyone visiting El Paso after lunchtime will find the sun is always in the right place, an unusual phenomenon!

FORT WORTH TX
FWH	KFWH	Carswell	7m/11km WNW

Carswell Air Force Base was once famous as the home of B-52s and KC-135s. It was due to be realigned as a reserve centre for the air force, marines and navy in 1994. The access road to General Dynamics, on the west side of the field, has always been a fine spot to view the action and take photos with the help of a 200mm zoom lens. Afternoons are best.

FORT WORTH TX
FTW	KFTW	Meacham Field	6m/9km N

With so many airfields around Dallas, plus DFW for quantities of airliners, it's easy to overlook Fort Worth itself. Meacham is a lively general aviation field and it has a few biz-jets and possibly still one or two other surprises in store. Literally in store were some old DC-8s and Convairs, all unlikely to find buyers. Page Avjet had a repair facility at the north end of the field, where interesting aircraft were regularly seen. It was closed late in 1994. Some of the Page inmates were stored in front of the passenger terminal, in the company of several flight schools. If anything of interest remains, permission for ramp access should be sought at one of the schools, where someone may be able to assist.

GALVESTON TX
GLS	KGLS	Scholes Field

Galveston is so close to Houston, its own airport generates no scheduled passenger traffic at all. But oil and gas rigs in the Gulf of Mexico mean some helicopter traffic. This is not Aberdeen, and expectations should not be too high. Possibly a couple of dozen Evergreen and Petroleum helicopters can be seen.

HARLINGEN TX
HRL	KHRL	Rio Grande Valley International	3m/5km NE

As an airport, there are Southwest and American Airlines scheduled services, both these airlines being seen readily in many other places, but Harlingen's reputation was founded on the Confederate Air Force collection. That was then; this is now. Most of the aircraft to be seen on the flying days were privately owned, and flown in for the occasion.

For someone who is happy to stand by the fence and take a souvenir photo of one of the airliners visiting, Harlingen is pleasant enough, but the only warbirds to be seen are a Catalina, a Skyraider and the fuselage of a B-23.

HOUSTON TX
EFD   KEFD   Ellington Field   15m/24km SE

By taking Highway 13 south east from Hobby, the trip to Ellington offers variety to a Houston log. UPS and Continental Express offer the only real airline interest, but there are other delights. Such an active Air Force base as this is bound to feature large numbers: mostly F-15s and F-16s, but there are a few T-43s. The proximity of the Space Center means that some NASA aircraft are always present.

HOUSTON TX
IAH   KIAH   Intercontinental   16m/25km N

The airport has all the features, including traffic, to justify the impressive name. The double bank of terminals are spread out and linked by an automatic People Mover, complete with recorded messages to tell travellers which terminal they are arriving at. They are now becoming accepted as the best means of ground transportation at many large airports.

Each of the three terminals has island departure lounges attached and these are occupied by one or two airlines, though Terminal C is used by Continental, with the new Mickey LeLand Terminal reserved for international flights. Terminal B, now used by Delta, TWA and American, has seen its international arrivals area closed, when the new terminal was opened. The terminal at the north end, A, is shared by United, USAir and Northwest, plus a selection of less regular operators. At its centre is a multi-storey car park, the top level of which is the only place to get an impression of what is going on.

The view from the car park is of the thresholds of Runways 8 and 14L/R and, in this respect, it is well placed. Sadly, wind directions can mean that aircraft land on Runway 26, which is long enough for the many Continental movements to stop and taxi to their stands, without having come into view. Assuming favourable winds/runways, a spell on the car park will result in a good quantity of interesting movements being logged and the quiet spells can be used to squint through binoculars at the more remote parts of the field. The terminal area, aligned east/west, has Runway 8/26 to the north and many of the more interesting stands are also on this side, making good photographs possible through the glass, especially on sunny days. The southern side has virtually no airlines of real interest to a seasoned traveller in the USA, but it does overlook the cargo ramp where a Burlington Express DC-8 is often parked.

Leaving the car park, with a varied collection of reasonable quality photos, a trip round the terminals can result in close-up views of some of the airlines and the only real opportunity to get shots of commuter carriers. Because the airport approach road, John Kennedy Boulevard, is more or less parallel to Runways 14/32, and because the majority of the executive terminals and hangars are lined up between the road and runway, these facilities are all but invisible from the car park. Only a small collection of hangars on the far side of 14L/32R are within sight and these are so far away that the LearJets parked outside Garrett's re-engine facility may be difficult to identify.

To appreciate the rest of the field, transport is really essential as the facilities are spread out. John Kennedy Boulevard leads to the terminals and turns east, as Will Clayton Boulevard, with a loop, Wright Road, allowing a view of The Delta hangar and the UPS freight apron. To the south of the terminal, leaving on Kennedy, two right turns lead to the various executive terminals, all of which can be seen at close quarters, and the FedEx terminal at the southern end, close to the threshold of 32R. Following the perimeter road, with its right angle turns, one corner reveals the Garrett apron and the threshold of 32L, both reasonably close but the latter unlikely to result in photographs. Another right turn leads to more executive hangars and the tour is complete. If the number of biz-jets logged is impressive, it should be borne in mind that there is another airport in the area where greater numbers are seen . . .

HOUSTON TX
HOU   KHOU   William P Hobby   12m/19km SE

The ability to drive around the perimeter and get very close to almost every aircraft is a feature at Hobby which few other airports in the world can match. A car is, however, absolutely essential. Air-conditioning is rarely an optional extra and it is needed. The range of airlines is limited but, for all that, Southwest and Delta 737s can be seen easier here than at most American airports. It's quite reasonable to expect at least fifty different Southwest 737s on an average weekday. The changes taking place in the airline world mean that Frontier, Ozark, PeoplExpress and TranStar, all of which were regular users of Hobby, are now absorbed into the rationalised operations following de-regulation.

A tour of the perimeter is interspersed with stops to photograph passing airliners at ridiculously close quarters, and telephoto lenses are unnecessary. Hobby may not handle TACA 737s or Aeromexico DC-9s, like its big brother, but it has many, many other delights for compensation.

For those without a car, but determined to log some Southwest Airline(r)s, there is a bus service from Intercontinental. It costs $11.50 each way, and tickets are purchased in the terminals.

LAREDO TX
LRD   KLRD   International   8m/13km NE

Though there isn't a lot of airline activity, TAESA's daily 737 service spends most of the afternoon on the apron. Other operators include Conquest, Continental Express and American Eagle. Two Laredo Air Convairs were still present in May 1994, their colours fading, but propliner enthusiasts will no doubt keep to to date with the changing situation. The staff at American Air Cargo are friendly, and usually allow access to the ramp.

LUBBOCK TX
LBB   KLBB   Regional   6m/9km N

The new terminal, now believed to be called Lubbock International, is on the east side of the field. It resembles a slice of DFW, being semi-circular with close kerbside access to the gates. Apart from the ASA ATR-72s, there isn't much of any interest to be seen here. The west side of the airport, the old Lubbock Regional, can play host to something worthy of inspection, one or two of Martinaire's air courier aircraft being the most likely.

McALLEN TX
MFE   KMFE   Miller International   2m/3km SW

A new passenger terminal is open; a splendid modern building that harkens back to the golden age of air transport. It faces south towards the runway but windows in the concourse allow reasonably good photography in the mornings. Metros, operated by Conquest and AeroLitoral, are part of the fare but DC-3s also fly cargo to and from Mexico.

For an alternative perspective, leave the terminal and walk towards the control tower. A parking lot, south of the tower, offers an excellent view of the runways, the general aviation hangars and the main terminal. Photographers will note that the morning sun favours the runway and terminal, while afternoons are best for the general aviation. A car is essential to reach the DC-3 apron. From the terminal, turn right onto Wichita Street, and right again on 10th Street South. You can't miss it, and photos over the fence are easy to take.

PARIS TX

PRX   Cox Field   8m/13km W

With only three or four Lone Star Metro movements each day, Paris Texas is not in quite the same league as its French namesake. Apart from that, there is just the general aviation, none of which is out of the ordinary. However, nearby Toco offers a sight to justify the journey, especially when travelling from the west. Rounding a bend, a Proair Martin 404 comes into sight, parked alongside the road. It's in full colours and in good condition, and shares a converted truck stop with a few warbirds, as Junior Burchenall's Flying Tiger air museum. The other aircraft include T-33s from Italy and Canada plus an A-26 and an F-86D.

SAN ANTONIO TX

SAT   KSAT   International   7m/11km N

The proximity of the Mexican border gives San Antonio its international status and two Mexicana Fokker 100s visit daily. Few aircraft exceed this size, and all movements can be enjoyed from the edge of the apron or from the glazed viewing deck. Other Mexican airlines include six or seven AeroLitoral Metros, an occasional Aeromar ATR-42 and TAESA LearJets on package express services. There are few other American airports where these movements can be seen.

The perimeter road leads to West Cargo, where the TAESA LearJets can be seen early in the morning and it is also a fine vantage point for action shots on Runway 3/21, for anyone with a 300mm lens. This offers also the closest view of Fairchild's factory ramp, without official access. Merlins and Metros are assembled.

The far side really needs a car. Taking the road marked 'Car Rental Return' the Dee Howard hangars can be seen on both sides. The Sunjet terminal is sure to be of interest. Aircraft undergoing, and awaiting, conversion are numerous. Some of Dee Howard's cast-offs reach 707 size. They are found, in a compound, on Jones Maltsburger. To get there, turn left at the general aviation and then watch for a right turn.

The area around San Antonio has other attractions: Stinson Field has mostly light aircraft. The Marriott Riverside Hotel has a heliport on top of its car park, and Lackland Air Force Base has a museum. Many of the exhibits are out in the open but a large number of them are not. Official permission is possible for anyone who wants to see the lot.

About forty miles west is HONDO, Texas. The Municipal Airport is three miles west of town. It's here that many of the ex-Florida Express BAC 1-11s were stored (still present in May 1992). The airport's main user is the USAF's Officer Training School (OTS). Their T-41A Mescaleros, wearing civil registrations, are very much in evidence. An aircraft painting facility has been known to handle aircraft up to 747 size but what is to be seen is obviously a matter of luck.

Hondo, Texas must not be confused with Hondo, New Mexico, but there are good reasons why it happens. Hondo NM, between Alamogordo and Roswell, is on the edge of the Mescalero Apache Reservation. The names of Hondo and Mescalero go together easily (not by coincidence) but you could drive around the New Mexico desert for ever in search of the OTC!

SHERMAN-DENISON TX

F39   Grayson County   10m/16km NW of Sherman

Forty miles or so north of Dallas, this airfield might be of interest to enthusiasts staying in the area, even though it has no scheduled operations. Previously a military base, the terminal side was occupied by M & M Aircraft Services, whose Convairs and DC-4s/6s brought cheer to propliner enthusiasts' hearts. The other side of the field is, however, another story . . .

The International Airline Support Group (IASG) operates a salvage centre on the west side of the field. Forests of tails can be seen from a distance, enough to quicken the heart of anyone. What's more, the facility is accessible from public roads. From Highway 82, take the Grayson County Airport exit (FM1417) and drive north for about a mile and a half. After the veterinary clinic, hang a left to go west on Plainview Road, (even the name sounds tempting!) as far as the first marked street, Hardenburg. A right here leads to the tails!

There are twenty or so aircraft to be seen and enthusiasts (there aren't many) are welcome to have a look around and take photos, after checking in at the office during business hours. Prior notice for a visit isn't necessary but the phone number, for those who need it, is (903) 786 9538. Mail should be addressed to IASG, PO Box 1056, Pottsboro, TX 75056.

WACO TX
CNW   KCNW   TSTI Airport

This used to be known as James Connally Airport and it is well-known to aviation specialists for a variety of reasons: Chrysler Technologies took over the former Elsinore Aircraft Support hangar, where a number of aircraft were stored. The Novair DC-10s, and almost everything else, have gone. What remains is the ex-Northwest CV-580 fleet. The airport manager should be contacted if access is required. Pointing a camera in the direction of Chrysler is not a good idea! The many security notices are necessitated by the work Chrysler does on EC-135s and NKC-135s.

Buffalo Airways maintenance base was at the north end of the ramp, where a couple of 707s could usually be seen. They have vanished, leaving no trace of their previous occupancy.

WACO TX
ACT   KACT   Regional/Madison Cooper   8m/13km NW

This is Waco's main link with the rest of Texas, but its services are strictly limited to a few ASA Brasilias and American Eagle Jetstreams each day. There is little to keep someone on the move from heading for the other field, which has more on offer.

PRICE UT
PUC   Carbon Emery   3m/5km

Utah is a beautiful state, but much of it is quite remote. Communities work hard to develop, as this is still genuine frontierland. The only scheduled passenger link with the outside world is offered by Alpine Air, whose fleet is best seen early in the morning at Provo. Apart from the chance of finding yet another of those elusive FedEx Caravans sitting in quiet corner, there is little reason to call in. A short detour in Utah can mean a hundred miles or more!

PROVO UT
PVU   Municipal   3m/5km SW

Of the more remote towns in Utah, Provo is perhaps the only one which warrants a stop. Being on I-15, it seems close to civilisation, though the impression is misleading. A few miles each side of the highway are miles and miles of wasteland. The airport sits on a promontary, with Utah Lake on the western and southern sides, and hills on the others. Alpine Air's base of operations is the biggest thing on the airfield, and it's small. Arrival during the middle of the day can reveal nothing more than a handful of light aircraft, possibly including one or two Alpine Navajo Chieftains.

SAINT GEORGE UT
SGU   Municipal   1m/1.5km N

A touring itinerary of the West often includes the scenic splendours of Bryce Canyon, Zion National Park and Lake Powell. Travelling from Las Vegas, St George is a possible staging post on the road east. Interstate 5 runs north to Salt Lake City.

The city nestles in the lee of the red bluffs, on the edge of a flat plain, its Mormon temple shining white and visible from miles away. With so much flat land around, it is strange that the airport wasn't built on some of it. It will be a long time before St George can boast a sophisticated, modern passenger terminal. What is there serves a number of Skywest Metro movements.

SALT LAKE CITY UT
SLC   KSLC   International   5m/8km NW

The city straddles the north-south I-15, where it joins with I-80. This Interstate heads west to Reno and passes the airport, as do almost all roads west of town. Delta's western hub was acquired when Western Airlines were bought, and many of the aircraft which pass through still retain their Western-derived registrations. 75% of all movements are Delta, so anyone in search of variety could be excused for disregarding Salt Lake City. It is fortunate that the remaining 25% does contain some quality.

The terminal facilities may pass unrecorded, because there is an excellent observation facility at what is probably the best location, most of the time. In the southwest corner of the field, close by the approach road, is a reservation designed with the needs of enthusiasts in mind. By taking the road to the cargo terminals, and turning right at the two T-junctions, the car park is reached. Next to it is a grassy bank rising clear above the perimeter fence, with views of much of the airfield.

Directly in front are the runway thresholds with the general aviation terminals and hangars on the far side, and the ANG base with its KC-135s at the far end. To the left is the holding point used by the majority of scheduled traffic and, further round to the left is the cargo apron with the main terminal area beyond. Use of the 34L/R runways is normal but not necessarily the rule, so there are days (or part thereof) when trying to make the most of Salt Lake City airport can be a waste of time. Sightseeing at Saltaire (flies permitting) or the excellent museum at Hill Air Force Base in Ogden are alternatives.

The constant stream of Delta movements through the day does comprise the complete range of types operated, and in good numbers. Skywest, the Delta Connection, offers the only variety apart from a handful of other flights. Photography is best after lunch, when the sun has passed the centreline of the runways, and anything of 737 size or larger makes portraits easy as it taxis to the hold. The evenings offer a splendid mixture of cargo traffic, and operators are as varied as the aircraft: Ameriflight with Navajos and Beech 99s, half a dozen FedEx, UPS with DC-8s and 757s and, star attraction, a Union Flights Caribou.

The east side has its own runway, which sees much use during the average day and evening. There are several access roads to the individual fixed base operators, with Majestic Air occupying space close to I-80. Parked here are mostly Beech 18s and DC-3s, and the red T-33 in one of the hangars looks familiar to most British eyes. Views of the various ramps need patience but few of the executive aircraft go unrecorded. Parked on its own, next to waste ground, is a rather derelict Viscount, possibly N7411, ex-United. The road passes the Utah ANG base entrance, with an F-105 on display outside, and continues north where close views of the field are impossible.

By making left turns, Delta's maintenance base is reached, north of the passenger terminal. The road offers an unobstructed view of the ramp, though the quality of photos taken from here is moderate due to the busy background. Another left turn leads to the central terminal area. What becomes apparent, after some time at the international airport, is the relatively small amount of light aircraft to be seen. These are all based, in number, a few miles to the south at an airport known officially as Salt Lake City II. Anyone who decides against a visit to Salt Lake City because of the large number of Delta movements will miss the opportunity to sample an interesting corner of the aviation world.

NEWPORT NEWS VA
PHF   KPHF   Patrick Henry   16m/25km NW

Virginia is a state quite remote from most itineraries but it receives a lot of aviation enthusiasts for the Oceana Open Day in autumn. The Chesapeake Bay metropolitan area is known as Tidewater, comprising Virginia Beach, Newport News, Norfolk, Portsmouth and Hampton.

Features in this part of the world are the F-15s at Langley and a small museum nearby, the guided tours of Norfolk Naval Base, to see which carriers are in port (their aircraft being at Oceana) and, not too far up Interstate 64, RICHMOND (q.v.) with a chance to see the Air National Guard A-7s.

Between Langley and Richmond, immediately to the east of I-64, is Patrick Henry Airport, almost on the edge of Williamsburg - hence the alternative name of Williamsburg. Not quite in the same league as Norfolk, this is mostly a commuter airport, offering scheduled feeder links to most regional cities. Patrick Henry is a spoke in many systems. Occasional US Air DC-9s visit but generally the largest aircraft are Henson Dash 8s. Photographs around the terminal area present no problems and access to the airport is best from Morris Boulevard, intersection 9 on I-64. From here, the large amount of general aviation is readily apparent.

NORFOLK VA
ORF   KORF   International   9m/15km NE

The civil enthusiast is well catered for at Norfolk, though not in the passenger terminal which has no worthwhile views. The 'old' side of the field has some interesting aircraft with an occasional commuter airliner on extended stay. To keep a close watch on a varied selection of eastern seaboard airlines, a visit to the Norfolk Botanical Gardens is highly recommended. This quiet backwater has been separated from the noise of the airport, immediately adjacent, by a high grass bank or berm, from which the viewing and photography are very good.

Regardless of which direction the runway is used, a 200mm lens will yield results which justify the small entrance fee into the gardens. The sun is at its best late in the afternoon. Anyone who intends to spend time here can find snacks and drinks at the cafeteria/shop, next to the parking lot, at the foot of the berm.

Photography in the morning requires a trip to the water's edge, at the other end of the field. Close to the naval base, north of the airfield, is a small parking lot. It is favoured by anglers, and jetties are provided to get them to deeper water. With a 200mm lens, good landing photos (of aircraft, not fish) are possible. If standing on dry land gets boring, you can always rent a canoe and row to a place which suits best.

RICHMOND VA
RIC   KRIC   Byrd International   8m/13km SE

Whilst not particularly busy, Richmond always seems to boast something of interest. The passenger terminal has been modernised and good close-ups of visiting airline traffic should be possible through the large windows overlooking the ramp. Most of the common American airlines serve the airport in reasonable quantities. A maintenance facility along from the terminal is the Washington area base for the SD3.60s of Air Wisconsin/United Express. Some of their aircraft can be idle here and ramp access for a portrait or two should present no problems.

Richmond is also well served by the overnight express companies, which means that the usual array of UPS, DHL and FedEx 727s etc can always be found spending the daytime in the sprawling cargo area. Photography is surprisingly good, with less clutter than normal for most cargo terminals.

There are surprisingly large quantities of executive aircraft and the spread-out nature of the field makes a car essential if they are to be seen. The far side of the field (and this means a long way away) is occupied by the Virginia ANG unit with its unit of A-7s. Unless they are on the move, identification on the ramp is difficult and written arrangements for a visit to the base are essential for any serious military enthusiast.

ROANOKE VA
ROA   Regional   6m/9km NE

Whilst this regional airport is unlikely to be on most itineraries, its growth in traffic volume is largely due to USAir's activities, which in turn leads to competition from other carriers. The new terminal has open car park areas next to the taxiway, from which movements can be witnessed. There is a reasonable amount of general aviation, though nothing exceptional has been reported.

BURLINGTON VT
BTV   KBTV   International   3m/5km E

This small, but very attractive, airport has many points in its favour. The view from the terminal isn't one of them, however, as it is restricted to the darkened glass next to the gate onto the small apron. Jet airline traffic is minimal but there is adequate compensation in the variety of commuters and feeder liners. Local airlines are Commutair, with Beech 1900s, and Metro Air Northeast, better known as Trans World Express, as their Metros and SF.340s are seen widely throughout New England. Their maintenance base has a good sized hangar, and part of its apron is seen from the fence. As is often the case in these less hurried backwaters, asking for a look can be more sensible than running the risk of being caught helping one's self.

The runway normally in use is served by a taxiway which passes very close to a chainlink fence, and open ground next to this allows a perfectly acceptable view of passing aircraft. The road which leads to the airport continues past the terminal, and a turning in the housing estate leads to this much-used observation point. Anything which passes is photogenic, especially in the mornings, when the sunlight is good. Even a King Air makes an excellent portrait without recourse to a long lens.

Not only is the taxiway close but the runway is near enough for reading off the serials of the active Vermont Air National Guard aircraft, based on the other side of the field. Known as the Green Mountain Boys, they are friendly, and written permission for a visit may be worthwhile. It is quite a long drive round past the end of the runway to get to the base and there is no gate to define the entrance. Spontaneous visitors may find themselves in a car park right next to the apron, by mistake, if they aren't careful!

Another military operator to use the field, though not particularly actively, is the Army National Guard unit whose hangar is at the intersection of Highway 2 and the airport approach road. Some difficulty may be experienced in finding someone to give permission for a look around. This may involve entry into the hangar and walking through it, past the UH-1s and OH-6s, to find someone in authority. In the unlikely event that permission is not granted, it's then necessary to walk through the hangar again, on the way out.

BELLINGHAM WA
BLI   KBLI   1m/1.5km NW

The largest scheduled airliner to be seen here will probably be a Dash 8, in Horizon's colours. Apart from the occasional Air Pac Navajo, there isn't much else to make the detour worthwhile. The residents will only be of interest to number crunchers, and they won't crunch many.

EVERETT WA

PAE   KPAE   Paine Field   4m/6km SW

Also called Snohomish County, but not by the local population, a left turn off Interstate 5 leads there but, from Renton, it is easier to take I-405 and then Highway 525. The Boeing 747, 767 and now the 777 production facilities have very little to do with the rest of the airport, and the only problem about getting a free tour of the plant is the amount of time it will be necessary to wait. The two mid-morning tours are usually heavily over-subscribed but they do include a look into the assembly plant, normally the 747 side, and the ramp, passing aircraft on the flight line. Note that the bus doesn't stop on the ramp and that its windows are likely to be very dark. A feature of this part of the world is that the sky is either grey . . . or dark grey, so Kodak ASA25 will not be the best choice of film!

Tours are only offered during the week, and it is possible to book beforehand. To do so, contact The Boeing Aircraft Company at PO Box 3707 (OA-65), Seattle Washington 98124, or phone (206) 342 4801.

The rest of the airport is quite separate and the only aircraft guaranteed to be of interest is the BOAC Comet (4C!), though TRAMCO may be fitting hush kits to an interesting 707. Due west of the general aviation terminal, across the main runway, is an air tanker base. The only other feature of the field is an Army Reserve base with some helicopters. Paine Field hosts an air show in August but don't expect too much from it. Apart from demonstrations by an F-16, an F-18 and a CH-47, the high spot might have been Teresa Stokes doing her wing-walking act!

FRIDAY HARBOR WA
FRD   0.5m/1km SE

Friday Harbor is on the south side of San Juan Island, between Victoria and Bellingham, and is part of the Natural History Park. When the US government gives an island special treatment, there is a good chance it is something out of the ordinary. It is, without doubt, extremely scenic, though not the sort of place to visit solely to take photos of floatplanes. That is just a bonus. Kenmore Air operate mostly Beavers but there are other aircraft to see. A remote spot to choose for a photo but there are few others to compare with it. Anyone flying from here into Seattle's Lake Union will remember the trip, and descent into the city, for a long time. Take lots of film but don't expect too much sunshine.

MOSES LAKE WA
MWH   Grant County   4m/6km NW

This is prairie land; open, dry and very hot in summer. The airport is north of I-90, on State Highway 282. The few commuter flights make little impression on what is clearly a rather major airfield. A distant hangar, bearing a Japan Air Lines logo offers one clue. Inside the fire station, numerous photographs of JAL 747s also suggest something. Clearly, most of the commuter

aircraft have little need of a 13,500 feet long runway, one of the longest in Washington State.
Unless information is gleaned from Boeing, it would be unwise to travel such a long way in the hope of seeing half a dozen 747-400s doing circuits and bumps. Testing might take two or three days at the most, and nothing happens for another six months. Settle instead for the sight of SLAFCO's Catalinas, which are based here. There is also a B-23 Dragon and a stored C-97.

OLYMPIA WA

OLM	Municipal	3m/5km S

Lovers of Washington State scenery and its national park may find their way to Olympia, in the vain hope that a state capital may generate a reasonable amount of traffic. Disappointment awaits, with only a few aged UH-1s, operated (rarely) by the Fire Department.

OMAK WA

OMK	Municipal

A visit here at the wrong time of the year can give a completely wrong impression. The field is on a plateau between the mountains and the Okanogan River (not the Okanagan), and difficult to find. Persevere! Leave town on Highway 97 and look for Old Riverside Highway. For most of the year a dozen or so light aircraft await their owners flying around at weekends. In summer it becomes an operational, and often very busy, water bomber base. Wenatchee occasionally suffers from being smoked in when the fires are at their worst, and Omak is used instead.

When it's good, it's very very good. A visit in August 1994 gives some idea of what can be seen: a couple of Skycranes, several C-130s, Neptunes, a C-54 and a DC-7. Activity can be intense, so a request for a look round might not be a good idea. Settle instead for watching the action from the terminal. Fully laden, these aircraft have a job getting airborne and make superb subjects for a camera.

Enthusiasts who pursue water bombers, smoke jumpers, air tankers and propliners in general, tend to know a thing or two which might not be common knowledge to the rest of humanity. The first rule is: Stick to the highway or dirt roads. Don't drive on grassland and NEVER park on it. Hot exhausts and dry grass don't mix. Well, they do, but it often ends in flames, one of the most common causes of fires.

PASCO WA

PSC	Tri-Cities Municipal	2m/3km NW

Together with Pasco, Richland and Kennewick make up the tri-cities, many miles inland on the Columbia River. Horizon Air provides the staple diet, including several F.28 movements during the day, though two or three Delta jets call. Photography, over the low fence next to the terminal, of taxying aircraft is about as easy as it gets, especially on sunny afternoons. With an 80-200mm zoom lens, almost anything makes a good subject. General aviation activity is slow.

PORT ANGELES WA

CLM	William R Fairchild International	3m/5km W

The Strait of Juan de Fuca separates the relative sophistication of Victoria in Canada with the forests of the Olympic National Park. They are worlds apart, and Port Angeles is on the American side. The sight of a 'Fairchild' sign can lead the unwary to the belief that bombers are close at hand, but this isn't the Air Force base. It is a quiet little airport which used to be the home of San Juan Airlines. Their Cessna twins and, less so, Islanders, used to be a regular sight at Sea-Tac. Only the occasional arrival of a Metro now breaks the peace and serenity.

SEATTLE/TACOMA WA

SEA   KSEA   International   14m/22km S (bus 50 minutes)

The busiest airport in a relatively small area reaching north to Vancouver, Sea/Tac has piers which are accessible with only a security check. Of the two piers which project out into the apron, the left hand offers extremely good views, especially from gates B5 and B7 or the area around C10/C12. Assuming the movements land from the north, these two lounges are very well placed for the photographer, especially in the mornings. What can be seen from here are the two parallel runways and the taxiway, with all Alaska and United traffic doing a U-turn commendably close before heading back to the northern half of the terminal.

Until lunchtime, the sun is behind the viewer, so photography is at its best, and only the occasional Cessna Twin or Navajo pass outside the range of most lenses. Much of the glass through which everything is seen is tinted but it soon becomes apparent, walking along the pier, that some areas of the glass are clear. Gates B5 and B7 are among them. Walking around the pleasant, modern terminal, there are all sorts of chances to get close to some of the smaller types, Horizon's fleet of Dash 8s, Metros and F.28s for example, but the fastidious will still seek other viewpoints for different angles to take photos. One of these is found by walking north to the end of the terminal buildings and then down a bank onto one of the approach roads. Being at the same height as the apron, with only an underpass between the viewer and the aircraft, some very close encounters can be had with the many United aircraft, and one or two of the Alaska fleet as they taxi, or park, very close.

A carefully negotiated crossing of the busy highway here leads through a hotel car park to Pacific Highway (99) and a good selection of moderately priced hotels and eating establishments. Old hands will not need an introduction to Denny's, one of which is just across the road here. Since it is just a short walk up South 160th Street to the perimeter road and the cargo area, it becomes apparent that a car is not essential to enjoy Sea/Tac.

Traffic is not at its peak, in fact far from it, in mid afternoon and it is a good time, if in possession of a car, to leave the terminal and seek an alternative vantage point. Having discovered that the very top level of the multi-storey car park only offers a limited view of proceedings, the car can be driven north along Perimeter Road, where some of the activity on the cargo ramps can be seen, though views are very restricted. Viewpoint Park still exists, having survived threats of redevelopment: to get there, take a left turn onto South 156th Way. After passing under the rather elevated thresholds of 16L/16R, the first permissible left turn is 121st Avenue South. The area is exceptionally hilly and climbing back to the top of a severe dip, a gated road on the left leads to Viewpoint Park. It is open between 6:00am and 8:00pm. Staying too late in the evening invites the interest of the police, who know it is used by local youngsters for purposes of which their parents would not approve and the law doesn't permit.

Vantage points at the southern end of the field are irrelevant if 16L/16R are in use but, if the opposite direction is being used, South 188th Street passes under the end of 34R and close to the threshold of 34L. Certainly a busy airport for scheduled passenger movements, Sea/Tac is not really noted for surprises but some traffic to watch out for includes Hawaiian Air DC-8s and TriStars, departing quite early in the morning, and the rather elusive Weyerhaeuser Lumber Co Citations which live in the hangar on the west side of the field.

SEATTLE WA

BFI   KBFI   King County/Boeing Field   4m/6km S

Not too far south of downtown Seattle, King County (or Boeing Field) is under the flightpath to

Sea/Tac's 16L/R runways, and much traffic flies overhead, most of which bears no registrations under the wings. There are two distinct sides to this long, narrow field: to the west, by Interstate 5, is a perimeter road with innumerable hangars and, between them, views across to Boeing's ramps. The terminal is of no use at all to the enthusiast but, just to the north of it is the Aviator's Store, an excellent bookshop with a vast selection of books, postcards and souvenirs. What will be seen on the east side is a fine assortment of aircraft but most visitors here will be more concerned with what can be seen from the east side. There is usually a selection of 737s and 757s in their full colours, and ready to go. All are seen from the tail end and many registrations are hidden by blast screens. The perimeter road continues round the southern end of the field and back up towards Boeing but the loop is strictly 'No Entry'.

To get round to the west side, leave the perimeter road and head south on Airport Way to the aptly named Boeing Access Road. Another right onto East Marginal Way leads back up to Boeing. At the south end, the new museum has been opened around the Red Barn, where it all started. The Museum of Flight has a Great Gallery, from the roof of which is suspended a formation of interesting aircraft, led by DC-3 N138D. The large expanses of glass make photography easy, and the $4 admission is extremely good value. Opening hours are 10am to 5pm, and further details are available from the museum, 9404 E Marginal Way South, Seattle, Wa 98102, or telephone (206) 764 5720.

At weekends particularly, the vast car parks are empty and unattended. It is possible to get reasonably close to some of the aircraft but photographers will be extremely frustrated, especially if something really special is to be seen. There is absolutely no reason why all registrations can't be obtained by the patient, as there are a good few nooks and crannies. With luck, one of the aircraft will be airtested and it is only then that photos of any quality are likely . . . but probably taken from the eastern side of the field.

For anyone without transport, but wishing to visit Boeing Field, there is a regular bus service which cost between 85 cents and $1.10, depending on the time of day.

SEATTLE WA

LKE   Lake Union Seaplane Base   3m/5km N

Just north of the city centre is Lake Union, with the seaplane base in the southwest corner. Access is by way of West Lake Avenue North, where Lake Union Air Service operate several Beavers and a Twin Otter, all on floats of course.

SEATTLE WA

RNT   Renton   10m/16km SSE

From Boeing Field/King County, Sunset Hiway (900) leads to Rainier Avenue North and a left turn here heads for Renton. At an intersection, the airport is suddenly visible on the right, with tantalising views of Boeings on the ramp. Behind the trees and a bank/berm is a very small airport with one or two Boeings nearing completion and, with luck, something exotic ready to go. Opposite the south-west corner of the field is a restaurant with a good-sized car park; a walk across Airport Way and up to the top of the bank, and one or two photographs should be possible.

Rainier Avenue (167) passes the west side of the field and offers good views of assorted general aviation, though there is nothing out of the ordinary. A turn onto the perimeter road leads back around the south side, and past the end of the short runway to the Boeing complex. By progressing up the east side, it is possible to get quite close to the new 737s and 757s but finding any on the apron, without clutter, is difficult. Halfway up the east side is a bridge over the creek and this is the link between Renton Field and the assembly plant.

On the other side of the bridge is an apron which normally contains half a dozen or so aircraft, all more or less complete with only their rudders painted, and all bearing the same registration. N1786B is easy to remember, and it has featured on many a 737. Careful notes of which rudders are seen followed by some research will usually reveal the identities of these aircraft.

SPOKANE WA
GEG   KGEG   International   6m/9km SW

Many miles inland, this is Twin Peaks country. This airport handles the scheduled services, and the International tag derives from the services to Calgary and Vancouver. Jet traffic, up to 727 size, is regular and the array of commuter feeders makes Spokane an interesting destination. The views from the passenger terminal are not as good as from the rather neat little mutli-storey car park. Salair's base normally has one or two DC-3s in evidence, though Convairs are more so, and Federal Express colours are a familiar sight here.

WENATCHEE WA
EAT   Pangborn   5m/8km SE

Generally known as East Wenatchee, as it's on the same side of the Columbia River as that town. On the other side of the river is Wenatchee, its big brother. This small airport is only mentioned because it becomes an active fire-fighting base in summer. Those dedicated to the relentless pursuit of DC-7s, P-2Vs and C-130s will consider the journey to be worthwhile.

APPLETON WI
ATW   Outagamie County   3m/5km W

This small airport has a modern passenger terminal but views from it onto the apron are few. This is not really a problem because there are plenty of places around the terminal which are adequate, and good enough for the photographer. The home of Air Wisconsin sees but a small proportion of the airline's movements, as they are concentrated elsewhere to match United Airlines' feeder traffic needs.

Other scheduled traffic here is minimal, with a handful of competing commuter flights operated by Express/Northwest Airlink Jetstreams. The daytime Federal Express resident is a 727 here, and at least one hangar-ful of biz-jets can be expected and inspected.

MILWAUKEE WI
MKE   KMKE   General Mitchell International   10m/16km S

Most international visitors to the Oshkosh spectacular will be familiar with Mitchell Field. To be sure that travellers know it's Mitchell Field, there's a B-25 at the main entrance.

The passenger terminal is modern, offering from its windows enough views of aircraft parked on stands to satisfy the casual observer. The serious head north, to the public car park by the executive aircraft hangars. Taxying aircraft pass close enough for good photos, but they do not include the 126ARS KC-135s which use their own runway, beyond the reach of most cameras. Note the AFRES base is on the opposite side of Runway 1L from the ANG facility.

Opposite the passenger terminal entrance, on South Howell Avenue, is a turning to the cargo area. The usual array of UPS, Emery and FedEx aircraft spend their daytime here, with Federal Express offering a decent selection. At the far end of the cargo area is a small Midwest maintenance base. Beside it is a car park and observation area, overlooking the cargo ramps. A 200mm lens should ensure a reasonable collection of photos. For anyone with a car, a perimeter tour involves taking a series of left turns from the cargo area. The road heads south, past the threshold of Runway 7R, to a T-junction. After a left turn, the AFRES base and the end of Runway 1L are passed, after which the road swings away from the perimeter, before returning to the northeast corner and the car park next to the end of Runway 19R.

Midwest Express and their commuter feeder, Skyway Airlines, offer pretty colour schemes, and there is also the usual assortment of airlines visiting. Commuter traffic is particularly good, with a fine selection of operators and types. Northwest and Northwest Airlink are, as to be expected in this part of the world, strongly represented.

OSHKOSH WI
OSH   Wittman Regional   3m/5km SW

The name is synonymous with one of the most famous events in the aviation calendar but, outside Convention time, the field reverts to its sleepy ways. A few commuter flights are operated by United Express F.27s, TWA Express Saab 340s and Beech 1900s, and Midway Commuter Do228s.

The main terminal is less use for photography than the car parks or the Basler ramp. Their DC-3s, of various types, are very much in evidence. Basler have two aprons, the old one being next to the terminal, and used as the executive ramp. The new hangar complex is on West 35th Avenue, reached via the perimeter road. Up to ten DC-3s can be accommodated inside the hangar (that's one extremely large hangar), where turbo conversions take place. With such customers as the Ecuador Air Force, Basler offer the chance to see something exotic.

Whilst at Oshkosh it is worth looking out for the EAA museum, as it holds many interesting, and some unique, aircraft.

GREYBULL WY
GEY   South Big Horn County

The name of Greybull means only one thing to many enthusiasts: Hawkins and Powers. A visit here takes commitment, as it's very remote. Only a small portion of the large fleet can be seen, but it still amounts to a lot of aircraft. Work is carried out on an extremely interesting assortment: older C-118s and P-2Vs share the apron with KC-97s, C-130s and now P-3s. Some of the airframes will take to the skies on their fire-fighting missions, while others are there just to provide the spares.

The cannibalisation of large aircraft provides many interesting photographs, as well as the airworthy machines. Because it is so far off the beaten track, visitors to the field are small in number, and usually very keen. Enthusiasm counts for a lot, and a letter beforehand usually results in reasonable hospitality.

JACKSON WY
JAC   Jackson Hole   8m/13km N

This winter resort has become established as a year-round gateway to Grand Teton and Yellowstone National Parks, just to the north. The valley floor is almost perfectly flat, with spectacular mountains rising at the west. The airport is some way out of town, indicating forethought, and easily seen from a distance. The terminal is delightfully modern, though it offers no views, and handles some commuter traffic. For ramp access at this informal field, a request should be made at Jackson Hole Aviation, to the left. Apart from them being aware that photos showing tail numbers on biz-jets lead to sensitivity from their owners, there are no problems.

AGUADILLA PR
BQN   TJBQ   Rafael Hernandez   65m/104km W of San Juan

At the north west corner of the island is an airfield, generally known as Borinquen, that conjures up rather more nostalgia than can be gleaned at Luis Muñoz Marin. Along the north side of the runway, and facing the Ramey base, is a line of buildings with a distinctly Caribbean feel. The passenger terminal is a modest affair and, to its left is a hangar used for cargo by Trans-Air-Link DC-6s. Beyond this is the US Coastguard base with a couple of C-130s and a Dauphin. At the right of the terminal are two disused hangars, adding greatly to the flavour, after which are buildings which see regular use.

First is that used by the Police, where a couple of GAF Nomads might be present. A Blackhawk was also there, according to the last report. An Aerial Transit DC-6, standing outside the next hangar, usually keeps company with Salair Convair 440s. The last hangar in the line is occupied by Fed Ex.

The road passes round the end of the field and returns to reveal a scrapyard and a general aviation facility. Nearby are parked Tradewinds CL-44 N100BB and L-1049 N1542CT. The airfield is far from inactive, as it is used by a variety of charter traffic. Tradewinds' TriStar is a regular visitor and 727s (anything from Fed Ex and American to Carnival) are not uncommon.

Since Aguadilla is a holiday resort, hotels are reasonably plentiful and quite affordable. The nearest hotel, La Cima, charges about $60 for a room but others, slightly further away, cost less.

ARECIBO PR
ABO   36m/57m W of San Juan

West of San Juan, just off Route 2, along the north coast of the island is another airfield which offers a taste of how aviation used to be. It's small time and it's quiet and, if anything moves, it carries cargo rather than passengers. What action there is takes place at night, as the field is used mostly for mail and packages.

SAN JUAN PR
SJU   TJSJ   Luis Muñoz Marin   9m/15km E

The major US airlines, operating scheduled services, make San Juan seem like an average American airport. American and American Eagle are, with TWA and Delta, now the standard fare. FedEx underline this impression by basing a couple of feeder Caravans here.

Propliner activity has dwindled to the occasional DC-3, C-46 or Constellation from the Dominican Republic. To add a positive note, rather more exotic traffic is supplied by Aeropostal DC-9s, Air Guadeloupe ATR-42s, Air BVI HS748s and LIAT Dash 8s.

The terminal's superb terrace has been closed for some years, with little chance of re-opening in the foreseeable future. There are, however, one or two spots on the approach road between the almost intersecting runways where photos of taxying and landing aircraft are possible. The hire car is useful to get to the spot but disposing of it next to a busy highway then becomes the problem! Good photos can only be taken clear of the fence on the busier northern, 8/26, runway and taxiway, so unobstructed shots need aid from one of the bunker-like structures, or the car bonnet/roof! For anyone wishing to park the car and walk somewhere for a view, there is a shopping mall and cinema car park on Laguna Avenue, just off the busy Highway 26. It is a short walk from the car to the bridge, from where Runway 10 is seen, but care should be taken (and patience used) when trying to cross the highway. It does get very busy.

A reasonably disused car park faces the taxiway to, and the threshold of, Runway 10. The improved view is of less movements, and into the sun. Access to the central cargo area (and the ANG base) is via a very long road parallel to the southern runway. Also to be found here is a general aviation terminal, directly opposite the international pier, where photography is good in the afternoon. What stored aircraft now remain are to be found next to the Executive Air/American Eagle facility. Tolair and Dodita Air Cargo have C-47s and CV-240s, normally parked on the ramps next to American Eagle and the Air National Guard F-16s. Driving parallel to Runway 10, take the first slip road which leads down to a roundabout and the access road.

Luis Muñoz Marin now looks like any other American airport but a more local type of aviation is still to be found (for how much longer?) at other fields. Having made the effort to get to Puerto Rico, it's worth hiring a car and seeing more of the island.

SAN JUAN PR

| SIG | TJIG | Isla Grande | 5m/8km NW |

A real taste of the Caribbean is much easier to experience at Isla Grande, on the way to old San Juan town, by the docks. From Luis Muñoz, follow Highway 26 (Baldorioty de Castro Avenue) towards Old San Juan, and the airport is on the left, just before crossing the bridge. It's here that Vieques Air Link and Sunaire Express can be seen. Islanders and Twin Otters evoke much more of the local feel than can be enjoyed at the busier main airport. The pace is more relaxed and casual. Photos present no problems, and ramp access is possible after a little nogotiation at quieter times. At Isla Grande most times are quiet times, except when Hurricane Hugo comes calling. It caused tremendous damage which will take time to repair. A few damaged and derelict aircraft litter the field: a couple of Islanders and a Piaggio won't fly again. Keeping them company is an engineless C-117, still in US military colours.

Flamenco Airways use their C-47s mostly for night-time cargo flights, so they are usually in evidence during the day, in the company of one or two Islanders.

OB PERU (Republic of Peru)
LIMA

| LIM | SPIM | Jorge Chavez International | 10m/16km NW |

This is a fascinating airport, with a fine selection of international carriers. It would be a good idea to get as many photographs as possible from the taxying aircraft because there will be no more chances. An important military presence here is the reason for the closure of the observation deck, though the smoked glass does allow views from the terminal. Cameras are definitely excess baggage . . . only to be used by the reckless. The report which best summed up Lima was, "stay in the terminal or get ready to answer questions." An honours degree in Spanish will be useful.

The perimeter is enclosed by a high screen, allowing only the occasional view, and even the semi-derelict aircraft should be avoided. The remains of L-749s OBR-833 and N22CS may no longer be present at the end of the field. The naval and army facilities can be seen through gaps, with Mi-8s and S-2s being strange bedfellows.

By venturing from the terminal to some of the operators' aprons, it may be thought that photos are possible. Both AeroPeru and Aeronaves are known to be friendly enough to interested parties but the authorities are still watchful, and capable of confiscating film at the slightest provocation. The possibility of this trouble means that a trip can only be recorded in the notebook. To travel so far without some pictorial record suggests that Lima will only figure incidentally in holiday plans which feature the Incas.

Municipal blue buses Nos 35 and 56 serve the airport from Plaza Dos de Mayo, but beware of colectivos buses, which will only run once five people have boarded. Travel on these can sometimes take longer!

OD LEBANON (Republic of Lebanon)
BEIRUT
BEY   OLBA   International   10m/16km S

The city is gradually returning to something like normality after many years of strife. American readers can forget about visiting as entry visas are not granted. It is possible this might have something to do with the many pictures of the Syrian President, which are very much in evidence. The airport area goes one step further, being situated in a Hezbollah neighbourhood: pictures of Ayatollah Khomeni decorate most of the street lamps.

It's essential to make hotel reservations by fax or in writing before leaving for Beirut. Failure to pre-book means queueing to use the airport's one telephone! Worse, it could mean paying $130 for a night in the Carlton. The ABC Hotel & Travel Index offers details of other downtown hotels, where a single bed costs about $60. Ask your travel agent for a little assistance.

The passenger terminal is 1950s vintage, from the days when Air Liban Caravelles stood on its apron (pause for older readers to sigh) but two new piers are slowly being constructed. Security is still very tightly controlled. About half a kilometre from the terminal is a roundabout, where heavily armed militia man check points. Straight on, south, is the passenger terminal. To the left is MEA and to the right is TMA. In other words, whichever way you turn, there are going to be Boeing 707s. A thorough search of belongings is required before proceeding to any of the facilities, and it may be necessary to surrender the passport, if visiting either MEA or TMA. Aviation photographers are not discouraged. Within the terminal, there is no observation deck but the coffee shop on the second floor overlooks the main apron, between the two piers.

Outside the perimeter, the afternoon sun favours a walk along the coastal road, parallel to Runway 18/36, the north end of which is surrounded by shops and housing. To the south is the beach, still undeveloped, and at more or less the same level as the airfield.

As Lebanon strives to get back to normal, foreign visitors are made very welcome. Someone with a specialist interest might expect a warm welcome, if making himself known to officialdom. This is a nation famous for its politeness and hospitality. Anyone with an enduring passion for 707s would do well to consider a trip to Beirut but time is running out.

OE AUSTRIA (Republic of Austria)
GRAZ
GRZ   LOWG   Thalerhof   15m/24km S (bus 30 minutes)

A very small airport in the south of the country. Most of the scheduled movements are local but the occasional Lufthansa or Air Malta makes a change. In the car park is an An-2 and the passenger terminal overlooks the small apron and the main, surfaced, runway 17/35. To the left, seen from landside, is a general aviation apron with a few light aircraft and a glimpse of the military base, tastefully hidden in the trees, on the far side of the runway. There are plenty of locations around the perimeter where the movements can be seen and photographed with a variety of backgrounds. Until it's realized there are also a cuple of grass strips, some of the light aircraft movements can cause some concern!

INNSBRUCK
INN   LOWI   Kranebitten   3m/5km W (bus 15 minutes)

Innsbruck is surrounded by the breathtaking scenery of the Tyrolean mountains, and the local operator is named after the region, its Dash Sevens and Dash Eights being equally photogenic.

The small terminal has a cafeteria but self service is only available on Saturdays in winter and

216

spring, when charter flights are normally operated. Access to both the balcony and the cafe is related to the purchase of a coffee or a snack. Since quantities of each can be expensive in Austria, a prolonged stay here is rare. This is a pity, as the glass front of the cafeteria offers an excellent view of the apron, where most of the aircraft are parked. The balcony runs along the front of the entire terminal, faces north and therefore offers photographers an ideal and unobstructed view all day long.

Photos of aircraft on approach can be taken from the low hill at the eastern end of the apron, to the right of the terminal, thereby keeping the fence out of the picture. Since most landings take place on Runway 26, this is a very satisfactory location. If the wind changes direction in th afternoon (as it is prone to do) and Runway 08 is used, the levée beside the river offers an alternative, equally good vantage point. The restricted zone between the river and the fence is closely watched, and trespassers face the prospect of trouble. Construction work around the hangar area may have reduced the appeal of a good spot for taking photos of taxying aircraft.

With careful planning of a visit, to coincide with a busy period, the terminal can be used to record scheduled movements, before investigating the rest of the field. Winter weekends bring plenty of charter traffic mostly from Britain and Scandinavia but there are also visits by such airlines as Corsair and Eurocypria plus, of course, Lauda Air and Austrian. Even when traffic gets slow, as it can during the summer, there is always the chance of a good quality photo of a couple of Tyrolean Dash Eights. Occasional exotic Dash 7/8s call in at Innsbruck on their delivery flights to Asia.

KLAGENFURT
KLU   LOWK   Woerthesee   2m/3km NE (bus 10 minutes)

Anyone visiting this quiet little airport might consider doing so in the morning, when the sun is at its best. The bus service F leaves from Anabichl, in the town. The passenger terminal sits at the western end of the field, to the north of the runway. The passenger terminal is modern and occupies the north side of the apron, with a couple of large general aviation hangars to the left.

Seen from the car park, a flight of steps at the left-hand end of the terminal leads to a small balcony where landing aircraft can be seen and photographed. On the roof a circular cafe opens onto a roof garden, where for the price of a nice beer (equivalent to the cost of a small house in Britain) the occasional Austrian Airlines Fokker 50, MD-87 or A320 can be seen sharing the apron with a dozen or so Cessnas.

LINZ
LNZ   LOWL   Horsching   9m/15km SW (bus 20 minutes)

The modern terminal building is served by only a handful of scheduled movements each day and, because the periods when nothing happens can be long, anyone paying a casual visit may see no activity whatsoever. Even the general aviation presence is minimal. The roof terrace is ideally placed, as is often the case with so little to witness, though it fulfills its intended purpose: friends and relatives do await arrivals there. Traffic peaks at weekends in summer, when charter movements to the sun are more frequent. Even so, Saturday's visitors are unlikely to exceed a dozen. Cargo operations are developing, which means a visit by the occasional Fred Olsen Electra or BAe 146 (or F.27) operating for TNT.

SALZBURG
SZG   LOWS   Maxglan   3m/5km SW (bus 15 minutes)

Salzburg was renowned for its free roof terrace, with its panoramic view of the field, but times have changed. The view is now somewhat restricted and entry costs 5 schillings. The turnstile accepts only these coins. Whilst prior knowledge of charter operations from Europe is difficult to obtain, it is worth studying scheduled operations beforehand, to ensure that a visit coincides with one of the busier times.

In summer, scheduled links are mainly Austrian Fokker 50s to Vienna and Zurich but there are also a few flights to London and Paris, most of which are operated for the businessman. Times of departure and arrival are therefore tailored to suit their needs, so the middle of the day, especially during the week, can be quiet. The general aviation centre is to the north of the passenger terminal, containing about thirty residents.

A walk along the road by the perimeter reveals, on the other side, the rather scenic castle, Hohensalzburg. Aircraft on the runway are close enough to make good photos and, with the castle behind, they are undoubtedly rather special. Weekday visits in summer are good but the festival in August usually means many additional biz-jets can be seen. Traffic in winter is busiest at weekends, when the many charters arrive, mostly from Britain and Scandinavia.

VIENNA
VIE   LOWW   Schwechat   11m/18km SE (bus/train 30 minutes)

Austria's main gateway has been compared with Frankfurt, and with some justification. The layout of the airport is generally very similar, though scaled down to suit the needs here. The roof terrace (zuschaur) area has re-opened, its location being at the western end of the terminal complex. There is also a lounge in the new building, next to the American Bar on the top level, which offers a good view of the apron and runway.

Also like Frankfurt, the terrace features a selection of museum exhibits, including a Viking and a Ju-52. The southerly aspect of the terrace means that photographers must make an early start, at 8am, when it opens. By noon on a sunny day, photographs of any quality become almost impossible to take. Admission costs 15 schillings, which does not allow re-admission. Planning a visit should include the purchase of food and drink which, once again like Frankfurt, are available in the basement supermarket. The deck closes at 6pm. Movements on the runway are distant, needing at least a 300mm lens, and those on Runway 16/34 are virtually out of sight. To the right of the passenger terminal is the cargo centre and, beyond that, the general aviation hangars and ramp, very close indeed to the taxiway to Runway 12. The pleasure flight office has always been noted for its proximity to the action and this should be investigated by any photographer who wants some high quality portraits. At the end of the road, past the general aviation centre, is the Austrian Airlines maintenance base.

East meets west at Vienna; a good variety of carriers complements the various Austrian fleets. Kuwait and TWA 767s, Royal Jordanian 747s and TriStars, Turkish DC-9s, El Al and Egyptair 737s are all regular scheduled visitors.

The railway service is the quickest and cheapest way of getting between the city and the airport, though trains only run hourly. The alternative is to take a bus from the Sudbahnhof or the City Terminal.

OH FINLAND (Republic of Finland)
HELSINKI
HEL   EFHK   Vantaa   12m/19km N (bus 35 minutes)

The Finnair coach from the city costs 20 Markka and serves both halves of the airline terminal, close to the intersection of the two runways. Domestic flights use the right-hand end and international flights the left. Both extremities are available only to passengers, so only the middle section offers a view of the apron, through the windows. The observation deck might be open in summer. If this is so, the view is excellent, with only Runway 15/33 being largely hidden from

218

sight. The TV monitors are also of some use, as they show the last three letters of the aircraft, as well as all the other usual details.

Alternative vantage points are also worthwhile, since they offer useful spots for the local specialities. To the right of the terminal, and just around the corner, is Parking Lot 11, where the fence is close to the domestic ramp. To be seen from here are Finnaviation SF.340s and Karair ATR-72s, neither being regularly seen outside the country. This parking lot also overlooks Runway 15/33 and just down the road are Finnair Cargo and some general aviation ramps, with the terminal at the far end. As this is the main airport for Finland, a good variety of operators and aircraft are guaranteed.

The other good location is at the opposite end of the terminal area, close to the Finnair maintenance base, and right next to the police station! This spot is handy for a wide-body on pushback, so attention to timetables is necessary, to ensure that the timing is right and the chance isn't missed.

The aviation museum, close to car park P50, is served by a shuttle bus for those too lazy to walk the 300 metres. Amongst its many military exhibits are a Karair DC-3 and the ex-Finnair Convair Metropolitan OH-LRB. Finnair's DC-3, OH-LCH, is kept in one of the hangars to the left of the terminal, which might be accessible if a request is made in writing prior to leaving for Finland.

HELSINKI
HEM   EFHF   Malmi   4m/6km NE

Helsinki's other airport, being closer to the city, is now strictly for general aviation, most of which can be logged from the car parks. Most of the time, the largest inhabitant could be an Islander used for para-dropping. The passenger terminal, painted white and dating from a time when beehives were the fashion, has a snack bar on the upper floor which offers a general view of the field. Do buy something - they don't get many visitors!

Apart from that, the two big hangars to the left of the small terminal are worth close inspection as they contain a considerable number of helicopters. From the city centre, take Lahti Road, and the entrance to the field is on Nordostra Motorvagen.

OK CZECHIA (Czech Republic)

PRAGUE
PRG   LKPR   Ruzyne   17m/27km W (bus 30 minutes)

Prague is radidly establishing a reputation as one of Europe's loveliest cities and one which has become increasingly attractive to tourists. When Czechoslvakia divided into two, this is the half that elected to develop a wester-style economy.

The bus service to the airport leaves every 30 minutes from the CSA office in Prague. Arrival at the North Terminal area reveals a splendid open observation deck, to the front of the International Terminal. For a nominal admission charge, there is an amazing view (probably one of the best in Europe) of the ramp, and the rest of the field. Immediately in front, requiring a wide angle lens, are stands used mostly by Il-62s and foreign arrivals. A normal 200mm zoom lens is adequate for all other occupants of the ramp.

The domestic terminal, to the left, also has a deck which is open all year round, from 7:00am to 7:00pm (and 9:00pm in the middle of summer). For most purposes that on the international terminal is adequate. All airliners in service park diagonally on the ramp, and those closest to the terminal are nose-out (to the right) and nose-in (to the left). The smaller Turbolets may pose a problem to the photographer, as they often taxi some distance away, rarely passing within range of even a 300mm zoom. The Air Koryo (ex Chosominhang) Il-62, however, usually parks very close indeed. Photos are best in the morning, before the sun moves round sufficiently to spoil things in the afternoon.

By walking away from the terminal, to the north, the fence by the taxiway offers an ideal location for photos, and on the far side is grassland which also allows close up views of traffic on Runway 25. On the far side, it is tempting, though perhaps unwise, to use some sort of aid such as a hard camera case to see over the fence.

Apart from the military visitors and government jets, there is an interesting selection of visitors, with Central Europeans still forming a predictable majority. Most of this interest is generated around the South Terminal area. A reasonably long walk passes the CSA maintenance apron, where several redundant aircraft are stored, including Il-62s and four Tu-154s plus an assortment of remains.

The Police hangar has, like the CSA fleet, acquired a western look. Their Mils have been joined by Bell 214s and Bo105s. On the south side of this terminal area is another ramp where some cargo and charter aircraft are usually to be seen at close quarters.

OM SLOVAKIA (Slovak Republic)
BRATISLAVA

BTS   LZIB   M R Stefanik   5m/8km N (bus 30 minutes)

The end of 1992 saw the division of Czechoslovakia. The Czech republic, following western ways, is rather different from the Slovaks, whose progress into modernity will take a different path. Bratislava, as the Slovak capital, clings to its old Central European character. The airport is still generally known as Ivanka. The passenger terminal's small terrace has, in the past, been quite adequate for watching and photographing the scheduled movements, but extensions and alterations to the terminal may have jeopardised its continued existence.

There is a choice of buses from the city centre. From the railway station, service No. 24 takes half an hour, whilst the airline bus from the City Air Terminal is a little quicker.

Ongoing political changes are bound to have consequences for the airport's traffic. The introduction of a western-style economy meant that many domestic services were no longer viable. The limited amount of services saw drastic reductions though, as compensation, there is a reasonable range of cargo flights and occasional charters.

POPRAD

TAT   LZTT   Tatry   3m/5km W

Visitors to the Slovak Republic will almost certainly want to see the Tatras, a range of splendidly picturesque mountains. Eight miles from the slopes is this small international airport, with a rather old-fashioned terminal, at least when seen from the outside. The interior is, however, modern but the enthusiast will probably settle for the view from gates at the side of it.

The apron rarely hoilds many aircraft at one time but those which can be seen include CSA Tu-134s and ATRs bound for Prague, and Air Ukraine An-24 operating from Kiev. In summer, the pace picks up, with increased general aviatio activity, many of which are helicopters. This is the main base of Air Transport Europe, the country's biggest helicopter operator, so movements by Mi-2s and Alouette IIIs are regular. The fleet also contains a number of fixed wing aircraft, used for charters. Slov-Air operate a nightly postal service flight, using a Turbolet.

As Central Europe becomes an increasingly attractive summer destination for tourists, this airport is likely to get its fair share of visitors. Anyone touring by car will be able to spend at least a couple of hours beside the terminal, taking satisfactory photos with even the most basic equipment.

OO BELGIUM (Kingdom of Belgium)
ANTWERP
ANR   EBAW   Deurne   3m/5km SSE (bus 20 minutes)

Despite the small size of Belgium, it has three airports (excluding Liège) but only Brussels handles any real quantity of movements. The proximity of Antwerp to major commercial centres has meant increased scheduled services, particularly with England. Since there are good connections to Brussels, this is now a convenient gateway for the businessman. The Delta Air Transport hangar is close to the terminal, though anything inside may be difficult to identify.

Since it is a very small airport, and its buildings are crammed into one corner, Antwerp offers a chance to see commuter airliners at very close quarters, and the cafe has a terrace at the apron's edge. Antwerp is also one of the centres of European enthusiasts, so the authorities are used to dealing with requests to have a look around. Deurne is reported to have a museum, understood to be at the other side of the field.

BRUSSELS
BRU   EBBR   National   8m/13km NE (bus/train 20 minutes)

Also known as Zaventem, enthusiasts generally find it most frustrating. Anyone without a car is restricted to the central terminal area. It is virtually impossible to follow all the movements, as there are three main runways, and various spots may be selected to watch individual parts of the activity. The original terminal has a glazed wall overlooking a part of the apron, with a dozen or so stands in view, but the glass is usually fingermarked and unsatisfactory for photographers' use. The cafeteria, to the right, offers a similar prospect but movements on the far side of the right-hand pier can also be seen, though even a coffee here is extremely expensive.

The multi-storey car park is too low to overlook the terminal buildings but it does face Runway 07R/25L, the circular satellite and, to a limited extent, the Sabena wide-body hangar.

Leaving the terminal area, the Sabena maintenance hangars on the right offer an impenetrable prospect but, just beyond, the general aviation terminal is very close to the taxiway to 07L and the view from the small car park will reward the patient, subject to wind direction, of course.

It can be a tricky business finding a way round to the Melsbroek side of the airport, and the use of main highways is the simplest, with first exits being used repeatedly. The north side houses the cargo complex, more general aviation and the inaccessible Belgian Air Force base. The patient enthusiast can circumnavigate the field and find a few places to photograph landing aircraft, as there are roads which pass close to the thresholds of 25L/R and 02. The road passing Steenokkerzeel is close to the taxiway and hold for Runway 25R. This is in regular use, and it is possible to reach the fence, for some good photos. If Runway 02 is used for departures, Zeven Tommen (previously Molenstraat) in Zaventem offers a rare chance to take good photos.

Brussels has developed as a European hub for distribution of overnight parcels delivery. From 8pm, over thirty aircraft arrive from various parts of the continent. A FedEx DC-10 and bizjets from Spain and Portugal are included, though many of the movements are British or Belgian. Anyone standing close to the general aviation area at night should be able to log these visitors.

LIEGE
LGG   EBLG   Bierset   5m/8km W

Sabena now provides a regular link to just about anywhere else in the world from Liège, though from the town centre by bus to Brussels. It is also very close to Maastricht, in the Netherlands, so scheduled services have proved uneconomic. A visit may still form part of an itinerary, as the small number of light aircraft share the field with Belgian Air Force Mirages.

OSTEND
OST   EBOS   3m/5km SW (bus 20 minutes)

This airport depends on cargo traffic, which can include some interesting aircraft. The ramp usually contains something to justify the detour on the way past, but a protracted stay is unlikely to yield worthwhile results. Due to the quiet nature of the runway, Sabena use it frequently for Xingu training flights and these aircraft can be seen sharing the ramp with one or two unusual aircraft or, sometimes, very little. The roof terrace offers an elevated view of the field, with the occasional cargo carrier within range of the camera.

Almost the entire perimeter is accessible for the photographer, with the threshold and holding point for Runway 26 offering the best possibilities. From the terminal, Duinkerkseweg leads east to the end of the runway, and a turning to the right leads up the southern side. This is reached before the T-junction with Torhoutsesteenweg. The main road past the airport, Nieuwpoortsesteenweg, passes close to the threshold of 08, and a left turn here on Kaklaertstraat offers a close view from the south side.

OY DENMARK (Kingdom of Denmark)
AALBORG
AAL   EKYT   4m/6km NW (bus 15 minutes)

The peace of this quiet little airport is only occasionally shattered by the arrival of a SAS DC-9 from Copenhagen or the Muk Air Bandeirante, though the odd ATR-42 and Aalborg Airtaxi movement can also be seen. The glazed front of the terminal overlooks a large apron, with a couple of dozen light aircraft parked. The runway is normally busier, as it is used by air force fighters during the week.

Several miles to the west, on the opposite side of Jutland, is THISTED. Anyone touring in this part of the country may wish to visit, in order to take a souvenir photograph of a Jetair Metro, operating a weekday feeder to Copenhagen.

AARHUS
AAR   EKAH   Tirstrup   25m/40km NE (bus 50 minutes)

Served by a handful of ATR-42s and SAS DC-9s, Tirstrup is a long way from anywhere else and hardly worth the effort. This is essentially a military field but the commercial terminal, north of the runway, does have views of the ramp from the first floor, and some of the hangars can also be seen.

BILLUND
BLL   EKBI   1.5m/2km E

Few maps even show the town, situated in the middle of Jutland, but the location is important because it is so centrally placed. The road from Esbjerg to Vejle passes through Grindsted and a right turn in the town leads to Billund. This has been Denmark's main charter airport for some time, served by all the Danish airlines as well as a few from other parts of Europe. The recent investment in the airport has been followed by regular scheduled services to Copenhagen by Maersk Air 737s and Dash 7s.

Billund, a departure airport for charters to the sun, is now becoming established as a destination in its own right. Just next to the terminal is Legoland: the children can enjoy the park while dad watches the aircraft from behind the glass of the viewing gallery. Visible on the grass is what remains of an EAS Cargo DC-8.

Activity is moderate, though much of it is generated by general aviation. Initial confusion by the vacant hangars (in aviation terms) next to the terminal is resolved by taking the access road to the west, which leads to the main hangar area. This may be Denmark's second busiest airport but it's a long way behind Copenhagen!

COPENHAGEN
CPH   EKCH   Kastrup   6m/9km SSE (bus 25 minutes)

Denmark's premier airport has one of the most frustrating terminal complexes in Europe for the enthusiast. The domestic terminal offers the best chance for the spotter. By passing the security check to the boarding area, access to the departure lounges has been possible without a boarding card. Most of the movements can be seen but good photography is difficult.

Another location inside the terminal is the snack bar at the end of Aamager Landeves overlooking Runway 22R, and photos with a 200mm zoom are possible. A patient spotter may be rewarded by the sight of the SAS wide-body fleet, in time, as most of the airport can be seen from here.

The SAS bus from the railway station in the city costs Kr28 and the cheaper alternative, only Kr13.5, is to take the service bus No. 32 from Radhuspladsen. Without a car to get to Kastrup South, there is not much alternative to walking between the terminals and glimpsing various parts of the ramp.

Kastrup South is on the far side of the field, and here are maintenance facilities for Conair, Maersk and Sterling. A drive round to this area may reveal little or nothing but the series of right hand turns from the main terminal will involve driving under Runway 04L/22R. At either side of the runway are turnings to the north, where good locations are found. The first, on the west side, is popular enough to warrant a burger bar. Aircraft departing on 22 are quite photogenic, but photos of landings on 04 have to wait until summer evenings, when the sun is more helpful.

On the eastern side of 04R, morning departures make ideal portraits, and anyone with a hard camera case, or something similar, to see clear of the fence will be pleased with the results.

COPENHAGEN
RKE   EKRK   Roskilde   21m/33km W (train/bus 35 minutes)

Known locally as Copenhagen West, Roskilde specialises in air taxi, executive and commuter operations. There are no scheduled services but there is steady traffic operating flights which are the next best thing. Fleet operators abound, including Ikarosfly, Jetair, Deltafly and Copenhagen Airtaxi, and it is fortunate that access to the aprons is easily achieved. Many hangars and aprons offer a range of aircraft, in a quantity unrivalled throughout Denmark. Any disappointment experienced at Kastrup is compensated by the packed ramps of Roskilde.

The No. 210 bus from Roskilde railway station supposedly goes to the airport (lufthavn) but it is a mile walk to the field. Before getting involved with aircraft, it is prudent to check the bus timetable. Timing the walk from the bus stop is also sensible. The service is infrequent, and lack of planning can result in a two-hour wait! Permission for ramp access should be sought at the airport's administrative office.

ESBJERG
EBJ   EKEB   5m/8km NE

The airport terminal is pleasant, and handles mainly occasional Maersk Air business movements. All parked aircraft are visible from the cafe, lounges etc but through glass, and the fence at each end of the terminal also offers limited views of the ramp. The Maersk hangar contains the company's Bell 212s, and other hangars are famous for their clean windows which allow the occupants to be identified with ease.

ODENSE
ODE   EKOD   Beldringe   8m/13km NW

Beldringe is the base of Falck Air, who operate ambulance services for the Danish Rescue Corps, and things are usually quiet enough for a visitor to be offered some hospitality, though the Islanders may be away on ambulance duties. The hangars can all be visited and it may be possible, on a pleasant afternoon, to enjoy the trip in one of Falck's golf buggies.

SOENDERRBORG
SGD   EKSB   4m/6km NW

Soenderborg is best remembered for the presence of Cimber Air, and the chance to see an ATR-42 on its home ground. A few scheduled flights are operated from here to Kastrup but there are only a couple of dozen other residents to note.

STAUNING
STA   EKVJ

Stauning's name has become synonymous to many general aviation enthusiasts as the home of the annual KZ Rally, where Danish aviation has a well deserved feast of home-grown produce. It is also one of the few places where a Metro Airways Metro can be seen at close quarters. Apart from a variety of old and interesting types to be seen, there is also a museum.

GREENLAND

Greenland, a Danish dependency, occupies a similar area to Saudi Arabia, although its total population is a mere 50,000. A number of small communities exist on the coastline, often for reasons of exploration or NATO defence. They are linked, virtually exclusively, by Gronlandsfly or Greenlandair, as all other means of transportation are restricted by the weather or geography.

SONDRESTROM
SFJ   BGSF   Kangerlussuaq

Flights between Denmark and Greenland operate to Sondrestrom (also known as Sondre Stromfjord), with SAS staff being helpful to visitors. The airport shares the runway with the USAF base on the opposite side of the field. Whilst a telephoned request for a base tour is normally welcomed, few enthusiasts would be foolish enough to make the long trip without making some tour arrangements beforehand.

GODTHAAB
GOH   BGGH   Nuuk

This is the main Greenlandair base, and the airport has a helipad for six aircraft. Visiting enthusiasts are so rare that they are welcomed, as is anyone who makes the trip. The opportunity to take memorable photographs of some very rare helicopters, Twin Otters and Dash 7s, makes for an interesting first day. There is, however, very little excitement afterwards.

NARSSASSUAQ
UAK   BGBW

Narssassuaq is like the two other fields which might feature in a rather specialised Greenland itinerary: these are IQALHUIT and NARSSASSUAQ, both of which amount to little more than a hut and a landing strip. Close scrutiny of sporadic movements presents no problem. To be realistic, there is little to be seen here that can't be seen just as well, or indeed better, at Sondrestrom.

PH NETHERLANDS (Kingdom of the Netherlands)
AMSTERDAM
AMS   EHAM   Schiphol   19m/30km SW (bus/train 25 minutes)

This large airport has an extensive terminal area at its heart and the facilities attract much attention from foreign enthusiasts because of the selection of aircraft to be seen. Plans are under way to turn Schiphol into a major trading and transport centre, Mainport 2000, by the turn of the century. Construction work has finished at Stationsgebouw West, with the new Pier G, and all the other piers were redesignated.

Assuming first that the visitor will make use of the extensive roof terrace at some time, guidance notes are worthy of attention. The terrace, or Wandelpier, is open between 8:45am and 6:00pm and can get very busy throughout the summer. When the weather is not at its best, the cafeteria, open all day, offers an alternative. Arrival by rail might mean stocking up with sensibly-priced food and drink for the day, and the ground floor shop next to the station is the place to go. The model planes in the window identify it, and also suggest that it stocks more for the enthusiast than just food. It carries an impressive selection of aviation books, so it could be somewhere to browse when things go quiet and the weather is poor.

A detour into the terminal before going onto the roof may be worthwhile as the ground floor information desk has lists of the day's flights: the yellow Aankomsten sheet shows arrivals and the blue Vertrekken/departures completes the picture. Whilst the registrations are shown for Dutch aircraft, these should not be taken too literally as they have a habit of being unreliable.

Most of the aircraft seen from the Wandelpier are less interesting than those using other parts of the airport, though good photographs are possible. To be sure of seeing all the movements, the eastern (far) end of the multi-storey car park is used, though everything is too far away for the camera. The busy Runway 06/24 is where serious photgraphers often settle, despite the fact that movements on the opposite runway are too far away to log. Bus services Nos. 173 and 176 go to Schiphol Oost, where activity is increasing.

Among the facilities at Schiphol Oost are KLM Helicopters and KLM's maintenance base, plus Fokker's assembly plant. There is usually some demonstrator or pre-delivery aircraft to be seen outside Fokkers, and guided tours are arranged for those who want to see what is produced there. Cameras are, incidentally, allowed on these visits. A close look at the aprons of Schiphol Oost also reveals a fair selection of general aviation, and often a cargo DC-8 or 707.

Continuing southeast along the road from Schiphol Oost, past the threshold of Runway 01R, a right turn on Oude Meer Weg leads to one vantage point very close to 06/24. Not far down this lane is the village of Rozenburg and a bus service operates here, for those without their own transport. Since this is one of the few places where the occupants of the new Schiphol Zuid cargo terminal can be seen, the road became very popular indeed. Peak times, such as sunny weekends, attracted so many visitors that the crowds and cars were cleared by the police. The most recent reports, still unconfirmed, suggest that permanent steps have been taken to stop the use of this vantage point.

Another road leads out of Rozenburg, bound for Badhoevedorp, and this runs parallel to 01L/19R, as well as being close to the threshold of Runway 09. Schiphol is a good airport for the enthusiast and offers a range of vantage points to reward the adventurous. KLM and other Dutch traffic obviously dominates the action, though it must be said that the international operators don't really amount to anything special that can't be seen at many other airports. Nevertheless, even the spotter who merely wishes to stay on the terrace will find a couple of days here enjoyable. The Aviodome Museum is close to the airport entrance and, for anyone who wants to take some ground level photos of the commuter carriers, the ramp to the right of Pier A handles this traffic, and a walk past the multi-storey car park will reveal a number of streets leading to the edge of this ramp. Patience will be needed because the apron is much used, and the view is foreshortened.

EINDHOVEN

EIN   EHEH   5m/8km W (bus 20 minutes)

The single storey passenger terminal building has a roof garden which is open in the summer, and a ground level external viewing area at its left. From this terrace it is difficult to see the Philips aircraft unless on the move, their hangar being to the right of the terminal, but all visitors are reasonably close, many being photogenically so. The staple diet is Cityhoppers but there are other attractions. The military base has F-16s and F.27Ms and, in 1994, KC-10s were stationed here. Throughout the year, the local Jetstreams of BASE Business Airlines are very much in evidence, their movements being complemented by the occasional Air Engiadina and Alsair service.

Aerofurn's painting and refurbishing shop means that one or two interesting arrivals can be expected during the year, and Fokker use the field for aircraft storage, rather than Ypenburg which is now closed. Additional storage space is still used at WOESDRECHT. Charter traffic in summer raises the tempo, with airlines such as Sun Express, Pegasus and, of course, Transavia.

ENSCHEDE

ENS   EHTW   Twente   4m/6km N

A tiny terminal is served by Twente Airlines Caravans and the car park to the right overlooks the (empty usually) apron. The F-86 mounted on a pole indicates that this airport may have more relevance to the military minded. Whilst the runway is distant from the terminal, it can be seen from other dead-end roads around the perimeter, but the taxiway to the hangars passes very close to the terminal car park, and good portraits of the F-5s or F-16s can be taken with ease. In summer, charter operations do liven things up a little.

Some 120 km from Twente is the SOESTERBURG Air Force Base: well worth a visit because there are good facilities for the large band of enthusiasts who congregate here. Quite close to the runway is an enclosure, where good portraits of F-15s can be taken as they take off and land. A visit here should include time for the museum, which houses some beautifully restored aircraft, though not necessarily with enough room around them.

GRONINGEN

GRQ   EHGG   Eelde   5m/8km S

Only the dedicated will consider a trip here to be worthwhile. On the southern edge of the town, just off the A28, is the home of the RLS and its fleet of Citations etc. A written request can result in a visit to RLS, during the week, but it should be noted that the airport is no longer served by scheduled flights. The area reserved for viewing is at the apron's edge, so good quality souvenir photos are a compensation, but it would take luck to be present in summer when a charter aircraft occupies the apron. Forty miles to the west is LEEUWARDEN, and its F-16s.

MAASTRICHT
MST   EHBK   Beek   4m/6km NNE (bus 20 minutes)

Maastricht is still really only a small regional airport, but it handles an increasingly interesting amount of traffic. Air Exel Brasilias, and BASE Jetstreams operate most of the commuter flights but there are charter services, mostly Transavia and Sultan Air, throughout the year. Royal Jordanian 707s have been regular visitors en route between JFK and Amman.

Between the terminal and the hotel is a terrace providing excellent viewing facilities for the taxiway and the runway. Almost any camera sets good results here, and above it is a cafeteria with an equally good view. Cargo charters are seen almost daily, frequently involving a Balkan An-12 or an Il-18 but various Russian operators have started to appear. GPA Expressions is the paintshop and refurbishment facility which guarantees an assortment of interesting visitors.

ROTTERDAM
RTM   EHRD   Zestienhoven   5m/8km NW (bus 20 minutes)

For anyone without a car, access to the airport is by bus from Rotterdam's Centraal Station. The passenger terminal is modern and features an open terrace at the apron's edge. Whilst it is ideally placed for many of the movements, traffic is increasing at Rotterdam and the most interesting aircraft may no longer occupy the most photogenic stands. There is now a chainlink fence separating the terrace and the apron, though photographs are still possible. To the right of the terminal and the car park is another vantage point, but only used for seeing incoming aircraft taxying to the apron. The expanse of apron to the left of the terminal is normally occupied by smaller aircraft, and it is often here that something out of the ordinary may be parked, usually within range of the average zoom lens.

One operator which may be of interest is KLM Aerocarto, whose Cessna 207 and Navajo are used for mapping and aerial photography. Their hangar is at the side of the approach road and the other end of it is used by Quick Airways. Without permission for access to these hangars and ramps, the presence of so much greenery can preclude an adequate view of the residents. Hamburg Airlines Dash 8s are regular visitors and it is always possible that some interesting, and unusual, visitor will arrive here.

PJ NETHERLANDS ANTILLES
SINT MAARTEN
SXM   TNCM   Prinses Juliana   7m/11km W of Philipsburg

This is the Caribbean for real jet-setters: white sand, turquoise water and very expensive indeed. A jewel is Maho Beach, at the end of the runway, which must be classed as an enthusiast's paradise. With only a few hundred feet separating beach and runway, aircraft can taxi to the end, turn (when they are photographed) and then set off down the runway. One small catch is the combination of aviation fuel and sandblasting which comes next! Even aircraft using the runway from the opposite end are within reach of a telephoto lens as they come over the beach.

Information strictly for the rich (courtesy of Genie online services): the Beachside Villa Resort is located very close to the airport and on the beach. The rooms are soundproofed and, in addition to the great photo opportunities, the beach is clothing-optional.

Many visitors are small: Winair base their three Twin Otters in the hangar next to the terminal, LIAT's largest movements are HS748s, Air St Barthelemy Trislanders and Air Guadeloupe ATR--42s are common visitors. Trans Air Link DC-6s offer variety, and the well-heeled arrive for the sun in a wide range of chartered jets, from TriStars to Express One 727s, and scheduled wide-bodies once a week from Air France, KLM and Lufthansa. The busiest time is between January and April, when winter is at its deepest in Europe.

The airport is small enough for all its facilities to be within reach of the average photographer, and the Leeward Islands are small enough for other islands to be within reach of St Maarten. The French island of ST BARTHELEMY is nearby, only ten minutes away by Air Guadeloupe Do228. The airfield is small, and highly photogenic, being next to the beach. The Trislanders of Air St Barths and Winair's Twin Otters are frequent visitors, shuttling to and from St Maarten.

PK INDONESIA (Republic of Indonesia)
BALIKPAPAN
BPN   WRLL   Sepingan   5m/8km E

Undoubtedly, this is Indonesia's second-ranking airport for aviation interest. It is on the eastern seaboard of Kalimantan (Borneo), an island shared between Indonesia, Brunei, Sarawak and Sabah. This may not be a rich country but there is an active oil industry, much of which is found on the edge of Balikpapan and nearby Pasar Baru. Oil-related flights dominate the traffic, and lunchtime is hectic as people transit through this hub.

Since the runway length restricts the size of aircraft, F.28s are the largest (and therefore most numerous) to be used. Bouraq movements abound, though there is no shortage of Merpati, Pelita and Garuda traffic. Apron space is limited, and peak time here is an experience never to be forgotten. The quantity of movements is more than adequate but the real interest lies in the frantic activity as passengers are transferred between flights.

If staying in Balikpapan, a visit to Lembah Harapan (the Valley of Hope) makes an interesting, and affordable, change from other tourist sights.

DENPASAR
DPS   WRRR   Ngurah Rai   8m/13km S

This airport is Bali's commercial field and has been undergoing expansion to cope with the tourist traffic. The international terminal was completed in 1992. International movements are still relatively limited: few aviation enthusiasts would travel to Bali for a photo of a KLM or Qantas 747! The last report from Denpasar said that only passengers in the international terminal get to see any of the aircraft from inside the building.

Arriving at the airport from Denpasar town on the dual carriageway, the bemo (cheap) bus passes a single storey cargo shed and the Merpati Nusantara hangar. Between these two buildings is a view of the taxiway through the chainlink fence. Photos of the Merpati CASAs are possible through the fence but it is not an ideal place to pass a full day in such an exotic location. To the left are normally a few helicopters and the occasional visitor, which can be as exotic as a Lloyd Aviation aircraft from Australia. Beyond the cargo shed are the domestic and international terminals. There was once a modest viewing area in the domestic building but this is now only available to departing passengers.

Some time around 5:00pm, local people start to arrive, to pass the time watching the aircraft. So does a vendor to supply snacks and drinks. Unless foreigners have unusually strong digestive systems, buying local produce in this way can result in close inspection of a bathroom for a few days . . . not recommended!

The Bali Beach Hotel at Sanur is where most airlines have a ticket office. The weekly roster of flights is shown there. Failure to book local flights there can sometimes be resolved by a visit to Garuda's office. Flights may not be as full as they say.

Bali may be an idyllic holiday spot but few other airports in Indonesia offer so little to the enthusiast. For an inexpensive change, the island of Lombok is less than a half-hour away by Merpati HS748, F.27 or CASA 235. The airport, MATARAM Selaparang, is served by these inter-island flights, most of which stop at Denpasar en route. The return fare is about £25.00.

JAKARTA
CGK   WIII   Soekarno Hatta   12m/19km NW (bus 45 minutes)

Anyone who has visited this airport will confirm that it is a memorable experience. One of the main reasons is the stifling heat . . . humid and very tiring. With the necessary walks between the various observation decks, it is fortunate that this airport holds one other treat: very cold draught Carlsberg! At each side of the approach road, and between the two runways, are two banks of three triangular terminals arranged in an arc. At the extremity of each terminal is an observation deck, each with its own view of the movements. To get from one to another, and it is a long way, stairs have to be negotiated to ground level and then back up. A few trips between decks in the really intense heat make the prospect of a beer very welcome indeed.

Much of the traditional-style terminal area is open, with check-in desks on the plazas, though covered from the sun by splendid ornamental roofs. There is an air of bustle, especially in the morning, and everywhere is perfectly clean. Shade is important, and each observation deck has some, plus a welcome breeze (with luck).

European enthusiasts will be drawn initially to the complex on the south side, the domestic terminals, as it is here that the more interesting movements can be seen. The three original passenger terminals are now the domestic passenger terminals, used by anybody that isn't Garuda. Viewed from landside, Sempati (A) to the left, Merpati (B) in the middle and Mandala/Bouraq (C) on the right. Redundant Viscounts, Electras and HS748s have occupied a ramp opposite Terminal C for a number of years.

Mesh fencing encloses the viewing decks, which makes photos extremely difficult. This side of Soekarno Hatta is fine for watching but that's about all. What can be seen is nevertheless an interesting procession of airline movements but photographers will be frustrated.

Morning and lunchtime witness a constant procession of domestic traffic, and the quantity of ex-Garuda (now Merpati) DC-9s and F.28s is still quite remarkable. However, the volume of traffic has reduced to the point that about twenty or so of these aircraft are now stored on the apron behind Garuda's maintenance base, clearly visible from the deck at the end of Terminal C. Garuda movements are still among the easiest to photograph at almost any time of the day, because they use Terminal F, at the eastern end of the new complex. The waving gallery here is accessible and is not enclosed by wire mesh. A shuttle bus operates between the terminals, the cost of which is a trifling 500 Rupyah, about 20 pence, as an alternative to walking in what can be very intense, and enervating, heat. Naturally, only one side of the airport can be monitored at any one time, so the shuttle bus might be used several times by anyone spending an entire day here.

Prior to leaving for Indonesia, it is wise to be familiar with the aircraft on the register. Busy though Soekarno-Hatta is, one must bear in mind that several airlines never visit. Merpati Nusantara, Bouraq, Sempati and Mandala are all present, plus the occasional Pelita movement but it becomes apparent that there must be a huge number of aircraft in Indonesia which only operate elsewhere. Pelita, for example, has traditionally had a major presence at Halim.

JAKARTA
HLP   WIIH   Halim Perdana Kusuma   8m/13km SE

Because there are now so few scheduled movements, Halim is no longer regularly served by the Damri link bus from Soekarno-Hatta. For those who feel a visit is essential, taxis offer affordable transport. The viewing deck has been closed, probably for ever, and there are no views of aircraft from public areas of the terminal.

With no viewing facilities, it may come as something of a relief to know that traffic is slow, with only Merpati operating regular flights. The balance is made up by Pelita, IAT and Eastindo, though access to see some of the helicopters at close range would be welcomed by most, if possible.

The modest traffic is as its peak, not saying much, in the early morning. A visit to Halim on the way to Soekarno-Hatta would be worthwhile, if only to ensure that an essential part of the national aviation scene is witnessed and that nothing is missed.

JAKARTA
JAK   WIID   Kemayoran   3m/5km NE

The last visit, reported in 1992, revealed a closed terminal, with only an engineless Viscount to be seen through the front gate. Nothing has been received by March 1995 to say whether or not redevelopment (the likely fate) has yet started.

JOGYAKARTA
JOG   WIIJ   Adisucipto   6m/9km NE

Java's cultural capital is a major tourist centre, being close to a number of famous ruins, including Borobodur. Pronounced Joag-jah, Jogya is equivalent to Japan's Kyoto, the Kraton and Taman Sari palaces dominate the heart of the town. The mini-bus which serves Solo calls at the airport, leaving from Terminal Terban, in the town centre.

Traffic is limited mainly to tourist flights from Jakarta. The small, and perfectly adequate, terminal has a central viewing area where good photographs are possible, especially in the afternoon. Only a low boundary wall separates the viewer and traffic, though candidates for the camera are limited. DC-9s are the staple diet, though Bouraq HS748s and Merpati F.27s do visit.

MEDAN
MES   WIIM   Polonia   1.5m/2km

The international terminal at Medan only has windows for passengers, and these overlook the car park! Attention is therefore focussed on the domestic terminal, where the interesting aircraft arrive. Here is what is described officially as a 'Waving Gallery'. Access requires a modest payment and there are catering facilities on the deck . . . waving isn't compulsory, incidentally!

The exotic palm trees enhance the tropical feel but they do obstruct the view of the apron. A zoom lens and some skill are the two ingredients for a photographic record. As aircraft taxi across the apron, a well-timed click should produce more than just trees. Not only is the resident C-47 still used regularly but there is also a good selection of regional carriers. Fokker 100s and F.28s are much in evidence as well as the occasional Dash Seven.

PADANG
PDG   WIMG   Tabing   5m/8km

This is an international airport but almost all its traffic is domestic. As with Medan, it is the domestic terminal (part of the only terminal, in fact) which offers a chance to see the aircraft. It is at the extreme southern end of the field, next to the runway threshold, so landing aircraft can normally be seen. Trees make photography of landings practically impossible.

The departure lounge is really the best place to be, and from here a few Sempati, Merpati and, of course, Garuda movements can be seen. Perhaps the most exotic visitor to be seen regularly is the Pelangi Air Do228, all the way from Kuala Lumpur. Telephoto lenses are essential without ramp access. Both require discretion. This is not Frankfurt, London or Denver . . . the security forces are trained to be sceptical of sophisticated equipment. Talking to someone can ensure that problems don't occur and open up the possibility of a walk onto the ramp.

PP BRAZIL (Democratic Republic of Brazil)
BELO HORIZONTE
PLU   SBBH   Pampulha   6m/9km N

When all the jet traffic was moved to Confins, Pampulha became the airport for regional, prop-driven traffic. In Brazil both halves of the picture are interesting but, when traffic is split into two, the old airport takes on a desolate look for a while. The crowded, noisy, hectic days of Pampulha are over, and the pace is now more relaxed. It should not be assumed that, because Lider Air Taxi are based at Pampulha, there will be a ramp crammed with LearJets. They operate from satellites all over the country.

The latest report from Belo Horizonte suggests that even the regional carriers are being moved out of Pampulha. To what extent this is true remains to be seen. Few passengers are going to welcome the prospect of a thirty mile drive to the airport, on Brazil's crazy roads, for the privilege of a short commuter flight. Time will tell.

BELO HORIZONTE
CNF   SBCF   Tancredo Neves/Confins   28m/44km N

This is another part of Brazil's investment in its future. Beautiful new passenger terminals have sprung up almost as fast as the rain forest is being destroyed. Confins has all the right facilities that are now expected in Brazil. The passenger's needs are not those of the enthusiast: pile it all onto one or two runways and fill the aprons to capacity. By splitting the traffic between two airports, life is more civilised but the pace at each airport is now very slow. For strangers, the name of the city is pronounced Bayo-orri-zonch.

BRASILIA
BSB   SBBR   International   7m/11km S

Like many federal capital cities, where the centre of commercial activity is elsewhere, Brasilia is not bustling with scheduled airline traffic. Like almost anywhere else in Brazil, the number of airlines to be seen is rather limited but Brasilia is one of the best places to see them. The terminal is set to one side of the runway, at a right angle, close enough for movements to be identified normally.

The passenger terminal faces east and good photography is possible at almost any time except early morning. The roof of the entire building is an observation deck with a view of all the stands to the front and the general aviation behind.

The general aviation and executive aprons can both be seen but the air force base is screened from view. However, the movements are plentiful during the week and, if Runway 09 is in use, they can also be inspected at very close quarters. A short walk from the terminal leads to the Transbrasil maintenance hangar and a right turn here passes the ramp, with a good view of any 727 which may be undergoing checks in the open air. The road ends at Lider Air Taxi's car park and this spot is very close to the taxiway. Any aircraft, no matter how small, can be photographed as it passes and photos of landing airliners are just distant enough to provide a side view as they flare out for touchdown.

Apart from Lider LearJets, there are several operators to be seen on the executive ramps, including those used by FUNAI, the indian development agency. Even though the traffic is limited, most of the Brazilian airlines are regular visitors and a couple of days in the warm sunshine should allow representative shots of each to be obtained.

CAMPINAS
VCP   SBKP   Viracopos   60m/92km NW of Sao Paulo

Viracopos was used for many years as Sao Paulo's main international gateway. This was where all the European flights arrived. The opening of Guarulhos meant that all flights could be transferred there, leaving Viracopos to lead a quiet existence as the regional airport for the city of Campinas. With so little traffic, it is improbable that anyone would tear themselves away from the bustle of Guarulhos, for the sake of a couple of Bandeirantes or F.27s.

CUIABA
CGB   SBCY   Marechal Rondon   5m/8km

Like so many other regional airports in Brazil, the verdict is the same: excellent but slow. With only twenty or so light aircraft on the ground, it takes more than six scheduled movements a day to make Cuiaba worth the journey.

CURITIBA
CWB   SBCT   Afonso Pena   12m/19km SE

Few visitors will stay here but it is a stop between Sao Paulo and Iguassu. The airport is small but, like most others in Brazil, it has been developed to the most modern standards. The apron is shared by airline visitors and a squadron of MB.339s which operate training flights. The short stop en route will allow time to get off the aircraft and take a few photographs of the other aircraft here. Purists will need to make a note of the different squadron markings, and the serials, which are quite small, also feature the 'last two', painted a little larger, on the nose.

FOZ DO IGUASSU
IGU   Cataratas   7m/11km NW

The name of the airport is Foz do Iguassu and should not be confused with Iguazu Cataratas, on the Argentine side of the border. What separates the two countries are the waterfalls, among the greatest sights in the world, comparable with the Grand Canyon, especially in the spring, when Niagara Falls pales into insignificance.

The airport, like most Brazilian examples, caters for waving off friends and there are actually two small observation decks here. Either allows a good view of the ramp and anything which uses the airport can be seen reasonably well. Airliners like TABA F.27s and Varig A300s are normal everyday traffic here but they do seem a little tame after seeing the spectacular waterfalls.

When at the falls, a pair of binoculars should always be kept close by, as one of the bonuses of a landing here is the chance to overfly, while turning onto approach. This could be the only chance to log something truly outstanding, as Austral 1-11s and Aerolineas Argentinas F.28s overfly, on approach to their destination, on the other side of the border.

Contrary to popular fears, Argentines have never been particularly hostile to Britons, and a day trip from Brazil is possible, even without a visa. Anyone who wants a passport stamp may encounter unexpected difficulties, as the bus does not normally stop at the border checkpoint! The short journey to Argentine Iguazu could result in a memorable souvenir photo.

JACAREPAGUA

24m/38km SW of Rio

Next to the old Grand Prix circuit is an airfield, included because it is also one of the maintenance bases for Votec. Enthusiasts are not common here, and anyone showing an interest can expect to be shown round, for the purposes of taking a few photographs.

What is immediately apparent is that there is a distinct lack of S-61s as Votec operations are from MACAE, some miles north of Rio and Niteroi. Anyone with a hire car and some dedication would be advised to investigate Jacarepagua, and obtain the name of a contact at Macae, to ensure some hospitality before making the journey.

Other activity at Jacarepagua is varied and includes some locally built single-engined types used to train Air Force Reserve pilots, as well as Prospec Islanders and a selection of stored aircraft, both civil and military.

MANAUS

MAO   SBEG   Eduardo Gomes   11m/17km NW

Signs of past glories abound in Manaus but the city is generally very run down now. The airport represents a major investment and is suitably modern, to attract tourists and investment into the area.

The passenger terminal faces the runway and has eight jetties for airliner use, though views from it are hard to find. Almost any other airport in Brazil offers better viewing facilities than Manaus, and the range of movements is fairly typical. Immediately left of the terminal area is a visitors ramp, where one or two executive aircraft park, all easily seen from the fence. Beyond this is a cargo ramp of some size, reflecting the proportion of cargo which arrives here by air, and its inmates range from Rico's fleet, largely redundant, to visiting aircraft of VASP and Varig.

MANAUS

SBMN   Ponta Pelada   4m/6km SW

Primarily a military base, Ponta Pelada is used mainly by the FAB Buffaloes, though the occasional TABA FH-227 can be seen from the main airport, while on approach to this field. It is located relatively close to the city centre, and might be worth exploration. The authorities may be reasonably welcoming to anyone who approaches the matter sensibly.

RECIFE

REC   SBRF   Guararapes   6m/9km SW

Photographs taken at Recife have a very distinct look to them because of the hill on the opposite side of the field from the terminal. A first floor open observation deck gives a perfect view of any traffic here and almost any airliner will make a fine subject for the camera as it taxis in to its stand. The international flights which refuel here do so during the night, though they are all generally airlines which are readily seen on many European trips.

Outside the passenger terminal is a preserved B-17 in FAB markings and to the north is the general aviation area, with a hangar used by Western Air Taxi, and there are other facilities around the field, including a small military presence at the far end of Runway 36.

RIO DE JANEIRO
GIG   SBGL   Galeao   9m/15km NW (bus 40 minutes)

This is very much a major international airport in every sense of the word, being extremely modern and handling a varied range of airlines from different countries. Sadly, it doesn't offer any real quantity and, even more sadly, the superb open air observation deck which once fronted the semi-circular terminal, has also been a victim of progress.

What remains is a rather small room on the third level, occupying the right-hand corner of what was once the deck, now glazed and smeared so that photography of any quality requires more than good luck. Essential equipment for the photographer is now a bottle of Windowlene and and wash leather. What is most frustrating is that the deck doesn't really face in the right direction. It overlooks the threshold of Runway 15 and, to a certain extent that of Runway 09 also, but if 27 and 33 are in use, which is quite often, trying to see the action is extremely frustrating.

The airfield is shared by a substantial FAB base. The C-130s can be seen in number from the terminal, identification being easiest from the approach road, and there are HS125s and HS748s in some quantity, also. As the base is quite close to the causeway road, it is very tempting to stop and take a portrait shot of a military transport but the guards tend to keep an eye out for this activity, so it involves some risk.

The long runway, 27/09, behind the original main terminal, created for the use of Air France Concordes, is still used for many flights and the Varig maintenance base is next to it, accessible only via a security gate. Some arrangement to pass this should be sought by anyone wishing to acquire a photograph of the preserved DC-3 (PP-ANU) and possibly one or two of the wide-body fleet undergoing checks. Access might be easier by expressing an interest in the Rapide, PP-VAN, which is stored inside.

RIO DE JANEIRO
SDU   SBRJ   Santos Dumont   2m/3km E

Located downtown, Santos Dumont is on a peninsula, surrounded on three sides by Guanabara Bay (Rio Harbour), with the Sugar Loaf at the end of Runway 18L. The airport is, in fact, a collection of various facilities of which a passenger terminal is one. There is a small, upper level, observation deck with a cafe, and the Punta Aereas airliners park in front, offering themselves very photogenically. Activity is slow, though all movements are worthy of attention. The Punta Aerea, or Air Bridge, was once Varig's exclusive territory but is now operated by VASP and Varig 737s with additional competition from the F.100s of TAM.

Enthusiasts with some interest in military aviation will enjoy Santos Dumont as it handles a good number of FAB movements, with Bandeirantes being operated by many different squadrons, each with its own distinctive scheme. The military base is spread along the roadside and a walk reveals hangars/ramps containing HS125s and a selection of trainers, as well as a fair number of Bandeirantes. Closer to the terminal are the facilities of Lider Air Taxi and Cruzeiro Aerofoto, where a variety of aircraft can always be seen but rarely photographed, unless on the move.

Being downtown, Santos Dumont handles executive movements in some profusion and the field can be seen to hold a variety, parked on the many stands in the middle of the field. Attempts to obtain a tour of the airside may involve some unofficial discussion regarding money, with large sums being considered reasonable. This is based on the assumption that photographs will be sold at a profit (to be shared), so the 'private collection' angle should be mentioned at a very early stage!

RIO DE JANEIRO

SBAF   Campos dos Afonsos   11m/17km WNW

The inclusion of this field in a book about airports may seem incongruous but it would be a shame for someone to visit the area and miss one of the most interesting parts of the aviation scene here, especially since it isn't world famous.

Apart from being an active military base, with Pumas, C-130s and Buffaloes, the museum houses an outstanding collection of aircraft each of which warrants a mention in its own right. The drive from Rio is horrendous, except for the brave, and approach from Jacarepagua is far more leisurely, with the aid of a good road map. A variety of these can be purchased in the shop at Santos Dumont, and the best value is the most expensive, as the cheaper ones are, effectively, useless.

SALVADOR

SSA   SBSV   Dois de Julho   22m/34km NE

Not one of Brazil's more interesting airports. Apart from the occasional Cruzeiro wide-body, most of the traffic is restricted to 737s. The heavies tend to pass through at unsociable hours on their way to Rio. The Nordeste apron, in front of their hangar, usually holds a few Bandeirantes.

SAO PAULO

CGH   SBSP   Congonhas   5m/8km S

Now very much a domestic airport, time has taken its toll on a downtown location and all scheduled traffic has been moved to Guarulhos. Still worth a visit, even if the huge quantities of movements have been severely trimmed, the observation deck offers an adequate view of most of the Air Bridge traffic (even some of this now uses Guarulhos).

All that remains is a row of hangars along the taxiway, out of sight from the terminal. Rather than wait for the occasional movement, it's now necessary to walk down to the hangars and see what's there. Congonhas may be a mere shadow of its former self but it still has some exotic machinery.

SAO PAULO

GRU   SBGR   Guarulhos   15m/23km (bus 50 minutes)

Guarulhos is now established as a very major airport, as is to be expected when it serves such an enormous city. All Sao Paulo's interesting scheduled movements, like Aerolineas Argentinas and Ladeco 727s, and Pluna 737s, use this airport. Transatlantic services, too, have been transferred here, so the pace and variety are enough to satisfy any enthusiast.

The passenger terminal does have an open observation deck, with good views of the scheduled traffic. Cargo facilities are found at both sides of the terminal and the Varig/Cruzeiro maintenance base is on the far side of the runways.

There are bus services between the city and the airport, and it is possible to catch the Metro to Bresser (on the Linha L'Este-Oueste/East West Line) and take a bus from there, which saves a little time. More important, it saves experiencing the awful downtown traffic . . . not much fun, even in a bus!

RA RUSSIA

The Soviet Union is no more. In its place is the Commonwealth of Independent States. Aeroflot, at the break-up, was worse than bankrupt and operations continued in a chaotic way. The international flights continue, as long as profit margins are there. Domestic flights have witnessed upheaval and many have been suspended, probably permanently. Many remote communities depended on Aeroflot for their very existence. Many of the changes appear to be merely cosmetic. Freedom of movement may be slightly more relaxed but it is still a difficult country for the lone traveller to make his way, particularly in search of aircraft. Escorted tours offer good value and some assurance of seeing as much as can be seen. They are easier for the authorities to control. As the purpose of this book is to offer guidance on where to go without official help, entries for Russia and its neighbours are largely meaningless, as most enthusiasts will be guided in their parties past security checkpoints and onto ramps.

BRATSK
BTK　　UIBB　　　　Yurba

Mainly a military field, with lots of MiG-25s to be seen in the company of several An-2s and Yak-40s. A pair of Tu-154s, damaged after an accident, found their way here, and the rear portions of their fuselages can be seen. On the opposite side of the road is an enormous helicopter base.

MOSCOW
MOW

Central Moscow is adorned with some of the most wonderful buildings to be seen anywhere in the world. St Basil's Cathedral, in Red Square (red means great, incidentally) is an example. The Russian people are rightly proud of their heritage but almost everything that has been built since 1917 is indescribably ugly: concrete boxes are everywhere. The enormous scale of apartment blocks and power stations is something the visitor gets used to, after a while.

The many airports and airfields around the city are becoming increasingly well known. Two years ago, this book offered some thumb-nail sketches in the hope that the quantity of information would increase. Below, the reader will be able to decide whether that has happened.

Apart from the airports, the enthusiast can consider this city to be interesting, and occasionally exciting. Several city parks have aircraft for the enjoyment of youngsters. Effectively, they are now enjoyed mostly by vandals. There is no money to keep the aircraft in good condition, so each year's passing means the situation gets worse. Frunze has one park worthy of inspection.

Entry to the Museum of the Armed Forces costs about US$10. It has one significant foreign item on display: Gary Power's U-2B 56-6693, shot down on May Day 1960. The aviation museum to beat all museums is located at Monino. It's the Russian equivalent of Wright-Patterson, only moreso. If the Russians flew it, this museum has it. Large quantities of time and film are needed. There is a lot of ground to cover. It is neither necessary nor possible to list what can be seen, though civil aviation enthusiasts will no doubt find such exhibits as the Tu-144 and the An-22 to be outstanding. The Tu-22 is, however, an amazing spectacle. More routine, but worthy of photos are the Tu-104, Tu-114 and Tu-124, plus the ever popular Il-18.

To reach the main airports from the city centre, public transport is good, if rather spartan. Buses leave from Leningradski Prospekt and trains to Vnukovo go from Kievski station. It might be possible to travel by taxi between a few of the airports in the south but, before parting company with your Lada and its driver, it is essential to ensure that means of leaving are available. Very little is yet known about public transport linking the airports with each other. Sheremetyevo is all alone on the north side of the city and should be treated separately.

MOSCOW

BKA   Bykovo   12m/19km E

The last few miles of the road to Bykovo give a constant impression that it must be the wrong way. Do not be fooled into thinking that just because the road looks like it must stop at any moment, it will. Bykovo is, to put it simply, out in the sticks. When the hovels and kiosks, the peddlers and the whores stand by the roadside, you're almost at the airport entrance.

Anyone who speaks good Russian could probably negotiate the purchase of an Il-76 with an old woman standing by the road. If she can't get you one, she could probably get enough parts to make one, and within a few hours. Failing that, she'll know someone who can.

Bykovo has an Il-14, CCCP-91484, on display at the far end of the car park, at the right-hand end of the terminal. Directly behind are the Il-76s. There is a rampside spectators area but this doesn't allow much impression of what can be seen by an organized tour. The terminal building, now almost defunct, has a tunnel through its middle which leads to the official observation area. Visible from here are assorted Antonov turboprops directly in front and Yak 40/42s to the right. The range of colour schemes now being applied to the Yaks is interesting but many of them are being stripped down for parts.

To be blunt, Bykovo has seen better days, but we can't be sure if it actually took part in them. Weeds grow, in abundance, through the concrete and the hangars seem to be semi-derelict. This can also be said for many of the Il-76s, few of which are now fully intact. This is a major maintenance base for Il-76s, often used by foreign air forces. Ramp access is essential, as it allows not just close encounters with these impressive aircraft but also the chance to see one or two less common aircraft: for example there is an Il-18 in good condition, plus another that has been reduced to its airframe.

Russia has more than its share of problems and nowhere are they more evident than at Bykovo. It can be a shock to see such squalor, especially around an airport but that is a major part of what makes a visit to Bykovo such a memorable event.

MOSCOW

DME   Domodedovo   25m/ SE (bus 80 min)

A moderately active airport, dominated by Il-62s, Domodedovo still looks superficially modern. Closer inspection reveals things are otherwise, however. The passenger terminal has a huge glass frontage, overlooking the central apron where many aircraft (mostly parked Il-62s) can be seen. The car park offers an additional, and also partial, view.

Displayed on a plinth, and in good condition, is Tu-114 CCCP-76464. This is the very large and impressive, four-engined, passenger propliner with contra-rotating propellors. It still makes a fine subject for the camera.

To each side of the terminal are runways, though only that on the left is used. Most of the movements are Tu-154s, rather than Il-62s, and many of them are operated by CIS airlines, so a welcome range of colour schemes passes through. Long fingers project from each side of the terminal, obscuring from sight anything parked on the far side, though registrations can be read off the Tu-154s. Be thankful that it is traditional to place the registrations on the central air intake, rather than below the cheat line. A few Il-76s and An-12s are parked on the far side of the central apron so that they appear nose-on. They are difficult, if not impossible, to identify.

The Aviatrans cargo ramp forms the remote left-hand corner of the main apron. To the left of the main terminal is another building, clearly seen from the car park, behind which is hidden a ramp. Before entering the passenger terminal, or certainly before leaving, it is worth investigating this ramp, because it isn't visible from inside. If exploration seems appropriate, then the opposite side of the car park is really worth a look . . .

A few hours spent in the terminal can give the impression that Domodedovo is an interesting airport. This would mean departing in complete ignorance of its star residents. Parked around the corner, to one side and completely out of sight, are several Il-96s. Without a ramp tour, they are inaccessible. Whether or not these aircraft are visible between the hangars is for others to discover. Caution is strongly advised.

MOSCOW
Myatchkyvo

This airfield is strictly for tour groups. If you think Bykovo is out in the sticks, then Myatchkyvo is more so. It's down a dirt track, in the woods. Little can be seen, and nothing heard, from the perimeter fence and one would be foolish to try taking a look. Not much moves here, mostly because there is no longer any reason for it do so. The days when aerial reconnaissance were needed (or could be afforded) are long gone. Parked here are plenty of An-30s, the ones with the glazed noses. They wear Aeroflot colours but their primary purpose wasn't as civil airliners.

Access, by prior arrangement, allows close encounters of a rotary kind. Long rows of helicopters, many derelict, offer much of interest to lovers of wrecks and relics. Add an Il-14 on its last legs and a few rows of An-2 biplanes, many covered by tarpaulins for some reason, and it's like one of world's best car boot sales. For non-British readers, Americans call them yard sales or garage sales.

Believed to be close to Myatchkyvo is another field, Lybertski. Most of it is reported to be hidden behind a high wall. On the other side are Mi-26s and much, much more.

MOSCOW
SVO   UUEE   Sheremetyevo   18m/ NW (bus 50 min)

Sheremetyevo is effectively two separate airports, located on either side of the two parallel runways, only one of which appears to be in use. To the north is the domestic terminal, Sheremetyevo 1: a long low building with an upper floor level balcony along its front, and a circular satellite with a wide, overhanging roof. The balcony is closed but this is not much of a problem because movements at Terminal 1 are few and far between.

On the south side, Terminal 2 has a restaurant on its fifth floor. This is not too high for phographers and it does ensure that many (but by no means all) of the distant aircraft parked on the north side, can be identified. There are rather a lot! The international movements dominate proceedings here, so Terminal 2 is the best place to be. Traffic is reasonably brisk, featuring a good assortment of ex-Soviet bloc and western types. Visitors from the USA are notably absent, apart from the daily Delta A310 from Frankfurt.

The restaurant has tinted glass, which can make life difficult for the photographer, especially when travelling alone. For example, it might be rather conspicuous to take from the gadget bag a decent-sized screwdriver, and remove the screws which keep a window closed. It easily done but the increase in aircraft noise is noticed by all apart from the stone deaf. Tour groups, however, have been known to do this sort of thing. Nobody seems to care enough to interfere with a large number of people but they might be easily moved to do something about a single person. Safety in numbers, as they say.

The principal aim of a restaurant is normally to serve food and drinks. Steak and fries might look a good bet, at US$5. Wait until you see what you get! If it moves, hit it. This is one of the few restaurants where you can count all your chips in less than half a minute and still have time left over. Times, it must be remembered, are hard in Russia. They are doing their best with what they've got. Your steak and chips might look less appetising than would be laid on your table in other parts of the world but it is considerably better than what the local folk get to eat.

The first sight, from these windows, is indeed impressive. On the far side are rows of Il-86s, Il-76s, Il-62s and Tu-154s. It is best to be contented with what is recorded, rather than be frustrated by what is not. After even half a day at Sheremetyevo, there will be plenty to remember. Subsequent visits, however, involve the law of diminishing returns.

MOSCOW
VKO UUWW   Vnukovo   19m/ SW (train 75 min)

On arrival here by road, the preserved Tu-104 at the entrance catches the eye. Stopping to take a photograph is the last time the air is filled only by the sound of jackdaws. This is Moscow's main national airport, handling flights from all over Russia. It gets very busy indeed. Chaotic might be a better description.

If Sheremetyevo is Moscow's JFK, then this is its LGA. Seasoned travellers argue that Vnukovo is better, as the two airports are moving in opposite directions, from the enthusiast's point of view. LGA once offered National Airlines DC-10s, Eastern Airbuses, Southern DC-9s, Empire F.28s and many, many more colour schemes. Vnukovo only had the blue and white of Aeroflot. It used to be wonderful for number-crunchers but one photo of a Tu-154 looked like any other. Now everything's changed: if the variety on display at LGA is reducing, new colour schemes are appearing, almost daily, at Vnukovo.

The upper floor has a snack bar at the front of which is an open terrace. In fact, there are two open terraces, side by side. Both can be accessible without problems but the scene can change as quickly as the airline colour schemes. It would be bad luck if both were closed. To be seen from here is pandemonium - people walking all over the apron between the many Tu-154s, yellow buses transporting passengers to and from their aircraft, and yellow tankers doing the refuelling. Most of the ground transport appears to have been designed in 1950 at the latest.

Apart from the many Tu-154s, Il-86s also abound though they move less often. Many of the Il-86s are stored, awaiting an uncertain future. Anyone old enough to remember spending mornings on the La Guardia roof terrace before heading to JFK will also recall the feeling of real action, the noise and the smell of aviation fuel. Vnukovo is where the sheer excitement of it all comes flooding back.

MOSCOW
Zhukovsky   15m/24km SE

Zhukovsky is close to Bykovo but it's not for the intrepid solo traveller. No matter how much Russia is opening up to the west, and very much to market forces, this airfield is still used by the Flight Research Institute, so it can't be assumed that interest by foreigners is harmless. The Russians have to be fast learners, if they are survive and prosper. A little entrepreneurial skill is essential. They have discovered that the appeal of this airport has a high price on its head. Even if tours are promised, don't be surprised if the arrangements are not finalised. Zhukovsky offers lots more than Il-76s and, reportedly, stored Tu-144s.

Expect the price to be raised at the last minute. Even when it's agreed, it can still be raised. Getting to this airport will be a matter of luck, until the going rate is established. Charging so much that a visit is cancelled is in nobody's interest. It will all be sorted out, in the course of time.

NOVOSIBIRSK
OVB   UNNN   Tolmachevo

Novoskibirsk is a major regional capital in eastern Russia. Scheduled airline activity here is best described as leisurely. A connection onwards might make a stop necessary. Anything seen on the field is unlikely to move during a short stay of an hour or two. The huge military base can be seen from the aircraft when taking off (or landing, if the wind is not in its prevailing direction). An Il-86 is to be seen, dumped, probably as the result of some landing accident. The selection of airliners is nothing exceptional, with a few examples of most types to be seen.

The other field is called Severnij, which is used mostly by local traffic. Apart from a lot of helicopters, the other aircraft are Turbolets and An-24s.

SINT PETERSBURG

LED	ULLI	Pulkovo	11m/17km S (bus 45 minutes)

The LED code tells us that, until recently, this was Leningrad. The local spelling of Saint is Sint, so the title block is not a typographical error! Despite being Russia's second city, airline activity is decidedly slow. There are very few international flights, and these can only be seen from the terminal by passengers, after passport control.

To be seen on the right from the international area, some parked/stored An-12s rarely move. What interest is generated by a visit to St Petersburg will be found at the domestic terminal. For anyone who is prepared to walk, the best views are from the approach road. There is also an officially approved viewing park next to one runway but details about it are vague.

Another airfield, closer to the city, is Rshevka. It may be small but it houses a considerable number of helicopters and An-2s, many of which are present for maintenance.

ULYANOVSK

ULY		10m/16km

Until very recently, the city of Ulyanovsk was officially rather important: it was Lenin's birthplace. But times have changed! The old city of Ulyanovsk lies on the west bank of the River Volga and has recently come to our attention as being the site for Aviastar's assembly plant. The airport is an entirely separate location, and of interest not for the very few scheduled flights during the average day but for its Civil Air Training Centre. Aeroflot's jet pilots are trained on all fleet types here, from Yak-42s to Il-76s.

On the east bank of the river is Ulyanovsk new town, with the Aviastar plant on its outskirts. New towns in this part of the world are rarely beautiful. The Russians usually have good reasons for some of their seemingly strange decisions. Locating the assembly plant nine miles from the runway is an interesting example!

Visitors to the city are almost sure to be in a guided tour party, so the civil aviation museum might be on the itinerary. At different locations in the east bank new town are displayed Tu-134 CCCP-65618 and Il-62 CCCP-86685. Financial resources to preserve them in good condition are non-existent.

RP PHILIPPINES (Republic of the Philippines)
MANILA

MNL	RPMM	Ninoy Aquino International	8m/13km S (bus 30 minutes)

Unless one has a definite objective, there is little incentive to spend time at the international terminal, where the activity is not particularly brisk. Likely exceptions are Continental 727s, Qantas 767s and 747 Combis, Cathay Pacific TriStars, and assorted A300s, any of which may be enough to encourage the average photographer. Visitors are fewer than at Hong Kong or Singapore and the opportunities for photography are limited. Visible from the international terminal is 707 RP-C911, previously used by President Marcos but now used as the very static Club 707. The airport is now named in memory of his political adversary, whose widow was subsequently elected to rule.

Heading towards Manila, on the Love Bus or in a (very cheap) taxi, the old domestic terminal is seen, very shabby and overcrowded but which now hosts A300s on the Cebu flights as well as PAL Fokker 50s. Photography of these taxying aircraft is possible from either side of the terminal but some care should be exercised: the police and military personnel can be unpredictable.

The old terminal is located opposite the threshold of Runway 13 and may no longer be in use. Next to it is the largest of the general aviation areas: that of the PADC (Philippine Aerospace Development Corporation), with the other general aviation area directly opposite. The walk to either of the aprons isn't too long, even in the humid heat, and both offer a wide selection of very interesting aircraft, as would be expected in this part of the world.

The PADC facility is quite accessible, with a wide taxiway separating the rows of hangars. It is a reflection on the economic situation that many of the aircraft rarely leave their hangars but there are good numbers of locally-built Islanders, quite a few Beech 18s and most of the nation's biz-jets to be seen. Access to the taxiway, and therefore the hangars, is straight-forward, via an entranceway from the main road next to the domestic terminal. The aprons feature a collection of derelict and (just) operational DC-3s, seven being seen in September 1992, and a number of other types including a YS-11 and the T-29.

The photographer is unlikely to meet with problems taking shots of these aircraft but a modicum of caution and politeness should be exercised when seeking access to hangars. Each has its own guard and there are always numerous hangers-on, all of whom will be wary of a westerner in their facility. Unless permission has been sought from each operator, the use of a camera may lead to trouble.

The smaller general aviation ramp across the runway is also easily accessible and, apart from many more exec types, a derelict Air Manila F.27 was dumped here. Next door is PAL's domestic maintenance base, though this is not so easily visited without prior permission. As well as Fokker 50s and stored 1-11s, the locally based US Embassy C-12 lives here, and a couple of PAF F.27s should also be in evidence.

The sizeable PAL training fleet of Seminoles and Tomahawks, all in full airline scheme, is parked on the runway side of one of the hangars, close to a few derelict PAF C-47s minus their wings. These Daks mark the transition of the civilian airport to Nichols Air Force Base so further walking along the apron is unwise in the extreme.

Access to PAL's widebody hangar is via the security guard at the entrance to Nichols AFB, so it may be possible to transit the base by having business with PAL. Air Force transports to be seen would normally include Maritime and ex-PAL F.27s, Islanders, the (civil) VIP F.28, the occasional Nomad, Hercules and even a C-123, plus numerous helicopters. Photography and conspicuous note-taking are definitely injudicious.

In summary, Manila offers probably as many as two hundred executive and light aircraft, with perhaps up to fifty military machines (if you can see them) plus the resident and visiting airline traffic. Manila also offers, for those who like that sort of thing, its very own, spectacular brand of night life to round off the day!

SE SWEDEN (Kingdom of Sweden)
GOTEBORG

GOT   ESGG   Landvetter   15m/23km E (bus 40 minutes)

The international traffic to be seen is probably the least attractive aspect. A handful of 737s and DC-9s from Europe's major capitals, none of which would warrant more than a passing glance at Frankfurt or Schiphol, are supplemented by SAS flights, several of which are operated by Fokker 50s.

The view of the apron is through the large windows but more than one visitor on the ramp at any time is an unusual event. Smaller aircraft provide occasional interest, Metros being regular in airline service. Landings on Runway 21 can be photographed but the walk is long and hiking boots are recommended. It is unlikely that anyone would venture this far off the beaten track in pursuit of aircraft but anyone on a business trip could pass a couple of hours and see something out of the ordinary.

GOTEBORG
GSE   ESGP   Saeve

Any visitor with time to spare would do well to investigate Saeve, as it is quite a busy little general aviation field. Several air taxi and other fleet operators base their operations here, and it's normal to see a number of Citations and King Airs.

MALMO
MMX   ESMS   Sturup   20m/32km E (bus 35 minutes)

The majority of Sturup's flights are domestic but SAS no longer operate F.27s to Copenhagen: the SAS hovercraft services from the City Hoverport are the quickest means of getting there. The modest traffic was best seen from the (free) observation deck, where a summer evening could be passed taking quality photos. This was before the construction of the new passenger terminal extension. Since its completion, in 1993, no reports have been received regarding the new situation.

There is a Swedair base here, and a varied collection of residents but this is little more than an airport where Swedish light aircraft will be logged (and possibly photographed) before moving on. A protracted stay will be dull to anyone other than a dedicated photographer with a specific subject in mind.

MALMO
JMM   ESHM   Heliport

It is unlikely that anything will be seen at the heliport, as movements are infrequent. The adjacent hovercraft terminal, operated by SAS, provides quick links between Malmö and Copenhagen.

NORRKOPING
NRK   ESSP   Kungsangen   3m/5km E (bus 10 minutes)

The Syd Aero SD3.30 flights supplement the usual Fokker 50s, operating their regional schedules. The based Calibrator C-53 and Kungsair's modest base are other marginal attractions, though it will be a dedicated enthusiast who heads for Norrköping. The general aviation apron, on the far side of the runway, is accessible upon request.

STOCKHOLM
ARN   ESSA   Arlanda   25m/40km N (bus 45 minutes)

The observation deck, above the international pier, is open but during the summer months only. When this is the case, Arlanda is a good airport to visit, and an early start is advised. Access to it is at the right hand side of Terminal 5, as seen from the road. There is no admission charge, and only photographers will be unhappy with the facilities, as the glass doesn't help. Apart from the apron, the threshold of Runway 26 can also be seen from here. Subject to the observation deck being open, Arlanda poses no problems.

Alternative possibilities exist: the cafe in the international terminal has a view of sorts, of some of the domestic gates. To the right are the SAS and Transwede hangars, and to the left is the domestic terminal with, beyond it, the new domestic terminal. A shuttle bus links the five terminals. The commuter carriers, which comprise some of the more interesting movements, use the pier most remote from view but they can be seen on the taxiway.

As this is the main airport for the country, it handles much international traffic, and is rated as Europe's fourth busiest airport. There are, however, few movements significantly different from what can be seen elsewhere. It is the local traffic, SAS and Skyways especially, which are of most interest but representative portraits will probably be restricted to landing shots taken beside Runways 01 and 26. During Arlanda's quiet times, in the early afternoon, exploration should reveal a few withdrawn SAS and Swedair aircraft. The domestic terminals also have accessible windows where most of the interesting local traffic can be seen.

STOCKHOLM
BMA   ESSB   Bromma   5m/8km W (trai/bus 20 minutes)

Closer to the city centre than Arlanda, Bromma handles little or no scheduled traffic. The field is now used for air taxi and general aviation operations, as well as much maintenance, so it is worth a visit. A written request for access to the ramps is normally successful, and a few hours spent here can compensate for any disappointment at Arlanda. One of the interesting residents is the derelict hulk of CV-440 SE-CCX, used by the fire crews. It last saw service with Linjeflyg.

The Metro railway station at Alnik is connected to the city, and its bus station is where service No.110 operates to the airport.

SP POLAND (Republic of Poland)
GDANSK
GDN   EPGD   Rebiechowo   9m/15km NW

Rather more like old Poland than Warsaw, Gdansk is an industrial city. It lacks charm! LOT ATR--72s operate there from Warsaw, as do occasional split-load flights to Heathrow. Traffic is extremely slow, and hardly worth the effort, when there is more to see and do in Warsaw.

WARSAW
WAW EPWA   Okecie   6m/9km S (bus 30 minutes)

With the changes taking place in central Europe, many enthusiasts are turning their attention in that direction. Okecie (pronounced Oh-ken-chi) has a new passenger terminal to match the country's active interest in the rest of Europe. Scheduled traffic is still moderate but there is usually something to keep the mind occupied whilst waiting for something to taxi past.

Every effort has been made to encourage travellers to visit Warsaw. The prices, by western standards, are an incentive in themselves. There aren't too many ancient European capital city centres where a coke and a burger cost less than a pound. The airport is still awaiting its own express bus service and, in the meantime, the traveller can get his act together in the airport's main concourse. Hotels to suit all budgets can be booked at the travel agency, and tickets for the bus can be bought at the kiosk marked 'RUCH'. They are so cheap, it's worth buying a few, to save inconvenience later.

The new terminal, called Okecie II, is as modern as any in Europe, the only difference being that the pace is relaxed and civilised. Few passengers have said that about Heathrow. On the roof of this building is the observation deck, accessible by going outside, turning right and

walking a few metres. Open between 8:00am and 8:00pm, entry costs Zl12,000 (not much!)
Arrival by plane allows sight, normally while taxying, of the extensive aprons to the north, which are bound to excite interest. For the best view of this area, the roof of the new multi-storey car park is good. From here the many Yak-40s can be seen, usually in the company of both Polnippon Cargo Il-18s. One or two Aeroflot Mi-8s are sometimes present, often in the company of a few Polish military examples of the same type.

The domestic terminal is the farthest building beyond the maintenance hangars and anyone who has visited the old Olympic terminal at Athens will see a similarity, though there are less passengers. The apron may contain one or two biz-jets. In front of it are parked the ATR--72s, awaiting duties. Most of the Tupolevs are to be seen in front of the hangars, whilst the Tu-154s which are ready for service have their own ramp. The Tu-134s in use are parked in front of the old terminal.

Some of the Yak-40s are painted in military colours, and others in a basic LOT scheme, though without titles. They have three-digit serials, unlike SP-GEA which lurks in its own small hangar. At around 4:00pm, when most of the scheduled traffic gets quiet, is when the Yaks and Turbolets tend to move. From the deck, a leisurely perusal of the perimeter reveals, sooner or later, a couple of Il-14s. One, SP-LNE, bears Aeropol titles and sits behind the fire station. the other, SP-LNB, is next to the control tower. At the northern edge of the field are some unsold PZL crop sprayers and, just to the right of them, a MiG-15 is derelict. The domestic terminal is barely visible from this new deck, though it could be seen from the old one, some way to the south.

Airline traffic is interesting, and most European carriers visit during the week. The new airport has been made inviting, and the officials are friendly but efficient. It will take some time for westerners to be understood. After so many years, a young officer may be alarmed at the sight of a telephoto lens, as these are beyond the means of the average Pole. Covert activity is bound to raise attention. It is so much easier to make contact with someone beforehand and explain your presence, and the purpose of your activities.

The nearest hotel to the airport is the Novotel, on the main highway to town, called Zwirki i Wigury. It is more expensive, and less convenient, than those in town. The Metropol and Polonia are both very affordable, though the late night trams make a noise. Only a two-hour flight from London, Warsaw is within easy reach. The weather in summer will come a pleasant surprise, as will everything else, to anyone who thinks Warsaw is a cold and inhospitable city.

The service bus into the city is No.175, though No.114 also goes there. Be sure to punch the ticket in the machine, as penalties for free-riding are severe. An express service into the city might now be operated. At the crossroads a few hundred metres from the airport is a road called 17 Styeznia. A left turn here leads past the backs of the hangars to the domestic terminal, and there is a bus service. The journey is hardly worth the effort. It might be possible to identify one or two visiting biz-jets, but everything will, sooner or later, pass the main terminal on its way to Runway 33.

Signs of the times in Warsaw are the monumental Palace of Culture, behind the main railway station, part of which has been converted into the Queen's Casino. On the other side of the building is a market where famous brand trainers are sold at ridiculously low prices by western standards. Duty free shopping is expensive compared with downtown Warsaw!

WARSAW
EPBC   Babice

The ability to watch, log and photograph aircraft at Okecie is one thing, but to be seen doing so at Babice may arouse rather more unwanted interest. On one side of the runway is a military base with a couple of MiGs and several Mi-8s. The civilian operations are dominated by Aeropol, though activity is rare. The many An-2s and Mi-2s share the field with one or two Turbolets. If guidance can be offered in this book, it would be to treat Babice with some caution. Making

244

contact with officials could prove better than allowing them to make the first move. In five years' time, it might be a different story. It won't be hastened in the right direction by too many unfortunate, and avoidable, incidents.

SU EGYPT (Arab Republic of Egypt)
CAIRO

CAI	HECA	International	14m/22km NE

Any opportunity to transit through Cairo should be welcomed, though a stay of any length is another matter. As there are no air jetties, all passengers need to take a bus between the aircraft and the terminal. Arrival by air always means a long taxi to the apron, so the opportunity to see a splendid array of aircraft is thus presented. Inactive and withdrawn aircraft include some An-12s. The most recent reports suggest that these are now reduced to two in number: SU-APA and SU-APX. Close by, Petroleum Air Services Twin Otters and a few DC-3s are also to be seen.

The selection of commercial flights is interesting, though traffic is quite slow. Terminal One, for domestic flights, has a viewing gallery, and the International Terminal has a cafeteria, where most of the action can be also be witnessed. Security is strict in much of Africa and the Middle East. Cairo can be classed as both, so it gets a double helping!

The Movenpick Hotel is up-market, and its location so close to the airport allows prices to rise even further. Even if a stay there isn't planned, it is worth a look, for anyone with transport. The remains of a 707 are to be found outside it.

LUXOR

LXR	HELX		4m/6km SE

Awakening to the commercial possibilities of tourist traffic, several charter flights to Egypt arrive at Luxor, to take their passengers to the Valley of the Kings. A scenic detour before landing is almost obligatory. Air traffic has been slow to develop, and there are very few movements each day. Military activity on the field is mostly with Mil helicopters, though they are difficult to see from the terminal.

SX GREECE (Hellenic Republic)

ATHENS

ATH	LGAT	Hellenikon	6m/9km S (bus 30 minutes)

Situated at the northern edge of Glyfada, this is one of the best destinations in Europe for the enthusiast who seeks a compromise between a summer holiday and an aviation feast. There are three runways in existence but only 15L/33R normally sees any use. Facilities sharing this runway are the Hellenic Air Force base, the Olympic terminal and the International terminals.

The appeal of Athens has diminished little, in spite of the security precautions necessitated by terrorist activity, though the front portion of the observation deck is closed and the perimeter is closely monitored by the police. This can result in photographers being arrested for 'anti-tourist' activities, though all are released after some muscle-flexing. It should be borne in mind that using a camera at the edge of the airport is NOT an offence, though it is very unpopular with those who have to be seen to be coming to grips with present day security requirements. Most of what people in uniform do is harass, the intention (usually quite successful) is to deter.

Considering first the Olympic terminal and its viewing facilities, these can be dismissed as being virtually non-existent. There are no windows in the terminal, so the movements of the smaller Olympic aircraft cannot be seen. The small observation deck at the north end has been closed. At the extreme northern end of the terminal, large windows offer some view of the Olympic training aircraft, Cessna 152s and Cherokees, and the air taxi Ecureuils and Aztec. Reasonable photographs can only be obtained by negotiation with Olympic Aviation, on the other side of this small apron. It is necessary to walk across this apron to talk to the people who can give that permission!

The International Terminal is split into two buildings, for departures and arrivals, and facilities are different at each. The arrivals building has a lounge fronting the apron, approached via a corridor at the right hand side, though the part of the ramp it overlooks only has a limited amount of traffic. The glass and the westerly aspect should be borne in mind in the afternoons.

The departures building was famous for the backpackers who slept on the roof overnight but the police have taken a negative stance on this activity as part of the clampdown. At the same time, they also sealed off the front of the deck, where photographs of all movements were quite easy to take. The remaining part of the roof looks down on the north ramp (quite busy) and diagonally across the stands in front of the arrivals building.

Photographers will be frustrated by these facilities at the terminal, especially when there are so many interesting movements. Consequently, the perimeter of the field will continue to be investigated, no matter how much it conflicts with officialdom. Since many of the airport workers live in Glyfada, a gap in the fence at the edge of the coach park has been created, allowing them to take the short cut, and this has been used by enthusiasts for many years. The 'wrong' side of the fence has some waste land (due for redevelopment) and a road, all immediately adjacent to the executive ramp, taxiway and the threshold of runway 33R. The old fence along the southern perimeter has been replaced by a new one (and the old one may also remain) but the gate next to the 33R holding point has always yielded impressive results for the average photographer. The presence of El Al aircraft usually entails at least one Israeli security vehicle being somewhere in the vicinity and, since they can make life difficult, caution is advised if confronted. Sensible behaviour helps, of course.

The attraction of this corner of the field is increased by its proximity to two hotels much favoured by spotters: the Fenix roof is closed, and the only view is from inside the building, for residents. The Emmantina has better facilities to compensate for being a little further out. The roof here has a bar and a pool . . . and a very good view. The Emmantina has been quick to realise its potential, even advertising in aviation magazines. There are instances when security personnel have paid visits, but nothing unpleasant has been reported. It must be borne in mind that the local weather pattern is changing, resulting the prevailing winds being increasingly from the south. This means that Runway 15L sees greater use, with a corresponding reduction in the amount of aircraft which approach over Glyfada. In other words, it can now be more a matter of luck.

Athens has much to offer the enthusiast, and the weather is probably best in May, June and September (mid summer being very hot); the attractions of the holiday resort of Glyfada on one side and historic Athens on the other, and aircraft in delightful profusion. March weather can be, at best, unpredictable and, at worst, unspeakable. Only the top class hotels are allowed to use power for heating at colder times. The others await the sunshine to power the solar panels. As a general guide, a visit to Athens before the middle of April could invite disappointment.

Intercontinental flights between Western Europe and the Far East make stops here (though many are at unsociable hours), European scheduled traffic is attracted by the world of commerce and holidaymakers, and charter flights are abundant from all over the rest of Europe. Airlines from all the Middle East countries fly here in quantity and executive movements are also plentiful throughout the year. To list the traffic in detail would take up unnecessary space but visitors can expect an assortment of movements unmatched by any other airport in Europe.

The USAF, who once operated surveillance flights from Hellenikon, were extremely unpopular with the local community. Now that they have gone, the radio on the roof of the Emmantina no longer plays AFN. Military activity hasn't been completely curtailed: the Hellenic Air Force operate crew training sorties by C-130s, YS-11s (though both break off approach early) and there are occasional visits by C-47s, F-104s and T-33s.

Hellenikon isn't normally busy, by any stretch of the imagination, but the weekends see plenty of German charters, when scheduled traffic is quietest. Any attempt to woo the enthusiast away for a tour of the Acropolis or the Plakka shops will surely be followed by some rare aircraft: a civilian on delivery or military staging through!

Car hire is expensive and unnecessary, as walking to Hellenikon from Glyfada is good exercise, buses are regular from the city and taxis are cheap. Most of the buses go to the Olympic side of the airport, though an irregular yellow bus service links both sides. From Athens, the Olympic buses are quick and comfortable, leaving from the terminal on Syngrou Avenue, while local buses leave from Syntagma Square, cost less but take longer. Athens is at the crossroads of Western Europe and the Middle East, has unparalleled tourist attractions and good weather, so no serious enthusiast should overlook this as being one of the best destinations for an aviation-related holiday. Restrictions imposed by the authorities are for a very good reason and the sensible spotter will be able to enjoy the facilities without undue conflict.

Notable by its absence from Hellenikon is general aviation, though a few visiting (mostly foreign) light aircraft can be seen tucked in one corner. This is to be found at MARATHON, though the journey there by bus takes time . . . a lot of time, and a passport will be useful. A street map of Athens is also handy, to locate the bus stops before setting off. Most of Athens buses use Zappio (an official building in a large park) as the terminus. Tickets should be bought beforehand, and punched into the machine. False economy is running the risk for a few pennies, as the penalties are strict. The No.122 from Glyfada passes the coastal side of the airport. A brisk walk from Zappio along Vasilissis Sofias to Leoforos Alexandras, where the country bus for Kato Souli leaves, is followed by a pleasant journey to Marathon.

Asking the driver to say when the bus reaches Aerodromo Marathon helps missing the stop. It's a fifteen minute walk to the field, where the passport can normally be exchanged for a walk around the ramp.

HERAKLION
HER   LGIR   Nikos Kazantzakis   3m/5km S (bus 40 minutes)

Crete is a major tourist island in the Mediterranean and its airport handles a predictably large amount of charter traffic. Scheduled links with the rest of the world are via Athens, so the traffic is dominated by Olympic aircraft, mainly A300s. The terminal faces the runway, and the A-7 dispersals on the far side, with a few air jetties restricting the view of proceedings. The balcony is for departing passengers only, though other views can be had from the restaurant. The road leading to Heraklion curves around the edge of the apron, with shuttle buses and ground handling equipment in the foreground, but it does allow quite a decent chance to see the movements on the apron and runway, sufficiently so for the authorities to have posted 'no photography' signs here.

The main car park overlooks a military apron where two or three C-130s are often noted, with the hardened A-7 shelters, on the far side of the runway, directly behind. The beach, to the east of the airport, is close enough for photographs of movements to be taken with a 200mm lens, except for the SD3.30s and Do228s, which are too small.

KERKYRA
CFU   LGKR   I Kapodistrias   1m/1.5km S (bus 10 minutes)

Anyone staying in Athens for a week or so might fancy a change. Olympic's domestic flights price structure makes Corfu an extremely interesting prospect. It gets quite busy in summer, with over thirty movements to be seen, few of which are Olympic. British and Dutch charters make up a good proportion of the traffic (it should be remembered that not all readers of this book are British or Dutch!) but the passenger terminal is not the place to watch or photograph them. The delapidated little terminal has a coffee shop with a bit of a view - the windows can be opened - but it is neither the nicest nor the quietest of places. Try instead the Imperial Hotel, in Perama, opposite the threshold of Runway 35. Leave the terminal in the direction of the end of Runway 17, the only direction possible, then make a couple of right turns onto the road which passes the cemetary. There is a choice of roads, both of which lead to the hotel. Along the front of the building is a deck which faces west over the lagoon to the runway. A landing 757 needs about 100mm focal length. Photography from here is obviously best in the mornings.

The causeway across the lagoon can be used only by pedestrians, and is much favoured by the local population. On the far side of the causeway, beside the lagoon, is a cafe which offers a good view all afternoon, as it faces east. Photography here does require concentration. The beach here features large numbers of topless sunbathers which, if nothing else, mean that it shouldn't be necessary to take a book when airport movements go quiet.

MYKONOS
JMK   LGMK   3m/5km

Mykonos is one of the more interesting islands, though its airport offers only one exciting moment: if arriving direct on a charter jet, the landing requires what is described as more rapid retardation than usual! A balcony to the left of the terminal is useful for the occasional portrait. Most of the movements, and there aren't many, tend to be small Olympic Aviation propliners doing their lifeline service to Athens. What can be seen at the airport comes a distant second to what can be seen on the beach.

RHODES
RHO   LGRP   Paradisi   10m/km SW (bus 30 minutes)

This tourist airport handles plenty of traffic, but the terminal has no viewing facilities. Anyone wanting to monitor every movement will stay at the hotels between the airport and Trianda: these are the Sunflower, Blue Bay and Sun Beach. An indication of the proximity of this area to the threshold of the runway may be gleaned from the fact that visual aids are sometimes not essential to note under-wing registrations! The mention of 'every movement' is a reminder that sleep can be interrupted by arrivals in the night. Light sleepers would do well to stay elsewhere on the island and catch the bus to the airport from Mandraki Square.

SANTORINI
JTR   LGSR   Thira   5m/8km

Crete's Minoan culture came to an abrupt end over two thousand years ago, when this volcano exploded. What remains is a crescent-shaped island which once formed part of the volcano's rim: civilisation steeped in tradition and culture. The airport's passenger terminal is modern but only compared with the island's history. It is primitive and enjoyable. The departure lounge is out in the open and the baggage reclaim is the trolley behind a tractor.

The runway is shared by the small civil facility and an Air Force presence, mostly peaceful until the occasional commuter flight arrives. Anyone visiting will spend little time here, being content with three, at the most, photos of the Olympic Aviation island hoppers. Olympic 737s are not unknown, however. Charters from Scandinavia, Germany and Austria add to the occasional British aircraft. Military activity is, under normal circumstances, subdued but it can include anything from a C-130 to the pilot of an F-104 or F-5E showing off to the holidaymakers.

248

THESSALONIKI
SKG   LGTS   Makedonia   10m/16km S (bus 25 minutes)

In northern Greece, on the mainland, is where another military base shares the civilian runway. Enthusiasts who have visited for a day, taking advantage of the attractive air fares, have occasionally been allowed a tour of the base, though no photographs are allowed.

THE GREEK ISLANDS

The Olympic fleet of SD3.30s, Dornier 228s and ATR--42s are used as the lifeline between Athens and the many islands in the Aegean. These flights are extremely cheap but tend to be fully booked well in advance. A flight on one of these services can be a memorable experience, weather permitting, but the destination may be a rather primitive airport. There are many dotted around the Cyclades and the Sporades, each of which may be visited for the experience of a quiet day trip.

S7 SEYCHELLES (Republic of Seychelles)
MAHE
SEZ   FSSS   Seychelles International   6m/9km SE of Victoria

Without doubt a romantic destination but the airport is not going to be one of the main reasons for visiting. The runway is built on reclaimed land to be capable of taking 747-400s (which it does). British Airways and Air France are the operators but Kenya Airways, Air Europe (Italy), Condor and Air Seychelles also operate wide-bodies. The USAF operate the occasional 707 or C-130, related to a satellite tracking station on the island. Regular inter-island activity keeps the pace ticking over all day.

The international passenger terminal is a simple two-storey affair, offering no views of the aircraft until into the departure lounges. A few yards to the north is the more modest inter-island terminal. At either side of the main terminal are grassed areas where the apron can be seen but the fence can make some angles difficult for photography. This is not too much of a problem as there are other places to go at both ends of the field.

When Runway 31 is in use, try a shop called Butcher's, about a mile south of the terminal. Movements using the opposite direction runway, 13, can be seen from a similar spot, on reclaimed land to the north. It must be borne in mind that Seychelles is a socialist single-party state, which has its own ideas about security. The police appear to show no interest in spotting activity but it would be wise to be discreet when in the presence of someone wearing a military uniform.

PRASLIN
PRI   FSPP

If any reader ever dreams of taking the perfect photo of a Twin Otter or an Islander, this is the place to visit. The island is small and its airport handles the regular inter-island flights from Mahe, its only air-link with the outside world. The passenger terminal is as modest and delightful as the rest of the island, ideal for seeing the movements arrive every 45 minutes or so. Only four or five aircraft are involved, however. The Indian Ocean is a stunning crystal blue, over which the aircraft come in to land. If you can't take good pictures here, you can't take good pictures at all! Praslin is the sort of place to get away from aviation, and everything else associated with a normal way of life, so aviation could take a back seat for a couple of days.

TC TURKEY (Republic of Turkey)
DALAMAN
DLM   LTBS

Security precautions in the Middle East are so well documented, anyone who gets into trouble is certain to have ignored several warnings. Turkey has a reputation, ill-deserved it must be said, because of the film 'Midnight Express'. If the West wants drug smuggling stopped, it must expect appropriate action closer to the source.

This is a modern airport, built a few years ago to handle the tourist trade being developed along Turkey's beautiful coastline. Open scrubland surround the field, where views are possible. This is more than can be said for the passenger terminal, inside which the only windows onto the apron are from the departure area. An early check-in at peak charter times allows a few British aircraft to be seen, in the company of a TUR 727.

Doubtless, other days see mostly arrivals from other countries, Germany and Scandinavia particluarly. As Turkey continues to invest in its tourist trade, Dalaman will handle visitors in greater numbers and variety.

ERCAN
ECN

Holidays in Cyprus normally involve travel to the Greek portion of the island, though the Turks are also keen to develop the tourist trade. Flights to this side use Ercan, and few enthusiasts faced with the choice between here and Larnaca would select the Turkish side. Charter and scheduled international traffic is much lighter, with only 737s of Noble and Istanbul Airlines, plus the Caravelles being regular (if not frequent) movements.

IZMIR
ADB   LTBJ   Cumaovasi-Adnan Menderes   16m/25km S

Izmir is seeking to earn its share of the tourist trade, and the airport handles a small amount of charter flights from Europe. Condor and EAS are seen from the terminal's glazed frontage, as is the military base. Caution and common sense could result in a photograph or two but plain clothes and armed patrols are meant to be taken seriously as a deterrent. Discreet noting of registrations and serials is wise, and the best opportunity to see the military aircraft is probably from the taxiway.

TF ICELAND (Republic of Iceland)
AKUREYRI
AEY   BIAR   3m/5km SW

Outside Reykjavik, this is the next most probable destination for a foreign visitor. Akureyri is on the scenic north coast, and can be reached by regional services from Reykjavik. The cost of the air fare from Reykjavik may seem expensive compared with overland transport but a bus takes ten hours, compared with one hour by Flugfelag Nordurland Twin Otter. Their small fleet includes some Piper twins and they are based at the airport.

The occasional visitor on the ramp can be seen with ease from the fence, and the pace is slow enough for ramp access to be possible after short negotiation. June is the best moth for visiting and, to a lesser extent, May and July.

REYKJAVIK
REK   BIRK   3m/5km S (bus 40 minutes)

The enthusiast who has been everywhere and seen everything may consider Iceland as a destination which offers something different. The capital city nestles in the warmer southwest corner, with an airport for domestic traffic and general aviation, and another for international flights. The domestic field is close to the city, with a small terminal building handling the F.27 flights. Views of these movements are more than adequate from inside the building. Variety is supplied, though not in quantity, by Norlandair Twin Otters, Eastair Navajos and Odin's Jetstreams.

The Loftleidir Hotel overlooks the commuter apron, and the variety seen from its rooms is interesting. Movements are modest but unusual, by most standards. The coastguard base can also be seen.

KEFLAVIK
KEF   BIKF   32m/50km SW of Reykjavik

Some thirty miles southwest of the city, on a promontory, is Keflavik where Icelandair operate their international hub and spoke operations. 737s and 757s arrive in the afternoon, all visible from the approach road next to the modern terminal building. The 737s arrive from Europe, to connect with the 757s, mostly on their way between Luxembourg and a range of destinations on the USA's east coast. On the far side of the runway is the USAF base where C-130s and P-3s are most visible. Other movements are sporadic, featuring a few tech-stops and airline movements such as SAS MD-80/87s and Greenlandair Dash 7s.

TR GABON (Gabonese Republic)
LIBREVILLE
LBV   FOOL   Leon M'ba   8m/13km

This is, without doubt, West Africa's most interesting airport, with a surprising collection of about eighty light aircraft, half of which are twins. A long apron on one side of the runway has the passenger terminal more or less in the middle. To the left is the civil side, with the National Guard hangar at the far end, occupied by an ATR-42 and a Bandeirante, several T-34Cs and a few immaculate Harvards. The Guard's next door neighbour is the general aviation area, shared by Air Service and Air Affaires, the latter operating a varied fleet of Bandeirante, Lear Jet, HS125, King Airs etc, though their Transall is now out of service. With so many Frenchmen around this area, it is easy for a European to look part of the scene, and photos of some of the more unusual residents and visitors should present no problem, as access to the apron may be obtained.

The Air Gabon hangar is often empty, usually with an ATR-72 and 737 out on the ramp, in the company of the Air Service CASA 212s, and visible from the terrace, more or less opposite the domestic terminal building.

To the right/east of the terminal is the small cargo area and a large military compound. A selection of hangars spreads, seemingly at random, eastwards and the extensive transport fleet of the Gabon Air Force is parked here. A French Air Force KC-135 sits on the cargo apron, nearer to the terminal, on rotational detachment.

The excellent terrace above the main terminal is normally packed with plenty of Gabonese, awaiting the arrival of a 747 or a DC-10 from Europe, and the odd gendarme is on duty to enforce the 'no camera' warnings, posted everywhere. With permission, good standard lens shots of civil airliners are possible. Traffic at Libreville is generally always interesting, though some of the European movements will have a familiar look to them. Really exotic visitors include the likes of a Lina Congo F.28 or 737. Nigerian 737s appear most days but the Air Zaire 737 rarely keeps its schedule, and Cameroon 737s visit about three times a week. Regular appearances are made by many of the Port Gentil-based Air Inter Gabon fleet.

TU IVORY COAST (Republic of the Ivory Coast)
ABIDJAN

ABJ	DIAP	Port Buet	13m/20km E

The passenger terminal sits at one side of the single runway. To its north are the six hangars used by Air Afrique and other carriers, and to the south is the parking area for general aviation. A few light aircraft are also parked at the front edge of the main apron. Most of Abidjan's visitors are making transit stops, which means restriction of movement once inside the terminal.

Normally there is little to see on the ramp, so most of it will be recorded when landing or taking off, as the airliner taxis by. Assuming the same runway direction is used for both landing and departure, a window seat offers one chance. Prior reference to a JP Airline Fleets list of Abidjan-based aircraft reveals that, apart from the governmental aircraft (TU-V..) almost everything carries TU-T.., so only the last two characters need to be recorded. With only one shot at a rather unusual array of machinery, it helps to be prepared beforehand.

UK UZBEKISTAN (Republic of Uzbekistan)
TASHKENT

TAS	UTTT	Yuzhny	6m/10km

When the Israeli Air Force paid their unexpected visit to Entebbe, they must have left it in a similar condition to Tashkent. The passenger terminal is now dirty, shabby, run-down and crumbling. The price of freedom and democracy can be seen here: once one of the greatest economic powers, this is now the Third World. It costs money to build but it costs more money to maintain them, hence the number of runways in the CIS states abandoned for lack of finance to make them operable.

Soviet jet airliners were built to keep people employed. Few of them flew much. Many of them now lie, like so much litter, around Yuzhny airport. Naturally, this makes it a number-cruncher's paradise. If an aviation enthusiast has to be stuck for four hours or so in a transit lounge, this would be the place to choose.

Binoculars can be used. Discretion might be wise. There is now such a general air of couldn't-care-less in the CIS that maybe nobody will take any notice of anyone writing down aircraft registrations. It seems more likely that you'd be offered a flight in one or, for a few dollars more, the chance to buy one. It must not be assumed that anybody actually owns anything. People here desperately need cash. If someone has an excuse to part a stranger from his passport, the motive could be money.

The quantity of ex-Aeroflot aircraft is extraordinary. Most of them sport hybrid Uzbekistan colour schemes and titles. There are Il-86s, Il-72s, Il-62s, Tu-134s and Tu-154s, plus an assortment of Antonovs. Aviation fuel (and possibly paint) seems to be more valuable than the aircraft, and certainly more difficult to get. Most of the aircraft at Yuzhny will disintegrate at an alarming pace, such is the climate. Parts will be stripped from most in order to keep some in flying condition. This, is must be added, does not necessarily mean airworthy as interpreted by western authorities.

Virtually the entire Uzbekistan fleet can be recorded in a single day. Turkmenistan and Kazakhstan Airways are frequent visitors, and Aeroflot can seen be seen in large numbers. Yuzhny, for all its faults, is still somewhere to make the pulse race.

252

UN KAZAKHSTAN (Republic of Kazakhstan)
AKTYUBINSK
AKX   UATT

Remote from almost everywhere, on the central Asian steppes, it seems like this is the end of the world. Ask the locals and they'll say it isn't . . . but you can see it from there! This large industrial city has an airport which possesses a military feel, despite there being no fighters in sight. The passenger terminal is small, and offers good views of the apron. Most of what is to be seen on the stands are passing Yak-40s.

Most of Kazakhstan's allocation of ex-Aeroflot aircraft is parked about a mile north of the terminal. There are rows and rows of Yak-40s, Tu-134s, Tu-154s and An-2 biplanes, all idle, and most of them unlikely to move ever again.

UR UKRAINE
KIEV
KBP   UKBB   Borispol   24m/38km E (bus 55 minutes)

This is Kiev's main airport, with its passenger terminal between the two parallel runways which are aligned north/south. It would appear that only one runway is in regular use, but this could be an isolated report which coincided with maintenance work. More likely, they can't afford the repairs. The terminal's first floor windows offer a good view of the proceedings. Traffic is mostly Tu-134s and Tu-154s, as is to be expected, though there are plenty of inactive Il-76s to be seen.

On the far side of the unused runway is an apron where the Il-76s are parked, possibly up to twenty at one time.

KIEV
IEV   UKKK   Zhulyany   2m/3km S (bus 10 minutes)

Historically this was a domestic airport, where operations linked the regional capital with its surroundings. For this reason, the majority of aircraft to be seen are Antonovs (24s and 26s). It is possible to see some of the movements from the terminal but the facilities are not ideal, by any stretch of the imagination.

Kiev has two other airfields: Gostomel, some 20 miles to the northwest, is used by Antonov for testing purposes. What can be seen is without doubt extremely interesting. To what extent it is wise to investigate in depth or take photos is another matter. The new way of doing things is fine in theory but it is in situations like this when the enthusiast realises that security will take a while to be relaxed. CHAIKA is also known as Kiev West, and is nothing more than a grass strip used for general aviation.

SIMFERAPOL
SIP   UKFF   8.5m/14km

This city is in the Crimea peninsula, so it attracts plenty of tourists heading for resorts along the Black Sea coast. Domestic flights, still operated mostly by Aeroflot, use one terminal and tourist traffic goes to the other. There are no viewing facilities in either, mainly because this is an active (a strange term, under the current circumstances) military airfield. The MiG-25s can be seen at a distance from the moving aircraft.

VH AUSTRALIA (Commonwealth of Australia)
ADELAIDE
ADL   APAD   5m/8km W (bus 30 minutes)

Vickers Vimy G-EAOU arrived in Australia in 1919, when the journey from England was more of an adventure and travelling time was rather more than a day. Keith and Ross Smith left England on November 12 and arrived in Australia on December 10. Their Vimy is now housed in its own museum building in the terminal area.

Both international and domestic terminals are good enough for viewing and photography. Access is possible, through a security check, to the departure lounges. The international terminal is, by far, the least interesting part of this airport. A walk down the road to the old part of the field, towards the domestic terminal, reveals first the general aviation ramp to the right of that used by international movements. Beyond the domestic terminal are hangars and aprons, where some of the more interesting aircraft can be seen at close quarters. Among these smaller are operators: Air Charter, Sky-Link, Lloyd Aviation and Rossair have facilities, though there are few aircraft above Cessna 402 size.

ADELAIDE
APPF   Parafield   5m/8km NE

This is home to most of Adelaide's general aviation, and there are some small fleet operators are also to be found. Because it is to be regarded as an airfield, there is little in the way of security measures which would prevent a sensible enthusiast from passing a useful half-hour here.

ALICE SPRINGS
ASP   7m/11km S

There are few places in the world as far in the Outback as Alice Springs. It would be easy to imagine a rickety old terminal, with old fashioned facilities, like the stage set for Crocodile Dundee's Walkabout Creek. That's Alice Springs! More remarkably, this airport is the new one. Whilst there is a garden in front of the terminal, it doesn't offer much of a view through the security screen. There is so much planting, vehicles and other paraphenalia to obscure the view, photography is practically impossible.

The old airport is now the Central Australian Aviation Museum, to be found on Memorial Avenue, off Larapinta Drive. On a pole outside is Flying Doctor Service Drover VH-FDC. Entry to the museum is free and the exhibits include aircraft up to DH Dove size.

There is so little of interest at Alice Springs airport, mostly because the scheduled visitors can be seen just as easily, and certainly in greater comfort, at more accessible airports. Folks come here to see Ayers Rock, and there aren't too many reasons for prolonging the stay!

AYERS ROCK
AYQ   YAYE   Connellan   3m/5km

Any desire to imagine Ayers Rock as an exotic location is best maintained by not visiting it. Most of the services are operated from Alice Springs, where there is just as little chance of seeing them well. To the left of the terminal is a general aviation facility which is used by the many sightseeing flights.

BRISBANE

BNE	ABBN	International	7m/11km NE (bus 40 minutes)

The airport occupies a large area of land at the edge of Moreton Bay, between a canal and the Brisbane River. The original runways and terminals occupy the southern corner of the field, close to Gateway Arterial Road. Arriving by road from the city, the domestic terminal is reached first. A small building outside houses the Southern Cross museum, dedicated to that aircraft. Viewing from the departure area of the domestic terminal is quite adequate, though what can be seen is mostly (by local standards) standard fare, apart from the occasional IPEC DC-9. The road continues for several miles to the international terminal and passes on the left some hangars and a lay-by. This parking facility is officially recognized, and is ideal for watching and photographing the airliners as they taxi by. The general aviation ramp usually contains one or two Kendell and Lloyd aircraft.

Within the international terminal is a remarkably good observation deck, offering very close views of proceedings. However, there are only about eight stands, so close proximity to the aircraft can be a mixed blessing. When a Qantas 747 is one of the parked aircraft, the view becomes severely restricted. A wide angle lens may be required - good news if present when one of the international visitors arrives, such as an Air Niugini A310, or a 767 operated by either Air New Zealand or Air Pacific.

Brisbane can be quite busy early in the morning, and an airband radio is particularly useful. It has been practice for pilots to use the aircraft's registration, rather than flight number, when talking to the tower. To many enthusiasts, this would represent paradise, as movements can be identified from a rather greater distance than usual! For those who find it too hot, standing beside the road, cooler close encounters can be obtained by visiting the domestic terminal, passing through the security check, and watching from a departure lounge.

Temperatures do rise quite alarmingly during the day, so spending too much time walking along perimeter fences is not a good idea. The end of Runway 01 is only about a fifteen minute walk from the domestic terminal but the comfort of an air conditioned car is safer. It also allows "proper" clothes to be worn, which are adviseable if seeking access to the various hangars.

BRISBANE

	ABAF	Archerfield	7m/11km S

The lack of significant quantities of general aviation at the international airport is explained by a visit to Archerfield. It would be reasonable to expect one hundred or so light aircraft. Ipswich Road leads out of town, and a left turn after passing Rochlea at Granard Road reveals the field. The small terminal is to be found on the far side, on Beatty Road.

CAIRNS

CNS	ABCS		3m/5km NW

The Great Barrier Reef attracts increasingly large numbers of tourists each year. Because of the distances involved, most of them arrive by air, and Cairns is the airport they use. Across the road from the domestic terminal is a Bush Pilots Airways DC-3 on a pole, the only remaining link with the old days.

Everything else about Cairns is very modern and pleasant. The international terminal has an observation gallery, though the view is poor. However, it is from here in the mornings that an Air Niugini F.28 can be seen. Qantas movements tend to be mostly 767s and 747SPs. A covered walkway links the two terminals, at the far side of which is the ramp used by the regional carriers, all visible from the fence. Twin Otters, Bandeirantes, Trislanders and Islanders, operated by the local air services are usually in evidence.

On the far side of the runway is quite a varied collection of general aviation. This includes Customs service Nomads, Westwinds and Aero Commanders. Two Kamov helicopters were shipped to Cairns, for use by a local company. The deal fell through for some reason, and the ancient choppers, still bearing their Soviet markings, decayed slowly over the years. That decaying process is not yet complete, and the aircraft languish, partly covered, in the general aviation park.

When staying in Cairns, the Inn in the Tropics is recommended, being affordable and comfortable. Time should be taken, if possible, to explore the harbour where floatplanes are to be seen, plus a helicopter pad used by Jayrow.

CANBERRA
CBR ASCB   4m/6km E

This small airport handles a fair amount of traffic. All can be seen from the bar inside the small passenger terminal. On the far side of the field is an air force base, where a few of the based Falcon 900s can usually be seen. Canberra, being a planned city, has a very definite layout: at the centre is Capitol Hill, surrounded by State Circle. Leaving this ring road to the northeast, on King's Avenue, the next intersection after crossing the water is Morshead Drive, which leads to the airport.

DARWIN
DRW ADDN   5m/8km W

Technically, Darwin is closer to the real Crocodile Dundee country than Alice Springs. The movie, and its successor, have generated enough interest in the area for tourism to be growing. What they come to see is Kakadu National Park. The old passenger terminal was due to be closed some time in 1991, when the new one was completed, on the far side of the runway.

Whilst nothing has yet been reported from the new terminal, its traffic is a reasonable mix, comprising local general aviation of some interest, including a few Nomads, to supplement the usual domestic services.

DUNK ISLAND
DKI

Just off the coast, about halfway between Townsville and Cairns, this is becoming one of Australia's star tourist destinations. The airport, if it can be called that, is served by a couple of Australian Regional Twin Otters each day. Photographs present no problems, as long as you can guess which way they are going to taxi!

MELBOURNE
MEL AMML   Tullamarine   13m/20km NW (bus 30 minutes)

Approaching the airport from the city on the Sunbury road, the busy field of Essendon is passed en route. Little of Tullamarine is seen before arriving in the central complex, though the elevated road for departures traffic does allow a view of the Ansett ramp. The car park has an Australian feel, with its many eucalyptus, or gum trees as they are known, but the pendant DC-3 which used to be here is flying again.

The three terminals were arranged so that the central International facility kept the traditional domestic competitors, Ansett and Australian Airlines, apart. Deregulation allowed other competitors to enter the fray but to no avail. All that happened was there were more airliners chasing the same number of passengers for a while so that, in the end one airline, Ansett Australian, was the result.

There are still two observation decks, one of which is well signposted. The other, which still exists, takes more finding and offers better views. Behind the Ansett Australian check-in area on the departures level is a staircase which leads to the deck.

Because the right-hand deck faces only the threshold of Runway 09/27, it is the most remote from the intersecting main runway, 16/34. To the left/south of the now-Qantas deck are general aviation ramps, the cargo centre and, in the distance, the maintenance areas. From the windows at the end of the pier, reasonable photos are possible of the daily RAAF Falcon 900 whilst at the sides are close-ups of Kendell's SF.340s and Metros.

International movements feature mostly the regular range of European and Asian carriers, whose aircraft can be seen at almost any major airport, with Qantas dominating. Scheduled movements are busiest in the early morning and at tea time, though there is a small peak in the middle of the day. Between these times, the going is slow, only compensated by the occasional 737 of Air Nauru or Air Caledonie. The maintenance areas of Ansett and Australian are in a remote corner, and accessible via Melrose Drive and Link Road. Some out-of-service Fokkers can usually be photographed from the fence. General aviation activity is subdued, as much of the action takes place elsewhere . . .

MELBOURNE
MEB   AMEN   Essendon   7m/11km NW (tram 30 minutes)

Accessible by the No. 59 tram from the city, Essendon is only a few miles from Tullamarine. The Sunbury buses, Nos. 478 and 479, operate to Tullamarine, with the stop on Matthews Road, on the far side of Tullamarine Freeway. A walk over the bridge leads directly to the airport entrance on English Street, a few yards away.

The first impression is of a sprawling airfield, with lots of hangars. Even without ramp access, there are so many aircraft parked on the grass next to the various roads, the photographer with only an hour or two to spare can leave with an interesting selection. A car will undoubtedly save time, and Essendon needs time, more than anything else.

At the end of the street is the administrative building, well worth a call to let someone know what the visit is all about. Some help may then be available. In front is a large, crammed, apron with another to the right serving the passenger terminal. There are hangars to the left, on Wirraway Road, and more at the end of a short road, called Short Road. Nomad Road leads across English Street to the IPEC hangar and the rest of the main parking areas and hangars are on Bristol Street, facing one of the two runways.

A limited amount of Melbourne's third level traffic operates here. The small terminal handles it, and a few executive movements. A request for access to the ramps is normally successful, as the Australians are renowned for being fairly relaxed.

Twin-engined aircraft are numerous, though the two hundred or so residents include only two or three dozen executive types. The largest inmates were IPEC's Argosies, but these were cut up in 1990. They also operate two DC-9s, which are normally seen at Tullamarine.

MELBOURNE
MBW   Moorabbin   10m/16km S

A serious interest in the smaller aircraft on the Australian register will also necessitate a visit to Melbourne's third airport, Moorabbin. With two airports in such close proximity, it is inevitable that the third is on the other side of the city. The trip is worthwhile, however, as scheduled services are operated by Aus-Air Bandeirantes and Navajo Chieftains, and by Promair Navajos.

PERTH

PER   APPH   6m/9km E (bus 45 minutes)

The passenger facilities at Perth are placed on opposite sides of the runway. The smart, modern International Terminal has a wonderful (though glazed) observation gallery, spanning all six of the air jetties. The view includes the domestic movements on the far side but distance and heat haze hinder identification of the traffic. It would be an understatement to describe international traffic as merely slow. Five flights a day is normal, so Perth is well-placed to handle growth in the future!

From a separate approach road off Tonkin Highway, the domestic facilities offer a better prospect. The terminal has a rooftop bar, which overlooks the Ansett hangar and ramp. A couple of F.28s and BAe146s are to be expected here while, on the other side of the terminal, a general aviation ramp is home to thirty or so light aircraft, visible from the fence.

PERTH

JAD   Jandakot

By far the greater majority of Perth's smaller aircraft are to be found at the busy Jandakot field, named after a suburb on the Fremantle side of the Swan River. Leach Highway (7), which joins Tonkin Highway (4) just south of Perth Airport, heads southwest linking the two airports. The journey is essential for anyone with an interest in Australian aviation.

The Royal Flying Doctor Service has some aircraft based here, and there are other operators, such as Corpair and Central Air, to be seen. Since it is a long walk from one end of the field to the other, anyone on foot will need time . . . and a fly swat!

SYDNEY

SYD   ASSY   Kingsford Smith   5m/8km S (bus 30 minutes)

Despite its official name, the airport is still generally known as Mascot, after the suburb over which it spreads its noise and fumes. For many years, the only pier in front of the International Terminal was that in the middle, shaped like a Y. Expansion is well under way, with an additional pier being built to the side. There are two viewing areas, one on each side of the central pier. What can be seen is limited and, since the sun is often directly ahead, photography is difficult. Large scale construction work will prepare the airport for its big event: the Olympics to be held there in 2000.

International traffic is disappointingly modest, comprising mostly types and colour schemes that an enthusiast could see almost anywhere. The domestic scene is likely to be of greater interest. Because boarding cards aren't needed for access to the domestic gates, it is possible to get close enough for photos through the glass as airliners taxi onto their stands or when they are pushed back. Reflections, however, do make it hard work.

What was formerly the Ansett terminal is worth the visit, as it offers the best views. From the large lounge windows, aircraft landing on Runway 16/34 can be photographed taxying to, parked at, or leaving their gates. The newer right-hand pier allows virtually all movements to be seen. At the opposite end, there are views of smaller operators, such as Hazelton's Metros, SD3.60s and SF.340s, as well as a limited view of the maintenance ramp.

Even the domestic terminals can be quiet for much of the day, as the best of the action is over by 9:30am. The pace is sufficiently relaxed for access to be possible to some of the more remote areas. A request for accompanied viewing may yield worthwhile results.

Almost certain to be seen on such a trip is the enormous Qantas Jetbase. Anyone with a car will pass this maintenance facility on Airport Drive. Since work is carried out for the RAAF, some interesting aircraft are often seen. Behind the domestic terminal area is a multi-storey car park, from the top of which can be seen most of the movements and anything at the Jetbase. Anyone without a car, in need of a closer inspection of the Jetbase inmates must risk the scorn of the 'okkers' by reading the registrations through binoculars from a seat on the transfer bus which runs between Sydney and the international/domestic terminals.

Two miles or so around the perimeter, close to the control tower, is a spot from which movements on Runway 07/25 can be seen, but most Australian enthusiasts keep going. The threshold of Runway 34 projects into Botany Bay and this where to find the spotters with their barbies, as barbecues are known locally. It should be noted that, at the time of writing, the new runway was nearing completion. This extends out into Botany Bay, on reclaimed land but, as yet, nothing is known about what can be seen in the vicinity.

Considering that Sydney is one of Australia's prime cities, and a major international gateway, the quantity of movements can come as a disappointment. Between 9:30am and dusk, it is probable that only thirty or forty flights will be noted. Investigation into the timetable will ensure that the early departure of an Air Niugini Airbus is witnessed.

SYDNEY
ASBK   Bankstown

Enthusiasts with time to explore will wish to sample Bankstown, as it handles much of the general aviation, with about three hundred residents. Air taxi, executive and commuter traffic is modest. This is a substantial field, some way out of Sydney on Canterbury Road (Highway 54). Ramp access is hardly necessary to see, and photograph, the majority of the residents but requests are normally successful. For a pleasure flight over the city, and the harbour, it may still be possible to take a ride in a Tiger Moth from here. The far side of the field has a separate entrance and it is here that four DC-3s are normally parked. Access is granted cheerfully to photographers.

On the south side of Sydney Harbour, AU ROSE BAY (RSE) is the arrival point for air taxi flights from Palm Beach. There is generally nothing else to see, and even the sight of one aircraft takes luck.

SYDNEY
LBH   Palm Beach

Some distance north of Sydney on Broken Bay, next to the Ku-Ring-Gai Chase National Park, this is becoming a select suburb. Vic Walton's Aquatic Air Beavers are based here. It is normal to see at least one sitting on the water, awaiting duties. Anyone intent on making the trip out to Palm Beach should consider relative costs. As Vic Walton points out, his air fare is cheaper than a taxi . . . but it's still a little pricy. However, for the chance to sample a take-off and landing on water, it's one of the cheapest.

VR-G GIBRALTAR (UK Dependency of Gibraltar)
GIBRALTAR
GIB   LXGB   North Front   2m/3km N (bus 10 minutes)

They say in Gibraltar that, when a Hercules lands, the whole town knows about it. This is primarily because it's a small community, close to the airport and because lots of reverse thrust is needed on landing, as the runway is short. A ten minute walk from town, this a local airport in every sense of the word, served by Yogi, as the local airline is known. Yogi Bear . . . Yo-Gibair.

Handling a few charters and scheduled movements, Gibraltar has for a long time been a small civil airport with airspace restricted by Spain's political posture on its territorial claim. Its existence is dependant upon Britain's strategic needs, no matter how small they are these days, and it is now mostly a staging post for Nimrods and Hercs on their way to the Falklands.

The runway crosses the road to La Linea and photos at the barrier, next to the Vulcan, can be taken but few would find the long wait between movements acceptable. The terminal is on the north, remote, side of the field but it is hardly the best place for photos with so many other vantage points. The Tangier ferry pier is close to the western end of the runway and, at the other end, a footpath leads to the runway at Catalan Bay from Devil's Tower.

For elevated views, which are very photogenic, the Upper Galleries of the Rock itself are also worth considering. In reality, Gibraltar has little more than novelty value. After three or four hours with nothing to do, the novelty can wear off.

VR-H HONG KONG (British Crown Colony)
HONG KONG

HKG   VHHH   Kai Tak   4m/6km N of Kowloon (bus 40 minutes)

Arrival at Kai Tak in normal daylight hours is no matter to be taken lightly. The rugged terrain, covered with high rise development, is something to be enjoyed (or endured) as the aircraft turns onto final approach. The popularity of hair-raising rides at funfairs, for which people pay good money, is worth remembering as the aircraft is about to land. The safety record is good, so the only advice is: sit back and enjoy the ride. After dark, when the curfew on flights comes into effect, landings are from over the harbour, when the views of the millions of twinkling lights are memorable.

The observation deck is easy to find, and a modest outlay of 50 cents gains admission. The view is comprehensive, though somewhat restricted by the renovations and extensions, from the Haeco ramp on the far left to the runway threshold on the right. Other notable features are the cargo terminal to the left and, at the far side of the enormous apron, a small hangar and ramp used by the Hong Kong Auxiliary Air Force. This should be noted on arrival also, as some of the inhabitants may only be seen from an aircraft on the taxiway. Morning traffic is generally busy, though the contents of the South China Morning Post's daily published list of movements should not be taken too literally. This is largely an historical feature, dating back to a time when the comings and goings of ships in port was the norm.

The air jetties are used almost exclusively by wide body international flights. At peak times, only a very small proportion of movements get such a slot, the rest taking their place on the vast apron, for passengers to be taken to the terminal by bus. As traffic builds up, and more stands are occupied, the parked aircraft and lighting columns make quality photography virtually impossible. Any excitement at the impending arrival of, say, an Air Nauru 737 will gradually turn to disappointment with the realisation that it is going to park a long way out, and any record of its presence will have to be snapped as the aircraft makes its way between the other aircraft. It is axiomatic that, the more exotic the aircraft, the more distant will be its stand!

Photographers will need further advice concerning the deck: continuous viewing is adequate through the large, but dirty, glazed portholes. Some screening from the noise and fumes is offered. The rest of the deck is glazed above a wall.

In terms of movements, Kai Tak has few equals, especially in Asia, but it can be a frustrating place for those who want the best of all worlds. The deck is patrolled occasionally by guards who may show passing interest in an enthusiast. A friendly explanation has generally sufficed, and regulars on the roof gain nodding acquaintance with officialdom.

Two reports have noted that the observation deck was closed but this was connected to the new construction work being carried out. On such occasions, the cafeteria on the Third Floor level offers an alternative vantage point, almost as good and certainly quieter.

Alternative vantage points to the terminal are few, and warm weather (even in winter) can make exploration tedious. The Haeco hangar doors normally remain closed, though aircraft parked outside can be seen from the terminal. The only viable alternatives are the multi-storey car park and the Aviation Club, on either side of Runway 13's threshold.

The top of the car park offers the prospect of close encounters with landing aircraft, but sunlight conditions are best in summer. From lunchtime, the other side of the runway is better, occupied by the Aviation Club which, apart from a few light aircraft parked outside, looks unremarkable. Access to the bar (remembering that is a Club) may allow an exciting couple of hours. The proximity of the runway where large aircraft land regularly, a couple of pints of ice cold beer, and the chance of a souvenir photograph or two, all make the Aviation Club an ideal destination, subject to access. The fence is just high enough to feature in photographs of aircraft lining up for take-off. The landing aircraft suffer no such problems, of course.

As enthusiasts travel the world in increasing numbers, Hong Kong has become nothing special as a destination from Europe, just as Frankfurt was for Britons in, say the 1970s. The reputation of the Aviation Club made it more than somewhere to be visited by two or three people a month. It has become a serious headache to the management. The club manager, Ms Ruth Gordon, issued the following statement in November 1994:

"Visitors are not permitted to the Club's facilities on Saturdays and Sundays. You will be permitted to use the Club's viewing deck Monday to Friday, but the following rules will apply: (1) all visitors must register with flight operations staff on arrival at the Club; (2) each visitor will be charged a HK$100 admin fee and will be issued a visitors permit which must be displayed at all times when on the Club's premises; (3) visitors may only use the Club's bar area to purchase snacks and refreshments between the hours of 9am and 12:30pm and 2:30pm and 5pm. Visitors may not use the bar between 12:30pm and 2:30pm as the Club is busy between these times serving lunches to members; (4) visitors are not permitted to use the Club's restaurant and (5) all visitors must leave the Club's premises by 5pm."

In other words, the members have been complaining that they are unable to make use of their own facilities because there have, on occasions, too many visitors. It is, after all, their club! Beyond the Ferrari dealership is the FedEx building, with its own parking lot. Here, too, things have got out of hand, to the extent that being seen walking in the area with a camera is now enough to cause annoyance. Be warned in advance: aviation photographers are now considered a serious nuisance, so don't expect that people will sympathise because you've travelled a few thousand miles. It's not their problem. As they see it, YOU are becoming their problem! Maybe a few hours after dark could be spent, checking the staircases which give access to the roofs of nearby apartment blocks. Those on Sun Wong Toi Road and Ma Tau Ching Road might offer the best prospects.

Ma Tau Kok Road runs all the way to the water's edge, ending at a small pier. the runway is close but photographers will need very quick reflexes (as opposed to single lens reflexes, that is). Buildings obscure the northern half of the runway, so photos must be composed and taken in split seconds. Several blocks west is a ferry terminal. By walking out onto the arrivals walkway, the view is better, but even 747s need a 200mm lens.

Movements at the airport have always varied from good to mouth-watering: Royal Nepal 757s, the occasional Air India A310, and the ever-increasing variety of Chinese airliners ensure that Kai Tak stands among the great airports of the world for enthusiasts. The first visit offers many notable airliners, though subsequent trips reveal the same registrations with some regularity. It is easy, after a few days, to tire of Thai Airbuses!

The Kowloon Motor Bus Co, KMB, operates three airbus services. A1 serves Tsim Sha Tsui, the downtown area of Kowloon, A2 and A3 use the tunnel to provide a link with Central and Causeway Bay. Costs are reasonable, being HK$8 from the Star Ferry terminal and HK$10 from the island. Times of operation are between 7am and 11pm, but it would be sensible not to be in too much of a hurry, as traffic conditions can be terrible.

Views of airliners on the move, mostly arriving, aren't restricted to the airport itself.

Chequerboard Hill is a famous alternative, as it here that they turn onto final approach. The nearby Regal Airport Hotel, Mong Kok, has rooms which offer superb views. Binoculars ensure that all registrations can be read (in daylight, of course). To get to Chequerboard Hill, take the KCR train to Tong station and follow the noise. The view down the length of the runway is interesting and really long telephoto lenses can produce remarkable photos.

With so many affordable packages to Hong Kong, this destination is within the reach of many people but for those with more enthusiasm than cash, a stay at the YMCA should be considered. Accommodation, to the uninitiated, comes as a surprise: a suite in the new wing, with lounge, kitchen and two twin bedrooms, costs about HK$800. At the other extreme, a bed in the dormitory costs HK$70. Since food is not cheap in Hong Kong, the YMCA has one of the best value restaurants in the colony. The location is good, close to the Star Ferry terminal in Kowloon, and the next door neighbour is the prestigious Peninsula Hotel.

Make the most of it, while it lasts. The colony will become Chinese territory very soon, and work is now under way to build the new airport.

HONG KONG

HHP	Heliport	0.5m/1km S

Situated on the dockside, close to the Star Ferry Terminal, this is where to see an East Asia Bell 222 taking off for its trip to Macau. Without a timetable, the sight of one of these helicopters is strictly a matter of luck. Hong Kong offers so much of interest apart from the airport that one or two trips on the ferry are likely. Sooner or later, luck will win.

Also near the Star Ferry is the science museum. The entry fee is $HK25 and inside, hanging from the roof, is Cathay Pacific DC-3 VR-HDB.

It is worthy of note that Macau, apart from its helipad, does have a microlight field, where rides are offered to tourists. News of Macau's new airport, with a 10,000 feet long runway capable of handling modern jet traffic, is still premature. The opening date is believed to be 1995 at the earliest.

VT INDIA (Republic of India)
BANGALORE

BLR	VOBG	Hindustan	5m/8km SE

The airport's name suggests something other than passenger services might be seen here. This is indeed the home of Hindustan Aeronautics Ltd (HAL), whose hangars can be seen, on the opposite of the airfield from the passenger terminal.

The single terminal building is divided into two: Indian Airlines in Terminal One and the rest of the domestic carriers in Terminal Two. They are separated by a snack bar! One gate serves all aircraft parked on the apron and, because passengers walk to their planes, they park as close as possible to the terminal.

Stairs at the back of "Terminal One" lead to an observation gallery on the upper level, where the view is excellent. A prominently-displayed notice might need a second reading. At first glance, it appears to say no spotting but, in fact the restriction is against SPITTING. Whilst there is no glass at the front of the gallery, there are two other drawbacks instead: mosquitoes and a heavy mesh screen. Another matter to bear in mind is the gallery also serves as the corridor leading to the security office so, despite this being a rather informal place, attempts to take photos could lead to difficulties.

Next to the terminal can be seen a small general aviation ramp, which can be expected to contain some interesting visitors. On the far side of the runway, clearly visible from the gallery, is HAL. What can be seen outside changes, of course. It would be reasonable to expect some 748s, various MiG fighters and Mil helicopters, if the last report is any indication.

BOMBAY
BOM   VABB   Santa Cruz/J Nehru International   23m/37km N

The Indian government, like that of Pakistan, treats security very seriously indeed. Naturally, this means that international airports are tightly controlled. Most airports are considered as special security areas, meaning that the public needs a good reason to gain access. Although New Delhi is the capital city, Bombay is the country's main international gateway and has been one of Asia's main seaports for many years.

Santa Cruz is, effectively, two entirely separate airports. This being India, nothing is wasted when it reaches the end of one useful life. The original passenger terminal still stands (but only just) and is used by private domestic airlines. Sahara India, Jet, Modiluf, Vayudoot (Dorniers and HAL 748s) and East West Airlines are all regular movements. Next to it is the second passenger terminal to be built, originally for international traffic, now used exclusively by Indian Airlines. A small cargo ramp completes this complex, which more or less faces Runway 09/27.

The present international terminal is the newest, and is located some distance from the old complex, on the far side of Runway 14/32. The building is crescent-shaped and, once upon a time, had a roof terrace. Times have changed.

Few aviation enthusiasts report from India, so what can be seen, and from where, remains a matter of some conjecture. Transit passengers often arrive in the middle of the night, having little more than the chance to stretch their legs and admire (but not necessarily buy) the uniquely Indian selection of duty-free goods. Not everyone is moved to buy an electric toaster or steam iron! What transit passengers do not have is any view from inside the building.

Airworks India may be directly opposite the international terminal, though some way off, but the hangars are only likely to be seen from a window seat in a moving aircraft. DC-3s are still very much in evidence here, one or two being serviced for other operators. Beside the hangar are a couple of DC-3 wrecks and, also close by, the two redundant ex-Pushpaka Caravelles, a DC-4 and a CV-440.

Making contact with Airworks can result in what sounds like good news. Propliner fans can be welcome but Airworks' approval is only half the story. Obtaining a security clearance is another matter, not so easily achieved without prior written notification.

BOMBAY
VAJJ   Juhu   9m/14km N

The port of Bombay was built on a peninsula which juts south into the Arabian Sea. To its east is Bombay Harbour and slightly further north is Mahim Bay. Swami Vivekland Road heads north across the bay beyond which, another couple of miles away, is Juhu Airport. This is known to be one of India's main general aviation fields . . . but that's all that's known, apart from the fact that Pawan Hans and a few other operators have a presence here. A prolonged stay in Bombay might include further investigation - by rickshaw, of course!

CALCUTTA
CCU   VECC   Netaji Subas Chandra Bose International   17m/27km NE

Historically, Calcutta has always been synonymous with poverty and it is very much in evidence, right up to the airport's perimeter fence. Whilst there is nothing to stop anyone taking a trip around the perimeter, it can be quite a frightening prospect: teeming millions, living in wooden shacks, with sewage systems that are best described as being below modern standards.

The passenger terminal is, however, clean and roomy. The one building handles both international and domestic traffic, though there is very little of the former. Whilst no viewing area has been reported, it is possible to see the aircraft from the departure lounge. Indian Airlines predominate, as is to be expected, but Jet, Sahara and Damania are also in evidence.

DELHI
DEL   VIDP   Indira Gandhi International   9m/14km SW

Without a valid ticket, the armed guards at the doors will not allow entry. New Delhi is the nation's capital city, so it can be expected that security precautions are strict and maintained at a high level. Photography is, of course, prohibited.

There are two separate terminals, international and domestic, a long way from each other. The international terminal is, predictably, secure and there are no viewing facilities. Most of the visiting airliners are operated by Air India and the usual European carriers. There is little to see here, in any quantity, that can't be seen elsewhere with greater ease. Close links with the CIS mean that a number of Aeroflot (and ex-Aeroflot) aircraft visit.

The domestic terminal does have a viewing area. The corridor, leading to the restaurant, has ten or so narrow windows (all solidly locked) which overlook the apron. Most of what is to be seen are Indian Airlines Airbuses and 737s but the newer, privately owned, airlines are well represented. Beyond the domestic apron is a tempting line of Indian Air Force 707s, An-32s and some CIS cargo aircraft. Also stored here are several DC-3s.

DELHI
VIDD   Safdir Jang   6m/10km S

Anyone staying in the Delhi area for a few days might also consider exploring Safdir Jang (or Safdarjung), the other airport, though nothing has been reported about it. This is likely to yield a quantity of helicopters, as Pawan Hans is based here. It used to be the Helicopter Corporation of India. A number of other small operators are also based but it would be wise to make contact by telephone to arrange a visit before turning up in a taxi, hoping to see something. To find Safdir Jang from the international airport, take the main road towards the city, as far as Delhi Cantonment. Here, take the ring road east, as far as a major road called Sri Aurobindo Marg. The airport is on the left.

GOA
GOI   VAGO   Dabolim   18m/29km SSE

Formerly a Portuguese protectorate, Goa is rapidly becoming a major tourist destination, causing all the associated problems: drunkenness and prostitution are extremely alien to the local culture. The beautiful tropical beaches and cheap alcohol are probably more attractive than the airport, mostly because the Indian Air Force base Badger bombers here. If things are tightly controlled at purely civil airports, it takes little imagination to work out what would happen if caught investigating what is to be seen here. A perimeter tour can result in one or two approach shots, since Jet, ModiLuft, Damania, East West and Indian Airlines operate 737s, plus the occasional A320. The bonus is an increasing amount of international charter traffic.

V2 ANTIGUA (State of Antigua and Barbuda)
SAINT JOHNS
ANU   TAPA   V C Bird - Antigua   4m/6km NE

It's easy to imagine, without visiting this part of the world, that life is informal and unhurried.

Apart from important cricket matches, nothing really upsets the leisurely pace, and life is pretty good. VC Bird airport reflects this in every way. The passenger terminal has an open observation deck, and access is free. Wire mesh prevents security worries without making life particularly difficult for the photographer.

Much of the traffic is Caribbean-based general aviation, and an interesting selection it is. Scheduled traffic is mostly Leeward Islands Air Transport (LIAT) with mostly Dash 8s, HS748s and Twin Otters, and BWIA supply the MD-80s. Wide-bodies from Europe are regular without being frequent, and there are a few American arrivals on most days.

Most of what Antigua's airport has to offer can be seen just as well at Miami, but Miami isn't the West Indies, by any stretch of the imagination. A trip to this island is probably planned for relaxation, and a chance to get away from it all. One or two visits to the airport offer a nice change from drinking by the hotel pool . . . the best of both worlds.

V3 BELIZE
BELIZE CITY
BZE   MZBZ   Phillip S W Goldson International   10m/16km NW

A sign of the country's recent history is displayed at the entrance to the airport: a Harrier GR.3. The British Army base, with its Gazelle helicopters, is on the far side of the field from the passenger terminal, but barely visible.

An open waving gallery offers a fine view of the airfield, with the sun usually in the right position. Traffic is reasonably varied, being a mixture of American Airlines services from Miami, Continental, TACA, Trans Jamaica and the local Tropic Air. Even a short stay at the airport should result in seeing a few Twin Otters, plus the Islanders of Maya and Island Air. There is only one hangar, containing a couple of local Cessnas but a few visitors from neighbouring countries make the ramp look more interesting. Any biz-jets in evidence are normally from the USA or Mexico.

The cargo area is used sporadically, one of Kalitta's DC-8s being the most likely visitor. For a complete picture of the city's aviation scene, a visit to the Municipal Airport (TZA), on the edge of town, is essential. This is where much of the maintenance is carried out but, in this part of the world, Islanders are considered to be quite large aircraft.

XA MEXICO (United Mexican States)

Mexico is rapidly becoming an interesting country for the aviation enthusiast. To make the most of what is an increasingly tempting destination, some background knowledge might be of use. Virtually all Mexico's major airports are built and operated by Aeroportos y Servicios Auxiliares (ASA) a quasi non-governmental organisation. As Britons know, quangos are autonomous, and often quite dictatorial bodies: what they say goes. The ASA is reported to make life difficult for airlines as well as individual people, when requests of various kinds don't fit in with their plans. The usual story, the whole world over: "we are here to do our job, and you can help by not interfering." The lowest-ranking ASA security guard can order a major airline's station manager to get a photographer off the ramp, and his action will be backed by ASA management.

Times are, however, changing. What was once an implacable anti-photography posture is being slightly relaxed to the point that quite arbitrary decisions are now being taken. The future is therefore in the balance. Foreign enthusiasts are very much ambassadors, paving the way for others in the future. It will take only one or two minor incidents for much progress to be undone. Spotting is not seen as a problem but photography is still, officially, frowned on. Observation decks and points around airfield perimeters are a rarity. There are many reasons to visit Mexico but, for the present, it would be wise not to put aviation photography too high on the agenda, as it will almost certainly lead to frustration.

ACAPULCO
ACA   MMAA   General Juan N Alvarez International   16m/25km SE

Few holiday destinations have as much charisma as Acapulco, though it is nothing like the place it used to be. It's America's answer to the Costa Brava. The small airport has managed to cope with traffic, though its facilities are rather modest. Wedged in between a lagoon and the sea, it's all white concrete and palm trees, so arrival here is a pleasant experience. The back edge of the apron is an unbelievable assortment of rampside clutter, so it is fortunate that the restaurant's observation area is on the upper floor of the terminal.

Scheduled traffic is minimal, almost half of it from the States, and 727s are the staple diet plus Aeromexico DC-9s/MD-88s/MD-82s. Winter is high season, when wide-bodies operate charters from Canada and other cooler climes. Generally speaking, there is little out of the ordinary. Acapulco's name is sure to impress friends but photos of airliners on the ramp are less likely to do so. It takes time and patience for the number of movements logged to reach double figures, and there are other pleasures to be enjoyed elsewhere.

CANCUN
CUN   MMUN   International   15m/23km SW

Cancun now reigns supreme as the resort for Americans to take their holidays, especially in winter. The rest of the world has followed, so that the airport has had to expand at the same rate as the resort. International services are generally similar to those to be seen at MIA, though with the exception of smaller types operated by Ladeco, AeroPeru and Cubana's Yak-42s.

Domestic movements are plentiful and varied, with all jet-equipped carriers, except Aero California, making appearances on scheduled or charter flights. Saturdays are by far the busiest, though Wednesdays are not far behind. Opportunities for viewing are, however, rather limited and the chances of photography almost negligible. Travellers, both international and domestic, show their tickets and boarding passes to access the boarding concourses, after which only the international area offers any real panorama for an hour and a half or so before the plane leaves.

Non-travellers have a difficult time. The windows en route to the boarding area allow aircraft to be see but only through the ornamental vegetation. There is a single glass door which is unobstructed but, even here, the view is restricted.

Photographers will need ingenuity, and probably a formal request to at least one of the airlines for ramp access (rather than the ASA). This has been possible in the past. Hints for those considering this approach: you'll need a white short-sleeved dress shirt, black or dark blue slacks and leather shoes, in order to blend in with everyone else. Goodwill is on the increase and it helps to thank your hosts profusely, thereby helping to ensure that the relaxed atmosphere continues to improve.

One of the cheapest ways to visit Cuba is to book through Divermex, a local travel agency, which does inexpensive 2, 3 and 7 day trips to Havana in Cubana Yak-42s.

CHICHEN ITZA
CZA

An airstrip, built on the Yucatan to serve tourists visiting the famous archaeological sites from Cancun and Cozumel, most of the movements occur in the week. They comprise mostly TAESA and AeroCaribe F.27s, operating on a rather more ad hoc basis than the schedules suggest. Before making a trip to the airport, it would be wise to ring the airlines and ask for confirmation of their movements. The tarmac can be seen easily from the approach road, and it is only a short walk from the nicer hotels, near the ruins. Afternoons are definitley best for photography.

COZUMEL
CZM   MMCZ   International   2m/3km NE

Apart from a few Continental and Mexicana movements, this airport handles mostly regional types, operating from Cancun. The passenger terminal is, however, one of the country's typical examples, offering no views of the proceedings. The approach to the runway can be seen from the beach at San Miguel and satisfactory photos of aircraft can be taken, depending on the wind direction.

GUADALAJARA
GDL   MMGL   Don Miguel Hidalgo International   11m/17km SE

Though a considerable distance behind Mexico City, this is one of the country's busier airports, handling all sorts of scheduled traffic from DC-10s down to DC-3s. The Wings restaurant on the passenger terminal's upper floor overlooks the ramp. What can be seen is a lot of construction work and, beyond it, the main apron. The air jetties will reduce the amount of passengers being bussed around the ramp, but they will partially restrict the view.

The domestic stands are to the left and the international flights park in front. There are enough American carriers for Guadalajara to look like any airport in southern Texas. To the right, and almost out of sight, is the general aviation ramp. To see this at close quarters, it's necessary to walk out of the terminal past the control tower.

To the east of the passenger terminal are the cargo apron and Mexicana maintenance area. Most of the movements on the main runway can be seen from the terminal but there is another, away to the left. The road which serves the airport continues towards Chapala, passing the threshold of Runway 28. Photos from the road of aircraft on approach need a 200mm lens from here.

MERIDA
MID   MMMD   Lic. Manuel Crescencio Rejon   5m/8km S

This corner of Mexico, the Yucutan Peninsula, is famous for its Mayan remains which attract tourists, especially on charter flights from Canada and the United States in winter. Scheduled airliners are now mainly domestic, all of which are regular visitors to the USA. What little traffic there is can be seen adequately from around the terminal but most enthusiasts who visit will arrive for reasons other than the traffic.

MEXICO CITY
MEX   MMMX   Benito Juarez   8m/13km E (train 25 minutes)

Mexico may be one of the poorest countries on earth but its capital city has many rich people. Business traffic through the city's airport is brisk, be it scheduled or private. The two parallel runways are used by airliners, with a shorter diagonal runway for smaller aircraft. Because of the Spanish words for left and right, the runways are known 5I (left) and 5D (right).

The first reported ground level view at the perimeter was one solitary spot. It is probably one of the most unhealthy places on earth, but one of the best! Let into the concrete blocks which screen the taxiway and hold for Runway 5I is what can best be described as a cage. It looks similar to a dug-out, used by the manager, trainer and reserves at the average football game, apart from being fenced across the front. This is one of the officially approved viewing platforms, and there are supposed to be others elsewhere around the field.

The bare bench seat accommodates at most two dozen happy people, and there are no facilities, other than the view . . . but what a view. Hot, dirty and incredibly noisy, this is the place to go! Nothing else comes close. It really would be adviseable to check about photography before making rash assumptions.

The main elevated viewpoint is multi-storey Car Park 2, though the power of a telescope may be essential to note the executive movements. Spotters are bound to take the top floor, and that's where the guards look for them. The next floor down is just as good, but there is shade from the very hot sun, and less hassle.

Hotels in the area are affordable, $15 being reasonable in Zocala, but the Hotel Fiesta Americana has more to offer in return for its higher prices. Its roof garden is close enough to the runways for photography of some sort to be possible, an important consideration when the multi-storey car park displays several signs prohibiting photos. Rooms on the 7th and 8th floors offer the best views. The hotel management is getting familiar with people asking for rooms overlooking the airport.

The Aviacion General complex is busy, with its own terminal, well-stocked apron and several hangars. It has its own Metro rail station, called Hangares. Based here are many operators, and traffic is brisk throughout the morning and early evening. Apart from the many Mexicana and Aeromexico flights, the executive movements (including Banxico DC-9s) and visits by a variety of Latin American carriers, governmental and air force transport flights make Mexico City a very interesting airport. It would not be unreasonable to expect over a hundred biz-jets, and some reports suggest that double that number is possible.

It would be sensible at Benito Juarez to expect official hostility to spotting activities, and more so to photography. What takes place in (or from) the privacy of a hotel room in the Fiesta Americana is unlikely to meet with any opposition, but it could be too far away for quality photos. Mexico is not the free-and-easy (in theory, anyway) USA. The country's main airport handles many extremely important and influential people. Sensitivity about their movements is a matter for the government to decide. The rest of us are left to draw our own conclusions.

The pressure on slots at Benito Juarez has led to restrictions on general aviation there. Most prop-driven aircraft, with a cruising speed of less than 250 knots, will be (have been?) the first casualties. There are plans to build a new passenger terminal on the south side, which will mean the relocation of non-scheduled activities. The most likely beneficiaries will be Toluca, about forty miles west, Puebla which is the same distance east, plus Cuernavaca, Pachuca and Atizapan. Official information is minimal.

Airlines are opposed to moving from Benito Juarez, though cargo carriers will probably be among the first to reach agreement. Puebla could be their new home. Any visits to Mexico City should bear this fact in mind, and any visible reduction in general aviation movements at the main airport means a corresponding increase elsewhere. Validated information is yet to be received on the subject.

MONTERREY
MTY   MMMY   General Mariano Escobido International   15m/23km NE

An increasingly interesting airport to visit, this is the home base for AeroExo, SARO, Servicios Aerolineas Mexicanas (SAM) and VARSA, and is a major station for Mexicana's fleet of Fokker 100s. Add some Aeromonterrey FH-227s and AeroLitoral Metros, and a visit here is most enjoyable, mostly because the restaurant in the boarding concourse can be reached without a boarding pass.

The passenger terminal lies to the south of the east-west runway, with a ten-gate concourse reached via a tunnel, similar to those at LAX. The restaurant at the other end of this tunnel offers a good view of the runway. There is another on the upper floor of the main terminal which overlooks part of the general aviation ramp, to the east. Outside, the considerable AeroLitoral fleet can be seen from the fence to the west of the terminal.

Travellers should remember that Monterrey isn't one of the world's cheapest cities. A taxi from downtown costs about 50 new pesos (about $17 and rising) and a modest hotel near the bus station, where most of them are, can be $50 a night. Consolation is that travelling from the airport is cheaper, by taking one of the colectivo buses. Bear in mind it can be a long wait if you are the first to get on board, as these buses only move when there are enough passengers.

The general aviation airfield is called Aeropuerto del Norte (codes: NTR MMAN) so care should be taken if driving out of town. As the name suggests, the field is to the north, reached by taking Av Alfonso Reyes (Hwy 58) but anyone heading for the airport should head east along Av Miguel Aleman (Hwy 54).

PLAYA DEL CARMEN
PCM

On the east coast of the Yucatan peninsula lies the small island of Cozumel. Facing the island is this small town whose airstrip, within walking distance of the main plaza, plays host to Aerocozumel Trislanders and other small aircraft. Busy it isn't, but anyone visiting Cozumel might wish to check it out.

TIJUANA
TIJ   MMTJ   General Abelardo Rodriguez   4m/6km S

There seems to be a rule in Mexico that, the smaller the airport, the longer is its name! Tijuana is the most easily reached of all Mexico's airports, being just across the border from San Diego. The culture shock of the crossing is enormous, as the town is squalid, but the airport is modern and quite pleasant. To the right of the terminal is an executive ramp, where half a dozen or so business twins are usually parked. Once inside the terminal, the only views are through windows but an early morning arrival can ensure photos of Mexicana DC-10s, as they taxi to their stands, very close indeed to the terminal.

YK SYRIA (Syrian Arab Republic)
DAMASCUS
DAM   OSDI   International   18m/30km E (bus 30 minutes)

This is one of those strange airports where an excellent roof terrace has been kept open despite the mysterious nature of many of the visiting aircraft. There are, however, distinct warnings against photography.

The passenger terminal and ramp are located at right angles to the axis of the main runway and a taxiway leads in both directions to runways, though that on the left appears to be generally out of use. The observation area provides a good, if elevated, view of the main apron and there is room for four aircraft to park at the terminal's jetties. To the left, Syrianair's seldom-used Tu-134s are parked, though some may be seen at the remote parking area at the other end of the main runway. To the right is the cargo terminal, where some general aviation movements also park. Other aircraft park out on the ramp but particularly sensitive visitors, like Libyan Il-76s, stay out of reach near the threshold of the runway. On the far side of the taxiway, opposite the terminal, disused Syrian DC-6 YK-AEC sits, decaying, in the sun.

For those in search of nourishment while on the roof deck, the beer is recommended, being of a very acceptable standard, but the food is not, by some European standards.

At the far end of the runway is a military controlled parking area, where the Syrian Government Il-76s, An-26s, Yak-40s and Falcon 20s are to be found. Most carry Syrianair titles and can be clearly seen from the airport road. Enthusiasts visiting Damascus should ensure that they are sitting on the left side of the aircraft when they arrive, to content themselves with low-quality photos out of their (western) airliner rather than be tempted to try poking a telephoto lens through the fence. The Syrianair maintenance base is just around the corner from the terminal and successful negotiations at the security barrier, not easily achieved, result in meeting an extremely friendly airline staff who will be happy to show a visitor around one of their unwanted Tu-154Ms, subject to availability.

The extent of military activity at Damascus is unknown and detailed investigation is hardly encouraged. Hardened concrete shelters do exist next to the main runway but only (!) the occasional MiG has been seen overshooting. The inaccessible area behind the passenger terminal may be a military base and the runway beyond it may serve some purpose related to it, but details are sketchy.

Visiting airlines feature arab and mid-European carriers, though some visit at quite ridiculous hours. The demand to get to Budapest must be extreme if the only flight leaves at 0335 on Sunday mornings! The political status of Syria means that numbers of 'extra' flights are almost regular, both from Central Europe and arab countries. Swissair, Austrian and Air France come from the west and PIA pause on the way between New York and Karachi. Cyprus Airways also operate regular 1-11 flights from neighbouring Larnaca, though these may be classed as being some of the most mundane visitors in this part of the world.

YR ROMANIA
BUCHAREST
BBU   LRBS   Baneasa   6m/km N

With the fall of communist rule, Romania has suffered great financial hardship. It was never a rich country and times are now hard indeed. A network of heavily subsidised domestic flights was operated by Tarom's An-24s, to link the country with its capital, through Baneasa airport. Hard economics mean hard times, and the future looks bleak. The aircraft are now virtually unused and therefore so is the airport.

With so many Tarom Antonovs to be seen, in the company of Romavia's aircraft and a fair selection of older Soviet-built types, Baneasa is not without interest, and the short taxi ride from Otopeni should allow the logbook to be filled with plenty of aircraft at minimal risk.

BUCHAREST
OTP   LROP   Otopeni   10m/16km N

Bucharest's international traffic uses Otopeni airport, described as being inadequate to cope even in the bad years. The spectator's terrace has been closed for many years, and what could be witnessed was mostly a procession of airliners to be seen far easier at most other European airports. With negligible charter traffic, a day's movements are unlikely to exceed twenty or so arrivals.

CONSTANTA
COZ   MDCZ   M Kogalniceanu

This is a military airfield, used in summer by a handful of charter flights to the small civil passenger terminal. Spectators have never been encouraged because of the military presence and, now that the economy has slackened even more, there is even less reason to visit.

TIMISOARA
TSR   LRTR   Giarmata

Technically, Timisoara still survives as an international airport, though its movements were, at best, restricted to a BAC-111 to Frankfurt and an Il-62 or 707 to America. These weekly services are supplemented by two daily air links to Bucharest. If Romania is planned as a destination, only the military presence at Timisoara is likely to appeal.

YV VENEZUELA (Republic of Venezuela)
CARACAS
CCS   SVMI   Simon Bolivar International   13m/20km NW (bus 60 minutes)

Venezuela is easy to overlook as a destination for the aviation enthusiast. This should not be so, as Caracas has an extremely interesting, and quite busy, airport. Prices in Venezuela are also very low, by European standards. Good hotel rooms are affordable and, at a pinch, the YMCA is cheap. The local beer, called Polar, costs the equivalent of 17pence a bottle.

To the north of the airport, behind a low hill, is the Caribbean Sea. There are, effectively, two separate airports whose facilities overlap, but an explanation is complicated: to the west of the field is Runway 09/27 which has, to the south of it, an international and domestic terminal. East of this, but slightly overlapping, is Runway 08/26 with its general aviation, military and cargo terminals. That much can be seen from a basic map.

The international and domestic terminals, both of which have outdoor spectator decks, face Runway 09/27 but are also close to the threshold of Runway 08. Both decks were closed in March 1995. Windows (tinted and dirty) in both terminals allow aircraft to be seen but photographers will find this a frustrating airport. To make matters worse, many of the aircraft park so that they are either nose-on or tail-on to the viewer.

The international terminal is passed by most departing airliners and taxying international movements are seen at closer range than from the domestic terminal. There is, however, no view at all of Runway 08 or the other areas, and aircraft landing come into view so quickly as to make life difficult.

Windows in the domestic terminal overlook the general aviation and cargo areas. They also allow movements to be seen on Runway 08, which tends to be busy. The view is restricted and international movements are too distant for photography. In other words, it might be necessary to spend equal amounts of time at each terminal if a truly representative record of the airport's movements is to be made.

The Aeropostal and Avensa fleets can be seen in a day and there are plenty of other domestic airlines. International traffic is not particularly brisk, and many of the movements arrive at odd hours. Caracas does seem to specialise in one or two rather unusual visitors: Rentavion's Martin 404 is likely to please many enthusiasts, for example, but there are also one or two Servivensa and Aero Executive DC-3s and a good selection of biz-jets and governmental aircraft.

To the right of the terminals are the separate military, general aviation and cargo facilities, though it should be noted that cargo traffic is minimal and features no major indigenous carriers. There are multiple rows of hangars in the general aviation area where a vast array of biz-jets can be seen, including the government's Gulfstreams. Photographers might walk (a long way) west from the terminal area to where the perimeter allows views of landing aircraft. The best spots are much used by the locals, with whom close contact is not always a good thing. Note also that the use of long focus lenses can, and does, attract attention. With so many military and governmental aircraft around, careless photography can lead to misunderstanding and trouble.

Taxis are relatively expensive, so it might be necessary to sample the local buses. They stop on the highway, across the car park from the terminal area, and can be flagged down. The drivers speak little English but do their best to help.

CARACAS
SVCS   Charallave/O Machado Zuloaga International

This is the other airport for Caracas, some miles inland, and 2000 feet above sea level. With so much confusing information coming from one airport, it would be unwise to offer further speculation about the other. However, whilst there are no scheduled operations, the general aviation does include a number of fleet operators who have maintenance facilities here. Apart from Cessna twins and one or two Trislanders or Metros of Viajes Expresos (CAVE), a few of Aeroejecutivos DC-3s can be seen. Some working Spanish is useful, to gain access to the ramps for a close-up look.

CARACAS
SVFM   Generalisimo Francisco Miranda   3m/5km E

This is Caracas' military air base, generally known as La Colota. To reach it, travel east from town, towards Parque del Este or along the Autopista. The adjacent general aviation terminal is, rather optimistically, called Metropolitano Internacional. They are side by side, separated by a fence. The domestic airport (or perhaps even the domestic terminal only) is known locally, to confuse matter even more, as Caracas Maiquetia.

Aircraft arriving do so much the same way as they do at Kai Tak: avoiding the hills before turning onto tight finals over the city. Accidents do happen, and have happened, so the field is no longer open to single-engined aircraft, which could make it an attraction to many enthusiasts! Biz-jets and other executive types are extremely well-represented at this field, including those operated by the Aero Club. On the north side of the field is the small passenger terminal, used by visiting aircraft, none of which operate commercial services. Photography from the terminal is good, with the sun seemingly always in a good position. Permission should be sought to take photos of civilian aircraft for two reasons: it is usually granted and it helps reduce any chance of misunderstanding.

The western part of the field, occupied by the miltary base, holds Aravas, Skyvans, King Airs and a whole range of helicopters, from S-61s and Pumas to JetRangers and Bo105s. A walk along the perimeter fence might seem like a good idea but it will soon be discovered that very few aircraft can be seen, because of the hangars and other buildings which obstruct the view.

One of the most convenient local hotels is part of the nearby CCCT shopping mall/hotel complex, almost directly opposite the entrance to the National Guard base. For a good view, the top floor of the multi-storey car park is recommended. The Eurobuilding Hotel's swimming pool offers a reasonably good view of the runway, from where the movements can be logged in comfort. Most of the other hotels are located in the Macuto/Caribe area. Walking along the perimeter is not necessarily a good idea. The northern boundary might be effectively out of bounds and that to the south is about a mile and a half long.

CIUDAD BOLIVAR
CBL   SVCB

Some way inland, on the Orinoco River, is the regional capital of Ciudad Bolivar. There are, literally, one or two domestic flights each day, operated by Avensa and Aeropostal but most interest is generated by the various hangars and aprons used by a variety of operators, all of which are something special to European eyes.

This is an informal airport in many ways, where Big City pressures have yet to reach. An-2s are not common anywhere in the world, and they are certainly distinctive aircraft. They are an unexpected delight here, sharing the aprons area with plenty of DC-3s, plus a truly wonderful assortment of other types and colour schemes. Ciudad Bolivar doesn't warrant a long stay, but a visit here will be memorable, for sure.

CUIDAD GUYANA

PZO   Puerto Ordaz   8m/11km SW

The provincial town of Ciudad Guyana sits at the junction of the Orinoco and Caroni Rivers, some distance east of Caracas. The airport is served by Avensa, Servivensa and Aerotuy which operate regular services to Palomar and Ciudad Bolivar as well as the capital.

The passenger terminal is, by European standards, rather basic but the upper floor does have a cafe/bar with a view of the apron. For a good photo of a Servivensa DC-3, this is the place to be. Also visible are a couple of based CL-215s, several twins and a Polish-registered An-2 which has been resident for over a year. The Catalina once used by the Orinoco Mining Co now looks very sorry for itself.

Next to the apron are two hangars containing mostly Cessnas. By leaving the passenger terminal and turning left, a walk beside the boundary fence and the National Guard Camp will probably allow most of the residents (of the airfield, rather than the camp) to be identified. For a closer inspection, some working knowledge of Spanish will be essential. Puerto Ordiz is an interesting little airport, if you need to travel there on business. It is not, however, worth a detour as the airline traffic can be seen elsewhere.

Z ZIMBABWE (Republic of Zimbabwe)
GWERU

FVTL   Thornhill   5m/8km

Whether or not Gweru has two airports is not certain. The codes GWE and FVGW are supposedly allocated to Gweru/Gweru! Anyone with a passion for propliners might be tempted to visit this part of the world because two of Air Zimbabwe's Viscounts are located here. Apart from the chance to see a modest number of light aircraft and a few airline movements, just as easily seen at Harare in all probability, there is no reason to make the trip. Propliner fans will, of course, insist that is reason enough!

HARARE

HRE   FVHA   International   7m/11km S

As is often the case in Africa, maximum use is made of expensive runways, meaning that civil and military traffic often share the one facility. This is indeed the case at Harare, with the base situated to the north side and the civil complex on the south.

Air Zimbabwe made use, for many years, of one of the world's last Viscount fleets. Whilst these have now been withdrawn from use, they are still very much in evidence. Harare has two examples, one of which has been lovingly preserved and is displayed by the airline's hangars. The pace of events here is sufficiently relaxed, and the people friendly enough, for photos to be taken of Z-YNB. The other, Z-WGC, has suffered a less dignified fate and now lies, semi-derelict, on the far side of the runway from the passenger terminal, next to Boeing 707 Z-WKT. Both are used (or abused, depending on your point of view) by the fire department.

The passenger terminal is much loved by those who have used it, despite offering only very basic facilities. Compensation is offered by the observation deck which offers unrestricted views across the apron and the rest of the airfield. There is no glass to mar the view, so photography couldn't be better. Access to the deck costs a couple of Zimbabwe dollars (that is to say, almost nothing) and there is waiter service for the rather good food and beer.

The terminal is divided into two, domestic passengers using the left side, outside which is the small executive apron. Further round to the left are the Air Zimbabwe cargo and customs buildings, beyond which are the remains of a Beech Baron.

Clearly visible, on the far side of the field, is the military base, with at least ten or so C-47s out in the open. There are also Islanders, CASA 212s, Hawks and helicopters. Activity is not brisk, and it can be difficult to identify all the aircraft. One report states that, after six visits, only three of the CASAs have been identified. Compared with airports in other parts of the world, this can probably be considered an achievement.

An early start is recommended - 7:00am is about right, because Air Zimbabwe's 707s tend to arrive between 6:00am and 8:00am. The rest of the traffic includes heavy metal from Europe: Swissair MD-11s and KLM 747-400s make stopovers here, arriving from Johannesburg and returning there in the evening. British Airways 747s, Air Mauritius A340s are also regular visitors. The smaller scheduled visitors, likely to be of more interest to western eyes, are BAe 146s from Botswana and Malawi, plus a few 737 movements operated by Kenya and Uganda Airlines.

Rather than spend all day on the deck, consuming large quantities of cheap beer, a wander around the airport can be a welcome change (depending on how much you like beer). All the hangars, apart from those of Air Zimbabwe, are accessible by negotiation. The Catalina, Z-CAT, is no longer present but there are plenty of King Airs, United Islanders and an assortment of other types, including HS 125 Z-VEC, as some consolation. Worth looking out for is Jetstream 9Q-CFI, normally to be found in the Fields hangar.

Almost all the cargo is handled by Affretair, whose hangar is at the head of the maintenance ramp, closest to the runway. Due to cargo movements being slightly less regular than passenger traffic, what can be seen outside Affretair's facility is largely a matter of luck.

Harare's other airfield is Prince Charles, still officially an airport, but used almost exclusively by general aviation. A taxi journey from the city centre takes about twenty minutes and costs about £3, one way. For this, you get to see over 150 light aircraft in somewhat relaxed fashion.

HWANGE
HWN FVWN   National Park   45m/72km

Zimbabwe's economy is partly dependant on the tourist industry, and Hwange is a major centre of activity for anyone seeking wild life (big game). The airport is therefore closer to where the tourists want to go than it is to the town, which has its own airport (Hwange Town: WKI/FVWT). Most of the movements involve ferrying tourists in twin-engined comfort from either Bulawayo or Harare but there is nothing special to be seen, if locally registered Navajos and Aztecs can be considered ordinary, that is.

KARIBA
KAB FVKB   12m/19km

Lake Kariba was formed when the dam was built. It is becoming a tourist attraction in its own right, mostly because people don't seem to realise how hot it is here until they arrive. Traffic is, by local standards, uninspiring as it comprises mostly a few commuters.

VICTORIA FALLS
VFA FVFA   14m/23km

A single runway, with the apron and terminal placed to one side, is used by visitors to the spectacular water falls. Apart from the occasional South African or Air Zimbabwe movement, the airport comes a very distant second place for even the most ardent aviation enthusiast. It can hardly be expected to compete with one of the greatest sights on earth. There are no problems with either viewing or photography at the airport, apart from the fact that there is very little to see. It is usual to find at least one biz-jet, parked on the apron.

When staying in the area for more than one day, some spare time might be spent also at Spray View, Victoria Falls' other airport. This is nothing more than an airstrip, used mostly for sight-seeing flights.

ZK NEW ZEALAND (Dominion of New Zealand)

Despite the initial cost of a flight to New Zealand, and the great distance to be flown, New Zealand is fast becoming one of the most desirable of tourist destinations. An Ansett Airpass, bought in the UK, costs less than £150.00 and allows up to five sectors. Car hire costs little more than £10 for a day and longer rental periods are even cheaper.

With so much spectacular scenery in such a small area, much of which offers the variety of fjords and alpine glaciers on South Island, and the famous volcanic activity of Rotorua to the north, there is no shortage of sights. Time can be a problem, and three weeks are better than two. Hotel costs for long stays can mount up, but there is no shortage of good accommodation, often for no more than £10.00 per night.

AUCKLAND
AMZ NZAR Ardmore 20m/32km SE of Auckland

To visit this airfield near Clevedon, time and a car are essential, and what's on offer is very much a matter of taste. A couple of hundred light aircraft, including helicopters, may be what some people want to see. The staff are certainly friendly enough, so taking a look around is rarely a problem. After all, a company called Captain Al's Fantasy Flights can't take life too seriously. The New Zealand Warbirds collection includes C-47 ZK-DAK plus a couple of Devons and a few Harvards etc.

The visit to Ardmore might be something of a pilrimage, for a few years yet, for piston-power freaks. Easily missed by anyone not knowing what to look for, there is a company specialising in aircraft spares, where a couple of Bristol 170 Freighters (ZK-EPE/G) are still stored. Don't expect them to be in good condition after all these years. The moving surfaces and the engines have gone but the airframes are still pretty much intact.

AUCKLAND
AKL NZAA International 14m/22km S (bus 50 minutes)

This is the country's main international gateway, known locally as Mangere, after the prominent mountain just across the water. Anyone contemplating a visit to New Zealand should bear in mind that it is unlike Australia for its climate. Being further from the equator it is cooler, and most of the country is quite close to the sea. Thus it is rather more like Britain for its weather.

For this reason the popular viewing deck on the Jean Batten International Terminal is enclosed by a glass screen. The winds blowing off Manakau Harbour can be quite chilly, though less so in summer, of course. From the deck, at first floor level, there are good views of the international activity and the runway. However its angle and close proximity to many of the arrivals mean it can make life difficult for the serious photographer. A good zoom lens is essential. Inside the international terminal is displayed the Gull Six G-ADPR.

Of the regular visitors here, it is the Air Niuguini, Air Nauru and Royal Tongan aircraft which are most likely to please, the rest being mostly a selection of British and American carriers. It should be remembered that Air New Zealand's 767s use this terminal, so a premature walk to the domestic terminal could cause consternation. Most of the unusual airlines seem to arive between 5:00pm and 8:00pm. These include a Mount Cook 748 and a couple of NZ Air Freight

CV-580s. Before settling down to watch these, it's important to have a look around the freight terminal. The many NZ Post Metros get put to bed quite early. The shuttle bus links the terminals, but on most days it's a pleasant stroll taking no more than ten minutes. There are bench seats which offer some view of proceedings but they are of no use to anyone wishing to use a camera. The domestic terminal is divided into two, with Air New Zealand and its subsidiaries occupying one part, and Ansett New Zealand the other. Ansett's facility is strictly functional, with no viewing area. The ANZ part has a bar and an external view of the apron. When Runway 23 is in use, this is definitely the place to be. There are stands immediately in front, and taxying aircraft pass within range of a 70-200mm zoom lens. It is here that close-ups are taken of Bandeirantes, Saab 340s and Metroliners. Tranzair Beech 99s and Mount Cook Airline 748s are a bonus.

The chainlink perimeter fence is barely six feet high, so photos can be taken on tiptoe by taller people. Following the fence leads to the cargo terminal where action is slower. Normal visitors are Postal F.27s and Metroliners but Classic Air CV580 ZK-FTA is occasionally present. Larger international cargo aircraft do visit, such as a Singapore Airlines 747 twice a week, and a trans-Tasman 727 operates daily from Sydney. Sightings of An-124s and Il-76s are not unknown but should be regarded as exceptional.

A bus service runs between the airport and the city every half hour, at a cost of about £3.50. Car hire, like so many other services in New Zealand, is quite affordable. Most hotels operate courtesy buses to the airport, despite offering high standard accommodation for about £20 per night.

CHRISTCHURCH
CHC   NZCH   International   6m/9km NW (bus 15 minutes)

With only limited time to visit New Zealand, Christchurch would probably feature as the Number Three destination, after Auckland and Wellington. On the eastern coast of South Island, Christchurch has carved itself a niche as a tourist destination by becoming the gateway to the South Pole. The beautiful Canterbury Plains also attract tourists.

The domestic passenger terminal does have an observation deck. Access is on the first floor, but don't expect any direction signs. Scheduled traffic offers nothing which can't be seen just as well elsewhere but there is a USAF presence featuring the occasional C-5 and C-130. What is unique to Christchurch is Air New Zealand's storage area, where their F.27s await sale. From the passenger terminal, the compound is along Orchard Road. The ANZ maintenance base also carries out work for the RAAF, and sightings of C-130s are fairly common. Mount Cook also have a base here.

Christchurch has another attraction for aviation enthusiasts, to be found at WIGRAM aerodrome: the New Zealand Air Force Museum. South of the city, on Riccarton or Blenheim Road, the entrance is on Main South Road. Buses (Nos 8 and 25) go from Cathedral Square. Open from 10:00am through the week, and from 1:00pm on Sundays, the museum closes at 4:00pm.

HAMILTON
HLZ   NZHN   5m/8km (bus 15 minutes)

The town is on North Island, on the road between Auckland and Rotorua. A detour, for anyone in a car, is essential because it could be a once-in-a-lifetime opportunity. Eagle Airways base their Bandeirante fleet here, and their movements occasionally liven up the day, together with the odd Air New Zealand 737. Residents are unlikely to exceed two dozen, and the displayed Fletcher has no identification marks.

INVERCARGILL
IVC   NZNV   2m/3km(bus 30 minutes)

Served by a good selection of scheduled airliners, Invercargill is the least likely holiday destination in New Zealand. What can be seen at the airport is no different from most other places, with the exception of the Southern Air Islanders. The fence at either side of the terminal offers the chance to get close to ANZ 737s and Ansett 146s, but it is an expensive and time-consuming way of doing so.

LAKE TEKAPO

Not much more than a small airfield, Lake Tekapo is only reached from the outside world by road! A car is therefore essential. Air Safaris operate excellent, and affordable, scenic flights over one of New Zealand's most extraordinarily beautiful areas, in their Nomads and Cessna 207s from this field. Photography is no problem and the staff, in this backwater, are predictably friendly. It is only a short distance (in miles) from the beautiful Lake Tekapo to Glentanner, though the terrain which separates them is rugged and mostly undeveloped. The journey takes about five hours each way! Car rental insurance can mean that some routes, such as this, are not allowed without special high risk cover.

No designator has been found for this field, so it is possibly also known by another name which officially recognized. Further information on the matter would be welcomed.

MILFORD SOUND
MFN   NZMF

Located on the west coast of South Island, this is the heart of New Zealand's fjordland. It is unbelievably scenic, and on a magnificent scale. The quickest way to Milford Sound is by air from Queenstown but coach services are operated. The airport is a very distant rival to the scenery, even for the most commited enthusiast.

For about one hour each day, Milford's airport goes crazy as Mount Cook's various aircraft, and Waterwings Nomads and Cessnas, scurry about. For the rest of the day scenic flights boost the airport's movements, mostly operated by Twin Otters or Islanders.

MOUNT COOK
GTN   Glentanner

Glentanner, down on the shore where the Tasman River enters Lake Pukaki, has a small amount of general aviation and the operations base for The Helicopter Line's Ecureuil scenic flights over the glaciers and around Mount Cook. Anyone in need of something unusual for excitement should enquire at their office about bungee-jumping from a helicopter!

MOUNT COOK
MON   Hermitage

This is the more northerly of the two Mount Cook airfields, used by the Airline to ferry tourists into the spectacular mountain area, called the Southern Alps. For any aviation photographer, this is one of the most wonderful places on earth. Pilatus Porters, Cessna taildraggers and 748s can all be seen at close range, with glacial and mountainous backdrops.

NELSON
NSN   NZNS

As befits a small regional airport, the air is relaxed and informal. Not only are the movements, the biggest of which are SF.340s, easily seen from the terminal area, there are also a few hangars which contain local rarities. The Air New Zealand Link maintenance facility usually has at least one Bandeirante or Metro in evidence and the Helicopters New Zealand base features half a dozen or so inmates. Even without access to the hangar, the helicopters can be seen through the windows. A few other hangars contain a fairly standard selection of light aircraft.

PICTON
PCN   Koromiko

At the head of Queen Charlotte Sound, in the northeast corner of South Island, Picton is only a 30 minute flight across Cook Strait from Wellington in the Flying Dolphin (Float Air) Beaver. Picton, as a destination, offers the chance of an economical floatplane flight and scenery at the other end.

QUEENSTOWN
ZQN   NZQN   Frankton   5m/8km NE

Situated on the beautiful north shore of Lake Wakatipu, Queenstown has become the touring base for the Southern Alps and Fjordland. From a lakeside hotel, the airport is to the east, on the far side of Frankton: a five minute drive or an hour's walk along the picturesque lakeside track. Queenstown needs time, though not a lot of money. A pleasant, friendly hotel, like the Esplanade, charges only £10 a night.

Spectacular all year round, Queenstown is at its best in winter, when the mountains are covered in snow. The airport is not a disappointment. It offers variety, with plenty of operators and aircraft types. There is nowhere around the perimeter where good photos can't be taken. The scheduled 737s, 146s, 748s, Nomads and Cessnas are supplemented by the comings and goings of the flightscene helicopters, and a lot of general aviation. Possibly one of the more notable light aircraft to be found here is Mount Cook's Tiger Moth. Pleasure flights in Tiger Moths and Ag-Cats are big business in this part of the world.

ROTORUA
ROT   NZRO   Lakefront   1m/1.5km N (bus 5 minutes)

Very much one of New Zealand's most popular tourist attractions, Rotorua's volcanic activity is on North Island. Only domestic services operate into this municipal field, though they are Mount Cook 748s and Ansett Dash 8s/BAe 146s, so they have some appeal. More important, they are readily seen and photographed at close quarters from inside the rather basic terminal and around it. Photos are very definitely better in the mornings.

The chainlink fence has mesh large enough for a lens to be poked through. By standing at either side of the terminal, all airliners can be photographed successfully with little trouble. There is also a certain amount of general aviation to be seen. Look out for the fuselage of DC-3 ZK-BKD, opposite the airport entrance.

At the far side of the field is Lake Rotorua, at the edge of which normally sits the Cessna floatplane of Volcanic Air Safaris. JetRangers carry visitors up to the hot springs and geysers, and there is even a helipad on top of the volcano, Mount Tarawera.

Just across the water from the airport is Rotorua town harbour, where Volcanic Air Services operate their Cessna flights.

STEWART ISLAND
SZS

Stewart Island is New Zealand's outpost, off the southern tip of South Island. It is reached from Invercargill by Southern Air's scheduled Islander flights. Pretty though the island is, there is little else to see in aviation terms apart from the occasional Islander.

WANAKA
WKA

At the south end of Lake Wanaka, this is one of New Zealand's most scenic areas. In New Zealand, that means a lot. The airfield is reachable by road or by scheduled flights, mostly from Queenstown. It is from here that Aspiring Air operate their flightscene Cessnas and Islanders. The name is explained by the presence, some miles to the northwest, of the 10,000 feet high Mount Aspiring.

This is very much a ski centre, which means ski and, worse still, après-ski people in large numbers. There is plenty of hotel accommodation which, outside the season, is very affordable.

A new hangar houses the Alpine Fighter Collection, which includes a Spitfire, Corsair, Mustang and Kittyhawk. It's possible that all are airworthy, as the Spitfire has been seen flying. The Tiger Moth and Chipmunk, which also form part of the collection, need a lot of imagination to be considered as fighters!

WELLINGTON
WLG NZWN International 5m/8km SE (bus 30 minutes)

The single runway has water at both ends: Evans Bay to the north and Cook Strait to the south. The aprons to the east and west serve different functions, and it is to the Eastern Apron that scheduled airliners taxi after landing. The two terminals are linked by a covered way. The ANZ facility handles some international services, though most of the traffic is domestic, as at the Ansett building. Unlike Auckland, it is Ansett's terminal which offers a view from its observation deck. Good photography needs a good lens, as the taxiway is a little distant. Afternoons are better when the sun's aspect is much better. Further opportunities for taking photos are offered along the covered link between the terminals. The glass, in some places, can mean problems.

What can be seen from here, as well as from the deck, is the far side of the field. Used mostly by general aviation, it is worth looking out for the presence of the occasional military aircraft, as there is a small base at the left/south end of that ramp. Access to the Western Apron needs transport as it is a long walk. Not visible from the terminal, because it's tucked away in the southeast corner, is the Air New Zealand maintenance area.

The variety of scheduled operators is good, though exactly what constitutes 'busy' is rather subjective. Tranzair Bandeirantes, which rarely visit Auckland, can be seen here regularly. Postal F.27s and Classic Air DC-3s are to be found in the cargo area. One report stated that the domestic terminal teams with life at all times, day and night. This was probably relative to the international flight area, which is quite dead, except when a flight is arriving. Most of the real action at Wellington takes place after 4:30pm in the late afternoon, until about 7:00pm.

The approach road to the airport is called Calabar Road. For anyone with a car, it is perfect for photography. The fence is close enough to the taxiway for taking pictures of anything that approaches the holding point for Runway 34.

WELLINGTON
Porirua Harbour   7m/11km SE

Float Air operate a shuttle bus service from downtown for use by passengers. $NZ65 buys a single ticket on the Flying Dolphin Beaver to Picton, so it's good value. The flight takes only half an hour each way, and pre-booking is advised. The need to record all aspects of Wellington's aviation will involve a trip out to Porirua, and it should be noted that flights are infrequent.

A general aviation field in the Wellington area called PARA PARA is also reported, though it offers little of interest to be seen.

ZS SOUTH AFRICA (Republic of South Africa)
BLOEMFONTEIN
BFN   FABL   J B M Hertzog   6m/9km

A very pleasant airport indeed: apart from huge quantities of movements, it would be difficult to ask for more. The passenger terminal is very modern and comfortable, the cafe on the upper level serves enjoyable cheese & tomato sandwiches with a cold beer, all at easily affordable prices, the staff are extremely friendly and they will open the patio door to the balcony if you wish.

From here, anything that moves can be seen: SAA 737s, Airlink Metros and BAe 146s, and South African Express Dash 8s. Some care must be exercised when taking photographs because of Bloemspruit, the air force base on the far side of the runway. As long as it's made clear that your interest is in civil aircraft, there should be no problem. If you are tempted to take the binoculars (telescopes really aren't a good idea) to the Impalas, Dakotas and other communications aircraft, the situation might become complicated. Life here is suffuciently informal for some agreement to be reached with the security office. Bloemfontein is the sort of place which deserves to be remembered fondly, rather than for some unnecessary altercation with authority, which could have been avoided with a little thought.

When staying in the area, it might also be worth making enquiries about Bloemfontein's general aviation field, NEW TEMPE, of which nothing has been reported.

CAPE TOWN
CPT   FACT   D F Malan   14m/22km E (bus 20 minutes)

South African aviation centres upon Johannesburg but Cape Town supports its own operations, the airport being on the side of Table Mountain remote from the city. The Flitestar passenger terminal has the best facilities for viewing and photographing but lacks subject matter. The departure lounge for passengers travelling to Joburg is accessible, and there is a glazed terrace, where the movements can be seen. Apart from SAA traffic, which can be seen at Jan Smuts, National Airlines/Namakwaland are based locally, and a couple of Comair CV-580s are normally in evidence.

The general aviation area is home to about seventy aircraft, including several executive aircraft. On the far side of the field is a military area, where C-47s are housed. The storage area contains Super Frelons and Piaggio P.166s. Security in South Africa is tight, and applies particularly to their military aircraft. Any attempts at photography could prove counter-productive.

Colourful Court Helicopters moved their headquarters and maintenance base here from Grand Central. A number of the smaller helicopters can be seen being serviced but the S-61s are usually found at the coastal town of George, some distance to the east. In Cape Town, the two locations where Court helicopters are most likely to be seen are in dockland: Bay Road Base should have at least one S-61 and a few JetRangers, while the nearby Victoria & Albert Base often houses a JetRanger used for sightseeing flights. Ysterplaat, in downtown Cape Town, is a military facility which is accessible because of its museum.

DURBAN
DUR   FADN   Louis Botha   12m/19km SSW (bus 20 minutes)

Anyone based in Johannesburg would not find the trip to Durban really worthwhile, as its movements are virtually all 737s of SAA. Court (ex-Republic) Helicopters and Magnum Metros are based here, but action is very slow compared with the rest of the country. Traffic has increased with the opening of the international terminal but it is still unlikely to offer quality prospects for the enthusiast.

DURBAN
VIR   FAVG   Virginia   7m/11km NE

A short way up the coast, this is the main field in Durban for general aviation, which also features one or two local carriers. The large roof terrace allows excellent views of the ramp and runway. About one hundred aircaft are present.

JOHANNESBURG
JNB   FAJS   Jan Smuts International   15m/24km ENE (bus 30 minutes)

South Africa is a very security-conscious country, and anyone wanting to be sure of being able to take photographs at airports, considered to be security areas, should write to the Directorate of Civil Aviation in Pretoria. There are few airports in Africa which could be considered as anything like busy, by European or American standards. Jan Smuts is not an airport where anyone would wish to survey the movements for several days at a time. The area holds much interest, however, but best enjoyed by being on the move.

The general view from the observation deck, above the international terminal, is very good but a little too elevated to allow first class photos. Long focus lenses are essential if the aircraft are to be captured in anything approximating to a side view. Apart from the height, there are other reasons why this deck has not met with universal approval. The glass is normally dirty and a long stay means tired feet, as no seats are provided.

The apron in front of the observation deck is used by long-haul arrivals, with some long-stay aircraft being parked to the left. The SAA 737s park at the far side of the apron, and most other 'local' movements have to be logged while they are on the taxiways. Comair passengers are taken by bus to the cargo apron, where the aircraft are parked, and Air Botswana park close to the domestic terminal, out of sight from the deck.

There is a waving deck in the domestic terminal, essential for anyone wishing to record at close quarters some of the smaller aircraft. Joburg is one of the few airports in the world where spotters (and even photographers) really do have a better view of what's happening than the passengers do.

To the north is the cargo apron, which is visible from the SAA car park. Also to be seen from here are the Comair and Safair facilities, on the opposite side of the runway. The South African Government (DCA) apron is also visible from here, plus a small quantity of general aviation.

The other two areas worthy of note at Jan Smuts are the Atlas aircraft plant, inaccessible on the far side of the field, and the South African Airways museum. The Constellation at the southern end of the ramp forms part of the collection, but the Dove, Viking and Ju-52 are usually kept out of sight. The Junckers makes regular forays into the air: weekend flights on this aircraft, between Rand and Lanseria, can be booked.

Other local airports offer a good range of alternatives: RAND is a major executive and general aviation field, with several helicopter operators based. It should be remembered that many of the aircraft earn their keep on contract work, and South Africa is a very large country, so it would be optimistic to expect fleets lined up on the ramp. Nevertheless the average log for a day at Rand totals as many as three hundred light aircraft.

Rand used to be Johannesburg's main airport, before Jan Smuts was opened. The terminal retains some of its old facilities, including the observation deck, at first floor level. The more interesting aircraft at Rand, such as the military C-47s, C-54s and AT-6s, are in the company of large numbers of rather ordinary Cessnas and Pipers. Viewing from the road presents no problems. One hangar worth watching out for contains up to eight Tiger Moths. Closer inspection can sometimes pose a problem. Ramp access at South African fields generally requires some officially recognized reason.

JOHANNESBURG
HLA   FALA   Lanseria   11m/17km NW

One of Joburg's major general aviation airports, where several executive operators, and three hundred or so other aircraft, are based. These two fields share the majority of international business aircraft movements. A request at the gate for access to the museum collection allows an interesting variety to be seen, including three Vampires, a Lancashire Prospector and a Falcon 50. On the far side of the field is the air force base, whose resident aircraft are mostly Macchi 362/Atlas Impalas, used for training duties.

The main terminal has a restaurant with an outside terrace. Of the huge numbers of aircraft to be logged, there are lots of 3D- registrations, from nearby Swaziland.

JOHANNESBURG
GCJ   Grand Central

Though not an airport, Grand Central is an important general aviation field, also with a viewing area beside the apron. It is normal to see about a hundred aircraft on a visit. One other item of aviation interest is Vic's Viking Garage, which became well-known because of the Viking on display. Vic's Viking Garage would now be better described as Vic's Shackleton Garage, for obvious reasons.

KIMBERLEY
KIM   FAKM   B J Vorster   5m/8km

South African Express operate about eight Dash 8 services daily into Kimberley, which means this is not one of the country's most exciting airports. Whilst the passenger terminal is small and modern, it possesses no viewing facilities, apart from the chance to see what's happening on the apron and runway from inside the main hall. Close to the terminal area are some small hangars which contain military Pumas, some of which might be out on the ramp. For this reason, attempts to take photos would be extremely unwise.

NELSPRUIT
NLP   FANS   3m/5km E

Anyone passing through eastern Transvaal on the way to the Kruger National Park will also pass the town of Nelspruit. The airport is worth the detour, if general aviation and, in particular, South

African Thrush Commanders, are of interest. Larger aircraft are not numerous but the total to be seen is about eighty.

PIETERMARITZBURG

PZB   Oribi

Pietermaritzburg is in Natal province, 30 miles or so northwest of Durban. To find the field, take King Edward Road, off the N3 highway. Whilst there are no scheduled airline operations, the general aviation scene offers good numbers as compensation.

PORT ELIZABETH

PLZ   FAPE   H F Verwoerd   3m/5km S

At the time of the last reported visit, Port Elizabeth had little to commend it, save a rumour that a museum would be opening soon. The small military area has a few C-47s, one of which is almost certain to make the transition from semi-retired to the main exhibit.

PRETORIA

PRY   FAWB   Wonderboom   5m/8km N

Pretoria is only forty miles north of Joburg, so the wealth of aviation facilities in the area are used by both cities. Wonderboom is Pretoria's own field, being located on the north side of the city, remote from Joburg, and it is here that the many DC-3s of Wonderair are based. For access to this facility, a request at the security point in the main terminal should result in being escorted to the ramp.

3B MAURITIUS
PLAISANCE

MRU   FIMP   International   30m/46km E

An idyllic tropical island in the Indian Ocean is sure to attract tourists and the airport (correct name Sir Seewoosagur Ramgoolam International!) is extremely pleasant. The viewing area offers a cafe and shade, overlooking the apron and the runway. Modest photographic equipment produces good results here but a 300mm zoom lens does help. The tinted glass is normally appallingly filthy and only very tall people are able to take photos over the top. Rather than dismiss the airport as a waste of time, exploration will reveal an alternative viewpoint.

The old terminal is now used for cargo operations and served by a road, from which first class photos can be taken of jet aircraft about to touch down or turning before take off. The ATRs, needing less runway, have an unfortunate habit of turning and departing some distance away.

Movements are few but they are interesting. The shuttle to Réunion is operated normally by F.28s and ATR-42s. The Air Mauritius long-haul fleet of A340s, 767ERs and 747SPs call regularly, as is to be expected, and other schedules include an Air Zimbabwe 737. South African Airways make tech stops on their way to and from Asia, occasionally also visiting with 737s, and the French connection is served by a regular Air France flight from Paris.

The airport is remote from many of the resorts, in the southeast corner of the island, where the weather is occasionally not as pleasant as further north. As there are no regular bus services, the journey can be time-consuming, and disappointment at the weather is always a possibility. Worth watching for are the Air Mauritius JetRangers which ferry some of their first class passengers to the more exclusive and remote resorts.

4X ISRAEL (State of Israel)
EILAT

ETH   LLET   J Hozman   1m/1.5km N

Eilat is a resort at the north of the Red Sea, at the end of one of the two prongs which we see on the map, called the Gulf of Aqaba (or Gulf of Eilat, depending on one's political viewpoint). Where most towns might have a Main Street, Eilat has a runway. This is no STOLport: 757s land here, though Arkia Dash 7s provide most of the movements. General aviation does use the airport, ranging from light aircraft to biz-jets, and military Queen Airs visit occasionally.

The prevailing wind is from the north, off the desert, so aircraft make a fairly tight turn to approach on Runway 03, avoiding the airspace of Jordan, Saudi Arabia and Egypt in doing so. Final approach is low over the beach, with the threshold of the runway just across the road. The terminal is not worth investigating because of security restrictions and, anyway, viewing and photography are possible from almost anywhere around the perimeter, mostly through the fence but there are places where views over are possible.

The Hotel Dalia is the place for enthusiasts to stay. It's positioned on the coast with seaviews on one side. Why pay the extra, when the other rooms overlook the end of the runway and the passenger terminal? The view from an upper floor balcony is superb. At the far end of the runway, a road to the right leads to the border with Jordan, half a kilometre away.

OVDA

ETH   LLET   30m/48km N of Eilat

Also spelt Ouvda and Uvda, this is a military airfield in the middle of the Negev Desert, but used also by some civil flights, both scheduled and charter, from Western Europe. It should come as no surprise to read that it isn't exactly user-friendly to spotters. Access to the small single-storey terminal building is via a security gate, for passengers only. Say goodbye to relatives and friends here. Anyone without a ticket turns round and goes back. Passengers enter the security interview area before proceeding to passport control.

As well as the departure lounge there is also a patio where passengers can await their flights. The view is good and photography, stricty in theory, would be fine. Airliners are turned round in reasonably quick time, so the number on the apron is always small. Military transports, mostly C-130s and 707s share the ramp. The subject of this book is civil airfields, rather than detailed coverage of military air bases in politically sensitive regions. The rest of the field is of no consequence, as there isn't much to see. What is of interest is that airliners, when they have landed, shut down their engines whilst on the runway and await a tug to take them to the ramp. Restart occurs on the runway, thereby avoiding blowing half the Negev Desert into the terminal.

Be'er Sheva, some miles to the northwest, is worth the drive for military enthusiasts, as there aren't many other ways they can enjoy themselves in Israel. At nearby Hatzerim is the Israeli Air Force Museum where, for about £2.50, there is access to aircraft from the earliest days up to the current F-4, A-4 and Kfir plus a number of captured aircraft. There are no barriers, so it's rather like being the only person to arrive at a big air show, and having access to the flight line in (usually) perfect weather conditions. Even the scrapyard is worth detailed investigation.

TEL AVIV

TLV LLBG   Ben Gurion   9m/15km SE (bus 35 minutes)

If security in Arab countries is tight it is even more so at Israeli airports. Tel Aviv has two fields, Ben Gurion being the main gateway for international flights. The whole airport is in a security cordon and casual visitors are unlikely to gain access. It is not going to come as a surprise therefore to read that the viewing area has been closed for a long time. What vantage points there are should not be used for photography and, even if permission to take photos has been formally given, it could still lead to trouble. Ben Gurion can be considered as one airport which is definitely not for the enthusiast!

TEL AVIV
SDV   LLSD   Sde Dov   2m/3km N

This is a small field close to the city, with a military base sharing the runway. The majority of scheduled flights are Arkia Dash Sevens providing an air bridge to Eilat, though these are few in number. Arkia does have a maintenance base here, in the company of military helicopters and some army trainers. What general aviation there is in Israel can be seen as well here as anywhere else, and twenty or so light aircraft are visible from the perimeter. By asking permission of the security staff, registrations can be logged but, predictably, photography is out of the question.

JERUSALEM
JRS   LLJR   Atarot   5m/8km N

Another small field, a few miles north of the city, where a dozen or so light aircraft are based. By checking with security staff, watching and logging the movements is normally permitted but of course photography is not allowed. The Arkia Dash Sevens only provide one or two movements each day.

5B CYPRUS (Republic of Cyprus)

LARNACA
LCA   LCLK   5m/8km S

Larnaca is still the principal airport in Cyprus, despite the existence of Paphos. For the spotter, there are enough vantage points around the terminal to ensure that all movements are seen, but the photographer can find the going a bit tough. The terminal is protected from moving aircraft by large red blast screens, so there are no views from inside the building.

Two viewing points remain around the terminal: to the right, the staff car park overlooks the ramp and, on the opposite side, a gate close to the police station allows the Cyprus Airways movements to be seen. This spot is close to the taxi rank and the Cyprus Airways catering buildings. For at least ten years, DC-6 N19CA decayed slowly nearby but its continued survival has not been confirmed.

Cyprus occupies a position of strategic importance, and shares with Athens a hub status where European and arab traffic meets. The civil war in the Lebanon, only 150 miles away, also reflected Larnaca's importance. The Middle East is often politically unstable, so the changing pattern of events will continue to have an effect. Traffic using the airport is variable in quantity and consistency. Some reports note much military activity, and others almost nil. Aeroflot movements, too, range from a regular Tu-154 to a varied range of Il-76s and An-22s. Delivery flights, though irregular, do include a number of short-range airliners on their way from Europe to customers in the Far East.

Scheduled arrivals are nonetheless an interesting mix with 727s and 737s of Alyemda, Libyan, Gulf Air, Egyptair, Royal Jordanian, Yemenia and Saudia all normally featuring amongst the arab visitors. Like Athens, Larnaca is often used for refuelling when long distance flights are adversely affected by winds.

Elsewhere around the perimeter, the southeastern corner is close to the beach. The Flamingo Beach Hotel, despite its rooftop pool and view of the airport, cannot be compared directly with Glyfada's Emmantina, as aircraft pass to the south, and too far away for photography or even reliable reading of registrations. Walking towards the airport along the beach road leads to a row of tavernas and the perimeter fence. From here the Cyprus Airways hangar is seen, and much of the airport. Reports of conflict with the authorities in this area have been variable, and it is likely that regular use of these local bars by enthusiasts will lead to an a gradual relaxation of security measures.

PAPHOS
PFO   LCPH   International   5m/8km SE

Because the name of Paphos features on a few departure boards, it might be assumed to be an airport worthy of a visit. This is definitely not the case, unless a handful of Cyprus Airways and charter movements are sought. Despite the heavy investment that Paphos airport represents, it still appears to handle a minimal quantity of flights. The terminal can remain closed for most of the day if no arrivals are due but, if viewing facilities exist, the combination of the sun in the right direction and a mountainous backdrop would please most photographers. A Caravelle, possibly ex-Air Afrique, has been rotting away at Paphos for some time.

AKROTIRI
AKT   LCRA

Akrotiri, to the south of Limassol, is a relatively busy field, used for practice sorties, trooping flights and technical stops en route to the Middle East, and a Wessex flight is based here. There is also a Vulcan on the dump.

LAKATAMIA, about six miles north of Nicosia, takes some finding as there are no road signs pointing to it. A dirt track leads to the short runway and the majority of the island's fixed wind residents, including the National Guard Islander.

The rest of aviation activity in Greek Cyprus is strictly military, and RAF dominated. In the eastern corner of the Greek part of the island is DHEKALIA, home of the Army Air Corps Alouettes. The strip is close to the UN buffer zone and is one of the few places where these helicopters can be seen. The island's other registered field is GECITKALE (IATA code GEC) which has no aircraft because its purpose is electronic surveillance.

Note also another airport in Cyprus: ERCAN, used by the Turkish Cypriot community on the other part of the island.

5N NIGERIA
KANO
KAN   DNKN   Mallam Aminu International   5m/8km NE

The main terminal overlooks the scheduled airline ramp, which is still a paradise for lovers of BAC 1-11s. Gas Air and Kabo Air examples share the tarmac with Nigerian 737s and A310s. The balcony offers a good view but the use of binoculars and cameras is strictly prohibited because of the military traffic which shares the runway. As with most other parts of Africa, the amount of movements which use the airport on an average day is small.

To the left of the balcony are a few biz-jets and other general aviation twins. This area contains one or two stored aircraft. To the right, and rather more remote, are the other light aircraft. Behind the terminal, a mile or so distant, is the military base where a number of MiG-17s can be seen in rather delapidated condition.

5X UGANDA (Republic of Uganda)
ENTEBBE
EBB   HUEN   22m/34km S

Aircraft to be seen in this part of the world include the Uganda Airways fleet of course, plus Kenya Airways DC-9s and F.27s. Ethiopian 727s and Egyptair aircraft are other foreign visitors, and Sabena DC-10s are the only European airline to be seen three times a week. Safari flight Beech 99s and VIP movements are only occasional. A 'busy' day could see no more than five commercial arrivals.

An interest in recording registrations will be misunderstood, and binoculars should not be used. The use of cameras in Uganda is reported to be illegal, so the consequences of aviation photography requires little imagination.

Entebbe's terminal was built twenty years ago with Yugoslav help. Its moment of fame was when the Israeli Air Force made some unscheduled landings. Now described as being semi-derelict, work is about to refurbish it. Uganda is a poor nation, and the terminal is grossly oversize for its needs. The work will be costly and, even when it's finished, other European carriers might not be wooed to land here, as the runway is also in need of urgent repair.

Uganda's military activity, such as it is, takes place at Entebbe: the hangar area at the north end of the field contains the remains of the air force and the Uganda Police Wing, also defunct. Access is not recommended, as those in charge have been described as hostile. To end on a less serious note, visitors may be surprised to see a Uganda Airways Trislander still in use, as a home!

5Y KENYA (Republic of Kenya)
MOMBASA
MBA   HKMO   Moi International   8m/13km SW (bus 25 minutes)

The best way to get to the airport is to catch the Kenya Airways or No.6 bus from downtown, and the reward is an excellent view from the rooftop observation deck, next to the cafe. The security staff use this cafe for their breaks, so they are used to people showing an active interest in aviation.

Traffic doesn't match the interest however. Most of the few movements are Kenya Airways flights to Nairobi. All representative types can be seen here but the A310s, travelling to London, are rarely present in daylight hours. Most interest is generated by Air Tanzania F.27s, the only foreign carrier of regular note, and the F.27s and DC-9s of Kenya Airways, which are very much local to this part of the world.

NAIROBI
NBO   HKNA   Jomo Kenyatta International   8m/13km SE (bus 30 minutes)

Also known as Embakasi, this is a quiet but interesting airport. A visit should be timed to coincide with the several unusual scheduled movements, as there can be long periods during the day, especially in the afternoons, when nothing happens except the occasional movement by the resident Kenya Airways fleet. Apart from sporadic European traffic, which normally passes through at unsociable hours, there is a good selection of airline traffic to be seen.

The main terminal is semi-circular, with nose-in parking for most of the visiting airliners which use the jetties, if they are working. There is a good waving gallery atop the building but opening hours are erratic, to say the least; on some days it doesn't open at all. Access is via a door at the front of the terminal complex, which opens to a stairway. Photography is only possible when aircraft are on the move, as the viewing area doesn't extend to edge of the roof. Thus, most of the aircraft are semi-hidden from view by the roof when they park at their stands.

When either the police or military personnel are in evidence, photography should not be attempted. The consequences are usually protracted negotiations about what might be best described as on-the-spot fines, a.k.a. cash transactions, or sampling the pleasures of a cell for a short while. Authority, in this part of the world, can be surprisingly unsophisticated. Do not, for example, assume that someone in uniform knows the difference between a camera and a pair of binoculars!

Small visiting aircraft park to the right-hand side of the terminal, near to any long-stay airliners up to 727 size, and the Aeroflot Tu-154, Royal Swazi F.28, Airstar Zanzibar YS-11 and Air Madagascar 737 are usually found here. Unfortunately, many of these aircraft are not very photogenic when parked but reasonable shots can be obtained from the fence, next to the terminal. The YS-11, which arrives late in the day, possibly after the deck closes. In this event it is worth seeking out the restaurant which isn't in the terminal at all but in the administration block opposite. The view from here is excellent.

The cargo terminal has its own access road, some distance from the passenger facilities. There is often something of interest parked on the ramp, usually in the company of the more familiar (to European eyes) movements, such as German Cargo DC-8-73Fs and Air France 747Fs, which are regular visitors.

Irregular visitors, largely resulting from the strife in nearby Rwanda and Burundi, are the many United Nations flights operating through Nairobi (in early 1995). The USAF make up the bulk of the movements, mostly with C-5s and C-141s but the CIS states are doing their bit to help. An-26s are often to be seen.

Across from the passenger terminal (on the other side of the runway) lies the modest Kenya Airways maintenance base with a small military compound adjacent, containing about twenty Hughes 500s. The remains of the Tradewinds CL-44 have now gone but, as compensation, a Boeing 720 fuselage is used for crew-training. The derelict C-119 N3267U is parked near the terminal. It was abandoned by the aircrew when they didn't get paid, and has remained here ever since. The maintenance side of the field is hardly worth visiting, as both access and photography are difficult, but a Uganda Airlines F.27, sometimes parked inside the Kenya Airways hangar is worth watching out for.

The assortment of visiting airlines is good, with 737s of Air Madagascar, Air Tanzania, Cameroon Airlines and Air Zaire (with luck!), Saudia A300-600s, Uganda Airlines F.27s plus Air Malawi and Royal Swazi F.28s. Smaller visitors are quite limited in number but the interest factor is a compensation: the Malawi Citation is a regular, and foreign military visitors are often seen. It can't be stressed too strongly that any attempts at photography should be discounted totally if any police or military personnel are nearby. In several parts of Africa, the political scene is volatile. When times are tense, often unkown to a foreigner, there can be heavy clampdowns.

NAIROBI

WIL	HKNW	Wilson	2m/3km S

Some ten miles across the small but excellent Nairobi National Park from Jomo Kenyatta, lies the much smaller Wilson Airport. Just before reaching the city, a winding lane leads off the main road, up to Wilson which is only two or three miles from the city centre. There are probably over two hundred aircraft based here, so it is a good field for the enthusiast in pursuit of general aviation.

Hangars run almost the entire length of the 4500 feet runway and, with Kenya's climate, they are almost always open during the day (except at weekends). Access to the apron is normally possible, and permission should be sought. Achieved one way or another (!), an escorted walk will reveal a hive of activity, but the Kenya Police Air Wing should be given a very wide berth, as the local security personnel can be unpredictable. The Geosurvey hangar, at the far end of the field, should also be treated with some care, with permission being necessary to walk inside. Up to ten specially configured Cessna Titans, a Twin Otter and sometimes their Challenger are to be seen.

Star attractions abound here: numerous Islanders and Beavers of the East African Locust Control and rarer types, plus a wonderful selection of non-Kenyan residents undergoing major maintenance.

With the beautiful view down from Wilson, over the wildlife park and across to the Ngong Hills, there can be few better places to sit outside than the bar of the aero club as the sun goes down, while an endless stream of twin aircraft arrive home after their day out at safari camps. An alternative is to find somewhere in the Air Kenya terminal. Loitering around the perimeter road, around the hangar area is not a very good idea.

6V SENEGAL (Republic of Senegal)
DAKAR
DKY   GOOY   Yoff   11m/17km NW

Dakar boasts a sizeable airfield which gained some prominence and prestige when its runway was constructed to handle Air France Concordes on their way between Paris and Rio de Janeiro. This service is no more, but the runway remains, and is now the emergency landing strip for any Space Shuttle suffering problems a few minutes after lift-off from Florida!

The terminal is not very good for viewing, although a landside bar/ restaurant in the terminal offers a restricted view of the main apron. A small light aviation area, with about twenty or so residents, is located just along from the terminal and is usually accessible. Any airliner taxiing to or from the terminal passes this area and can be photographed with the average zoom lens . . . in theory.

An excellent panoramic view of the field is possible from the Meridien Hotel complex, a mile away from the terminal. A stay here allows the latest arrivals to be checked before heading to the terminal for a closer look. Frequent movements from Ouagadougou are a lone F.28, plus one or two Nord 262s and HS748s. In this part of the world, frequent means about three times a week! F.28s of Air Mauretanie, Air Guinée Dash7s/An-24s/737s call about twice a week but the Air Zaire flight has a habit of being cancelled.

The Ghanaian DC-9 and Nigerian 737s are regular, and the Air Afrique fleet is, officially, resident here. In reality, it spends much of its time at Charles de Gaulle, though Air Senegal's resident fleet includes a couple of HS748s and Twin Otters.

Military activity comprises resident F.27s, Twin Otter and Magister movements, and the derelict Air Force C-47s are still present. Regular visits are made by USAF C-141s, and RAF VC-10s refuel on their way to the Falklands, while French Jaguars and Transalls are based.

6Y JAMAICA
KINGSTON
KIN   MKJP   Norman Manley International 12m/19km SE

A spit of land stretches out into the bay, east of town, on which the airport has been built. The runway, 12/30, sits on reclaimed land and is almost entirely surrounded by water. At its northeast corner is the apron and terminal.

The view from the terminal's rooftop terrace is southerly, and very reminiscent of Newcastle: scheduled airliners park at either side of the central single-storey finger which is built out into the centre of the ramp. The fencing which encloses the terrace is, however, something of a major problem. People are kept at a distance from it, so it's impossible to take photos. Having been disappointed by the roof, photographers are bound to seek vantage points elsewhere. To save time and energy, they would do best to get on a plane and fly somewhere else.

Outside the terminal, landside, a right turn leads past Air Jamaica's maintenance facility, where nothing is visible from the road. Beyond it, however, is the rest of the old apron which is now used to store impounded aircraft. Drug smugglers have been caught using a DC-3, a Convair 440, a couple of Queen Airs and some Cessna twins. Behind the compound is the Defence Force ramp, with a brace of Islanders and a Cessna 210, but not within range of a camera lens. Next to the fire station is a US-registered DC-3, showing distinct signs of old age. For anyone who is determined to prove the findings wrong, it will be tempting to follow the road to Nelson's old barracks at Fort Royal, since it looks promising. Airborne movements are visible but they are too distant for photos.

Kingston's traffic is mostly Air Jamaica obviously but American, TACA, BWIA and British Airways appear in fits and starts. In other words, anyone who wants photos of Caribbean aircraft in exotic surroundings, Manley Airport is definitely the wrong destination.

KINGSTON

Tinson Pen   6m/9km NW

From downtown Kingston, head out towards Spanish Town and the airport is on the edge of Kingston, to the north side of the road. Of the sixty or so light aircraft on the field, many are US-registered. A dump contains half a dozen singles and a Beech 18. The passenger terminal offers the chance to see, at close quarters, the visiting Trans Jamaica Do228s. It is adviseable to seek permission before taking photos.

7O YEMEN (Republic of Yemen)
ADEN
ADE   OYAA   Khormaksar   6m/9km NE

Obtaining a visa to visit the Yemen is a difficult business, and possession of one doesn't even guarantee entry into the country! There has been internal strife for a long time and it would be a hardy enthusiast who set off in search of Alyemda aircraft at home. The squalid old terminal has been replaced by a new one, with just as few facilities for viewing proceedings.

Left of the new terminal is the old one and to the right is the open fronted Alyemda hangar with a few aircraft parked beside it. Some derelict DC-3s and DC-6s would make ideal subjects for first-hand research, if conditions were friendlier. The VIP Tu-154 7O-ACT is usually parked outside on the main ramp.

The only chance of realistic viewing will be fleeting, by sitting on the left of the departing aircraft and hoping it takes off to the east. The taxiway leads past the derelict machines, then past the Air Force transport ramp (with a dozen An-12s/An-26s) and the MiGs etc which live in the large, old RAF hangars. At the other side of the runway threshold is the military dump, which must contain a fascinating collection, but the road which passes all these facilities and the end of the runway, with the sea on the other side, will remain uncharted territory for many years to come. The only hope is to put a 100-300mm zoom lens on the camera and snap away on departure.

SANA'A
SAH   OYSN   International   8m/13km

At 7,000 feet above sea level, Sana'a is higher than Denver and the Yemenia publicity material makes a big deal about Sana'a being the oldest capital city in the world. The airport's passenger terminal seems to be one of the oldest too! Squalid it may be, but it does have an observation deck, with a good view of most of the proceedings.

The title 'International' is rather misleading to the unwary as it suggests a greater emphasis on foreign traffic than is really the case. Visiting airlines are few and far between, with occasional visits by Air France A300s and Aeroflot plus a handful of flights per week from middle eastern airlines: Saudia A300s and Gulf Air 737s, Ethiopian and Kuwaiti 727s and Egyptair 707 or 767 flights take place but mostly the airport can be considered as handling domestic traffic with the odd international movement.

The deck overlooks the 'domestic' ramp where the Dash 7s park. The heavy-weight traffic (everything else) parks on the apron to the right and can be easily seen, although at a greater distance. The 'No photography' signs are placed at strategic points along the balcony and, with machine gun-equipped guards to enforce the rule, it seems wise to comply. It doesn't say that binoculars are also out of the question but their use may also lead to a misunderstanding.

The prime reason for the sensitivity is the airfield's role as headquarters for the Yemen Arab Republic Air Force. MiGs, assorted Sukhois, F-5s, An-24s, An-26s and Mi-8s are all resident, bearing very small serials in arabic (if at all) so the military presence is a significant one.

The base is close to the terminal but hidden from view by several large buildings. From outside the terminal, a high concrete wall maintains privacy. If flying with an airline whose flight attendants are not concerned with Yemeni security (e.g. Air France) a window seat on the left-hand side of the aircraft should guarantee a closer inspection while taxiing out. The Antonovs and C-130s are normally within range of a 135-200mm lens.

At the other end of the field lies the Yemenia hangar and the civilian dump, sealed off by a security barrier which can be regarded as impassable. On the other side of the gate is a host of treats, such as the rare Yemenia VIP 727, the two immaculate DC-3s with Yemen Airways titles but flown for the air force, three DC-6s, an Alyemda DC-3 and the semi-derelict 707.

Anyone wandering around any part of the airport, including around the passenger terminal area, should exercise extreme caution. There are military personnel everywhere and they are particularly sensitive about Iraqi Il-76 flights, and others, which fly very mysterious missions into Sana'a. At the end of the runway lie the remains, almost complete, of an Il-18 which failed to approach in the correct manner!

TA'IZZ
TAI   OYTZ   Al-Janad (or Ganed)

Visitors to the Yemen should also remember that Ta'izz, to the south of the country, has another three DC-6s, two of which still bear Yemen Airlines titles and colours. In this part of the world it would be wasteful to build a runway without using it for military purposes. Apart from the hulks, the only aviation interest at Ta'izz would come from the air force, as almost all the airliners operate from Sana'a.

As with anywhere else in this country, active interest in aircraft is best confined to the departure lounge or the window of the aircraft.

7P LESOTHO (Kingdom of Lesotho)
MASERU
MSU   FXMM   Moshoeshoe International   13m/21km

As long as quantities of aircraft are not the reason for visiting airports, the trip to Maseru can be very worthwhile indeed. The setting is quite idyllic: a splendidly modern terminal nestling among the beautiful Lesotho mountains. There is an open air viewing gallery upstairs, with a glazed screeen which is kept perfectly clean. There appears to be no problem using a camera but the reason could be that there are only four Lesotho Airways F.27 flights each day.

7Q MALAWI (Republic of Malawi)
LILONGWE

LLW	Kamazu	14m/22km

Like many other African airports, only the supreme enthusiast would consider a visit here, as there isn't really enough activity to justify leaving Britain. The terminal is a beautiful building, modern in the extreme, with an open balcony at first floor level, though a little remote from the apron for really good photos. Traffic is extremely slow, and the Air Malawi aircraft visit South Africa and Zimbabwe, and so are better seen there.

8P BARBADOS
CHRIST CHURCH

BGI	TBPB	Grantley Adams International	7m/11km E (bus 30 mins)

Barbados is located just east of the Windward Islands, and its neighbours are nations in their own right. Grantley Adams is normally referred to as Bridgetown, although official sources differ, preferring to call it Christ Church. Movements at the airport may not be numerous but they do feature a very interesting array of registrations. The Leeward Islands are only 150 miles or so to the north, so LIAT's fleet of island hoppers are regular visitors. HS748s, Islanders, Twin Otters and Dash 8s operate the majority of scheduled services, though Air St Vincent/Mustique Airways Islanders are also much in evidence. Charter traffic features several American and Canadian carriers, as well as Britannia 767s, though exotic visitors can be very special indeed. Cubana operate Il-18s or Tu-154s twice a week, Varig 737s appear (but usually at night) and such rarities as Aerosucre Caravelles and smaller aircraft of the Brazilian Air Force can be seen.

   The terminal offers few vantage points and the apron can be too cluttered for photography, but LIAT and general aviation can be seen through the fence, between the terminal and the cargo sheds. Fortunately, anyone with a car can enjoy the perimeter. From the highway, a left turn onto Wilcox Road (at the garage) passes the holding point at the end of the runway before leading to the Aero Services hangar.

   The ground next to the airport's solitary hangar offers trouble-free viewing and photography, though the runway alignment means that quality portraits are best obtained, using 135-200mm focal length, in the morning.

9G GHANA
ACCRA

ACC	DGAA	Kotoka	6m/9km SW

A visit to Kotoka on a Monday, Wednesday or Friday evening reveals a fair number of European heavies passing through. They give the impression of a bustling international airport . . . it is misleading. At all other times, there is very little happening. A scattering of movements from Ethiopia, Nigeria and Egypt offer passing interest. Even the home-based Ghana Airways fleet is small. The cost of access to the roof terrace is negligible and the view is excellent, but everything else is bad news. Binoculars and cameras are forbidden by law, as a means of giving its enforcement officers the chance to supplement their income. Bribery is known as 'dash' and care should be exercised when trying to reach agreement. It's best to listen for the word, rather than suggest it. A smooth tongue is also crucial to successful negotiations.

   With aircraft such as an Air Afrique F.100 landing on the runway, time may be at a premium. The reason for the tight restrictions is the military presence at the far side of the runway, with mostly transports in evidence, from Skyvans to Fokkers, plus a sprinkling of MB 326s.

9H MALTA (Republic of Malta)
MALTA

MLA   LMML   Luqa   3m/5km W (bus 20 minutes)

The old terminal has become the cargo and executive terminal, having been replaced by a new passenger building. This is light and airy, with fountains in the courtyard between the arrivals and departures sections. The top floor is occupied by the observation deck, and fronted with glass. Refreshments are cheap enough and the view is first class. So, what's the catch? Apart from there only being a modest amount of traffic, and the glass making life a bit difficult for photographers, there is none.

One of the regular departures from the old terminal is the Mi-8, wet leased from Aeroflot (replacing LZ-CAP). It operates a ferry link with the nearby island of Gozo, and is also used for pleasure flights. The cost, starting at ten Maltese pounds, is extremely reasonable for a 25 minute flight.

Serious photographers nevertheless can still make their way along the road to the underpass which leads to the far side of the runway. A left turn after the tunnel leads to a good location. Depending on aircraft size, 135-300mm focal length allows moving aircraft to be photographed. Further along this road ex-Mauretanian Super Constellation 5T-TAF has just about reached the end of its life, being in extremely poor condition.

Also on this side of the field, reached by turning in the opposite direction after passing through the tunnel, is the Maltese Defence Force with its rather strange collection: an Agusta-Bell 47, a JetRanger and Ecureuil are hardly a rationalised fleet of helicopters, and Cessna Bird Dogs provide fixed wing assistance in times of need.

The occasional visit to Luqa by an Italian Air Force G222 is connected with their Agusta-Bell 212s which carry out sonar-dipping sorties in Mellieha Bay, north of the island. At the side of Runway 06/24, reached by passing this area (part military base, part disusued quarry) are the remains of an Air Malta 720, used for fire crew training.

The general aviation community is served by its own facility in the north eastern corner of the field, on the far side of Runway 06/24 from the other facilities.

SAFI
SFI

The field is close to Luqa, just to the southeast. From the airport it is a short distance past the remains of the Super Connie. Whether one would wish to walk there from Luqa's rerminal is another matter. In one corner are the Caribous of MIACO. They are visible, but only just, from the airport's observation deck. At least two appear to be airworthy and can operate from Safi's short runway. The others are slowly being dismantled. Also to be seen are a few light aircraft, including three camouflaged Bulldogs.

Hal-Far is now an industrial estate. The derelict DC-6 and three DC-3s from Safi are still present. At least two will be burnt but their remains will join those of Eisenhower's Beech 18 N946F, still to be seen. A scrapyard to the south of Hal-Far, known as Brolli-Lane, is the last resting place of two C-54s, a Beech 18 and the remains of Canberra WT482.

The small field which used to be worth a look was TA'QUALI, close to Mdina. This is now the site for the national stadium and serves in the meantime as a so-called craft market, if that name applies to a place where cheap and tatty goods are sold at offensive prices to gullible tourists.

The War Museum, to complete the picture of Malta, is at Fort Saint Elmo, in Valletta. It houses the wreckage of a Spitfire and a BF109 plus 'Faith', one of the three famous Gladiators. It carries the serial N5520 but is also reported in some publications as N5519.

9K KUWAIT (State of Kuwait)
KUWAIT

| KWI | OKBK | International | 10m/16km S |

No entry in this book for an airport illustrates more vividly the volatile nature of Middle Eastern affairs than Kuwait. Even before 1990/91 Kuwait was partly a military field, without observation facilities. Many of the scheduled flights pass through Kuwait mostly during the night. The only post-war report was succinct: the place is a dump!

9M MALAYSIA (Federation of Malaysia)
KUALA LUMPUR

| KUL | WMKK | Subang International | 14m/22km SW |

Visitors to Singapore soon realise that the air bridge which operates to Kuala Lumpur generates plenty of traffic and passengers. The distance between the two airports is relatively modest, by Asian standards, (the flight taking less than an hour) so this may be considered as a day trip from Singapore.

The larger Malaysian airliners which are to be seen at Singapore, A300s and 737s, are obviously also present on their home tarmac. The appeal lies more in the presence of Malaysian Air Charter Skyvans, Islanders and Do228s, and the colourful Pelangi Air Do228s/Fokker 50s.

Terminal 1, for international traffic, sits between the road and the runway, and beside it are Terminals 2 (closed for renovation) and 3, the domestic building. Beyond Terminal 3 is a taxiway over the road which leads to the cargo apron and maintenance hangars, effectively placed behind the terminal area. Between Terminals 1 and 2 is a hangar used by MAS for 737s and Fokker 50s. Directly opposite the terminals, on the far side of the runway and partially obscured by trees, is the military base where C-130s are regularly seen.

All movements can be seen from the windows of the newly renovated domestic Terminal 3 but photography can sometimes be difficult when aircraft are parked at it. For example, a fine photo of a Pelangi F.50 is possible but, once it is parked, the view of the runway is partially obscured. It may therefore be necessary to spend an equal amount of time in Terminal 3, which allows views and photos of all the other (larger) movements. A free shuttle bus operates between arrivals levels of the domestic and international terminals but walking allows a sight of the general aviation ramp, usually with a few biz-jets present. It should be remembered that it is over a mile between the two terminals, so walking can be hard work in the Malaysian heat.

Walking is, unfortunately, essential to see what Subang has to offer: the cargo apron and MAS maintenance facility are side by side, with a grassy bank handily placed for the photographer. The Airod Sendirian Berhad ramp should be treated with some caution, as some of their customers are military. C-130s are regular visitors (it's a Lockheed joint venture) as are exotic helicopters. Beyond the Airod area, the walk is parallel to the runway, with plenty of movements, though dominated by the MAS 737s.

To the south of the city is the old airport, now used as a helicopter field and the base for the Royal Flight. Close scrutiny is not recommended, as there is a significant military presence.

9V SINGAPORE (Republic of Singapore)
SINGAPORE

| SIN | WSSS | Changi International | 12m/19km E (bus 25 minutes) |

Widely regarded as the most sophisticated and civilised airport in the world, Changi is without equal. Because it was designed from the start to be able to cope with future needs, the airport is already too big for the enthusiast to have a relaxing day. The rapid expansion of Changi has not stopped with the opening of Terminal Two. Already an additional seventeen gates are being added to this terminal. A third terminal will be needed by 1997/8, and the CAAS are renowned for matching need with investment. By the next century, Singapore will be a very large airport.

The third storey viewing gallery was designed to face in three directions, but pressure for office space caused the loss of the east and west wings. What remains faces north onto only a small portion of apron space, though there are views at each end to the runways, and several stands. An airband radio is the only means of ensuring that some significant movements are seen during the day, but the observation area is not the place from which to see anything land on Runway 02R before it taxis to its stand, usually at Terminal Two.

As is common in the Far East, international traffic reaches its peak after dark. Qantas, for example, use Singapore as their Asian hub and there can be, in an average evening, two 747s and four 767s on the ground at once. A recipe for frustration is guaranteed, although the daytime movements should provide some exciting moments for even the hardened traveller. Royal Brunei and the Malaysian Air Bridge have, however, moved into Terminal Two.

Some consolation for the restricted views of stands is offered by Singapore Airlines' maintenance base, the long stay north apron and the cargo aprons, all north of the main ramp. It must be stressed that daytime traffic is not brisk, so patience, time and an airband radio are needed to get the most from Singapore.

At the perimeter, a turn off Airport Boulevard, the approach road, leads to Changi Coast Road. There are views of aircraft using runway 02R, and the road continues past Singapore Airlines' service base. This can be one of the few places offering a sight of the aircraft parked at the executive terminal, though the distance between ramp and road is substantial.

Terminal Two is served by the Skytrain, a monorail link with the original Terminal One. If the viewing mall stays open (which is in some doubt) what can be seen is, of course, restricted to just one side of the field, though photographers will welcome the chance of some different views of taxying aircraft, particularly when Runway 02R sees so much use. Because the view faces east, traffic landing on 02L and using stands on the west apron cannot be seen. The remote stands are out of sight from all internal vantage points, and busiest after dark. As Changi International grows, so does the frustration for the enthusiast, but what can be seen and photographed is still worth the trip.

There have been occasional instances where security personnel have expressed disapproval of photography. This is due to the presence of the military base, containing . . . hardly front-line combat aircraft. In the northwest corner of the field, off Upper Changi Road, and screened from the terminal by trees, is a ramp which usually contains four or five Skyvans but independent means of transport is essential to get close.

The cost of living, even for a tourist, need not be high in Singapore. Car hire, however, is not cheap. For anyone anxious to see as much of possible of the island, shopping around for a keen price is advisable. Bus service 390 from Orchard Road serves the airport, though the excellent rapid transit around town does not, as yet. The other 'civil' field of any note is located towards the north of the island . . .

SINGAPORE

QPG	Paya Lebar	11m/17km NE

The number 92 bus links Orchard Road with the community of Paya Lebar but the airfield is some way out, if on foot. The terminal facilities are closed, as are most of the associated buildings. It can be safely assumed that Paya Lebar is no longer an airport of any description.

Because there are several ramps used only, it would appear, for storing withdrawn aircraft, a pedestrian with a notebook, or worse, a camera and binoculars, would be bound to attract unwanted attention. The word 'bound' suggests a stronger treatment than may be the case, but it would be foolish to run risks, just to be able to log a handful of T-33s.

SINGAPORE
XSP   WSSL   Seletar   12m/19km N

To visit Seletar, a hire car is preferable. Arriving by taxi is not necessarily a good idea, largely because it will be difficult to find another taxi to take you out. Nominally under military control, it might be necessary to check in at the security hut. There are forms to fill in and, possibly, cameras to be handed over. In practice, the camera can be quietly retained but seeking out the military areas might be injudicious.

There is usually little or no movement at Seletar but there is usually plenty to be seen. AirFast have a maintenance base here, with an assortment of aircraft parked outside their hangar. Between the two Dowty hangars is a security hut, and requests for access to the ramp have been successful. What can be seen is anyone's guess. It's purely a matter of luck. The Bell Helicopters concession usually has an assortment of 212s and 206s in crates and various stages of assembly.

The military presence includes C-130s and a few trainers, though the US forces use Seletar as their main point of access to Singapore. The fire dump still contains the remains of what could be either a Convair or a Martin 404, and an unmarked fuselage next to the tower might be an ex-AirFast Grumman HU-16B (PK-AOH?). Speculation about aircraft identities is, however, hardly the purpose of this book.

AIRPORT RADIO FREQUENCIES

The publication in this book of airband radio frequencies must, on no account, be taken to mean that the use of portable airband radios is sanctioned or even recommended. It must be emphasised that local restrictions in several parts of the world can be strict, with penalties to match. Extreme caution must be exercised in some countries where security is taken seriously. If in doubt, ask.

The tables show basic information about most of the airports referred to in this book. The airport's name is often abbreviated and is shown with its IATA (3-letter) and ICAO (4-letter) codes, where applicable. Wherever possible, the exact location of the airport is given. Available information is variable. For example, the location for Ushuaia in Argentina is correct to within five miles but a 747, parked on Stand 12 at Buenos Aires Ezeiza can be pinpointed to within a few feet. (It's actually 34º 48' 9"S 58º 32' 4"W!)

The runway information is limited for reasons of space. That shown refers only to the longest runway, though in many instances it might be the only runway. Headings and lengths (in feet) are shown.

Radio frequencies are given for Approach and Tower only, for two reasons, the more important being space restrictions. Landing aircraft are normally told to contact Ground on 121.8 or 121.9. These are widely used, throughout the world, with only a few airports using different frequencies. Those variations can be heard locally. The number of radio frequencies which change throughout the year is appreciable, especially when there are several hundred airports in this book. Strict accuracy for a two-year period is therefore impossible.

Every effort has been made to supply the most comprehensive range of information at the time of printing and readers who wish to keep it up to date will need to invest in a number of publications. An example is the British Airways Aerad supplement: this is available in four volumes for the Western Hemisphere, Europe & Middle East, Africa, and Asia/Australasia & Pacific. When purchased from anyone other than British Airways, they are much cheaper because they are no longer current. Many of the changes will inevitably include radio frequencies.

#	IATA	ICAO	Town/city	Name	St/country	location	R/W	length	APPROACH		TOWER	
221	AAL	EKYT	Aalborg		OY	5706N 0951E	08L/26R	8694	123.875	120.7	118.3	122.1
221	AAR	EKAH	Aarhus	Tirstrup	OY	5618N 1037E	10R/28L	8885			122.5	
10	YXX	CYXX	Abbotsford		BC C	4901N 12222W	07/25	8000			119.4	
71	ABZ	EGPD	ABERDEEN	Dyce	G	5712N 0212W	16/34	6001	132.7		118.1	126.3
251	ABJ	DIAP	Abidjan	Port Buet	TU	0515N 0356W	03/21	8858	120.4		118.1	121.1
5		OMAD	Abu Dhabi	Bateen	A6	2426N 5427E	13/31	10500	119.9		127.5	
5	AUH	OMAA	Abu Dhabi	International	A6	2426N 5439E	13/31	13451	124.4		118.5	
265	ACA	MMAA	Acapulco	Juan Alvarez Intl	XA	1645N 9945W	10/28	10824	119.9		118.6	
291	ACC	DGAA	Accra	Kotoka	9G	0336N 0010W	03/21	9800	119.1		120.5	
253	ADL	APAD	Adelaide		SA VH	3457S 13832E	05/23	8294	124.2		124.6	
253	ADL	APPF	Adelaide	Parafield	SA VH	3448S 13838E	03R/21L	4429	118.7		118.7	
289	ADE	OYAA	Aden	Khormaksar	7O	1250N 4502E	08/26	10168	135.7		118.3	
213	BQN	TJBQ	Aguadilla	Rafael Hernandez	PR N	1829N 6708W	08/26	11700	125.5		122.1	
182	CAK	KAKR	Akron	Canton Regional	OH N	4055N 8126W	05/23	7600	122.1		126.0	121.5
285	AKT	LCRA	Akrotiri		5B	3435N 3259E	10/28	8994	118.1		118.7	
252	AKX	UATT	Aktyubinsk		UN	5015N 5711E						
249	AEY	BIAR	Akureyri		TF	6539N 1805W	02/20	6496	118.2		126.1	129.15
6	AAN	OMAL	Al Ain	International	A6	2416N 5536E	01/19	13123	119.85	121.8	120.6	
172	ALM	KALB	Alamogordo	White Sands	NM N	3250N 10559W		7005	125.0		118.3	
175	ALB	KALB	Albany	County	NY N	4244N 7348W		7200	121.1		118.3	
172	ABQ	KABQ	Albuquerque	International	NM N	3503N10635W	08/26	13375	125.35	123.9	118.2	120.3
74	ACI	EGJA	Alderney	The Blaye	G	4942N 0213W	08/26	2887			118.35	
253	ASP		Alice Springs		NT VH	2349S 13354E	12/30	8000			119.5	
188	ABE		Allentown	BethlehemEaston	PA N	4039N 7527W	08/26	7600			118.1	
43	LEI	LEAM	Almeria		EC	3651N 0222W	04/22	7874			119.8	
195	AMA	KAMA	Amarillo	Air Terminal	TX N	3513N 10142W	06/24	13500	128.9	124.4	118.1	
99	ADJ	OJAM	Amman	Marka	JY	3158N 3559E	08R/26L	10781	128.9		127.2	
98	AMM	OJAI	Amman	Queen Alia	JY	3143N 3600E	09/27	12008	121.2		118.6	
224	AMS	EHAM	AMSTERDAM	Schiphol	PH	5218N 0446E	05/23	11330	118.6	131.15	118.3	126.4
106	EDF	PAED	Anchorage	Elmendorf	AK N	6115N 14948W		10000	118.6	119.1		
106	MRI	PAMR	Anchorage	Merrill	AK N	6112N 14950W		4000				
104	ANC	PANC	ANCHORAGE	International	AK N	6114N 14948W	06L/24R	10900	124.6	119.1		
			Anchorage	International						126.4		
193	AND		Anderson	County	SC N	3429N 8242W	04L/22R	5000	127.5			
49	NCY	LFLP	Annecy	Meythet	F	4556N 0606E	11/29	5348				
220	ANR	EBAW	Antwerp	Deurne	OO	5111N 0428E		4839			121.4	119.7

	IATA	ICAO	Town/city	Name	St/country	location	R/W	length	APPROACH	TOWER
211	ATW		Appleton	Outagamie County	WI N	4415N 8831W		7000	126.3	
186	ADM	KADM	Ardmore	Airpark	OK N	3418N 9701W		7200	128.1	
213	ABO		Arecibo		PR N	1827N 6640W		3975		
130	ASE		Aspen	Pitkin County	CO N	3913N 10652W		7000	128.5	
244	ATH	LGAT	ATHENS	Hellenikon	SX	3754N 2344E	15L/33R	11483	119.1 121.4	118.1 119.3 122.1
150	PDK		Atlanta	deKalb-Peachtree	GA N	3353N 8418W	02R/20L	5000		
150	FTY		Atlanta	Fulton County	GA N	3347N 8431W	8R/26L	5800	121.0	
150	ATL	KATL	ATLANTA	Wm B Hartsfield	GA N	3338N 8426W	09L/27R	11889	118.35 127.25	119.1 123.85 119.5
274	AMZ	NZAR	Auckland	Ardmore	ZK	3702S 17458E	07/25	4800	118.1	120.1
274	AKL	NZAA	AUCKLAND	International	ZK	3701S 17447E	05/23	10797	120.5 124.3	118.7 124.3
151	AGS		Augusta	Bush Field	GA N	3322N 8157W		8000	126.8	
152	DNL		Augusta	Daniel Field	GA N	3327N 8202W		3877	126.8	119.3
130	FTG		Aurora	Front Range	CO N	3947N 10433W		8000		
195	AUS	KAUS	Austin	Robert Mueller	TX N	3018N 9742W	13R/31L	7200	124.9	
50	AVM	LFMV	Avignon	Caumont	F	4354N 0454E	17/35	4396		
253	AYQ	YAYE	Ayers Rock	Connellan	VH	2511S 13058E	13/31	6562		
7	BAH	OBBI	Bahrain	Muharraq Intl	A9C	2616N 5038E	12/30	13002	122.3 124.3	118.5 118.8
116	BFL	KBFL	Bakersfield	Meadows Field	CA N	3526N 11903W		10857		
227	BPN	WRLL	Balikpapan	Sepingan	PK	0116S 11654E	07/25	5905	120.4	118.3
163	MTN		Baltimore	Glenn L Martin	MD N	3919N 7624W		7000	119.0	
162	BWI	KBWI	BALTIMORE	Washington Intl	MD N	3911N 7640W	15R/33L	9519	119.0 123.5 124.55	121.3 119.4
261	BLR	VOBG	Bangalore	Hindustan	VT	1257N 7740E	09/27	10850	119.1 119.7	122.7
83	BKK	VTBD	BANGKOK	Don Muang Intl	HS	1355N 10036E	03L/21R	12139	118.3	118.1
32	BJL	GBYD	Banjul	Yundum Intl	C5	1321N 1640W	14/32	11810	119.1	121.3
43	BCN	LEBL	Barcelona		EC	4118N 0205E	07/25	10197	124.7 121.25	118.1 118.3
76	BSL	LFSB	Basel	EuroAirport	HB	4735N 0732E	16/34	12795	119.35	118.1 119.7
164	BTL		Battle C'eek	W K Kellogg	MI N	4218N 8515W		10003	121.2	118.3
33	BYU	EDQD	Bayreuth	Bindlacher-Berg	D	4959N 1138E	06/24	3461	119.9	118.45
50	BVA	LFOB	Beauvais	Tille	F	4927N 0207E	13/31	7972	129.0	119.9
7	BJS	ZBAA	BEIJING	Capital	B	4004N 11636E	18R/36L	10500	121.9	118.1 119.3
215	BEY	OLBA	Beirut	International	OD	3349N 3529E	18/36	10663	130.85 118.9	130.75 121.4
74	BHD	EGAC	Belfast	City	G	5437N 0552W	04/22	6000	120.0	118.3
74	BFS	EGAA	Belfast	International	G	5439N 0614W	07/25	9110		118.5
50	BOR	LFSQ	Belfort	Fontaine	F	4739N 0701E	04/22	9318		
264	BZE	MZBZ	Belize City	PSW Goldson Intl	V3	1732N 8818W	07/25	7100	118.0	121.0 120.3

#	IATA	ICAO	Town/city	Name	St/country		location	R/W	length	APPROACH	TOWER
207	BLI	KBLI	Bellingham	International	WA	N	4847N 12232W	13/31	5000	132.7	118.4
230	PLU	SBBH	Belo Horizonte	Pampulha	MG	PP	1951S 4357W	16/34	8325		118.2
230	CNF	SBCF	Belo Horizonte	Tancredo Neves		PP	1937S 4358W	11/29	9843	129.1 129.4	126.3
88	BGY	LIME	Bergamo	Orio al Serio		I	4540N 0942E	11/29	9186	126.5	119.1
99	BGO	ENBR	Bergen	Flesland		LN	6018N 0513E	18/36	8038	125.0	118.1 122.1
34	THF	EDBB	Berlin	Tempelhof		D	5228N 1342E	09R/27L	6942	125.8	118.3
33	SXF	ETBS	Berlin	Schoenefeld		D	5223N 1331E	07R/25L	9843		118.7
33	TXL	EDBT	BERLIN	Tegel		D	5234N 1317E	08L/26R	9918	125.8	118.9 119.7
77	BRN	LSZB	Bern	Belp		HB	4655N 0730E	14/32	4298	124.35	123.0
50	BZR	LFMU	Beziers	Vias		F	4319N 0321E	10/28	5971	121.075	134.8
61		EGKB	Biggin Hill			G	5119N 0002E	03/21	6017	129.4	118.5
44	BIO	LEBB	Bilbao			EC	4318N 0256W	12/30	8530	120.7	124.2
168	BIL		Billings	Logan Intl	MT	N	4548N 10832W	09L/27R	10500	125.075 6300	119.0
221	BLL	EKBI	Billund			OY	5544N 0909E	09/27	10171		118.6
175	BGM	KBHM	Binghampton	Broome County	NY	N	4212N 7558W	08/26	8000	118.25 124.5	122.3
109	BHM	EGBB	Birmingham	International	AL	N	3334N 8645W	05/23	7398	118.25 132.2	118.4
61	BHX		Birmingham			G	5227N 0145W	15/33		131.325 7500	124.3
117	BIH		Bishop		CA	N	3722N 11821W				118.1
61	BBS	EGLK	Blackbushe			G	5119N 0051W	08/26	4403	135.95	118.1
62	BFN	EGNH	Blackpool	Squire's Gate		G	5346N 0302W	10/28	6000	118.1	120.8
279		FABL	Bloemfontein	JBM Hertzog		ZS	2906S 2618E	02/20	8396		118.1
137	BCT	KBCT	Boca Raton		FL	N	2622N 8006W		5200		127.9
99	BOO	ENBO	Bodo	Eldorado		LN	6716N 1422E	08/26	9163	119.7	118.1
82	BOG	SKBO	Bogota	Gowen Field		HK	0442N 7409W	12/30	12467	119.5	119.1
155	BOI		Boise	Gowen Field	ID	N	4335N 11618W	10L/28R	9763	126.9	118.0
88	BLQ	LIPE	Bologna	G Marconi		I	4432N 1118E	12/30	8038	120.1 123.5	125.6 127.9
262		VAJJ	Bombay	Juhu		VT	1906N 7250E	08/26	3750	122.5	118.1
262	BOM	VABB	BOMBAY	J Nehru International		VT	1905N 7252E	09/27	11447	118.1 121.2 127.2	118.3
50	BOD	FLBD	Bordeaux	Merignac		F	4450N 0043W	05/23	10170	118.1 118.6	118.1
161	BOS	KBOS	BOSTON	Logan Intl	MA	N	4222N 7100W	15R/33L	10081	118.25 120.6	118.1 128.8
103	BOJ	LBBG	Bourgas	International		LZ	4234N 2730E	04/22	10499	125.1 119.65	119.1
62	BOH	EGHH	Bournemouth	Hurn		G	5047N 0150W	08/26	6030	119.625 119.7	118.0
230	BSB	SBBR	Brasilia	International	DF	PP	1551S 4754W	11/29	10496	125.1 119.625 120.2	118.3 118.3
			Brasilia	International							118.1
219	BTS	LKIB	Bratislava	Ivanka		OK	4810N 1713E	13/31	9678	120.0 119.5 120.9	118.3 119.9
235	BTK	UIBB	Bratsk			RA	5622N 10150E	12/30	10335	120.9 126.9	118.1

No.	IATA	ICAO	Town/city	Name	St/country	location	R/W	length	APPROACH		TOWER	
34	BWE	EDVE	Braunschweig		D	5219N 1033E	09/27	5315	125.65	119.45	119.35	118.575
34	BRE	EDDW	Bremen	Neuenland	D	5303N 0847E	09/27	6673		125.6	118.5	123.6
254		ABAF	Brisbane	Archer Field	QL VH	2134S 15300E	10L/28R	4855	124.7		118.1	
254	BNE	ABBN	Brisbane	International	QL VH	2223S 15307E	01/19	11680	132.4		120.5	
62	BRS	EGGD	Bristol	Luisgate	G	5123N 0243W	09/27	6598	119.0	133.75	133.85	
63	BZZ	EGVN	Brize Norton		G	5145N 0135W	08/26	10007			126.75	
196	BRO	KBRO	Brownsville	South Padre Island	TX N	2554N 9726W	13R/31L	7400	112.5	118.25	119.5	
220	BRU	EBBR	BRUSSELS	National	OO	5054N 0429E	07L/25R	11936	120.6		118.6	120.775
269	BBU	LRBS	Bucharest	Baneasa	YR	4430N 2606E	07/25	9843	120.6	120.9	120.8	
269	OTP	LROP	Bucharest	Otopeni	YR	4434N 2606E	08/26	10499	129.7		118.1	121.85
76	BUD	LHBP	BUDAPEST	Ferihegy	HA	4726N 1914E	13L/31R	12163	119.5		118.3	
101	AEP	SABE	Buenos Aires	Aeroparque	LV	3434S 5825W	13/31	6890	119.9		119.1	
102	EZE	SAEZ	BUENOS AIRES	Ezeiza	LV	3449S 5832W	11/29	10827	123.8	126.15	120.5	126.5
175	BUF	KBUF	Buffalo	Intl	NY N	4256N 7844W	05/23	8100	135.05		121.1	
117	BUR	KBUR	Burbank	Glendale Pasadena	CA N	3412N 11821W		6902				
206	BTV	KBTV	Burlington	International	VT N	4428N 7309W		7807	118.4		124.9	
254	CNS	ABCS	Cairns	International	QL VH	1653S 14545E	15/33	10489	119.05	119.55	118.1	
244	CAI	HECA	CAIRO		SU	3007N 3124E	05L/23R	10827	118.1		119.3	
262	CCU	VECC	Calcutta	NSCB International	VT	2239N 8827E	01R/19L	11900	128.7	133.3	118.4	127.9
11	YYC	CYYC	CALGARY	International	AL C	5106N 11401W	16/34	12675	123.6		122.2	
63	CBG	EGSC	Cambridge		G	5212N 0011E	05/23	6447	118.9		121.4	
231	VCP	SBKP	Campinas	Viracopos	SP PP	2300S 4708W	15/33	10630	124.5		118.7	
255	CBR	ASCB	Canberra		AC VH	3519S 14912E	17/35	8800	120.4		118.6	
265	CUN	MMUN	Cancur		XA	2102N 8653W	12/30	11484	119.7		118.1	
279	CPT	FACT	Cape Town	D F Malan	ZS	3358S 1836E	01/19	10500			118.1	
271		SVCS	Caracas	Chavallare	YV	1030N 6700W						
271		SVFM	Caracas	Francisco Miranda	YV	1030N 6655W						
270	CCS	SVMI	Caracas	Simon Bolivar Intl	YV	1036N 6659W	09/27	11483	120.1		121.0	
51	CCF	LFMK	Carcassonne	Salvaza	F	4313N 0219E	10/28	6398	123.85		125.0	
73	CWL	EGFF	Cardiff	Wales	G	5124N 0321W	12/30	7000			123.6	
63	CAX	EGNC	Carlisle	Crosby	G	5456N 0249W	07/25	6027				
117	CLD	KCNM	Carlstad	Palomar	CA N	3307N 11706W	6/24	4700	127.3			
173	CSN		Carson City		NV N	3911N 11944W		5900				
12	YCG	CYCG	Castlegar	Ralph West	BC C	4917N 11737W	08/26	5300			118.9	123.3
88	CTA	LICC	Cataria	Fontana Rossa	I	3728N 1504E		8366	120.8	122.1	118.7	
51	CMF	LFLB	Chambery	Aix les Bains	F	4538N 0553E	18/36	6627	123.7		118.3	121.1

#	IATA	ICAO	Town/city	Name	St/country	location	R/W	length	APPROACH	TOWER
110			Chandler	Memorial	AZ N	3500N 11200W		4005	124.1	118.1 126.4
111	P19		Chandler	Stellar Air Park	AZ N	3517N 11154W				
168	CLT	KCLT	CHARLOTTE	Douglas Municipal	NC N	3531N 8056W	18R/36L	10000	120.05 134.75	118.25
51	CHR	LFLX	Chateauroux	Deols	F	4652N 1043E	04/22	8366	125.1	
193	CHA	KCHA	Chattanooga	Lovell Field	TN N	3502N 8512W	02/20	7400	118.1	129.6
85	CNX	VTCC	Chiang Mai		HS	1846N 9858E	18/36	10171	122.3	126.2
85	CEI	VTCR	Chiang Rai	Ban Du	HS	1953N 9950E	18/36	5035	121.3	
156	CGX		Chicago	Merrill C Meigs	IL N	4151N 8736W		3947		118.4 121.3
158	MDW	KMDW	Chicago	Midway	IL N	4147N 8748W		6519	125.0	118.4
157	PWK		Chicago	Pal-Waukee	IL N	4207N 8754W		5137		119.9
265	ORD	KORD	CHICAGO	O'Hare Intl	IL N	4159N 8754W	14R/32L	13000	119.0 125.7	120.75 126.9
117	CZA		Chichen Itza		XA	2040N 8800W				
118	CIC	KCIC	Chico	Municipal	CA N	3945N 12154W				118.5
291	CNO		Chino		CA N	3358N 11738W		6222	135.4	118.7
275	BGI	TBPB	Christ Church	Grantley Adams	8P	1304N 5920W	09/27	11000	129.35 125.0	118.3
182	CHC	NZCH	Christchurch	International	ZK	4329S 17232E	02/20	10784	120.9	118.7
160	LUK	KLUK	Cincinnati	Lunken Municipal	OH N	3906N 8425W	2R/20L	6100	121.0	118.3
271	CVG	KCVG	CINCINNATI	N Kentucky Int	KY N	3903N 8440W	18L/36R	10000	119.7 123.87	118.3 118.97
272	CBL	SVCB	Ciudad Bolivar		YV	0807N 6631W				
137	PZO		Ciudad Guyana	Puerto Ordaz	YV	0818N 6244W			130.6	
51	PIE	KPIE	Clearwater	St Petersburg	FL N	2754N 8241W	09/27	7989	125.3	118.5
183	CFE	LFLC	Clermont Ferrand	Aulnat	F	4547N 0310E	6L/24R	9892	125.0	
183	BKL		Cleveland	Burke Lakefront	OH N	4131N 8141W	05/23	6200	125.35	124.3
182	CGF		Cleveland	Cuyahoga Co	OH N	4133N 8129W	05R/23L	5101	125.35	118.5
28	CLE	KCLE	CLEVELAND	Hopkins Intl	OH N	4125N 8151W	04/22	9000	124.0 124.5	120.9 126.55
155	CBB	SLCB	Cochabamba	Jorge Wilstermann	CP	1726S 6610W	7400	8202		
163	COE		Coeur d'Alene	Air Terminal	ID N	4746N 11649W				125.8
196	CGS		College Park		MD N	3850N 7655W		2740		119.85
52	CLL	KCLL	College Station	Easterwood	TX N	3035N 9622W	16/34	7000		120.4
35	CMR	LFGA	Colmar	Hussen	F	4807N 0722E	01/19	5282		119.0
	CGN	EDDK	COLOGNE/BONN		D	5052N 0709E	14L/32R	12467	121.05 126.325	119.075 120.5
130	COS	KCOS	Colorado Springs	Peterson Field	CO N	3848N 10442W		11000	124.2	118.5
184	OSU	KOSU	Columbus	Ohio State Univ	OH N	4004N 8304W	9R/27L	5000		118.8
183	CMH	KCMH	Columbus	Port Columbus	OH N	3959N 8253W	10R/28L	10700	124.2 132.3	120.5
184	LCK	KLCK	Columbus	Rickenbacker	OH N	3957N 8301W		12255	119.15	120.05
118	CPM	KCPM	Compton		CA N	3353N 11814W		3670		

No.	IATA	ICAO	Town/city	Name	St/country	location	R/W	length	APPROACH	TOWER
269	COZ	LRCK	Constanta	M Kogalniceanu	YR	4422N 2829E	18/36	11483	122.9	120.5
222	RKE	EKRK	Copenhagen	Roskilde	OY	5535N 1208E	11/29	4921	131.3	118.9
222	CPH	EKCH	COPENHAGEN	Kastrup	OY	5537N 1239E	04L/22R	11811	119.8 120.2	118.1 119.9 121.6
48	ORK	EICK	Cork	Cork	EI	5150N 0829W	17/35	7000	119.9 135.25	119.3 121.7
196	CRP	KCRP	Corpus Christi	International	TX N	2746N 9730W	13/31	7506		
63	CVT	EGBE	Coventry	Baginton	G	5222N 0129W	05/23	5300		
266	CZM	MMCZ	Cozumel	International	XA	2031N 8656W	11/29	8858	122.2 126.7	119.25
12	YXC	CYXC	Cranbrock	Kimberley	BC C	4936N 11546W		6000		
231	CGB	SBCY	Cuiaba	Marechal Rondon	MT PP	1539S 5607W	17/35	7546		
118	CVR		Culver City	Hughes	CA N	3358N 11824W				132.4
89	CUF		Cuneo	Levaldigi	I	4433N 0737E	03/21	6886		
231	CWB	SBCT	Curitiba	Afonso Pena	PR PP	2531S 4910W	15/33	7267		119.55 119.95
288	DKR	GOOY	Dakar	Yoff	6V	1445N 1730W	18/36	11450		118.1
249	DLM	LTBS	Dalaman	Mugla	TC	3642N 2847E	01/19	9843	129.5	118.5
196	ADS		Dallas	Addison	TX N	3258N 9650W	15/33	7200	123.9	121.1
196	DAL	KDAL	Dallas	Love Field	TX N	3251N 9652W	13R/31L	8800	123.9	118.7
197	DNE		Dallas	North	TX N	3301N 9658W				
197	RBD		Dallas	Redbird	TX N	3241N 9652W	13/31	5452		122.5
197	DFW	KDFW	DALLAS-FT WORTH	International	TX N	3254N 9702W	17L/35R	11388	120.3 123.9	124.15 126.55
268	DAM	OSDI	Damascus	International	YK	3325N 3631E	05R/23L	11811	119.05 125.8	118.5 121.9
255	DRW	ADDN	Darwin		VH	1225S 13053E	11/29	10906	126.2 134.1	133.1
12	YDA	CYDA	Dawson City	Municipal	NT C	6401N 13909W		6000		
184	DAY	KDAY	Dayton	James M Cox	OH N	3954N 8413W	6L/24R	9500	134.45	119.9
185	MGY		Dayton	Montgomery	OH N	3945N 8410W				
185	FFO	KFFO	Dayton	Wright-Patterson	OH N	3900N 8400W		7500		126.9
137	DAB		Daytona Beach	Regional	FL N	2911N 8103W				
263	DEL	VIDP	Delhi	Indira Gandhi Intl	VT	2836N 7707E	10/28	12500	123.9	127.9
263	DEL	VIDD	Delhi	Safdir Jang	VT	2835N 7712E	12/30	3870	118.1	
227	DPS	WRRR	Denpasar	Bali-Ngurah Rai	PK	0845S 11510E	09/27	9843	122.3	
131	APA		Denver	Centennial	CO N	3925N 10451W	16L/34R	10002	119.7	118.1
131	DIA	KDIA	DENVER	International	CO N	3951N 10440W	08/26	12000	124.3 132.35	118.9 133.3
131	DEN	KDEN	Denver	Stapleton Intl	CO N	3946N 10453W	17L/35R	12000	120.8 127.4	135.3 119.5
164	DET	KDET	Detroit	City	MI N	4224N 8301W	121.3	12000		118.3
165	YIP	KYIP	Detroit	Willow Run	MI N	4214N 8331W			118.45	120.0
164	DTW	KDTW	DETROIT	Metropolitan	MI N	4213N 8321W	03L/31R	12000	124.05 125.15	118.4 135.0
86	DHA	OEDR	Dhahran	International	HZ	2617N 5010E	16R/34L	12008	120.3 125.8 126.85	118.4 118.7

	IATA	ICAO	Town/city	Name	St/country	location	R/W	length	APPROACH	TOWER
52	DNR	LFRD	Dinard	Pleurtuit	F	4835N 0205W	17/35	7218	120.15	121.1
6	DOH	OTBD	Doha	International	A7	2516N 5134E	16/34	15000	121.1	118.9 121.1
35	DTM	EDLW	Dortmund	Wickede	D	5131N 0737E	06/24	3445		118.895 122.5
109	DHN	KDHN	Dothan		AL N	3119N 8526W		8500	125.4	118.0
36	DRS	ETDN	Dresden	Klotzsche	D	5108N 1346E	04/22	8202	119.7 127.7	120.9
158	DPA		Du Page	County	IL N	4154N 8814W		4000	133.5	118.75
4	DXB	OMDB	DUBAI	International	A6	2512N 5521E	12L/30R	13123	124.9	118.6
48	DUB	EIDW	DUBLIN		EI	5326N 0615W	10/28	8652	121.1	122.9
72	DND	EGPN	Dundee	Riverside	G	5627N 0301W	10/28	3609		
255	DKI		Dunk Island		QL VH	1759S 14614E				
280	DUR	FADN	Durban	Louis Botha	ZS	2958S 3057E	05/23	8015	119.1	118.7
280	VIR	FAVG	Durban	Virginia	ZS	2946S 3104E	05/23	3051		120.6
36	DUS	EDDL	DUSSELDORF		D	5117N 0645E	05R/23L	9843	119.4 120.05	118.3 128.85
64	EMA	EGNX	East Midlands	Castle Donington	G	5250N 0119W	09/27	7480	119.65	124.0
72	EDI	EGPH	Edinburgh	Turnhouse	G	5557N 0322W	07/25	8400	121.2	118.7
12	YXD	CYXD	Edmonton	Industrial	AL C	5334N 11331W		5860		119.5
13	YEG	CYEG	Edmonton	International	AL C	5319N 11335W	02/20	11000	120.5	118.3
283	ETH	LLET	Eilat	J HHozman	4X	2934N 3458E	03/21	6234	118.6 119.0	121.1 122.1
225	EIN	EHEH	Eindhoven		PH	5127N 0523E	04/22	9843	123.175	118.3
198	ELP	KELP	EL PASO	International	TX N	3151N 10619W	04/22	11012	123.85	
169	ECG	KECG	Elizabeth City		NC N	3615N 7610W		7219		
173	EKO		Elko	Municipal	NV N	4040N 11550W				
176	ELM		Elmira	Corning Regional	NY N	4209N 7653W		7000	133.35	
225	ENS	EHTW	Enschede	Twenthe	PH	5217N 0653E	06/24	8599	119.1	118.1
286	EBB	HUEN	Entebbe	Dr I M Obote Intl	5X	0003N 3226E	17/35	12001		
249	ECN		Ercan		TC	3530N 3355E				
37	ERF	ETEF	Erfurt		D	5059N 1058E	10/28		119.7	
189	ERI		Erie	International	PA N	4205N 8010W	06/24	6562		121.2
222	EBJ	EKEB	Esbjerg		OY	5532N 0833E	08/26	6500	121.0	
188	EUG	KPAE	Eugene	Mahlon Sweet	OR N	4407N 12313W	03/21	8530		120.15
207	PAE	EGTE	Everett	Paine Field	WA N	4654N 12217W	16R/34L	5251	128.5	119.6
64	EXT		Exeter		G	5044N 0325W	08/26	9010	128.15	120.2
107	FBK	PAFB	Fairbanks	Fort Wainright	AK N	6450N 14750W		6834		119.8
106	FAI	PAFA	Fairbanks	International	AK N	6458N 14734W	01L/19R	10300	118.1 126.6	118.3
176	FRG		Farmingdale	Republic	NY N	4043N 7324W	14/32	6827	127.4	118.2
30	FAO	LPFR	Faro		CS	3701N 0758W	11/29	8169	119.4	

#	IATA	ICAO	Town/city	Name	St/country	location	R/W	length	APPROACH	TOWER
110	FYV	KFYV	Fayetteville	Drake Field	AR N	3600N 9410W		4900		
193	FAY		Fayetteville	Municipal	TN N	3503N 8633W			125.6	
111	FLG		Flagstaff	Pulliam	AZ N	3508N 11140W	7000	128.45		
89	FLR	LIRQ	Florence	Peretola/A Vespucci	I	4349N 1122E	05/23	4600	118.3 122.1	122.2
13	YFS	CYFS	Fort Simpson		NT C	6145N 12114W		6000		
199	FWH	KFWH	Fort Worth	Carswell	TX N	3200N 9700W		7500		
199	FTW	KFTW	Fort Worth	Meacham Field	TX N	3249N 9721W		8000		118.1
110	FSM	KFSM	Fort Smith	Municipal	AR N	3520N 9422W		6400		119.25
139	FMY	KFMY	Fort Myers	Page Field	FL N	2635N 8152W	05/23	5000	126.8	
139	FPR		Fort Pierce	St Lucie County	FL N	2729N 8022W	14/30	8400		
139	RSW		Fort Myers	SW Florida	FL N	2632N 8145W		7219	126.8	
231	IGU	SBSI	Foz do Iguassu	Cataratas	PR PP	2535S 5429W	14/32	13123		
37	FRA	EDDF	FRANKFURT	Main	D D	5002N 0834E	07L/25R		118.5 124.2	119.9 124.85
119	FAT	KFAT	Fresno	Air Terminal	CA N	3653N 11949W		3400	119.6 132.35	118.2
207	FRD		Friday Harbor		WA N	4831N 12301W		6000		118.2
138	FXE	KFXE	Ft Lauderdale	Executive	FL N	2612N 8010W	08/26	9000		120.9
137	FLL	KFLL	FT LAUDERDALE	Hollywood Intl	FL N	2604N 8009W	09L/27R	7874		119.3
44	FUE	GCFV	Fuertaventura	Puerto del Rosario	EC	2827N 1352W	01/19	9186		118.5
93	FUK	RJFF	Fukuoka	Itazuke	JA	3335N 13027E	16/34	3121	118.4 126.2	119.1 119.65 120.7
119	FUL		Fullerton	Municipal	CA N	3352N 11758W		5600	124.65	119.1
30	FNC	LPFU	Funchal	Santa Cruz Madeira	CS	3241N 1646W	06/24	7500	118.1	119.2
139	GNV	KGNV	Gainesville	J R Alison	FL N	2941N 8216W		6022	134.4	
199	GLS	KGLS	Galveston	Scholes Field	TX N	2916N 9451W	09/27	4429	135.35	
49	GWY	EICM	Galway	Carnmore	EI	5318N 0856W	12/30	7000	133.1	122.5
158	GYY		Gary	Municipal	IN N	4137N 8725W		3500	125.35	126.3
169	0A6		Gastonia	Municipal	NC N	3512N 8109W		6000	122.3	
13	YND	CYND	Gatineau		QU C	4531N 7533W	11/29	9186		
242	GDN	EPGD	Gdansk	Rebiechowo	SP	5423N 1828E	05/23	12795	120.3 130.15	118.1
77	GVA	LSGG	GENEVA	Cointrin	HB	4614N 0607E	11/29	9925	119.6	118.7 119.7
89	GOA	LIMJ	Genoa	Sestri	I	4425N 0850E	09/27	6000	122.8	118.6
258	GIB	LXGB	Gibraltar	North Front	VR-G	3609N 0521W	07/25	5440	122.8	122.8 123.3 130.4
1	GIL	OPGT	Gilgit		AP	3555N 7420E		8720	119.1	118.8
72	GLA	EGPF	GLASGOW	International	G	5552N 0426W	05/23	11253	119.1	119.7
263	GOI	VAGO	Goa	Dabolim	VT	1523N 7350E	08/26	3117	118.1	121.3
223	GOH	BGGH	Godthaab	Nuuk	OY	6412N 5142W	06/24	8500		
114	GYR		Goodyear	Municipal	AZ N	3325N 11222W			134.1	

	IATA	ICAO	Town/city	Name	St/country	location	R/W	length	APPROACH	TOWER
240	GOT	ESGG	Goteborg	Landvetter	SE	5740N 1217E	03/21	10827	124.2 124.675	118.6 123.3
241	GSE	ESGP	Goteborg	Saeve	SE	5747N 1152E	01/19	6319	120.55 124.2	119.05 122.0 123.25
44	LPA	GCLP	Gran Canaria	Las Palmas	EC	2756N 1523W	03L/21R	10170	120.9 121.3 124.3	118.3 131.3
60	CFG		Grand Case	Esperance	F-O	1805N 6305W				
111	JGC		Grand Canyon	Heliport	AZ N	3615N 11220W				
111	GCN		Grand Canyon	National Park	AZ N	3557N 11208W		9000	124.85	118.1
132	GJT		Grand Junction	Walker Field	CO N	3910N 10838W		10500	119.7	119.3 125.65
215	GRZ	LOWG	Graz	Thalerhof	OE	4700N 1526E	17/35	9055	118.2	119.3
170	GSO		Greensboro	Piedmont Triad	NC N	3606N 7956W		10000	120.9	
193	GSP		Greenville	Spartanburg	SC N	3453N 8213W		7600		118.8
52	GNB	LFLS	Grenoble	St Geoirs	F	4522N 0520E	09/27	10007	120.4	119.3
212	GEY		Greybull	South Big Horn	WY N	4430N 10803W		6300	133.25	119.8
152	6AZ		Griffin	Spalding County	GA N	3313N 8416W	14/32	3300		118.7
225	GRQ	EHGG	Groningen	Eelde	PH	5308N 0635E	05/23	5906	120.3 128.5	119.45
133	GON		Groton	New London	CT N	4119N 7203W		5000		125.0
136	ILG	KILG	Gtr Wilmington	International	DE N	3945N 7532W		7165		119.1 128.3
191	PIT	KPIT	GTR PITTSBURGH		PA N	4030N 8014W	10R/28L	11500	123.95 124.15	118.1
266	GDL	MMQL	Guadalajara	Manuel Hidalgo	XA	2031N 10319W	10/28	13120	119.3 120.8	118.1
7	CAN	ZGGG	Guangzhou	Baiyun	B	2311N 11316E	03/21	11089		119.95
74	GCI	EGJB	Guernsey		G	4926N 0236W	09/27	4800	128.65	
8	KWL	ZGKL	Guilin		B	2508N 11019E				
168	GPT		Gulfport-Biloxi	Regional	MS N	3024N 8904W	13L/31R	9002	124.6	126.5
272		FVTL	Gweru	Thornhill	Z	1924S 2952E		7800	123.5	
14	YWF		Halifax	Downtown	NS C	4438N 6335W				
13	YHZ	CYHZ	Halifax	International	NS C	4453N 6331W	06/24	8800	119.2	118.4
14	YAW	CYAW	Halifax	Shearwater CFB	NS C	4438N 6330W	16/34	8200	119.2	119.0 126.2
39	XFW	EDHI	Hamburg	Finkenwerder	D	5332N 0950E	05/23	6325		130.35
39	HAM	EDDH	HAMBURG	Fuhlsbuttel	D	5338N 0959E	15/33	12028	120.6 124.225	121.275 126.85
275	HLZ	NZHN	Hamilton		ZK	3752S 17520E	18/36	5600	125.9	122.9
14	YHM	CYHM	Hamilton	Civic	OT C	4310N 7956W	12L/30R	8000	128.1	125.0
153	HNM	PHHN	Hana	Municipal	HI N	2048N 15601W	08/26	3605		122.1
39	HAJ	EDVV	Hannover		D	5228N 0941E	09L/27R	12467	118.05 119.6	120.175 123.55
272	HRE	FVHA	Harare	International	Z	1756S 3106E	06/24	15502		
272		FVCP	Harare	Prince Charles	Z	1745S 3055E	14/32	3035	119.1	118.1
199	HRL	KHRL	Harlingen	Rio Grande Valley	TX N	2613N 9739W				118.7
189	MDT	KMDT	Harrisburg	International	PA N	4014N 7701W		8300		120.7

#	IATA	ICAO	Town/city	Name	St/country	location	R/W	length	APPROACH	TOWER
189	HAR	KHAR	Harrisburg	Skyport	PA N	4014N 7701W	02/20	4418	123.85	
133	HFD	KHFD	Hartford	Brainard	CT N	4144N 7239W	05/23	13123	120.3	118.1
31	HAV	MUHA	Havana	Jose Marti Intl	CU	2300N 8225W		4956	124.5 121.1	122.3
119	HHR	KHHR	Hawthorne	Municipal	CA N	3355N 11820W				
14	YHY	CYHY	Hay River		NT C	6050N 11546W				
132	HDN	KHDN	Hayden	Yampa Valley	CO N	4031N 10718W		10000		
168	HLN	KHLN	Helena	Regional	MT N	4636N 11159W	09/27	9000	128.5	118.3
218	HEM	EFHF	Helsinki	Malmi	OH	6015N 2503E	18/36	4590	119.5	118.9
217	HEL	EFHK	HELSINKI	Vantaa	OH	6019N 2458E	04/22	11286	119.1	118.6 119.7
173	HSH		Henderson	Sky Harbor	NV N	3558N 11508W		5000		
246	HER	LGIR	Heraklion	Nikos Kazantzakis	SX	3520N 2511E	09/27	8793	119.85 122.1	120.85 122.1 123.6
153	ITO	PHTO	Hilo	General Lyman	HI N	1943N 15503W	08/26	9803	118.9 119.7	122.1 122.2
139	HWO		Hollywood	North Perry	FL N	2600N 8014W		3065	128.6	121.3 124.4
261	HHP		HongKong	Heliport	VR-H	2211N 11414E				
259	HKG	VHHH	HONGKONG	Kai Tak	VR-H	2219N 11412E	13/31	11130	119.1	118.7
153	HNL	PHNL	HONOLULU	International	HI N	2120N 15756W	08L/26R	12360	118.3	118.1
200	EFD	KEFD	Houston	Ellington AFB	TX N	2936N 9509W	17R/35L	9000	127.25 124.35	118.7
201	HOU	KHOU	Houston	William P Hobby	TX N	2939N 9517W	04/22	7602	120.05 120.8	118.1
200	IAH	KIAH	HOUSTON	Intercontinental	TX N	2959N 9520W	14L/32R	12000	120.05 124.35	118.55 121.85 135.15
64	HUY	EGNJ	Humberside		G	5335N 0021W	03/21	7218	124.675	119.9
273	HWN	FVWN	Hwange	National Park	Z	1838S 2700E	08/26	14764		119.2
162	HYA		Hyannis	Barnstable	MA N	4140N 7016W		5430	119.8	118.5
44	IBZ	LEIB	Ibiza		EC	3852N 0122E		9186	134.5	
156	IDA		Idaho Falls	Fanning Field	ID N	4330N 11204W	07/25	9000		
158	IND	KIND	Indianapolis	International	IN N	3944N 8617W	05L/23R	10005	124.65 127.15	120.9
215	INN	LOWI	Innsbruck	Kranebitten	OE	4716N 1121E	08/26	6562	118.95	120.1
276	IVC	NZNV	Invercargill		ZK	4625S 16819E	04/22	5997		118.5
73	INV	EGPE	Inverness	Dalcross	G	5732N 0403W	06/24	6191		
119	IYK		Inyokern	Kern County	CA N	3539N 11750W		7337		122.6
1	ISB	OPRN	Islamabad	Chaklala	AP	3337N 7706E	12/30	9000	119.7 121.8	124.9 123.7
75	IOM	EGNS	Isle of Man	Ronaldsway	G	5404N 0438W	09/27	5751	120.85	118.9
176	ISP	KISP	Islip	Long I-MacArthur	NY N	4047N 7306W		6020	120.05	
249	ADB	LTBJ	Izmir	Adnan Menderes	TC	3818N 2710E	16/34	10630	120.1 132.9	121.9 125.5
232			Jacarepagua		PP	2300S 4330W				
212	JAC		Jackson	Jackson Hole	WY N	4336N 11044W		6300	133.25	
140	JAX	KJAX	Jacksonville	International	FL N	3029N 8141W		8000	127.0	118.3

	IATA	ICAO	Town/city	Name	St/country	location	R/W	length	APPROACH	TOWER
228	HLP	WIIH	Jakarta	Halim P Kusama	PK	0616S 10653E	06/24	9843	119.7 120.0	118.3
229	JAK	WIID	Jakarta	Kemayoran	PK	0609S 10651E	17/35	8120	119.7 120.0	118.6
228	CGK	WIII	JAKARTA	Soekarno-Hatta	PK	0608S 10639E	07R/25L	12008	125.45 135.9	118.2 118.75
86	JED	OEJN	Jeddah	King Abdulaziz	HZ	2141N 3909E	16R/34L	12467	119.1 124.0	118.2 124.3
284	JER	EGJJ	Jersey		G	4913N 0212W	09/27	5597	120.3	119.45
75	JRS	LLJR	Jerusalem		4X	3152N 3513E	12/30	6447		118.8
229	JOG	WIIJ	Jogyarkarta	Adisucipto	PK	0747S 11026E	09/27	6070	120.2 123.4	118.1
281	GCJ	FAGC	Johannesburg	Grand Central	ZS	2559S 2809E	17/35	4000	128.65	122.8
281	HLA	FALA	Johannesburg	Lanseria	ZS	2555S 2756E	06L/24R	10000		124.0
280	JNB	FAJS	JOHANNESBURG	Jan Smuts Intl	ZS	2608S 2815E	03L/21R	14495	123.7 124.5 125.3	118.1 121.9
190	JST		Johnstown	Cambria County	PA	4019N 7850W		5486		121.2
93	KOJ	RJFK	Kagoshima		JA	3148N 13043E	16/34	9843	119.4 126.0	118.2 126.2
154	OGG	PHOG	Kahului	Maui Island	HI	2054N 15626W	02/20	7000	120.2	118.7
165	AZO		Kalamazoo	County	MI	4214N 8533W	06/24	6500	121.2	118.1
285	KAN	DNKN	Kano	Aminu Mallam Intl	5N	1203N 0832E	06/24	10827	119.0	126.8
166	MKC	KMKC	Kansas City	Downtown	MO	3907N 9436W				125.75
166	MCI	KMCI	Kansas City	International	MO	3918N 9444W	01L/19R	10801	120.95 132.95	118.3 128.2
167	JCI		Kansas City	Johnson Ind	MO	3851N 9454W			118.9	118.9
167	OJC		Kansas City	Johnson Exec	MO	3903N 9444W				118.4 126.0
154	JHM		Kapalua	West Maui	HI	2052N 14641W				125.3
1	KHI	OPKC	Karachi	Quaid-e-Azam Intl	AP	2454N 6709E	07L/25R	10500	118.3 121.8	118.3 121.3
273	KAB	FVKB	Kariba		Z	1631S 2853E	09/27	5413		119.6
250	KEF	BIKF	Keflavik		TF	6359N 2237W	11/29	10013	119.3	121.1
15	YLW	CYLW	Kelowna	Ellison Field	BC	4957N 11922W		5350		120.85
107	ENA	PAEN	Kenai	Municipal	AK	6034N 15115W	01/19	7575	121.3 118.9	118.7
140	TMB	KTMB	Kendall-Tamiami	Executive	FL	2539N 8025W	17/35	5002	118.1	119.2
246	CFU	LGKR	Kerkyra	I Kapodistrias	SX	3936N 1955E	17/35	7792	122.35	
140	EYW	KEYW	Key West	International	FL	2433N 8145W	18R/36L	4800		
252	KBP	UKBB	Kiev	Borispol	UR	5021N 3053E		11483	121.2 124.6 127.9	119.3 123.7
252	IEV	UKKK	Kiev	Zhulyany	UR	5024N 3021E	02/20	9843	130.6 132.6	
281	KIM	FAKM	Kimberley	B J Vorster	ZS	2848S 2446E	12/30	6831		123.8
112	IGM		Kingman	Municipal	AZ	3515N 11356W		8600		120.6
288	KIN	MKJP	Kingston	Norman Manley Intl	6Y	1756N 7648W	10/28	3346	121.6	
289			Kingston	Tinson Pen	6Y	1759N 7649W		8924	118.1	119.45
216	KLU	LOWK	Klagenfurt	Worthesee	OE	4639N 1420E				

	IATA	ICAO	Town/city	Name	St	country	location	R/W	length	APPROACH	TOWER
194	TYS	KTYS	Knoxville	McGhee Tyson	TN	N	3549N 8359W	4L/22R	9000		118.5 129.25
293	KUL	WMKK	Kuala Lumpur	Subang Intl		9M	0308N 10133E	15/33	12400		118.2
94	KMJ	RJFT	Kumamoto			JA	3250N 13051E	07/25	9840		118.7 126.2
293	KWI	OKBK	Kuwait	International		9K	2913N 4758E	15L/33R	11483	119.0 126.5	118.3
152	LGC		La Grange	Callaway	GA	N	3300N 8504W		5600	121.3 124.8	119.25
28	LPB	SADL	La Paz	El Alto		CP	1631S 6811W				
2	LHE	OPLA	Lahore			AP	3131N 7424E	18/36	9000	118.1	121.3
276			Lake Tekapo			ZK	4400S 17030E				
155	LNY	PHNY	Lanai City	City	HI	N	2047N 15657W		5000		
120	WJF		Lancaster	Fox Field	CA	N	3444N 11813W		5000		
45	ACE	GCRR	Lanzarote			EC	2856N 1336W	04/22	7874	129.1	126.1
201	LRD	KLRD	Laredo	International	TX	N	2732N 9927W	04/22	8201	127.8	120.7
284	LCA	LCLK	Larnaca			5B	3453N 3338E		8858	121.2	119.4
174	VGT		Las Vegas	North Air Terml	NV	N	3612N 11511W		5005		119.9
173	LAS	KLAS	LAS VEGAS	McCarran Intl	NV	N	3605N 11509W	07L/25R	12635	127.15	121.2
190	LBE		Latrobe	Westmoreland	PA	N	4016N 7924W		7000		119.15
52	LEH	LFOH	Le Havre	Octeville		F	4932N 0005E	05/23	7546	118.3	118.3 125.3
52	LTQ	LFAT	Le Touquet	Paris-Plage		F	5031N 0138E	14/32	7382	123.75	120.3
65	LBA	EGNM	Leeds/Bradford			G	5352N 0140W	14/32	7382	119.7 121.1	120.1
40	LEJ	ETLS	Leipzig	Halle		D	5125N 1214E		8202		
160	LEX	KLEX	Lexington	Blue Grass	KY	N	3802N 8436W	11/29	7000	120.75	118.7
159	LBL		Liberal	Geo Welch	KS	N	3702N 10057W	04/22	7100	134.0	119.7 122.1
250	LBV	FOOL	Libreville	Leon M'ba		TR	0027N 0925E	16/24	9843	119.275 122.5 123.05	118.9
155	LGG	EBLG	Liege	Bierset		OO	5038N 0527E	05R/23L	8839	126.5	118.55
53	LIH	PHLI	Lihue	Municipal	HI	N	2159N 15920W	17/35	6500	127.9	118.7
291	LIL	LFQQ	Lille	Lesquin		F	5034N 0305E	08/26	9268	128.0	118.9
214	LLW	FWKI	Lilongwe	Kamuzu		7Q	1347S 3347E	14/32	11614	119.75 129.625	118.55
216	LIM	SPIM	Lima	Jorge Chavez Intl		OB	1201S 7707W	15/33	11506	120.6	118.7
31	LNZ	LOWL	Linz	Horsching		OE	4814N 1411E	09/27	9219		118.8
110	LIS	LPPT	LISBON	Portela de Sacavem		CS	3846N 0908W	03/21	12483	119.85	118.1
65	LIT	KLIT	Little Rock	Adams Field	AR	N	3443N 9214W		7173		124.2
15	LPL	EGGP	Liverpool	Speke		G	5321N 0253W	09/27	7500		118.1
65	YXU	CYXU	London			C	4302N 8109W	15/33	8800		119.4 122.5
65	LCY	EGLC	London	City		G	5130N 0003E	10/28	3379	125.55	119.425
68	STN	EGSS	London	Stansted		G	5153N 0014E	05/23	10000	125.875	123.8
66	LGW	EGKK	LONDON	Gatwick		G	5109N 0011W	08R/26L	10364	125.875 134.225	124.225

#	IATA	ICAO	Town/city	Name	St/country	location	R/W	length	APPROACH	TOWER
66	LHR	EGLL	LONDON	Heathrow	G	5129N 0028W	09L/27R	12802	119.2 119.5 120.4	118.7 124.475 127.55
67	LTN	EGGW	London	Luton	G	5153N 0022W	08/26	7087	127.3 128.75 129.55	119.975
120	LGB	KLGB	Long Beach	Daugherty Field	CA N	3349N 11809W		10000	124.65	119.4
122	VNY		Los Angeles	Van Nuys	CA N	3414N 11829W			119.3	120.2
121	LAX	KLAX	LOS ANGELES	International	CA N	3356N 11824W	07L/25R	12090	124.5 124.9 128.5	120.95 133.9
201	LBB	KLBB	Lubbock	International	TX N	3340N 10149W		11500		119.9
78	LUG	LSZA	Lugano	Agno	HB	4600N 0855E	03/21	4429		122.55 124.55
102	LUX	ELLX	Luxembourg	Findel	LX	4937N 0612E	06/24	13123	118.45	118.1
244	LXR	HELX	Luxor		SU	2540N 3242E	02/20	9843		119.9 124.3
53	LYN	LFLY	Lyon	Bron	F	4544N 0456E	17/35	5971		118.1
53	LYS	LFLL	Lyon	Satolas	F	4544N 0505E	18R/36L	13123	119.45 125.8 127.95	120.0 128.0 128.5
226	MST	EHBK	Maastricht	Beek	PH	5055N 0547E	04/22	8202	119.25	119.475
152	MCN	KMCN	Macon	Mid Georgia	GA N	3241N 8338W		6500	123.975	119.6
122	MAE		Madera	Municipal	CA N	3700N 12006W		4500		119.45
46		LEUS	Madrid	Cuatro Vientos	EC	4022N 0347W	10/28	4921	118.7 122.5 139.7	121.6
45	MAD	LEMD	MADRID	Barajas	EC	4029N 0334W	15/33	13450	119.95 120.9 127.1	118.15 128.7
248	SEZ	FSIA	Mahe	Seychelles Intl	S7	0440S 5531E	13/31	9800	118.3	119.7
46	MAH	LEMH	Mahon	Menorca	EC	3952N 0413E	01/19	7710		119.65
46	AGP	LEMG	Malaga		EC	3640N 0430W	14/32	10500	123.95 118.45	118.15
241	JMM	ESHM	Malmo	Harbour Heliport	SE	5536N 1259E				
241	MMX	ESMS	Malmo	Sturup	SE	5533N 1322E	17/35	9186		118.8
292	SFI	GMMS	Malta	Safi	9H	3218N 0910E				
292	MLA	LMML	MALTA	Luqa	9H	3552N 1429E	14/32	11627	121.0 127.1	118.9
292	MAO	SBEG	Manaus	Eduardo Gomes	AM PP	0302S 6002W	10/28	8858		
232		SBMN	Manaus	Ponta Pelada	AM PP	0308S 5959W				
232	MAN	EGCC	MANCHESTER	International	G	5321N 0216W	06/24	10000	119.4 121.35	118.1 118.625
68	MNL	RPMM	MANILA	Ninoy Aquino Intl	RP	1430N 12100E	06/24	11004	119.7 121.1	118.1
239	MHG	EDFM	Mannheim	Neuostheim	D	4928N 0831E	09/27	3280		
40	MPD		Mansfield	Lahm Municipal	OH N	4049N 8231W	14/32	9000	119.25 134.9	119.8
185	MZJ		Marana	Pinal Air Park	AZ N	3230N 11119W		6860		
112	MTH		Marathon		FL N	2443N 8103W		5000		
140	MKY		Marco Island		FL	2600N 8140W		5008	120.8	
141			Marseille	Provence Intl	F					
53	MRS	LFML	Marseille	Provence Intl	F	4326N 0513E	14L/32R	11483	119.5 120.2 120.65	118.1 125.65 119.5
290	MSU	FXMM	Maseru	Moshoeshoe Intl	7P	2922S 2733E	04/22	10500	127.725	120.7
282	MRU	FIMP	Mauritius	Plaisance Intl	3B	2026S 5741E	14/32	8500	118.5 119.1	118.1

#	IATA	ICAO	Town/city	Name	St	country	location	R/W	length	APPROACH	TOWER
201	MFE	KMFE	McAllen	Miller International	TX	N	2610N 9814W	13/31	7100	121.0	118.1
229	MES	WIMM	Medan	Polonia		PK	0334N 9841E	05/23	9514	119.7	
82		SKMD	Medellin	Olaya Herrera		HK	0613N 7536W	01/19	8028		
188	MFR		Medford	Jackson County	OR	N	4222N 12252W		6700	125.3	
256	MEB	AMEN	Melbourne	Essendon	VI	VH	3744S 14454E	08/26	6300	124.7 135.7	125.1
256	MBW	AMMB	Melbourne	Moorabbin	VI	VH	3759S 14506E	17L/35R	4380		118.1 123.0
141	MLB	KMLB	Melbourne	Regional	FL	N	2806N 8038W	09R/27L	9481	125.1	125.1
255	MEL	AMML	MELBOURNE	Tullamarine	VI	VH	3741S 14451E	16/34	12000	124.7 129.4	120.5
193	MEM	KMEM	Memphis	International	TN	N	3505N 8958W	18R/36L	9319	119.1 125.8	118.3 119.7
266	MID	MMMD	Merida	Manuel Cresencio		XA	2056N 8940W	10/28	8858	121.2	118.3
113	FFZ		Mesa	Falcon Field	AZ	N	3327N 11143W		5100		119.2
266	MEX	MMMX	MEXICO CITY	Benito Juarez		XA	1926N 9904W	05R/23L	12796	121.2	118.1
144	OPF	KOPF	Miami	Opa Locka	FL	N	2554N 8017W	09L/27R	8002	118.6	120.7 125.6
144	MPB		Miami	Watson Island	FL	N	2550N 8010W				
142	MIA	KMIA	MIAMI	International	FL	N	2548N 8017W	09R/27L	13002	124.85	118.3 123.9
90	MXP	LIMC	MILAN	Malpensa		I	4538N 0843E	17L/35R	12844	126.3	119.0 128.35
89	LIN	LIML	MILAN	Linate		I	4527N 0917E	18L/36R	8005	126.3	118.1 119.25
276	MFN	NZMF	Milford Sound			ZK	4440S 16755E	11/29	2600		
211	MKE	KMKE	Milwaukee	General Mitchell	WI	N	4257N 8754W	01/19R	9690	118.0 126.5	119.1 125.35
165	MSP	KMSP	MINNEAPOLIS	St Paul Intl	MN	N	4453N 9313W	11R/29L	10000	119.3 126.95	123.95 126.7
82			Miraflores			HK					
94	KMI	RJFM	Miyazaki			JA	3152N 13127E	09/27	8200	120.1 121.4	118.3 126.2
109	MOB	KMOB	Mobile	Regional	AL	N	3041N 8814W		8527	120.95	118.5
122	MOD		Modesto	Harry Sham	CA	N	3737N 12057W		5911		
122	MHV		Mojave	Kern County	CA	N	3503N 11809W		9600		
155	MKK	PHMK	Molokai	Hoolehua	HI	N	2109N 15706W	05/23	4494	120.3	125.7
286	MBA	HKMO	Mombasa	Moi International		5Y	0402S 3936E	03/21	10991	133.5	118.6
123	MRY		Monterey	Peninsula	CA	N	3635N 12157W	10R/28L	6597	118.1	
267	MTY	MMMY	Monterrey	Mariano Escobido		XA	2547N 10006W	11/29	9843		120.4
176	MSV		Monticello	Sullivan County	NY	N	4142N 7447W		6300		120.2
54	MPL	LFMT	Montpellier	Frejorgues		F	4335N 0358E	13L/31R	8530	119.8	118.7
16	YMX	CYMX	Montreal	Mirabel	PQ	C	4541N 7402W	06/24	12000	125.15	119.1
16	YHU	CYHU	Montreal	St Hubert	PQ	C	4503N 7325W		7840	125.15	
15	YUL	CYUL	MONTREAL	Dorval	PQ	C	4528N 7345W	06L/24R	11000	125.15 125.4	119.9
194	MOR		Morristown	Moore-Murrell	TN	N	3611N 8322W		5700	125.05	
171	MMU		Morristown	Municipal	NJ	N	4048N 7424W		6000	127.6	

#	IATA	ICAO	Town/city	Name	St/country	location	R/W	length	APPROACH	TOWER
236			Moscow	Bykovo	RA	5500N 3700E				
236	DME		Moscow	Domodedovo	RA	5558N 3820E				
237			Moscow	Myatchkyvo	RA	5500N 3700E				
237	SVO	UUEE	Moscow	Sheremetievo	RA	5558N 3725E	07R/25L	12139	119.3 120.7 123.7	120.7 131.5
238	VKO	UUWW	Moscow	Vnukovo	RA	5558N 3725E	07R/25L	12139	122.3	118.3
238			Moscow	Zhukovsky	RA	5500N 3700E				
207	MWH		Moses Lake	Grant County	WA N	4712N 11919W			126.4	
276	GTN	NZMC	Mount Cook	Glentanner	ZK	4346S 17008E	13/31	13500		118.6
276	MON		Mount Cook	Hermitage	ZK	4336S 17009E		5748		
54	MLH	LFSB	Mulhouse	EuroAirport	F	4735N 0732E	16/34	12795	119.35 121.25	118.3
40	MUC	EDDM	MUNICH	F-J Strauss	D	4814N 1149E	08L/26R	11000		126.2
41	FMO	EDLG	Munster/Osbruck	Greven	D	5208N 0741E	07/25	7119	124.45	129.8
3	MCT	OOMS	Muscat	Seeb International	A4O	2336N 5817E	08/26	11762	121.2	118.4
247	JMK	LGMK	Mykonos	International	SX	3726N 2521E	16/34	4626		118.75
43	NAN	NFFN	Nadi	International	DQ	1745S 17727E	02/20	10500	119.1	118.7 122.7
94	NGO	RJNN	Nagoya	Komaki	JA	3515N 13656E	16/34	8990	120.3	118.7
286	NBO	HKNA	Nairobi	Jomo Kenyatta Int	5Y	0119S 3656E	06/24	13507	119.7	118.1
287	WIL	HKNW	Nairobi	Wilson	5Y	0119S 3649E	07/25	4800		
16	YCD	CYCD	Nanaimo	Cassidy	BC C	4903N 12352W		5000	122.1	
17	ZNA		Nanaimo	Harbour	BC C	4910N 12400W				
123	APC		Napa	County	CA N	3818N 12217W		5931	127.8	
90	NAP	LIRN	Naples	Capodichino	I	4053N 1417E		8661	124.35	118.5
145	APF		Naples	Municipal	FL N	2609N 8146W		5000		118.0
224	UAK	BGBW	Narssassuaq		OY	6110N 4526W		6004		118.1
195	BNA	KBNA	Nashville	Metropolitan	TN N	3608N 8641W	13/31	9240	120.6 127.3	118.6 128.15
277	NSN	NZNS	Nelson		ZK	4118S 17313E	02/20	4419	123.3 127.4	122.4
281	NLP	FANS	Nelspruit		ZS	2530S 3055E	04/22	2871		
161	MSY	KMSY	New Orleans	International	LA N	2959N 9016W	10/28	10080	118.1 123.85	119.5 125.5
161	NEW	KNEW	New Orleans	Lakefront	LA N	3002N 9001W	18R/38L	6700	120.6	
133	HVN		New Haven	Tweed	CT N	4115N 7253W		5600	126.95	
177	JFK	KJFK	NEW YORK	John F Kennedy	NY N	4039N 7347W	13R/31L	14572	127.4 132.4 127.05	119.1 123.9
179	LGA	KLGA	NEW YORK	La Guardia	NY N	4047N 7352W	13/31	7000	118.8 124.95 132.7 134.9	118.7 126.5
180	TSS		New York	E34th St	NY N	4045N 7400W				
180	JRE		New York	E60th St	NY N	4045N 7400W				
171	EWR	KEWR	NEWARK	International	NJ N	4043N 7410W	04R/22L	9300	120.15 127.6 128.55	118.3 135.35

No.	IATA	ICAO	Town/city	Name	St/country	location	R/W	length	APPROACH	TOWER
177	SWF	KSWF	Newburgh	Stewart Intl	NY N	4130N 7406W	09/27	11818	121.0 133.1	119.7 128.2
69	NCL	EGNT	Newcastle	International	G	5502N 0141W	07/25	7651	126.35	118.7
205	PHF	KPHF	Newport News	Patrick Henry	VA N	3708N 7629W		8003	125.7	122.1 123.4
69	NQY	EGDG	Newquay	St Mawgan	G	5026N 0500W	13/31	9894	126.5	118.5
180	IAG	KIAG	Niagara Falls	International	NY N	4306N 7857W		9125	126.15	118.7
54	NCE	LFMN	NICE	Cote d'Azur	F	4340N 0713E	05R/23L	9711	120.25 120.85	119.7 123.2
55	FNI	LFTW	Nimes	Garons	F	4345N 0425E	18/36	8005	122.1 124.9	120.8
205	ORF	KORF	Norfolk	International	VA N	3653N 7612W			118.9	120.35
241	NRK	ESSP	Norrkoping	Kungsangen	SE	5835N 1615E	09/27	7218		124.25
70	NWI	EGSH	Norwich	International	G	5241N 0117E	09/27	6043	119.35	118.5 128.0
238	OVB	UNNN	Novosibirsk	Tolmachevo	RA	5501N 8240E	07/25	11808	127.1 128.5 133.8	118.1 118.3
41	NUE	EDDN	Nurnberg		D	4930N 1105E	10/28	8858	119.475 119.525 124.775	118.3 127.2
123	OAK	KOAK	OAKLAND	International	CA N	3744N 12213W	11/29	10000	120.1 120.9 133.95 135.4	
223	ODE	EKOD	Odense	Beldringe	OY	5529N 1020E	06/24	5397	134.5 135.1	
95	OKA	ROAH	Okinawa	Naha	JA	2612N 12739E	18/36	9840	121.1 126.5 135.1	119.1 126.5
187	TIK	KTIK	Oklahoma City	Tinker AFB	OK N	3500N 9700W	17L/35R	7200	126.5	
187	PWA		Oklahoma City	Wiley Post	OK N	3532N 9738W		9800	124.6	
187	OKC	KOKC	Oklahoma City	Will Rogers World	OK N	3523N 9736W			126.65	120.1
208	OLM		Olympia	Municipal	WA N	4658N 12254W		5419		
208	OMK		Omak	Municipal	WA N	4828N 11931W		4650		
124	ONT	KONT	Ontario	International	CA N	3403N 11736W	08L/26R	12200	119.65 125.5 127.25 134.0 135.4	120.6
31	OPO	LPPR	Oporto	Francisco da Carneiro	CS	4114N 0841W	18/36	11417	121.1	118.1
146	ORL	KORL	Orlando	Executive	FL N	2830N 8725W	07/25	6000	119.4 120.15 121.1	120.15
145	MCO	KMCO	ORLANDO	International	FL N	2826N 8119W	18L/36R	12004	118.1 126.2 127.5	118.45
96	OSA	RJOO	Osaka	Itami	JA	3447N 13527E	14R/32L	9840	127.5	124.7 124.3
95	KIX		Osaka	Kansai Intl	JA	3432N 13526E			120.1	126.2
17	YOO		Oshawa		OT C	4353N 7855W				
212	OSH		Oshkosh	Wittman Field	WI N	4403N 8833W	18/36	8000	127.5	
100	GEN	ENGM	Oslo	Gardemoen	LN	6012N 1105E	01/19	10499	118.225 120.45 131.35	118.3
99	FBU	ENFB	Oslo	Fornebu	LN	5954N 1037E	06/24	7218	120.6	118.1 119.775
221	OST	EBOS	Ostend		OO	5112N 0252E	08/26	10499		118.7
17	YRO		Ottawa	Rockcliffe	OT C	4527N 7542W				
17	YOW	CYOW	OTTAWA	M-C International	OT C	4519N 7540W	14/32	10000	127.7 135.15	
283	VDA	LLOV	Ovda		4X	2956N 3456E	02R/20L	9843	129.9 127.4	118.8

Ref	IATA	ICAO	Town/city	Name	St	Ctry	location	R/W	length	APPROACH	TOWER
124	OXR		Oxnard	Ventura County	CA	N	3412N 11912W	16/34	5950	124.7	124.0
229	PDG	WIMG	Padang	Tabing		PK	0053S 10021E	06/24	6070	122.2	118.275
41	PAD	EDLP	Paderborn	Lippstadt		D	5137N 0837E		7152		
113	PGA		Page	Municipal	AZ	N	3655N 11126W		5500	124.2	
124	UDD		Palm Springs	Bermuda Dunes	CA	N	3344N 11616W		4030	128.15	
147	LNA	KLNA	Palm Beach	County/Lantana	FL	N	2636N 8005W		3485	127.35	
124	PSP	KPSP	Palm Springs	Regional	CA	N	3349N 11630W	8500		126.7	
47	PMI	LEPA	PALMA	Son San Juan		EC	3933N 0244E	06L/24R	10728	118.5	118.3, 118.45
124	PMD	KPMD	Palmdale	Municipal	CA	N	3438N 11805W	07/25	12002	126.1	119.2
108	PAQ	PAAQ	Palmer	Municipal	AK	N	6135N 14910W				
147	PFN		Panama City	Bay County	FL	N	3013N 8540W		6314		119.1
285	PFO	LCPH	Paphos	International		5B	3443N 3229E			120.8	119.9
202	PRX		Paris	Cox Field	TX	N	3338N 9527W		6000	124.8	
56	JDP		Paris	Issy les Moulineaux		F	4850N 0220E				
57	JPU		Paris	la Defense		F	4850N 0227E				
57	LBG	LFPB	Paris	Le Bourget		F	4858N 0227E		9843		119.1
55	CDG	LFPG	PARIS	Charles de Gaulle		F	4901N 0233E	07/25	11860	118.15, 119.85, 121.15	119.25, 120.65, 125.325
57	ORY	LFPO	PARIS	Orly		F	4843N 0223E	10/28	11975	118.85, 120.85, 124.45	118.7, 121.05, 135.5
3	PBH	VQPR	Paro			A5	2724N 8926E	07/25	6512	122.7	
208	PSC		Pasco	Tri-Cities	WA	N	4616N 11907W	15/33	7700	125.0	121.4
58	PUF	LFBP	Pau	Uzein		F	4323N 0025W	13/31	8202	120.6	118.5
18	YYF	CYYF	Penticton	Municipal	BC	C	4927N 11936W		6000	126.525	118.1
70	PZE	EGHK	Penzance	Heliport		G	5007N 0532W				
59	PGF	LFMP	Perpignan	Rivesaltes		F	4244N 0252E	15/33	8202	120.75	118.3, 121.9
257	PER	YPPH	Perth		WA	VH	3156S 11558E	03/21	11300	118.7, 123.7	120.5
257	JAD	YPJT	Perth	Jandakot	WA	VH	3206S 11553E	06/24	3698	122.9	118.1, 119.4
2	PEW	OPPS	Peshawar'			AP	3400N 7131E	17/35	9000		
18	YPQ	CYPQ	Peterborough		OT	C	4413N 7821W		5000		
191	PNE	KPNE	Philadelphia	Northeast	PA	N	4004N 7500W		7000	123.8	
190	PHL	KPHL	PHILADELPHIA	International	PA	N	3953N 7514W	09R/27L	10500	123.8, 123.7, 124.1	118.5, 126.9, 128.4
113	PHX	KPHX	PHOENIX	Sky Harbor International	AZ	N	3326N 11201W	08L/26R	11001	120.7, 126.8	118.7, 120.9
85	HKT	VTSP	Phuket	International		HS	0806N 9818E	09/27		118.1, 122.7	
277	PCN		Picton	Karamika		ZK	4118S 17403E		4840		126.7
282	PZB	FAPM	Pietermaritzburg	Oribi		ZS	2939S 3024E	16/34	4200		122.0
91	PSA	LIRP	Pisa	Galilei Galilei		I	4341N 1024E	04R/22L	9800	126.075	119.1

#	IATA	ICAO	Town/city	Name	St/country	location	R/W	length	APPROACH	TOWER
192	AGC		Pittsburgh	Allegheny County	PA N	4021N 7955W		6500		119.35
180	PLB		Plattsburgh	Clinton County	NY N	4441N 7331W		5000		121.1
268	PCM		Playa del Carmen		XA	2030N 8700W				
70	PLH	EGHD	Plymouth	Roborough	G	5025N 0406W	13/31	3839	133.55	122.6
59	PIS	LFBI	Poitiers	Biard	F	4635N 0018E	03/21	7710	124.4	118.5
147	PPM		Pompano Beach	Air Park	FL N	2615N 8006W		4420		119.7
219	TAT	LZTT	Poprad	Tatry	OM	4909N 2015E	09/27	8530	118.9	120.25
208	CLM		Port Angeles	Fairchild Intl	WA N	4807N 12330W		6349		118.1
282	PLZ	FAPE	Port Elizabeth	H F Verwoerd	ZS	3359S 2537E	08/26	6496	119.7	120.2
180	POU		Poughkeepsie	Dutchess County	NY N	4137N 7353W		5000		118.1
218	PRG	LKPR	PRAGUE	Ruzyne	OK	5006N 1416E	06/24	12188	119.0 119.7	118.1 121.4
248	PRI	FSPP	Praslin		S7	0419S 5542E	15/33	3993		
73	PIK	EGPK	Prestwick		G	5530N 0435W	13/31	9800	120.55	118.15 120.6 121.8
282	PRY	FAWB	Pretoria	Wonderboom	ZS	2539S 2813E	11/29	6000	134.8	120.6
203	PUC		Price	Carbon County	UT N	3936N 11045W		7300		
155	HPV		Princeville		HI N	2212N 15926W		3380		
203	PVU		Provo	Municipal	UT N	4012N 11143W		7091	124.3	118.0 120.3 121.9
81	POP	MDPP	Puerto Plata	La Union	HI	1946N 7034W	08/26	10102	124.3 127.85	
19	YQB	CYQB	Quebec City		PQ C	4648N 7123W	06/24	9000	124.3	
277	ZQN	NZQN	Queenstown	Frankton	ZK	4501S 16844E	05/23	5000		
81	UIO	SEQU	Quito	Mariscal Sucre	HC	0008S 7829W	17/35	10236	119.3	126.9 127.45
170	RDU	KRDU	Raleigh-Durham	International	NC N	3552N 7847W	05L/23R	10000	119.3	119.25
6	RKT	OMRK	Ras al Khaymah	International	A6	2550N 5605E				
192	RDG		Reading	General Spaatz	PA N	4022N 7557W		6350		118.1
232	REC	SBRF	Recife	Guararapes	PE PP	0807S 3455W	18/36	9846	119.0 119.7	118.5
19	YQF	CYQF	Red Deer	Industrial	AL C	5210N 11353W		3450	119.7	118.6
19	YQR	CYQR	Regina	Municipal	SA C	5026N 10440W	13/31	7900	120.1	118.7
174	RNO	KRNO	Reno	Cannon Intl	NV N	3930N 11946W	16R/34L	10000	119.2 120.8 126.3	118.0
250	REK	BIRK	REYKJAVIK		TF	6408N 2157W	02/20	5987	119.0	118.2
247	RHO	LGRP	Rhodes	Paradisi	SX	3624N 2805E	07/25	10696	120.6	121.1
205	RIC	KRIC	Richmond	Byrd Field	VA N	3730N 7720W		9000	119.9 126.3	126.4
91	RMI	LIPR	Rimini	Miramari	I	4341N 1024E	04R/22L	9800	119.1 122.1	126.075
234		SBAF	Rio de Janeiro	Campos/Afonsos	RJ PP	2252S 4322W				118.9 122.8
82	MDE	SKRG	Rio Negro	J M Cordova	HK	0613N 7536W	01/19	8028	8028	122.8
233	SDU	SBRJ	Rio de Janeiro	Santos Dumont	RJ PP	2252S 4309W				118.0
233	GIG	SBGL	RIO JANEIRO	Galeao	RJ PP	2249S 4315W	10/28	13123	119.0 119.7	118.2 120.3

	IATA	ICAO	Town/city	Name	St/country	location	R/W	length	APPROACH	TOWER
125	RIR		Riverside	Flabob	CA N	3359N 11724W		3200		
125	HMT		Riverside	Hemet-Ryan	CA N	3344N 11701W		4315	124.8	
125	RAL		Riverside	Municipal	CA N	3357N 11727W		5400	135.4	121.0
87	RUH	OERK	Riyadh	King Khaled Intl	HZ	2458N 4643E	15L/23R	13780	120.0 126.0	118.6 118.8
59	RNE	LFLO	Roanne	Renaison	F	4603N 0400E	02/20	4790		
206	ROA		Roanoke	Regional	VA N	3720N 7958W		6802	124.5	
19	YRM	CYRM	Rocky Mtn House		AL C	5225N 11454W		6400		
91	CIA	LIRA	Rome	Ciampino	I	4148N 1236E	15/33	7218	119.2	120.5 122.1
91	FCO	LIRF	Rome	Fiumicino	I	4149N 1215E	16R/34L	12795	119.2	118.7
173	ROW	KROW	Roswell	Industrial Air Ctr	NM N	3318N 10431W		13000		
277	ROT	NZRO	Rotorua	Lakefront	ZK	3807S 17619E	01/19	4500	119.5	121.2
226	RTM	EHRD	Rotterdam	Zestienhoven	PH	5157N 0426E	06/24	7218	127.025 118.2	119.7
41	SCN	EDRS	Saarbrucken	Ensheim	D	4913N 0707E	09/27	6562	118.55	129.475
125	SAC	KSAC	Sacramento	Executive	CA N	3830N 12130W		5503	127.4	125.7
125	SMF	KSMF	Sacramento	Metropolitan	CA N	3842N 12136W	16R/34L	8600	124.5 125.2 127.4	
20	YJN	CYJN	Saint Jean		PQ C	4520N 7350W				
166	STP		Saint Paul	Downtown	MN N	4456N 9304W		6550		119.1
167	STL	KSTL	Saint Louis	Lambert Intl	MO N	3844N 9021W	12R/30L	11019	121.2	118.5 120.05
202	SGU		Saint George	Municipal	UT N	3705N 11335W		6100	121.1 124.3	
204	SLC	KSLC	SALT LAKE CITY	International	UT N	4047N 11158W	16R/34L	12000	123.75 124.125 124.9	118.3 135.5
216	SZG	LOWS	Saltzburg	Maxglan	OE	4748N 1300E	16/34	8366	119.3	118.1
234	SSA	SBSV	Salvador	Dois de Julho	BA PP	1254S 3819W	10/28	9859		118.35
126	SDM		San Diego	Brown Municipal	CA N	3234N 11658W	8L/26R	8000		119.6
128	SPQ		San Pedro	Catalina	CA N	3346N 11814W				
202	SAT	KSAT	San Antonio	International	TX N	2932N 9828W	12R/30L	8500	118.05 124.45 125.1	119.8 128.05
214	SIG	TJIG	San Juan	Isla Grande	PR N	1827N 6606W	09L/27R	5332		
128	CSL		San Luis Obispo	McChesney Field	CA N	3521N 12038W	3402	127.3		
126	MYF		San Diego	Montgomery Fld	CA N	3248N 11708W				
127	SJC		San Jose	Municipal	CA N	3722N 12155W		8900	120.7	124.0
128	SBP		San Luis Obispo	Municipal	CA N	3514N 12038W		4800		119.05
127	SFO	KSFO	SAN FRANCISCO	International	CA N	3737N 12223W	10L/28R	11870	134.5 135.65	120.5
126	SAN	KSAN	SAN DIEGO	Lindbergh Intl	CA N	3244N 11711W	09/27	9400	124.35	118.3 125.6
213	SJU	TJSJ	SAN JUAN	Luis Munoz Marin International	PR N	1826N 6600W	08/26	10000	119.4 120.9	118.3
289	SAH	OYSN	Sana'a	International	7O N	1529N 4413E	18/36	10669	125.3	118.9
147	SFB	KNRJ	Sanford	Central Florida	FL N	2847N 8114W		8000		
79	SMV	LSZS	Sankt Moritz		HB	4630N 0950E				121.1

#	IATA	ICAO	Town/city	Name	St/country	location	R/W	length	APPROACH	TOWER
29	SRZ	SLCZ	Santa Cruz	El Trompillo	CP	1748S 6311W	15/33	6234		119.9 123.85 126.8
129	SBA		Santa Barbara	Goleta	CA N	3425N 11950W		6049	125.4	
128	SNA	KSNA	Santa Ana	John Wayne	CA N	3340N 11752W			132.8	
173	SAF	KSAF	Santa Fe	Municipal	NM N	3537N 10605W		8323		
129	SMO		Santa Monica	Municipal	CA N	3401N 11827W		4987	128.5	119.15 120.1
129	STS		Santa Rosa	Sonoma County	CA N	3830N 12248W		5115	127.8	
29	VVI	SLVR	Santa Cruz	Viru Viru Intl	CP	1738S 6308W	15/33	11482		
32	SCU	MUCU	Santiago/Cuba	Antonio Maceo	CU	1958N 7550W	09/27	13123	126.9	
81	STI	MDST	Santiago	Cibao	HI	1928N 7042W	12/30	5200		
82	HEX	MDHE	Santo Domingo	Herrera	HI	1830N 7000W				118.1
81	SDQ	MDSD	Santo Domingo	Las Americas	HI	1826N 6940W	17/35	11000	119.3	118.05
247	JTR	LGSR	Santorini	Thira	SX	3624N 2528E	16L/34R	6955		129.75
234	CGH	SBSP	Sao Paulo	Congonhas	SP PP	2337S 4639W	17R/35L	6362	119.4 119.8	118.1 118.4 126.4
234	GRU	SBGR	Sao Paulo	Guarulhos	SP PP	2326S 4629W	09L/27R	12140	119.9 120.4	120.1
147	SRQ		Sarasota	Bradenton	FL N	2724N 8233W	13/31	7003	118.4	118.3
20	YXE	CYXE	Saskatoon		SA C	5210N 10642W	09/27	8300		119.1
153	SAV	KSAV	Savannah	International	GA N	3208N 8112W	09/27	9351		119.2
114	SDL		Scottsdale	Municipal	AZ N	3337N 11154W	03/21	8251		
209	BFI	KBFI	Seattle	King/Boeing	WA N	4731N 12218W	13R/31L	10001		119.2
210	LKE		Seattle	Lake Union	WA N	4741N 12215W				
210	RNT		Seattle	Renton	WA N	4730N 12212W		5379		
209	SEA	KSEA	SEATTLE	Tacoma Intl	WA N	4727N 12218W	16L/34R	11900	123.9	119.9
114	SEZ		Sedona		AZ N	3450N 11147W		5142		
83	SEL	RKSS	SEOUL	Kimpo Intl	HL	3733N 12648E	14R/32L	10499	120.2 121.4	118.1
49	SNN	EINN	Shannon	International	EI	5242N 0855W	06/24	10500		118.7
5	SHJ	OMSJ	Sharjah		A6	2520N 5531E	12/30	12336		118.6
202	F39		Sherman-Denison	Grayson County	TX N	3343N 9640W	03/21	9000	134.15	125.4
70	ESH	EGKA	Shoreham by Sea		G	5050N 0018W		2703	123.15	
252	SIP	UKFF	Simferopol		UR	4455N 3403E		12402		
294	QPG		Singapore	Paya Lebar	9V	0121N 10354E	02/20	5354	119.9	118.05
295	XSP	WSSL	Singapore	Seletar	9V	0125N 10352E	03/21	5354		118.45 122.7
293	SIN	WSSS	SINGAPORE	Changi Intl	9V	0122N 10359E	02L/20R	13123	119.3	118.6
226	SXM	TNCM	Sint Maarten	Prinses Juliana	PJ	1802N 6307W	09/27	7073	128.95	118.7
79	SIR	LSGS	Sion		HB	4613N 0720E	08/26	6562		
108	SGY		Skagway	Municipal	AK N	5927N 13518W		3850		
2	KDU	OPSD	Skardu		AP	3521N 7532E	15/33	6500	119.7	118.55

#	IATA	ICAO	Town/city	Name	St	Country	location	R/W	length	APPROACH	TOWER
223	SGD	EKSB	Soenderborg			OY	5458N 0948E	14/32	4921	118.7	118.1 120.4
103	SOF	LBSF	Sofia	International		LZ	4242N 2325E	09/27	9186	119.5 123.7	126.2
108	SXQ		Soldotna		AK	N	6028N 15102W		4973	125.7	118.2
223	SFJ	BGSF	Sondrestrom	Kangerlussuaq		OY	6701N 5042W	10/28	9236	118.3	127.725
70	SOU	EGHI	Southampton	Eastleigh		G	5057N 0121W	02/20	5653	120.225 128.85	118.3
71	SEN	EGMC	Southend	Rochford		G	5134N 0042E	06/24	5265	128.95	120.7
211	GEG	KGEG	Spokane	International	WA	N	4738N 11732W	03/21	9000	124.7	118.1 118.7
185	SGH		Springfield	Beckley	OH	N	3950N 8350W	06/24	9000	118.85 126.5	118.2
239	LED	ULLI	St Petersburg	Pulkovo		RA	5948N 3016E	10R/28L	12408	125.2 129.8	
263	ANU	TAPA	St John's	VCBird - Antigua		V2	1708N 6147W	07/25	9000	119.1	
192	SCE		State College	University Park	PA	N	4050N 7751W		5000	134.8	
223	STA	EKVJ	Stauning			OY	5559N 0821E	09/27	4757	121.4	
100	SVG	ENZV	Stavanger	Sola		LN	5853N 0538E	18/36	8366	119.4 119.6	118.35
132	SBS		Steamboat Spr	Bob Adams	CO	N	4030N 10651W		3913		
278	SZS		Stewart Island			ZK	4658S 16754E				
241	ARN	ESSA	Stockholm	Arlanda		SE	5939N 1755E	01/19	10827	119.4 126.65	125.0 119.4
242	BMA	ESSB	Stockholm	Bromma		SE	5921N 1757E	12/30	5863	120.15	118.5 118.1
129	SCK	KSCK	Stockton	Metropolitan	CA	N	3754N 12114W	11L/29R	8651	123.85 125.1 127.75	120.3
59	SXB	LFST	Strasbourg	Entzheim		F	4832N 0738E	05/23	7874	120.7 121.35 125.875	118.7
133	BDR	KBDR	Stratford	Sikorsky Memorial	CT	N	4109N 7307W	11/29	4761		126.95
148	SUA		Stuart	Witham Field	FL	N	2710N 8013W	08/26	5300	126.6	118.8 122.7
42	STR	EDDS	STUTTGART	Echterdingen		D	4841N 0913E		8366	119.2	123.6
258	RSE	ASBK	Sydney	Au-Rose Bay	NS	VH	3400S 15000E	11C/29C	3648	118.1	
258			Sydney	Bankstown	NS	VH	3356S 15059E				
258	LBH		Sydney	Palm Beach	NS	VH	3353S 15110E				
257	SYD	ASSY	SYDNEY	Kingsford Smith	NS	VH	3357S 15110E	16/34	13000	124.4 126.1	120.5
181	SYR	KSYR	Syracuse	Hancock Field	NY	N	4307N 7606W	10/28	9005	124.2 124.6	123.0
290	TAI	OYTZ	Ta'izz	Ganed		7O	1341N 4408E	01/19	9843	118.5	126.5
10	TSA	RCSS	Taipei	Sung Shan		B	2504N 12133E	10/28	8547	119.7	118.1 126.18
9	TPE	RCTP	TAIPEI	Chiang Kai Shek		B	2505N 12113E	05L/23R	12008	119.5 125.1	118.7 126.18
148	TPA	KTPA	TAMPA	International	FL	N	2756N 8232W	18R/36L	11002	118.15 118.5	119.5
251	TAS	UTTT	Tashkent	Yuzhny		UK	4115N 6917E	08R/26L	13123	120.4	125.2 134.25
71	MME	EGNV	Teesside			G	5431N 0125W	05/23	7516	118.85	119.8
283	TLV	LLBG	Tel Aviv	Ben Gurion		4X	3201N 3453E	08/26	11998	120.5	118.3
284	SDV	LLSD	Tel Aviv	Sde Dov		4X	3207N 3447E	03/21	5709		122.6
48	TFN	GCXO	Tenerife	Norte/Los Rodeos		EC	2829N 1620W	12/30	11155	119.7	118.7

#	IATA	ICAO	Town/city	Name	St/country	location	R/W	length	APPROACH	TOWER
47	TFS	GCTS	Tenerife	Sur/Reina Sofia	EC	2803N 1634W	08/26	10500	120.3	119.0
171	TEB	KTEB	Teterboro		NJ N	4051N 7403W		7000	127.6	
248	SKG	LGTS	Thessaloniki	Makedonia	SX	4031N 2258E	10/28	8005	120.8	118.1 122.1
221	TED	EKTS	Thisted		OY	5704N 0842E	10/28	5249	120.3	119.3
268	TIJ	MMTJ	Tijuana	Abelardo Rodriguez	XA	3232N 11659W	09/27	8203		118.1
270	TSR	LRTR	Timisoara	Giarmata	YR	4549N 2120E	11/29	11483		
149	TIX		Titusville	Space Center Ex	FL N	2830N 8047W		6000		119.25
96		RJTF	Tokyo	Chofu	JA	3545N 13945E	15/33		119.1	
97	HND	RJTT	TOKYO	Haneda	JA	3533N 13946E	16/34	10007	124.4 125.8	118.1 118.8 124.35
97	NRT	RJAA	TOKYO	Narita	JA	3546N 14023E	07/25	13123		118.2 122.7
186	TOL	KTOL	Toledo	Express	OH N	4135N 8348W		8700	128.0 123.9	118.1
22	YKZ	CYKZ	Toronto	Buttonville	OT C	4356N 7919W				
22	YZD	CYZD	Toronto	Downsview	OT C	4345N 7928W				
22	YTZ	CYTZ	Toronto	Island	OT C	4337N 7923W		4000		
20	YYZ	CYYZ	TORONTO	Lester B Pearson	OT C	4341N 7938W	15/33	11050	125.4 124.3	118.35
130	TOA		Torrance		CA N	3348N 11820W	15R/33L	5000	118.9	124.0
59	TLS	LFBO	Toulouse	Blagnac	F	4337N 0123E	02/20	11483	121.1	118.1
60	TUF	LFOT	Tours	St Symphorien	F	4726N 0043E		7874	121.0	118.3
23	YTR	CYTR	Trenton		OT C	4407N 7731W				
92	TSF	LIPH	Treviso	San Angelo	I	4539N 1212E	07/25	7940	118.7 122.1	120.4
116	E14		Tucson	Avra Valley	AZ N	3224N 11113W		4200		
115	TUS	KTUS	Tucson	International	AZ N	3207N 11056W		11000		125.1
188	TUL	KTUL	Tulsa	International	OK N	3612N 9553W	18/36	10000		120.7
92	TRN	LIMF	Turin	Caselle	I	4512N 0739E		10827	120.15 121.1	118.5
239	ULY		Ulyanovsk		RA	5425N 4825E				
101	USH	SAWH	Ushuaia		LV	5450S 6818W				
181	UCA		Utica	Oneida County	NY N	4308N 7523W	01L/19R	6000	126.65	118.1
60	VAF	LFLU	Valence	Chabeuil	F	4455N 0458E		6890	125.7	
24	CXH		Vancouver	Coal Harbour	BC C	4920N 12310W				
23	YVR	CYVR	VANCOUVER	International	BC C	4911N 12310W	08/26	11000	120.8	120.1
32	VRA	MUVR	Varadero	J G Gomez	CU	2308N 8118W	06/24	11483		118.7
103	VAR	LBWN	Varna	International	LZ	4314N 2749E	09/27	8202		118.3
92	VCE	LIPZ	Venice	Tessera	I	4530N 1221E	04/22	10827	120.4 121.15	120.2
149	VRB	KVRB	Vero Beach	Municipal	FL N	2704N 8026W	11R/29L	7296		119.65
93	VRN	LIPX	Verona	Villafranca Veronesa	I	4524N 1053E	05/23	8717	118.65 124.5	124.45
273	VFA	FVFA	Victoria Falls		Z	1806S 2550E	12/30	7500		121.1

#	IATA	ICAO	Town/city	Name	St/country	location	R/W	length	APPROACH	TOWER
25	YWH	CYYJ	Victoria	Inner Harbour	BC C	4830N 12325W			133.85	119.1
25	YYJ	CYYJ	Victoria	International	BC C	4838N 12324W	16/34	11811	119.8 124.55 128.2	118.45 121.2
217	VIE	LOWW	VIENNA	Schwechat	OE	4807N 1633E				127.3
83	VVC	SKVV	Villavicencio	La Vanguardia	HK	0404N 7323W				119.3
203	ACT	KACT	Waco	Madison Cooper	TX N	3136N 9713W		6600		
203	CNW		Waco	TSTI	TX N	3138N 9706W		8600	133.3	
278	WKA	NZWF	Wanaka		ZK	4444S 16915E	11/29	3937		
243		EPBC	Warsaw	Babice	SP	5230N 2100E				
242	WAW	EPWA	WARSAW	Okecie	SP	5210N 2058E	15/33	12106	128.8	121.6
133	IAD	KIAD	WASHINGTON	Dulles Intl	VA N	3857N 7727W	01R/19L	11500	120.45 124.65 126.1	120.1
135	DCA	KDCA	WASHINGTON	National	DC N	3851N 7702W	18/36	6869	124.2 124.7	119.1 120.75
109	WWA		Wasilla		AK N	5950N 15012W				
278	WLG	NZWN	Wellington	International	ZK	4119S 17448E	16/34	6348	118.8	120.0
279			Wellington	Porirua	ZK	4119S 17446E				
211	EAT		Wenatchee	Pangborn	WA N	4724N 12012W		5500		
150	PBI	KPBI W	West Palm Beach	International	FL N	2641N 8005W		7989	124.6	119.1
181	FOK	KFOK	Westhampton	Suffolk County	NY N	4050N 7237W		9000		120.5
181	HPN	KHPN	White Plains	Westchester Co	NY N	4104N 7342W		6548	126.4	119.7
25	YXY	CYXY	Whitehorse		YT C	6042N 13504W	13R/31L	7200	118.3	122.5
159	CEA		Wichita	Cessna Aircraft	KS N	3740N 9729W				
159	IAB	KIAB	Wichita	McConnell AFB	KS N	3740N 9729W				
160	ICT	KICT	Wichita	Mid-Continent	KS N	3740N 9726W	01L/19R	10300	125.5 134.8	118.2
192	AVP		Wilkes Barre	Scranton	PA N	4120N 7543W	04/22	7500	124.5	
192	IPT	KIPT	Williamsport	Lycoming County	PA N	4120N 7646W		6450	124.9	
186	ILN		Wilmington	Airborne Park	OH N	3925N 8348W	04/22	9000	118.5	118.85
26	YQG	CYQG	Windsor		OT C	4216N 8258W	07/25	7900	126.85	124.7
133	BDL	KBDL	WINDSOR LOCKS	Bradley Intl	CT N	4156N 7241W	06/24	9501	125.8	120.3 125.65
26	YWG	CYWG	WINNIPEG	International	MN C	4955N 9714W	18/36	11000	119.5	118.3
170	INT	KINT	Winston-Salem	Smith-Reynolds	NC N	3607N 8015W		6655		120.9
8	WUH	ZHHH	Wuhan	Nanhu	B	3030N 11400E				
8		ZHWT	Wuhan	Wangjiaddun	B	3030N 11400E				
9	XIY	ZLXY	Xi'an	Xianyang	B	3426N 10845E	05/23	9843	123.0	135.8
27	YZF	CYZF	Yellowknife		NT C	6227N 11426W	14/32	7500	118.5	119.5
186	YNG	KYNG	Youngstown	Warren Regional	OH N	4116N 8041W	14/32	7500	120.2 127.5	120.0
116	YUM	KYUM	Yuma	International	AZ N	3239N 11436W		13299		118.1 127.75
79	ZRH	LSZH	ZURICH	Kloten	HB	4728N 0833E	16/34	12140	118.0 120.75	118.1

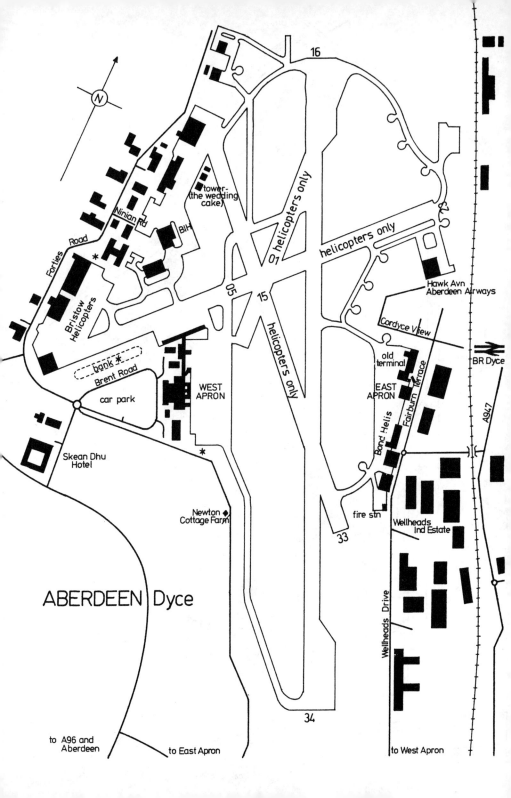

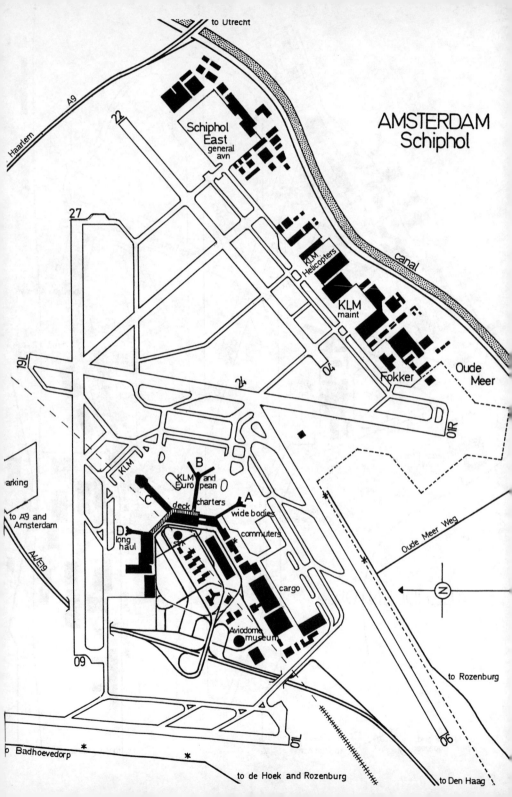

AMSTERDAM
Schiphol

to Utrecht

Haarlem

A9

22

27

19L

Schiphol
East
general
avn

KLM.
Helicopters

canal

KLM
maint

Fokker

Oude
Meer

01R

arking

to A9 and
Amsterdam

Av/eng

09

KLM

B

KLM and
European
charters

C

deck

D
long
haul

A

wide bodies

commuters

stn

cargo

Aviodome
museum

Oude Meer Weg

N

to Rozenburg

01L

to Badhoevedorp

to de Hoek and Rozenburg

to Den Haag

06

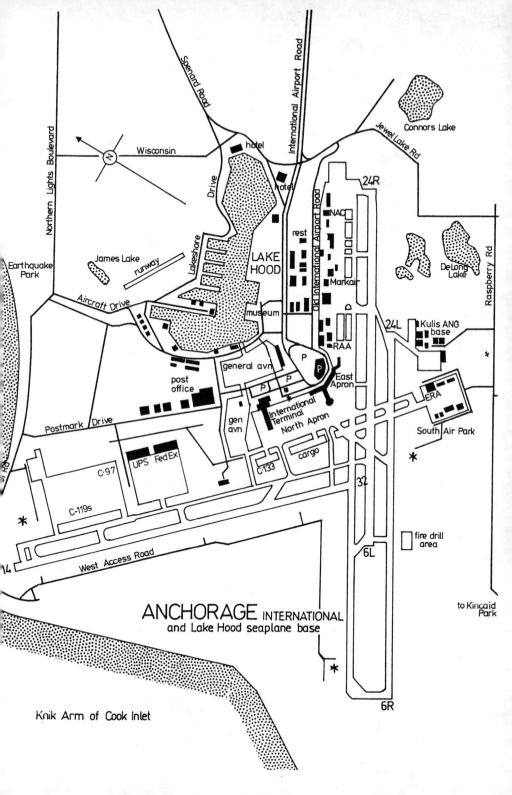

ANCHORAGE INTERNATIONAL
and Lake Hood seaplane base

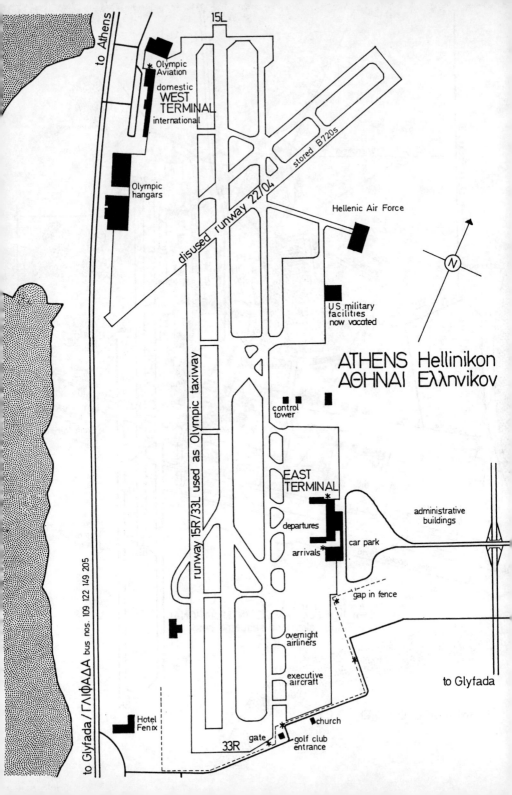

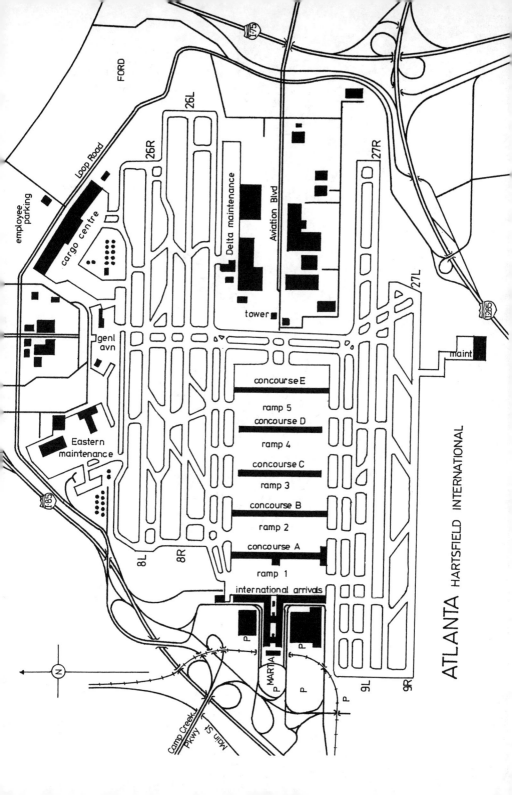

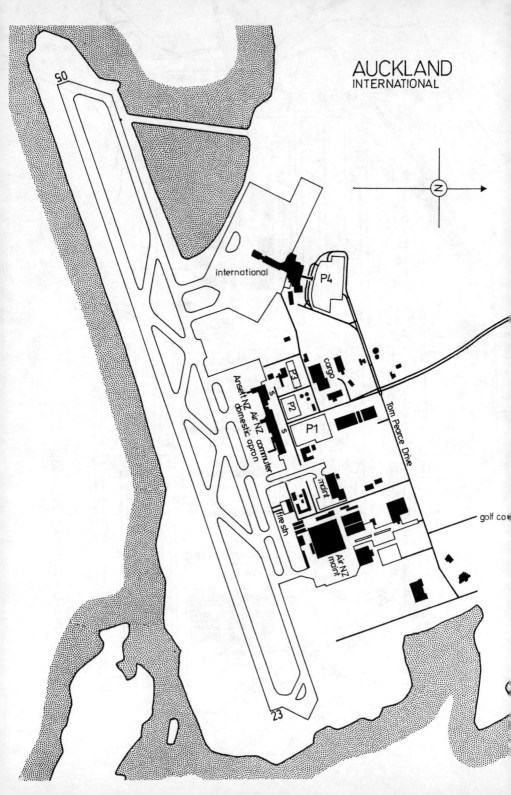

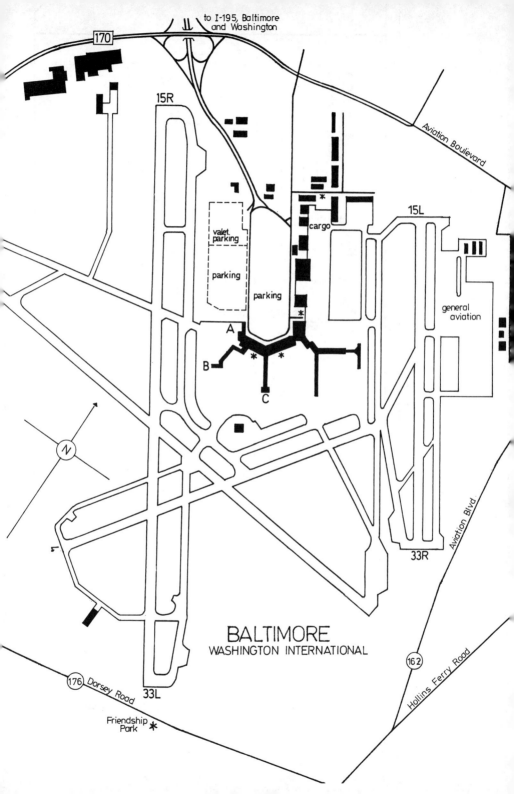

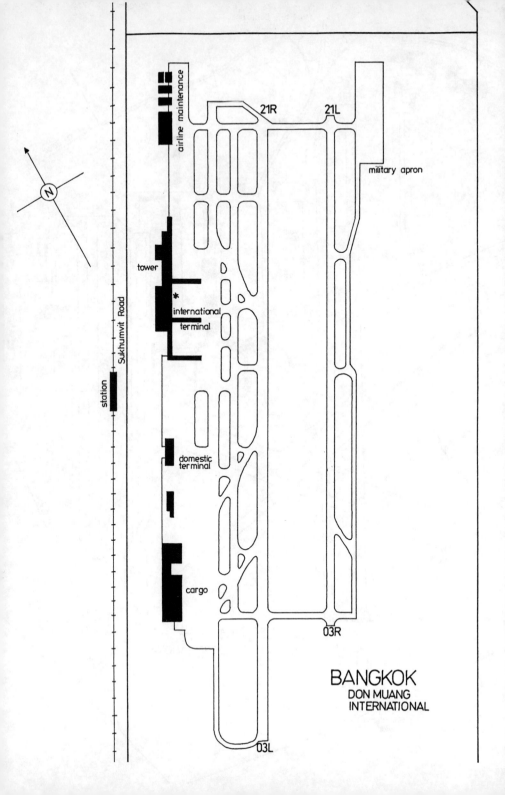

BANGKOK
DON MUANG
INTERNATIONAL

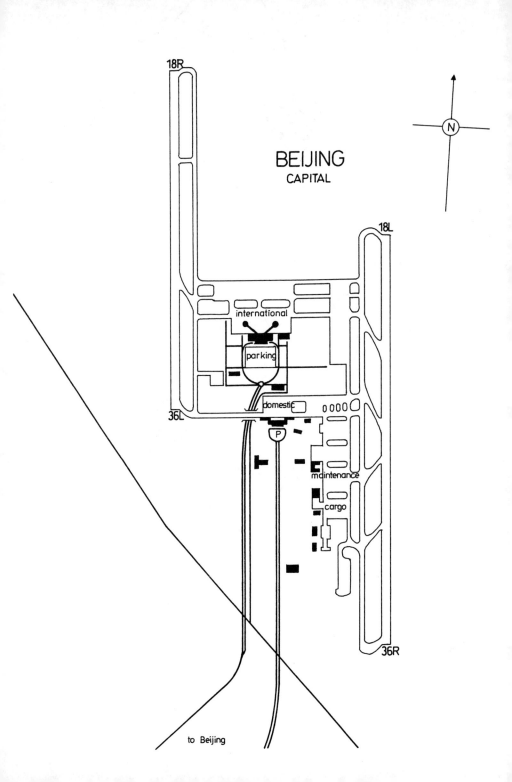

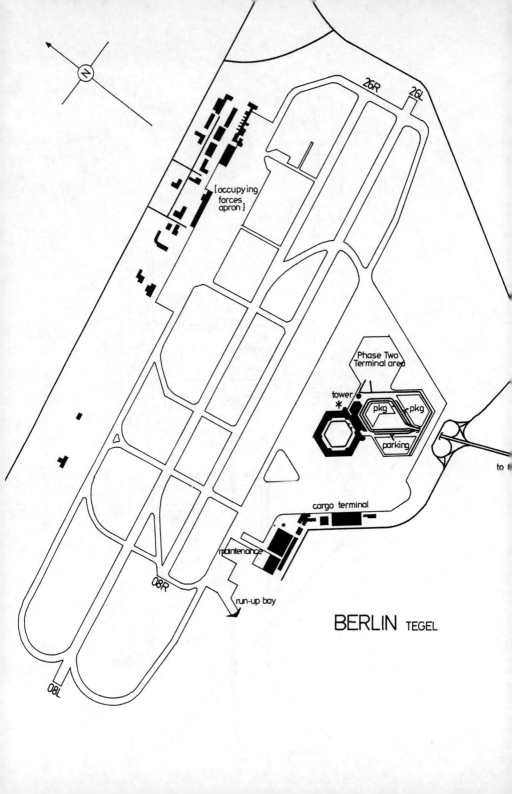

[occupying forces apron]

26R 26L

Phase Two Terminal area

tower
*

pkg pkg

parking

to

cargo terminal

maintenance

08R

run-up bay

08L

BERLIN TEGEL

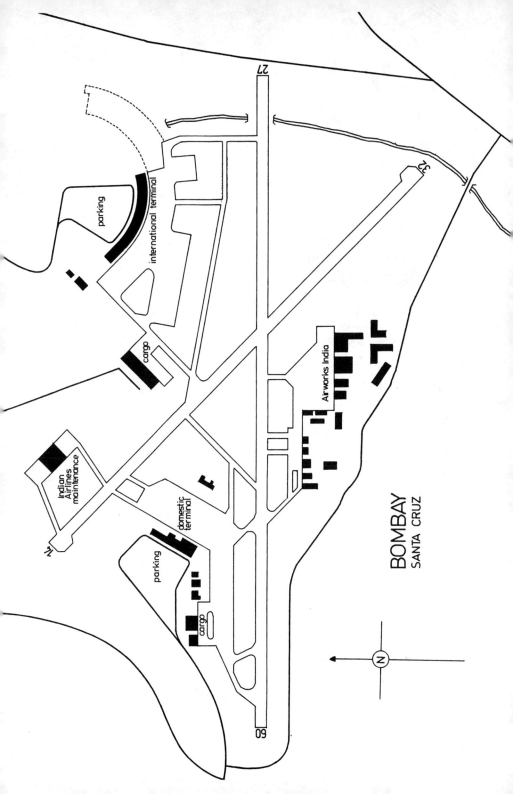

BOMBAY
SANTA CRUZ

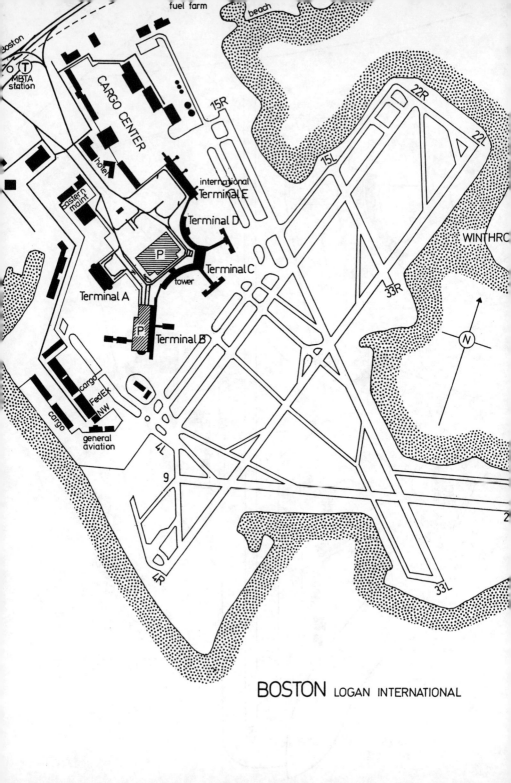

BOSTON LOGAN INTERNATIONAL

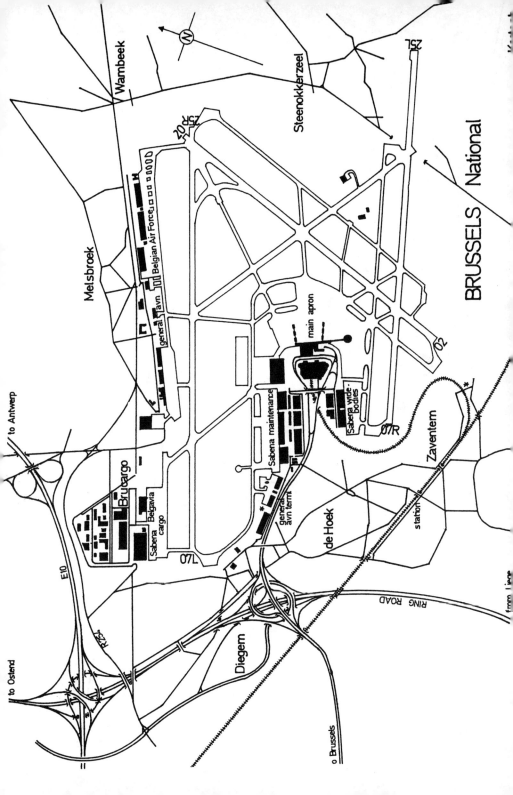

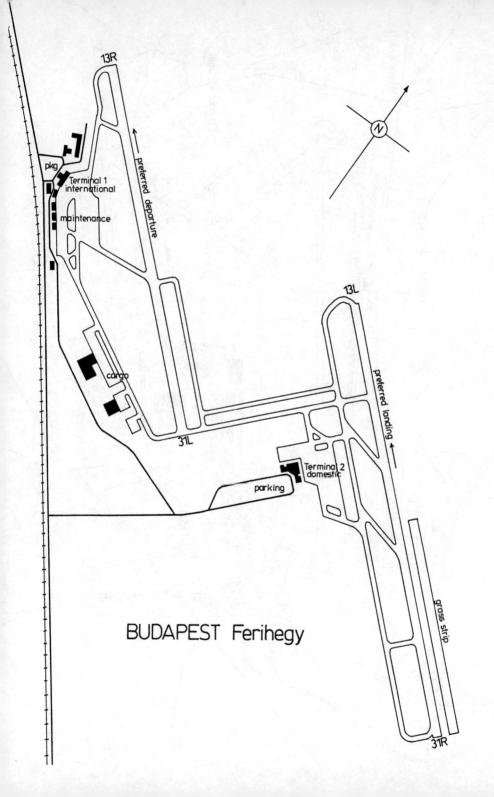

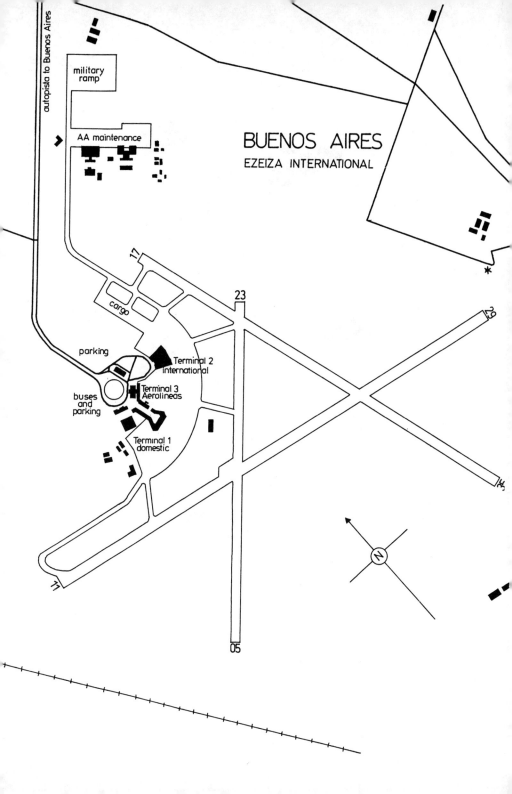

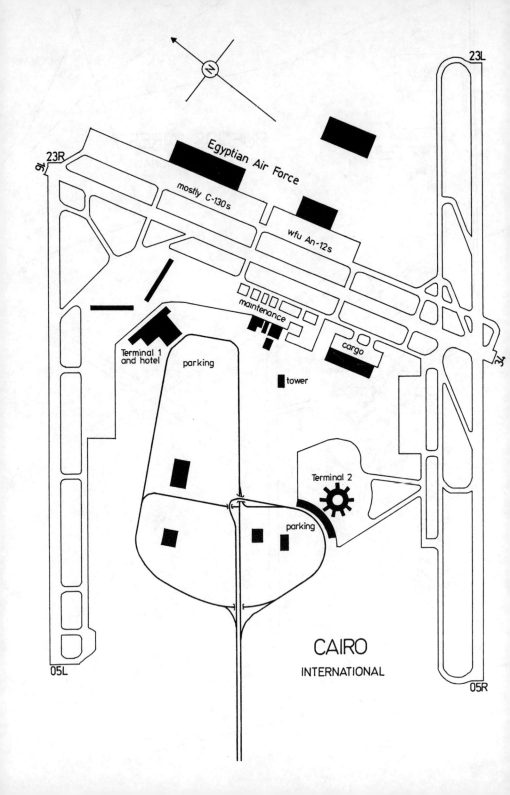

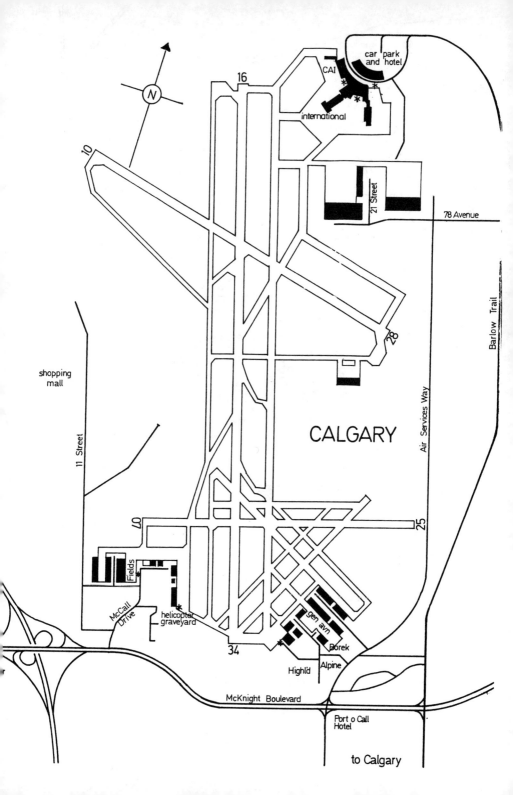

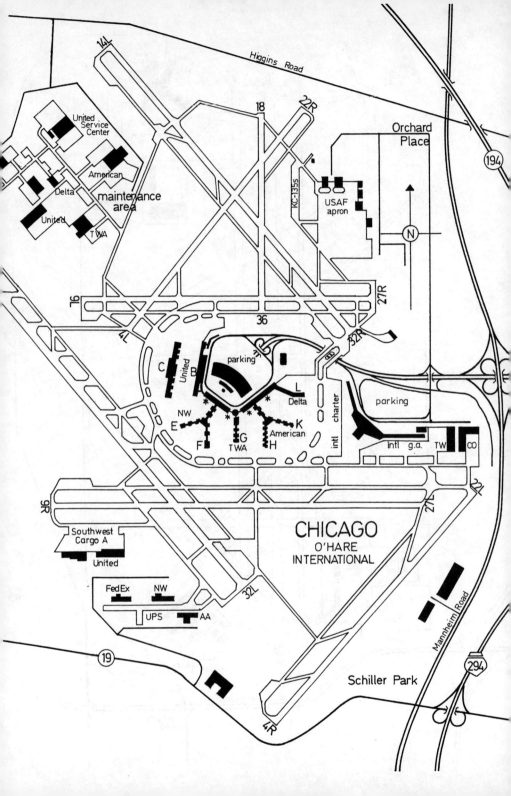

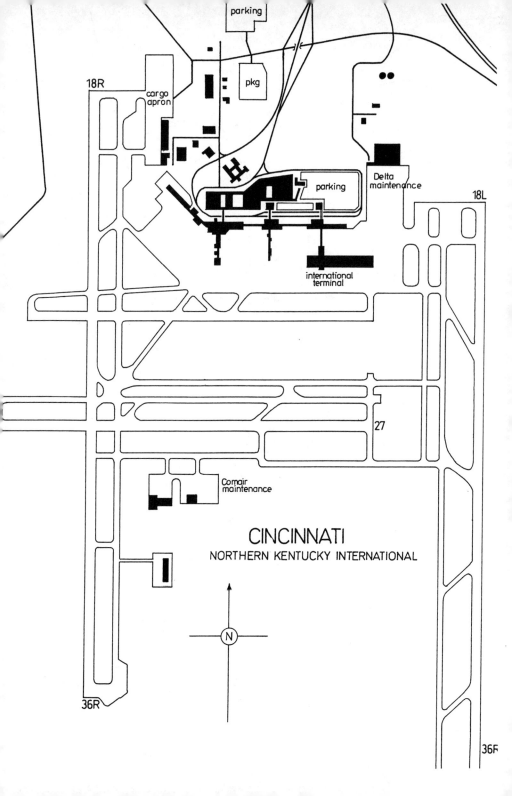

CINCINNATI
NORTHERN KENTUCKY INTERNATIONAL

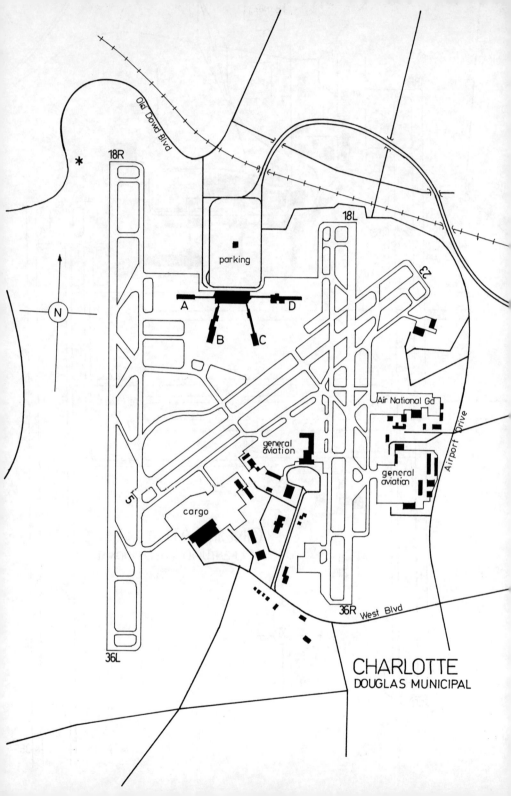

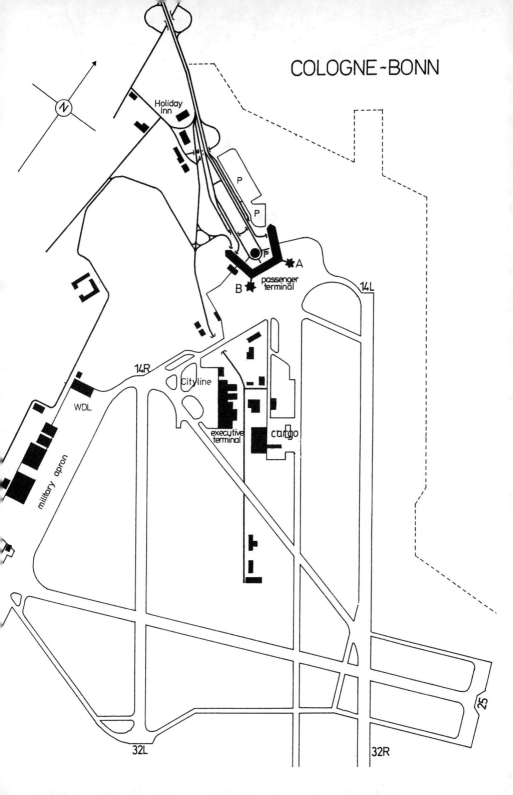

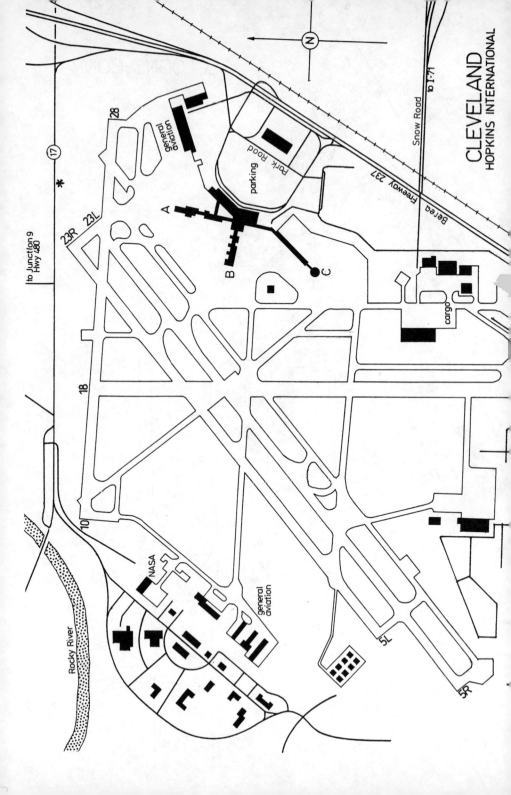

CLEVELAND
HOPKINS INTERNATIONAL

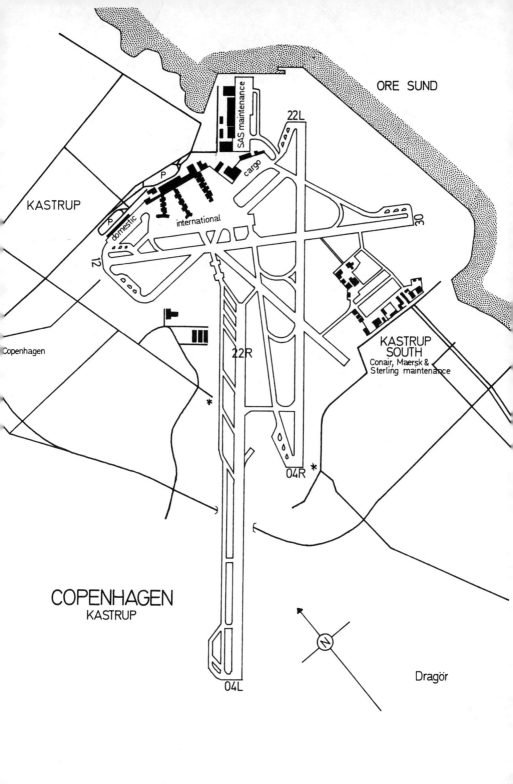

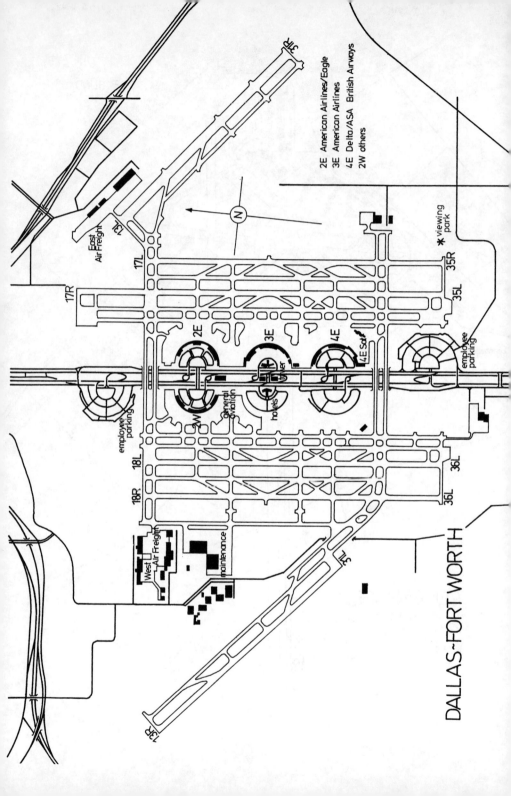

DALLAS~FORT WORTH

2E   American Airlines/Eagle
3E   American Airlines
4E   Delta/ASA   British Airways
2W   others

* viewing park

N

East Air Freight

West Air Freight

maintenance

general aviation

hotels

tower

employee parking

employee parking

2E
3E
4E
2W
4E Sat

17R
17L
13L
31R

18R
18L

35R
35L
36L

3L
13R

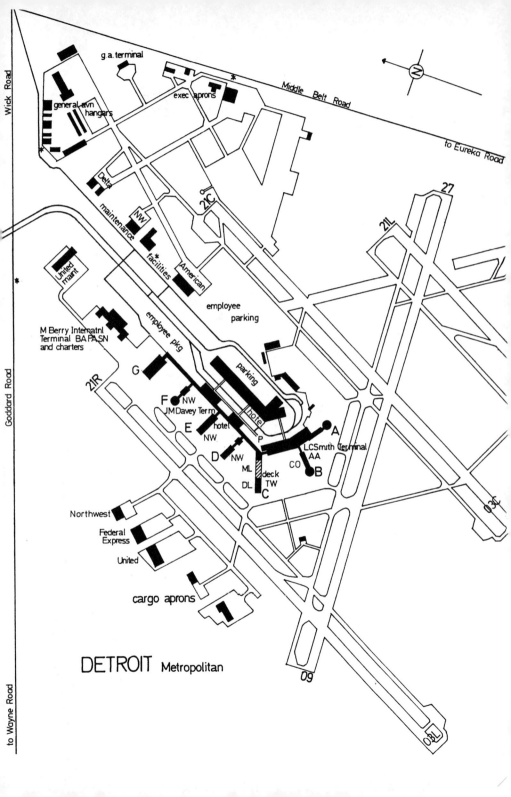

DENVER
INTERNATIONAL

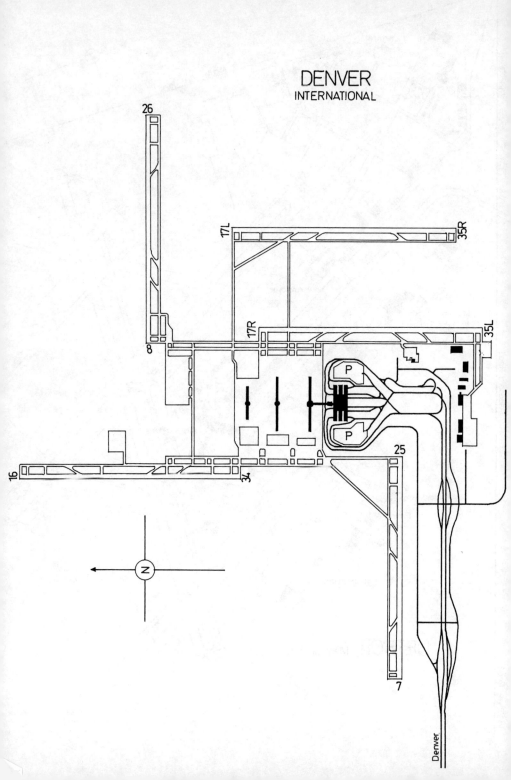

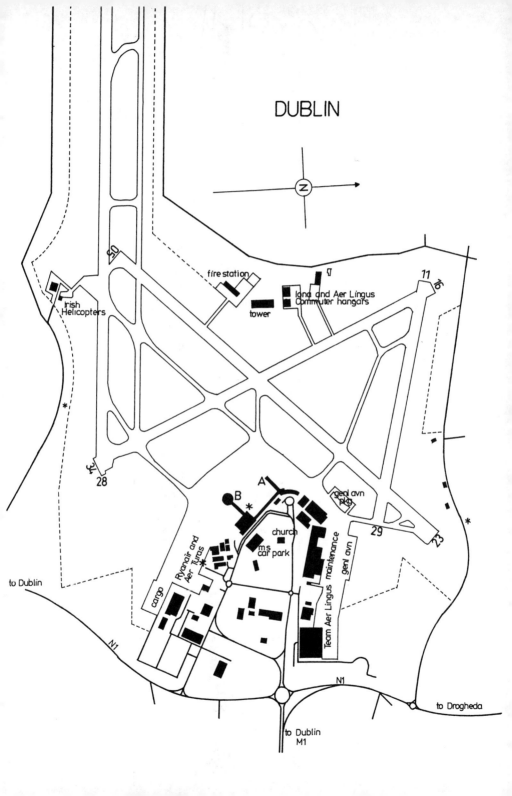

DUBLIN

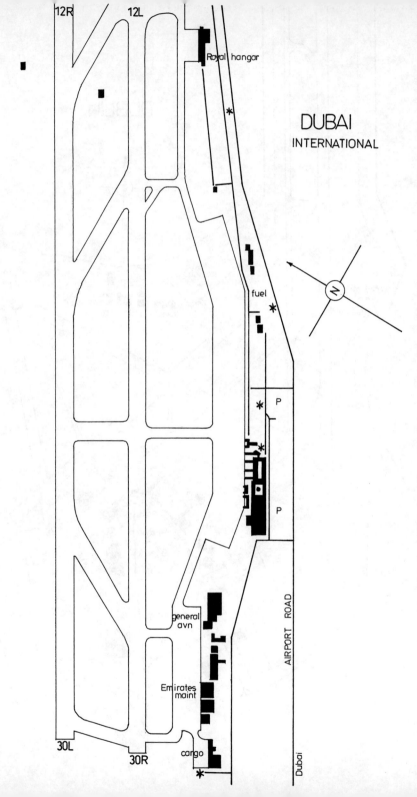

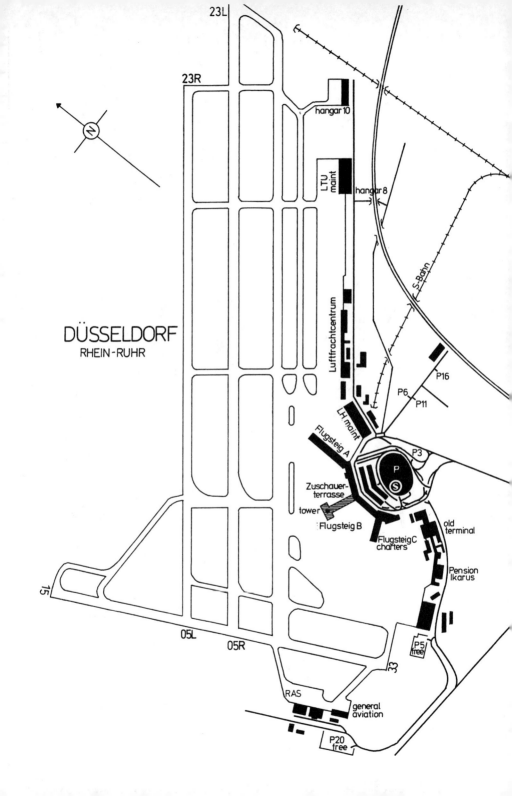

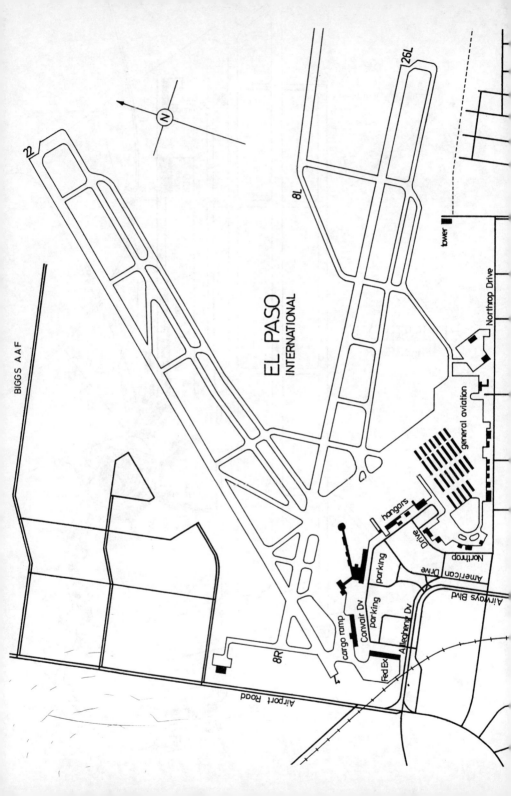

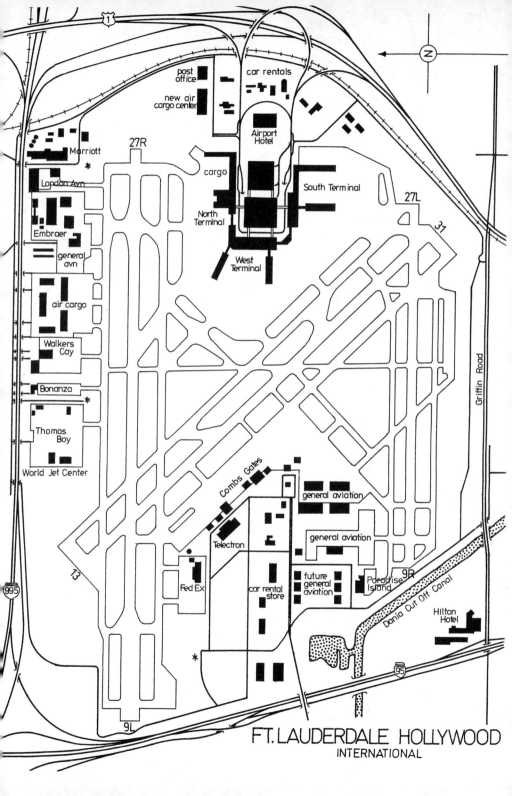

FT. LAUDERDALE HOLLYWOOD
INTERNATIONAL

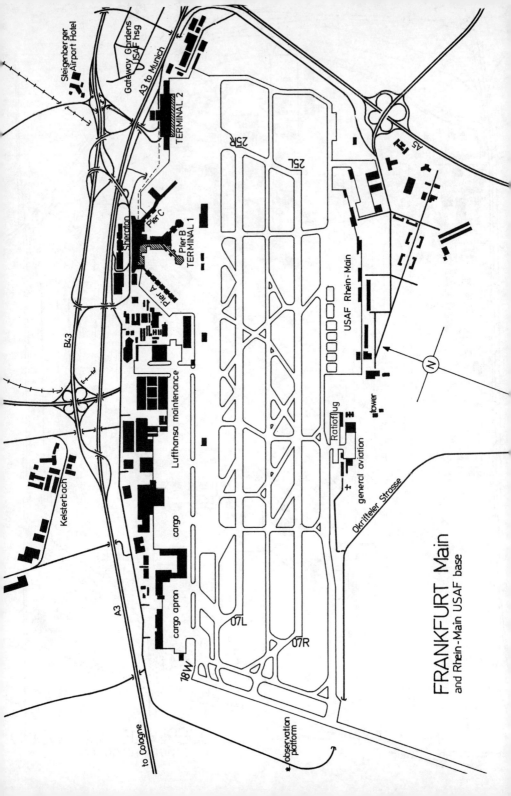

FRANKFURT Main
and Rhein-Main USAF base

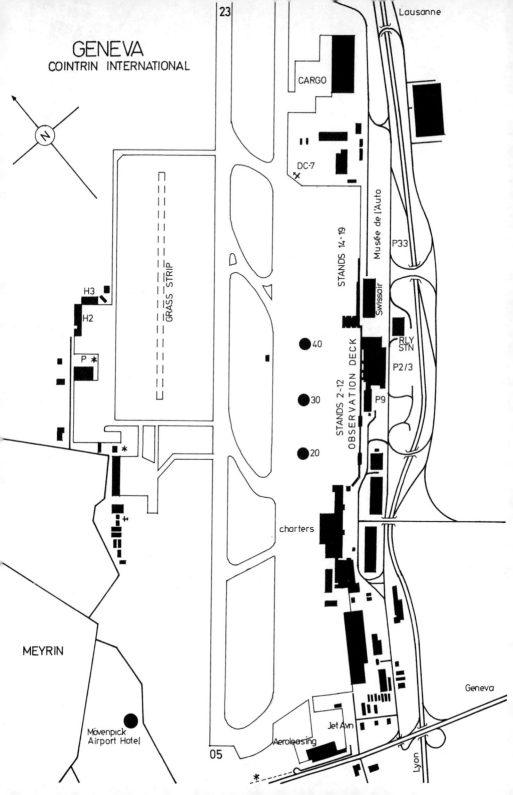

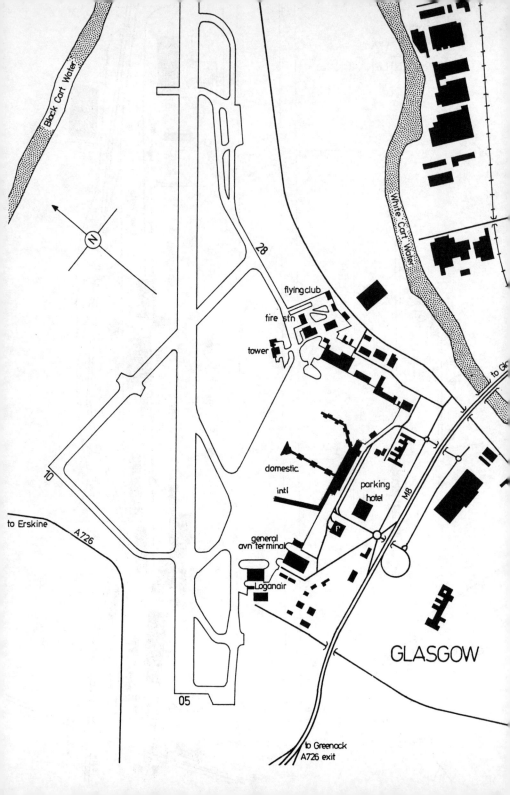

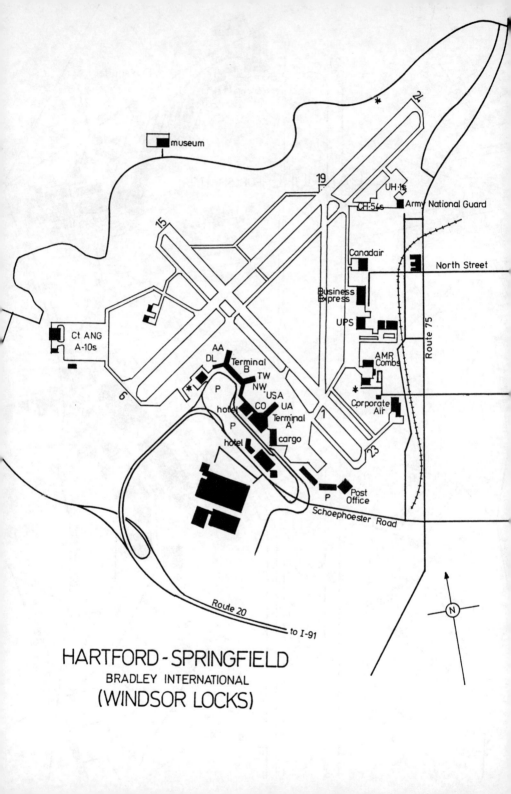

museum

24

*

19

UH-1s

CH-54s

Army National Guard

15

Canadair

North Street

Business Express

UPS

Route 75

Ct ANG
A-10s

AA

DL Terminal
B

TW

AMR
Combs

*

NW

*

USA

P

6

hotel

CO UA

Terminal
A

Corporate
Air

P

cargo

23

1

hotel

P

Post
Office

Schoephoester Road

Route 20

N

to I-91

HARTFORD - SPRINGFIELD
BRADLEY INTERNATIONAL
(WINDSOR LOCKS)

HELSINKI Vantaa

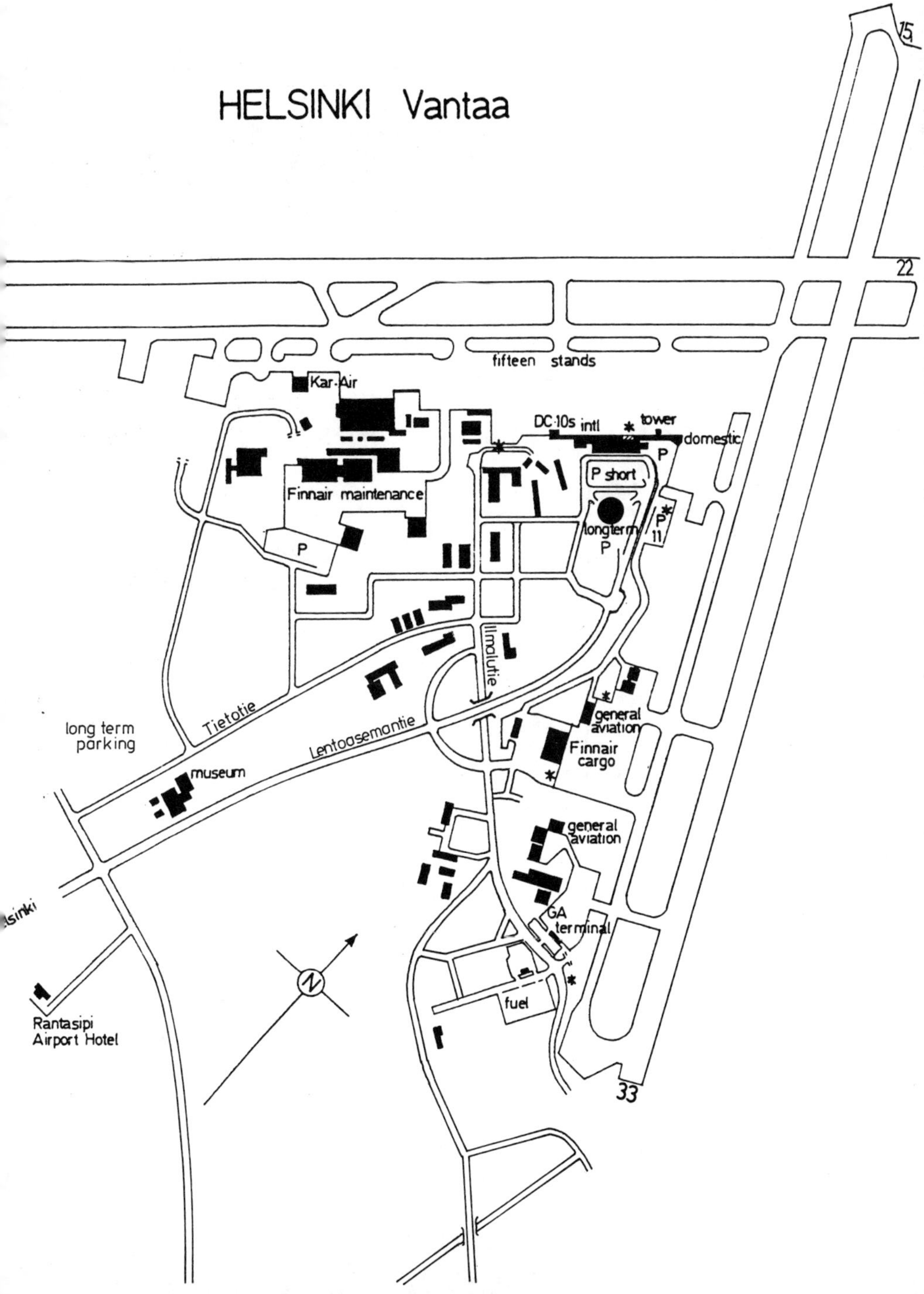

15

22

fifteen stands

Kar-Air

DC-10s intl
tower
domestic

P

Finnair maintenance

P short

longterm
P

P
11

P

Ilmailutie

Tietotie

long term
parking

Lentoasemantie

museum

general
aviation

Finnair
cargo

general
aviation

GA
terminal

N

fuel

Helsinki

Rantasipi
Airport Hotel

33

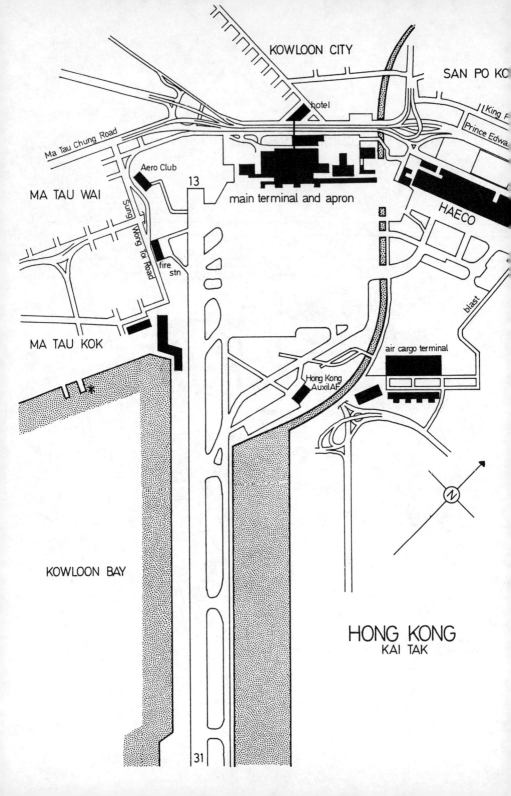

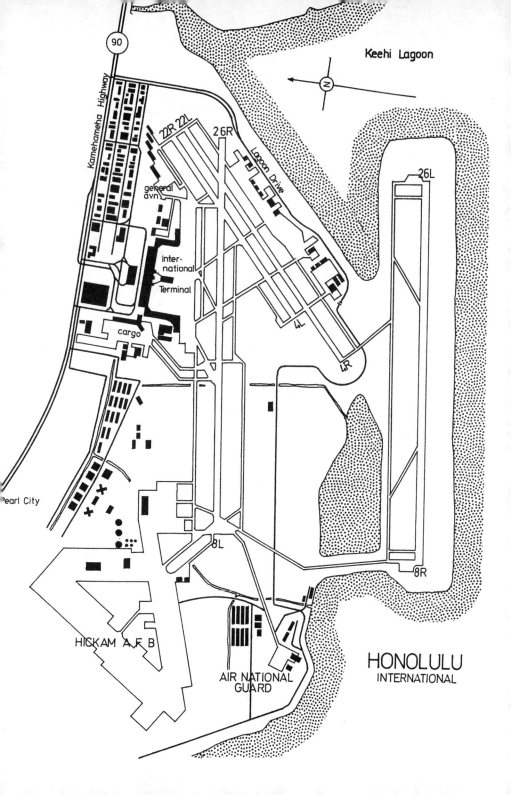

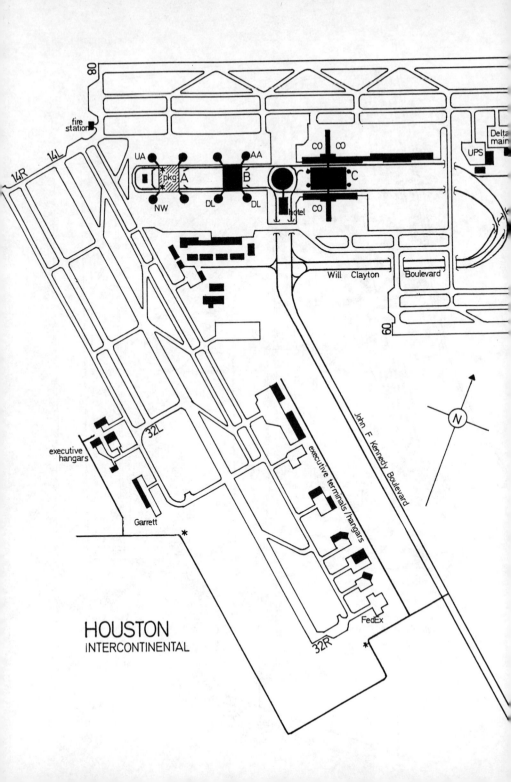

HOUSTON
INTERCONTINENTAL

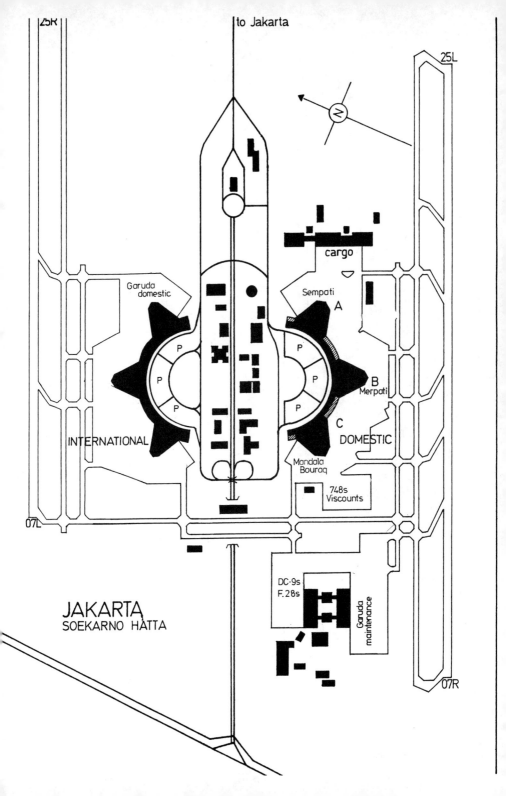

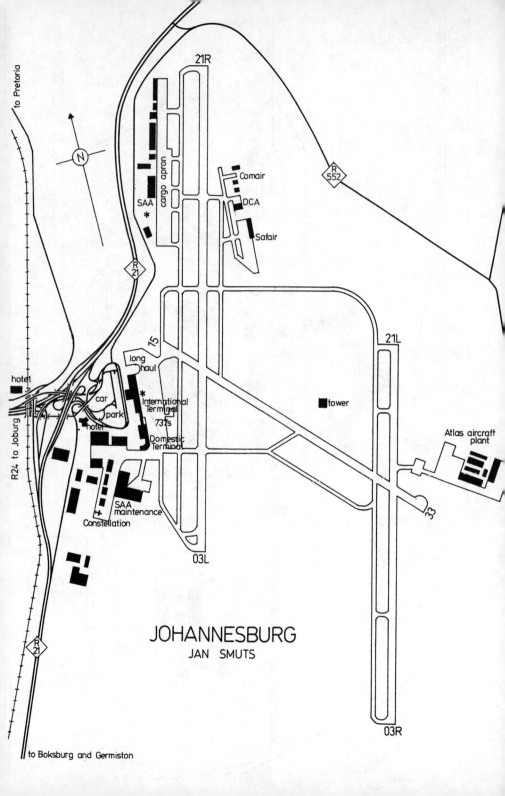

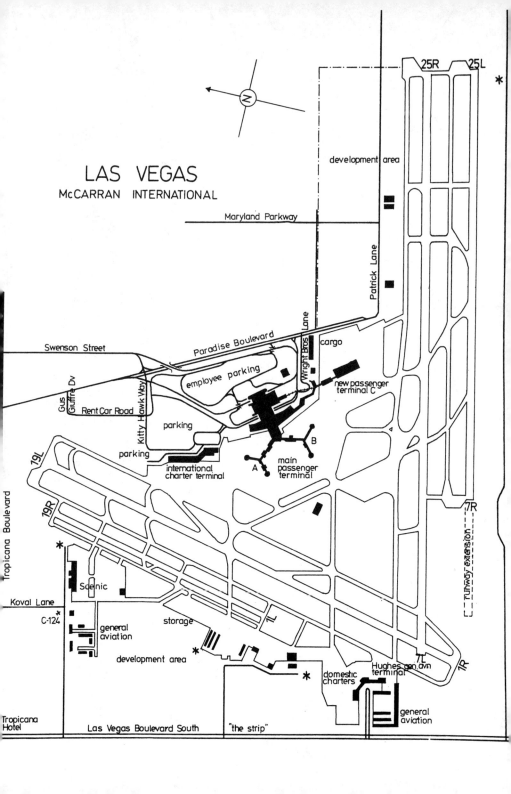

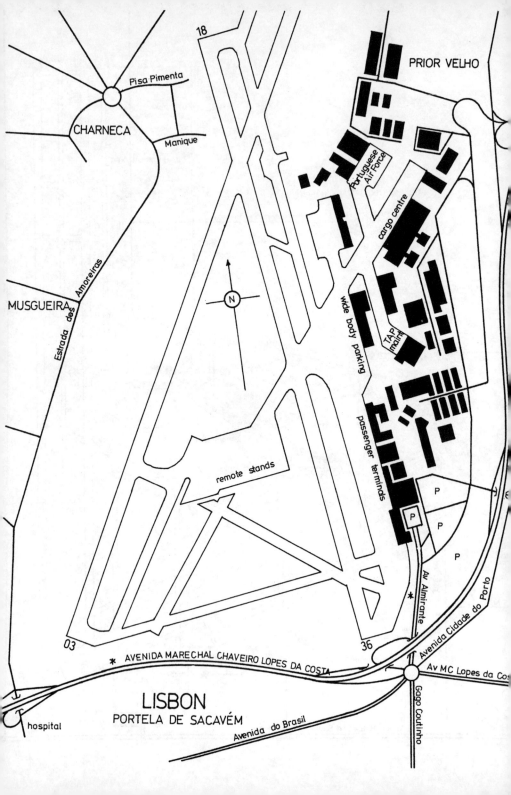

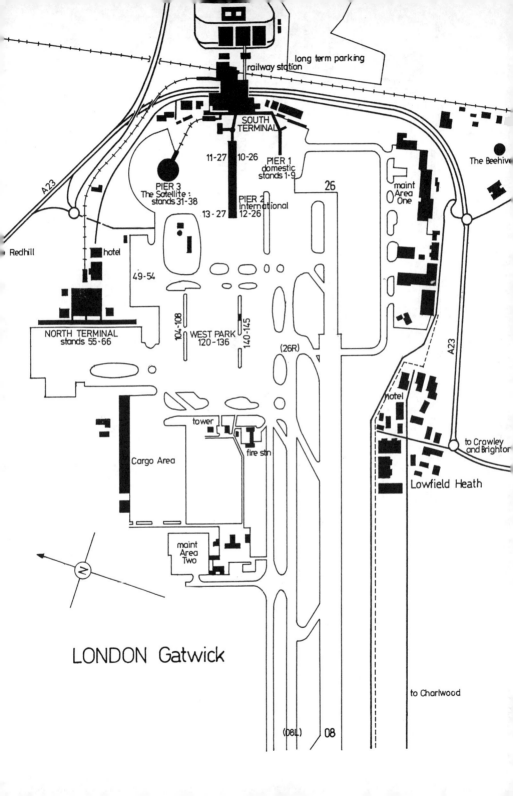

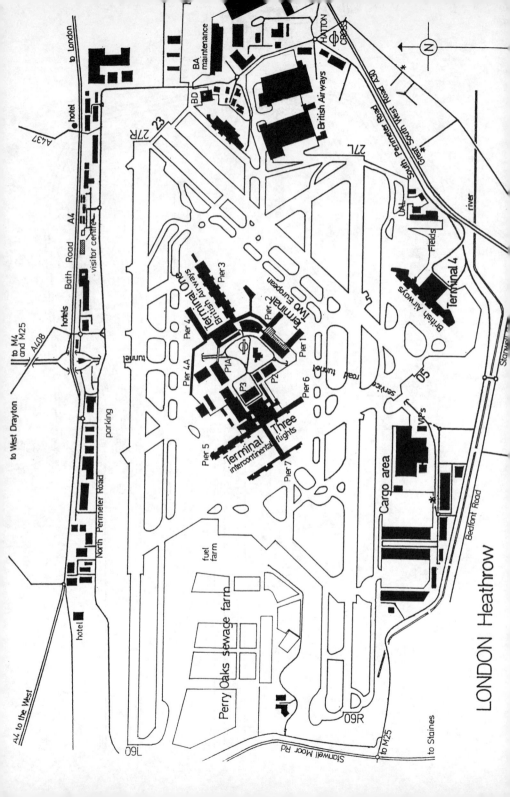

LONDON Heathrow

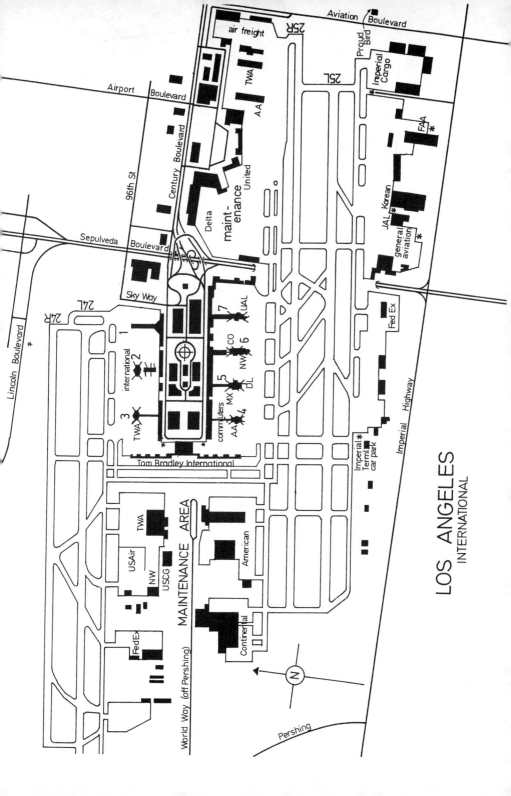

LOS ANGELES
INTERNATIONAL

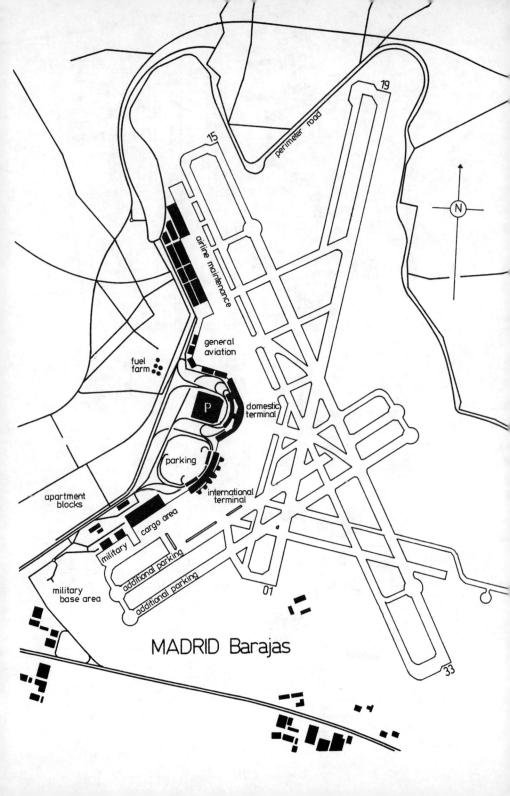

MADRID Barajas

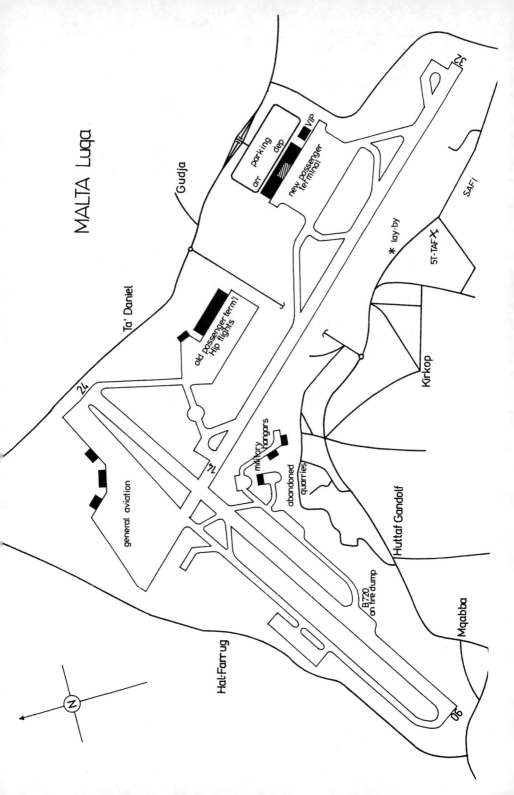

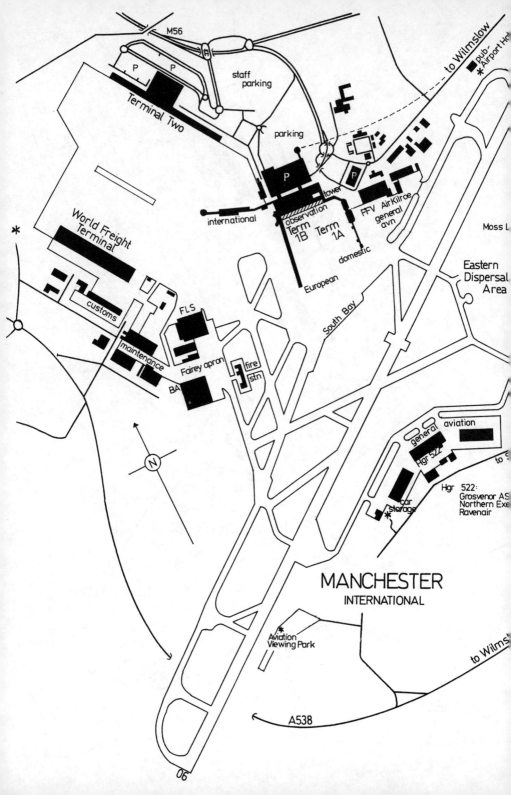

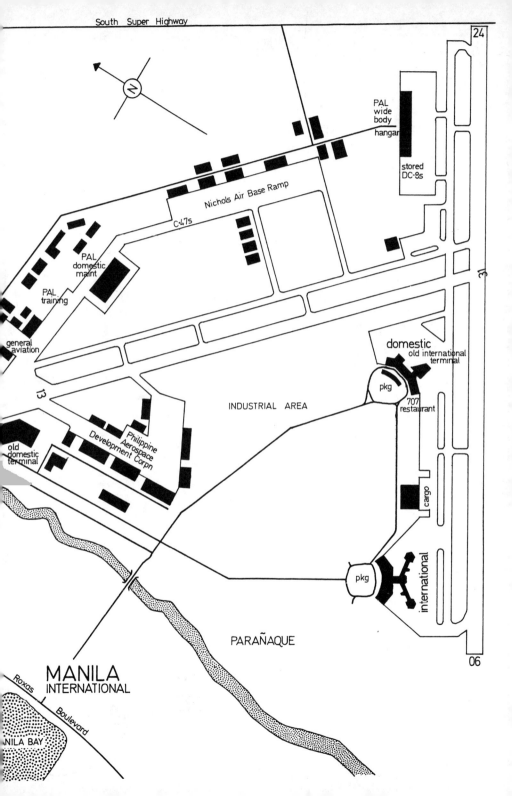

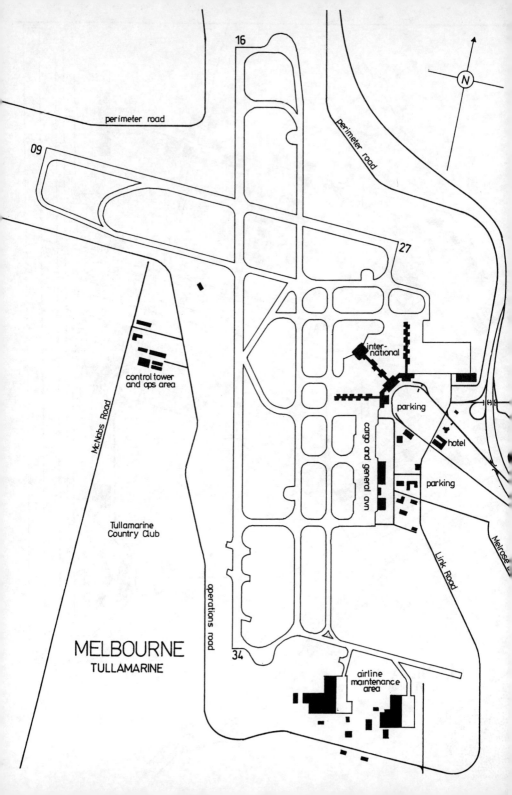

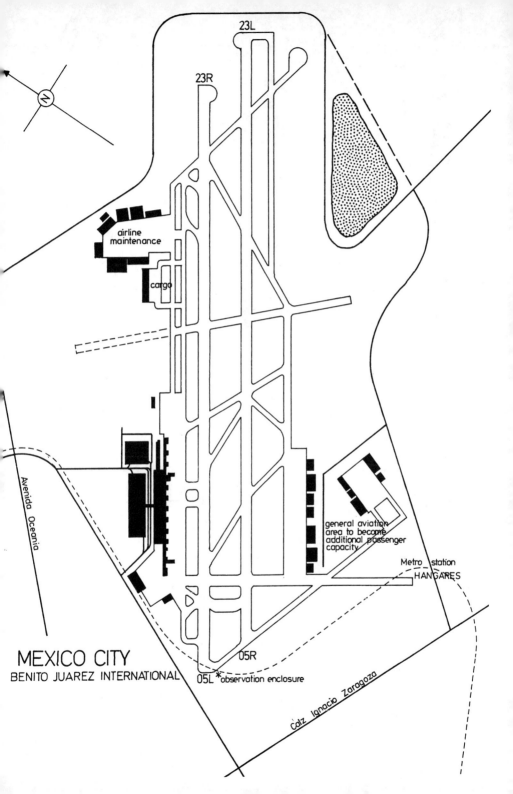

MEXICO CITY
BENITO JUAREZ INTERNATIONAL

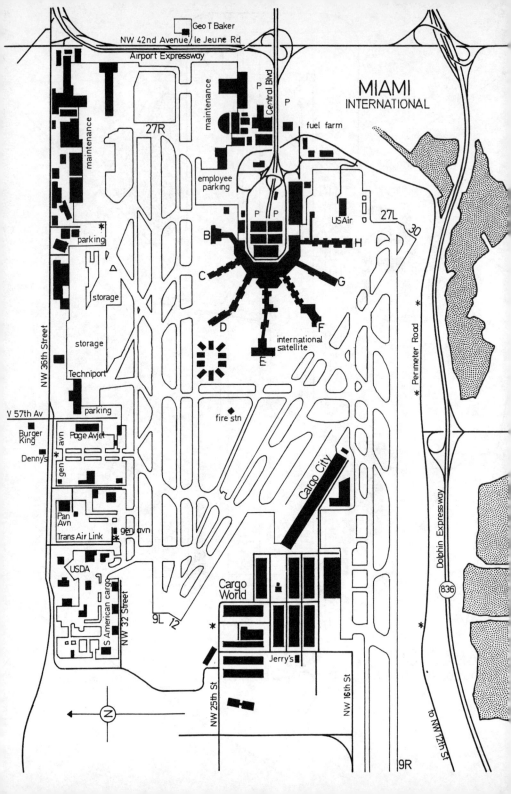

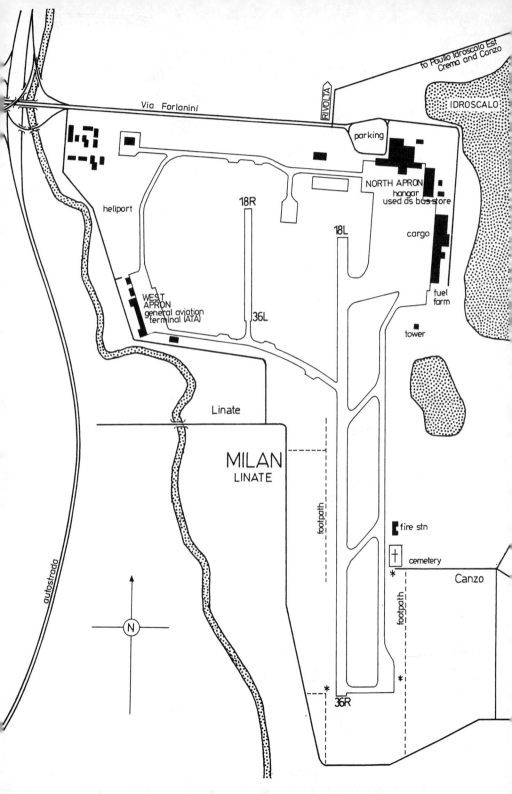

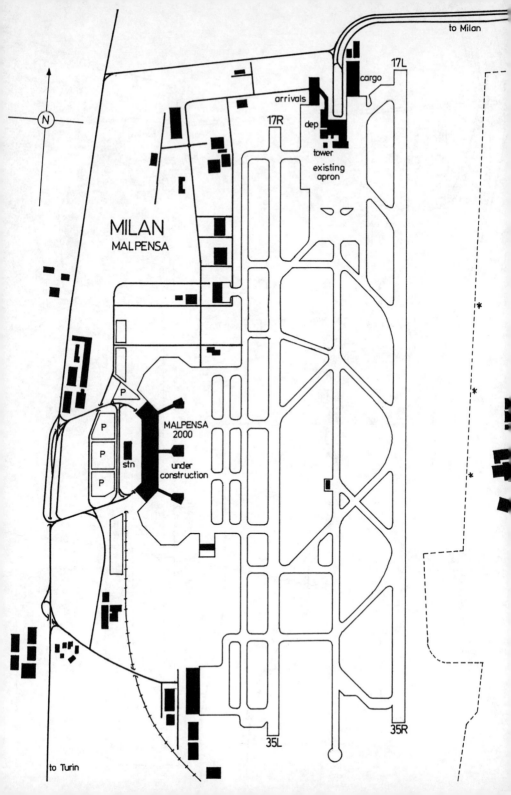

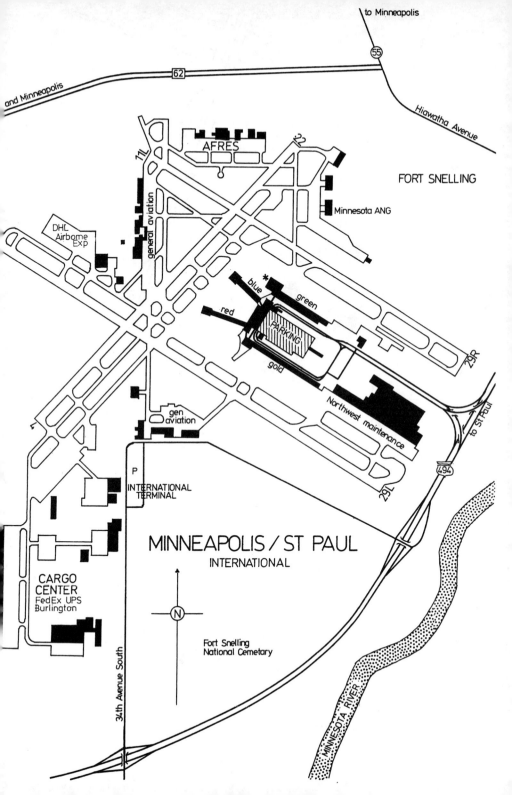

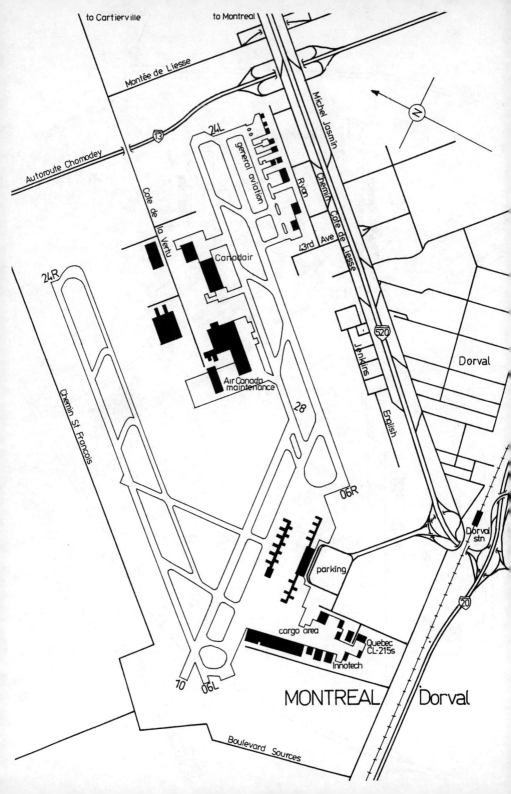

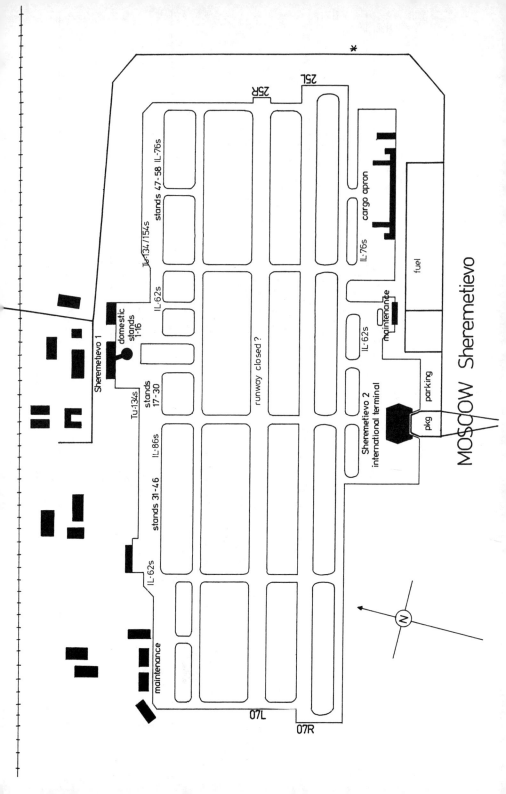

MOSCOW Sheremetievo

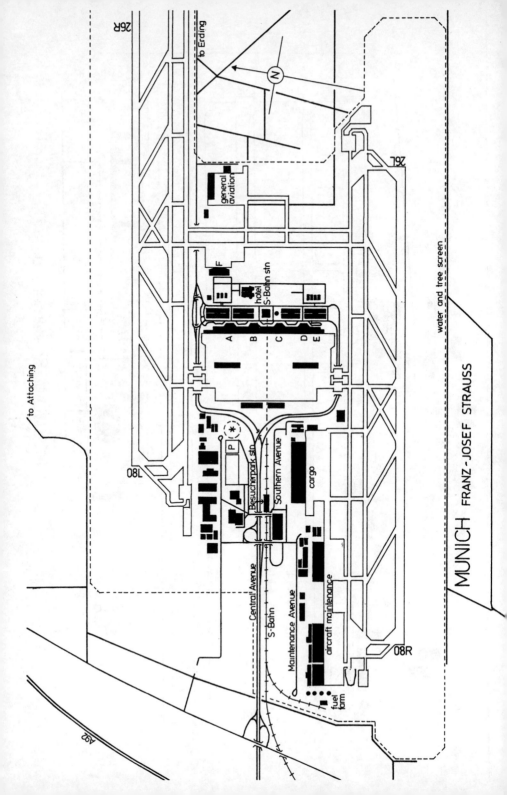

to Attaching

to Erding

N

26R

26L

08R

18R

general aviation

F

hotel
S-Bahn stn

A
B
C
D
E

P

Besucherpark stn

Southern Avenue

cargo

Central Avenue

'S-Bahn'

Maintenance Avenue

aircraft maintenance

fuel farm

A92

water and tree screen

MUNICH FRANZ-JOSEF STRAUSS

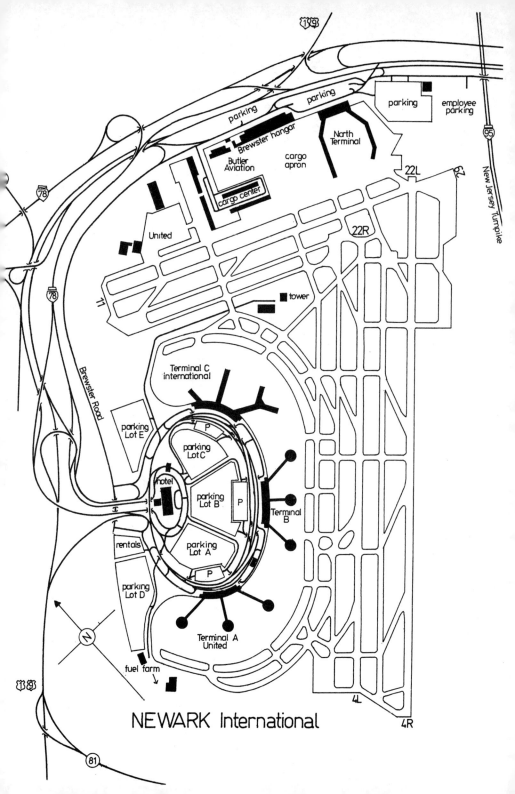

NEWARK International

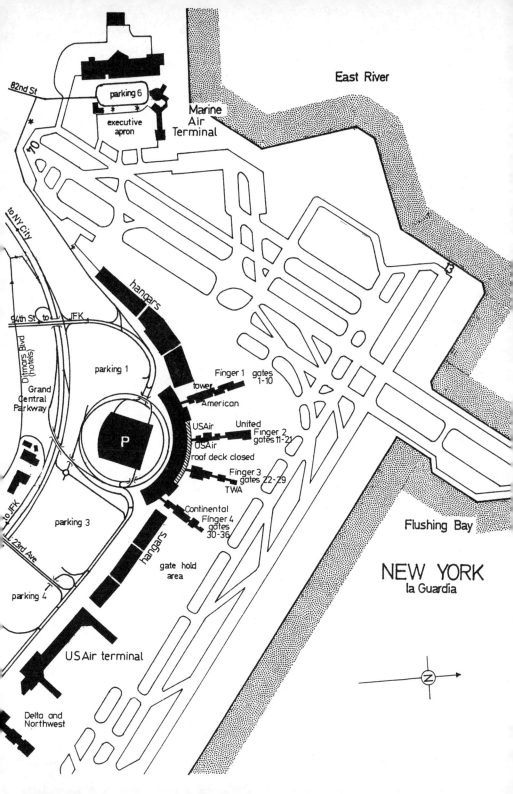

NEW YORK JOHN F KENNEDY INTERNATIONAL

JAMAICA BAY

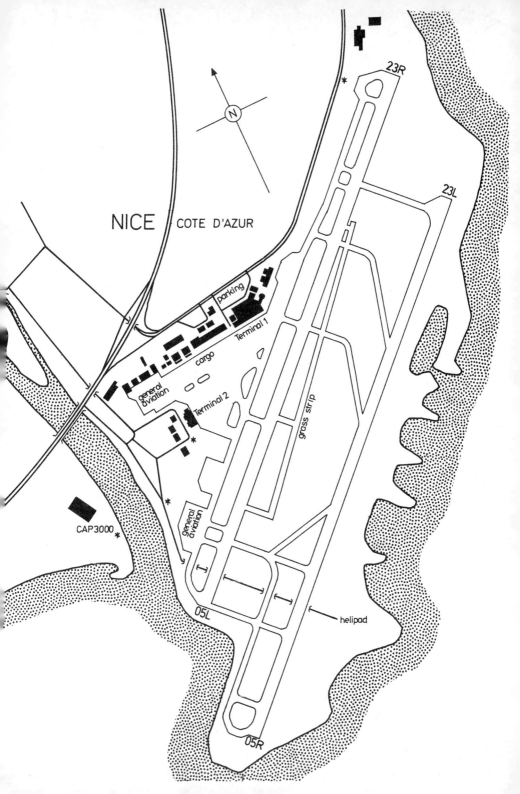

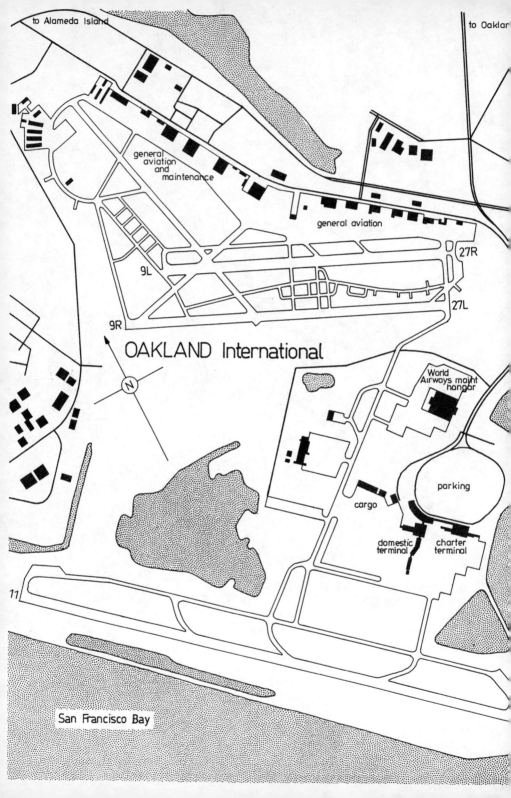

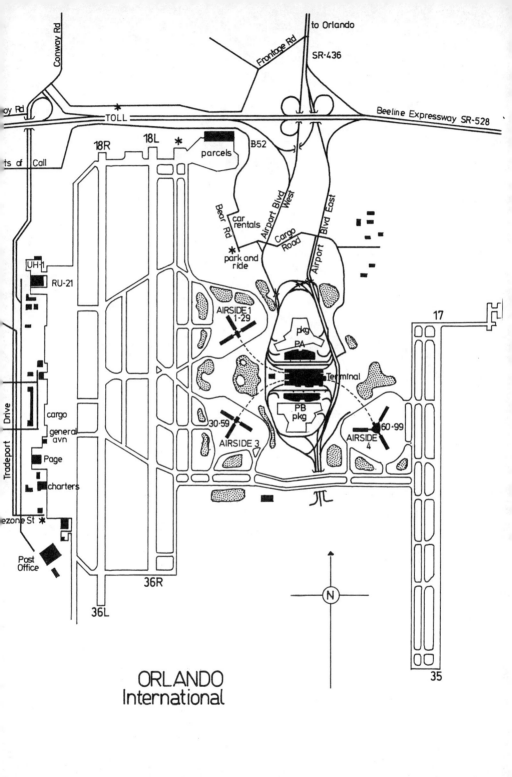

ORLANDO
International

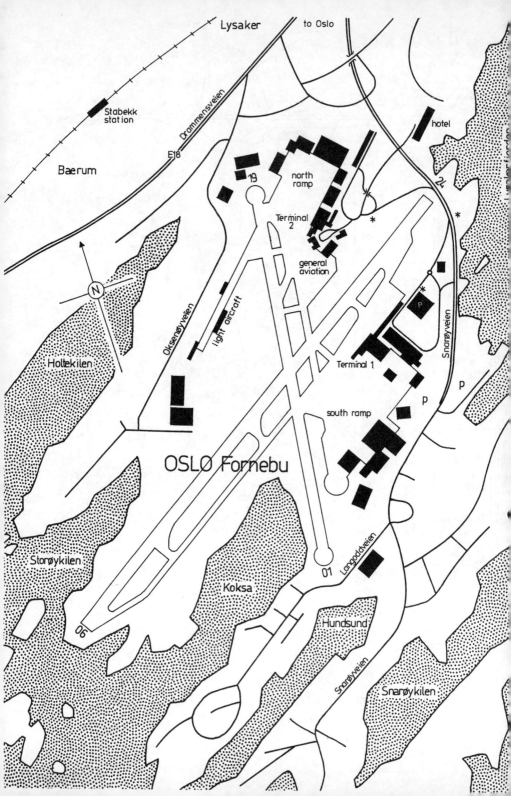

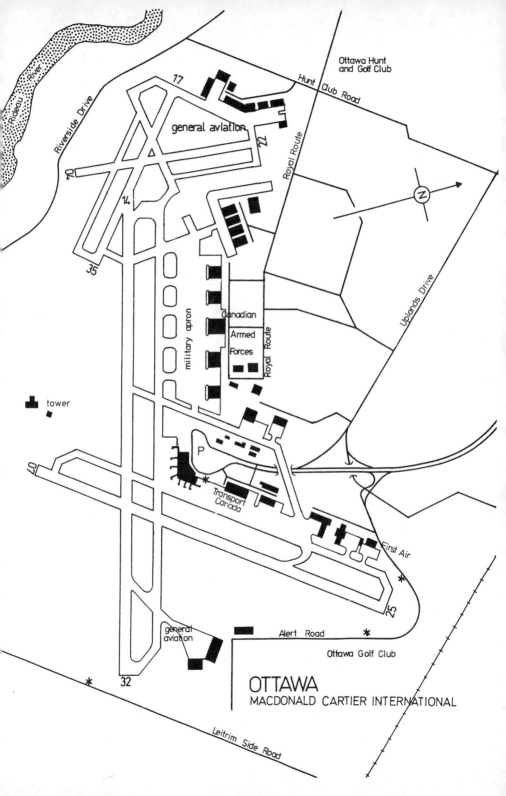

OTTAWA
MACDONALD CARTIER INTERNATIONAL

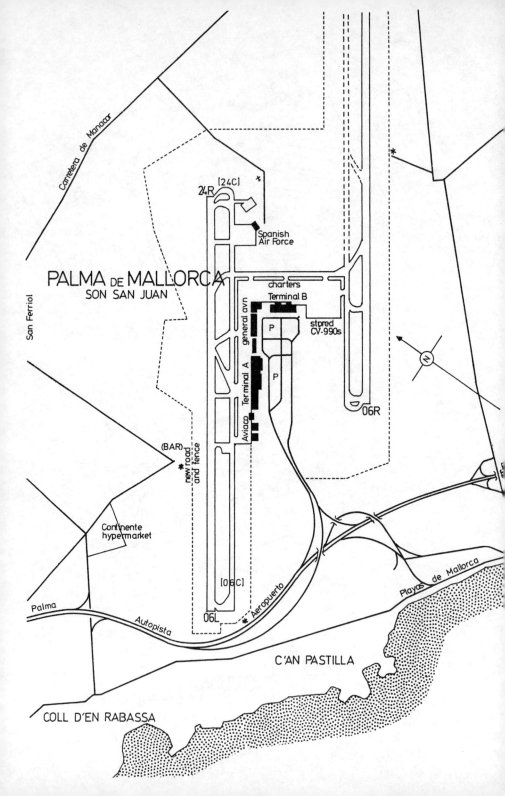

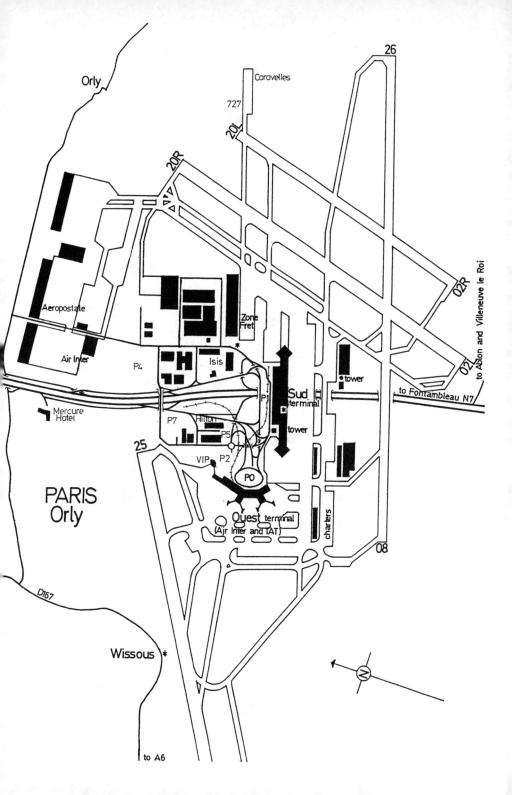

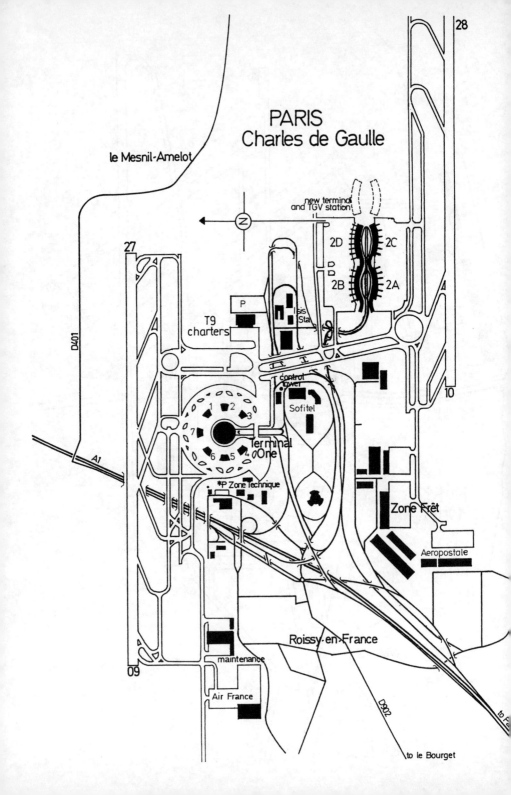

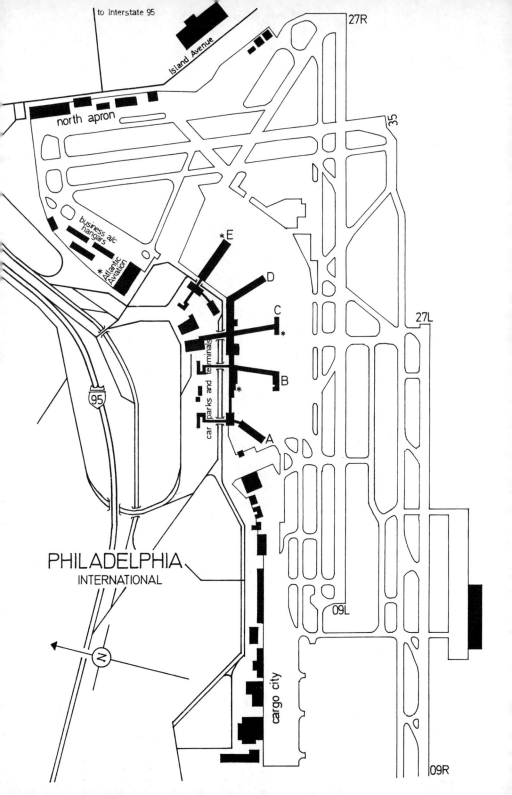

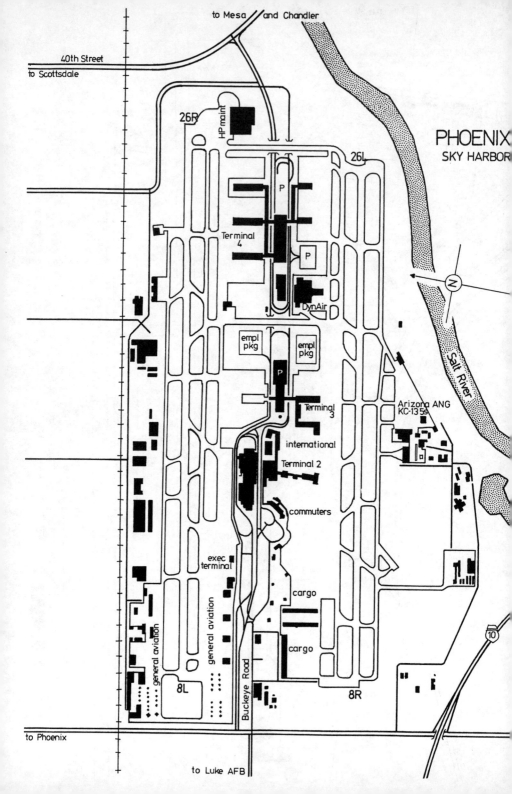

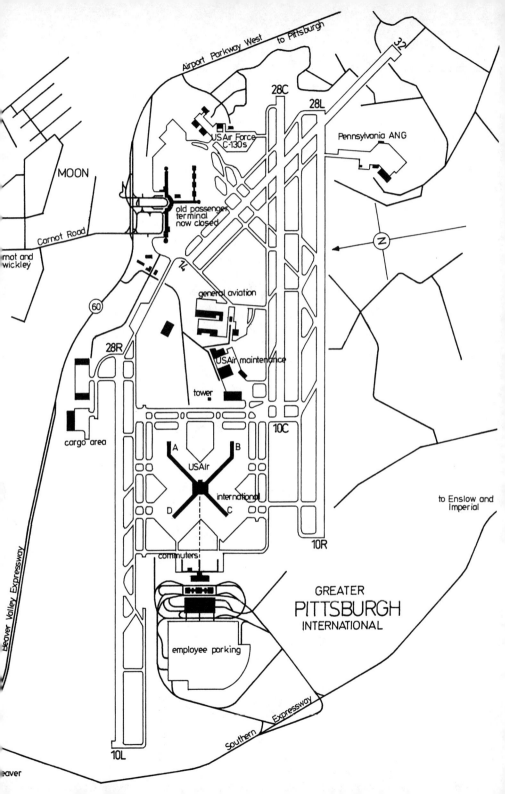

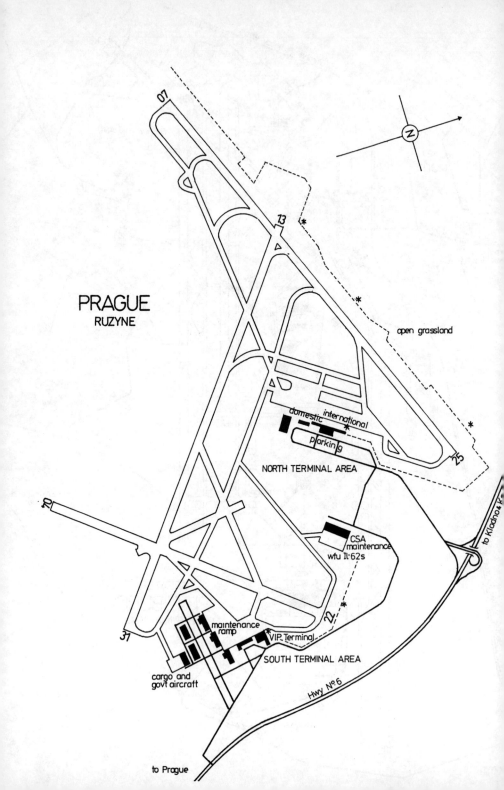

PRAGUE
RUZYNE

07

13

25

70

37

open grassland

domestic
international
parking

NORTH TERMINAL AREA

CSA
maintenance
wfu Il·62s

22

maintenance
ramp

VIP Terminal

SOUTH TERMINAL AREA

cargo and
gov't aircraft

Hwy Nº6

to Kladno & K

to Prague

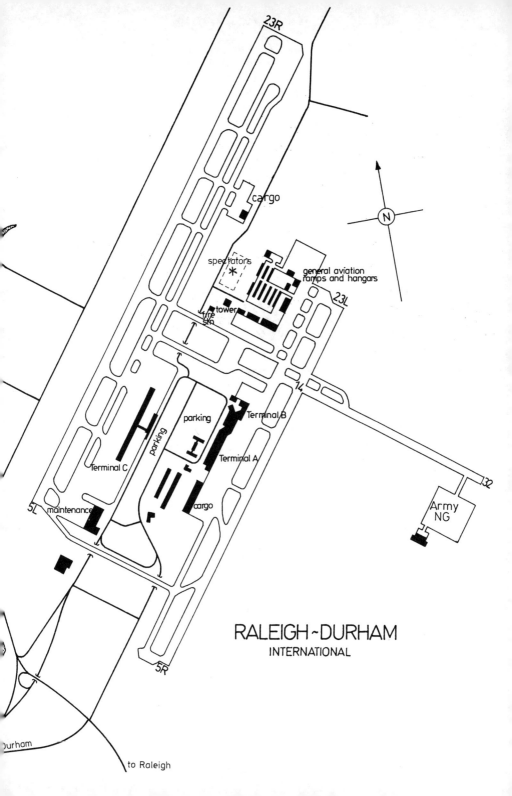

23R

cargo

N

spectators

*

general aviation
ramps and hangars

23L

tower

fire
stn

14

parking

parking

Terminal B

Terminal C

Terminal A

5L

maintenance

cargo

32

Army
NG

5R

RALEIGH~DURHAM
INTERNATIONAL

Durham

to Raleigh

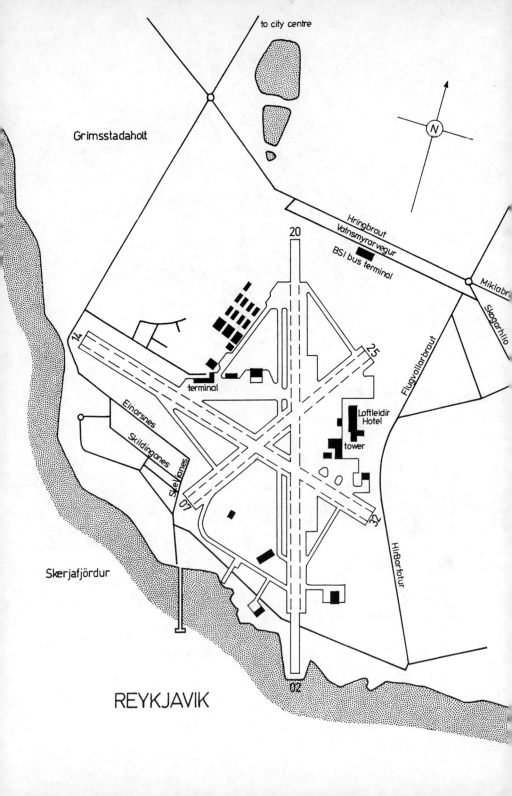

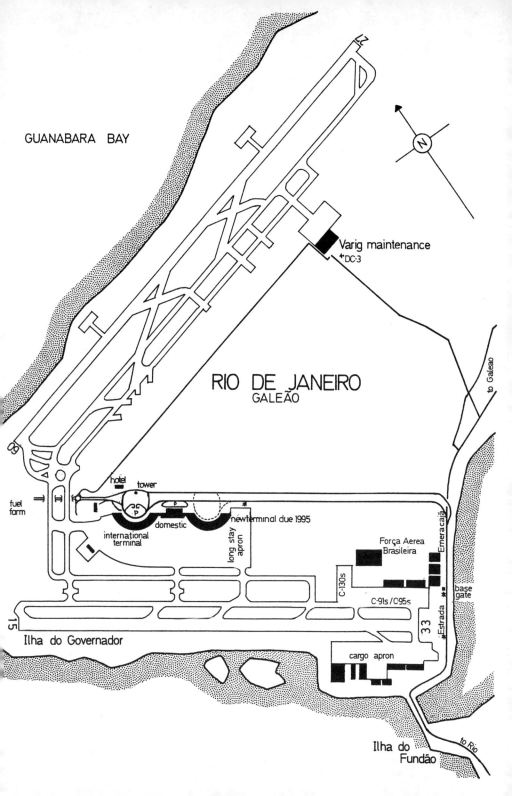

GUANABARA BAY

Varig maintenance
+ DC-3

RIO DE JANEIRO
GALEÃO

to Galeao

N

hotel
tower

fuel
farm

P
P

P

international
terminal

domestic

new terminal due 1995

long stay apron

Força Aerea
Brasileira

Emeracaia

C-130s

C-91s / C-95s

base
gate

Estrada

33

15

Ilha do Governador

cargo apron

to Rio

Ilha do
Fundão

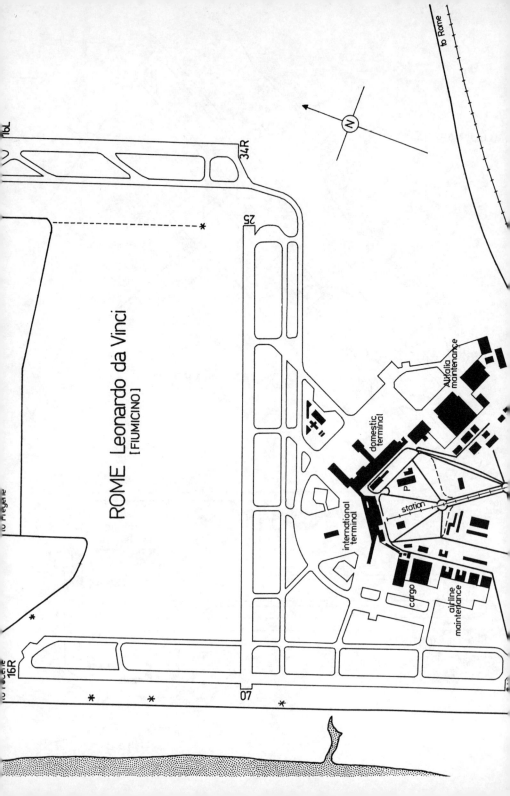

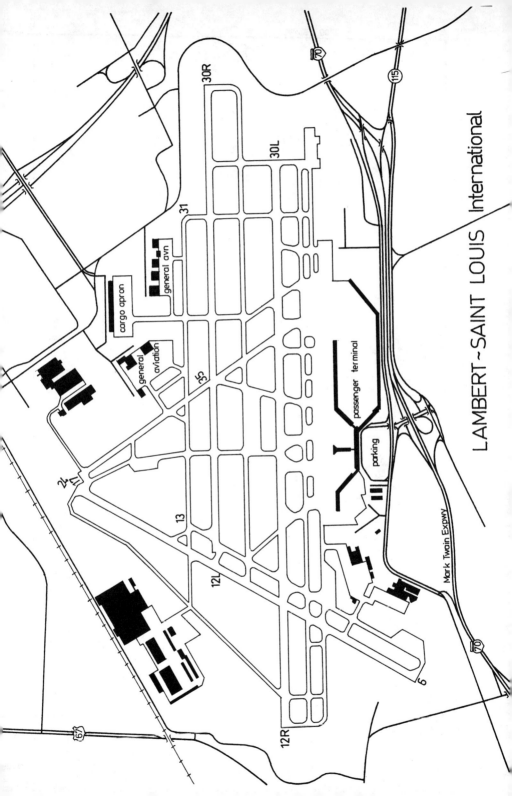

LAMBERT~SAINT LOUIS International

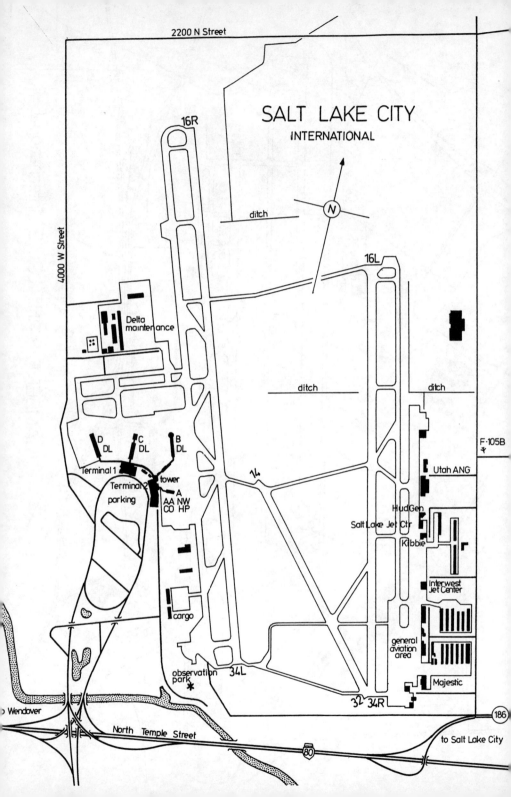

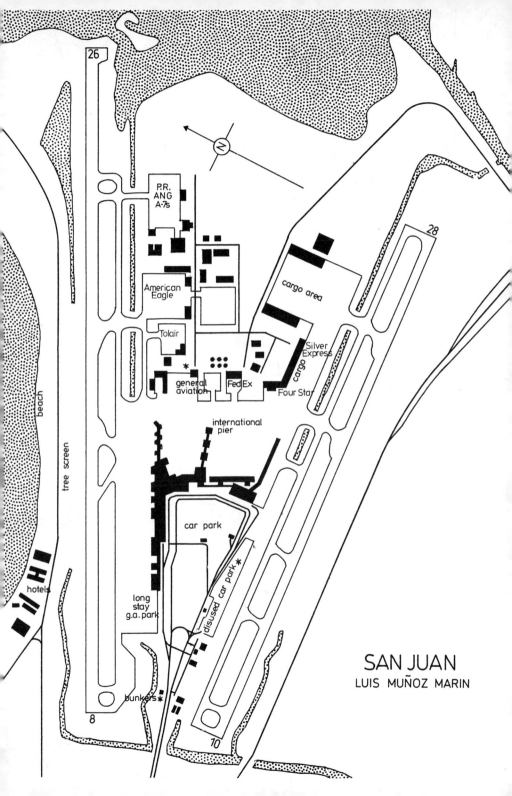

SAN JUAN
LUIS MUÑOZ MARIN

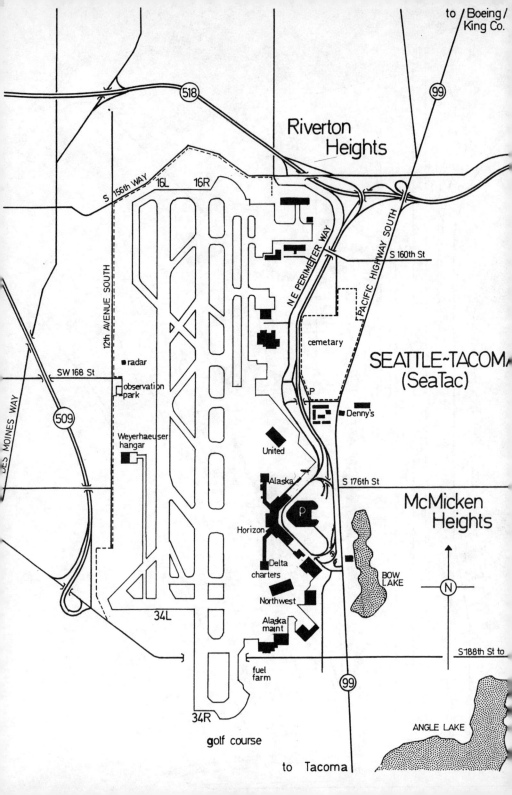

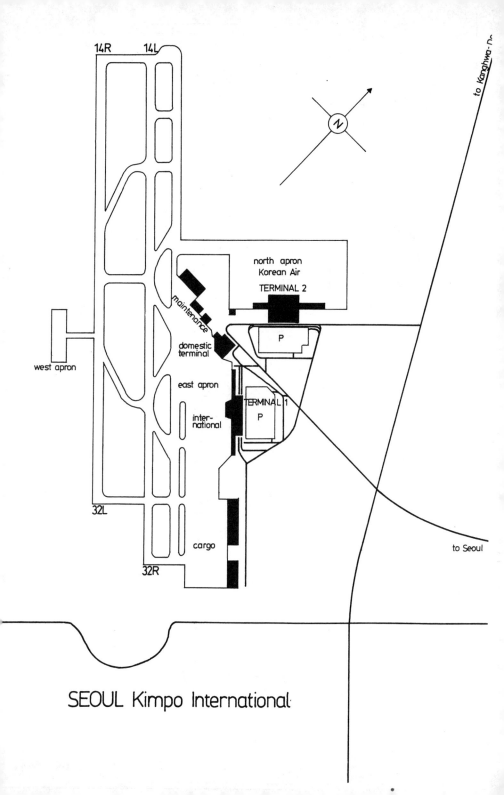

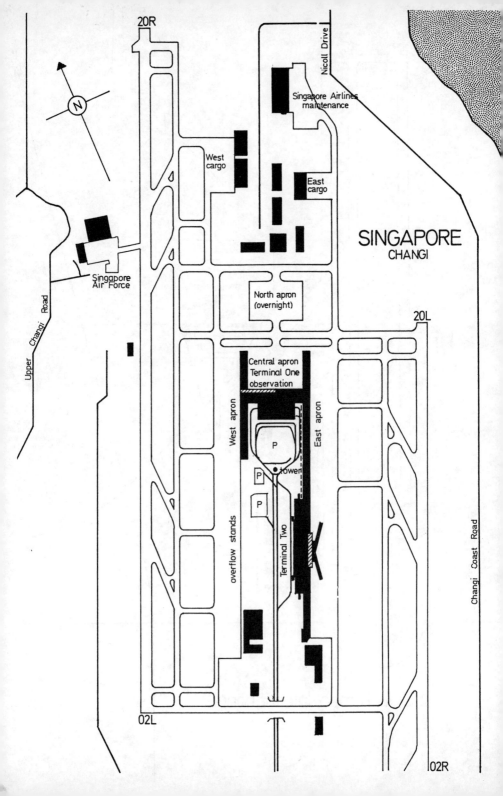

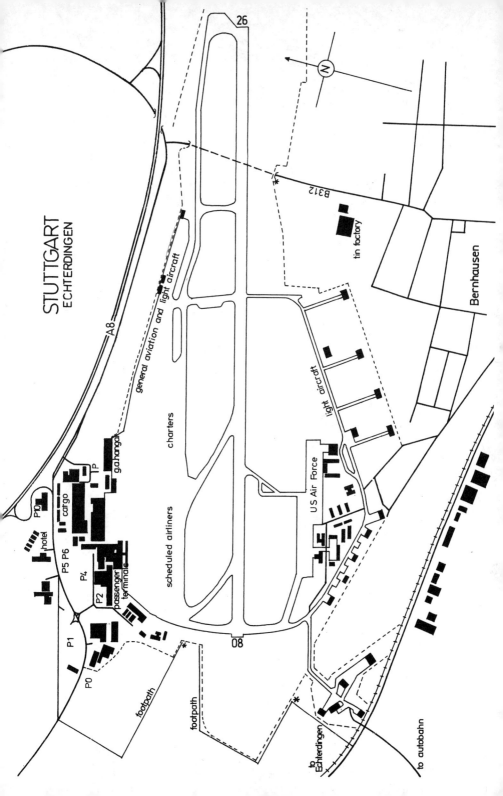

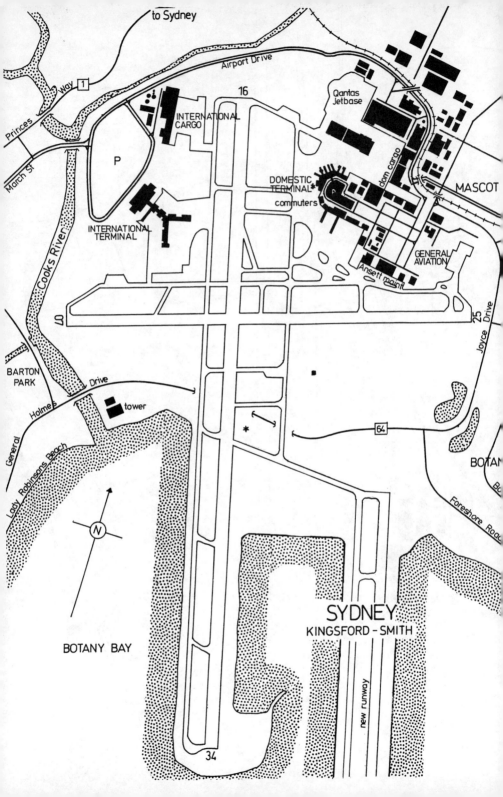

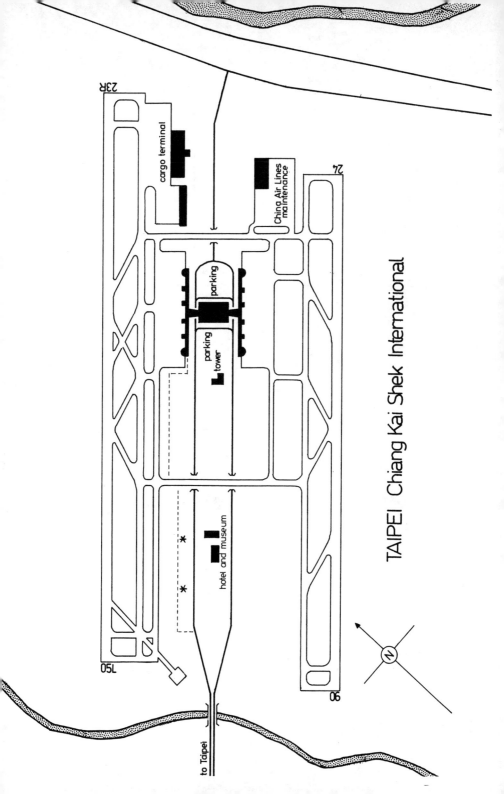

TAIPEI Chiang Kai Shek International

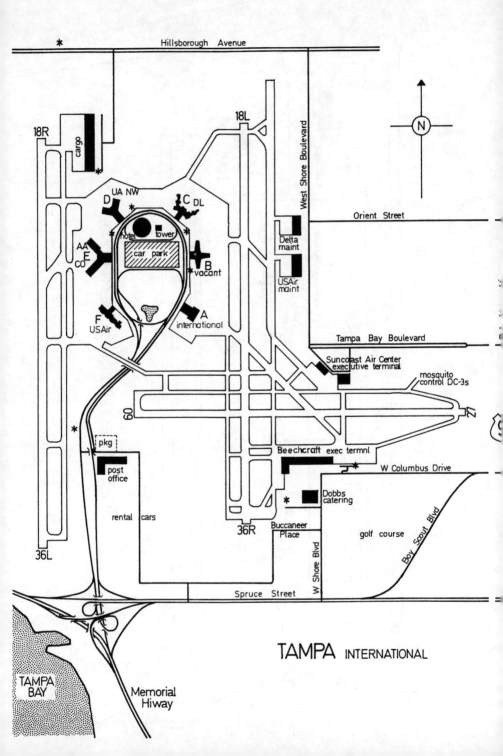

TAMPA INTERNATIONAL

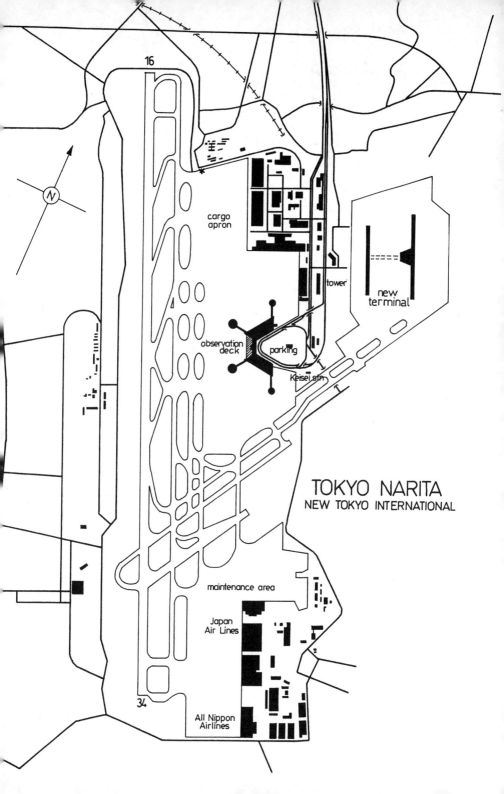

16

N

cargo
apron

tower

new
terminal

observation
deck

parking

Keisei stn

TOKYO NARITA
NEW TOKYO INTERNATIONAL

maintenance area

Japan
Air Lines

34

All Nippon
Airlines

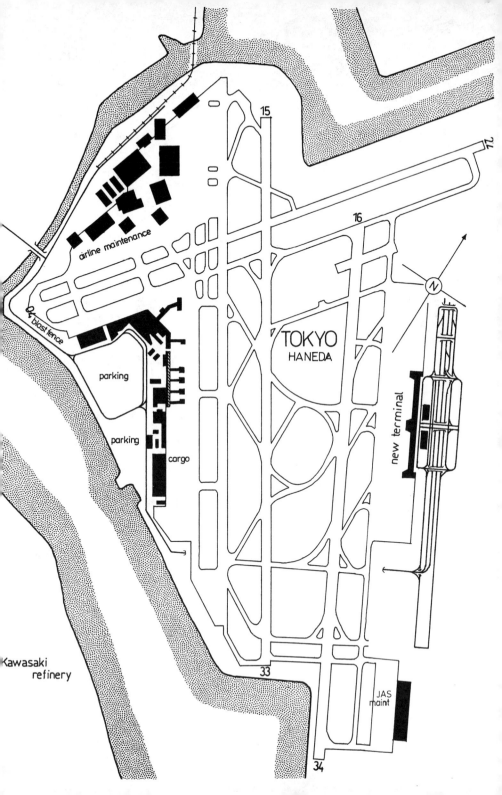

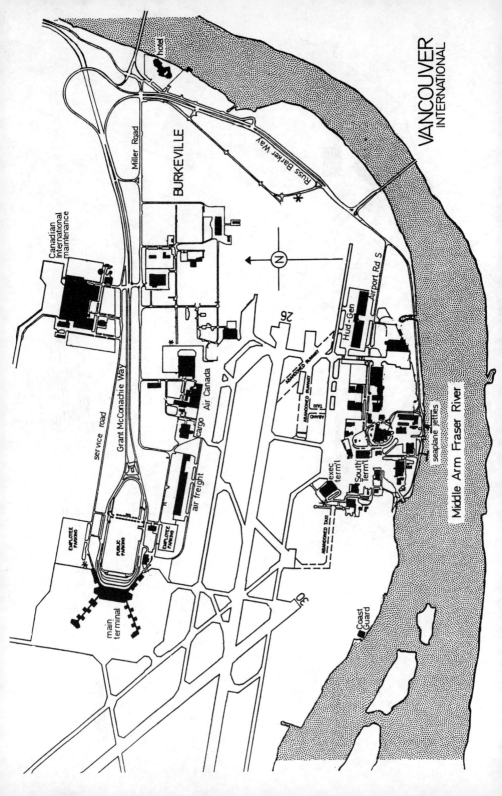

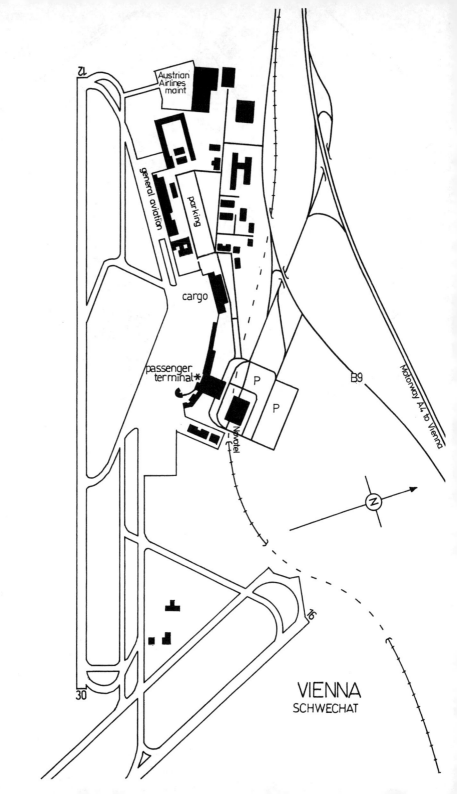

VIENNA
SCHWECHAT

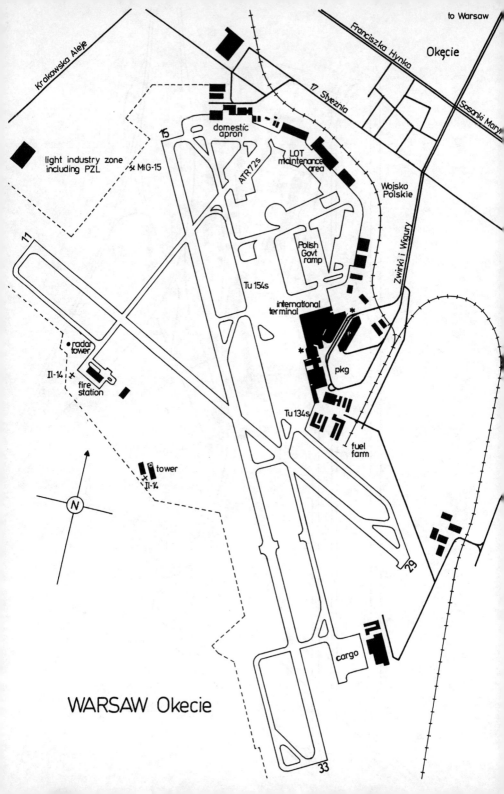

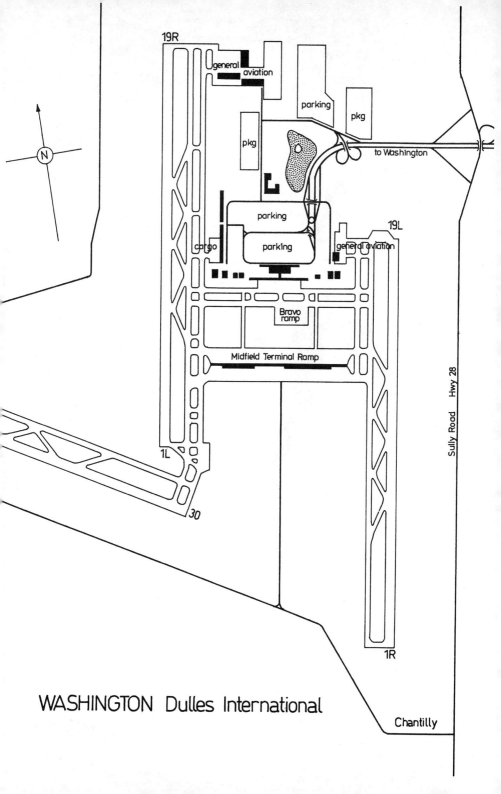

WASHINGTON Dulles International

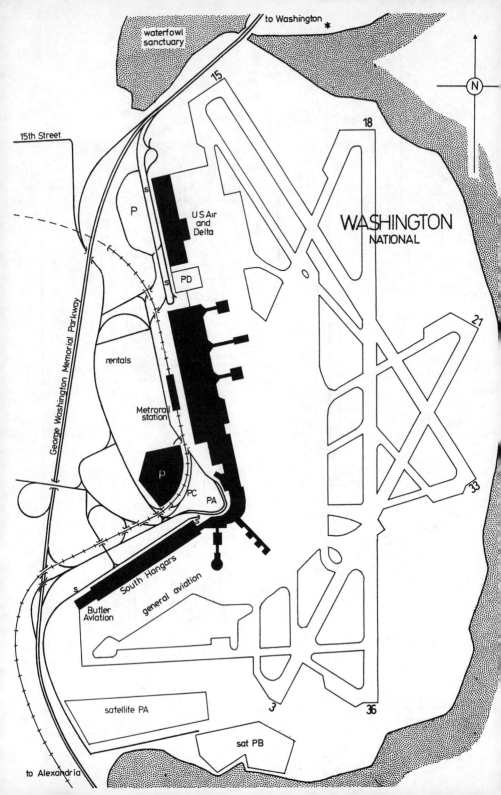

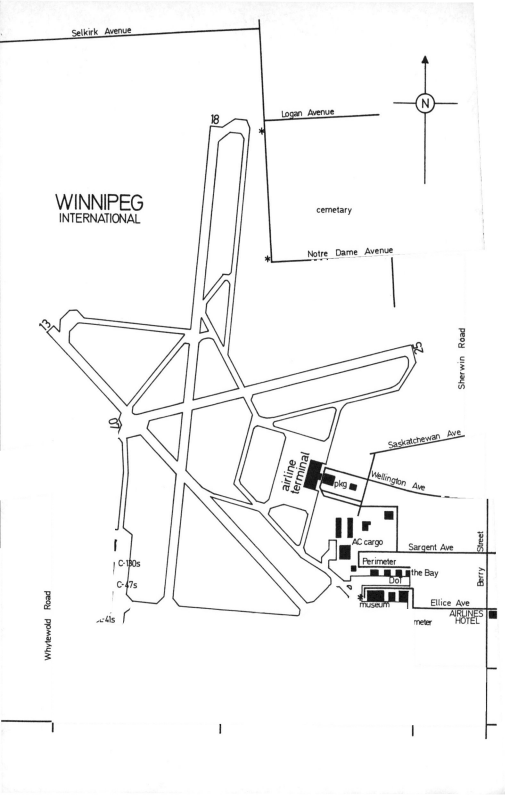

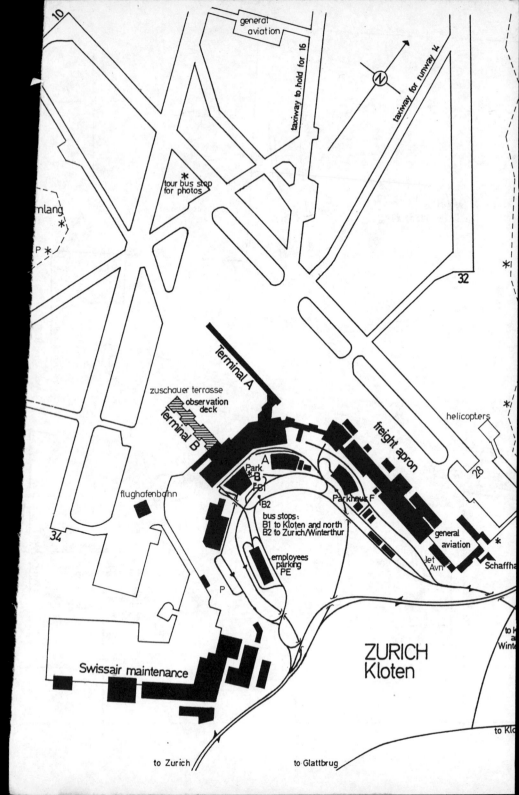